Oeuvre

DREW STRUZAN

Drew Struzan: Oeuvre

ISBN: 9780857685575

Published by
Titan Books
A division of Titan Publishing Group Ltd.
144 Southwark St.
London
SE1 0UP

First edition: October 2011
6 8 10 9 7 5

Book design by Drew Struzan.

EU RP (for authorities only)
eucomply OÜ Pärnu mnt 139b-14 11317
Tallinn, Estonia
hello@eucompliancepartner.com
+3375690241

ACKNOWLEDGEMENTS
Titan Books would like to thank George Lucas for writing the Foreword, Dylan Struzan for her time and support, and most crucially Drew Struzan for his time and patience, as well as for his keen eye.
Thanks also to Joanna Boylett, Stephen Saffel, Rodolfo Muraguchi, Natalie Laverick, Lizzie Bennett, Kevin Wooff, Bob Kelly, Tim Scrivens, Vivian Cheung and Nick Landau.

visit our website:
www.titanbooks.com

A CIP catalogue record for this title is available from the British Library.

Printed and bound in China.

Oeuvre

DREW STRUZAN

written by DREW & DYLAN STRUZAN

introduction by GEORGE LUCAS

TITAN BOOKS

My work is my letter of dedication to the Creator that gives all good gifts.
I am thankful for the spirit of creativity that is power and love.
Grateful for the Industry that gave me the opportunity to work, live, and create.
Humbled by the freedom I enjoyed to pursue my dreams.

This book is for everyone around the world who has appreciated my efforts.
To you, my friends ... with affection, esteem, respect and appreciation.
... and to my wife ... my life, my partner, my savior, and my love.

drew

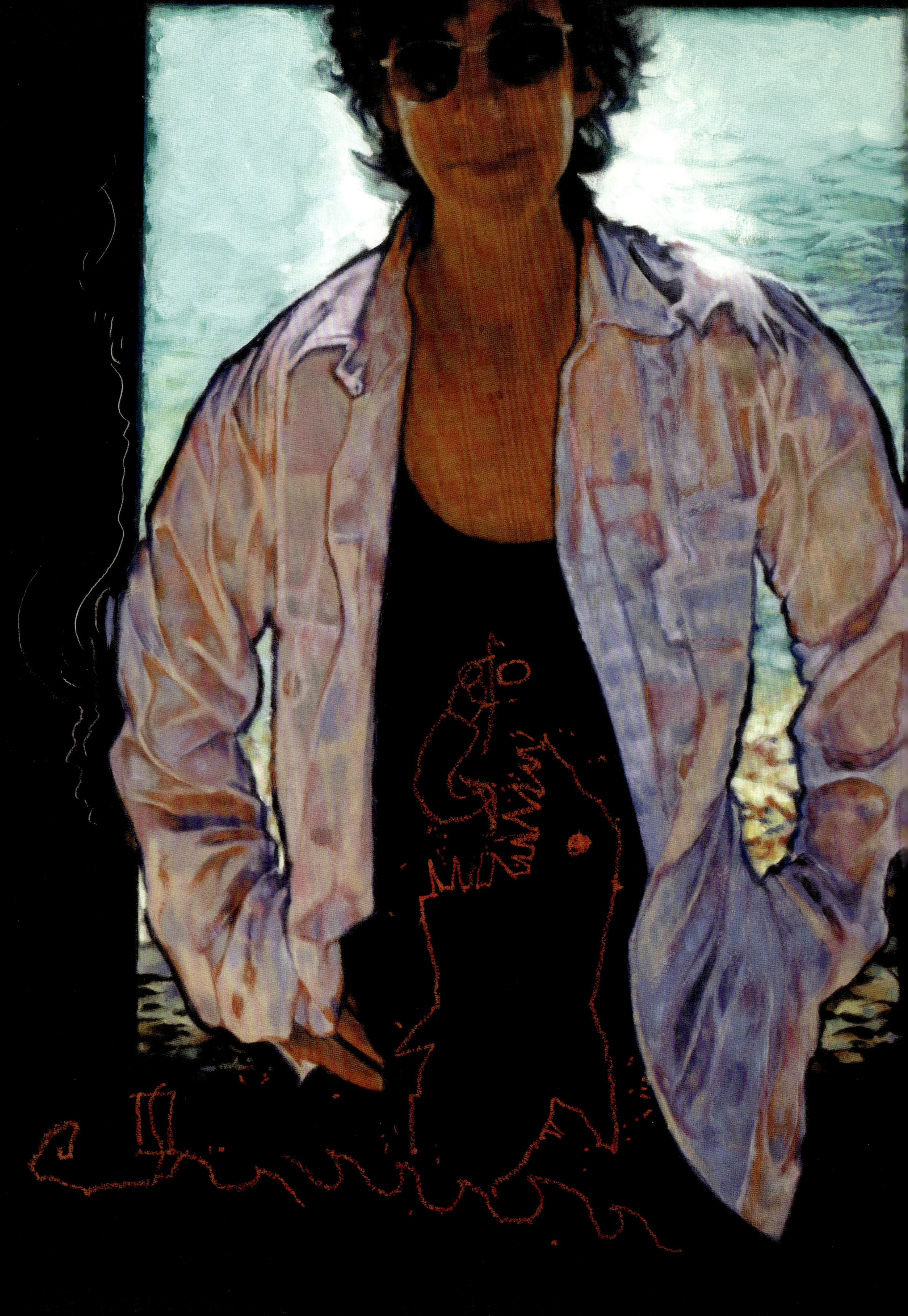

CONTENTS

FOREWORD BY GEORGE LUCAS

I don't think it will surprise many readers to know that I think visually. I always have. Even though I've become known as a storyteller, I am more enamored with communicating through images than words. In school, I made a serious study of art and at one point my ambition was to become an illustrator, not a filmmaker. Although I made filmmaking my career, I have never abandoned my love of art and images and those who create them. Art is not only a powerful means of communication, it has the ability to build ideas that go beyond the literal into the more spiritual nature of existence, in ways that are both profound and enlightening.

I collect the works of illustrators, though my focus has been illustrators from 1850 to 1950, artists such as N.C. Wyeth, Maxfield Parrish and Norman Rockwell. The artists I think of as social in nature, in that they depict or define the mood of the culture or some aspect of culture from their time period. A painting can show how a culture works, how society views itself, what the issues of the day might have been. This aspect of art has always fascinated me, in that it can be an anthropological tool, revealing certain aspects of a culture, preserving them and offering deeper insight into the way people think. Whether it's literature or music or film or painting or sculpture, to me it becomes an artifact, something left behind that is infused with emotion, or a particular feeling, or a cultural sensibility that is otherwise lost in time.

I like to think I am reasonably sophisticated about art—that I have an eye for what is good and for recognizing talent when I see it. When I first saw the illustrations of Drew Struzan, I knew that his work was special and conveyed a sensibility, artistic flair and dramatic depth that would fit perfectly with the characters and films that I had created, from *Star Wars* to Indiana Jones. Indeed, as soon as I saw his first works for Lucasfilm Ltd. in 1984, I thought that Drew's style and my films were a perfect match.

In the ensuing two decades, Drew's *Star Wars* and Indiana Jones illustrations have conveyed and furthered the stories not just on the movie posters, but on book covers, theme-park attractions and other beautifully detailed visual representations. His work does much more than show a few characters—it tells its own stories and serves as dramatic and memorable entertainment in its own right. Drew has the talent not only to capture the characters faithfully, but to enrich them with something a little grander, a little more glorious and more romantic than a photograph could ever convey. Creating a memorable movie poster is always a difficult task. Developing poster art that stands on its own as a compelling piece of art can be nearly impossible, but Drew has helped Lucasfilm do just that for our movies.

I like to think that Drew's illustrations for our *Star Wars* posters do even more than that. It is fun to think that *Star Wars* and the art associated with it have carved an anthropological niche—and that in time, art scholars will look at these pieces and contemplate what they say about our own culture and time. Maybe they will create their own theories about the images they see—the epic adventure that surrounds the characters in these illustrations—and glean unique insights into the artwork.

But I think it's safe to conclude one thing right now: they will immediately appreciate the artistry and amazing attention to detail that infuses these pieces. Drew Struzan brings an original and impeccable style to all of his work, and I hope you enjoy it as much as I do.

George Lucas

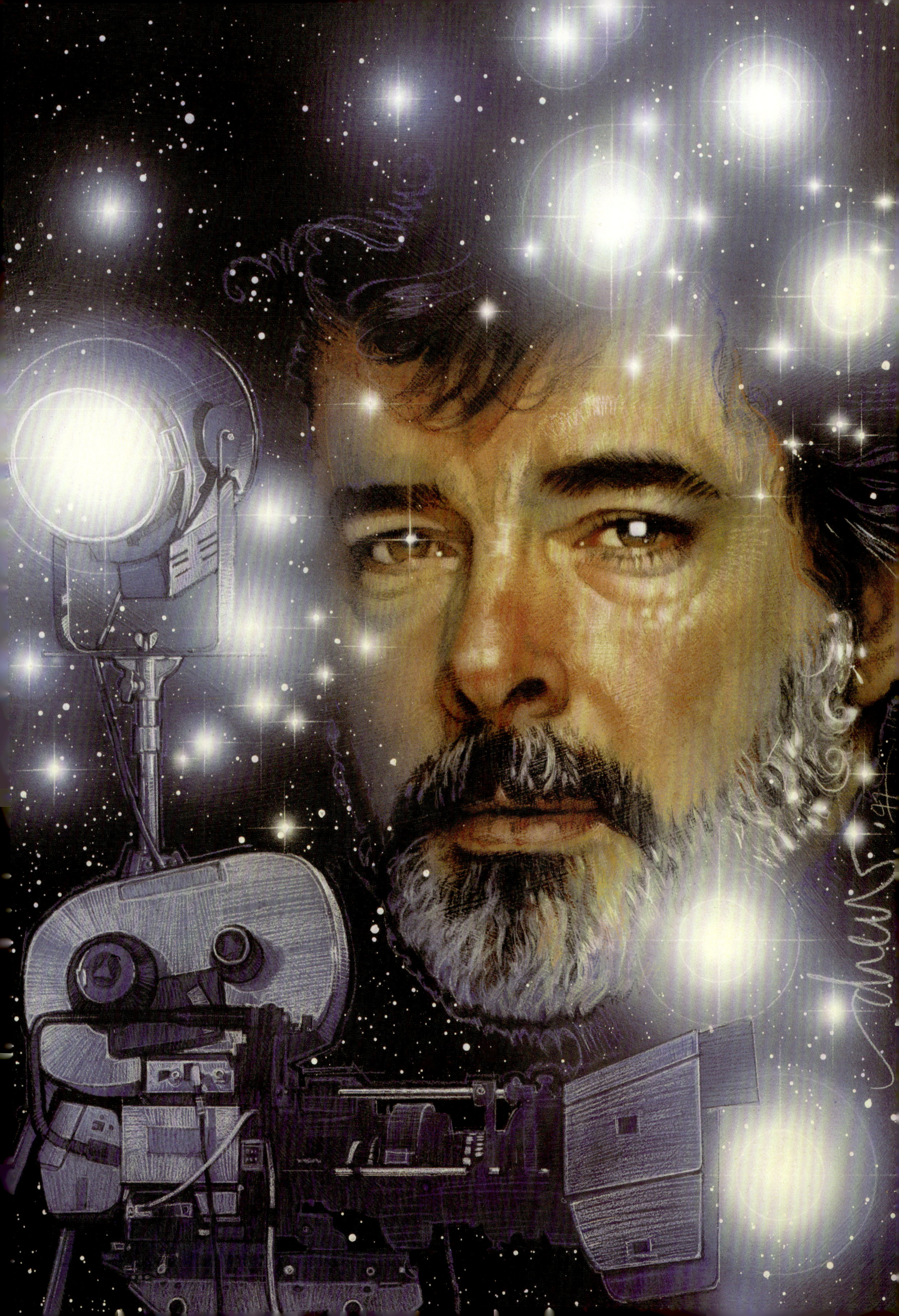

INTRODUCTION

My mind is always thinking about painting and creative possibilities. That's who I am. That's how I express myself. I don't have a hobby; I don't go skiing or boating. Art is what I do. That's what's on my mind. I look around and think, Would that make a cool picture? What if I did this or did that? *I love painting. My career gave me the chance to do what I do best. My personal work offers the freedom to explore and experiment, a chance to answer 'What if?'*

— Drew

Drew wasn't always so singularly focused. He started out as a typical kid riding his bicycle, building models, and watching *Hopalong Cassidy* on TV. He also drew, not because he wanted to become an artist but because drawing brought him pleasure. He was a quiet kid wrestling with dyslexia, more comfortable being alone with his feelings. He was, by nature, more suited for the studio than the playground and found drawing pictures a comfortable outlet for which he was rewarded both personally and publicly.

In the third grade, he functioned as the class artist. When Easter rolled around, his teacher asked him to fill the chalkboard with drawings. He drew bunnies and baskets and eggs using the colored chalk his teacher gave him. This was fine with Drew who was happy to escape endless mimeographed sheets of multiplication tables and other rote work.

Home life consisted of an endless series of moves from one town to another. This constant uprooting left Drew and his brother and sister with no friends, no attachments, and very little support for building a strong internal foundation. The closest his parents ever came to settling down was in 1957 when Drew was ten years old. His grandfather bought the struggling family a home in San Jose (Silicon Valley), California. The agricultural town was then a budding metropolis, but still one full of open groves. Rows of trees and old barns dotted the landscape.

"I found peace and contentment being alone among the trees," he says. Daily, Drew picked up his drawing tablet and disappeared into the quiet of the fields and drew subjects that interested him.

Something in those drawings must have sparked his mother's maternal instinct. She located a college student to come to the house to give Drew art lessons. Teacher and student began with a discussion on linear perspective, the technique of depicting volumes and spatial relationships on a flat surface. As a practical application, they walked across the street from Drew's house, sat on the corner, and, as the teacher watched, Drew demonstrated his understanding of the concept by drawing the intersecting streets and the rows of houses that lined them. His visual acuity was quite apparent to his teacher, who then assigned Drew to create a drawing from the painting of a favored artist to gauge how good his general drawing skills were.

In preparation, Drew headed off to the library. There he found a book containing a painting that struck his fancy, Paolo Veronese's *Venus and Mars United by Love.* With pencil in hand, Drew tackled the assignment. Line for line, shape for shape, and tone for tone, Drew created a fully rendered black and white pencil drawing of the painting. When the teacher returned, "he didn't have much to say," Drew remembers. "All I know is that he collected his five dollars and left. He never came back. I don't know why. He just didn't come back."

In Drew's family, you didn't ask why.

Before long, the family was on the move again.

By the time Drew entered high school, he was adept at painting and drawing for money, which was a good thing for a kid from an impoverished background. His peers hired him to create T-shirt designs. Parents hired him to paint matadors and friars and portraits of relatives. And for five dollars a pop, teachers hired him to paint their caricatures on 5 by 7 inch cards, which they wore to pep rallies.

At fourteen, Drew entered a national art competition sponsored by the U.N. To express the theme, "The Spirit of the United Nations," he painted a long line of men and women dressed in their respective ethnic costumes, all shaking hands. His effort earned him first prize and the novel experience of appearing on a local TV news program.

The painting was then exhibited along with those of the other honorees at an art show in San Francisco. Drew missed the show because his parents either would not or could not drive the fifty miles north. Consequently, the painting went wherever unclaimed paintings go and Drew lost an early, formative experience.

In Drew's family, you didn't complain.

As the high school years drew to a close and an uncertain future loomed on the horizon, Drew began to think about his career options. His art teacher took the liberty of pointing him toward Art Center College of Design, located in Los Angeles. At the time, the school was held in high esteem as one of the best in the country for art education. The founder, Edward "Tink" Adams, held the radical idea that working professionals should "teach real-world skills to artists and designers and prepare them for leadership roles in advertising, publishing, and industrial design."

Students were expected to have completed two years of basic college education before applying to Art Center for professional training. Nevertheless, Drew was one of the rare exceptions who applied directly out of high school and was accepted. Thus in 1965, after high school graduation, Drew packed a suitcase and, with a hundred dollars in his pocket awarded him by the Lion's Club scholarship fund, headed for Los Angeles.

Art Center offered him two choices for a major: Illustration or fine art. The counselor advised Drew that a fine artist paints what he wants while an illustrator paints for others to get paid. Drew was eighteen, alone, and without support. He chose to get paid. He was then placed directly into the third semester curriculum.

To survive, Drew often sold his class assignments to other students, but by and large, Drew remained the proverbial "starving artist," once landing in hospital for malnutrition only to be turned away because he was a minor and, thus, unable to be held accountable for the hospital bill. Undeterred by his meager status, he continued on.

By far, Drew's most influential teacher – and head of the Fine Art Department at Art Center – was Lorser Feitelson. Lorser was one of the founding fathers of California's "Hard Edge" painters, a movement that emphasized abrupt transitions between areas of color, the "hard edge" referring to the place where two colors come together. The white wave on the red Coca Cola™ can is a classic example of the art Lorser produced.

"Lorser taught history, composition, techniques, and taste, but most of all he taught freedom of thought, criticism, creative motive, and encouraged a search for truth," Drew says with fondness for the man who infused

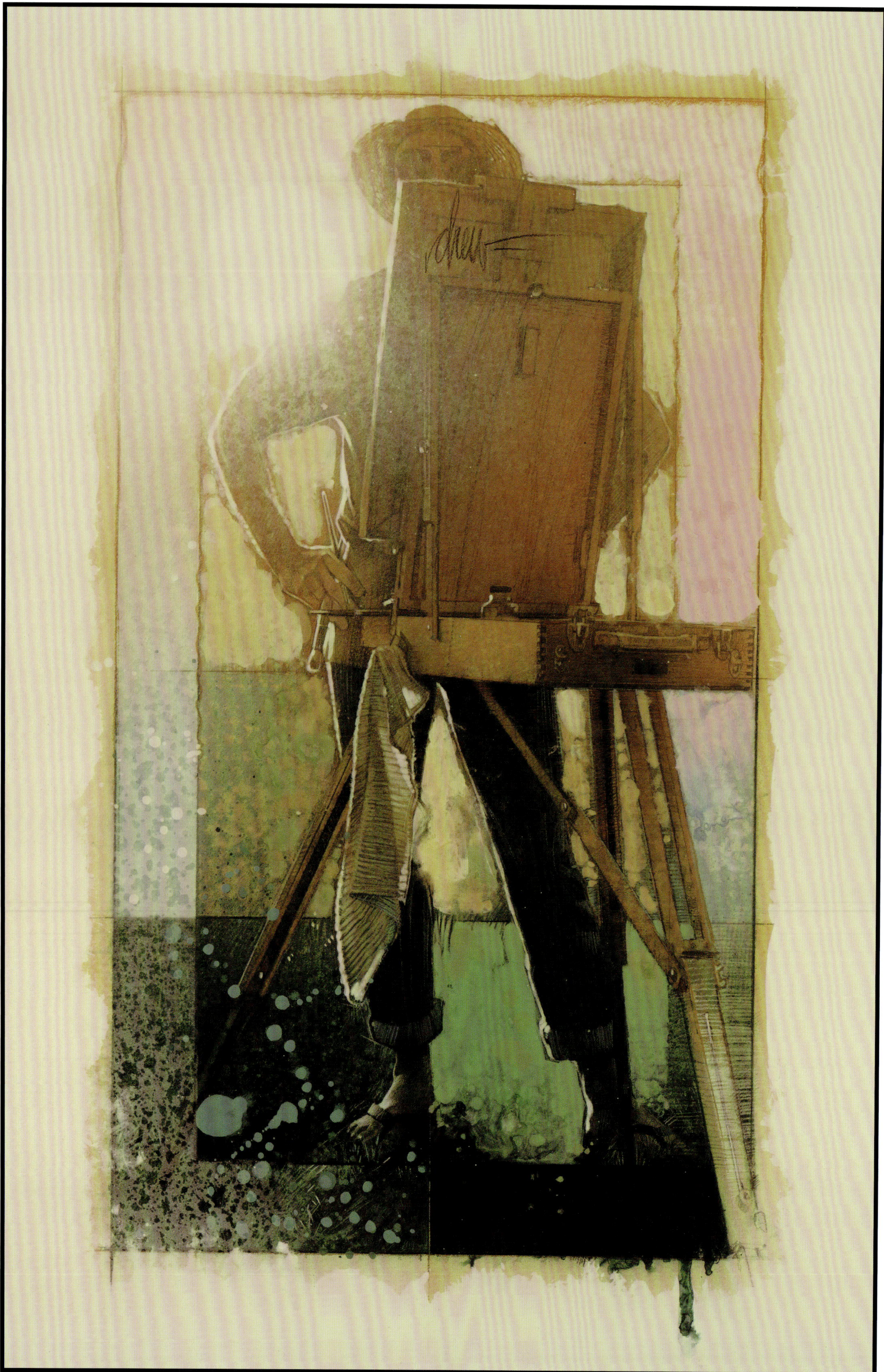

him with the spirit of an artist. For Drew and many of his fellow students, Lorser was Art Center's greatest gift second only to the tuition scholarship allocated him from his third semester on.

Drew graduated from Art Center with "Great Distinction." Whether by chance or circumstance, his talent was now solidly grounded in an extensive education of his craft. "In the end," Drew says, "the education for illustration and fine art was exactly the same."

He then embarked on a Master of Fine Art program with the intention of becoming a teacher. In the end, his work found favor in the eyes of the assessing committee but was denied his degree on the grounds that his thesis was not written in a scholarly fashion. Without the ability to explain his work satisfactorily, Drew was spun in a new direction, forced to put to the test "Tink" Adams' assertion that Art Center taught real-world skills that would take him into leadership roles.

The work came slowly. Newly married and pounding the streets for two years after graduation, Drew was frustrated that he still was not finding enough work to feed his wife and child. He hired on as a staff illustrator in a small Los Angeles design agency, Pacific Eye & Ear, which catered to the music industry. There, he painted such iconic album covers as Black Sabbath's *Sabbath Bloody Sabbath* (1973) and Alice Cooper's *Welcome to My Nightmare* (1975) for which he collected a modest weekly paycheck. As the work began to circulate in the mainstream, executives in the movie industry noticed and took an interest. Soon Drew was called on to paint movie posters. Drew left the agency and once again freelanced, this time with a reputation generated by his body of work.

The early movie posters he was called on to produce were quite diverse, everything from comedies (*The Black Bird* [1975]) to horror (*Squirm* and *The Food of the Gods* [both 1976]). Even then, a creative ethic prevailed in his work. "My approach to horror was very different from the art that was being done at the time. In *The Food of the Gods*, I avoided the gory depiction that would have been typical for the time and genre, choosing instead to give this 'B' movie a sense of depth, class, and dignity. I emphasized the situation between the girl and the rat because that was the element that sparked the emotion. I chose to build tension, using anticipation to evoke the feeling of what might be."

Drew was beginning to hone his feelings as a touchstone for his creativity, while also discovering the central emotions inherent to each film and, by his depiction, motivating interest in the subject. Dramatic choices governed his work and made it stand out, but he had not yet realized the full potential of his mighty talent. In yet another way, school had not prepared him for the real-world job of a commercial illustrator. "You have to learn how to shop yourself," he explains. "When someone is interested in hiring you, you have to learn to speak your client's language. They don't come to you and say, 'You're wonderful. Do something for us.' They want to use your skills to promote their product."

Before pencil ever hits paper, the illustrator has to understand the subject of the work he is to create, whether it is for a story, a movie, or a product. "I consider that it must have value," Drew says. "Something in the thing I'm illustrating had the power to motivate the maker. That's where I use my feeling side. I can go straight for the motivational foundation of the work, and I can put that into visual form immediately.

"School didn't prepare me for that," Drew notes. "That came later... in the real world when I had to please the client." Professionalism means asking the right questions, and that means becoming bilingual with the language of advertising.

"An illustrator does not paint according to his own desire. That's a change of mind and spirit that has to be made once one leaves school. It is a case of jumping into the fire and learning how to do it in order to survive the business. An illustrator has to get his or her mind around that simple fact. Understanding and sympathizing with the mind and purpose of the client is what creates a successful campaign."

Like a mad scientist with a test tube of impressions, Drew descends into his laboratory to throw the switches of education and infuse life into an otherwise dead body. Every element must work in harmony. The picture must be complete. Nothing escapes artistic scrutiny. What is added or subtracted is done by sheer instinct. "It could be a couple of touches of color. It could be moving something or making something a little freer or a little tighter. Those decisions depend on a mature understanding of visual composition and the ability to say it is not right until it breathes. The trick, the mystery and gift is the perception and power to create life where there was none."

When he emerges, he has in hand nothing less than a painting designed with the purpose of taking the viewer to the heart of a film's story, the core of a book's premise, or the essence of a commercial product. The journey is collaborative. The artist's single image has but seconds to capture and hold the viewer's attention. This requires masterful skill. As Michelangelo once said, "If people knew how hard I worked to get mastery, it wouldn't seem so wonderful at all."

Drew's focus has always been on the *creation* of art. And art, he insists, is a matter of intention. "The thing we call humanities, or the arts, has always been the highest and finest expression of what makes us human. It is the bohemian ethic set out in *Moulin Rouge*: love, truth, beauty, and freedom. I would add to that list peace and justice. Those are the qualities I try to encompass in my art. The values I live by prompt my artistic inspiration.

"I define my goals for each piece of art and am not satisfied with a piece until I accomplish what I set out to do. It matters not if the intent is romance, adventure, mystery, horror, or sci-fi. The design and execution must support the emotion. Art is consistency. The mark of great art is that everything in the work cooperates to generate the desired atmosphere or emotion. Since a painting is a universe with four sides, it is imperative that the creator enforce a consistent set of rules dependent upon his intent. The created world must be harmonious. Consistency creates peace, power, and success."

This truth clarifies why it is detrimental to the integrity of a piece of art when a computer jockey becomes involved, and introduces hackneyed elements or shifts a composition haphazardly according to marketing whims. The universe of the work of art, the consistency of the image, crumbles in ruin.

"If people without practical knowledge make changes," Drew says, "they destroy the composition, destroy the emotional impact of the art, and weaken the work. It pleases them to have a part in the action, but the better course would be to tell me what it is they wish to accomplish rather than use their fingers—or computer—to change it. Tampering with the art is an affront. The insensitivity of others can, and does, destroy the work. I'm trying to do more than make a picture; I'm trying to make art that connects with the emotions of people. You can't have somebody come in and rape the picture and expect it to continue to give you the gifts of balance and peace and beauty. The universe of the work is disrupted. You wind up with chaos."

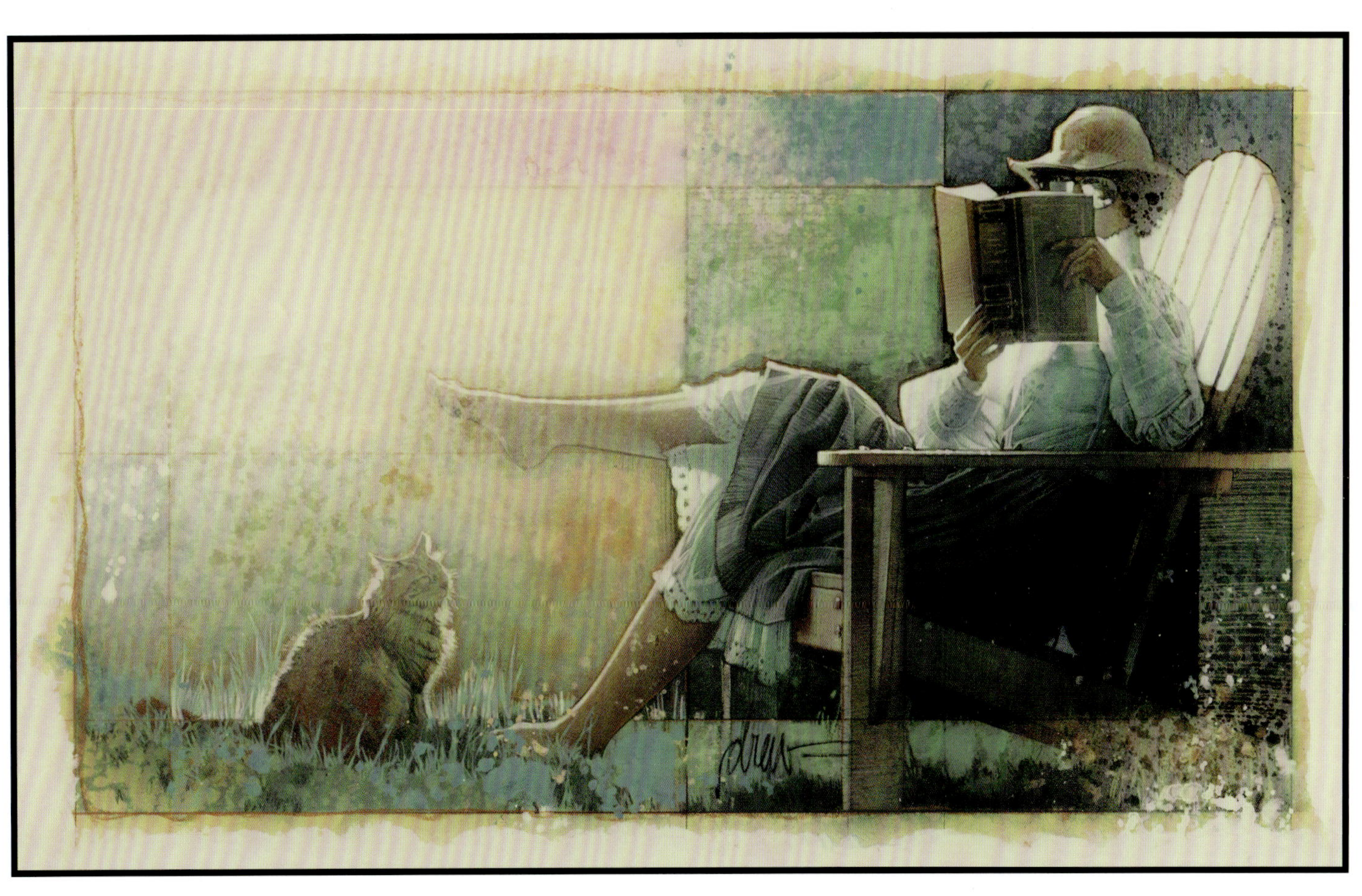

Love, truth, beauty, and freedom. How do these qualities manifest themselves in a poster that might otherwise appear to represent the opposing values of violence, destruction, and outright meanness?

To answer that question, one need only consider the artwork for *First Blood* (1982).

"In all my efforts as a commercial artist, I try to find what is good and true in the movie. *First Blood* tells the truth about a warrior returning home, worn, tired and displaced, but whose spirit for justice remains intact. I intended to capture the spirit of the character, so I painted Rambo in a blue and peaceful sky. He is holding a weapon. I wanted to bring beauty and power together in this piece. When I say beauty, I don't mean cute, fuzzy and cuddly. Beauty is his struggle for justice. Even the man of peace must pick up the sword when righteousness and justice are threatened. There is no gratuitous gore in the painting. It is an iconic figure that portrays love and power. Love is an act of power.

"As an artist, you *learn* your craft," Drew explains. "That's why it is said there are no geniuses in the field, because you have to be a mature person to do the real art of it. You get your tools and then you practice. It takes time to acquire the technical abilities to render, to paint, to see what's really there. You go through all the millions of processes of visual balance and beauty and thinking and representation and positives and negatives. You become very facile and no longer have to think about how to put down a line or how to interpret a shape or how to balance objects. You don't ask what colors to mix; you focus on *purpose.* You think about what you are trying to achieve with these tools. To do any less would be to halt the movement of the process and stifle creativity."

Feeling is the barometer. "American society often looks down on emotional acuity and promotes the intellectual aspect. This misguides people; it tells them not to trust their emotions. I'm speaking of emotions like love, compassion, sorrow, joy, or peace. You view art or experience art with these feelings. You can't put a letter to that law. You just can't do it. That's why it is hard for people to understand art in our society. When they look at art the first thing they often say is 'What is it supposed to mean? What is it supposed to be?' They don't feel the art with their hearts, with their emotions. They try to look intellectually at the work because that's what they've been told to do. What people don't understand is that the artist has done the intellectual work with the intent that it should be enjoyed emotionally.

"You have to put the analysis aside and just enjoy the work, live with it, look at it, feel it. Only then will you begin to understand the power of it."

Drew's big break came in the form of *Indiana Jones and the Temple of Doom...*

Perhaps the greatest leap forward in Drew's style came in 1984 when he was asked to create a poster for the second Indiana Jones movie. By that time, Drew was a polished professional. Experience made him confident in his abilities to interpret the client's needs without sacrificing artistic value. He trusted his creative instincts. "Somehow, the client and I met on that level," he says.

When Lucasfilm asked him to create a poster for the movie, which was already in theaters, Bruce Wolfe's poster was already in circulation. For whatever reason, Lucasfilm wanted a new look.

"I didn't go through the long process of endless meetings and hundreds of drawings," Drew recalls. "I wanted an emotional connection with the character so I designed a technique that was freer, crustier, more masculine. I designed edges that were sharp, hard, barbed, and threatening. I took the whole emotional response of the film and the character and tried to put it into the painting. Once they saw the piece they said, 'That's Indy.'"

Drew took quite a few creative liberties in that artwork. One such small venture was painting sharp the teeth on Mola Ram, the film's villain. George Lucas called Drew directly to ask why he did that. Drew replied simply that he thought it felt "right." Lucas agreed. Access to the director is always invaluable. Since this was the second Indy film, Drew knew the character and the style in which Lucas and director Steven Spielberg were telling the story. This information was integral to Drew's creative choices and from that time forward, Drew's distinctive design became part of Indiana Jones' hallmark. As reported by Ain't It Cool News, when Spielberg was asked if Drew would be doing the poster for *Indiana Jones and the Kingdom of the Crystal Skull*, he replied that he couldn't make an Indiana Jones movie without John Williams' score, Michael Kahn's editing, and Drew Struzan's poster art.

"Truth in advertising," Drew insists. "You have to know what the story is about and see what the director intended, not what some marketing maven wishes the movie was about or what they think they can sell. So much advertising today is about what's cute or what's fun, but not so much about the product. I want to create artwork that says, 'If you like the feeling of this painting, you're going to love the movie.'"

He contends that ultimately there is no difference between art and illustration. All art is created for a client, whether that client is purchasing the work for commercial reasons or for investment, pleasure, or appreciation for the art. The commercial artist brings the two worlds of art and the practical together. To do that, the creative impulse must be alive and well. Any artist worth his salt cannot afford to fall into a rut. The work must be and remain exciting. The universe of the canvas must be alive and well.

"The voice of the filmmaker speaks throughout the film as the story unfolds in a linear fashion. The artist must take that story and encapsulate it into a single image.

"I do far more than just translate what the filmmaker has done," Drew says. "I take the emotional content of the film and place it on the canvas in a way that speaks to the viewer. I wish each person to experience my art with the same involvement that I do."

On his deathbed, Michelangelo is reported to have said, "I regret that I have not done enough for the salvation of my soul and that I am dying just as I am beginning to learn the alphabet of my profession." The creative spirit is eternal, expansive. It thrives on what is new and different. It has to grow and experience new things in order to keep life exciting and valuable.

"I always want a new experience, even if it is scary," Drew says, "and pushing the limits. I want to solve the problem and make something new. That's the nature of the creative temperament. The growth is good. I remain open-minded, ready to search my soul, not afraid of my feelings, willing to change, and needing to find truth."

To quote a line from *Road to Perdition*:

"To be paid for what you love to do... ain't that the dream?"

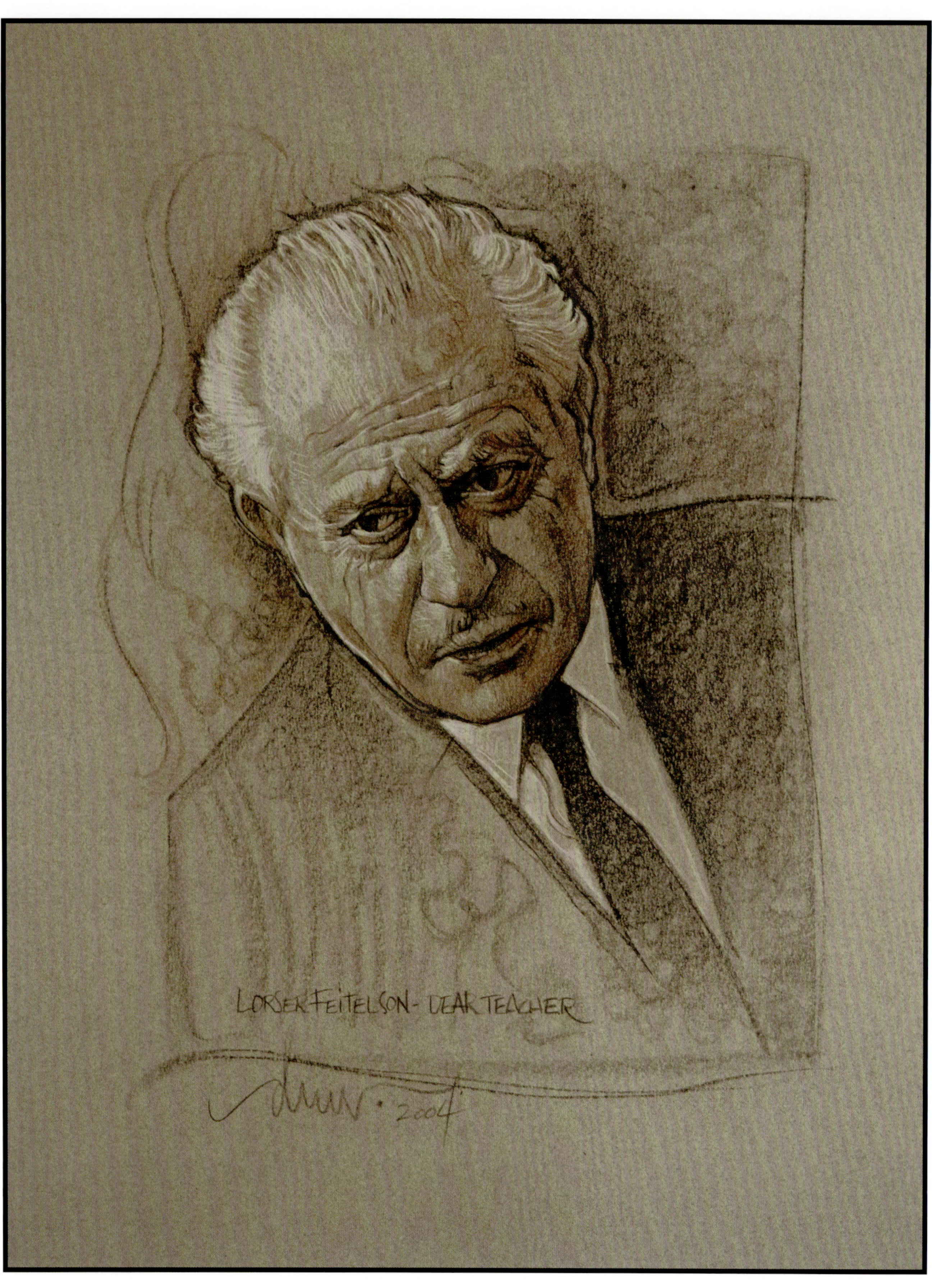
LORSER FEITELSON - DEAR TEACHER

CAVEAT

One dictionary definition of "oeuvre" is "the total output of a writer or artist (or a substantial part of it)." As you read through this book and contemplate the works presented herein, please dispense with the idea that this book is the ultimate and final word on Drew Struzan's career. He is, after all, still very much alive.

If you are aware of early works that are not included in this catalogue, please understand that tracking down those pieces for compilation is an impossible task. In the early days, Drew was a freelance illustrator. Once the artwork was handed over to the client, it simply disappeared. For all Drew knows, these originals were tossed into a trash bin or hidden away in someone's private collection. One thing is certain, the money he was paid for the job was appallingly slight, barely enough to buy food, let alone spring for the expense of a quality reproduction.

Even assuming the images could be collected, a truly definitive book of ALL his work to date would consist of postage stamp-sized images packed into about 200 pages. For these reasons, *Oeuvre* seeks to encompass the full *range* of work that has occupied Drew's career, rather than include the full complement.

MUSIC

In the 1960s and '70s, the music industry was unbelievably open-ended. It welcomed young illustrators and gave them a lot of freedom to create. But album cover work did little to offset the poverty of the early days of Drew's career. The pay was low and the jobs slow in coming. Even with the addition of his wife's salary, his young family still couldn't rise above poverty level, so Drew went to an employment agency to find steady work.

He interviewed at WED (Walter E. Disney) and a boutique design studio, Pacific Eye & Ear, that specialized in album covers. Both companies offered him a job. He chose to go to work for the design studio. "I liked the idea of painting album covers where my work would be seen rather than paint backgrounds for animated films where no one would ever take note.

"The music business was hot in the '70s and album covers were very prominent in the marketplace," Drew recalls, "A wonderful format for artwork, twelve inches square." A steady stream of musicians came through the studio in search of designs to grace their latest creations.

When Black Sabbath finished the tracks for *Sabbath Bloody Sabbath* (1973), Ozzy Osbourne came calling. He knew what he wanted—an illustration of a man dying. In those days artists had both the front and back covers with which to work, so the decision was made to create a study in contrasts. The front cover would be as hauntingly frightening as the band expected—a 'bad' man dying, replete with startling symbolism, like '666', a large skull, snakes, and demons. The back of the album portrayed a 'good' man dying, surrounded by friends—peaceful, even hopeful.

"I tried to have something to say," Drew comments. "It is the same people on the front and the back, just the setting is different. Life is a matter of choice. The covers remain a source of contemplation to this day."

Alice Cooper was a continuous client at the studio. Drew did two of his albums, *Alice Cooper's Greatest Hits* (1974) and *Welcome to My Nightmare* (1975). Alice came by every day to watch Drew paint. "I had more fun with Drew than I did recording the record," Alice recalls. *Rolling Stone* magazine ranked Alice Cooper's *Welcome to My Nightmare* as one of the top 100 album covers of all time.

When Mary Travers recorded her second solo album, *Circles*, in 1974, she hired the studio to do the album cover. "I want it to be photographic," she said. "I don't want an illustration. Every time somebody paints me, they make me look ugly." Undaunted, Drew painted her portrait and below it placed a photograph held in her hand.

Mary saw the artwork, boarded a plane to Los Angeles, and thanked Drew personally with a dozen yellow roses. It was a magical time as Peter, Paul and Mary loomed large on the folk music landscape. Their songs and activism resounded powerfully with Drew's idealistic nature. The artwork created a bridge between the illustrator and the musician. Drew often sent yellow roses backstage when she appeared in concert, and she always sent a fond reply.

Jefferson Airplane, the Modern Jazz Quartet, Iron Butterfly, Black Oak Arkansas, Earth, Wind & Fire, Canned Heat, Tony Orlando and Dawn. The list of musicians for whom Drew created artwork is long and memorable. The work got him noticed. As a result, it wasn't long before he was busy doing movie posters.

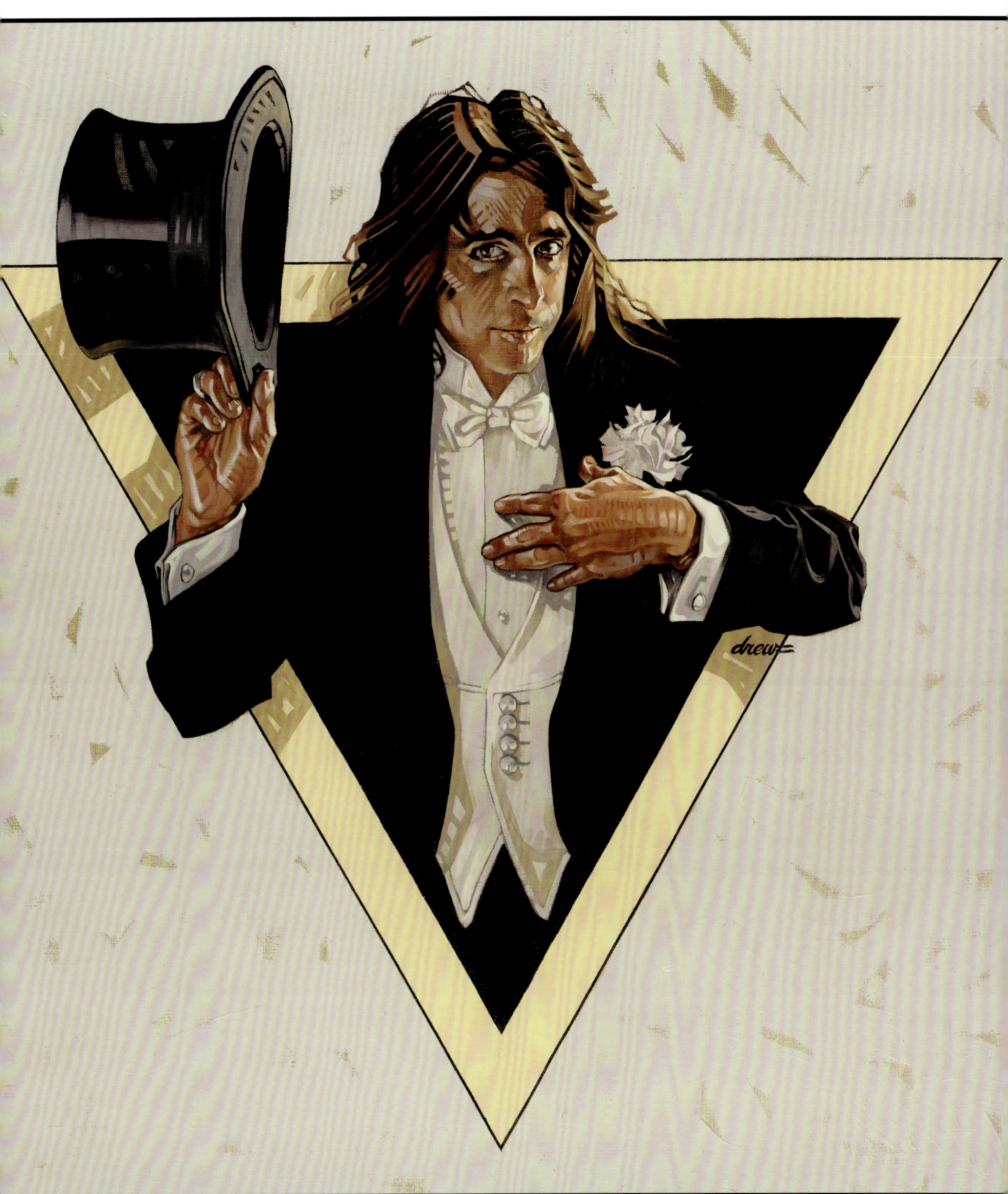
drew

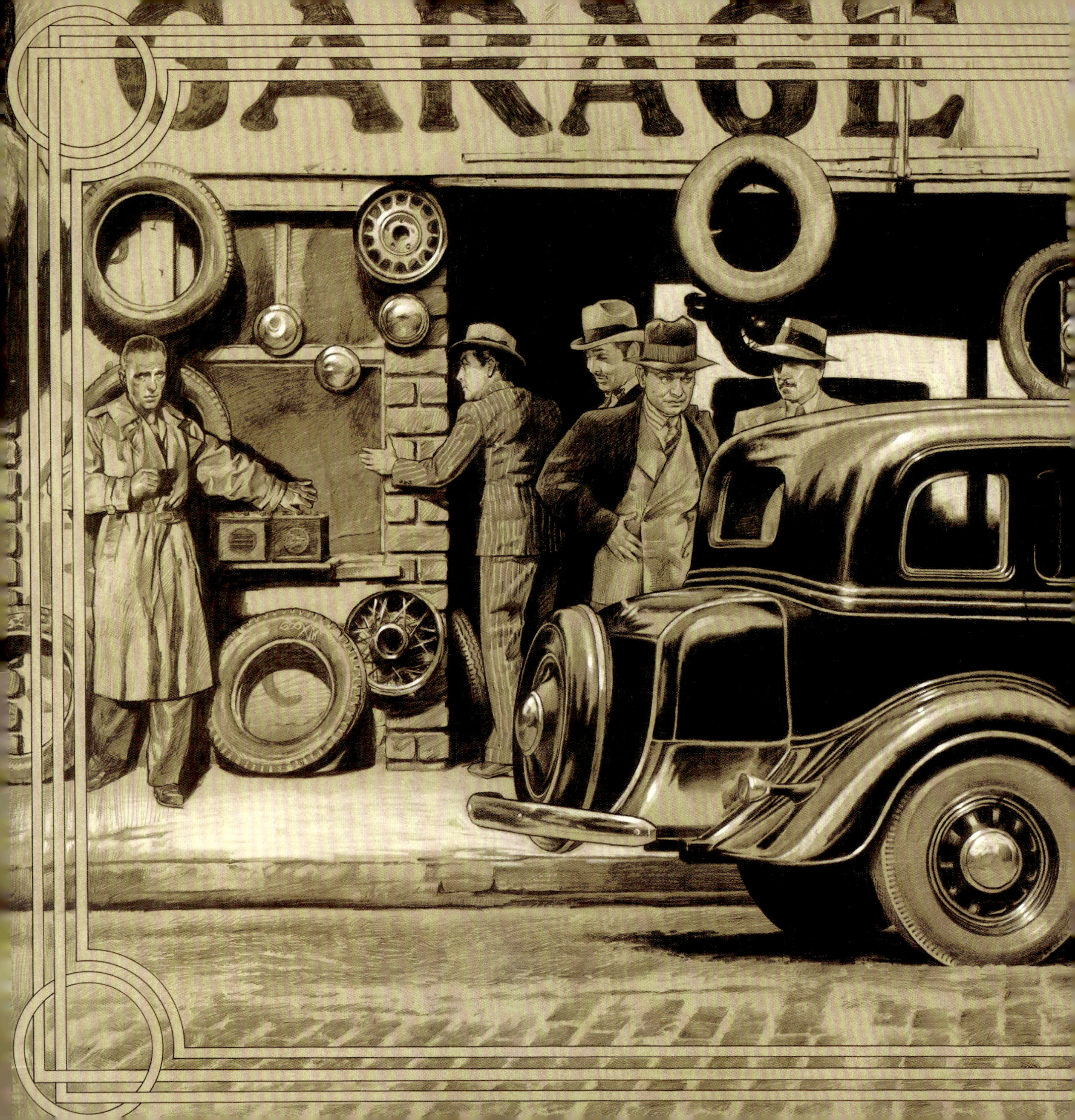
GARAGE

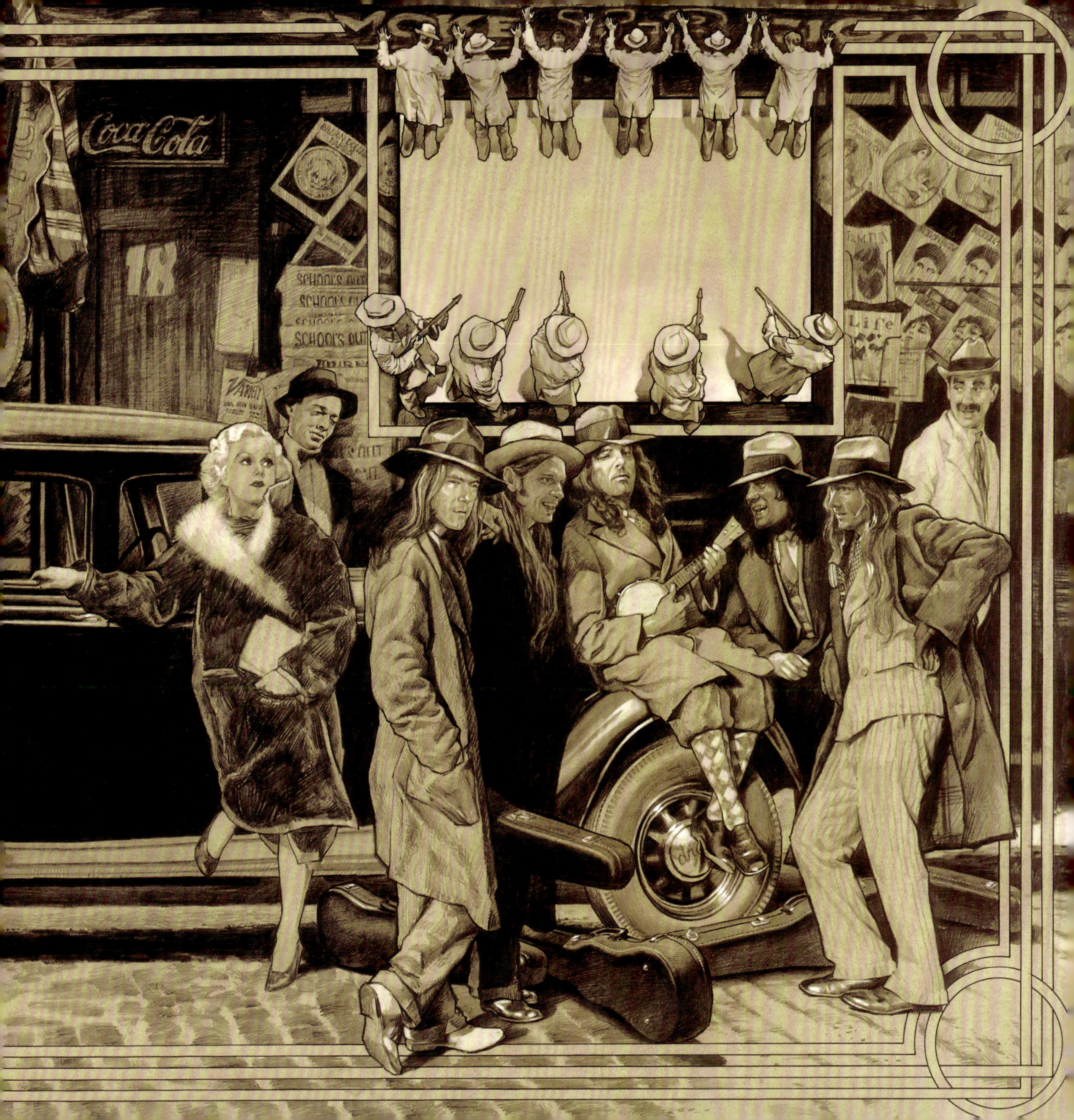

Coca-Cola
18
SCHOOL'S OUT
SCHOOL'S OUT
SCHOOL'S OUT
Life

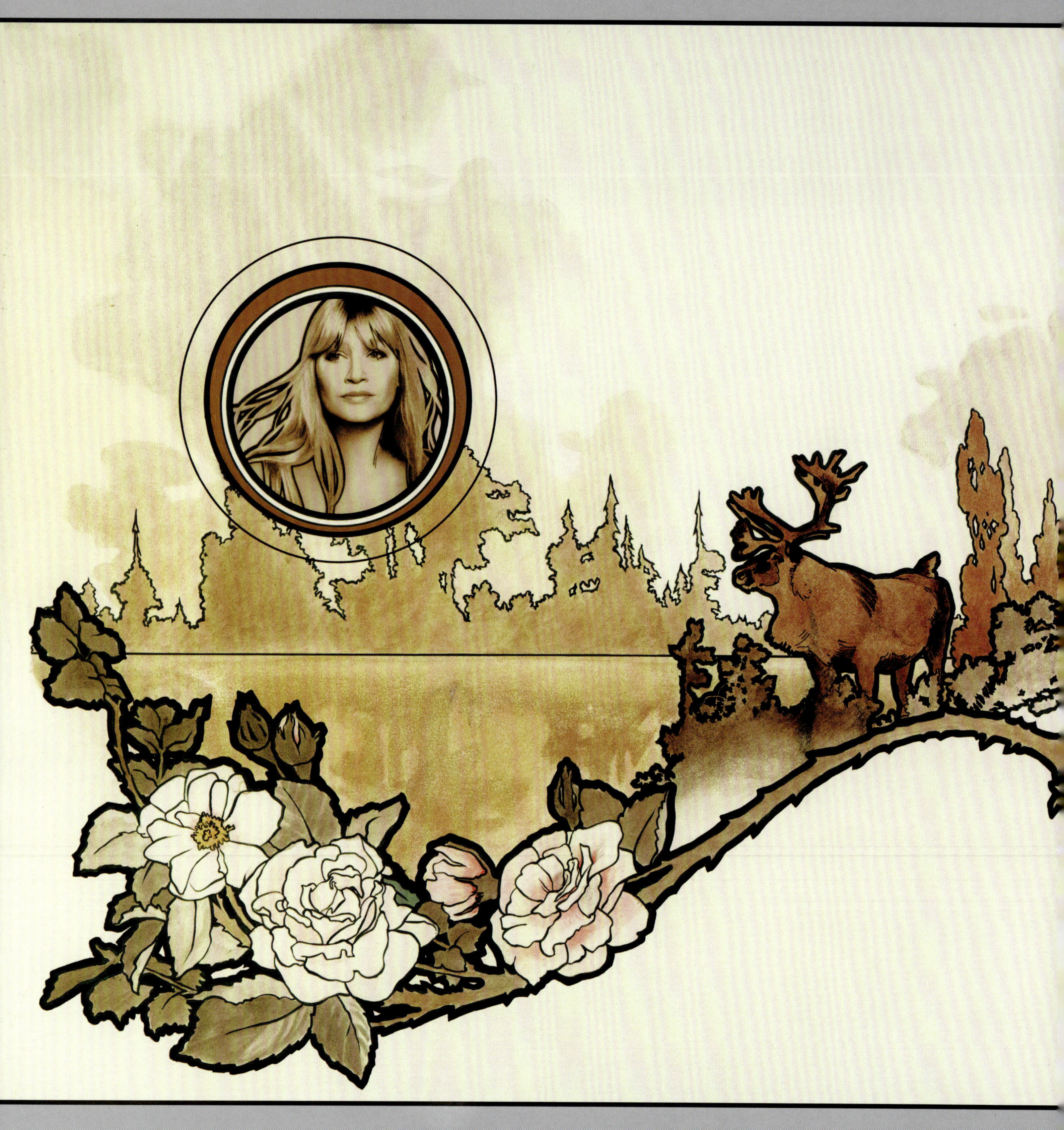

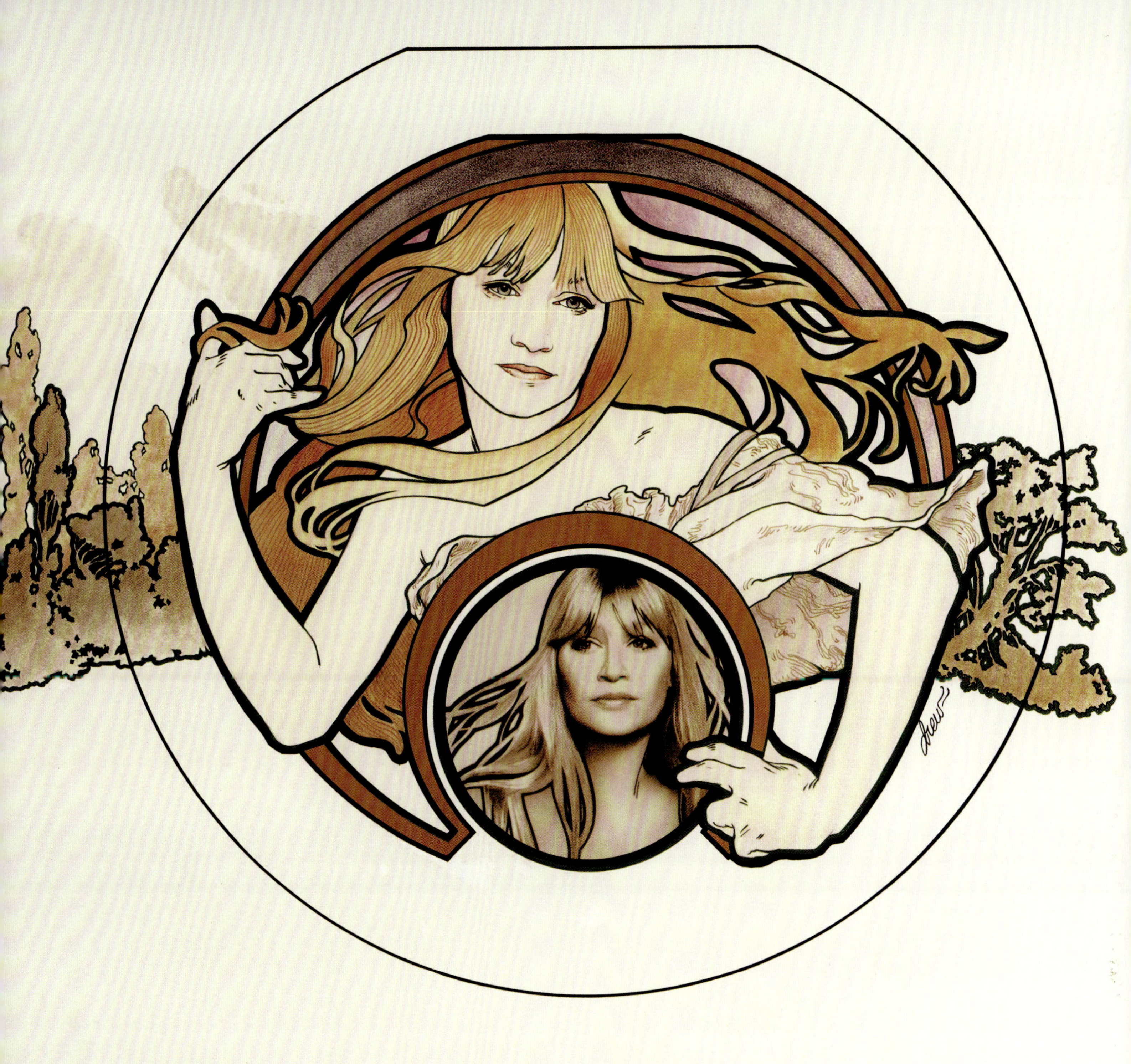

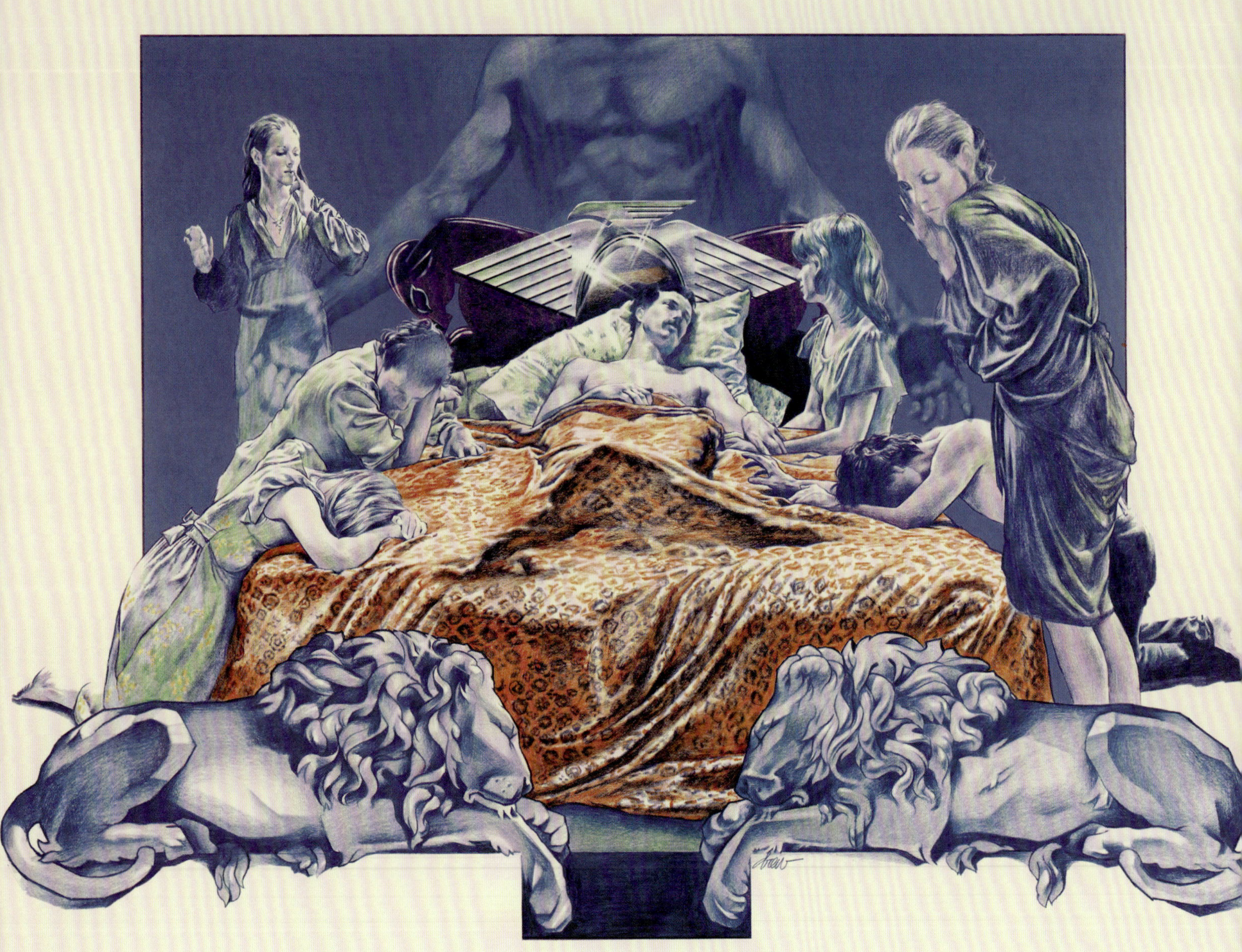

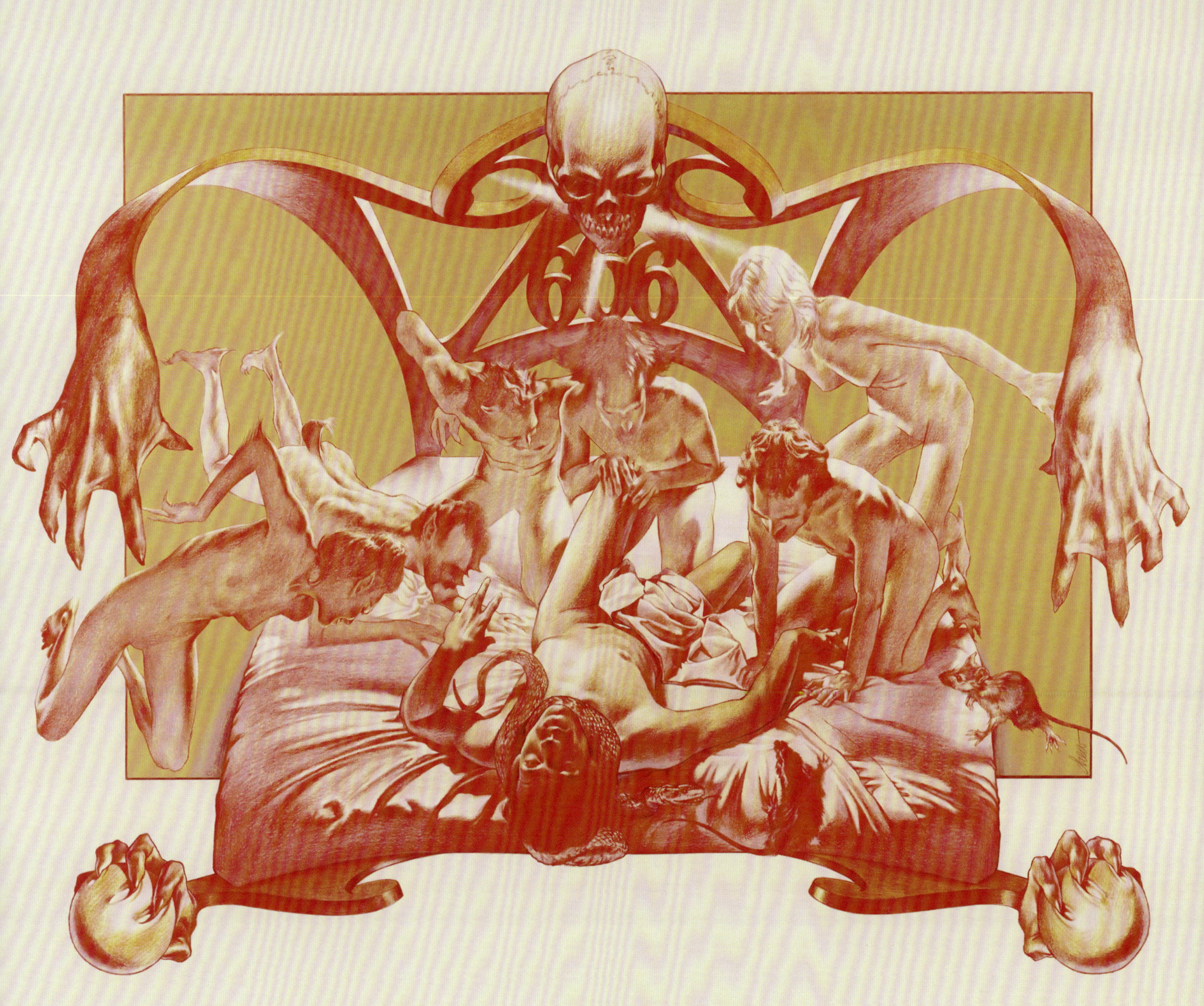
666

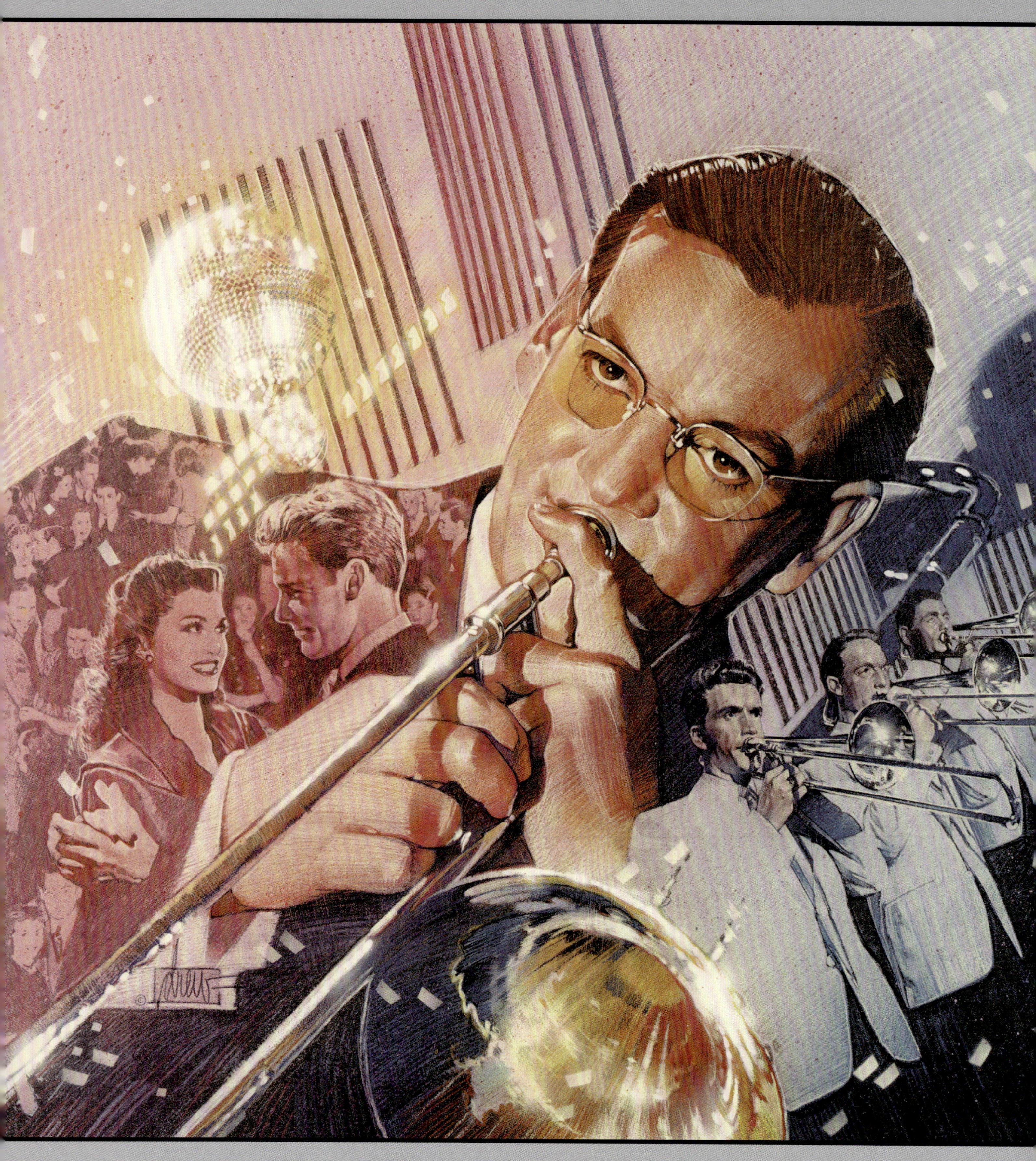

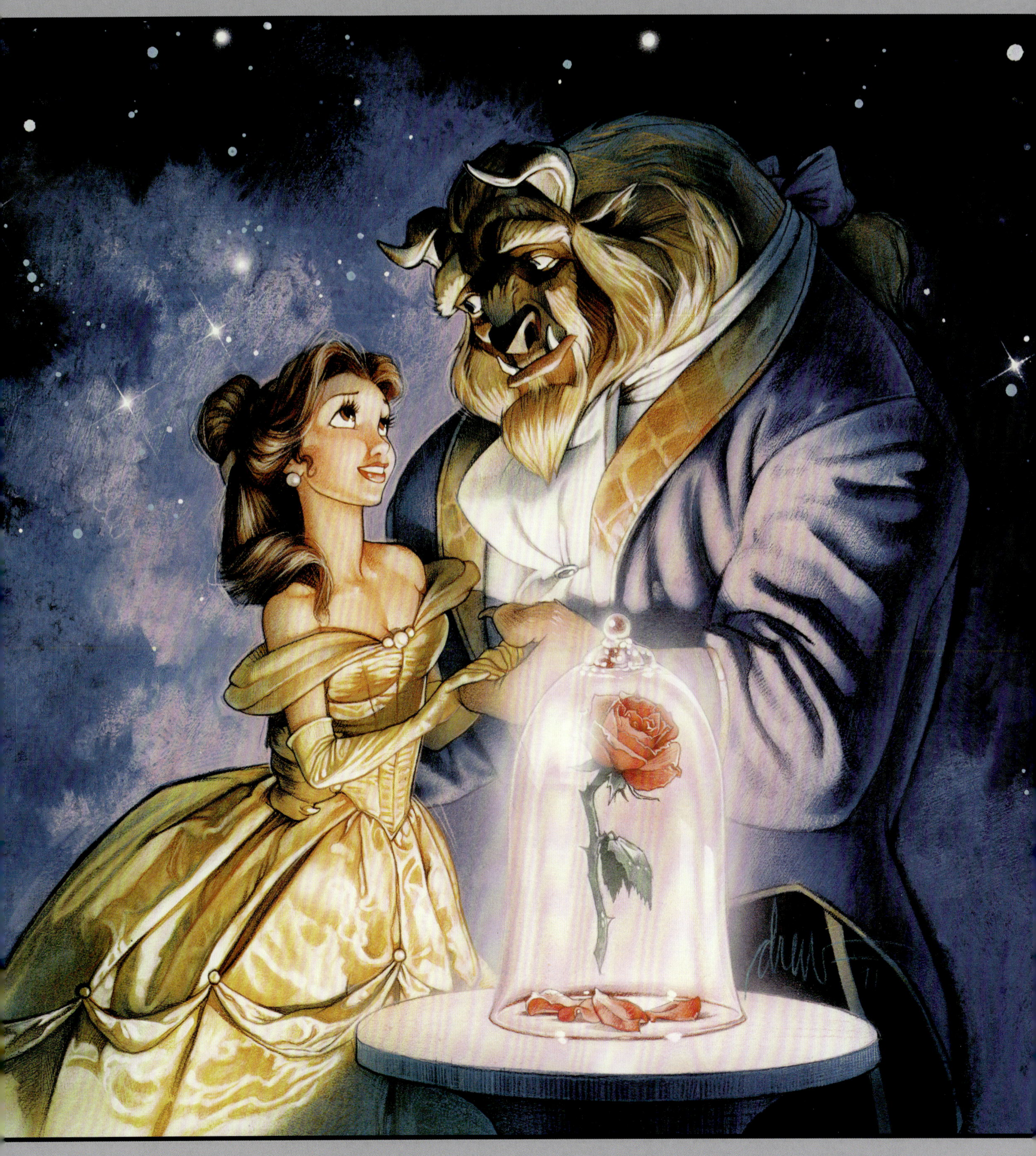

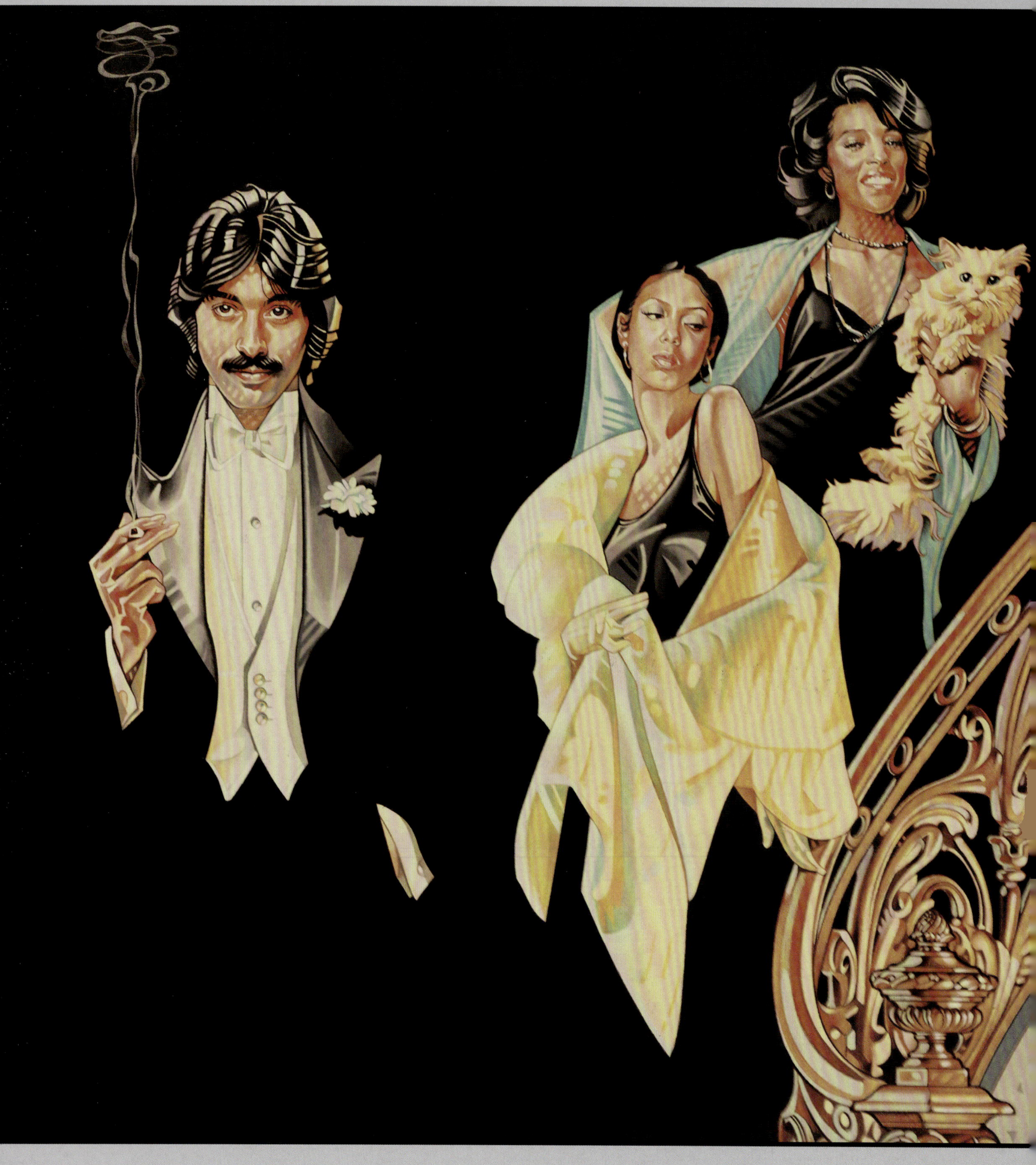

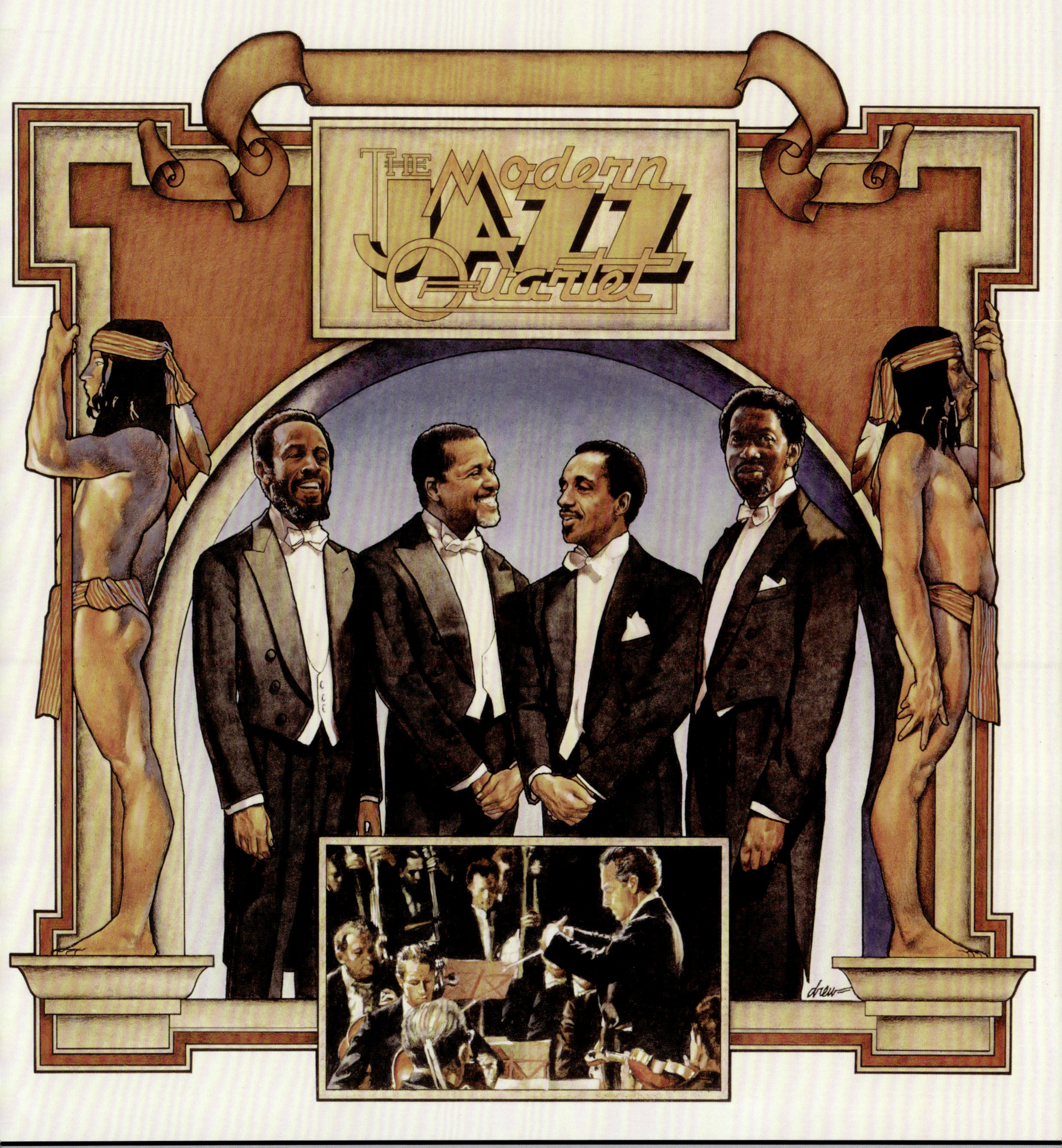
The Modern Jazz Quartet
drew

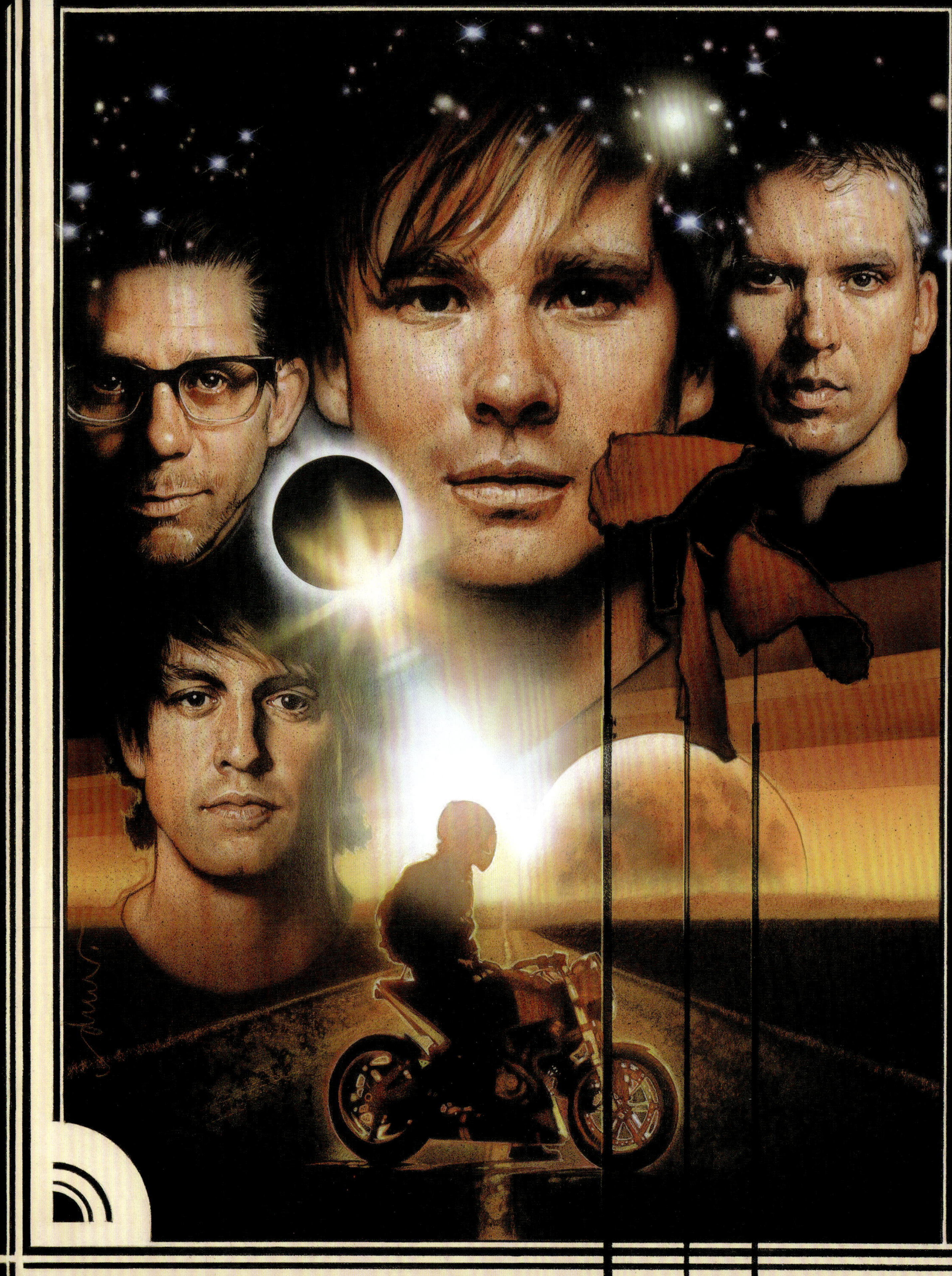

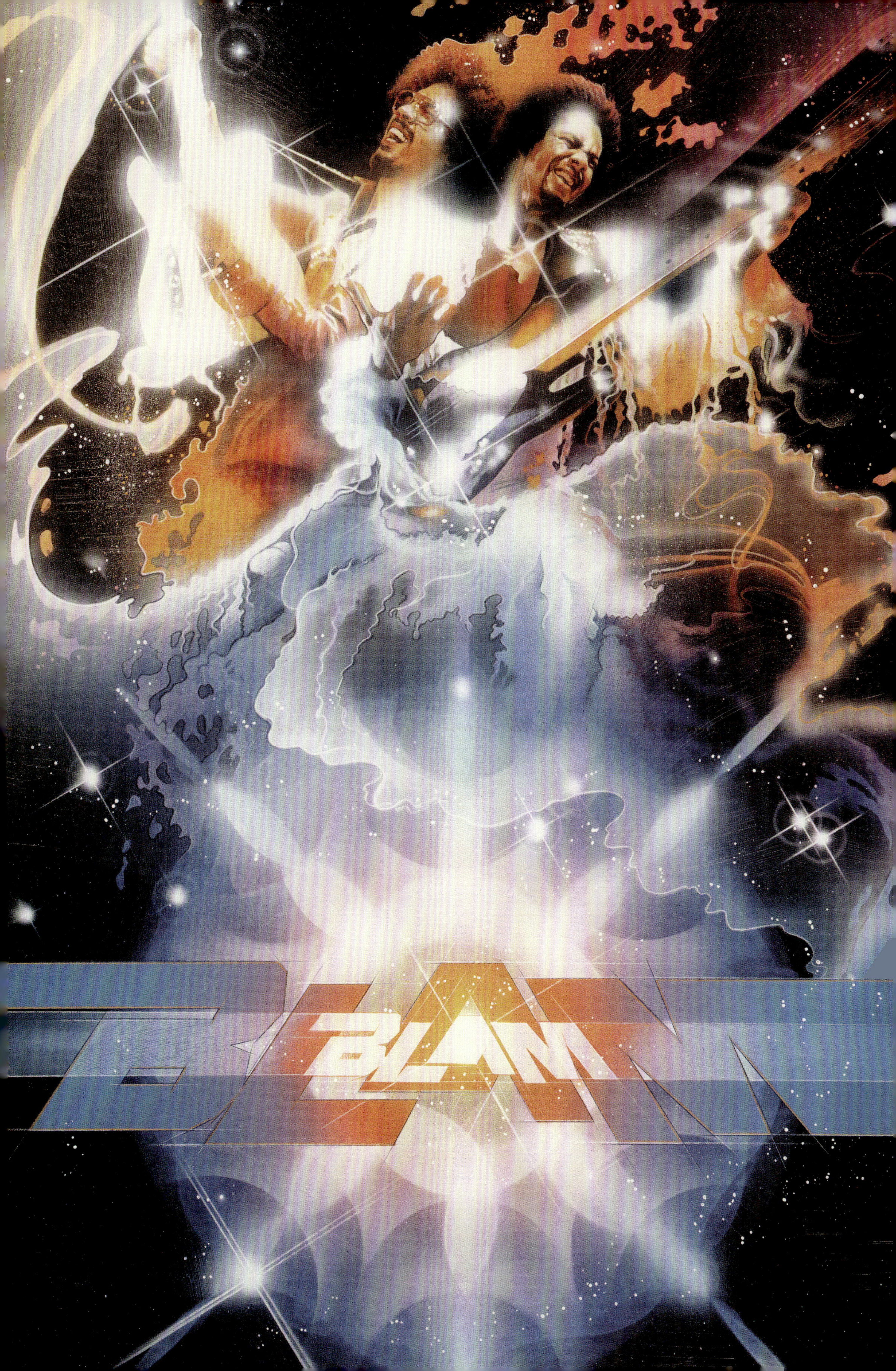
BLAM

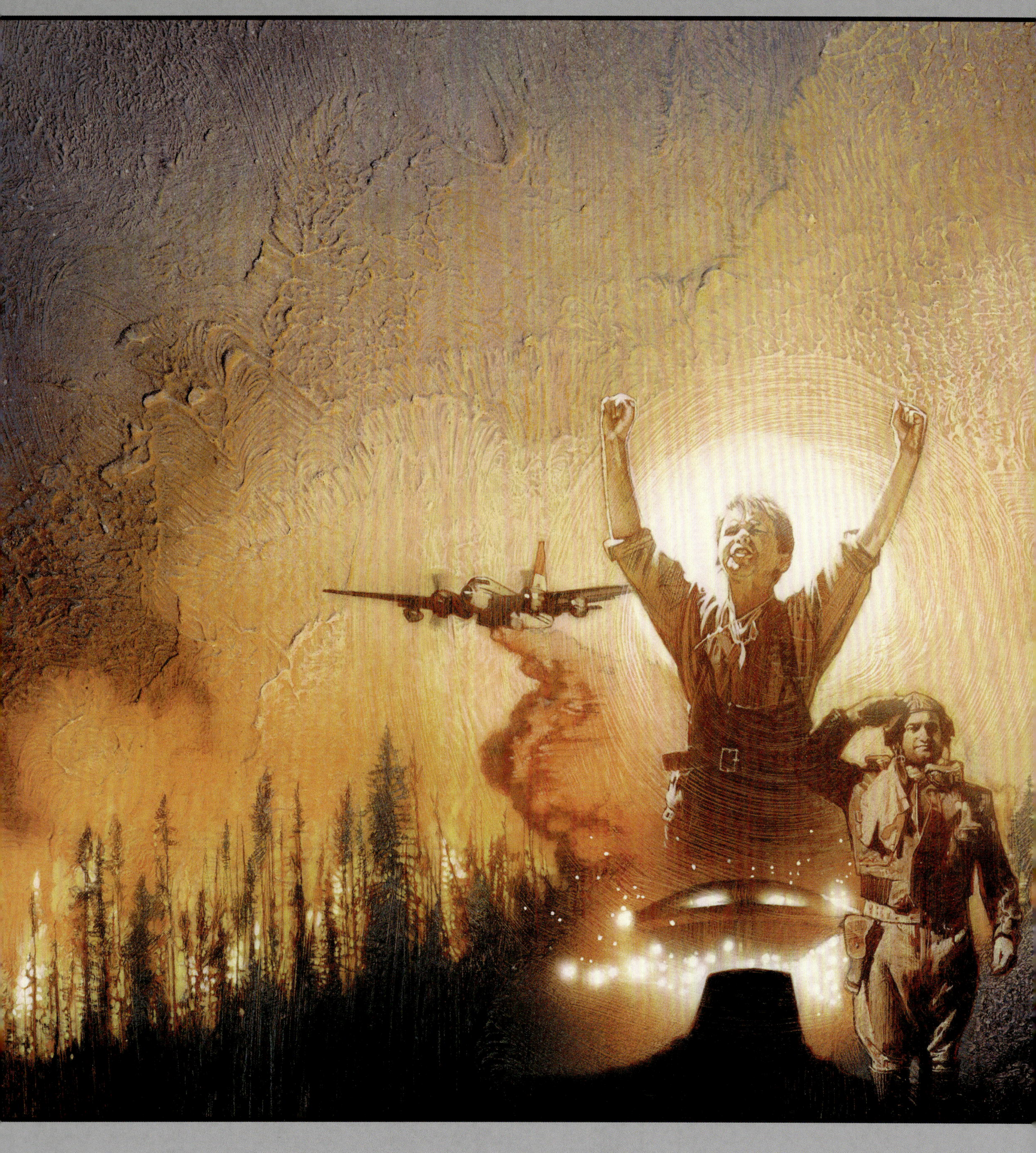

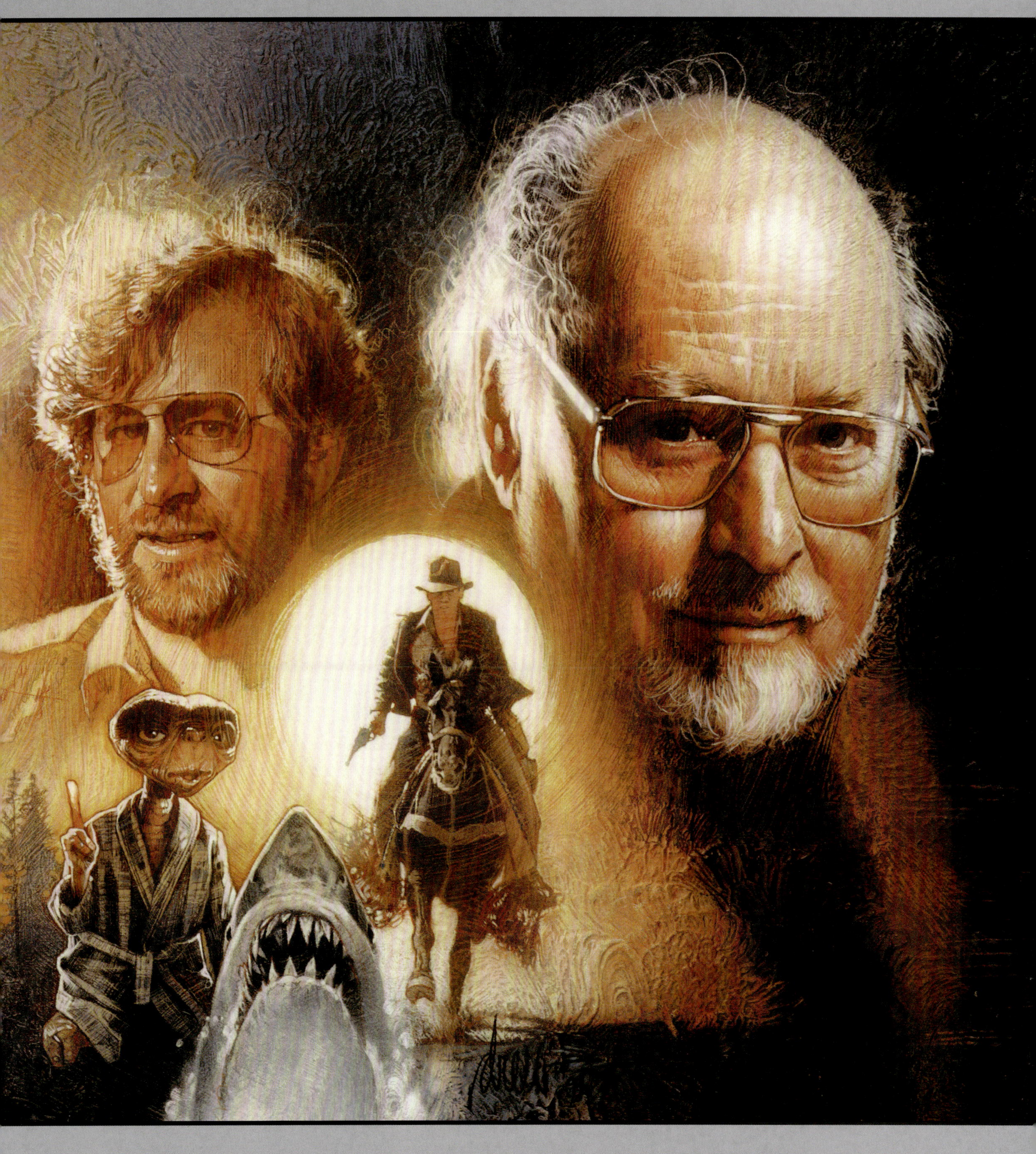

MOVIES

"Movie posters brought me out of the dark ages and into the light. Everybody sees movies and most of them see the posters. Painting for such a large audience means my work is seen around the world. Artists always wish for audiences, but seldom find them. Having my work seen by people everywhere has been the biggest blessing of my professional life."

The job of a poster illustrator, simply put, is to boil down two hours of story into a single image that will motivate people to go see the film. The deadlines are horrendous. It's not uncommon to work seven days and a hundred hours a week. Passion for the job and unrelenting diligence kept Drew going. His dedication was rewarded via the honor of working with some of the greatest talent in Hollywood.

Indiana Jones, who has been called "an ordinary man in extraordinary circumstances," remains one of Drew's favorite subjects. "Indy is hopeful because he's not a superhero," Drew says. "He is any one of us who is principled, who will face life, his own life. Indy didn't have to be a big story. He stands up and does the right thing. He gets hurt, banged, beat up, but he always sticks to what he believes. That's what makes Indy beautiful and powerful. That's what I tried to portray in the illustrations."

And there's another beloved movie series for which Drew created the iconic poster art. In *Star Wars*, "Vader is Luke's enemy, his foil. Luke saves the universe from the Empire and is forced to come to grips with the fact that his father had the opportunity to do the same, but blew it. Vader had the most power of any Jedi. He had the highest midi-chlorian count of any Force-sensitive by nature, but he didn't stick to his principles. The son put the father to shame. What a grand story. My art has to be about those things."

In 2004, Drew had the pleasure of creating two pieces of art for the tenth anniversary of the release of *The Shawshank Redemption*. One illustration features Red and Andy Dufresne behind bars, and Drew says, "I thought that was what the movie was about, the relationship between the two characters. Plus, I liked the earthiness of it. I put scratches on it to show that it was about real, hard love. When people talk about the movie, they understand that the two men were friends, *real* friends. In my poster, I didn't show the violence that happened to them. Rather, I wanted to show the hopelessness of their situation, but in that, their triumph of spirit. It was great when Andy escaped, but the ending of the film was the perfect fulfillment, freedom to live in peace and beauty. I tried to paint the situation where that's what you wanted for them.

"At this point in time I was asked to do artwork for many other things, but I turned most of it down. I was at my best doing movie posters and I recognized that. Movies made the difference in my career so I am utterly grateful to the industry in general for allowing me to be a part of it."

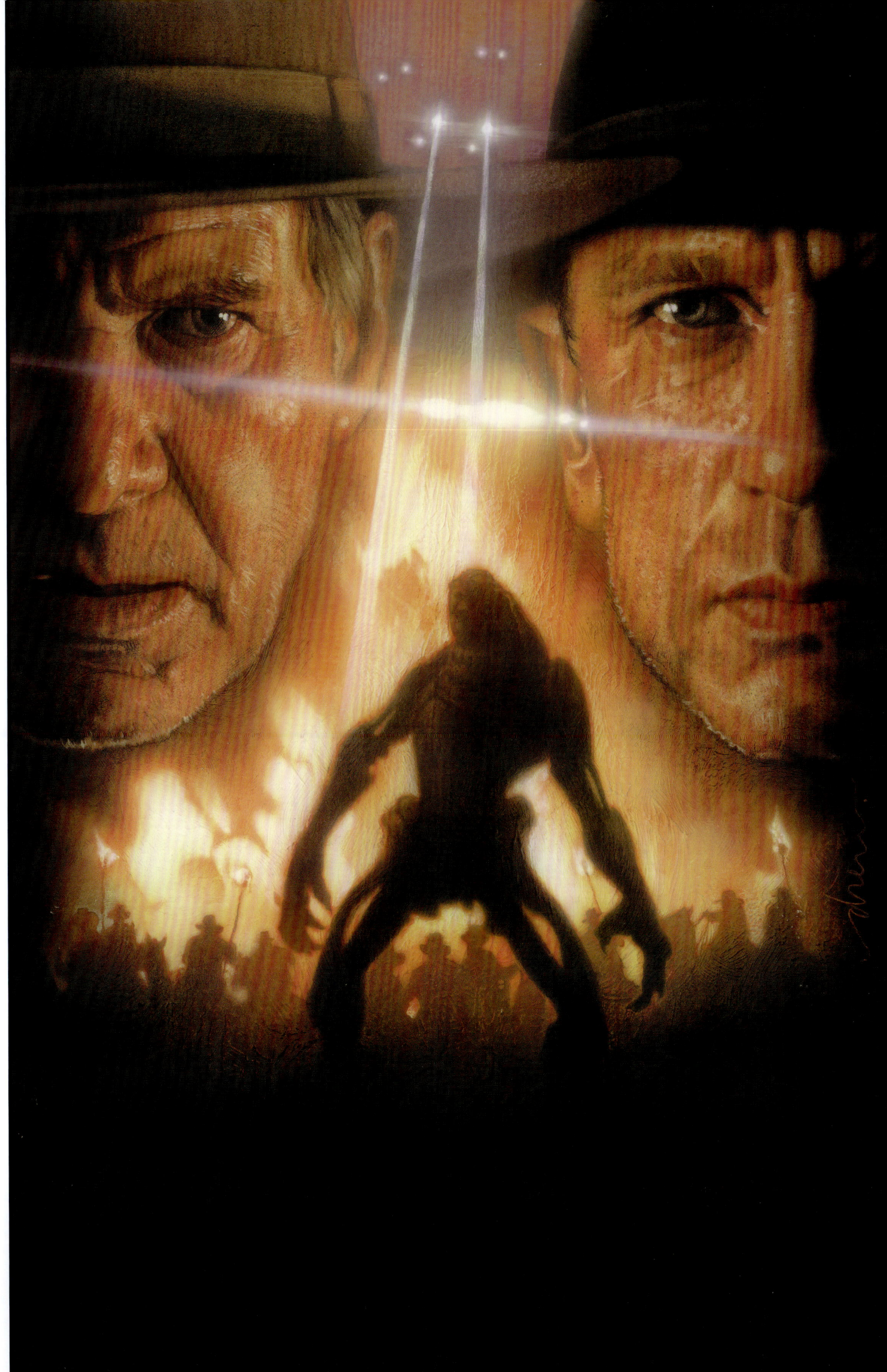

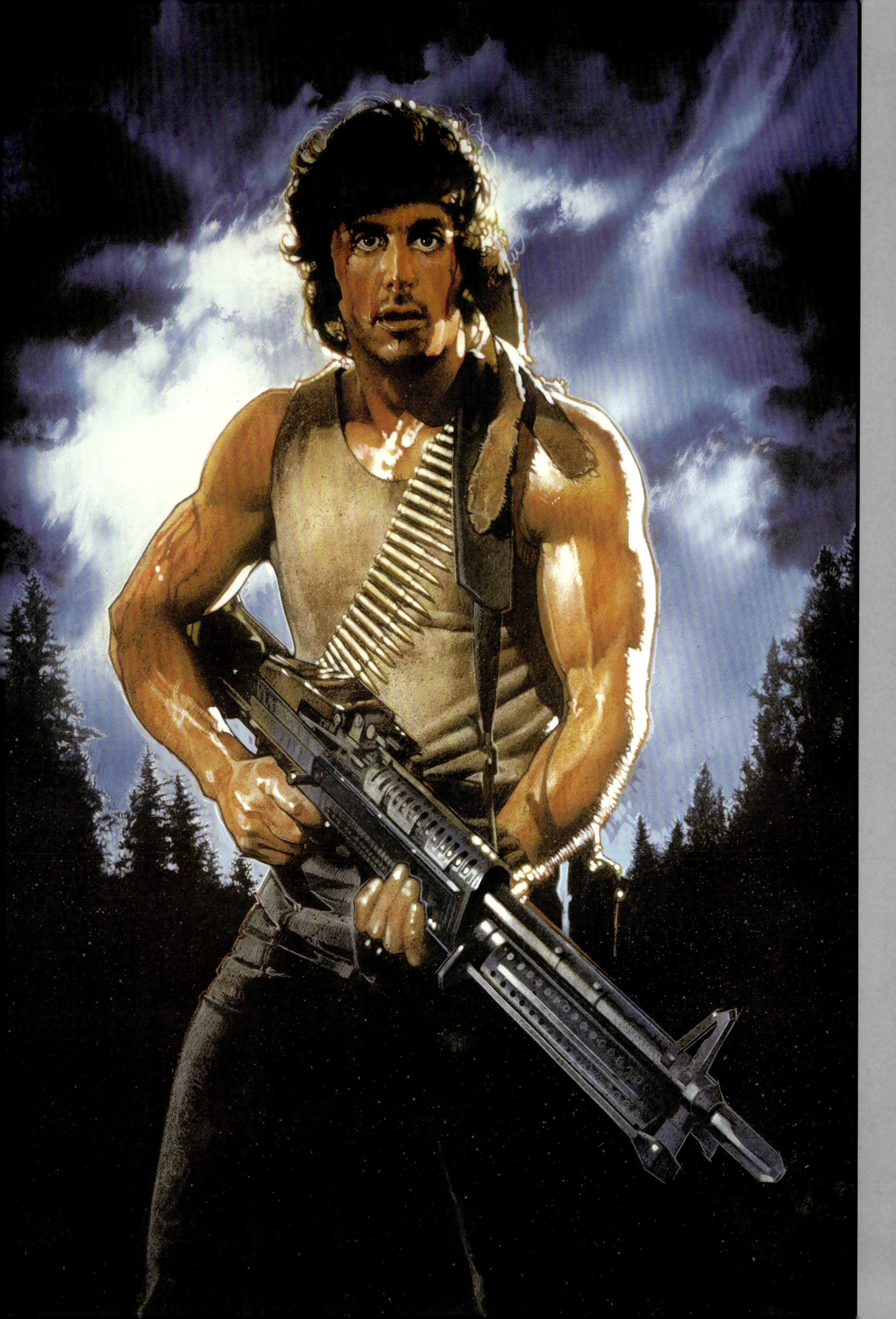

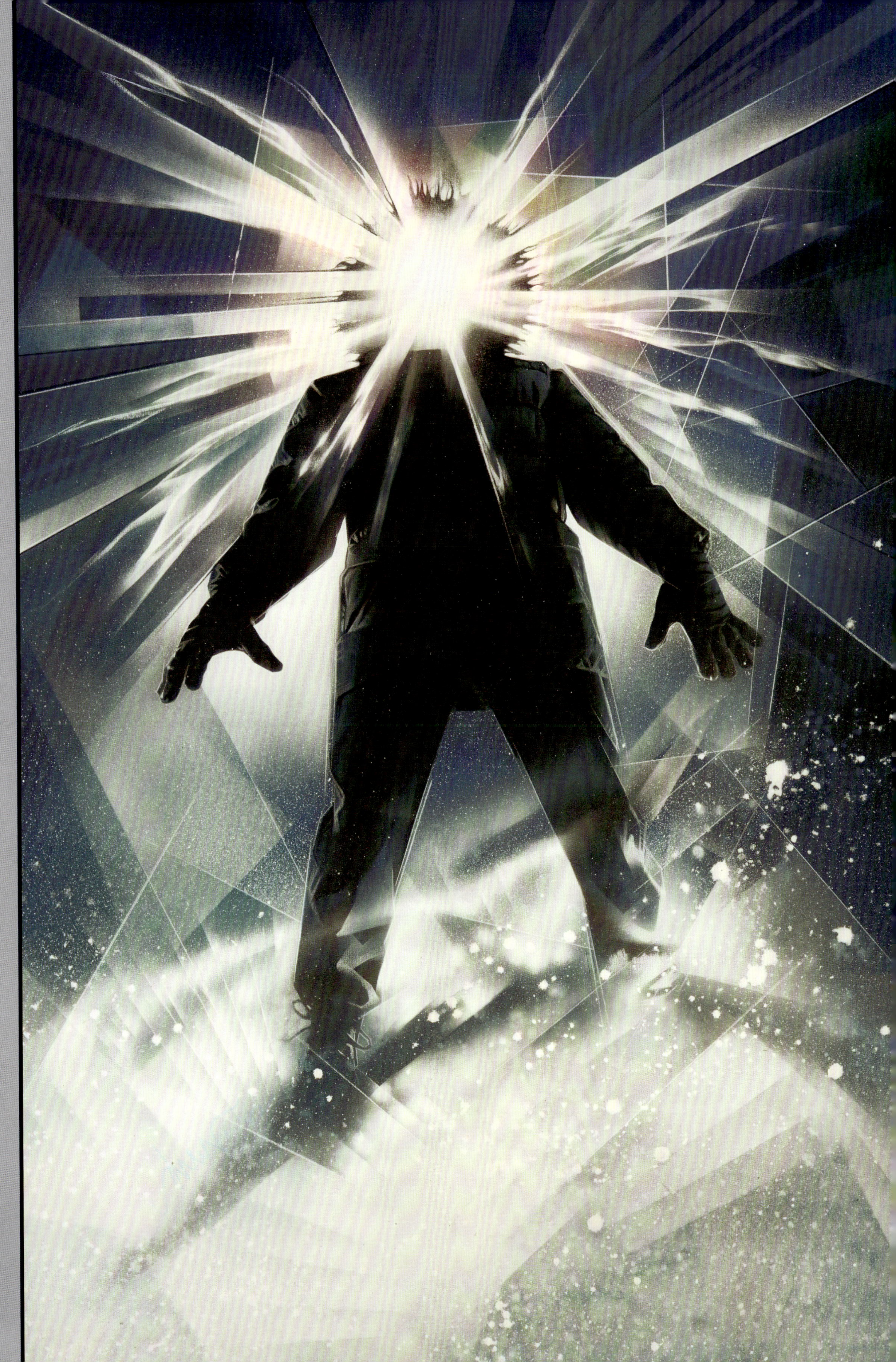

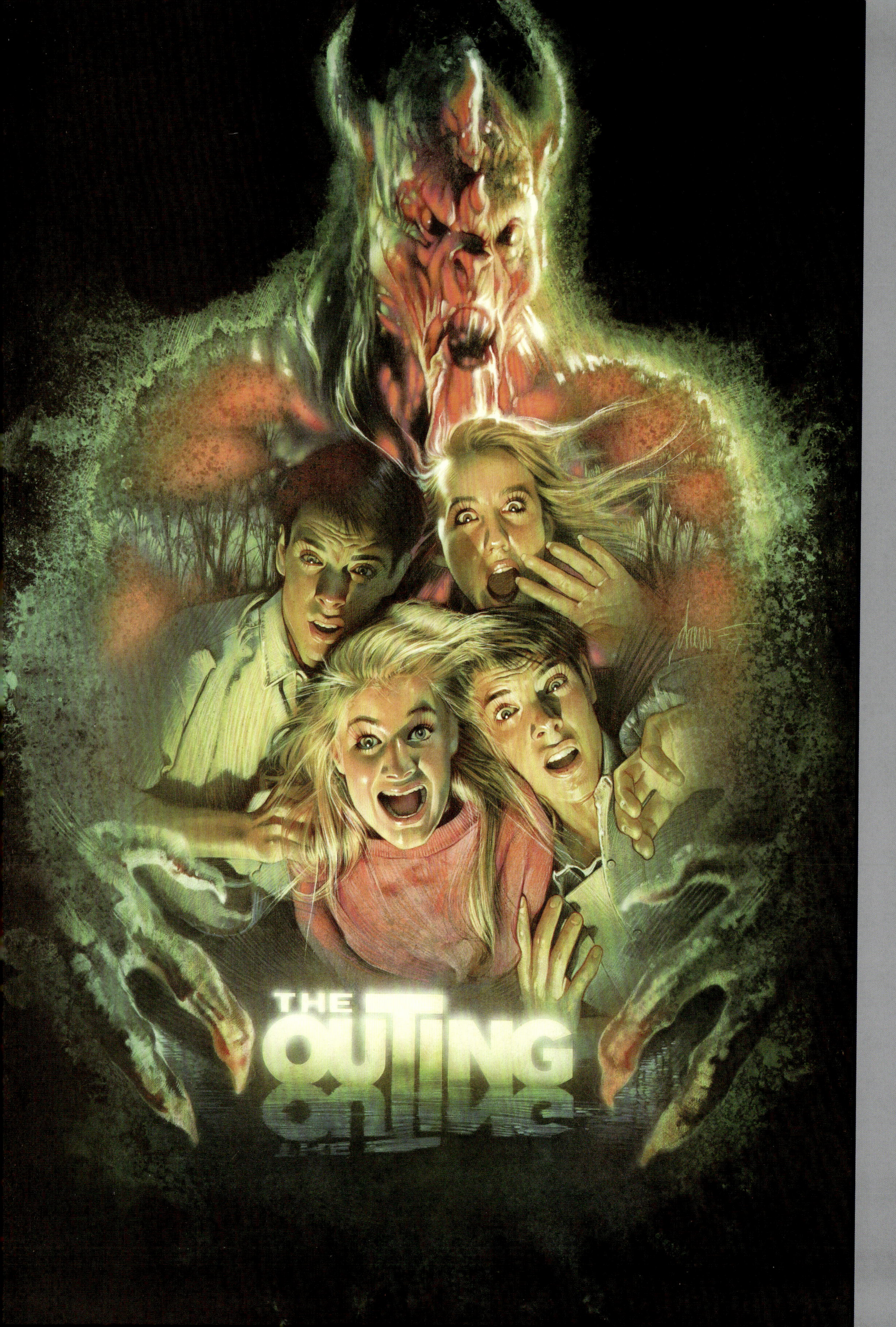
THE
OUTING

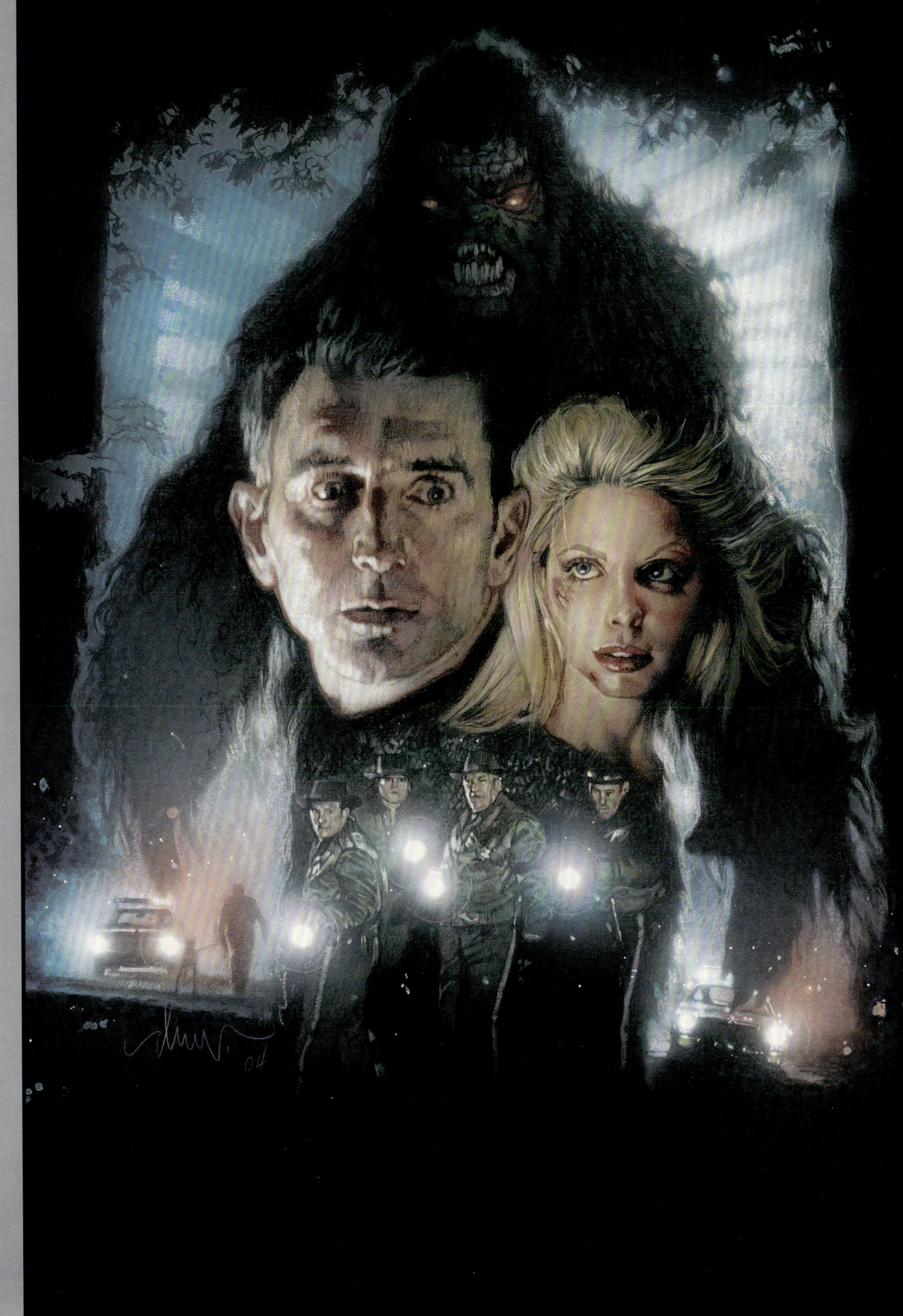

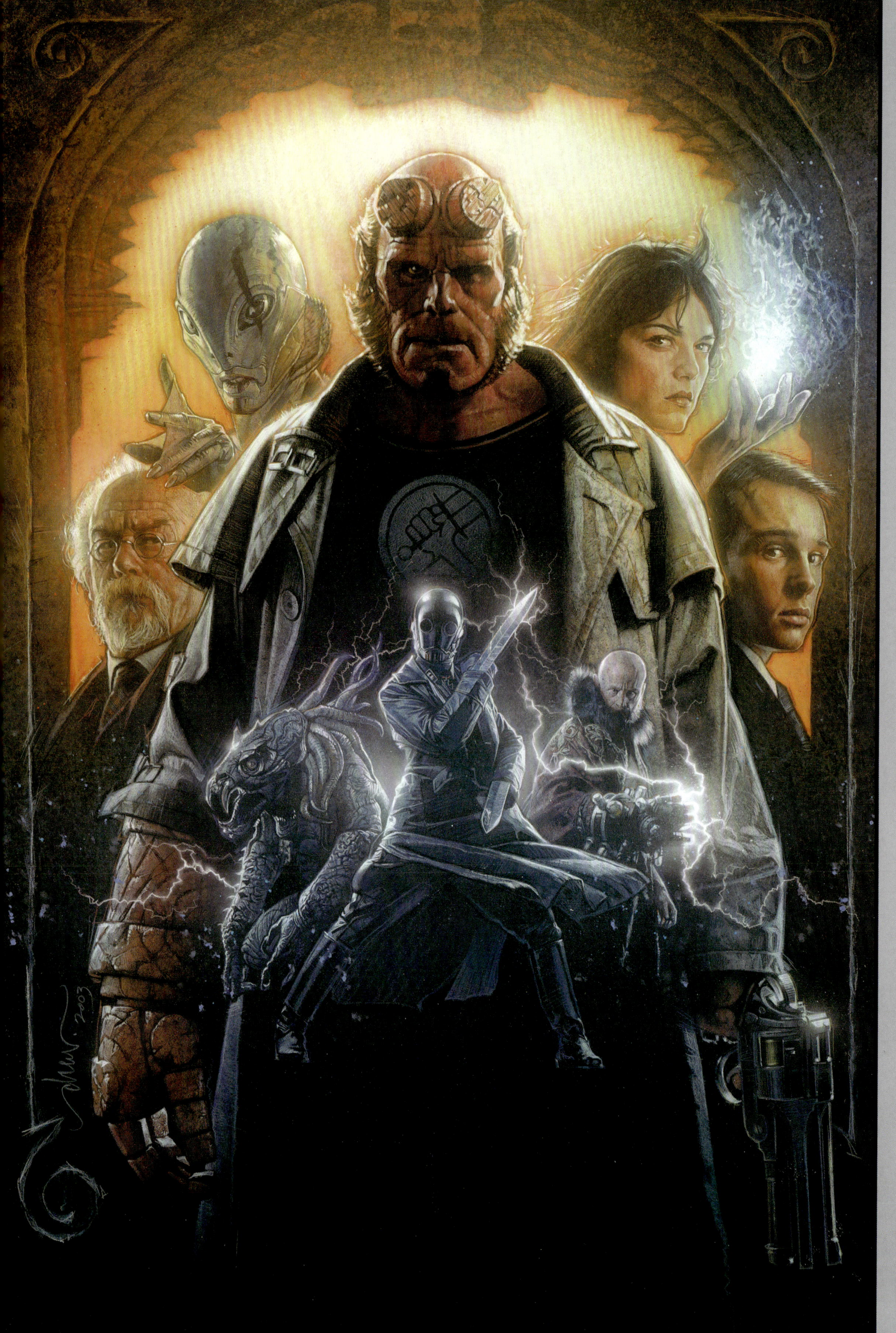

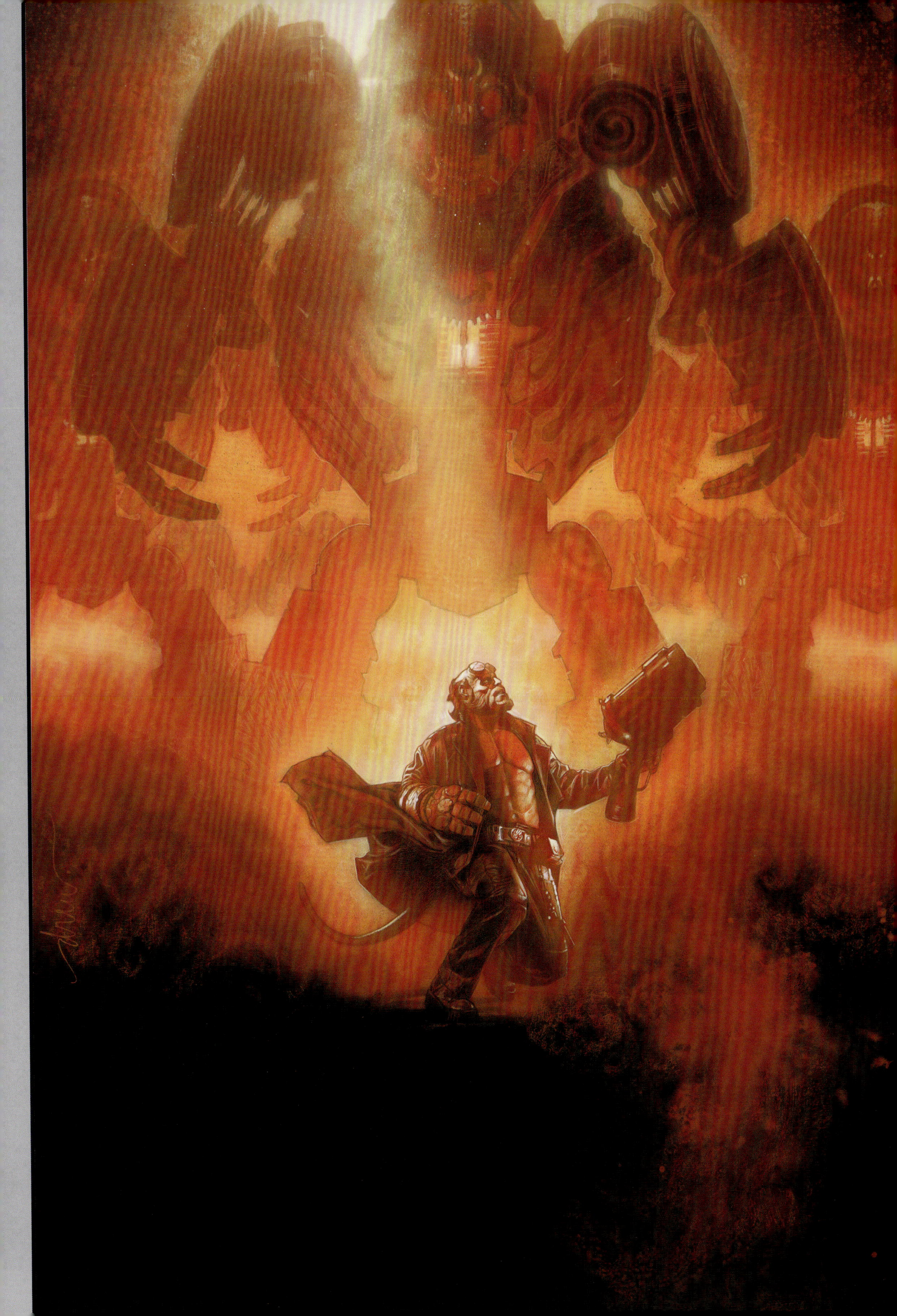

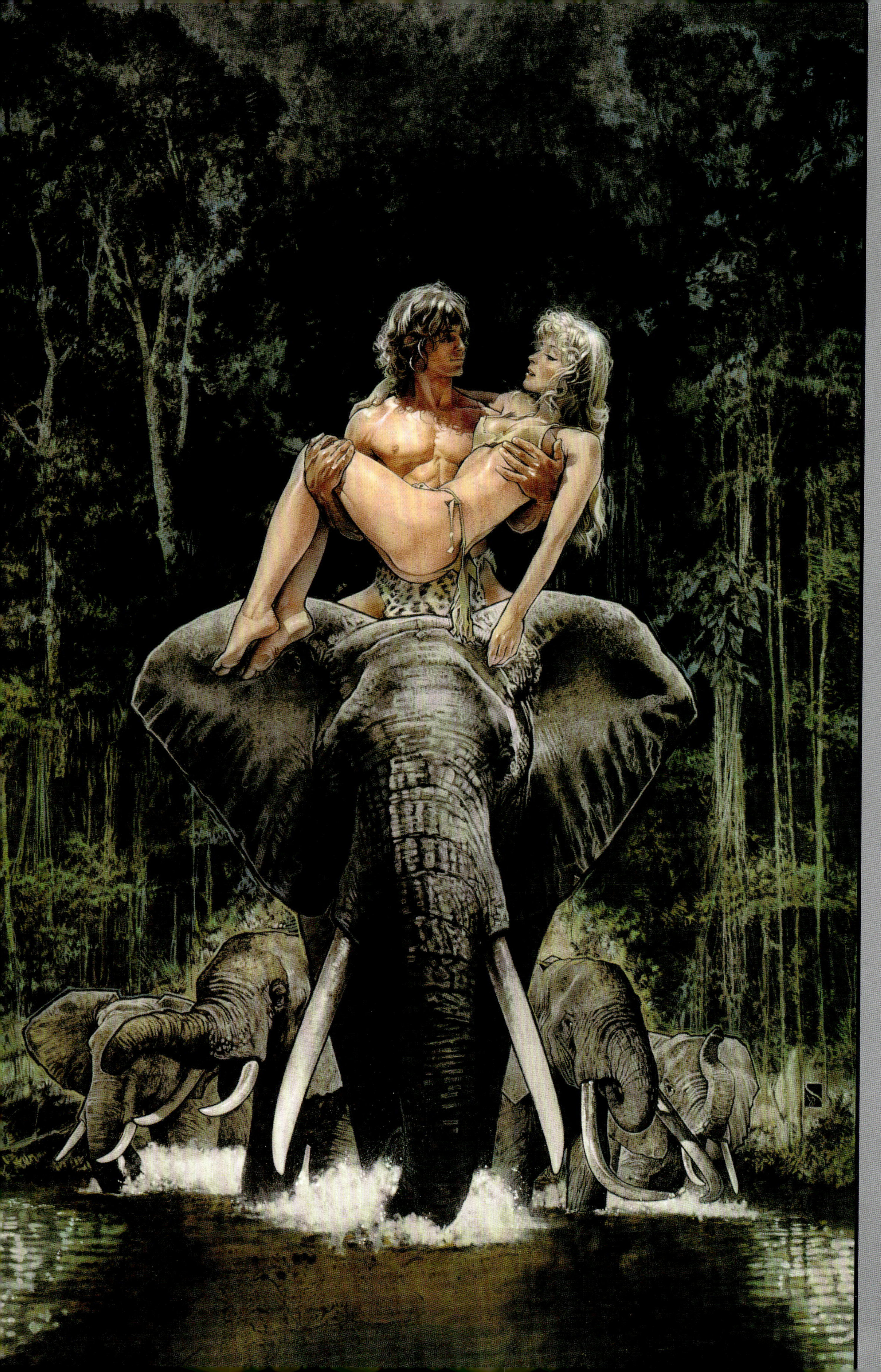

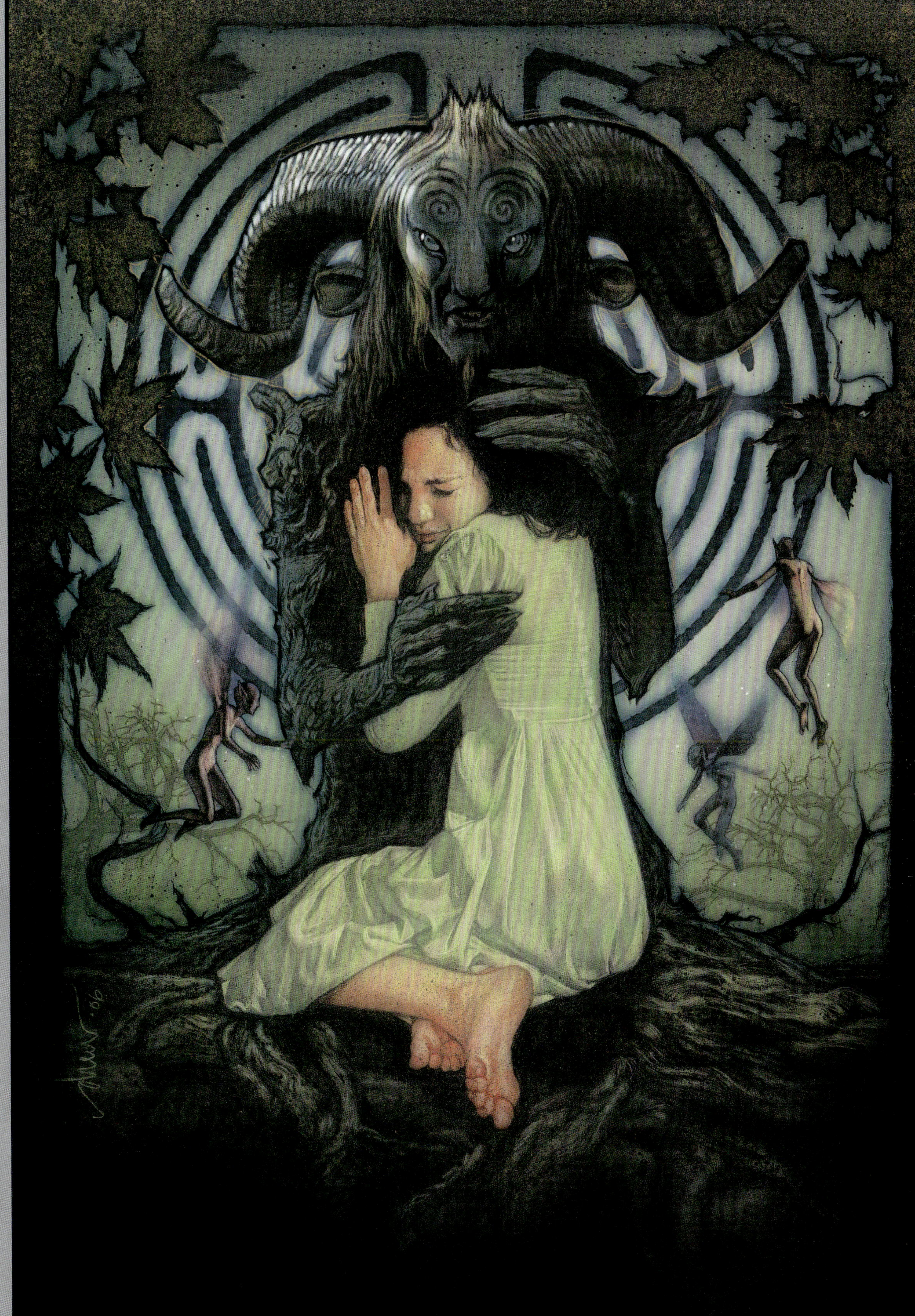

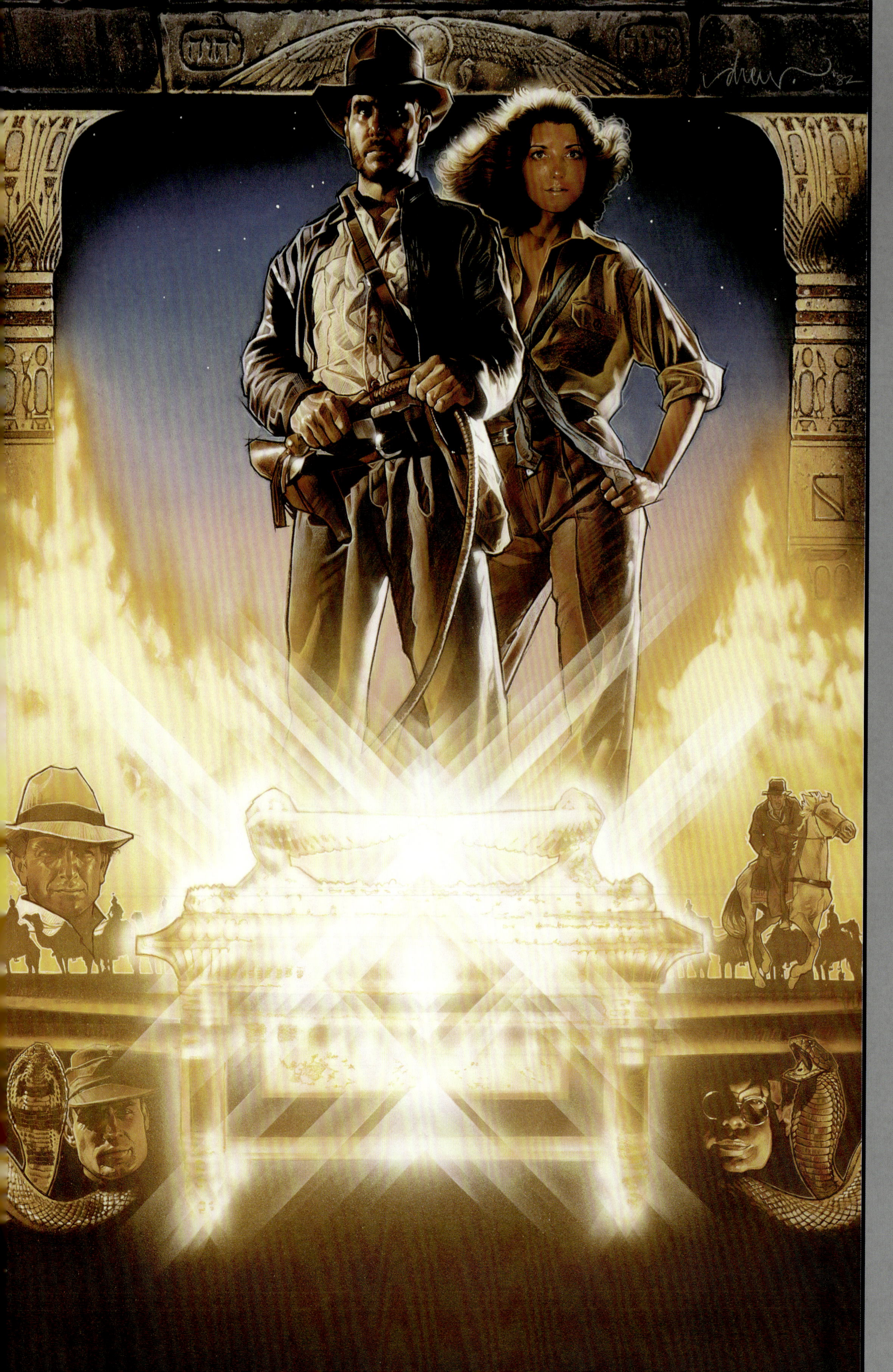

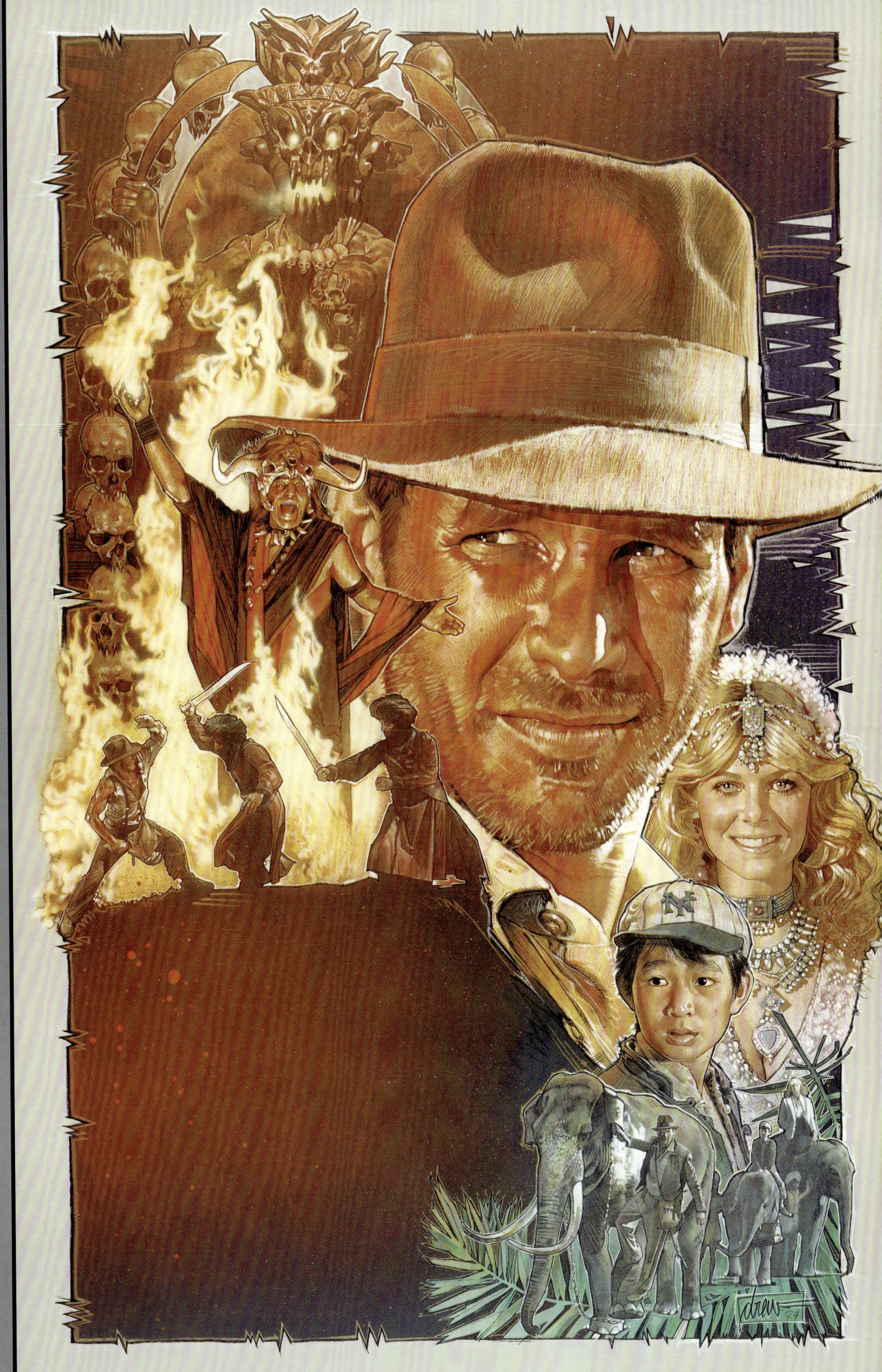
drew

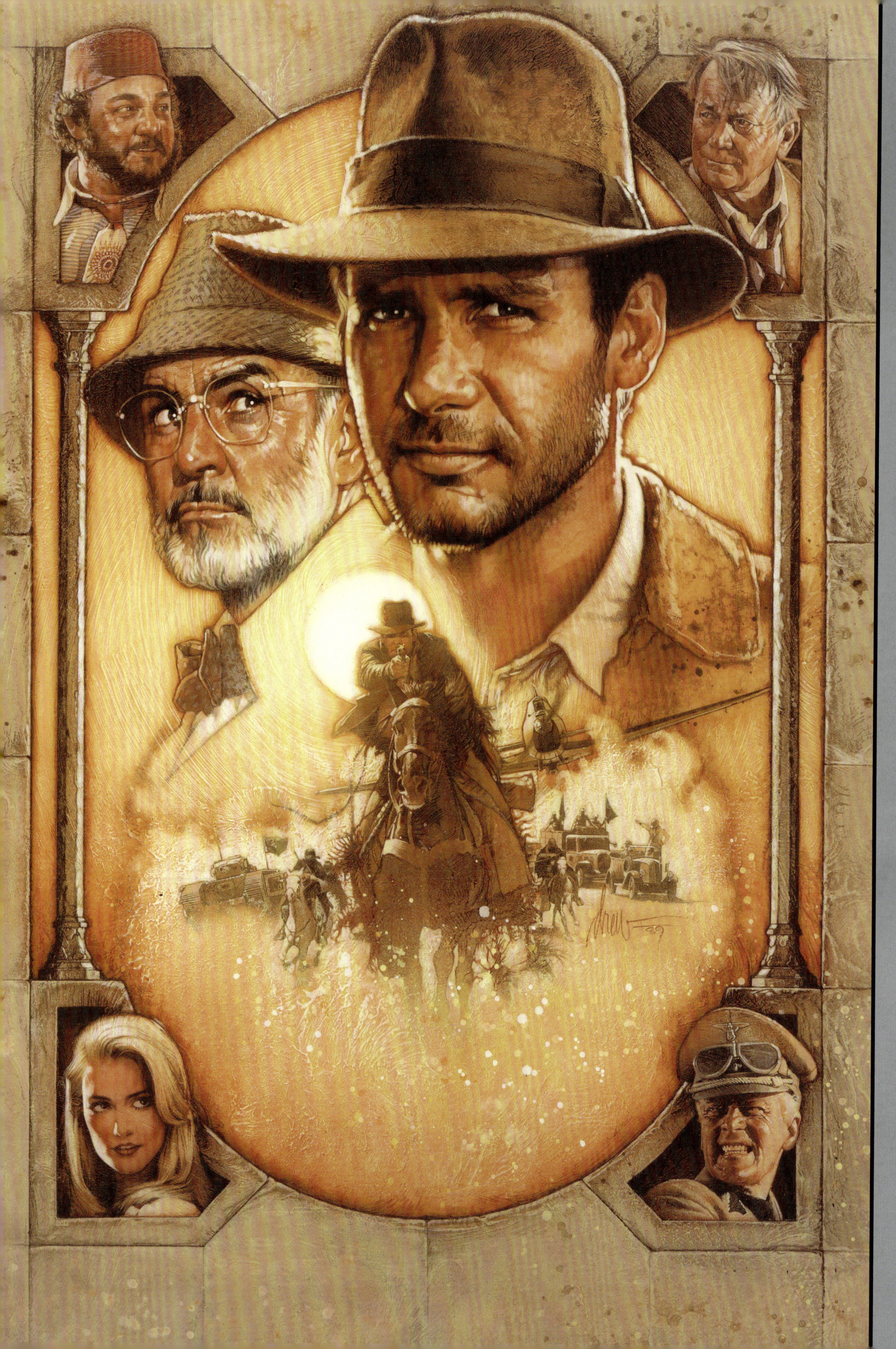

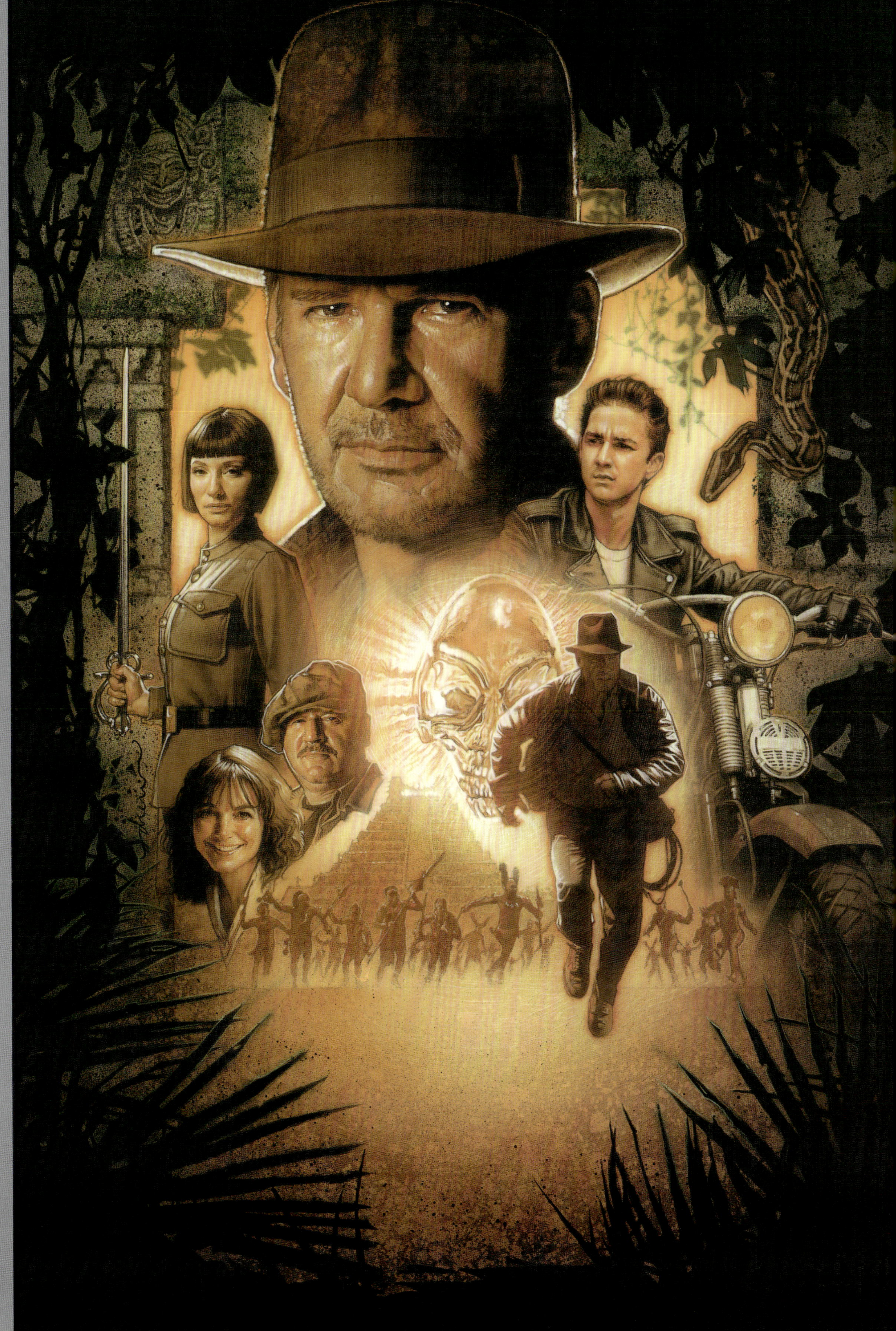

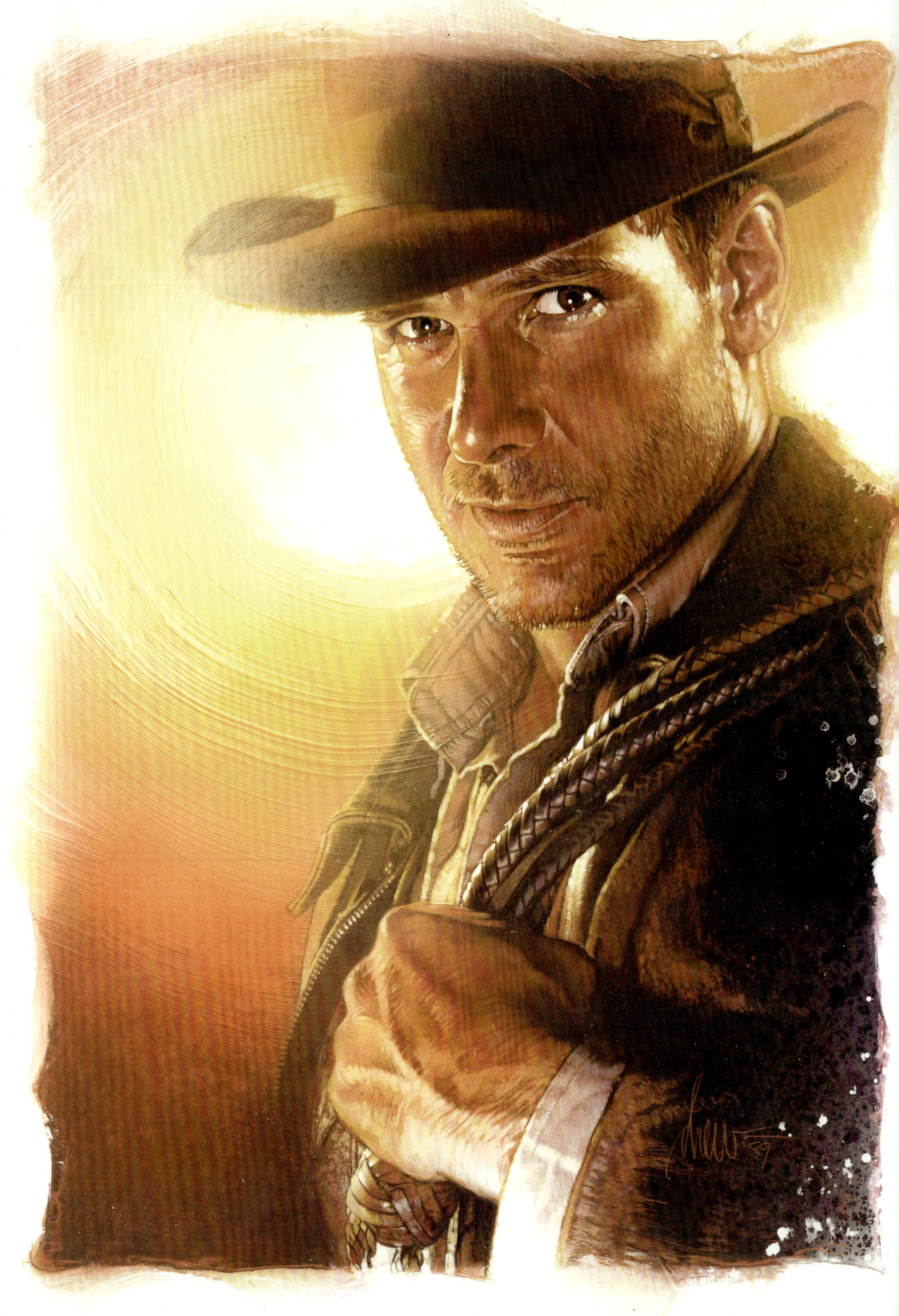

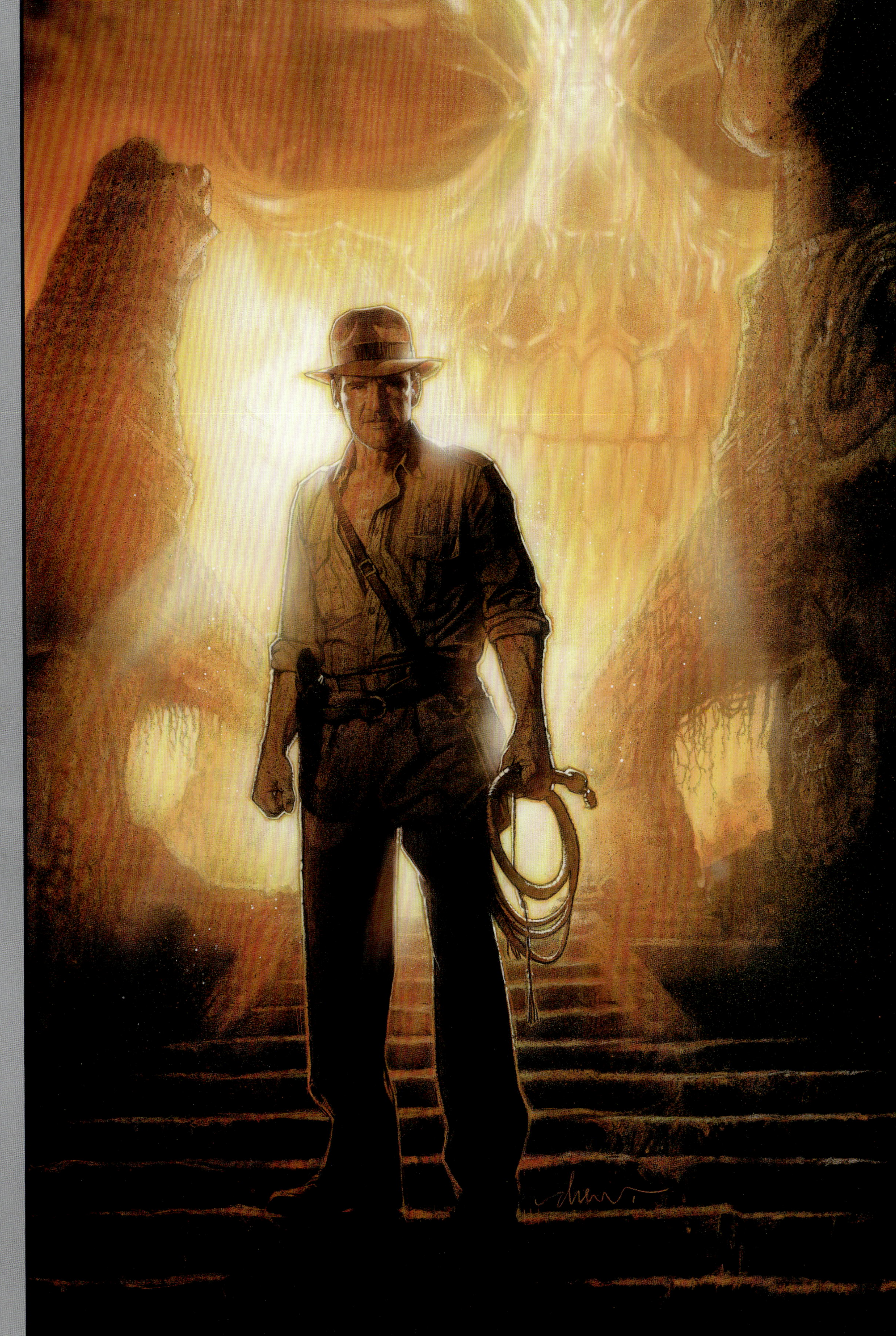

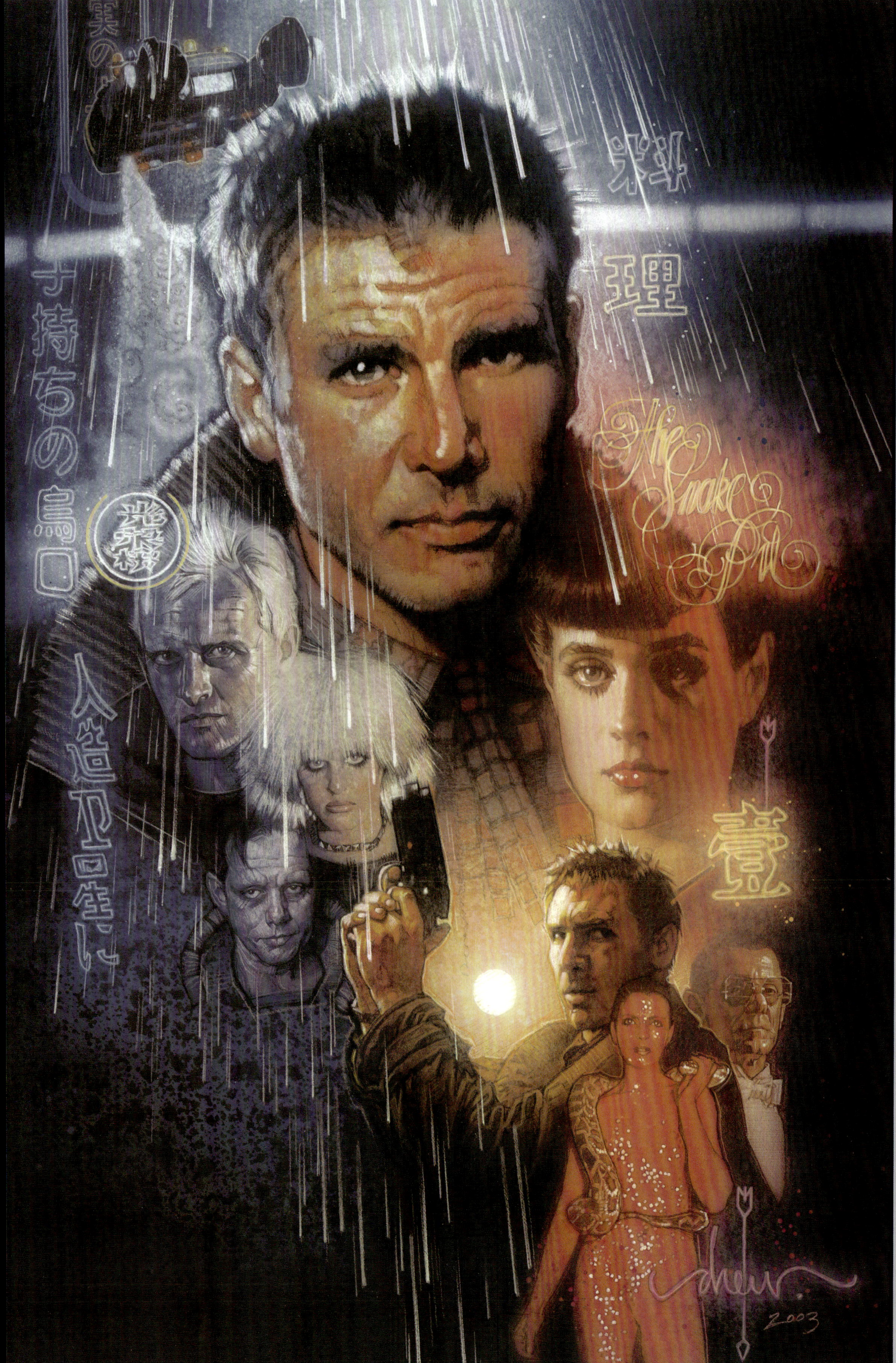

理
The Snake Pit
壹
2003

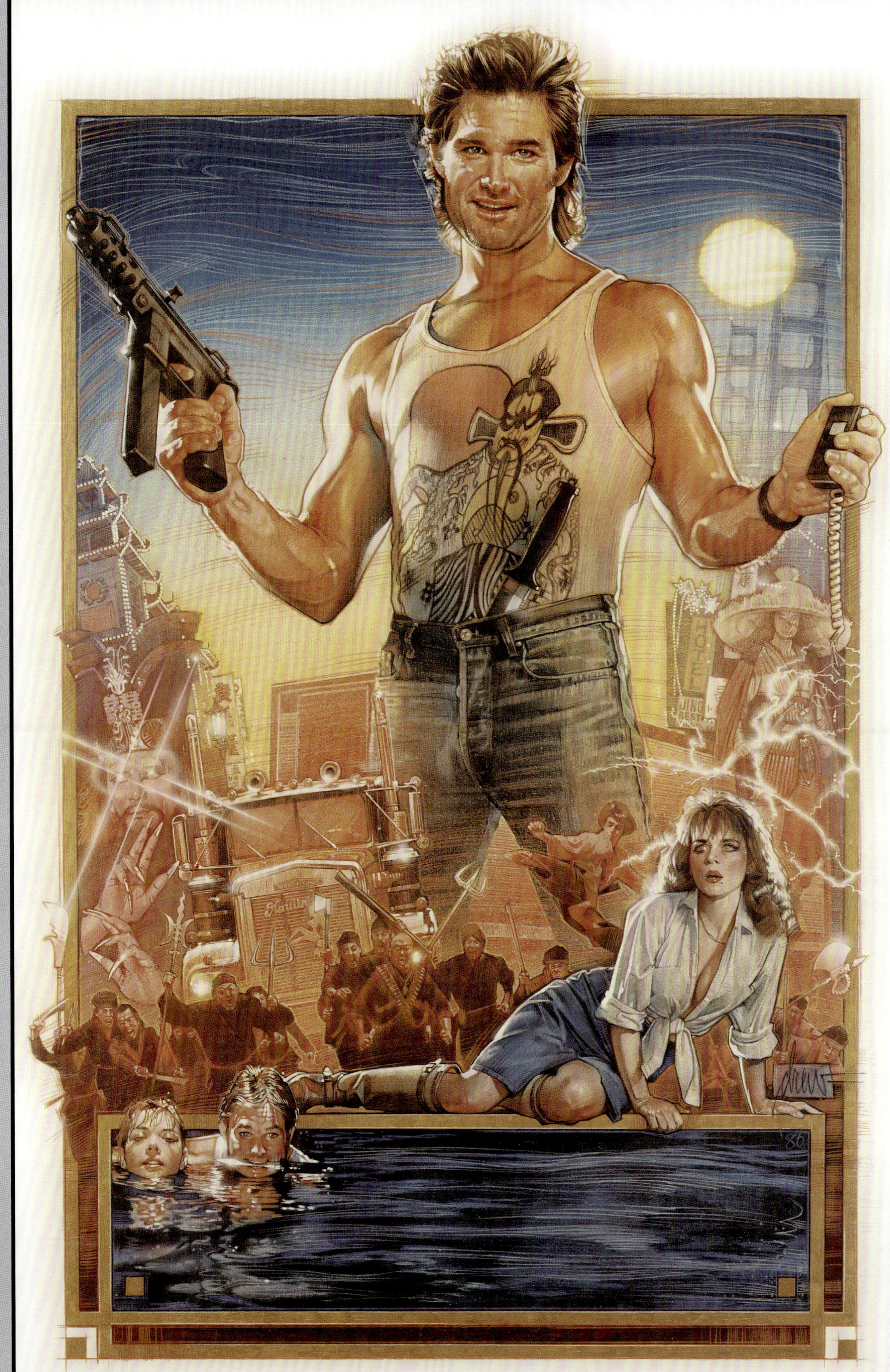
HOTEL

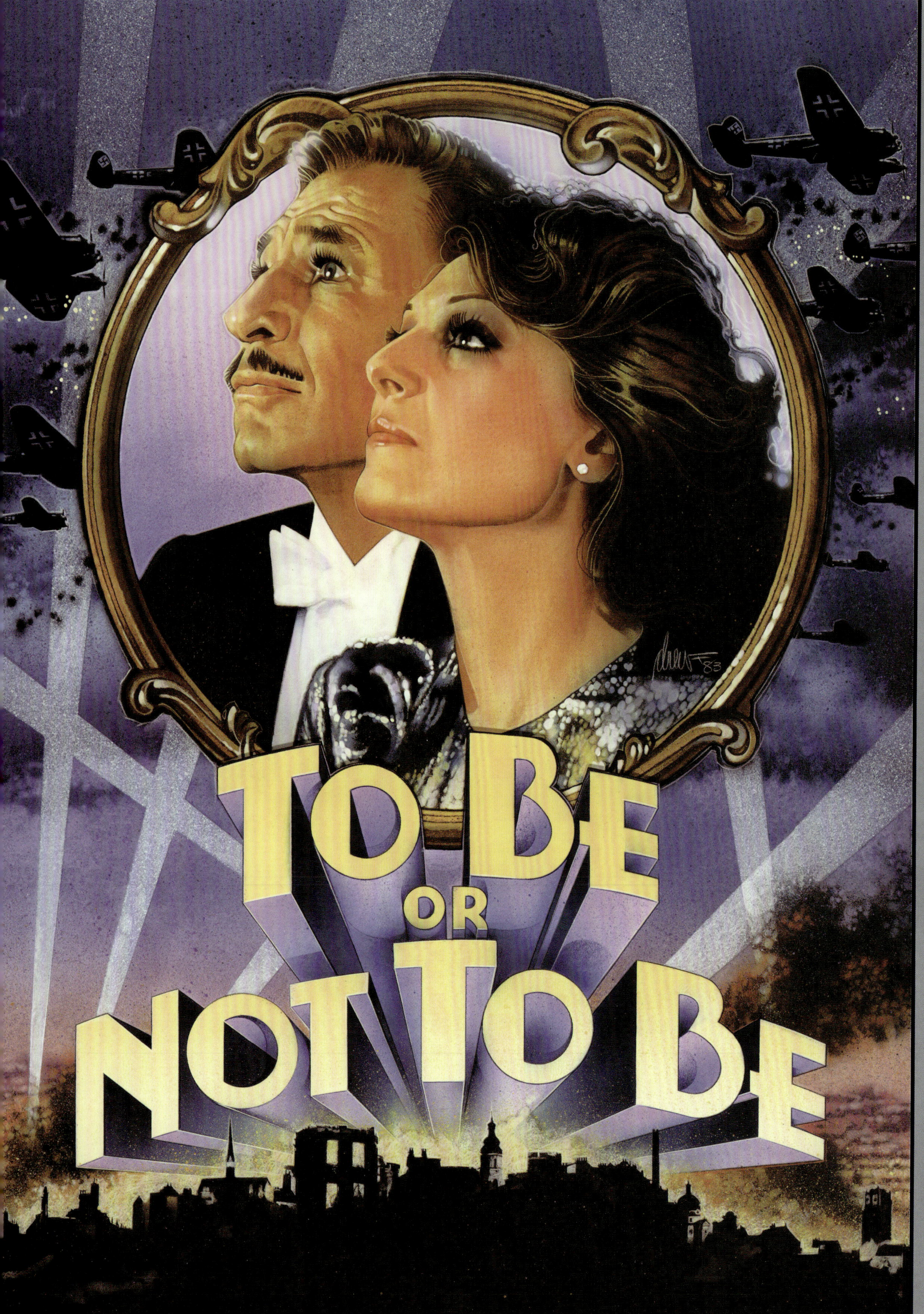
TO BE
OR
NOT TO BE

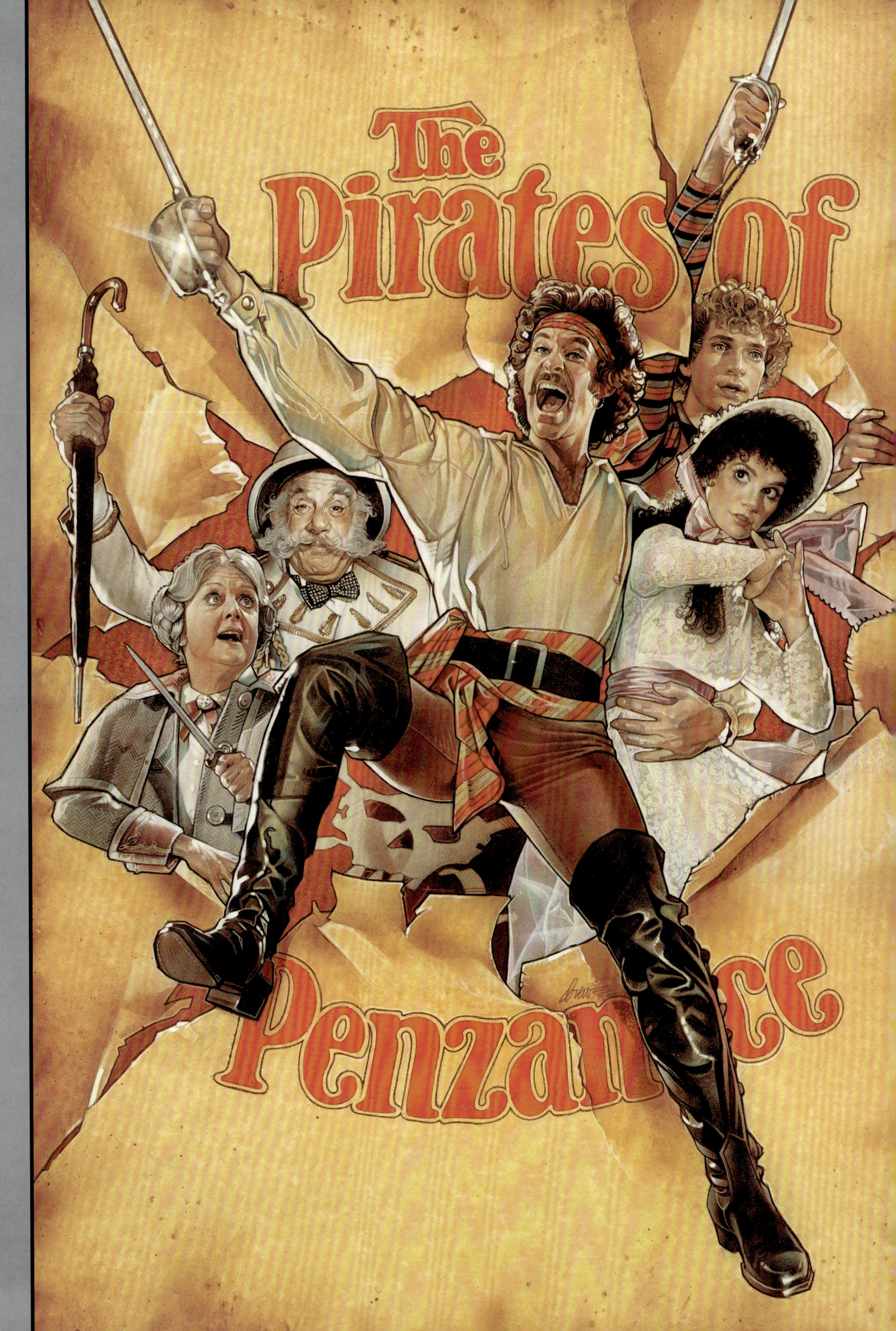
The Pirates of Penzance

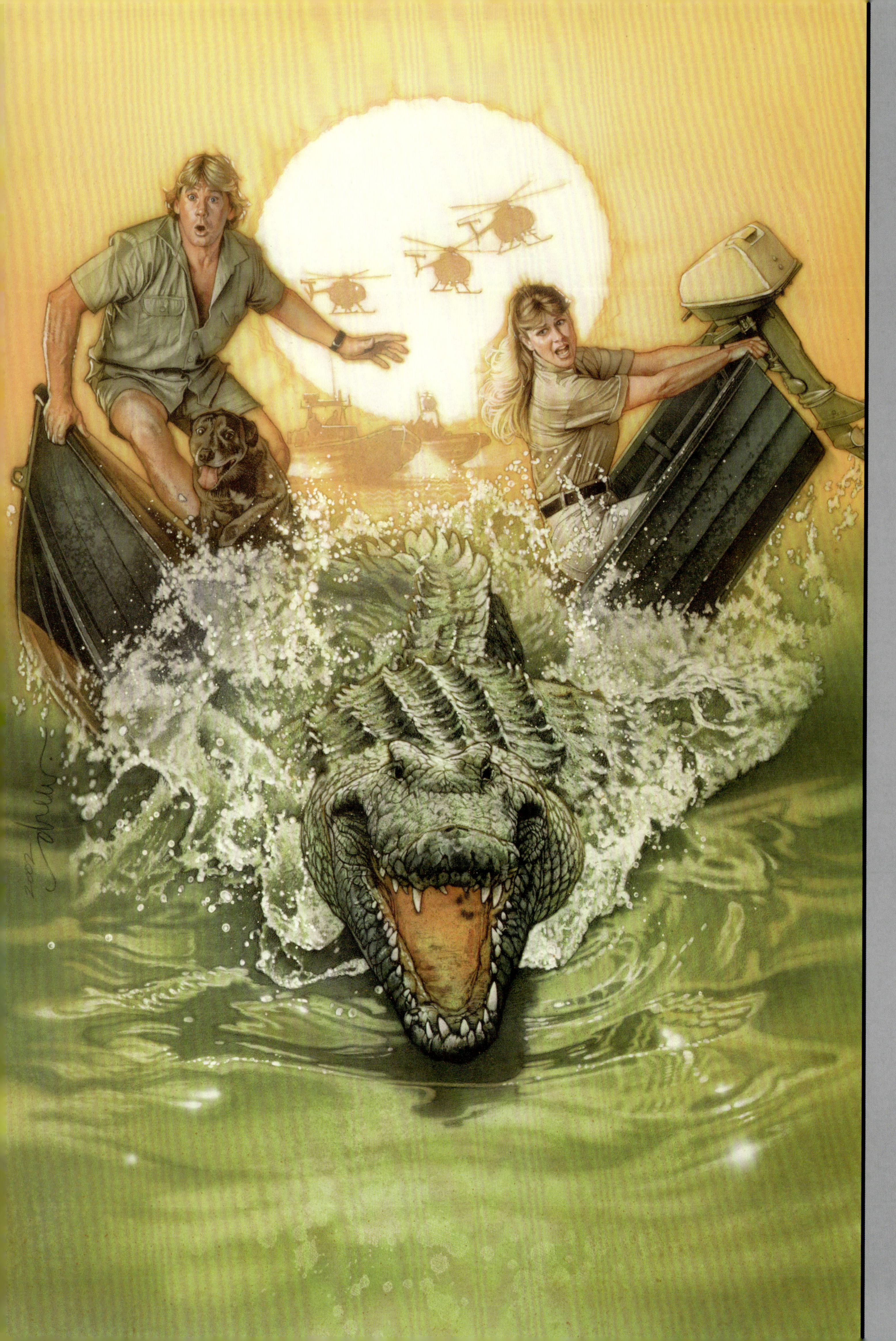

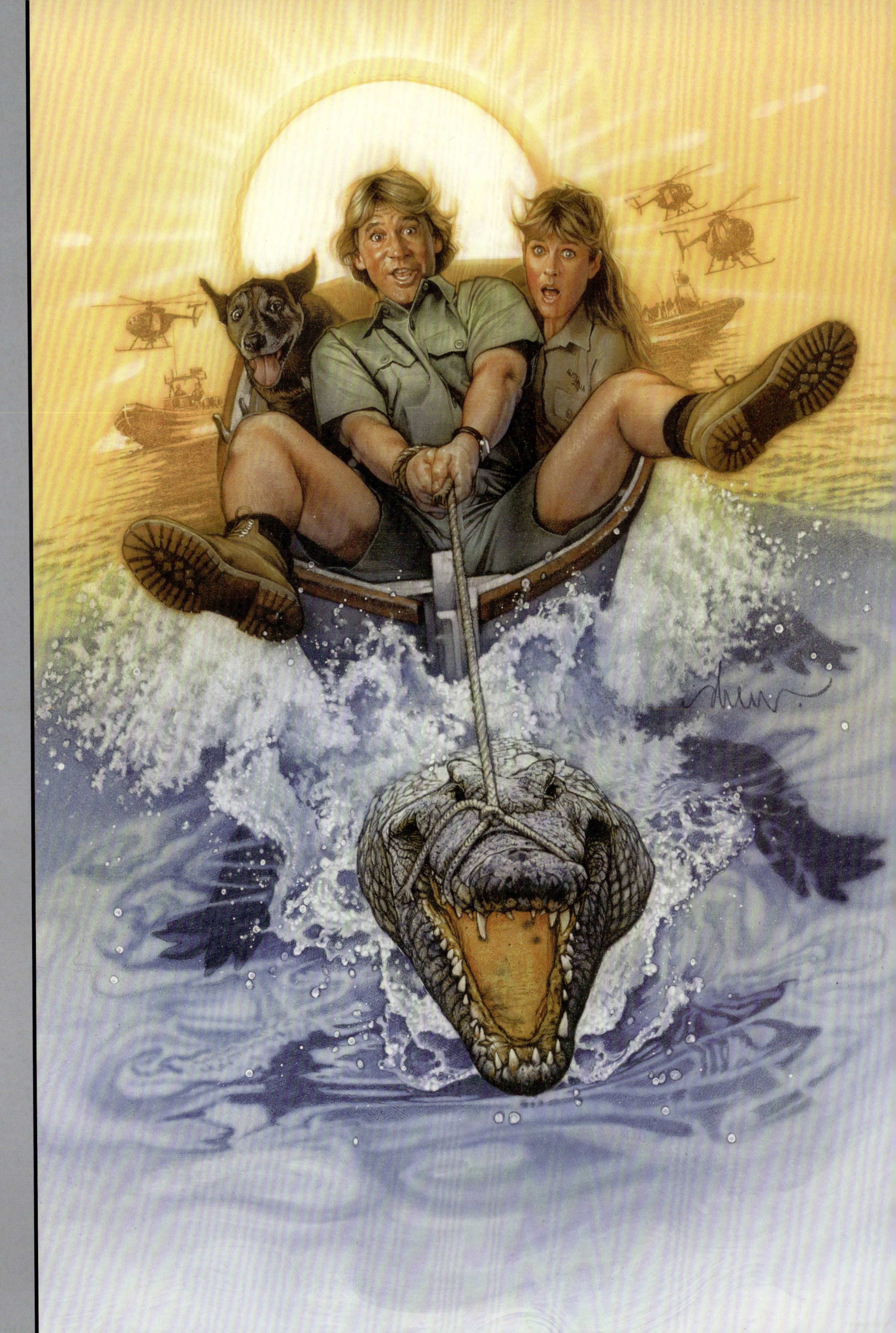

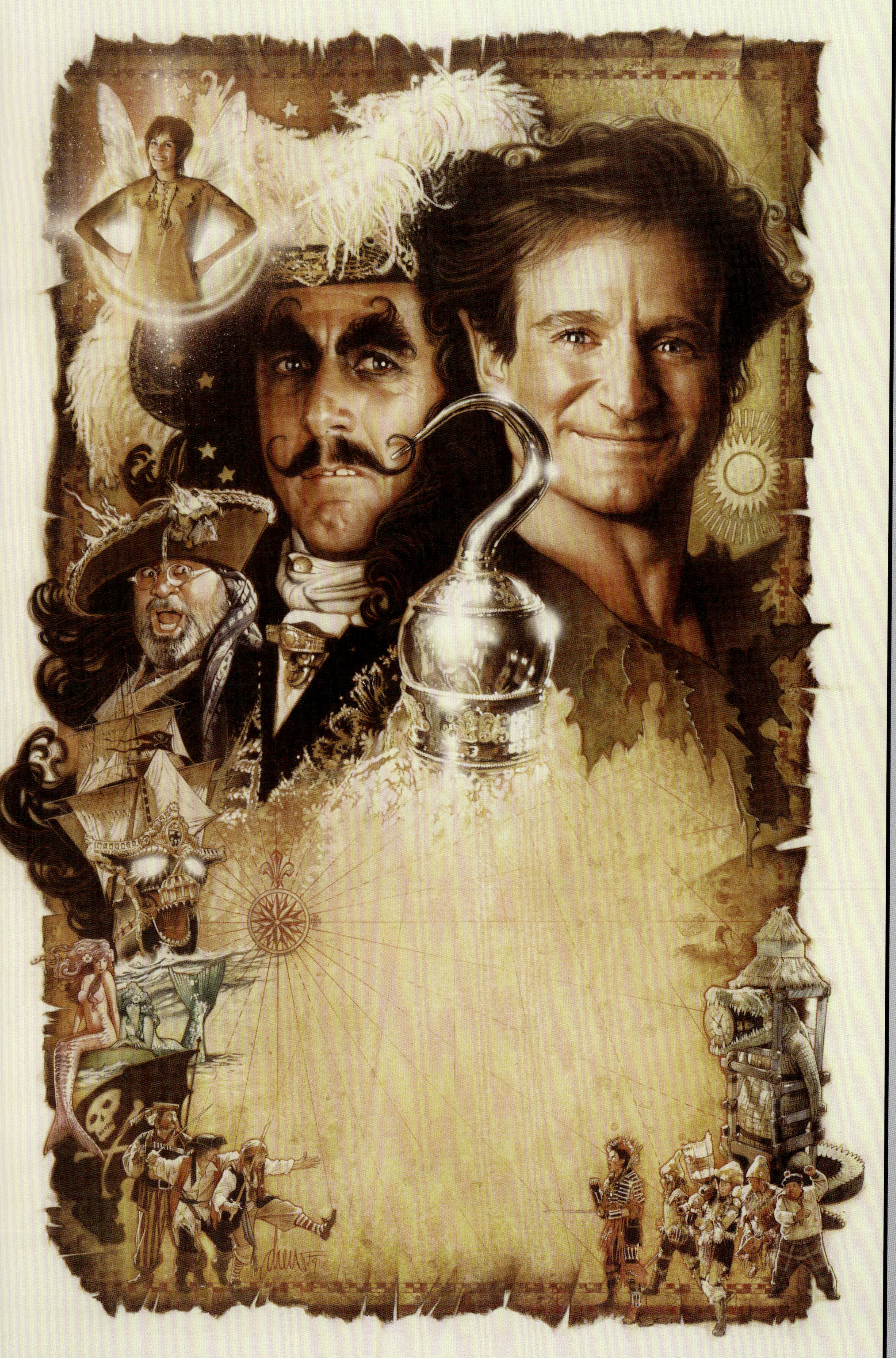

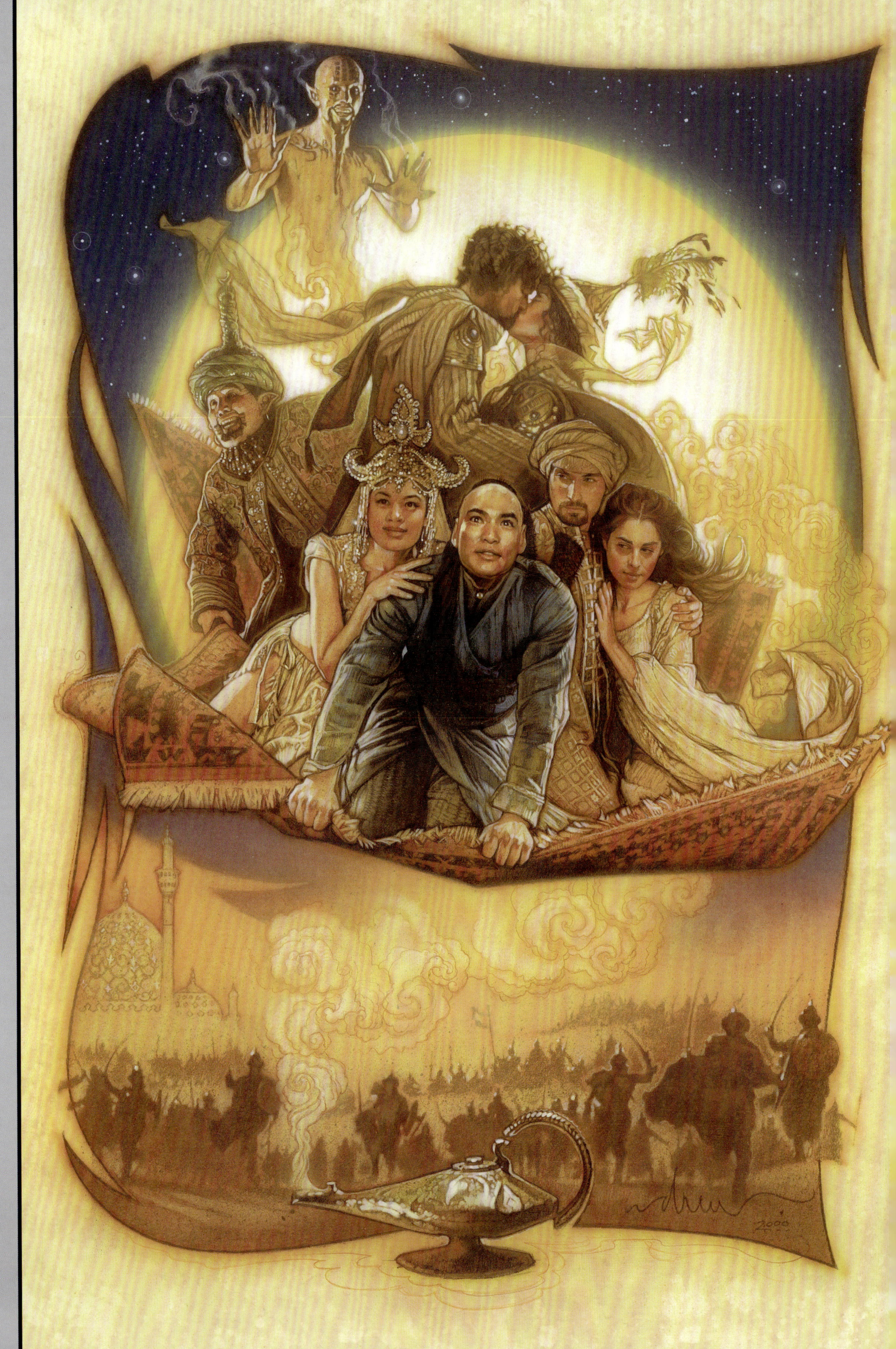

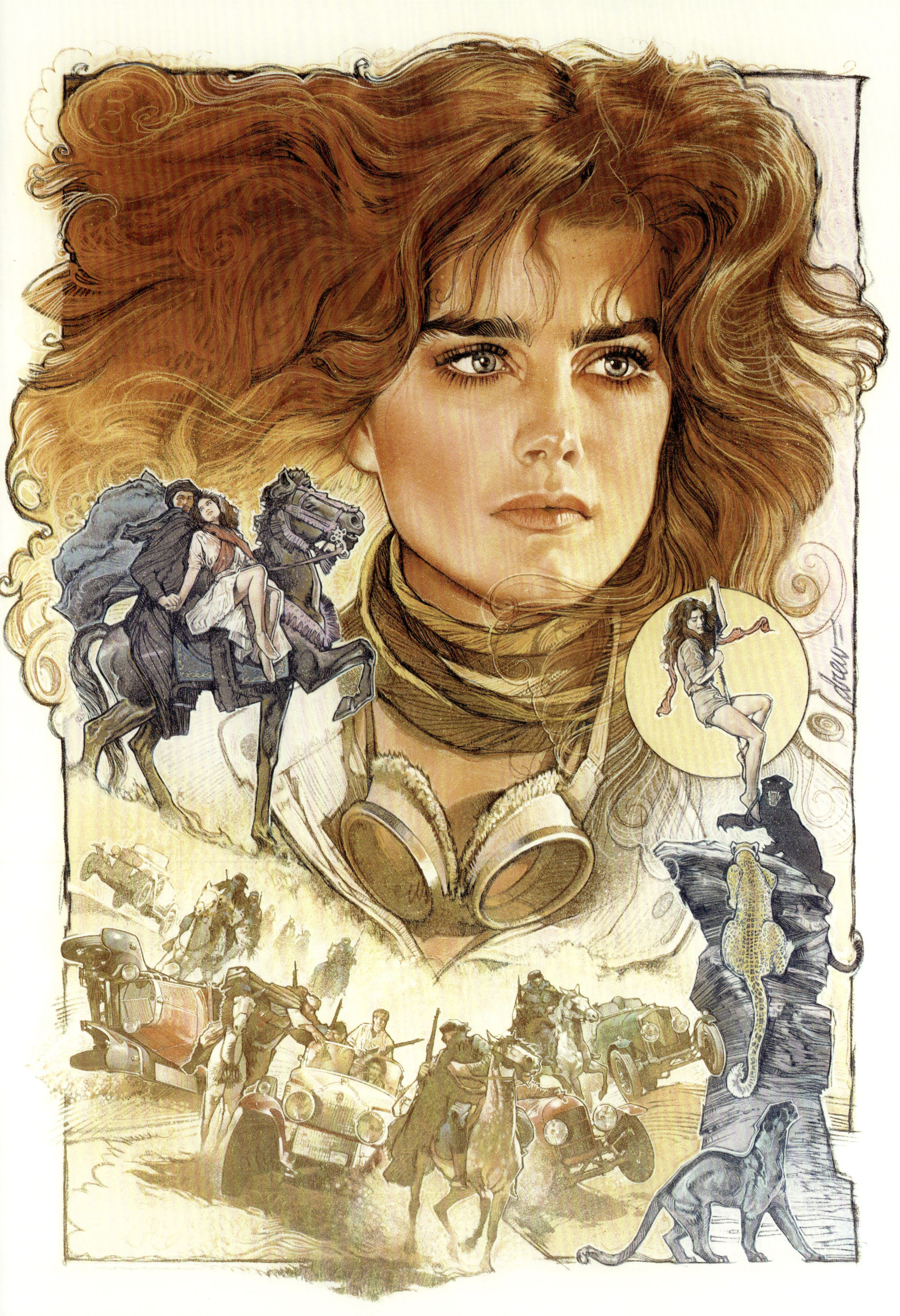

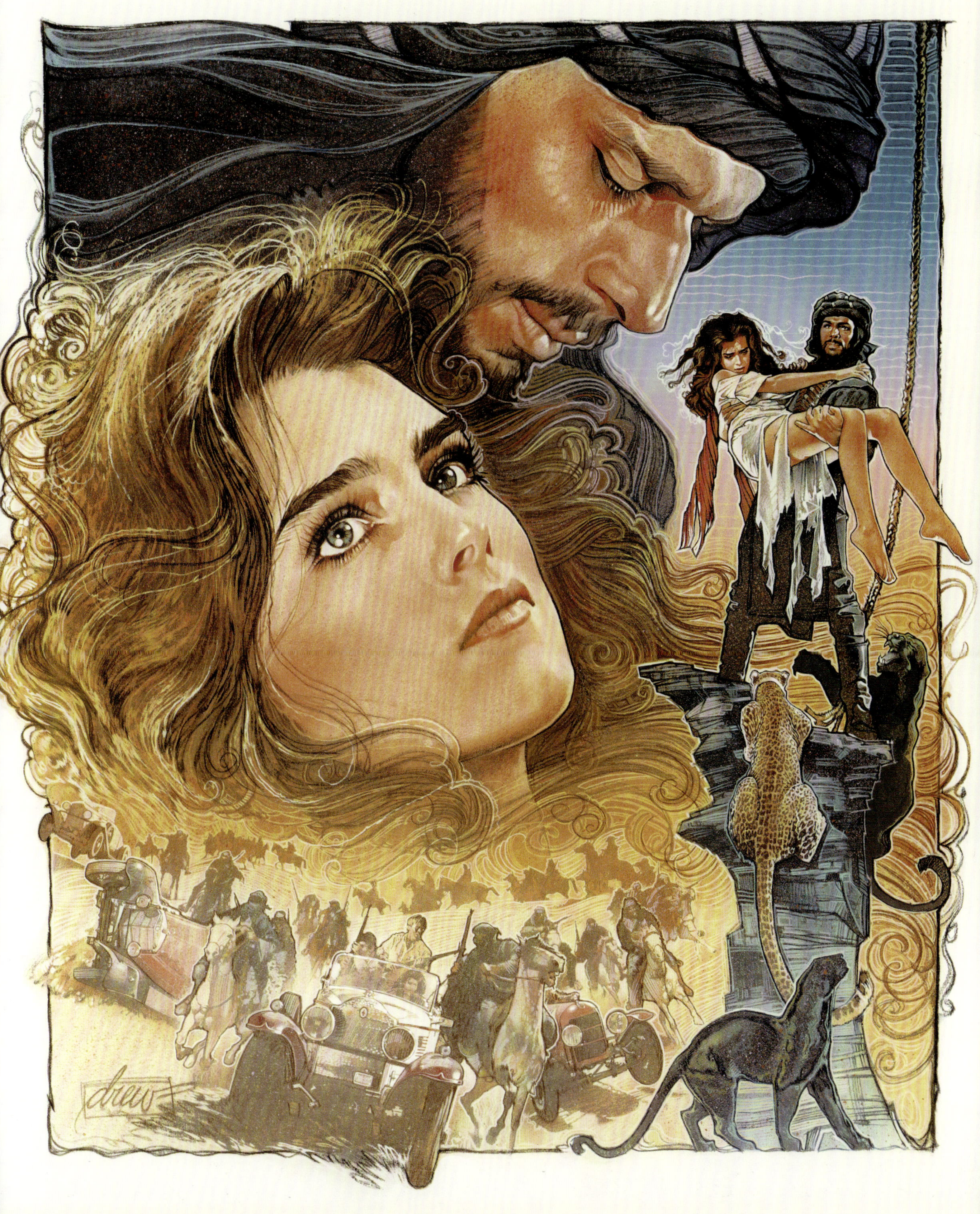
drew

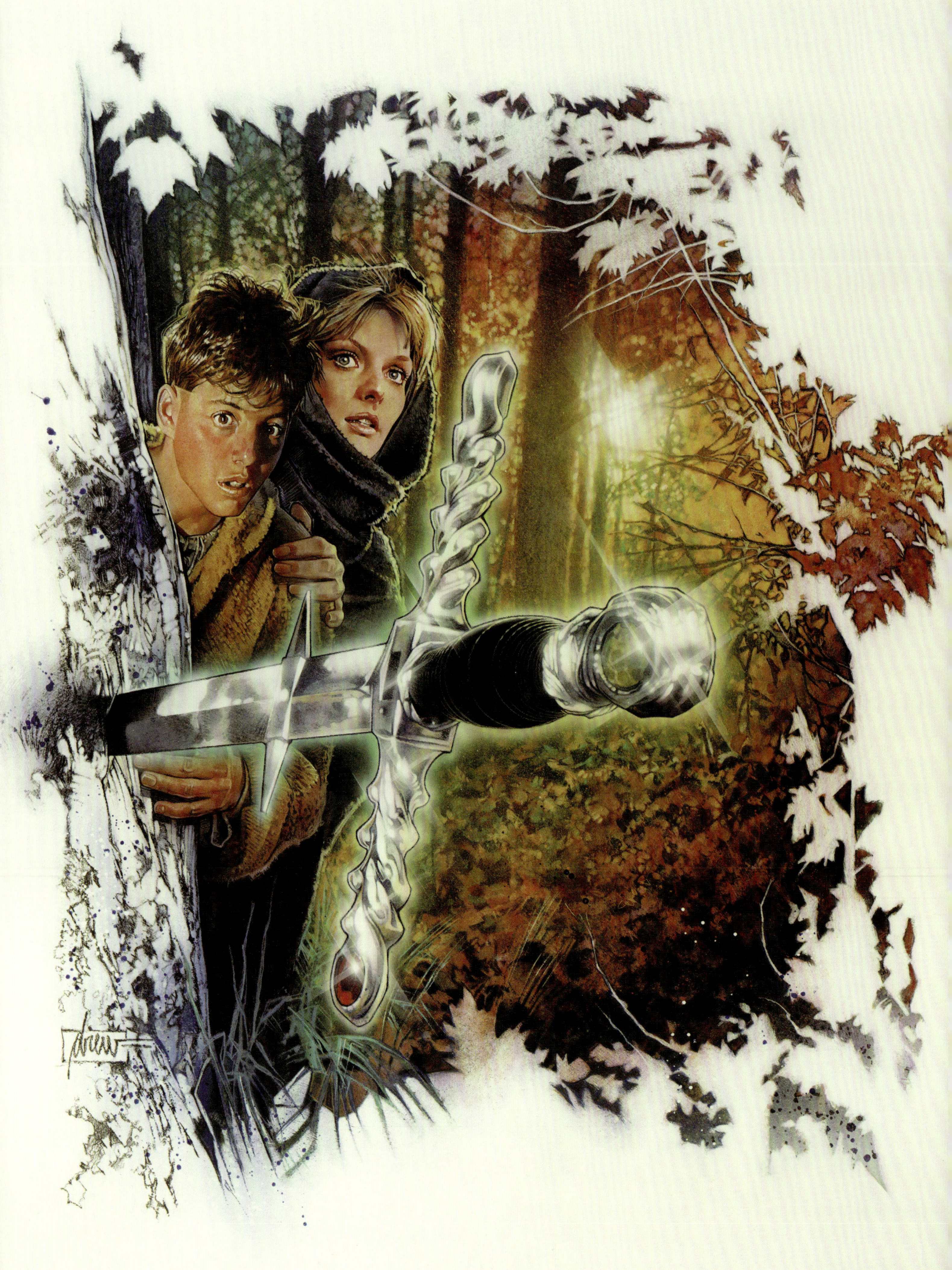

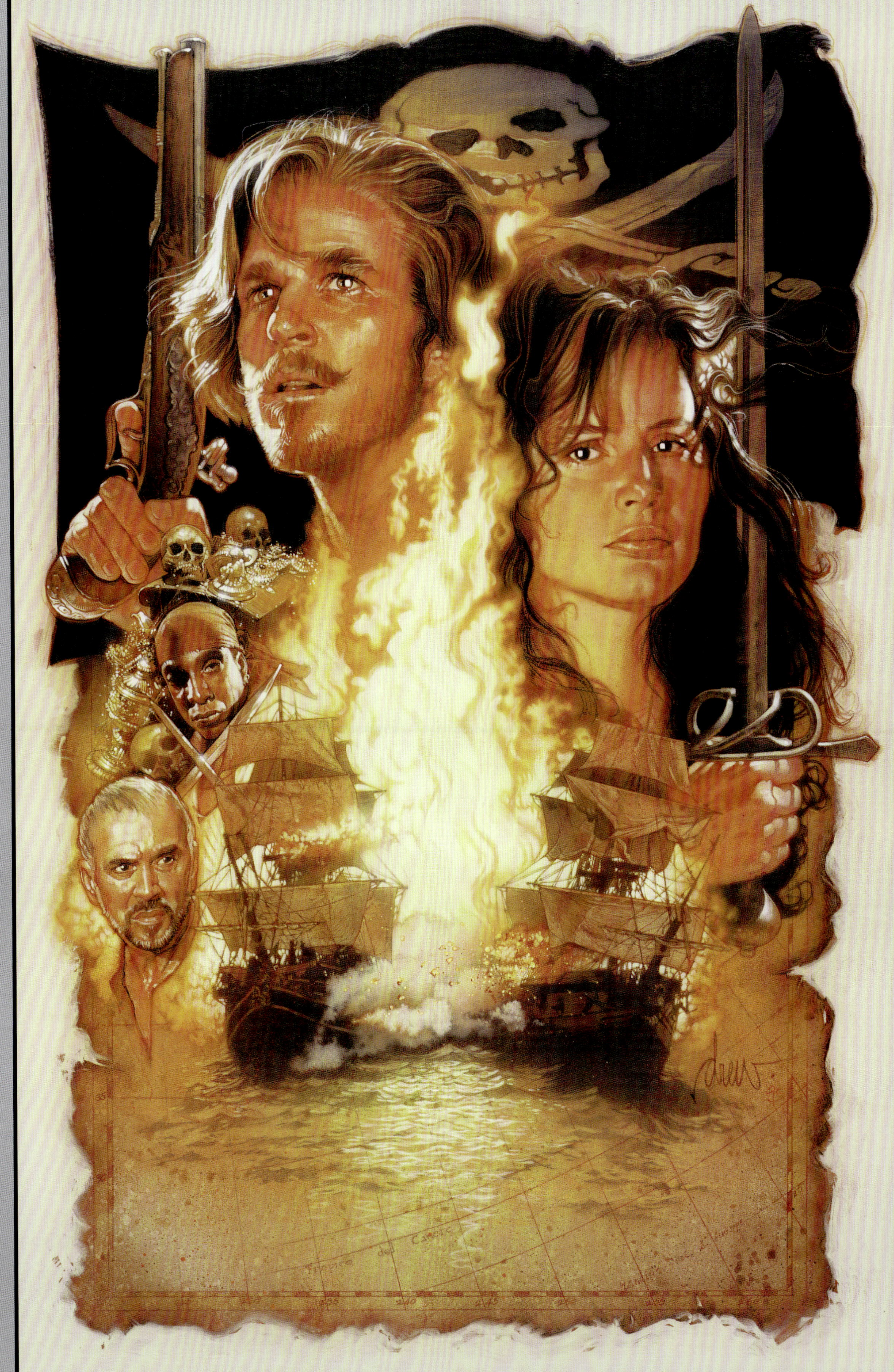

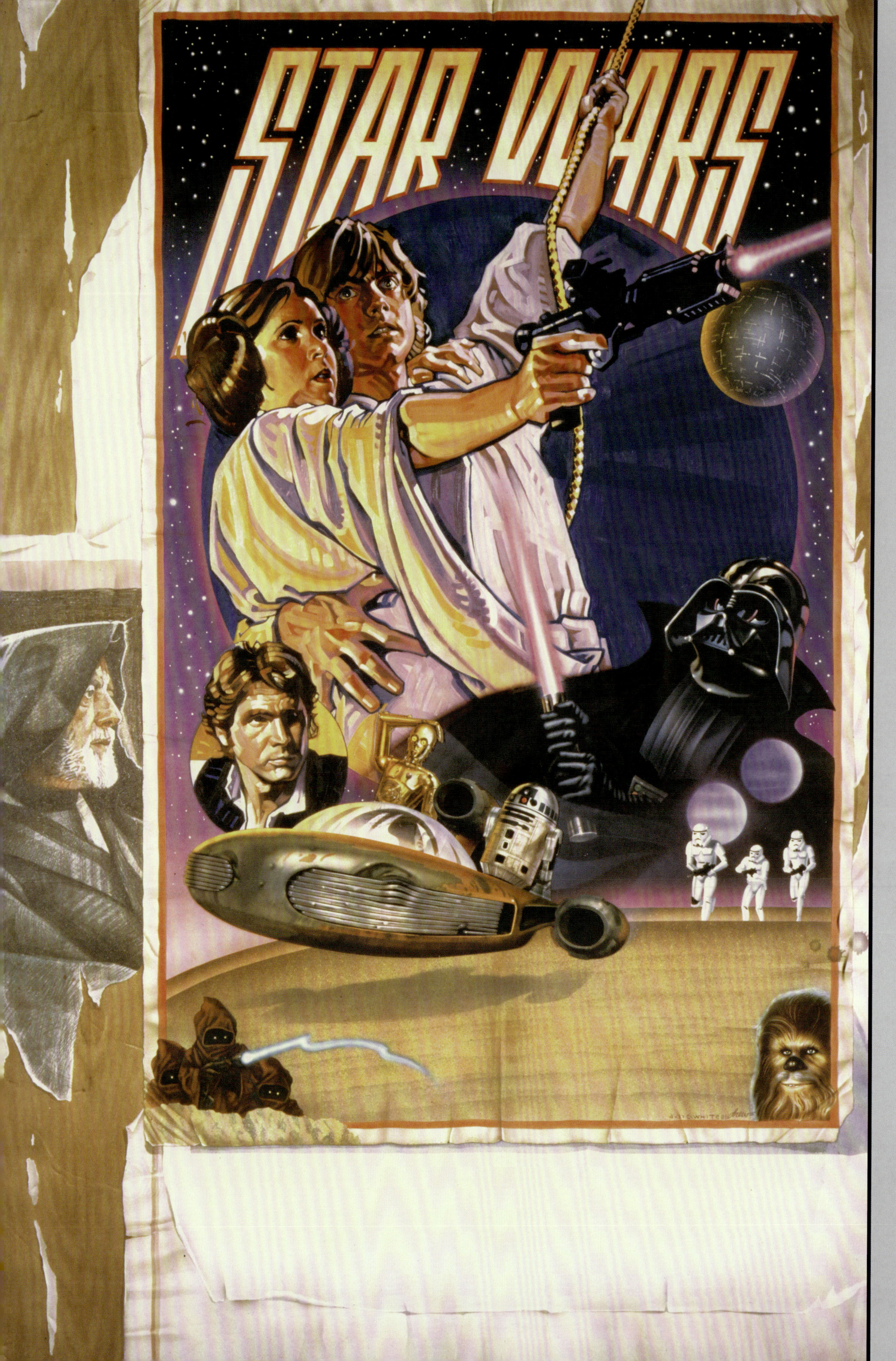
STAR WARS

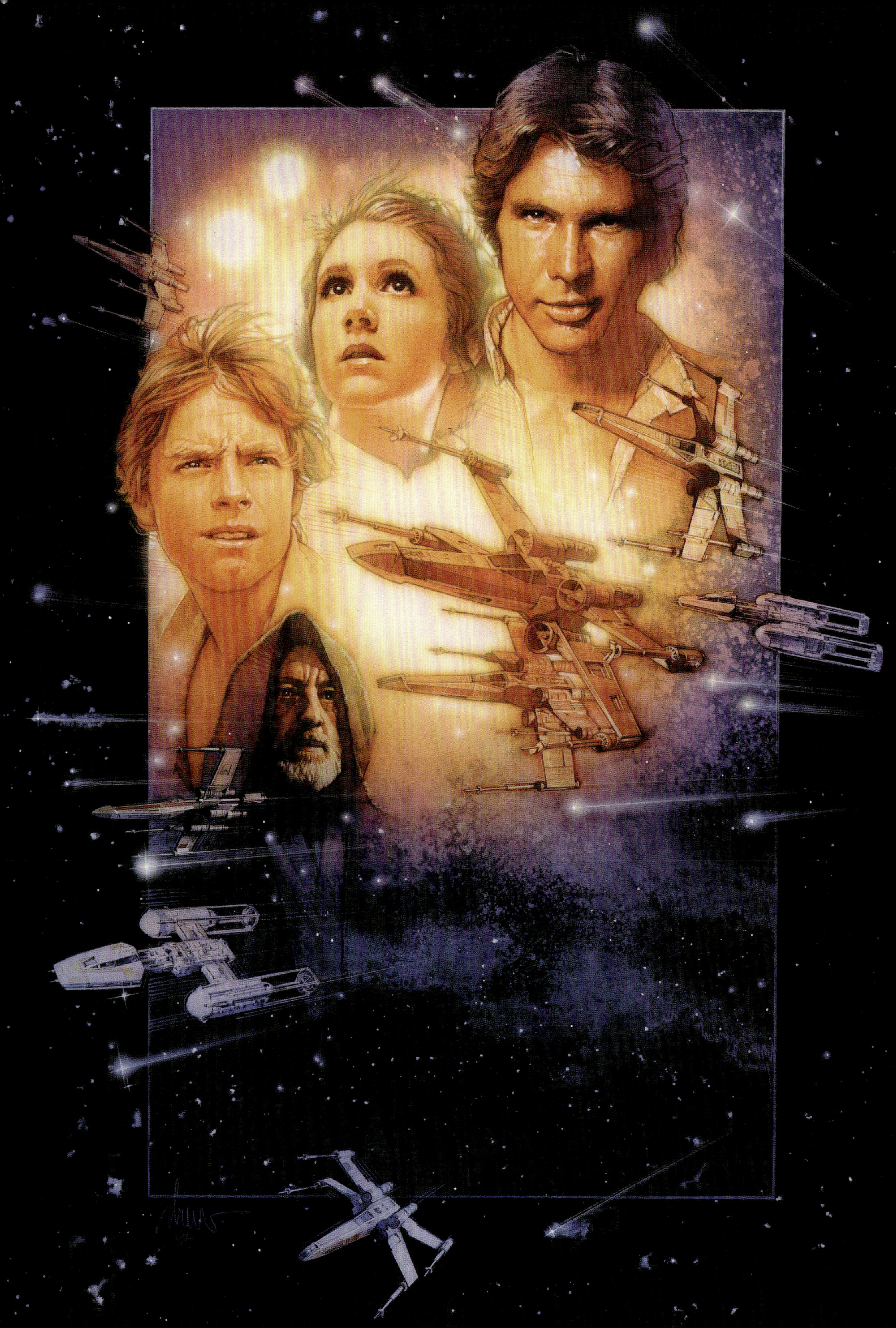

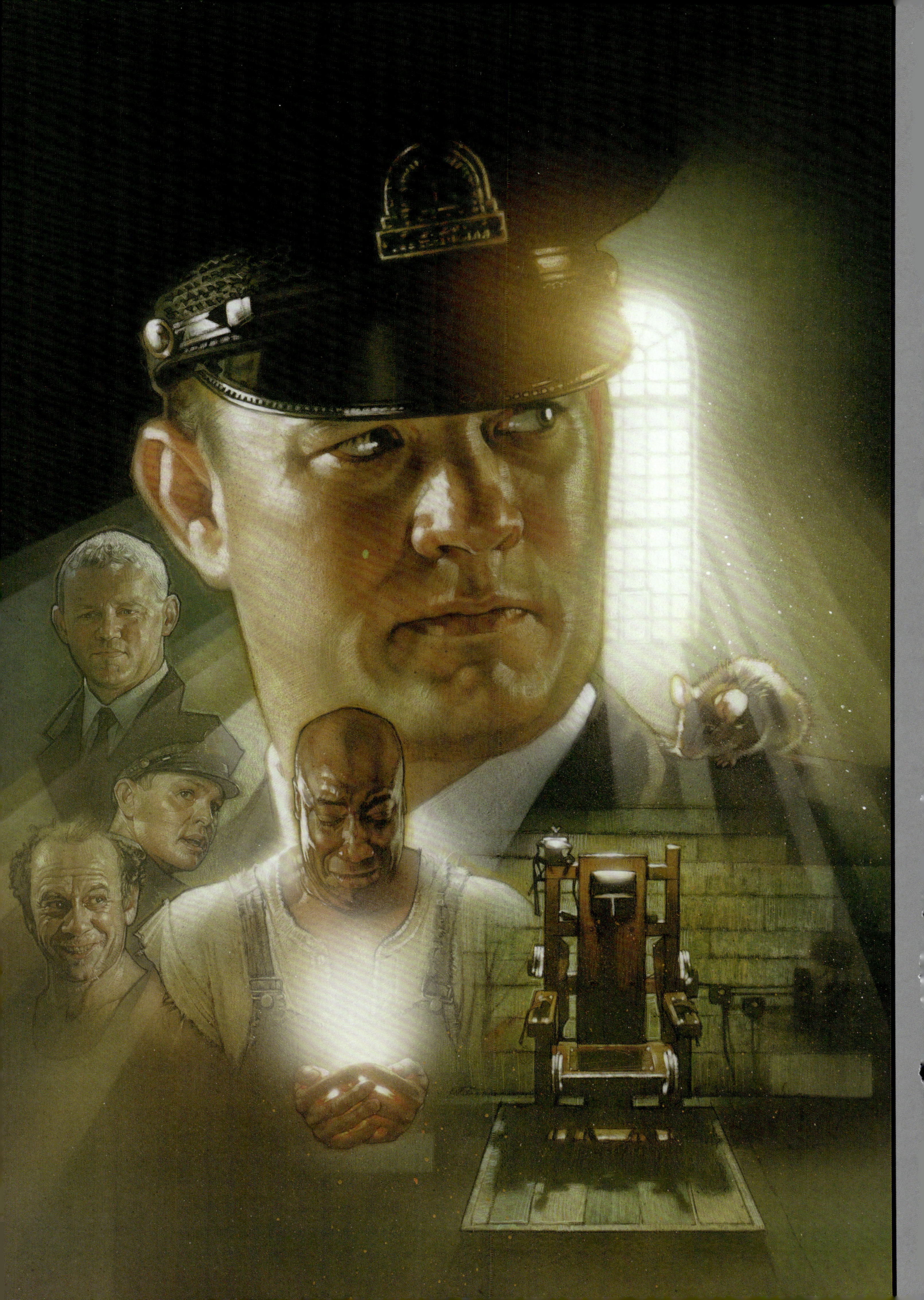

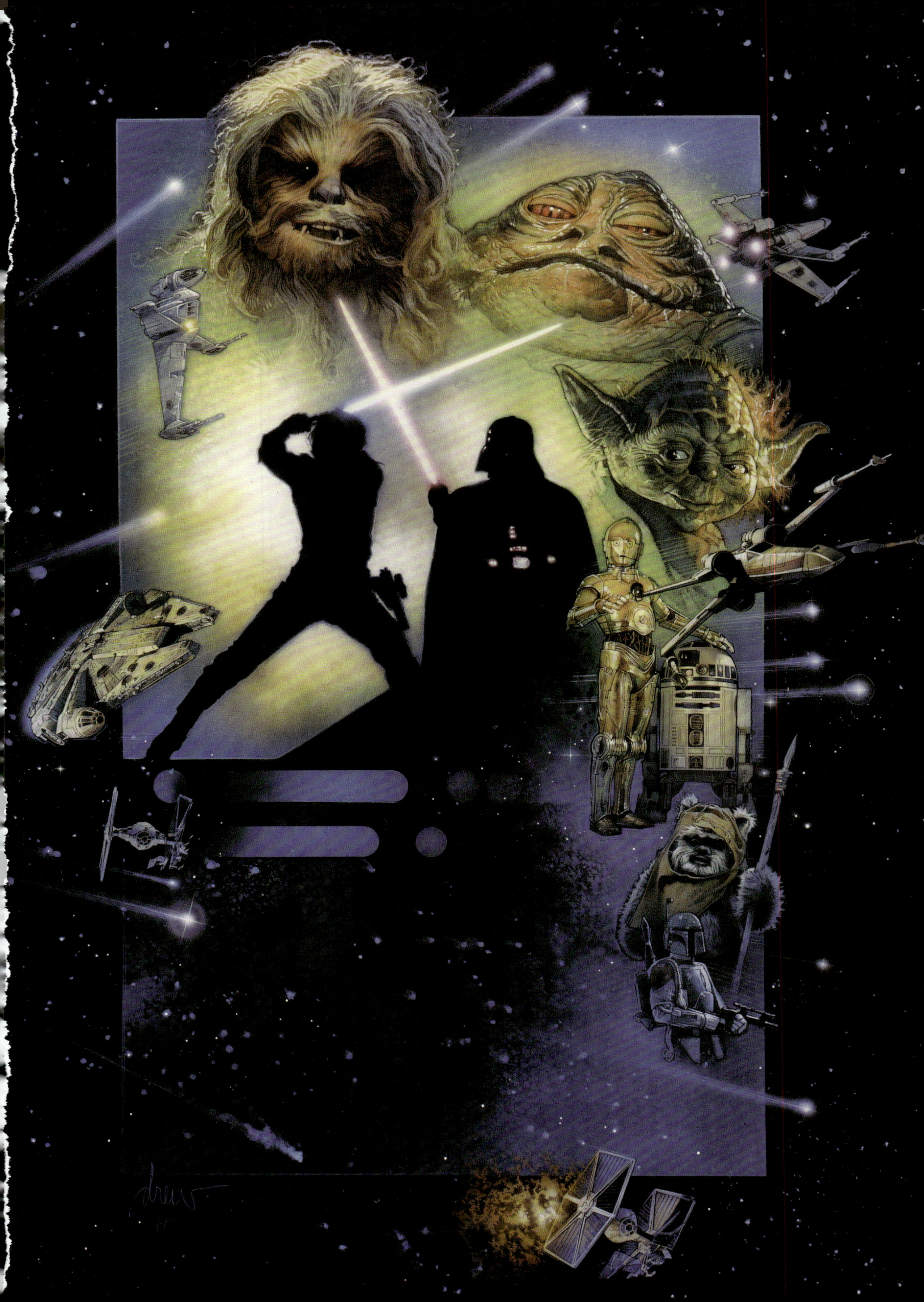

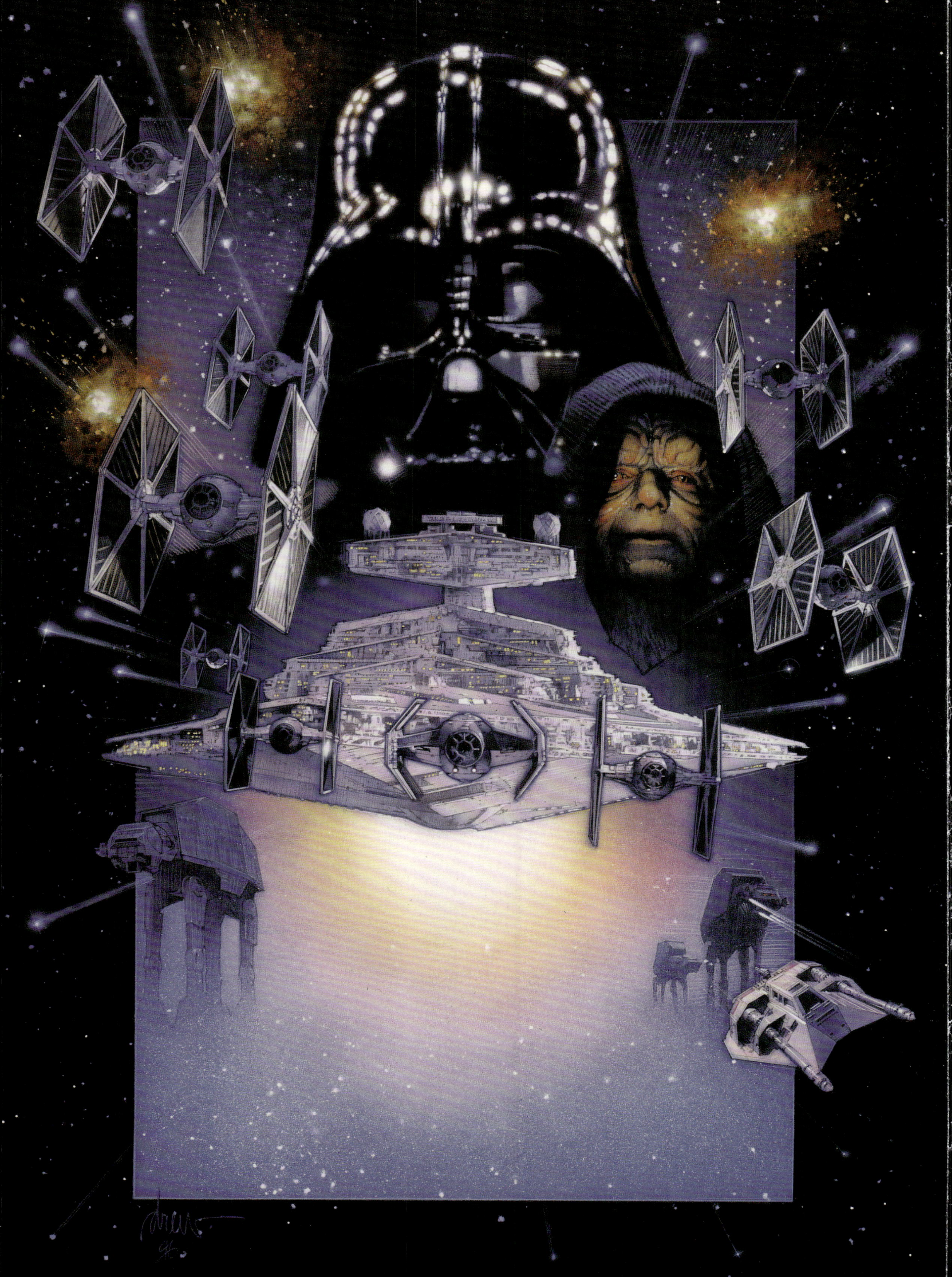

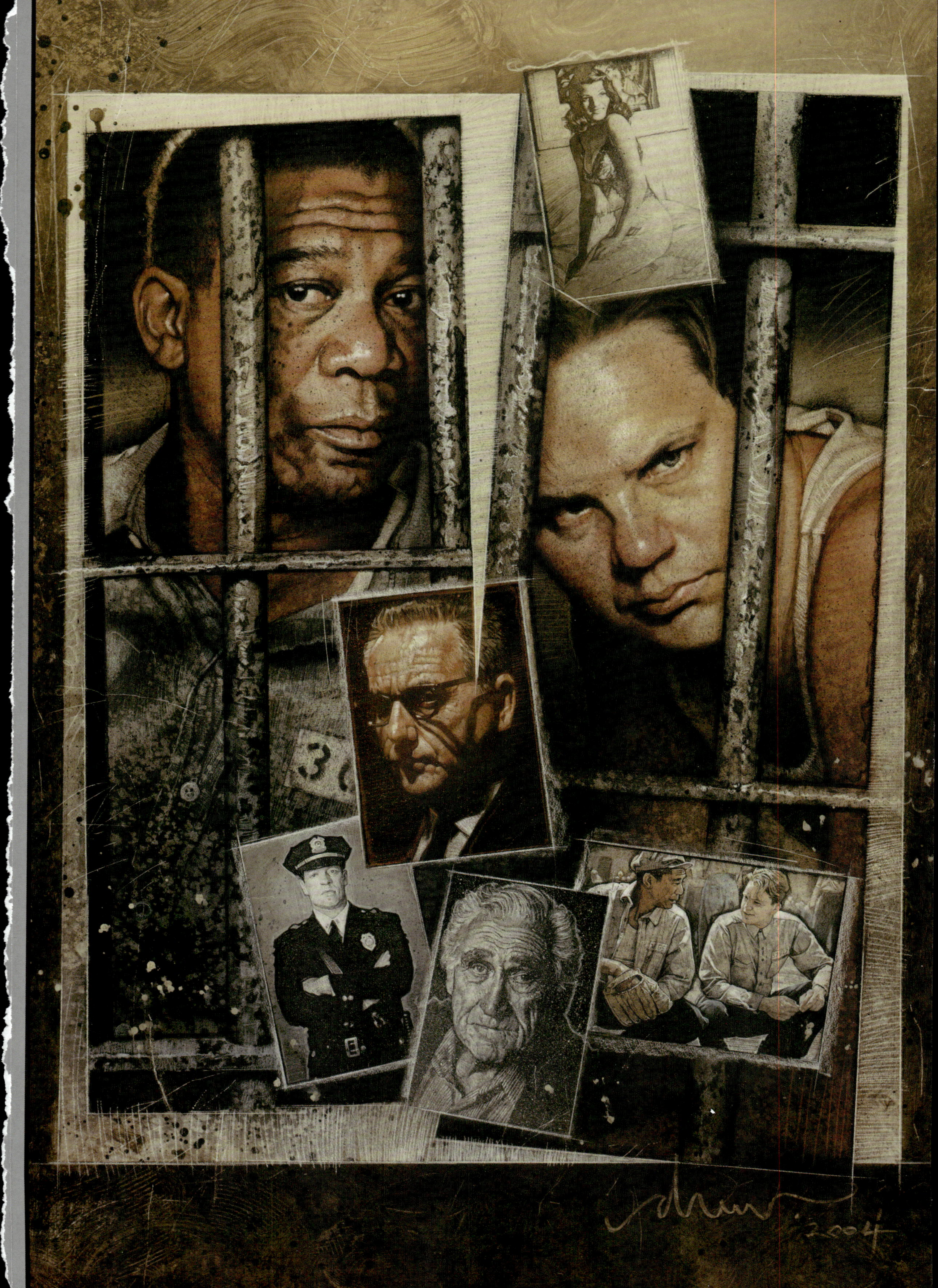
2004

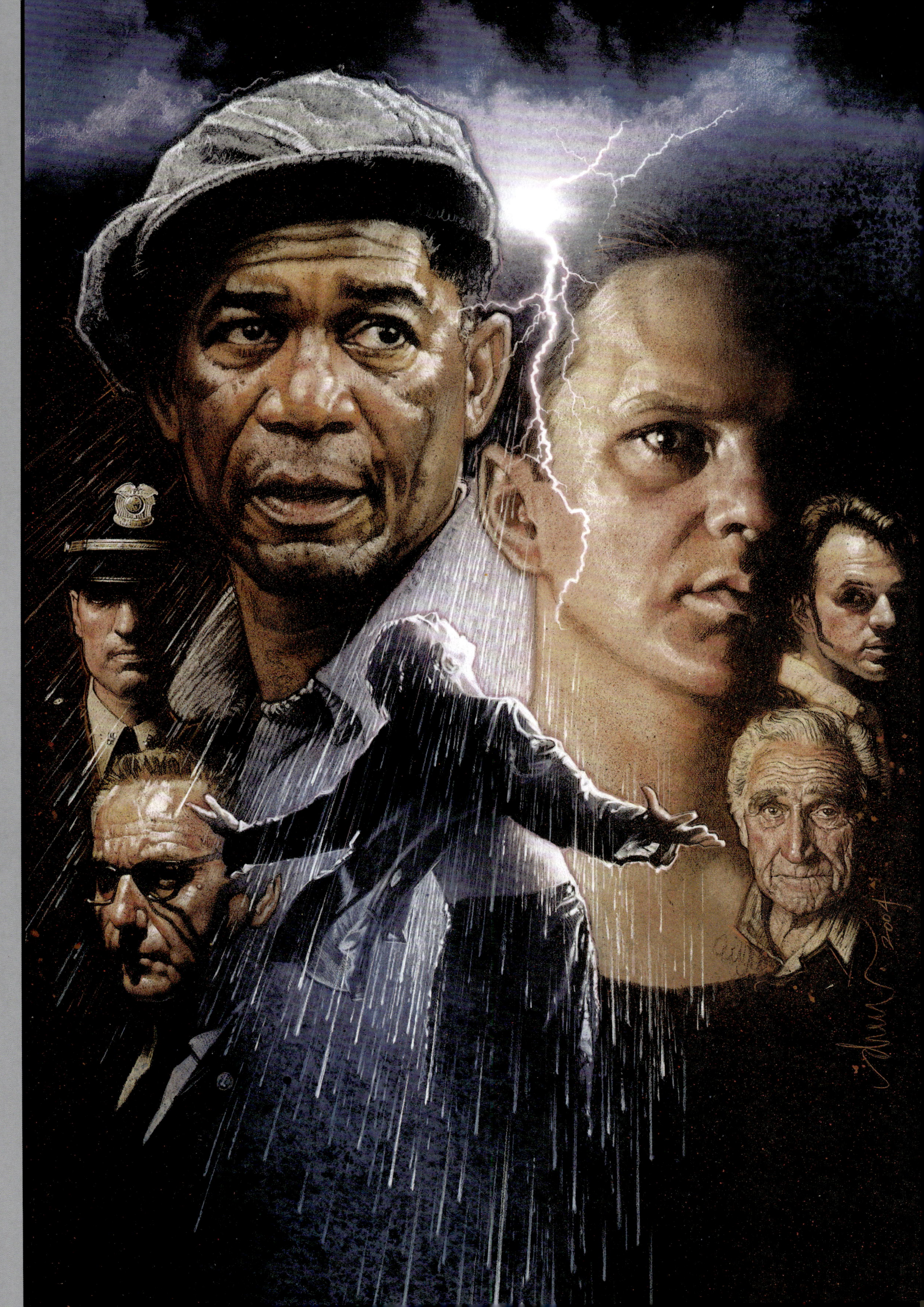

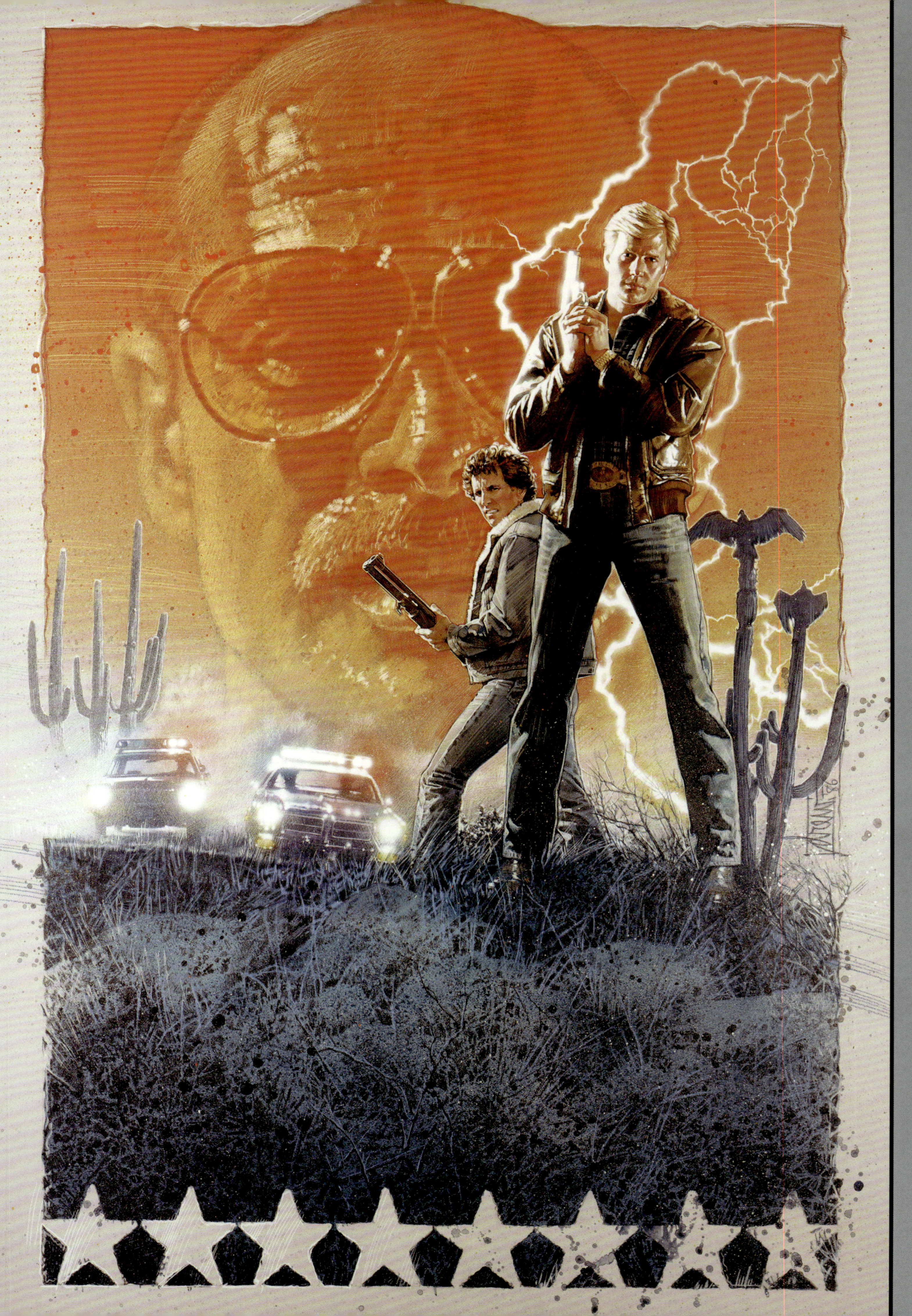

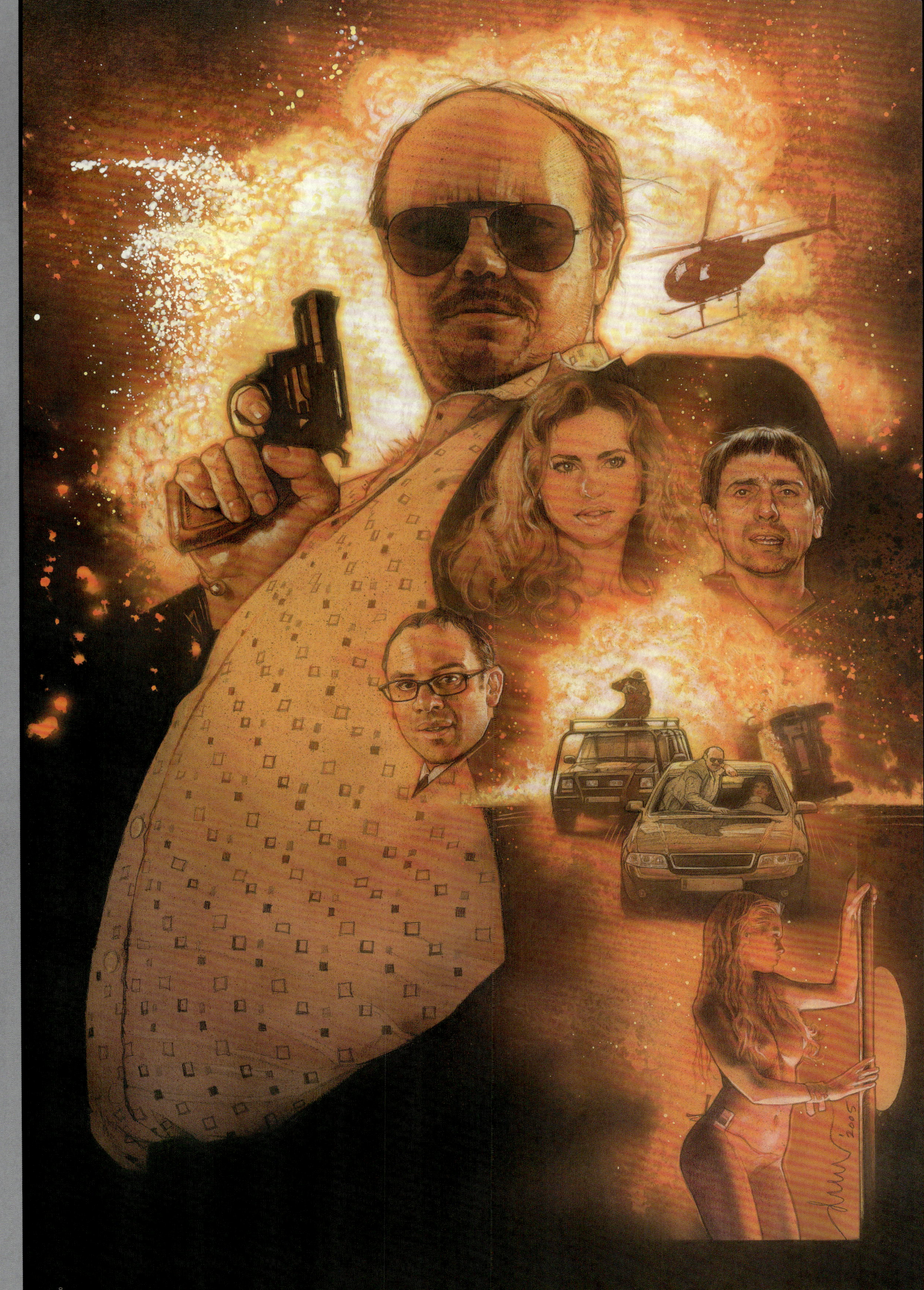

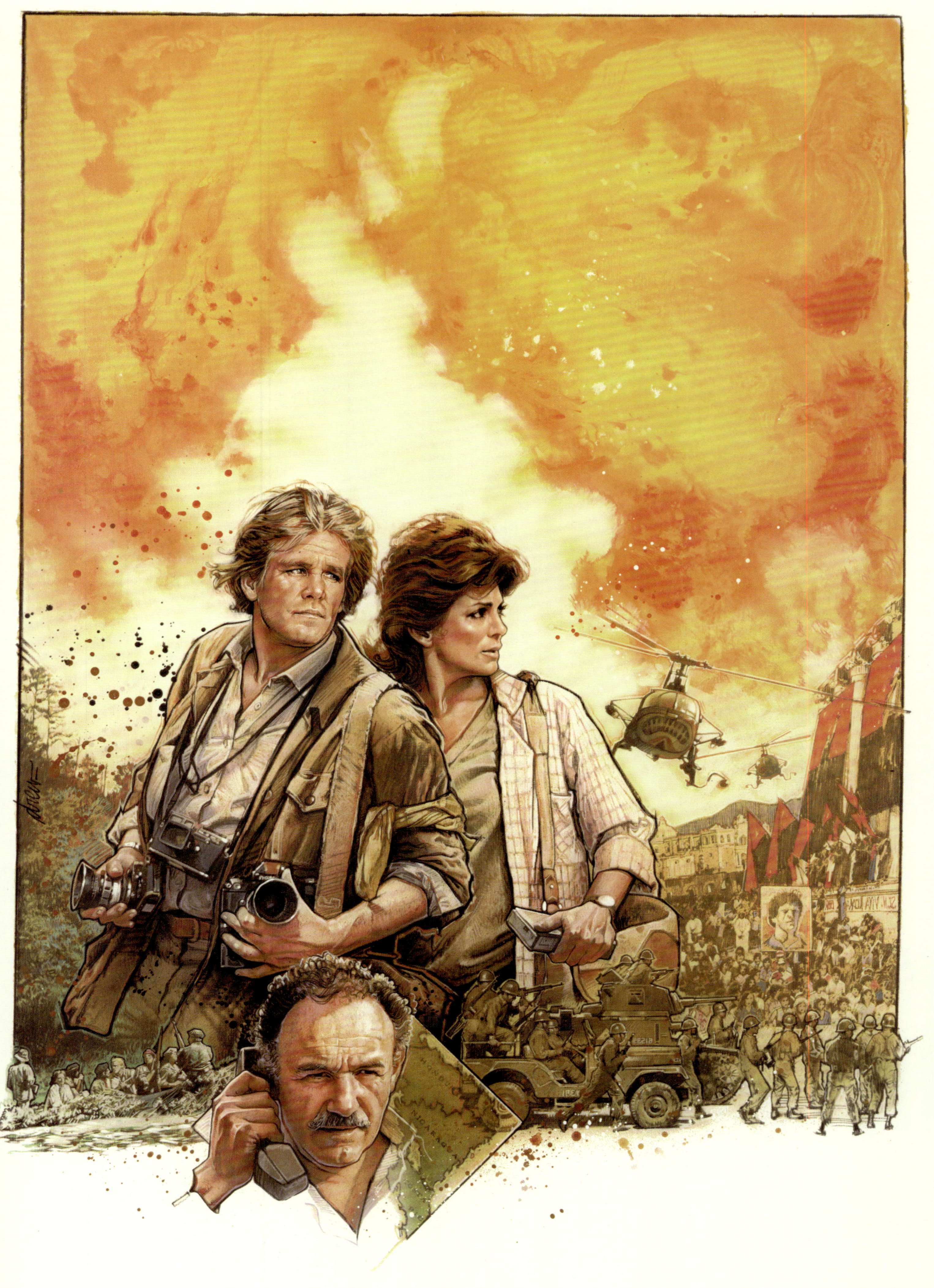

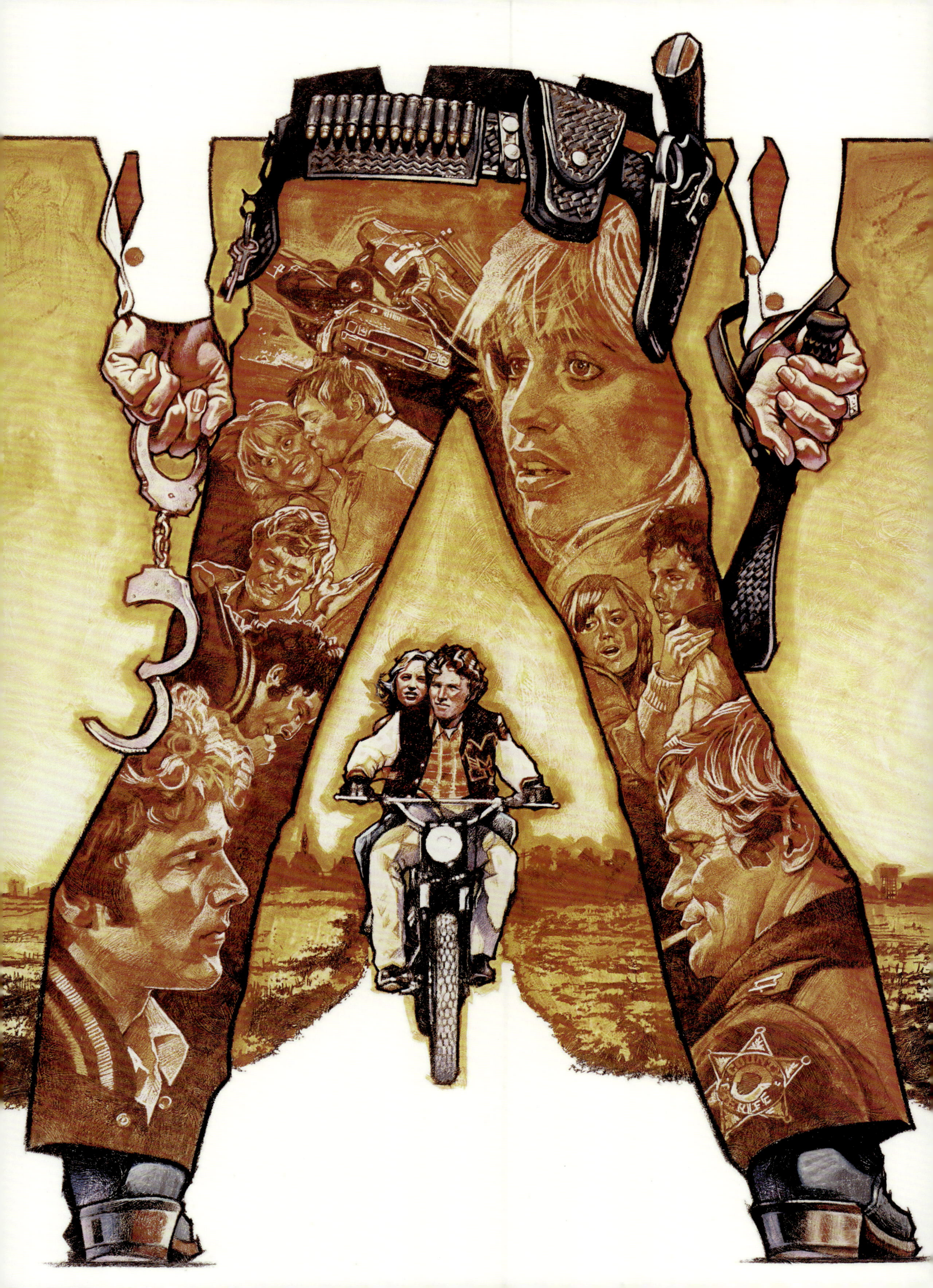

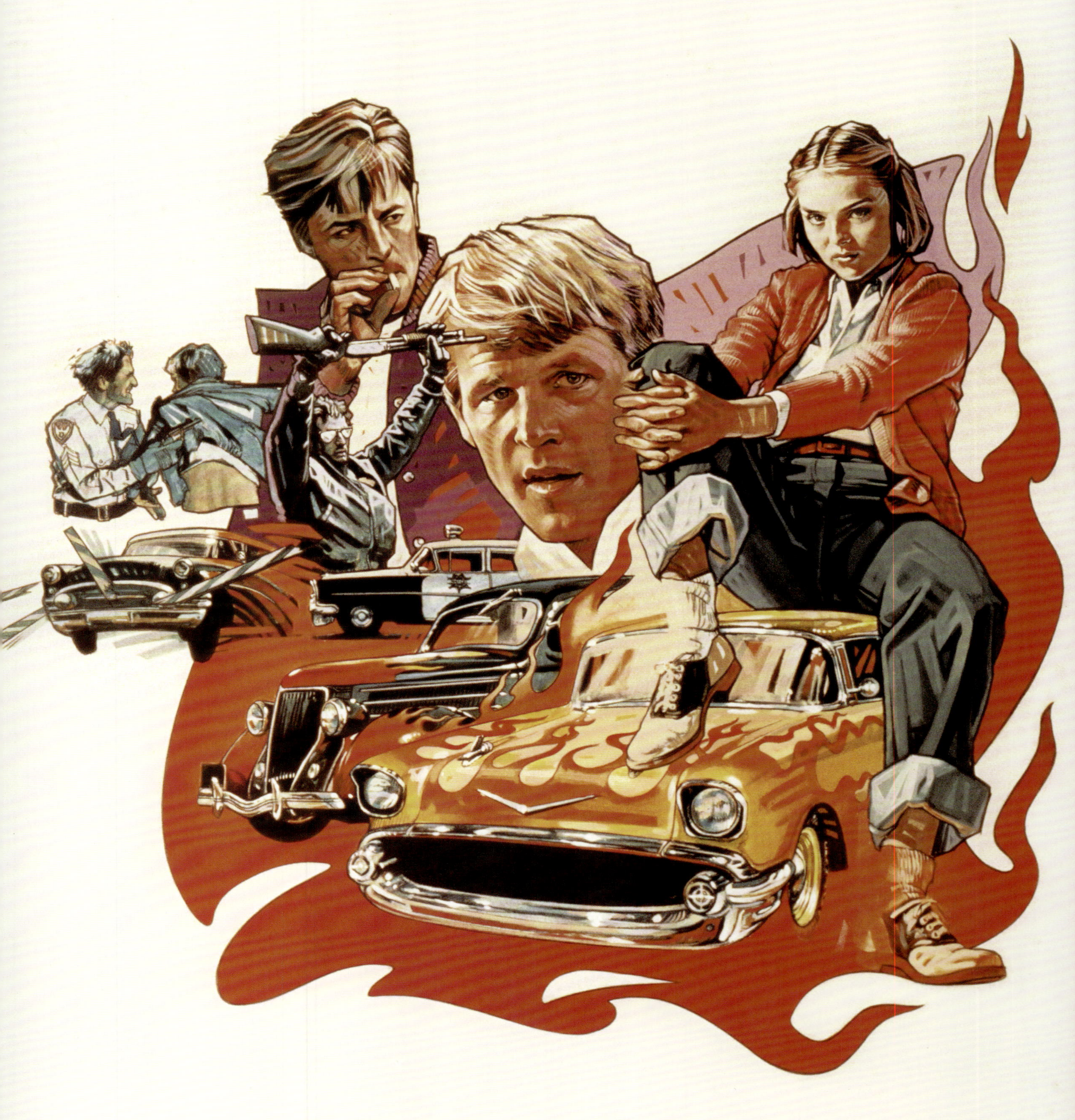

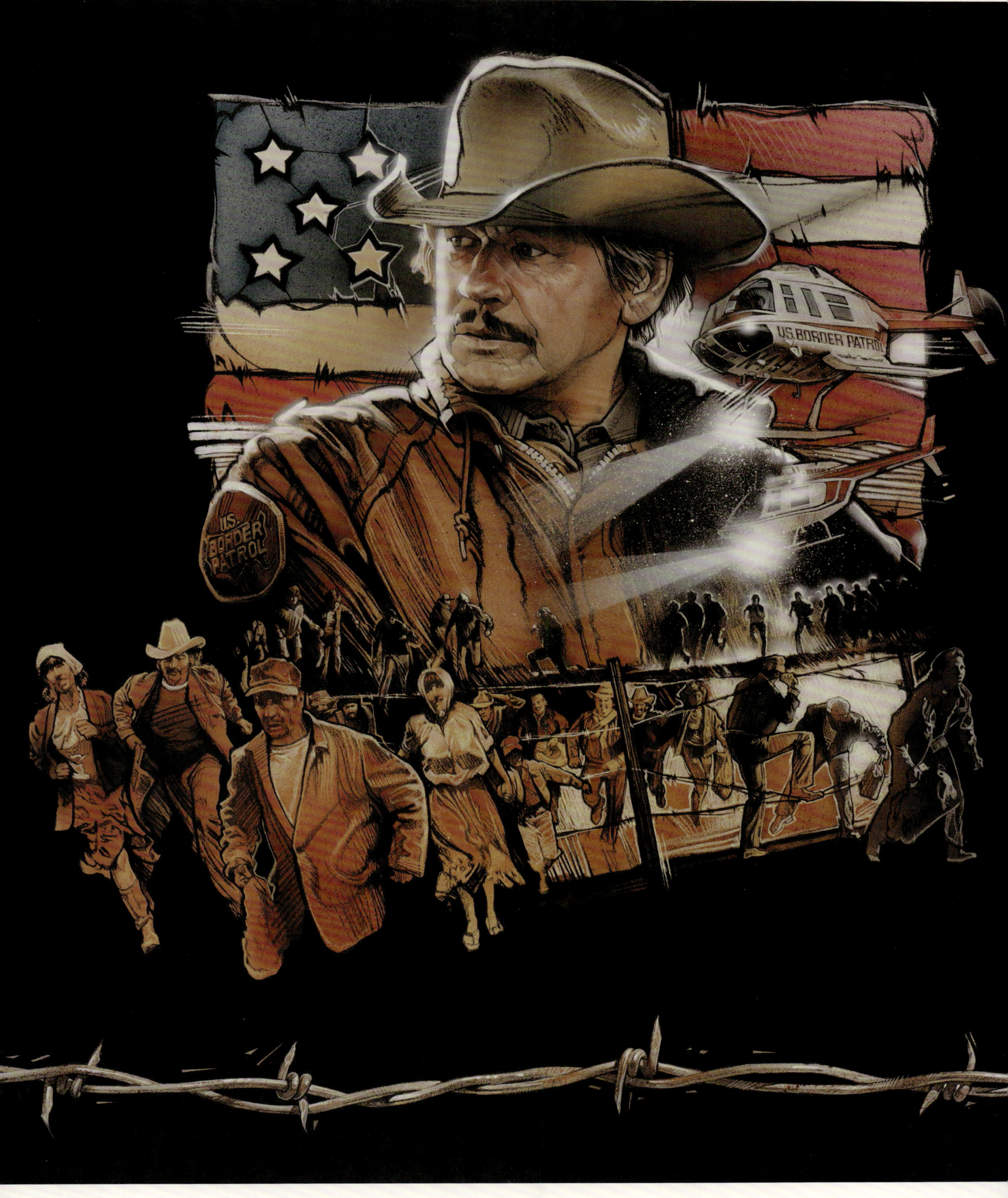
U.S. BORDER PATROL
U.S. BORDER PATROL

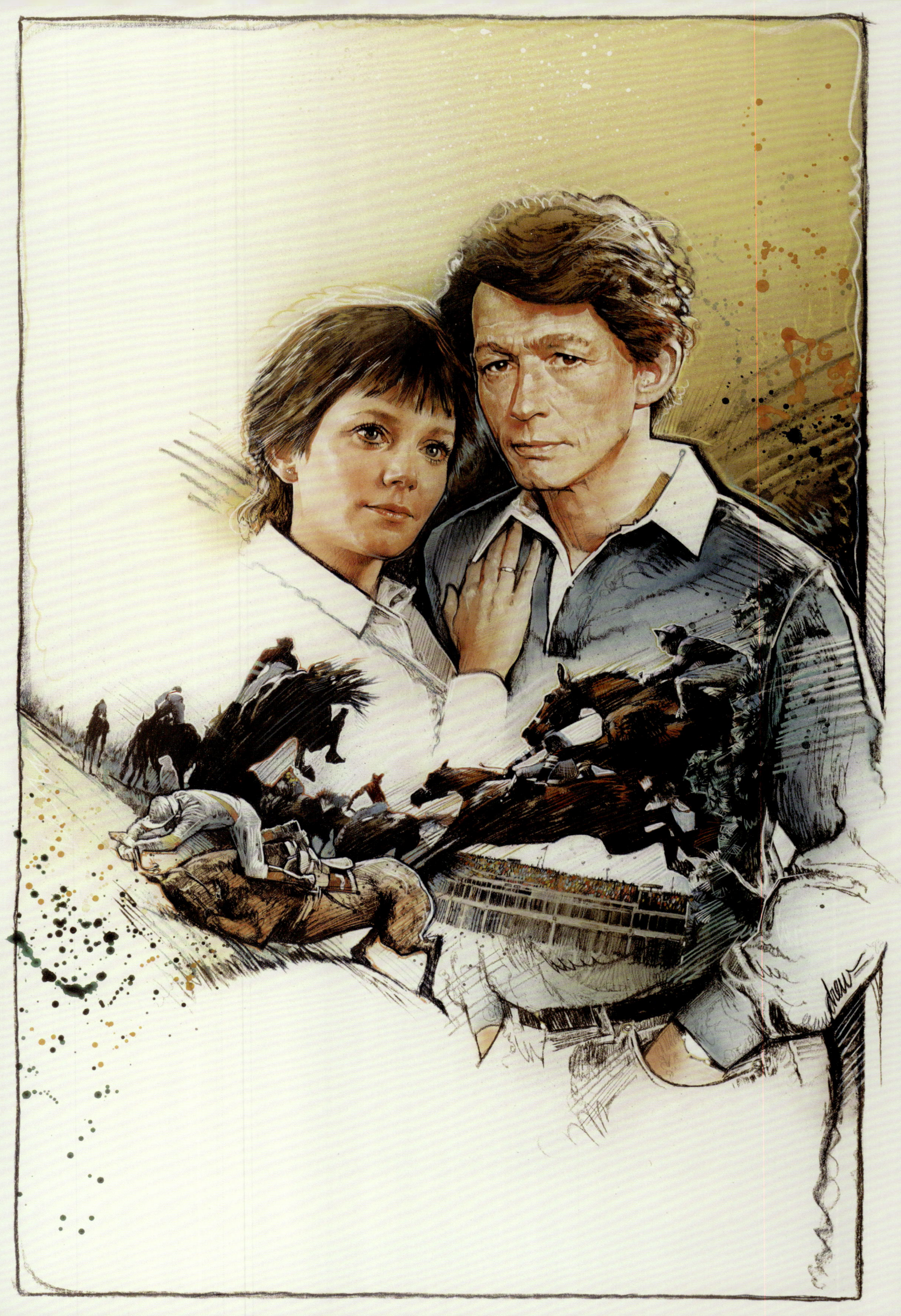

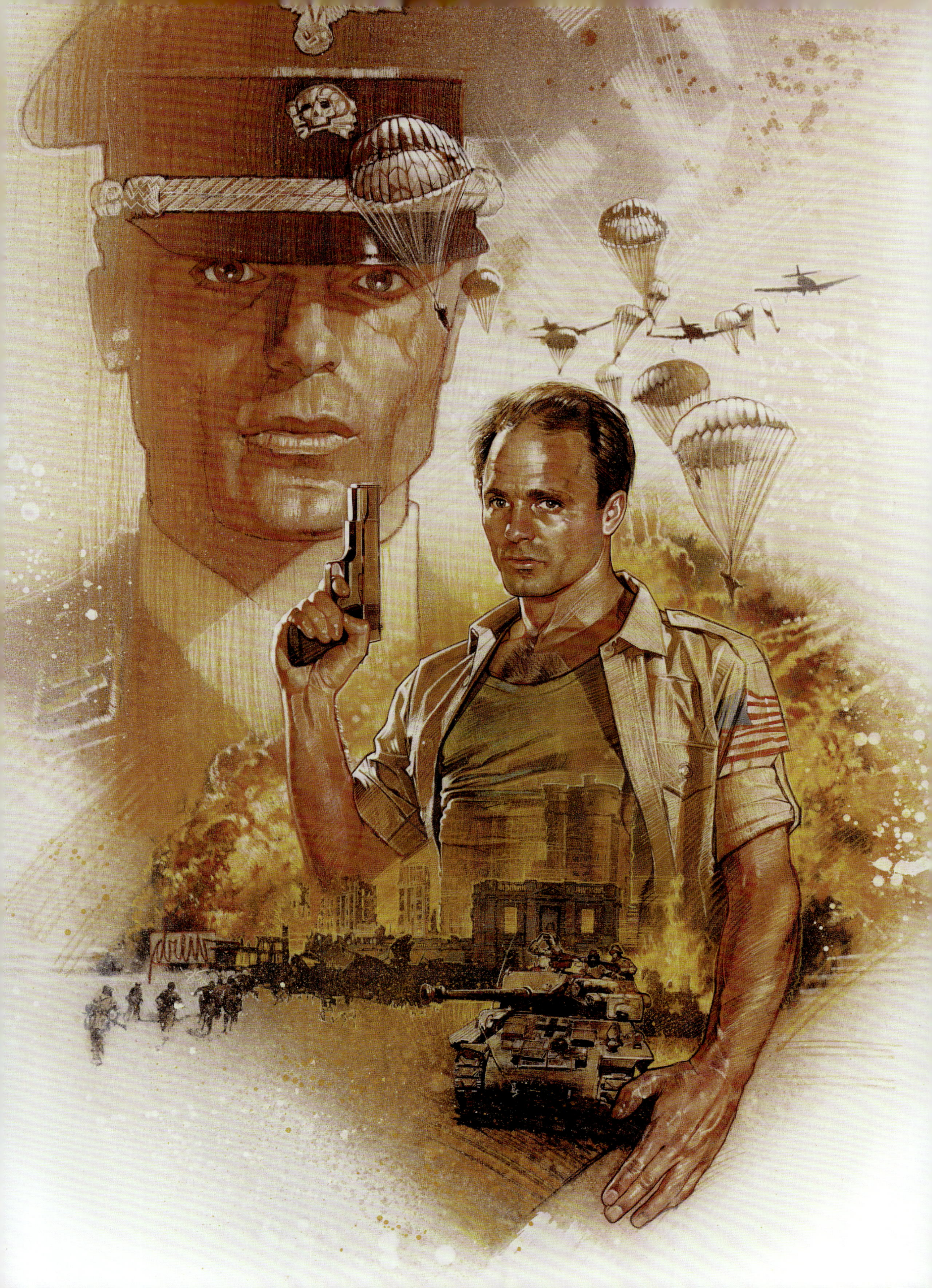

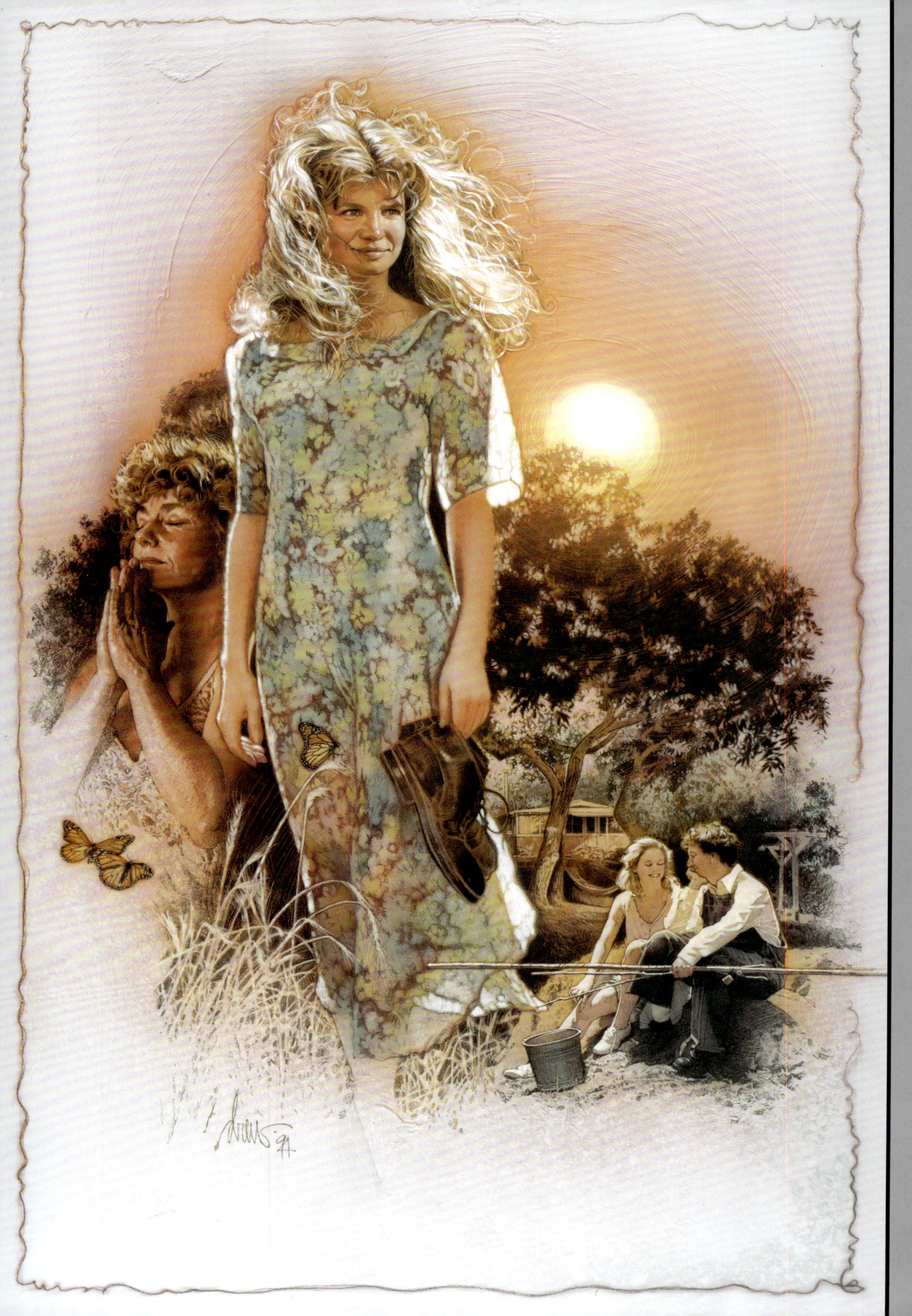

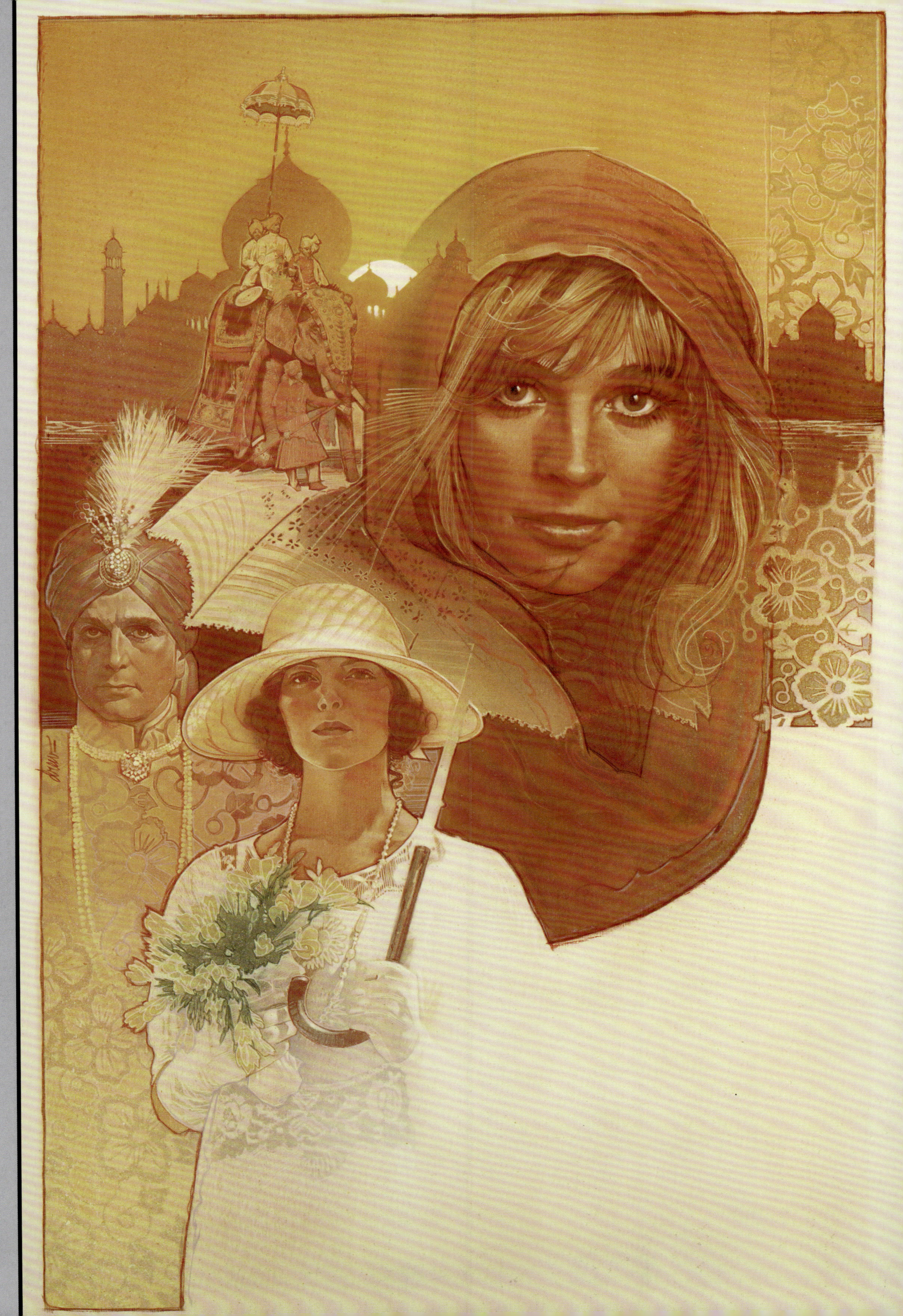

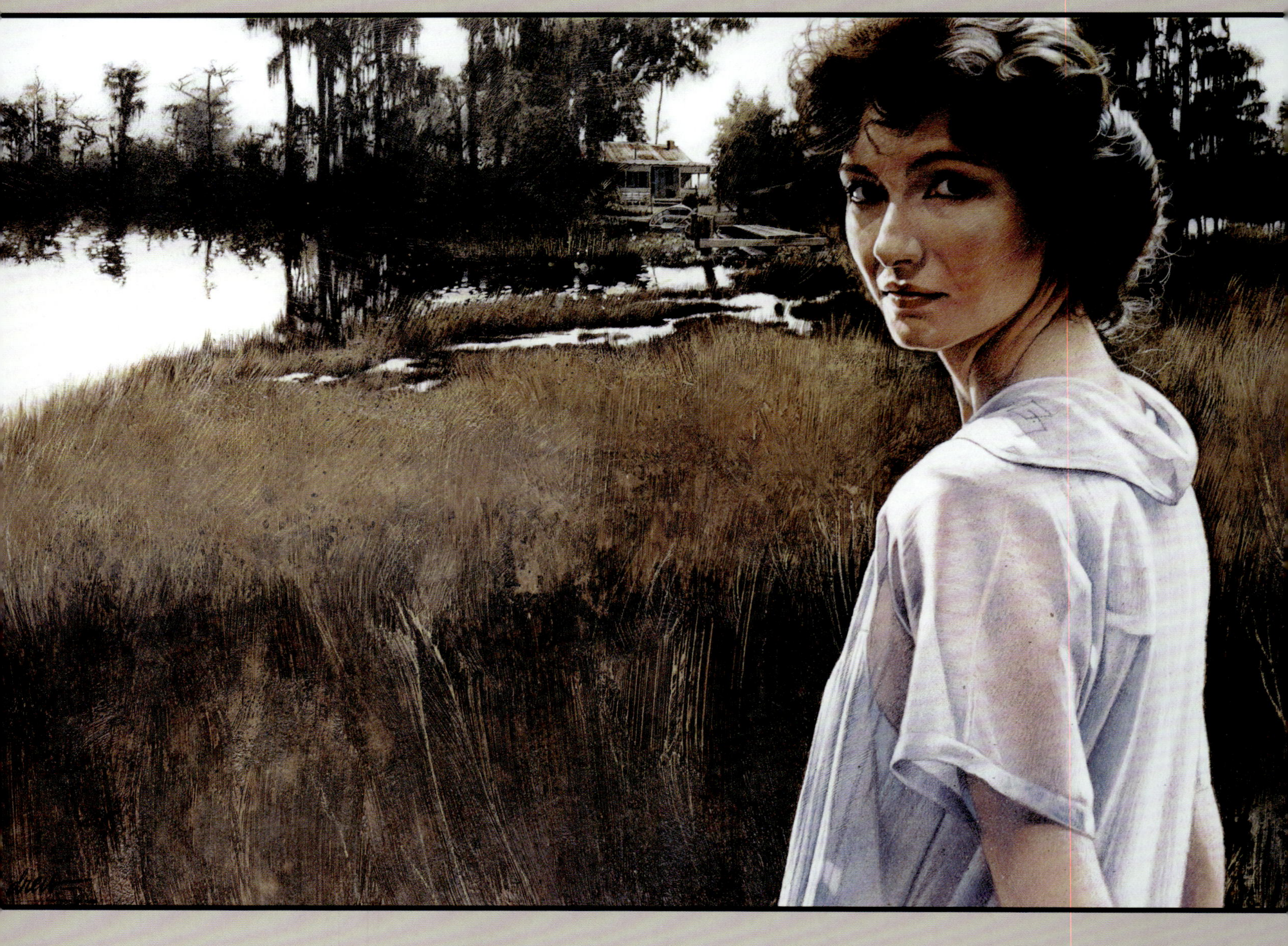

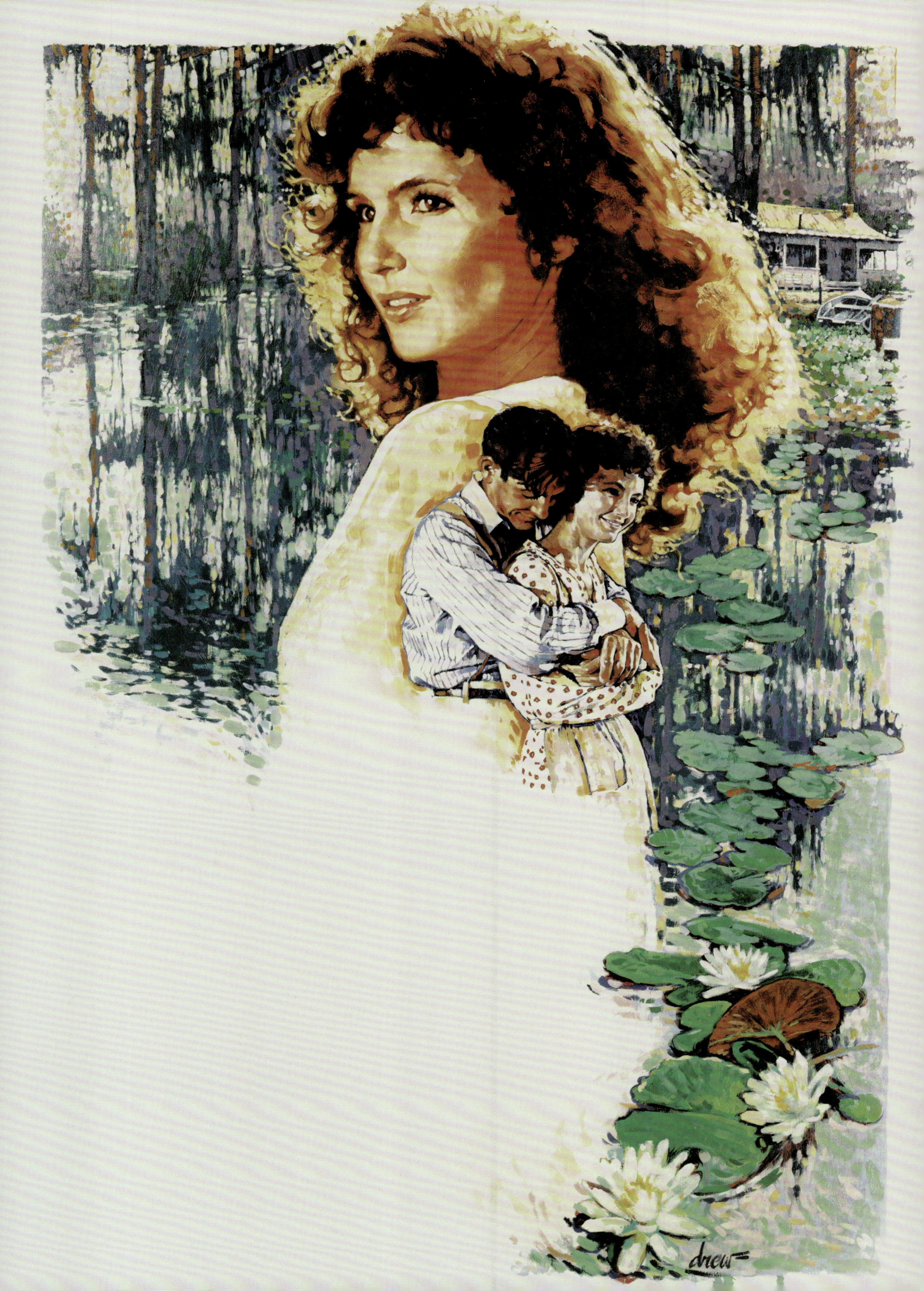
drew

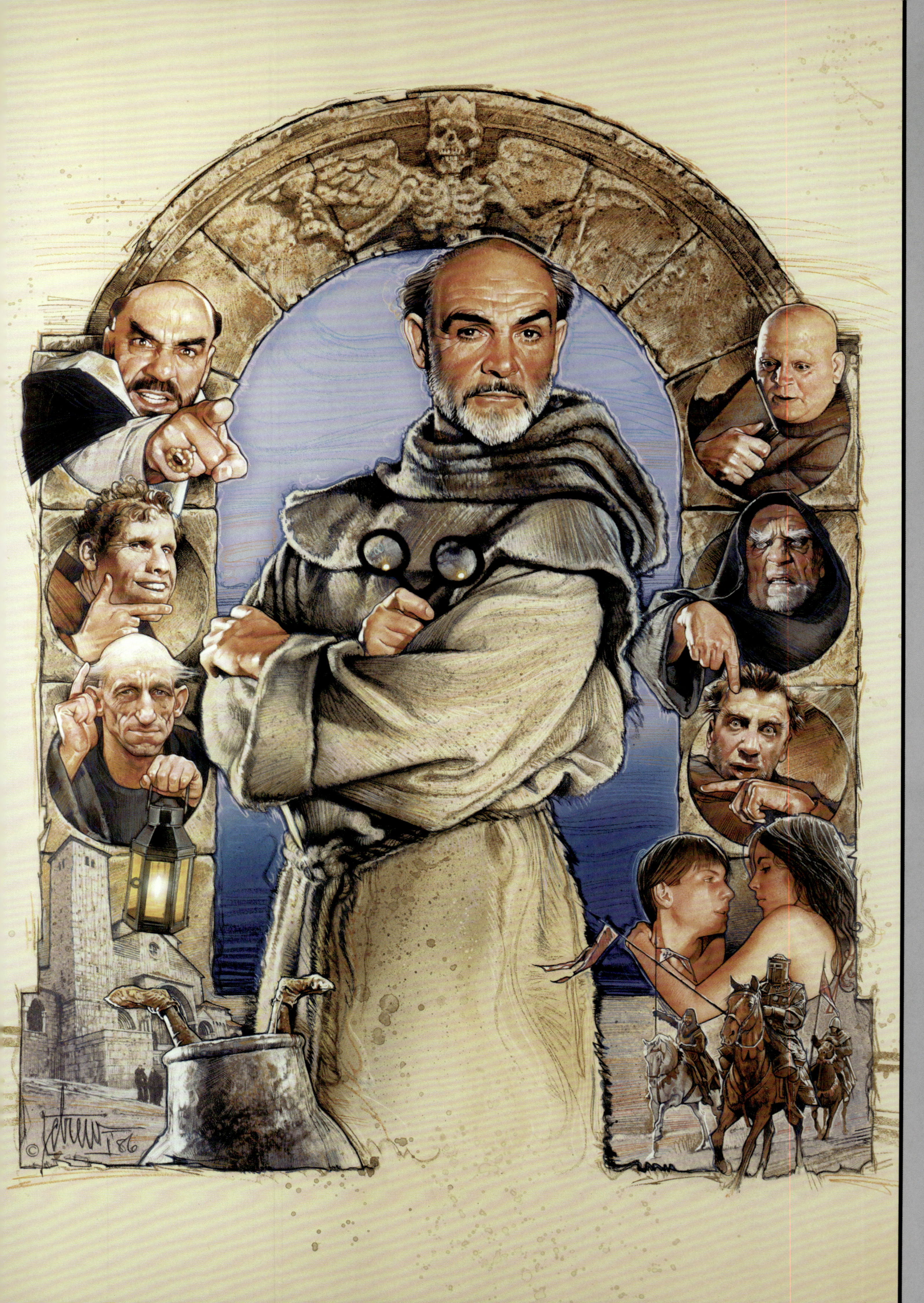
© Drew '86

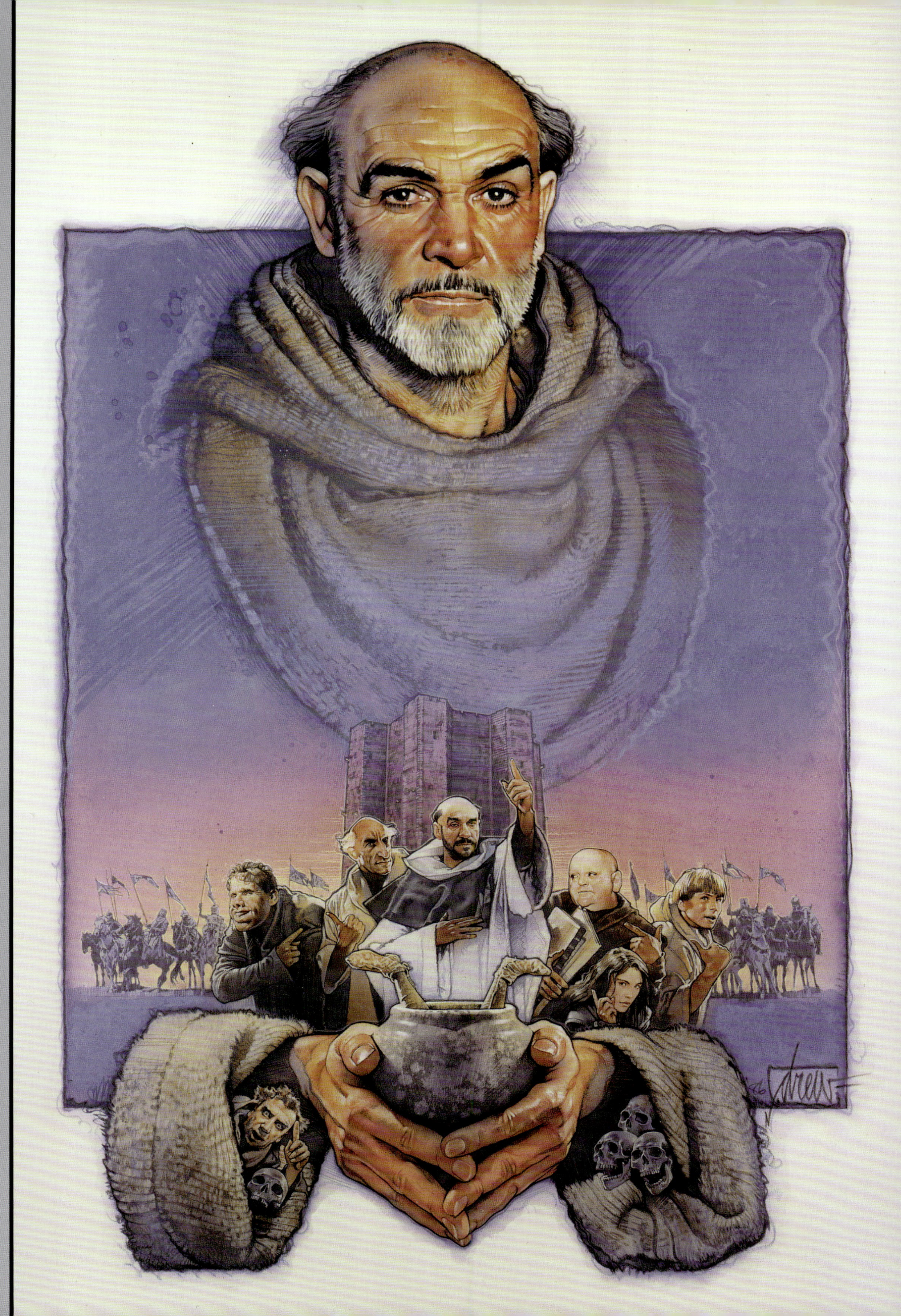

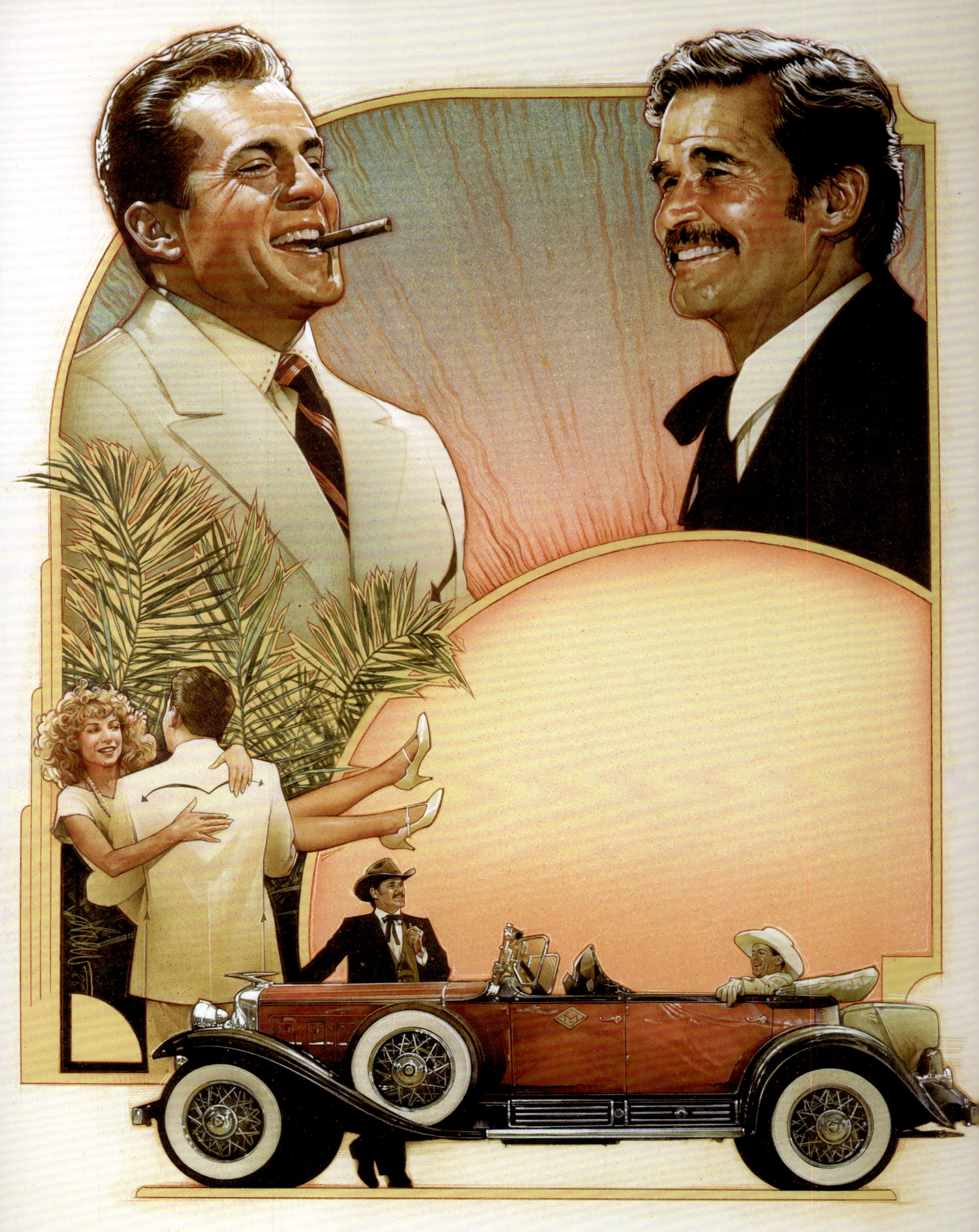

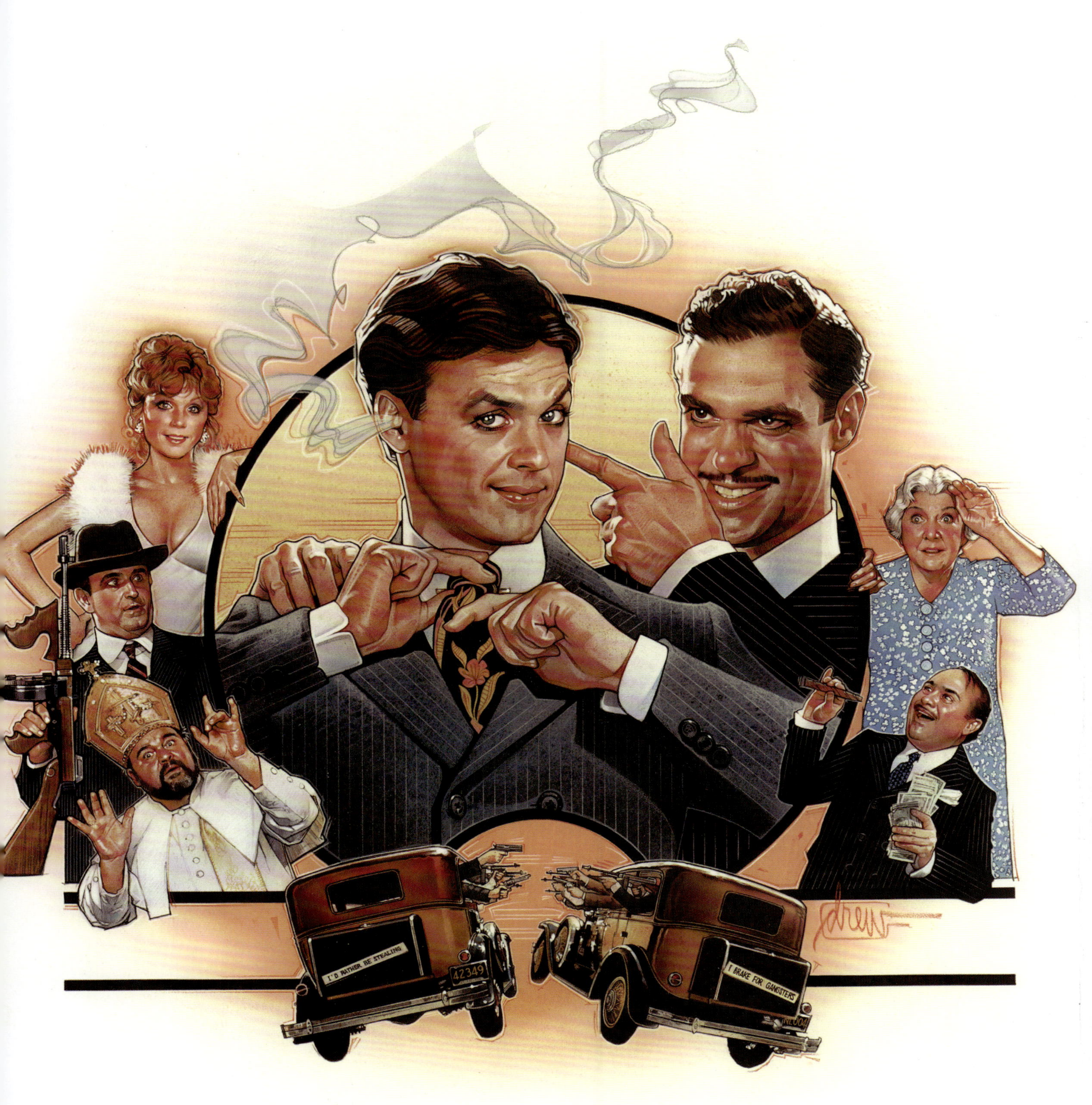

I'D RATHER BE STEALING
42349
I BRAKE FOR GANGSTERS
drew

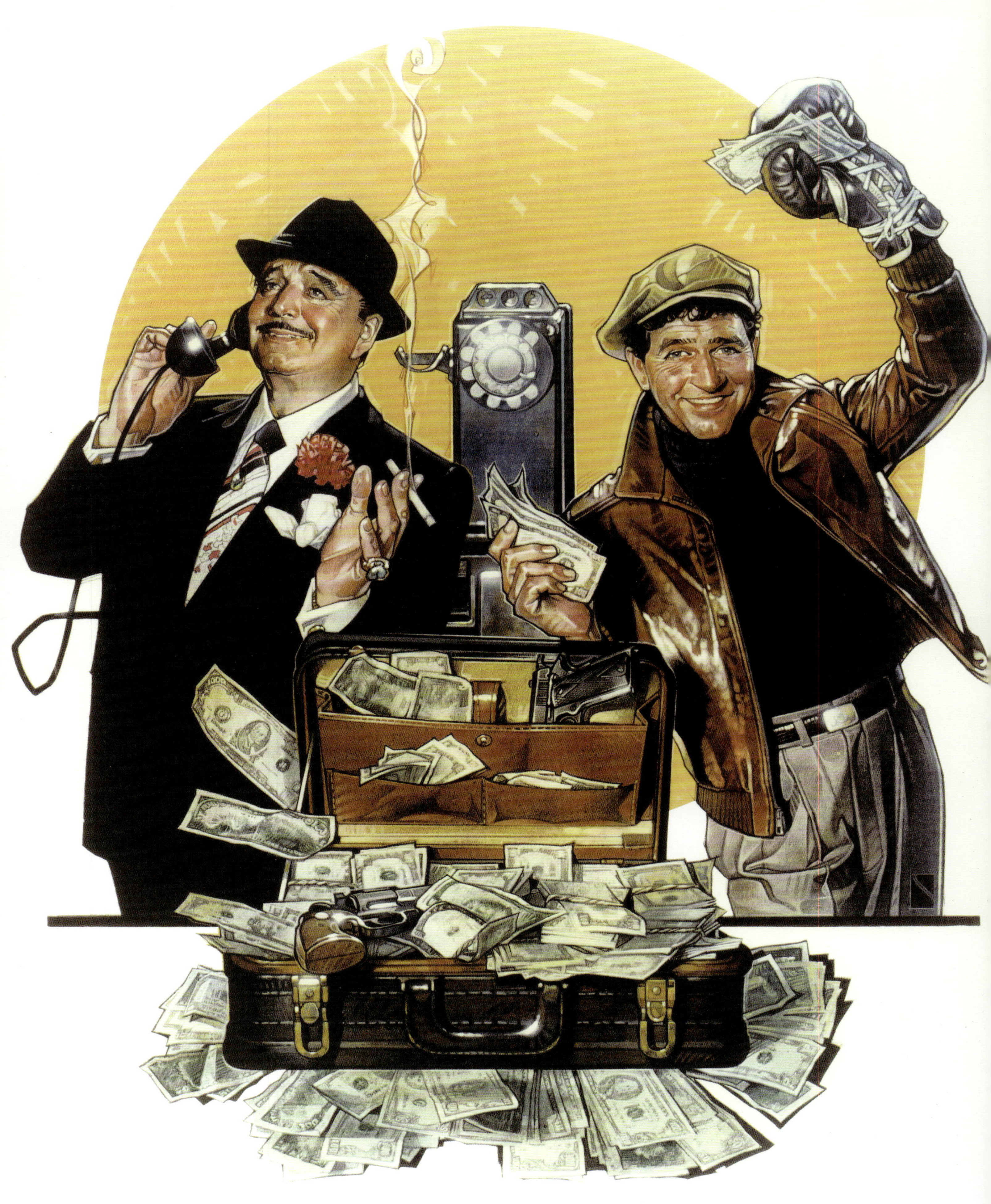

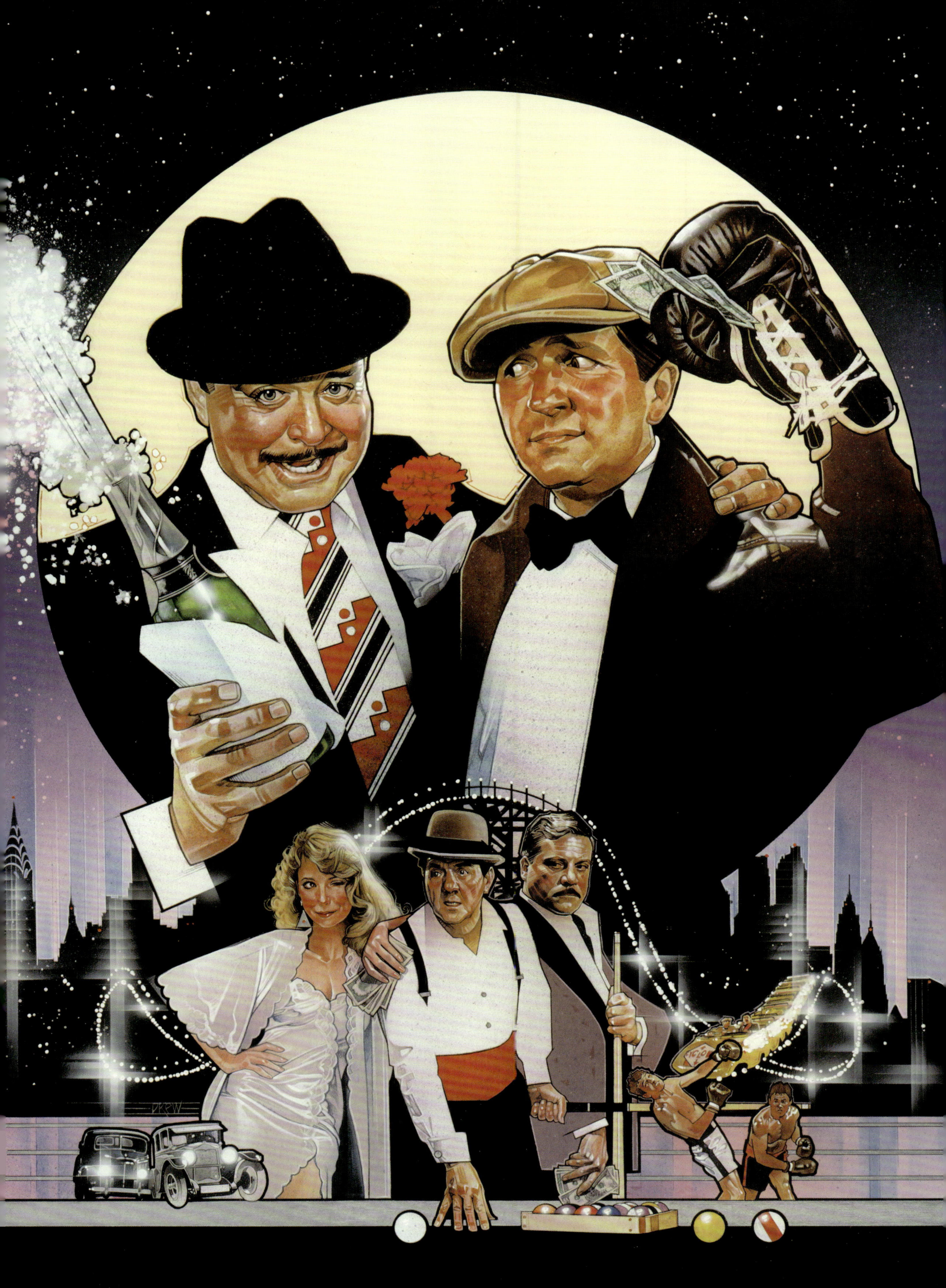
DREW

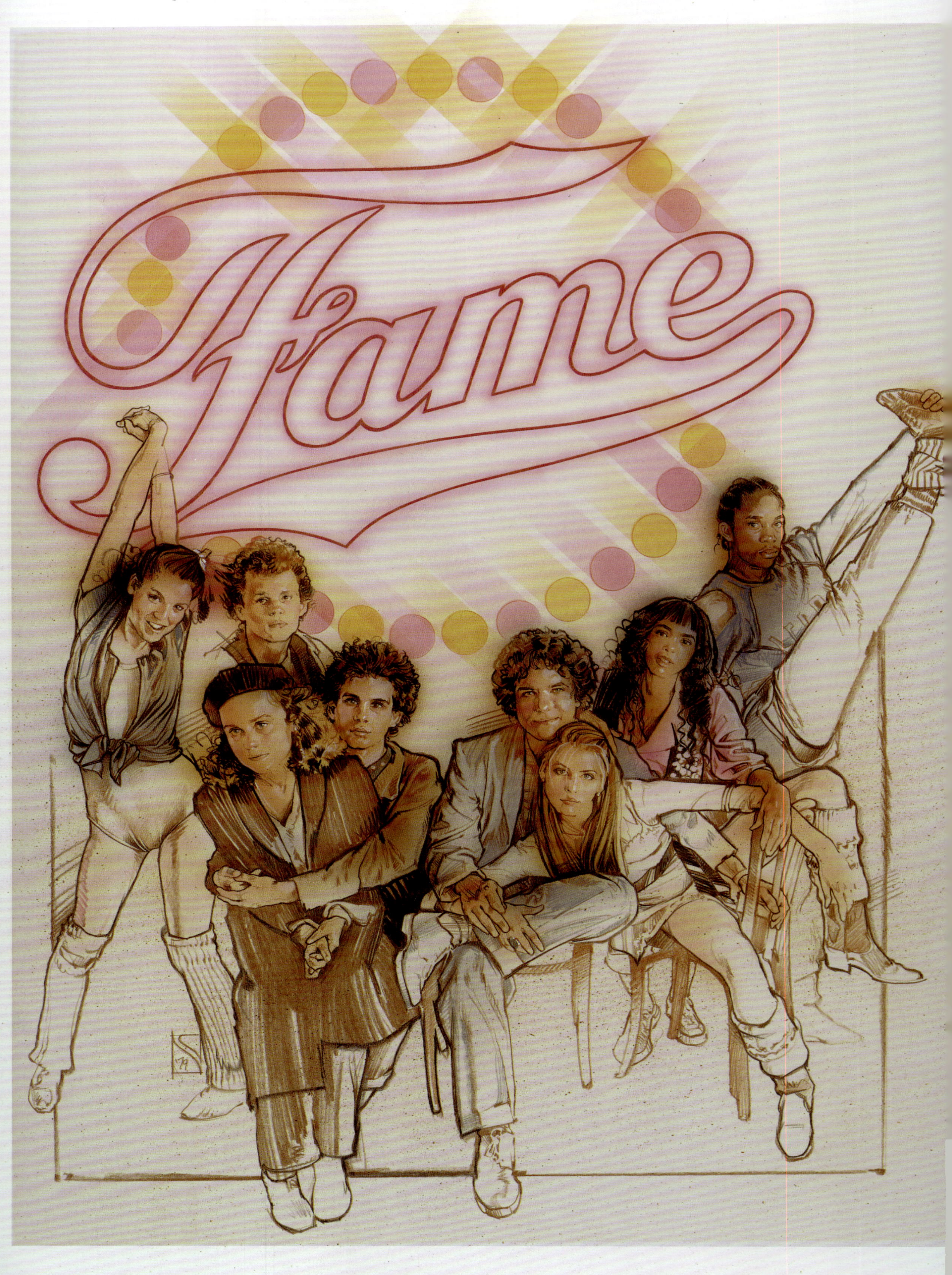
Fame

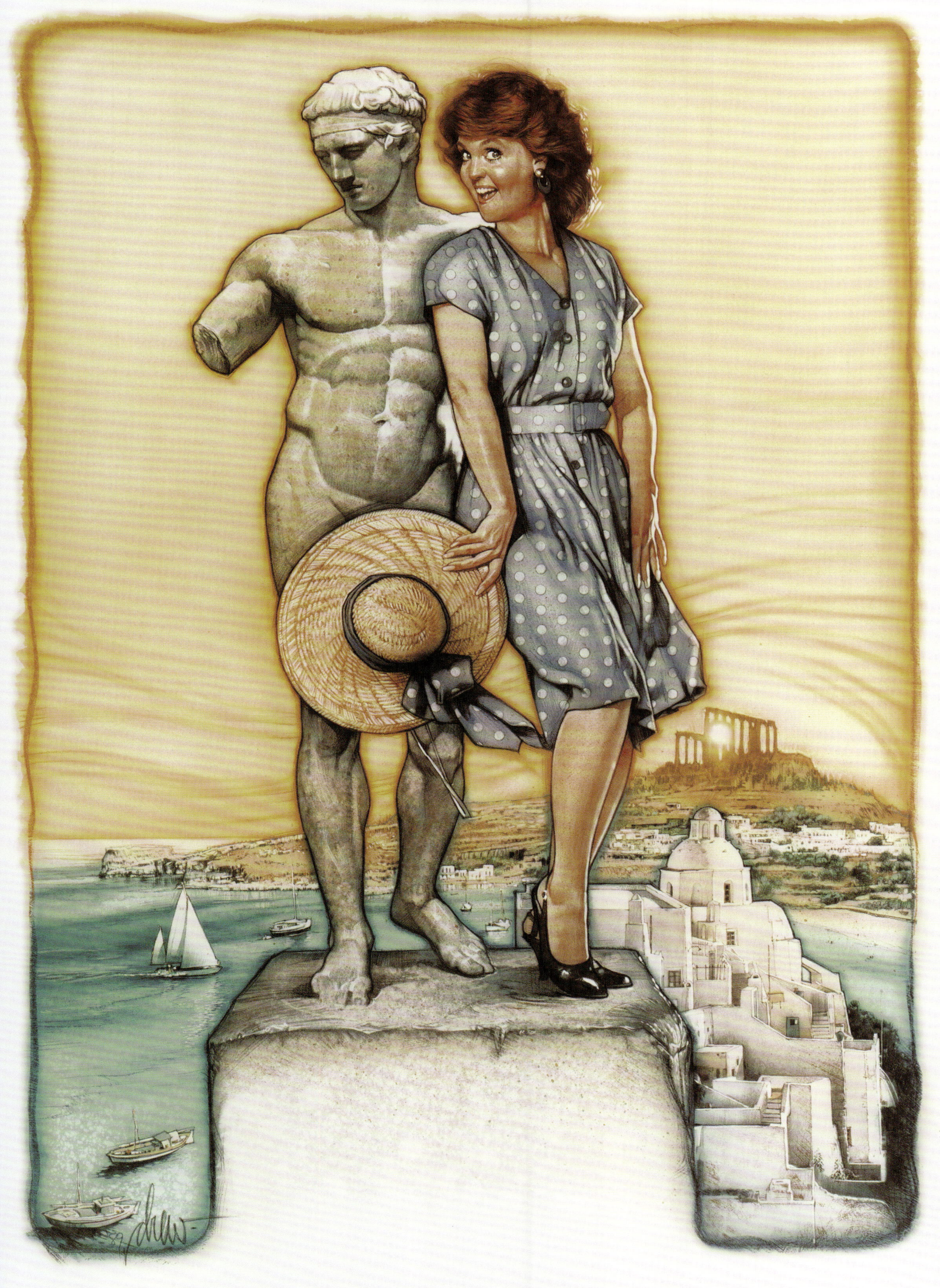

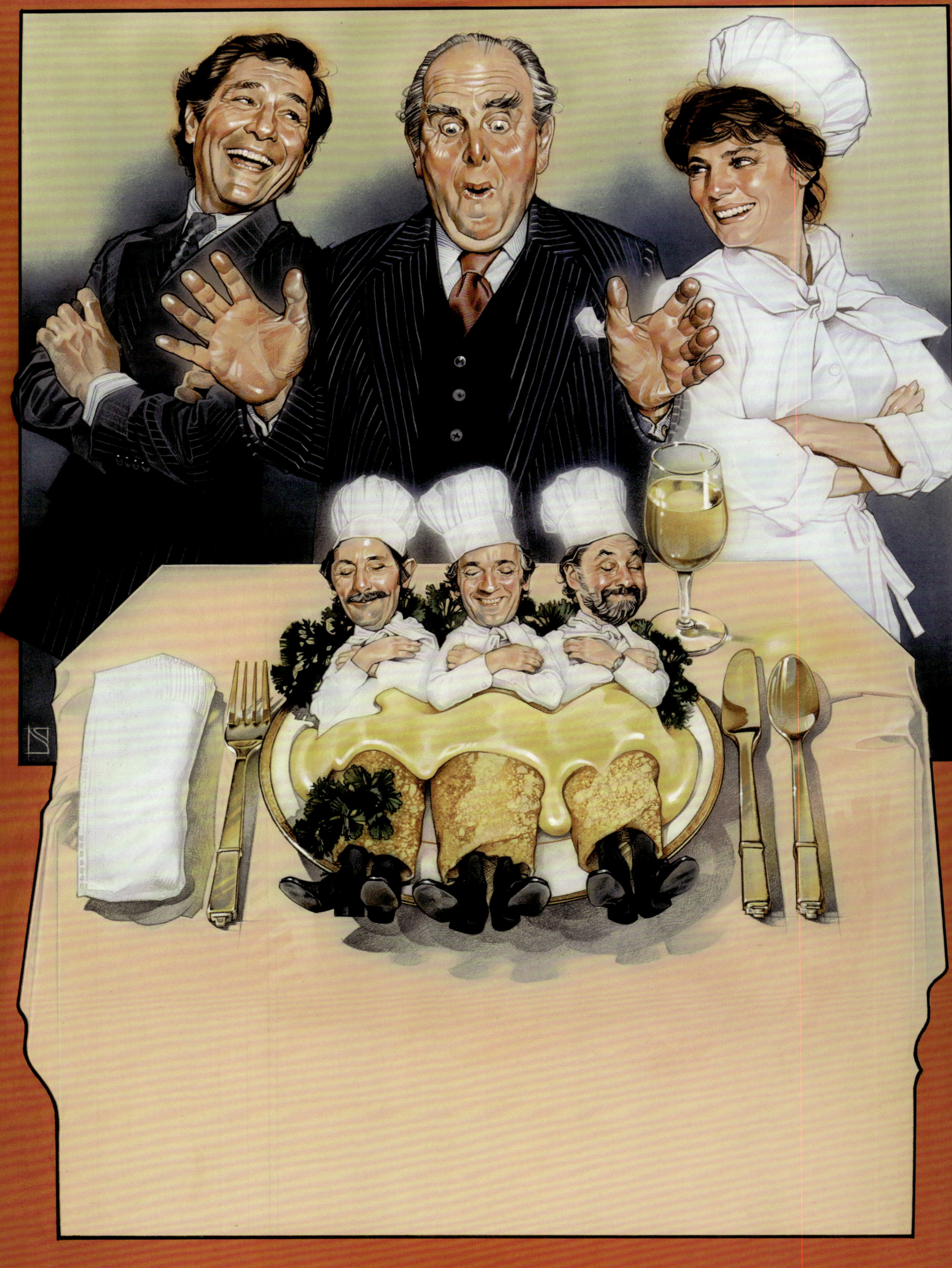

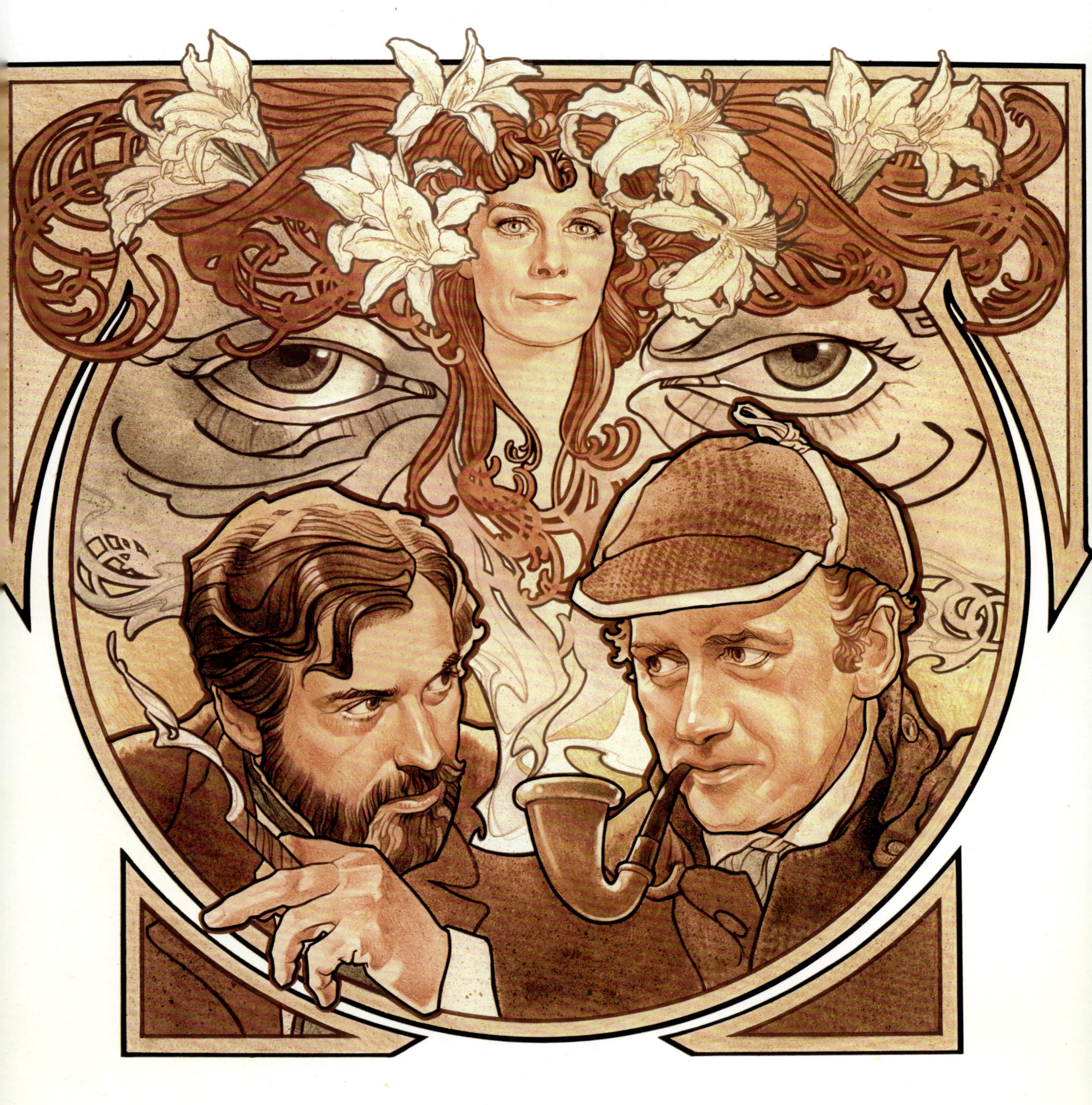

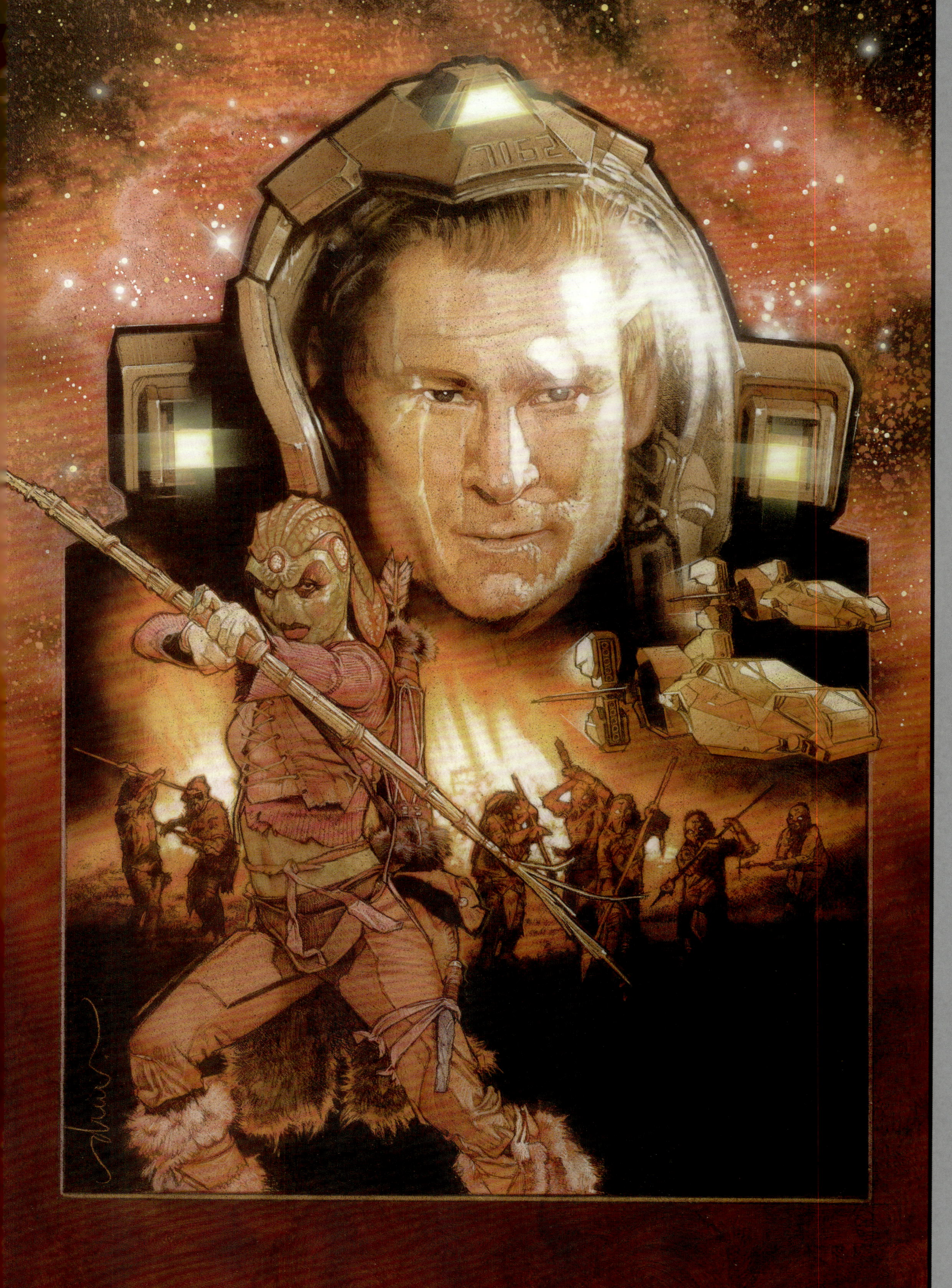

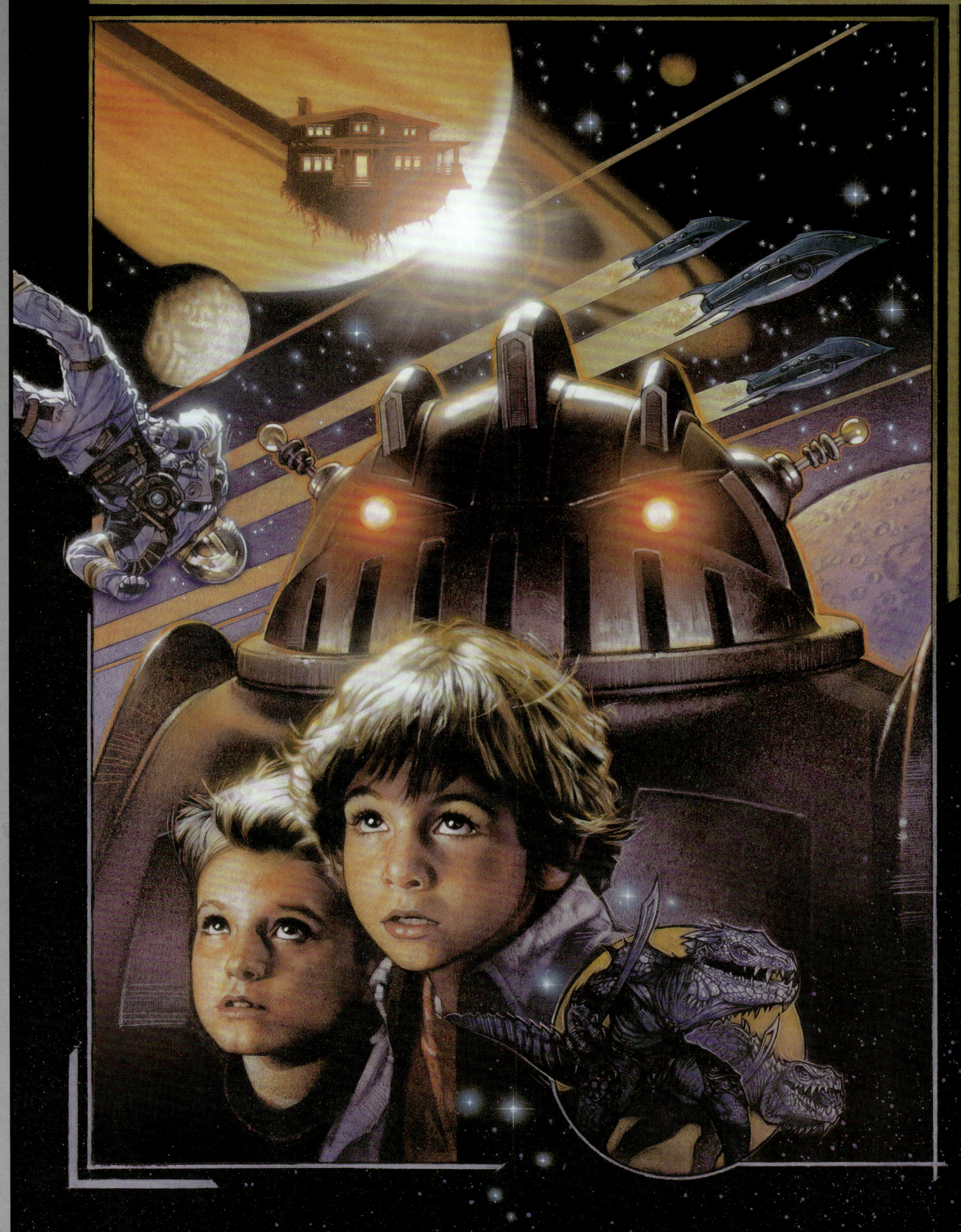

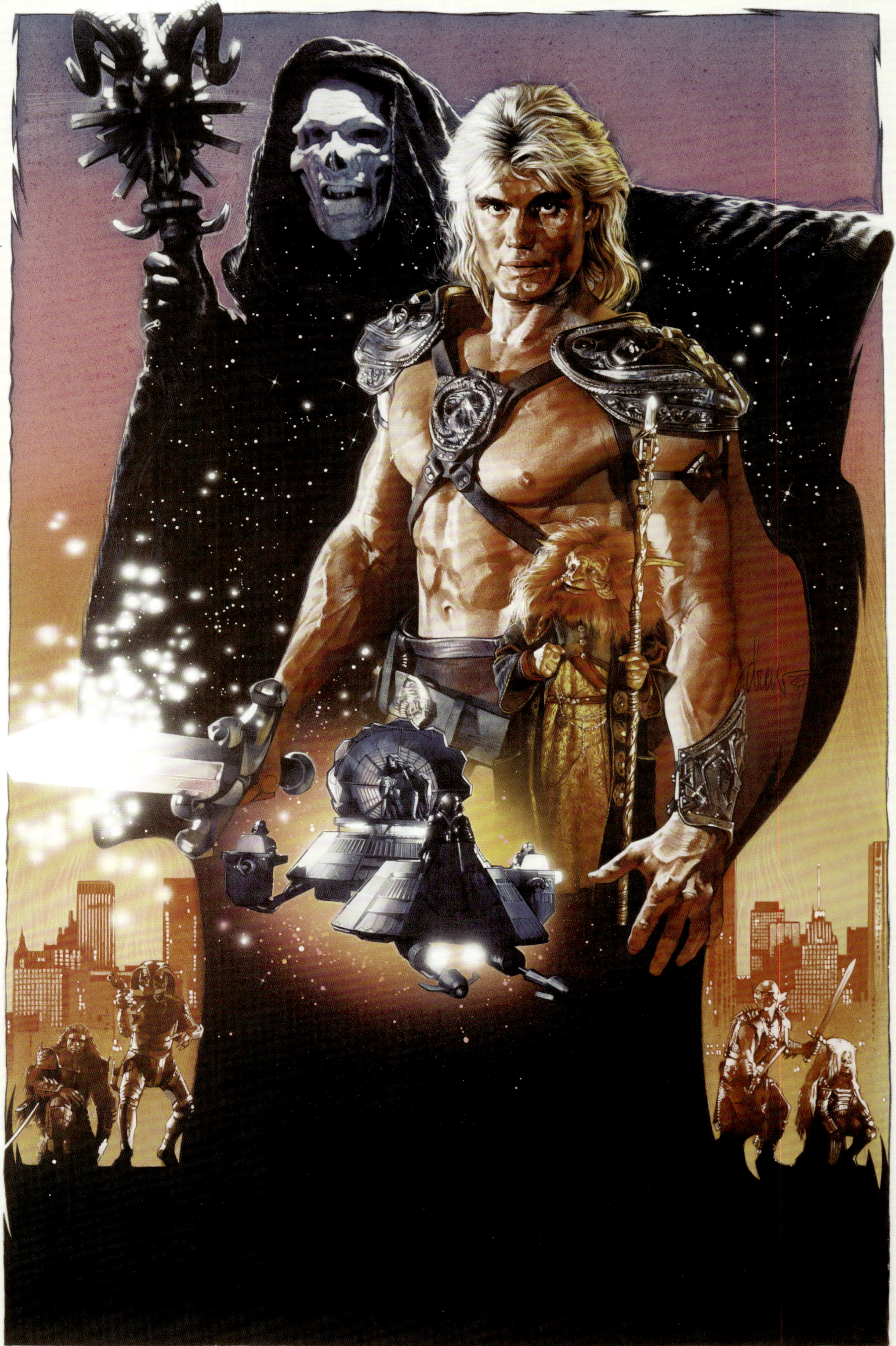

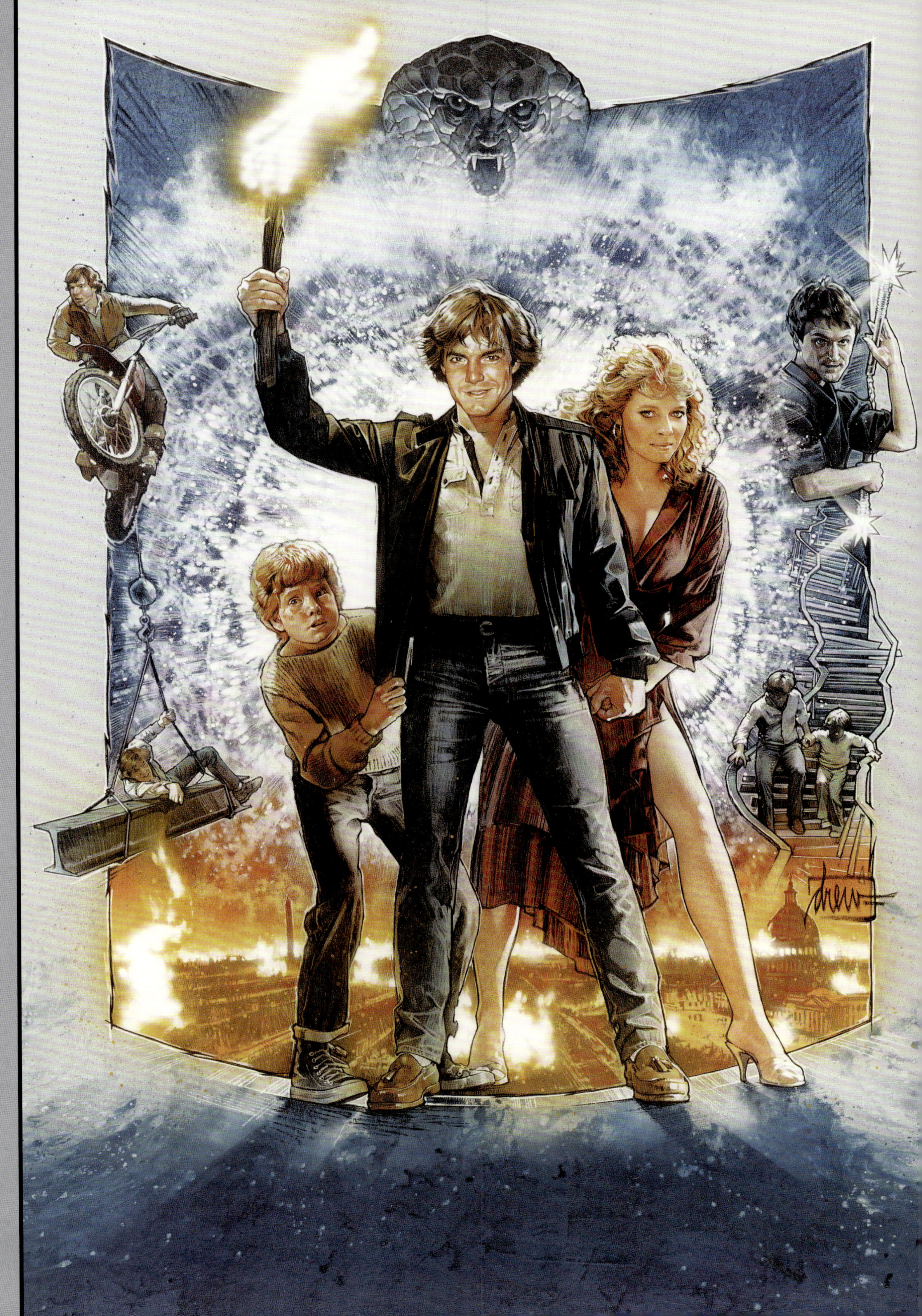
drew

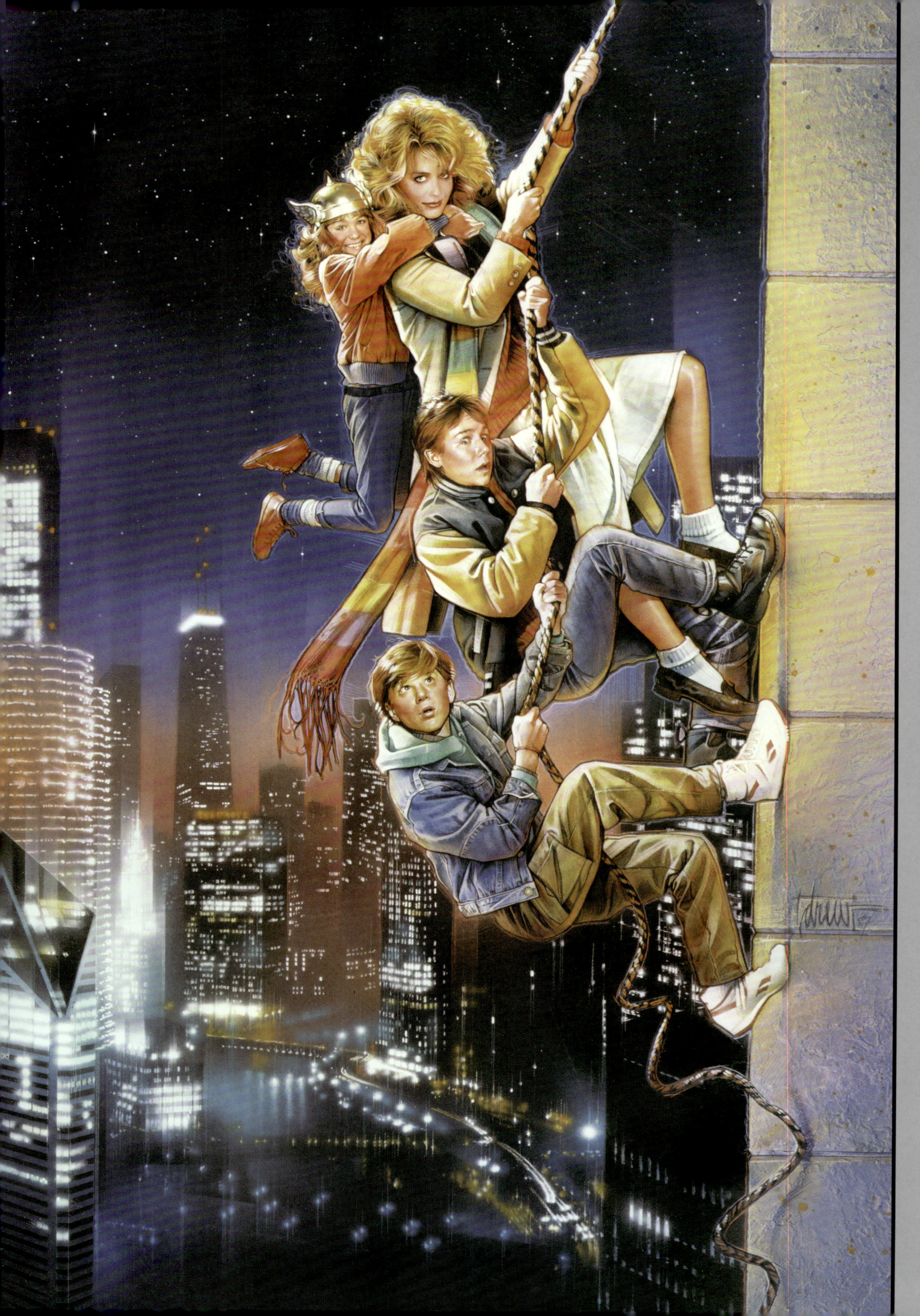

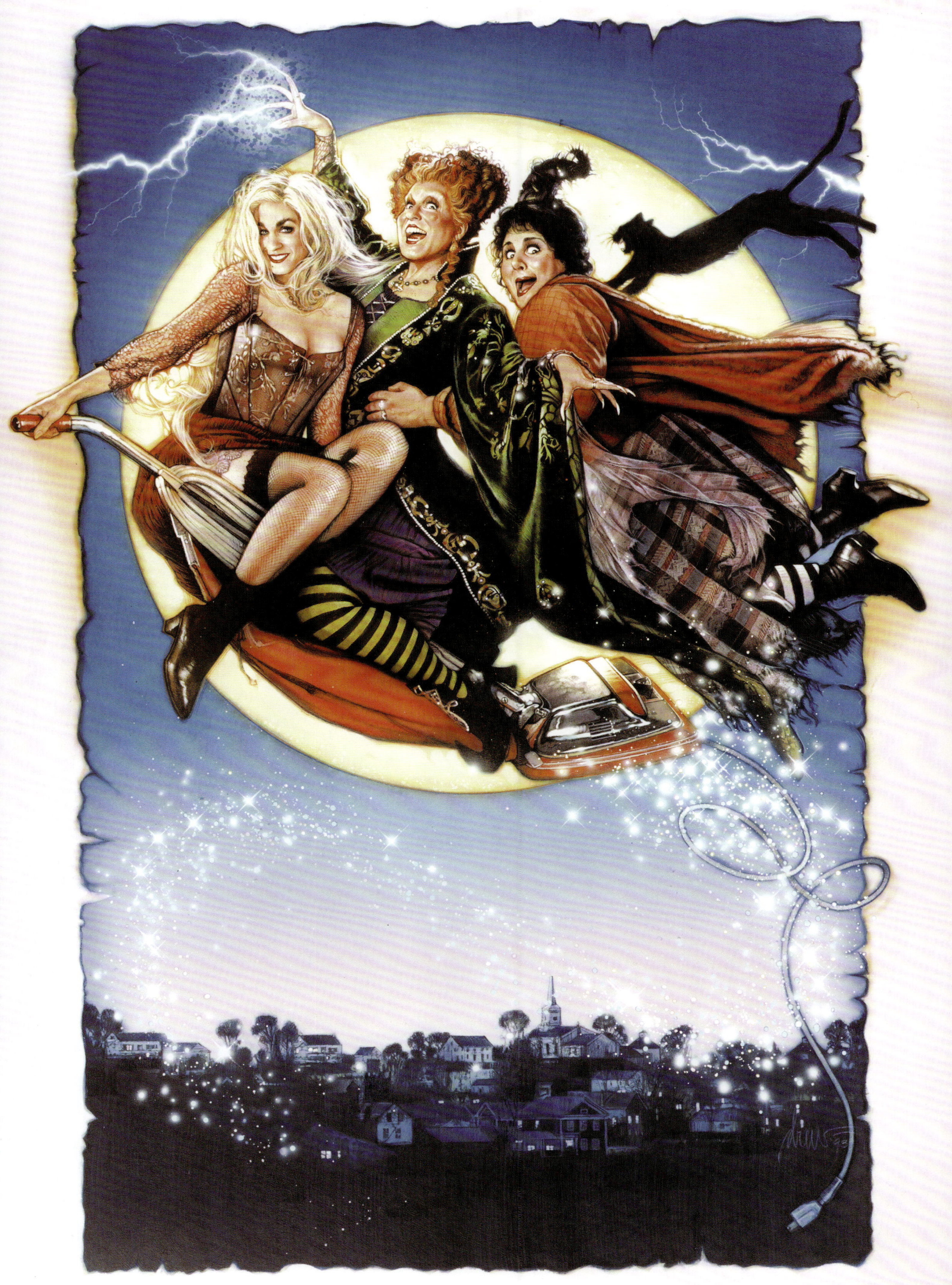

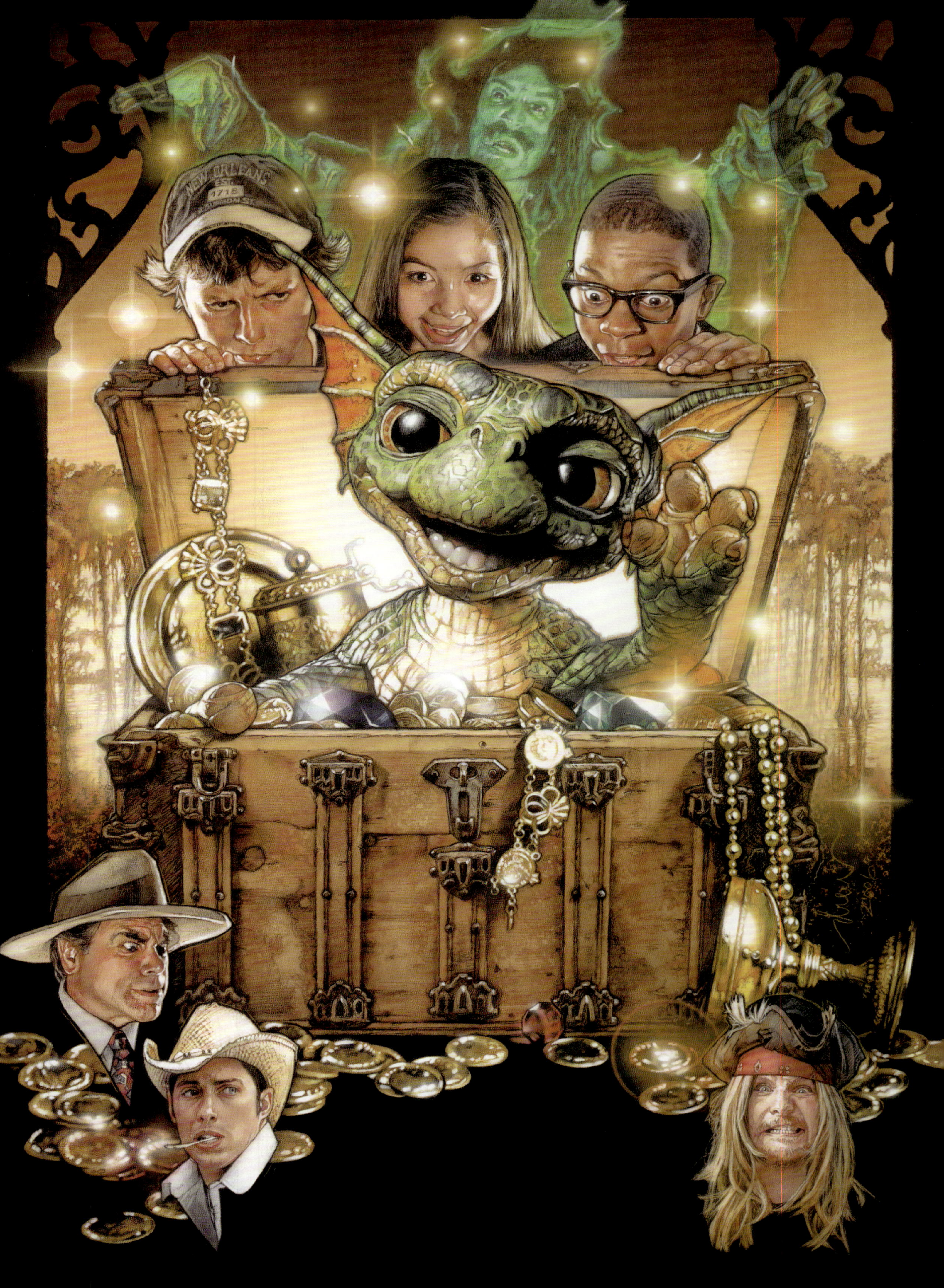
NEW ORLEANS
EST.
1718

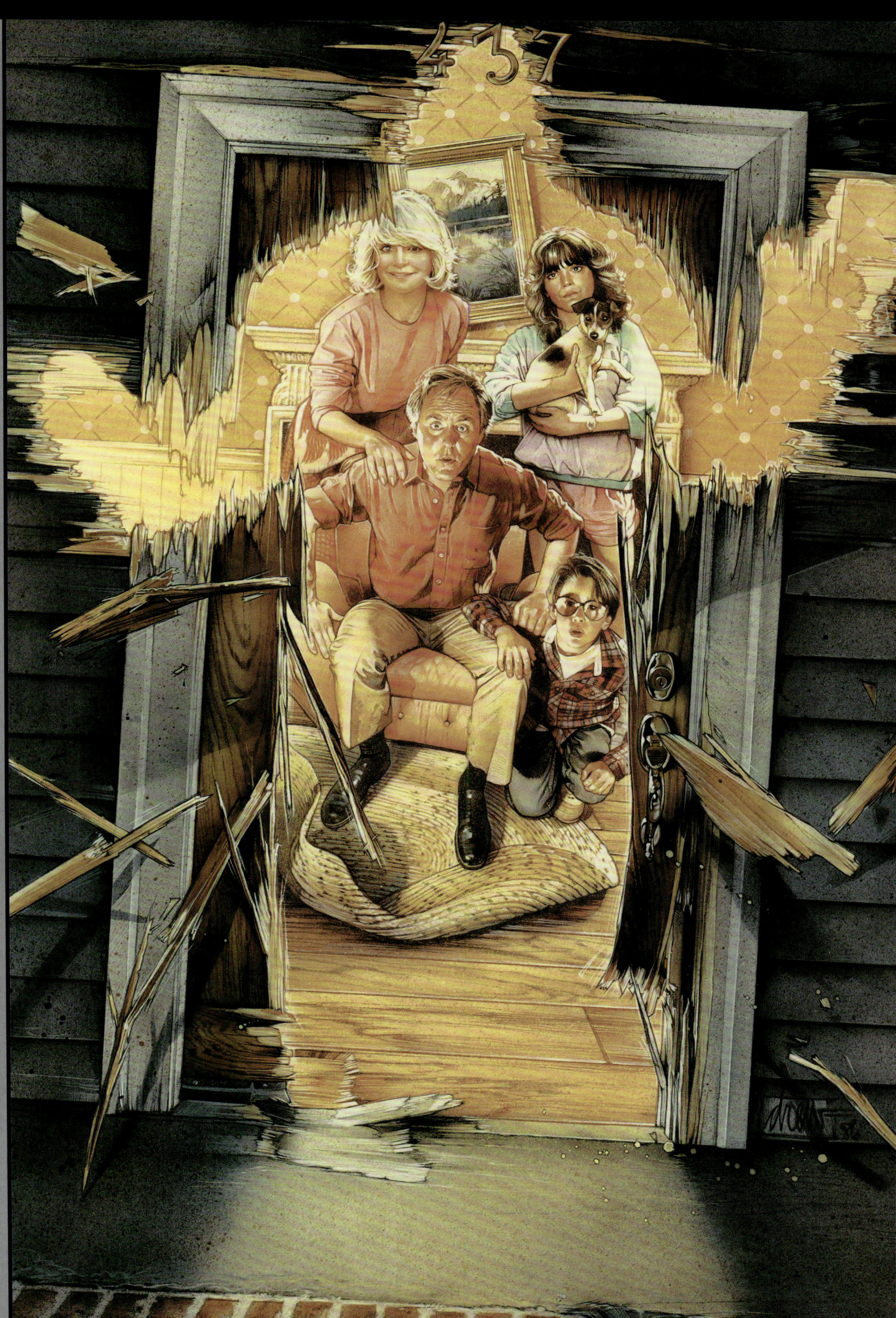
437

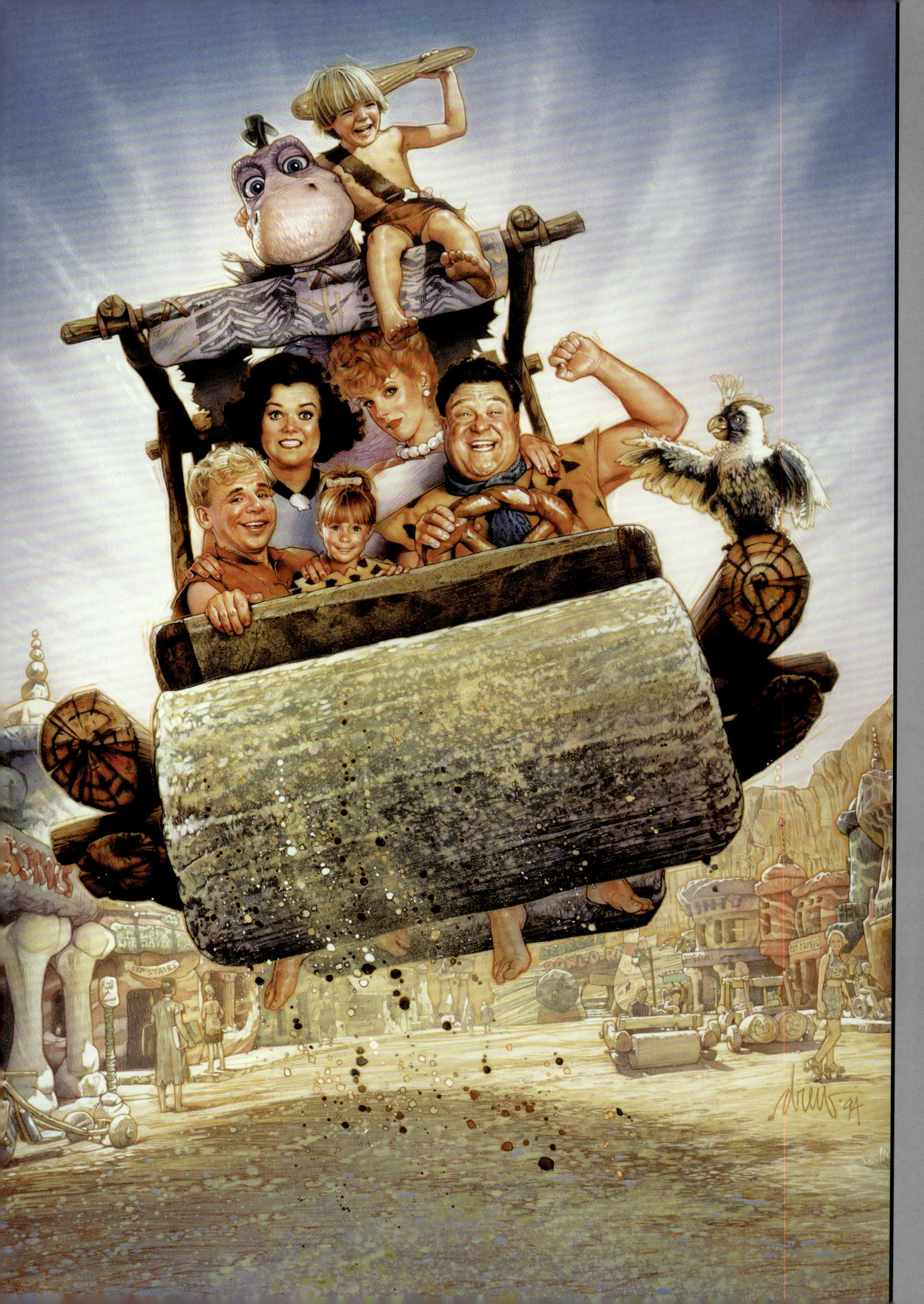
UP STAIRS

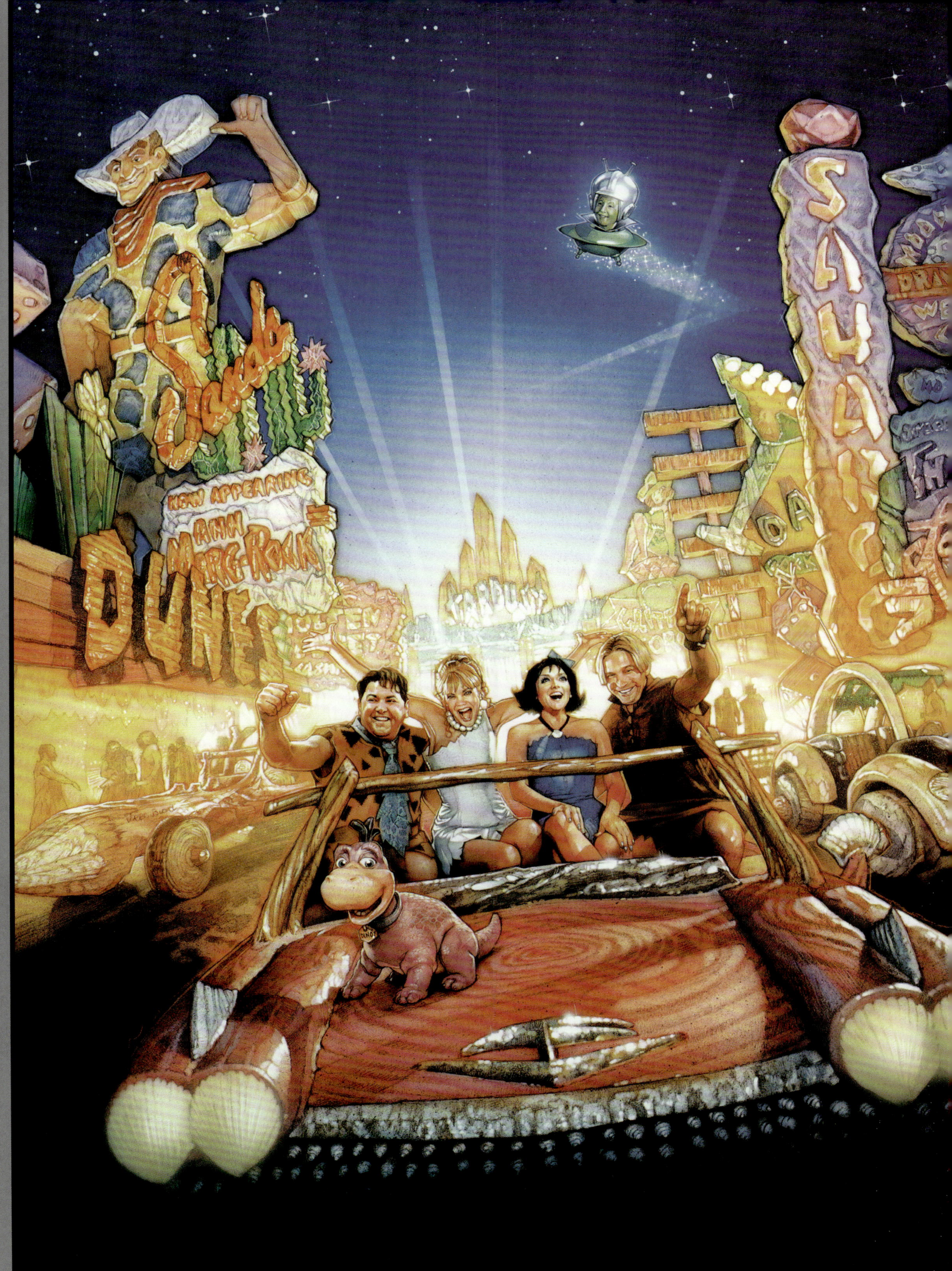
NOW APPEARING
ANN MARG-ROCK

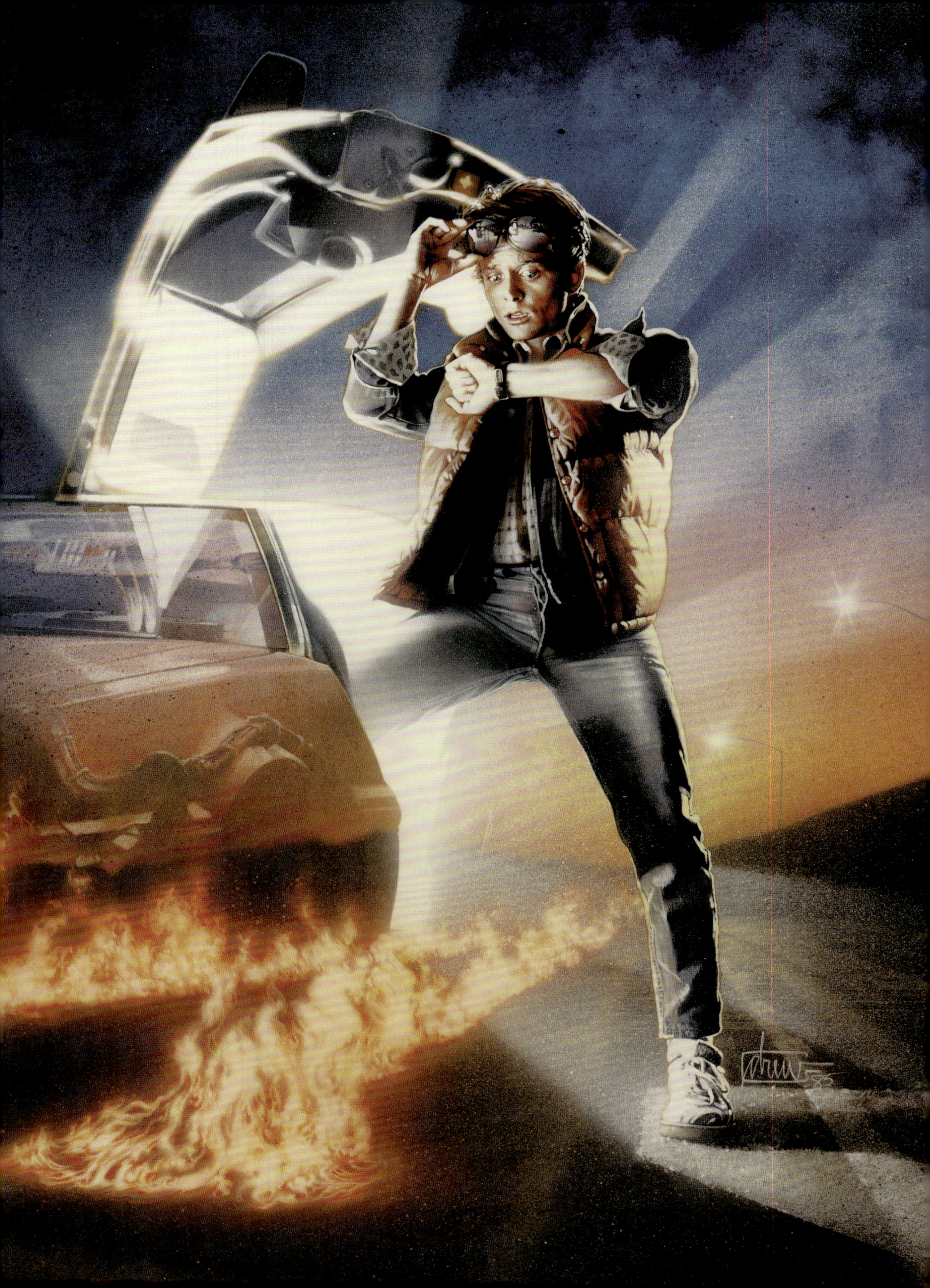

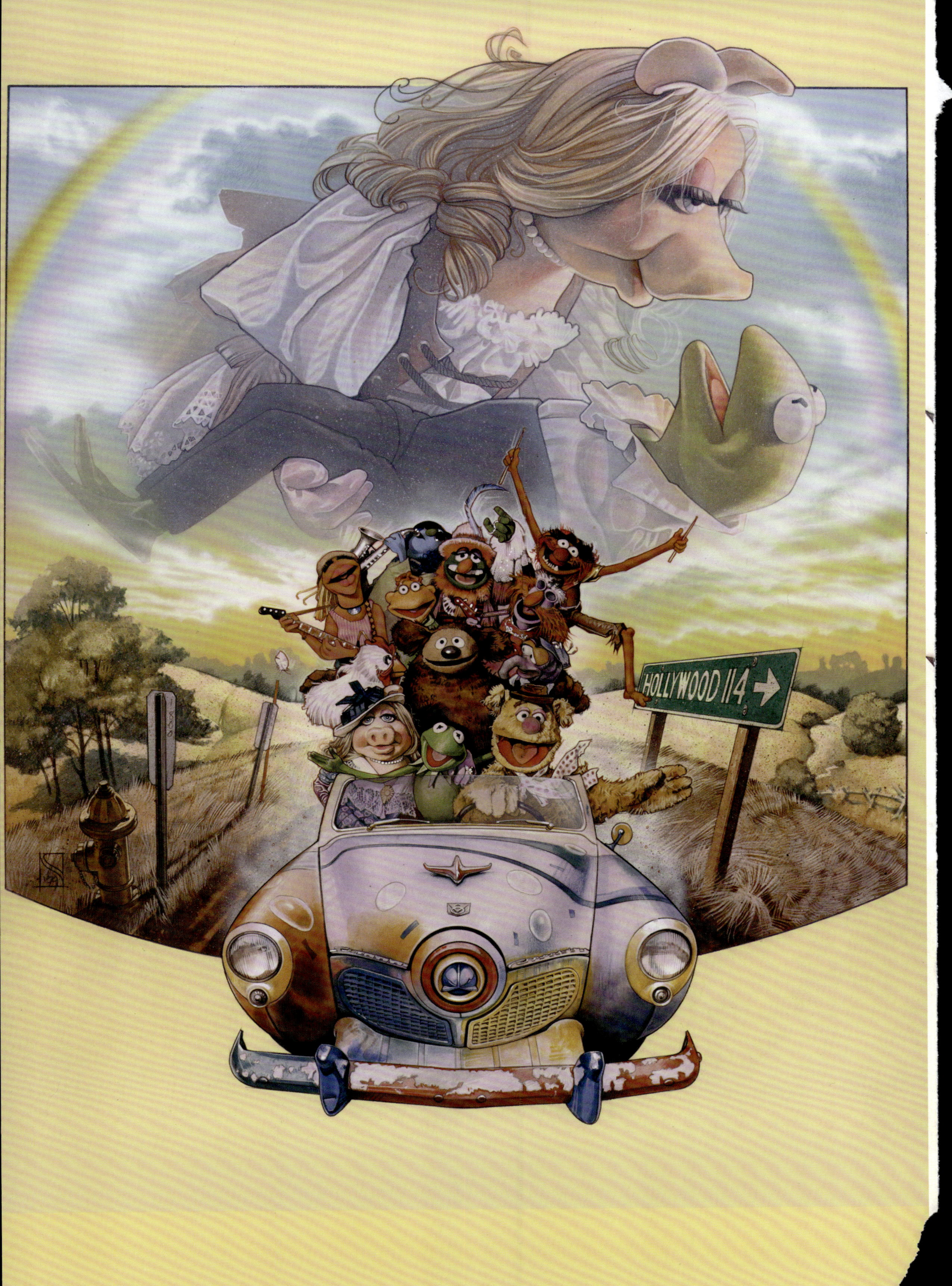
HOLLYWOOD 114

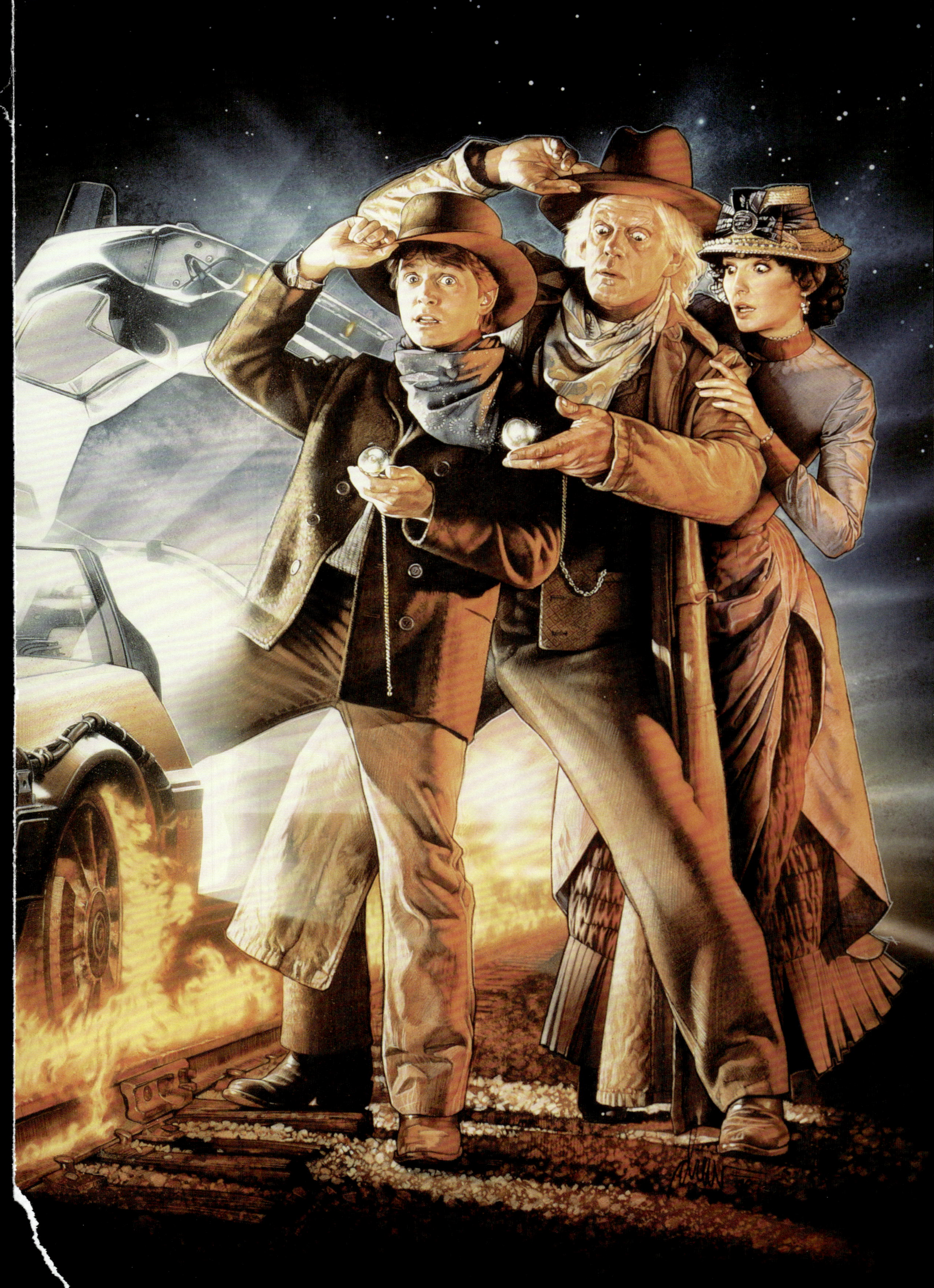

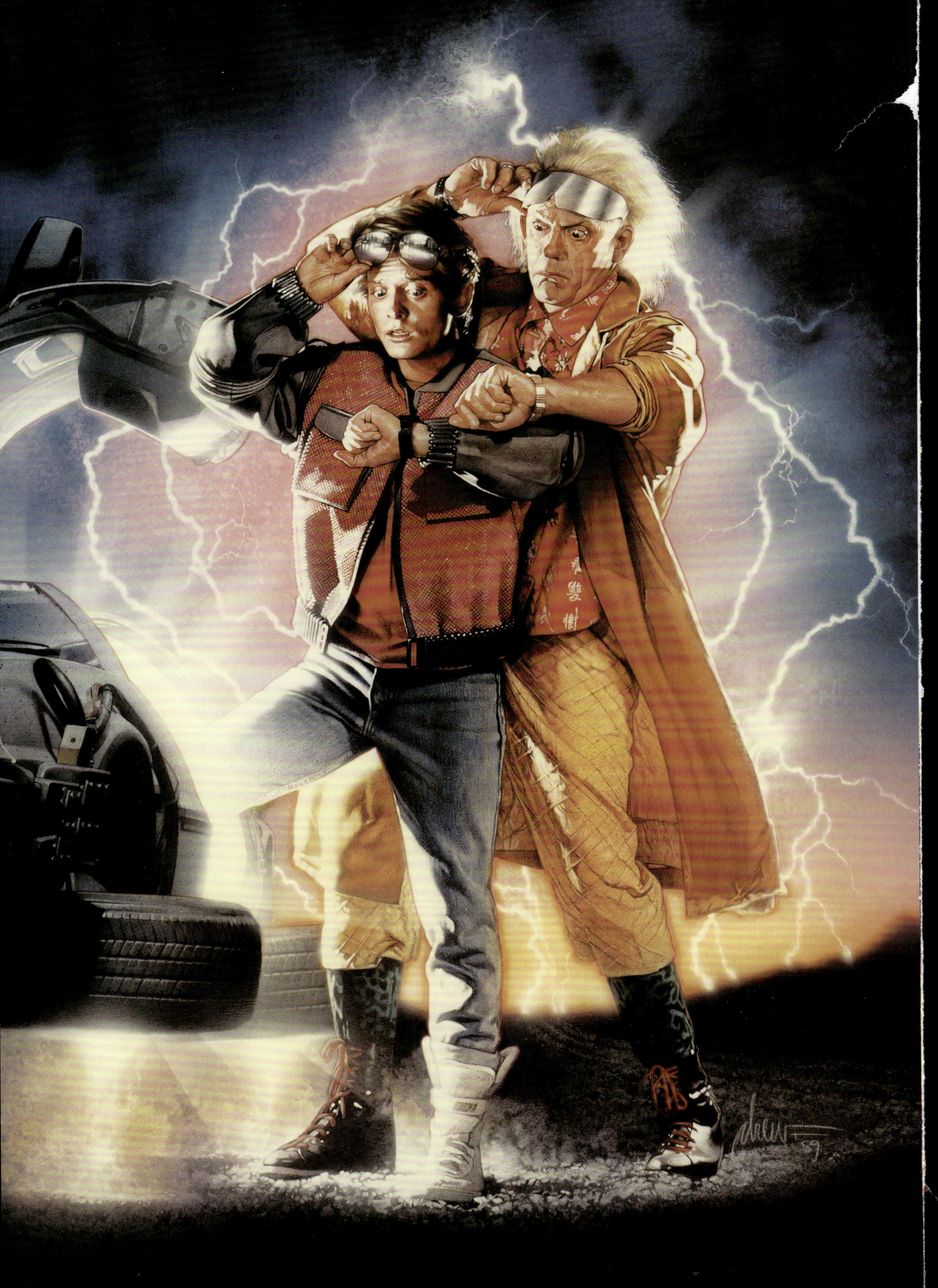

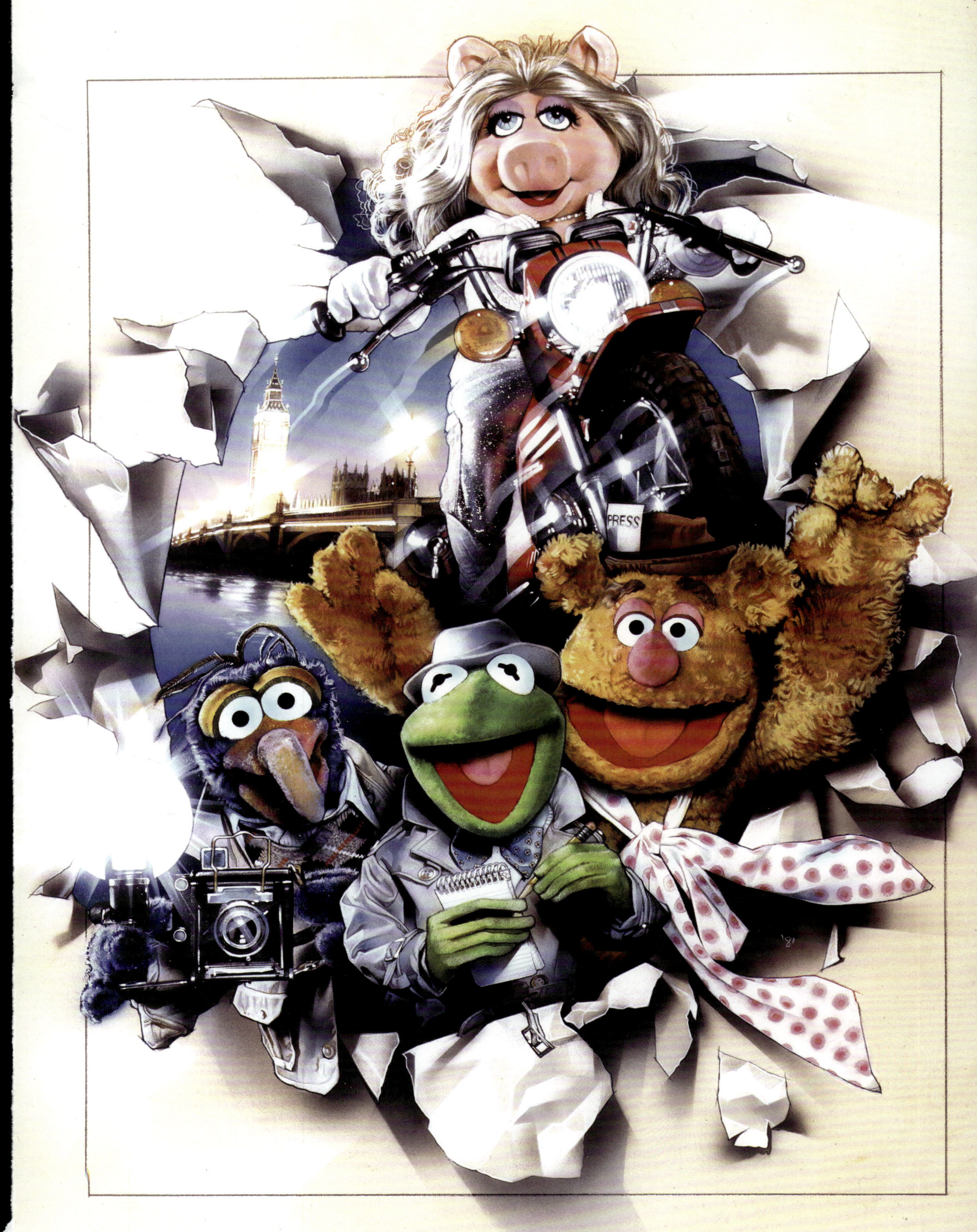
PRESS

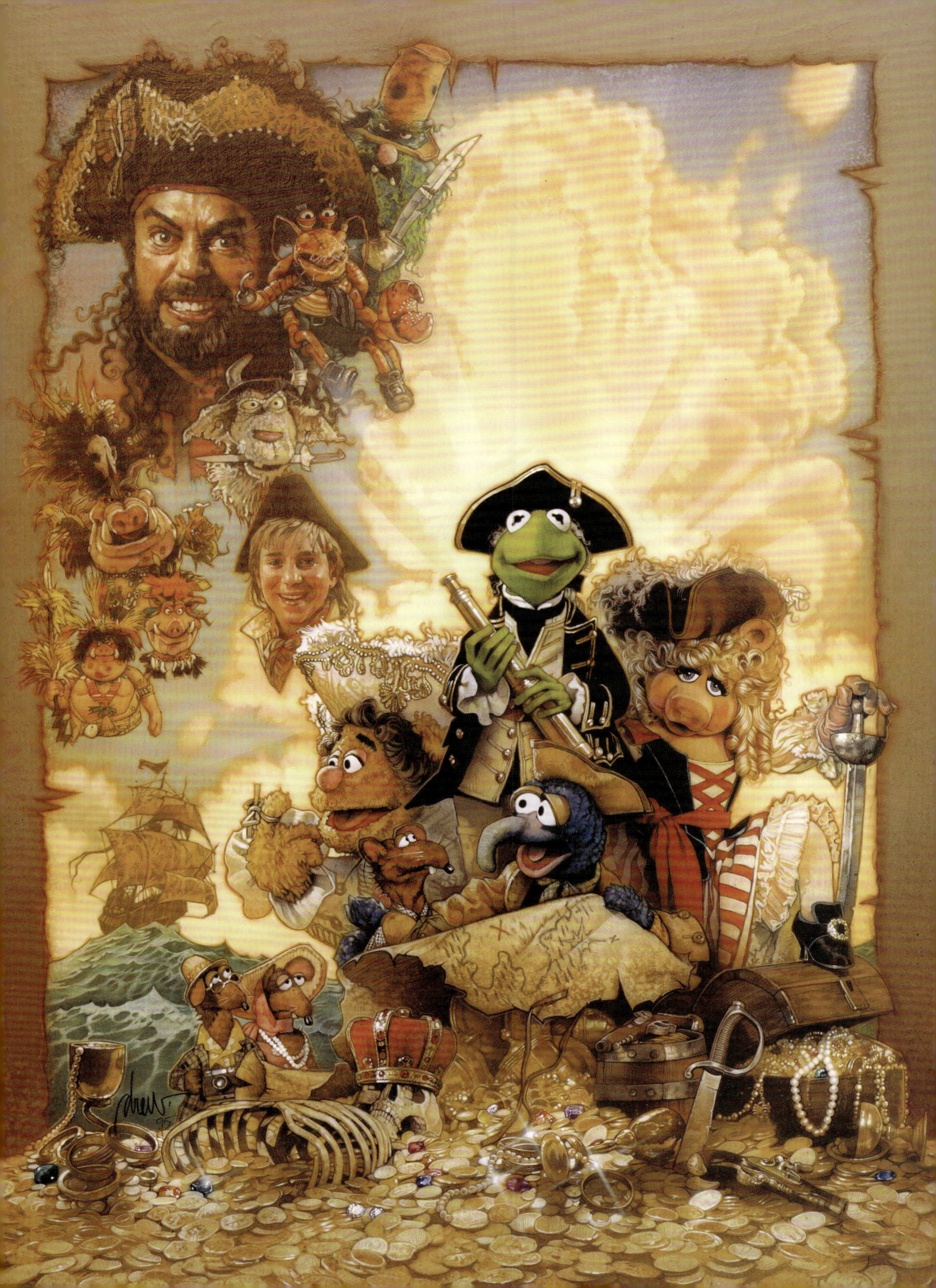

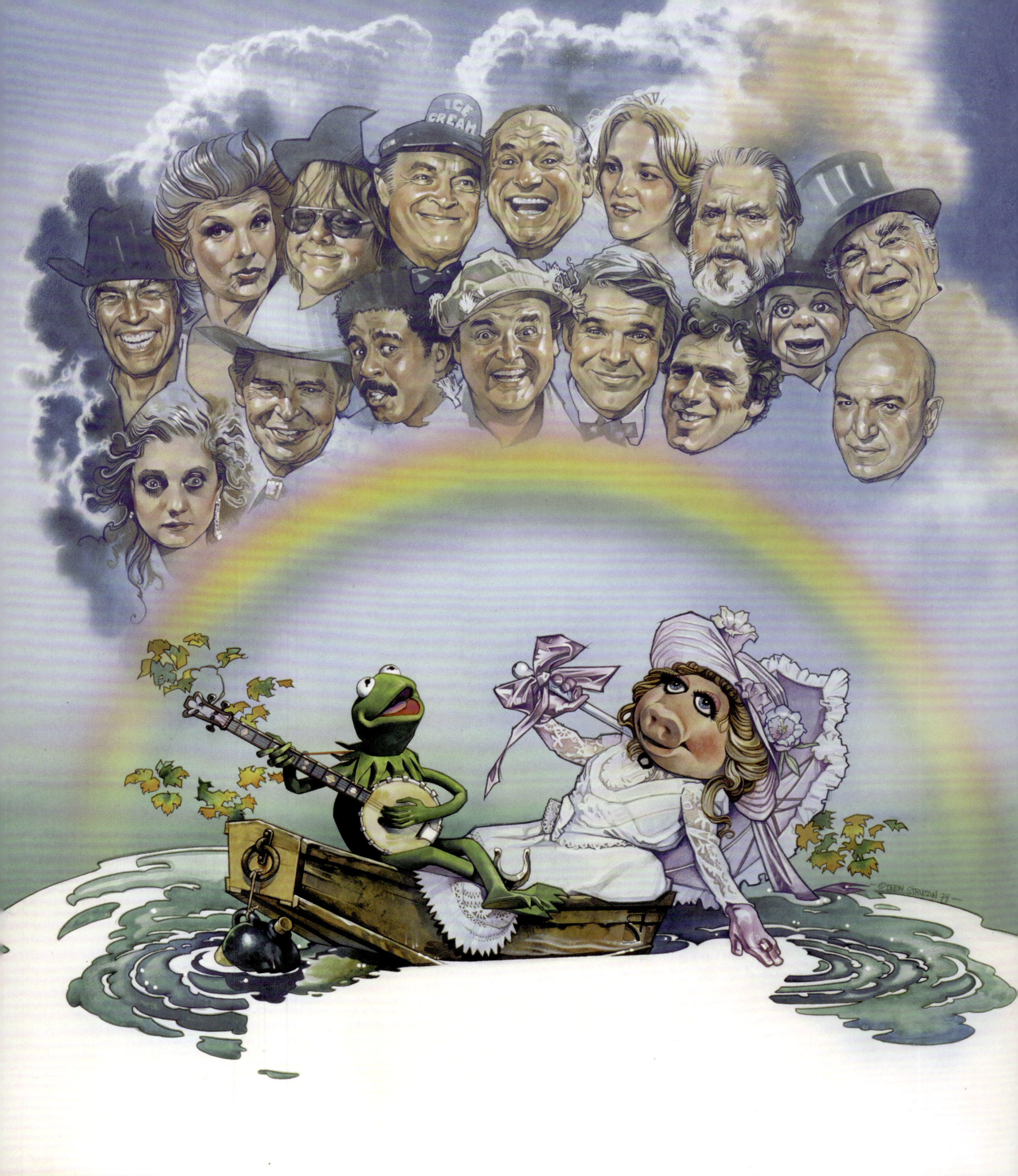
ICE CREAM
©DREW STRUZAN 79

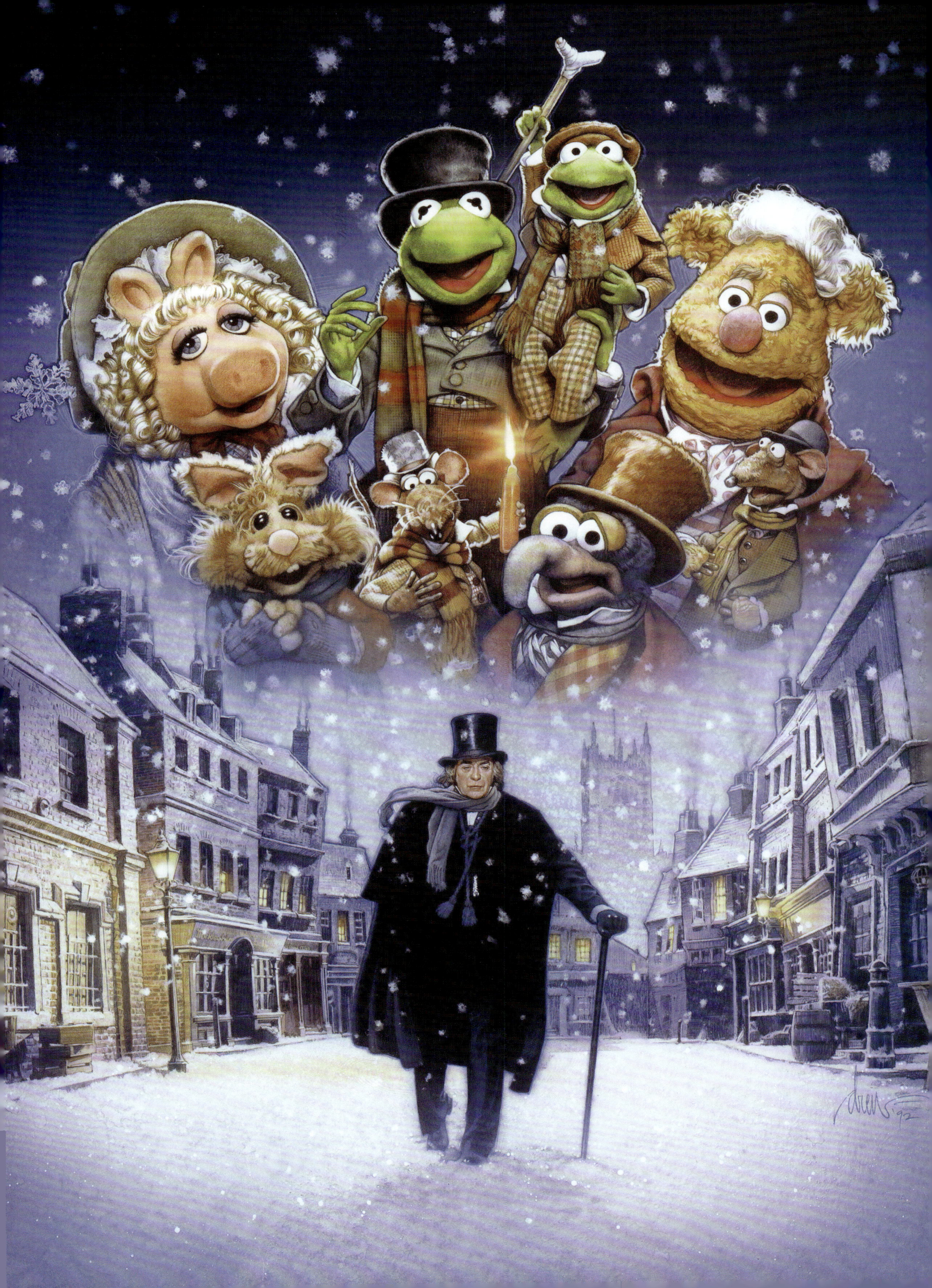

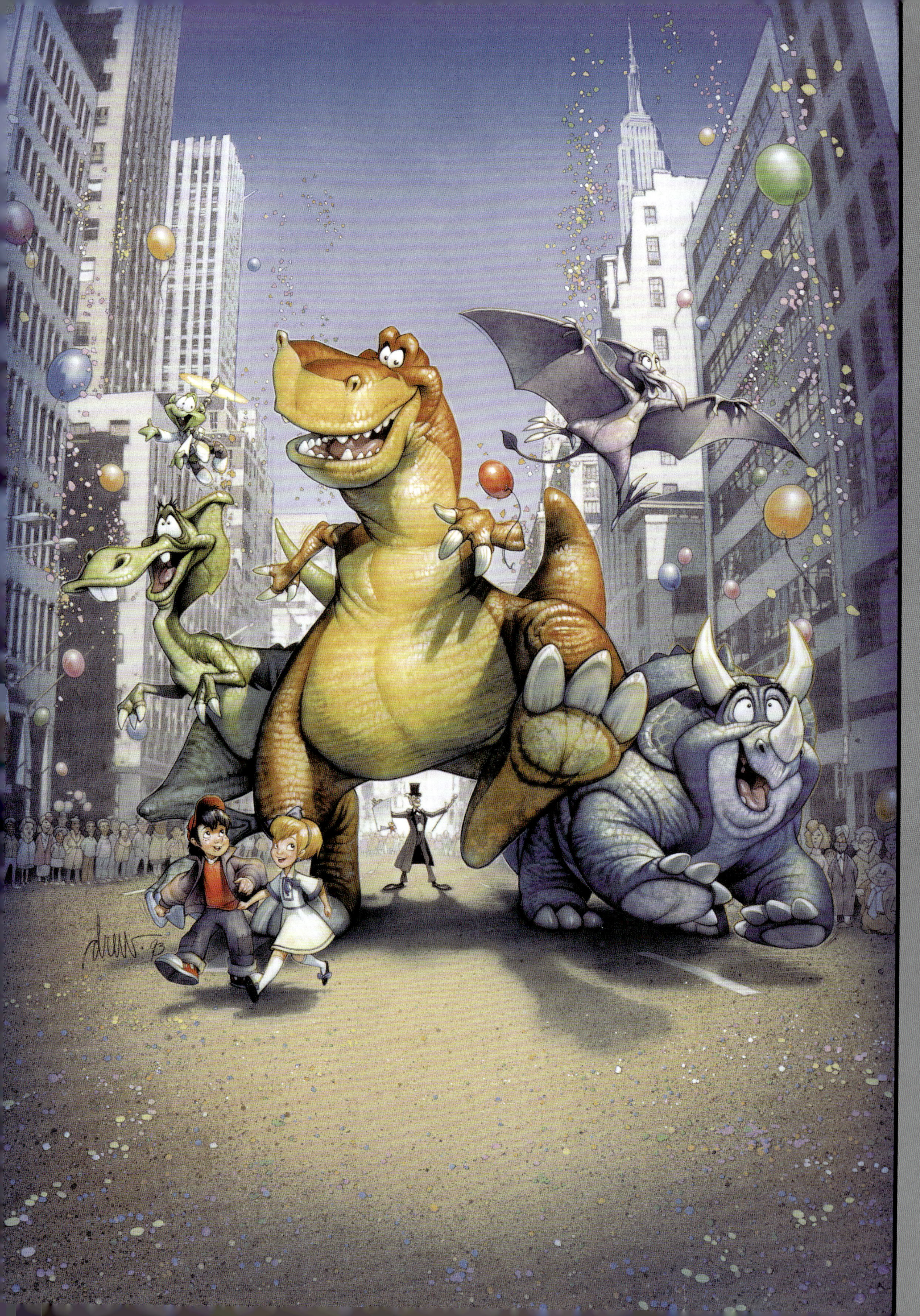

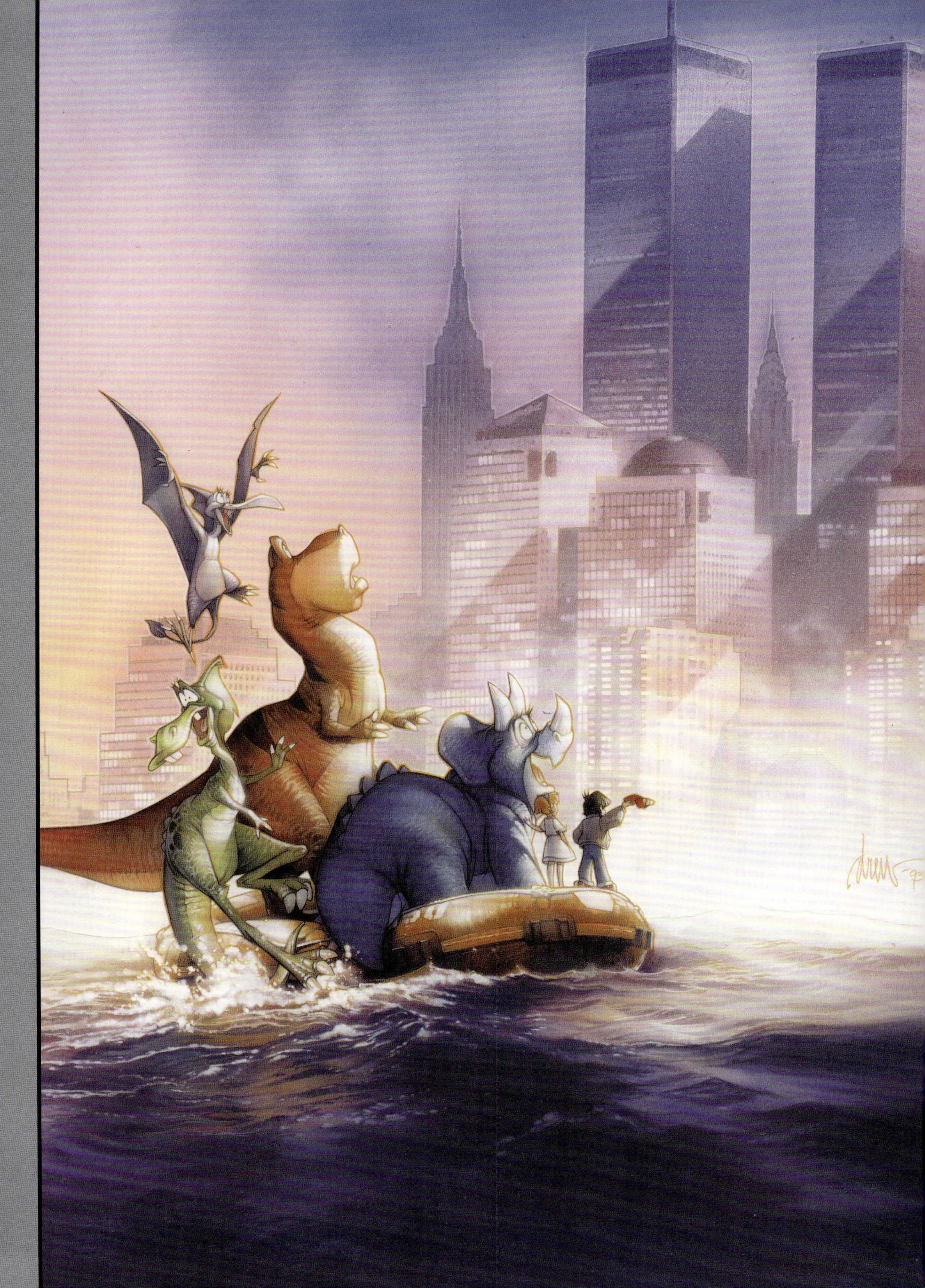

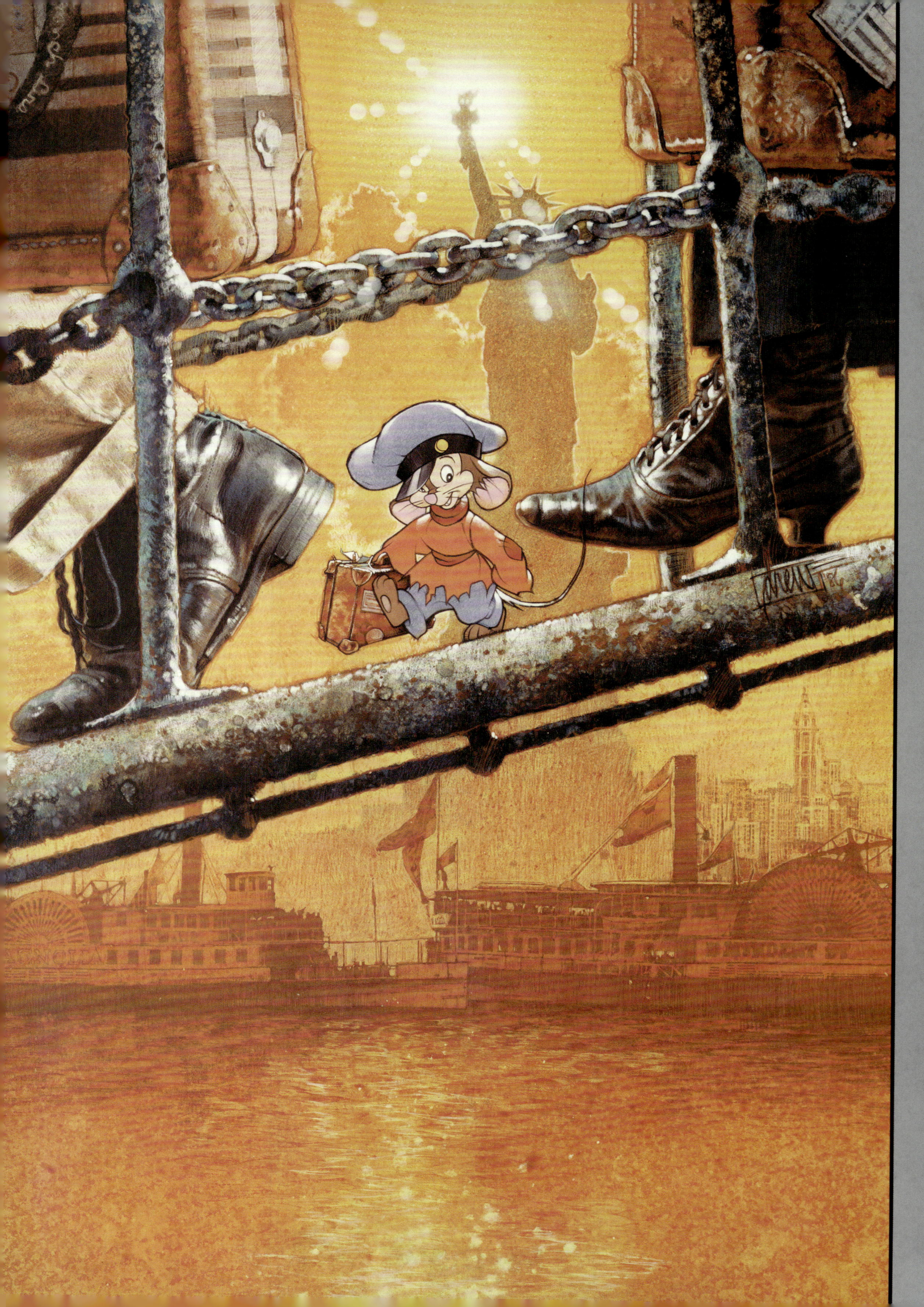

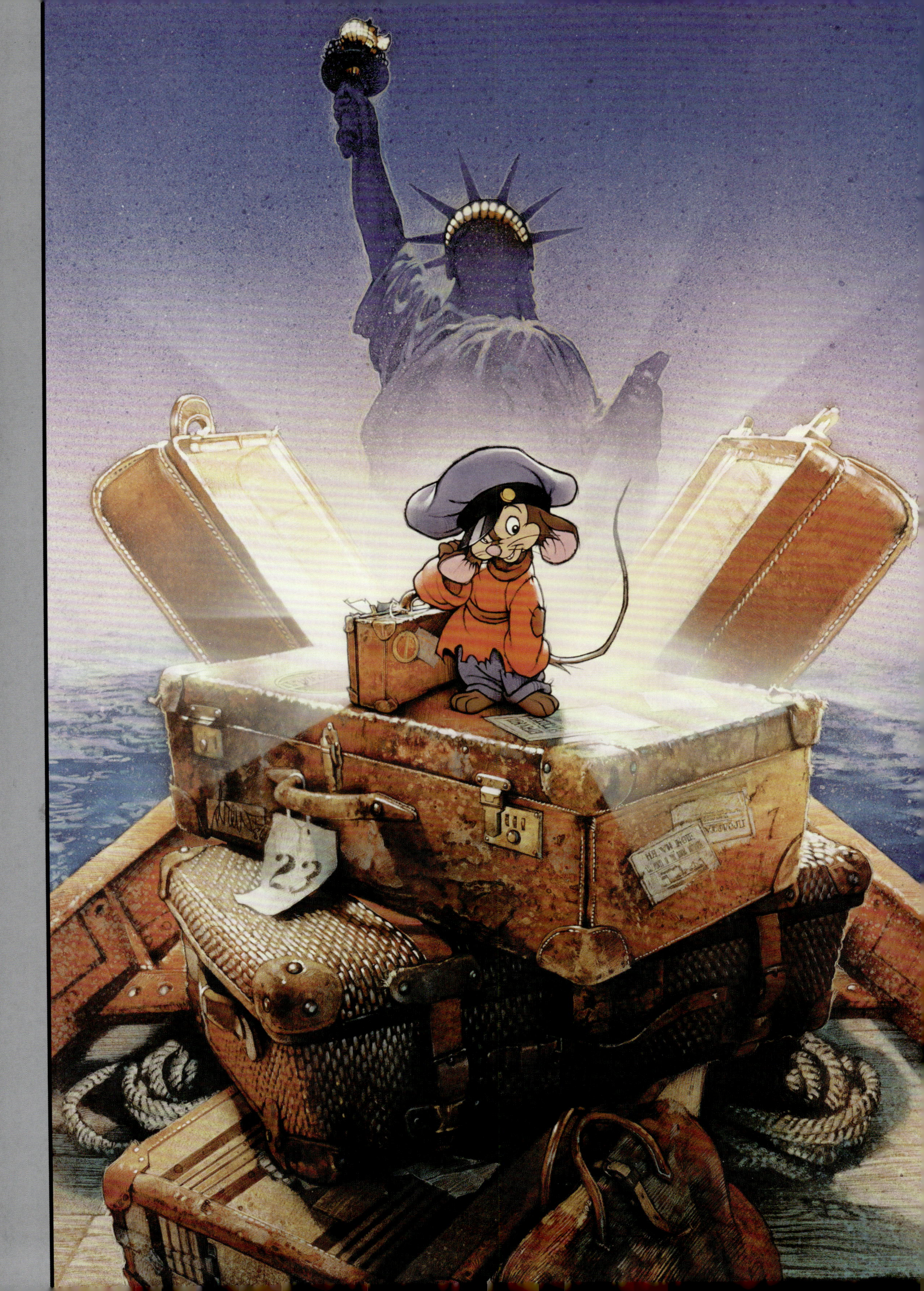
23

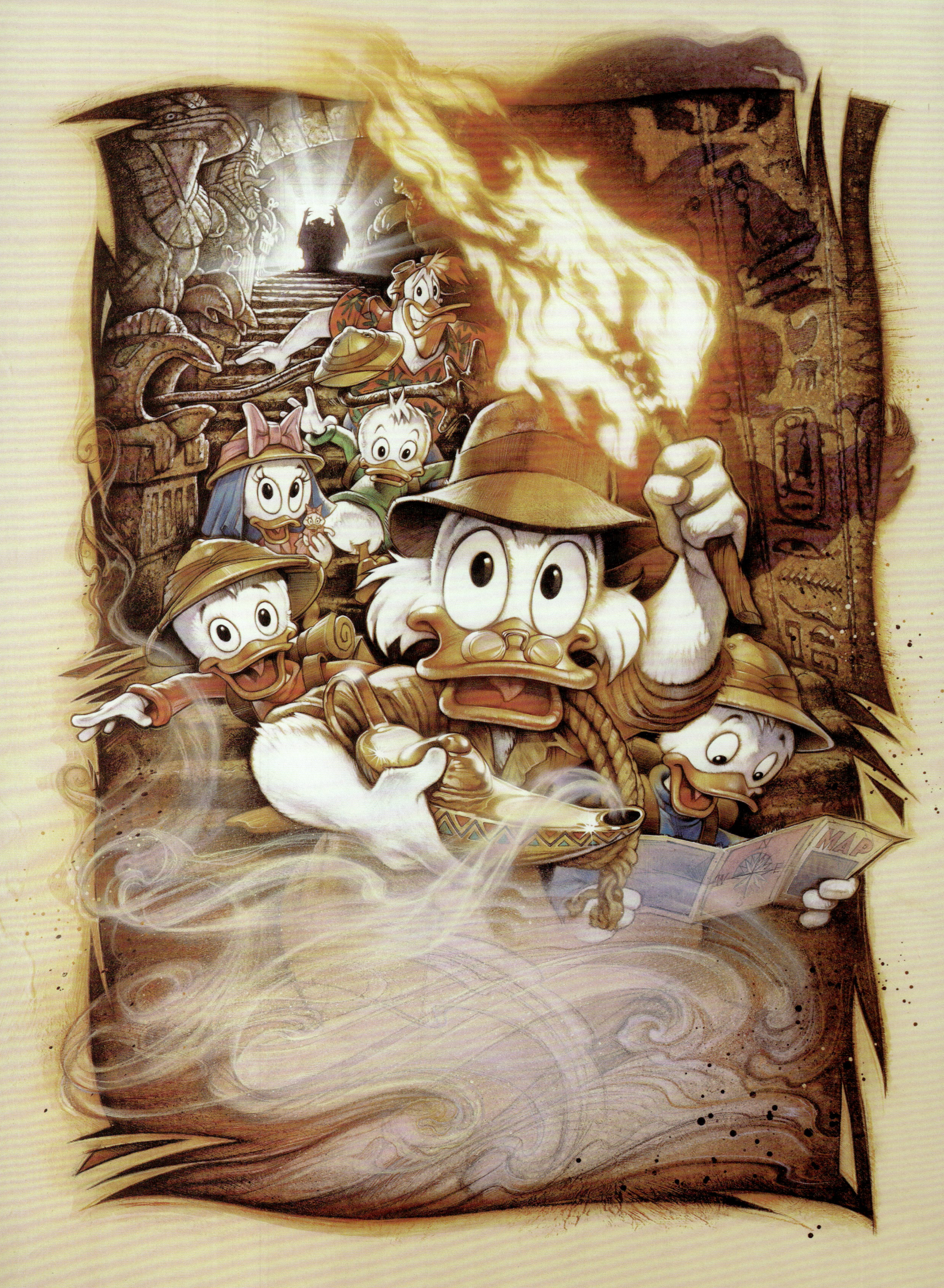
MAP

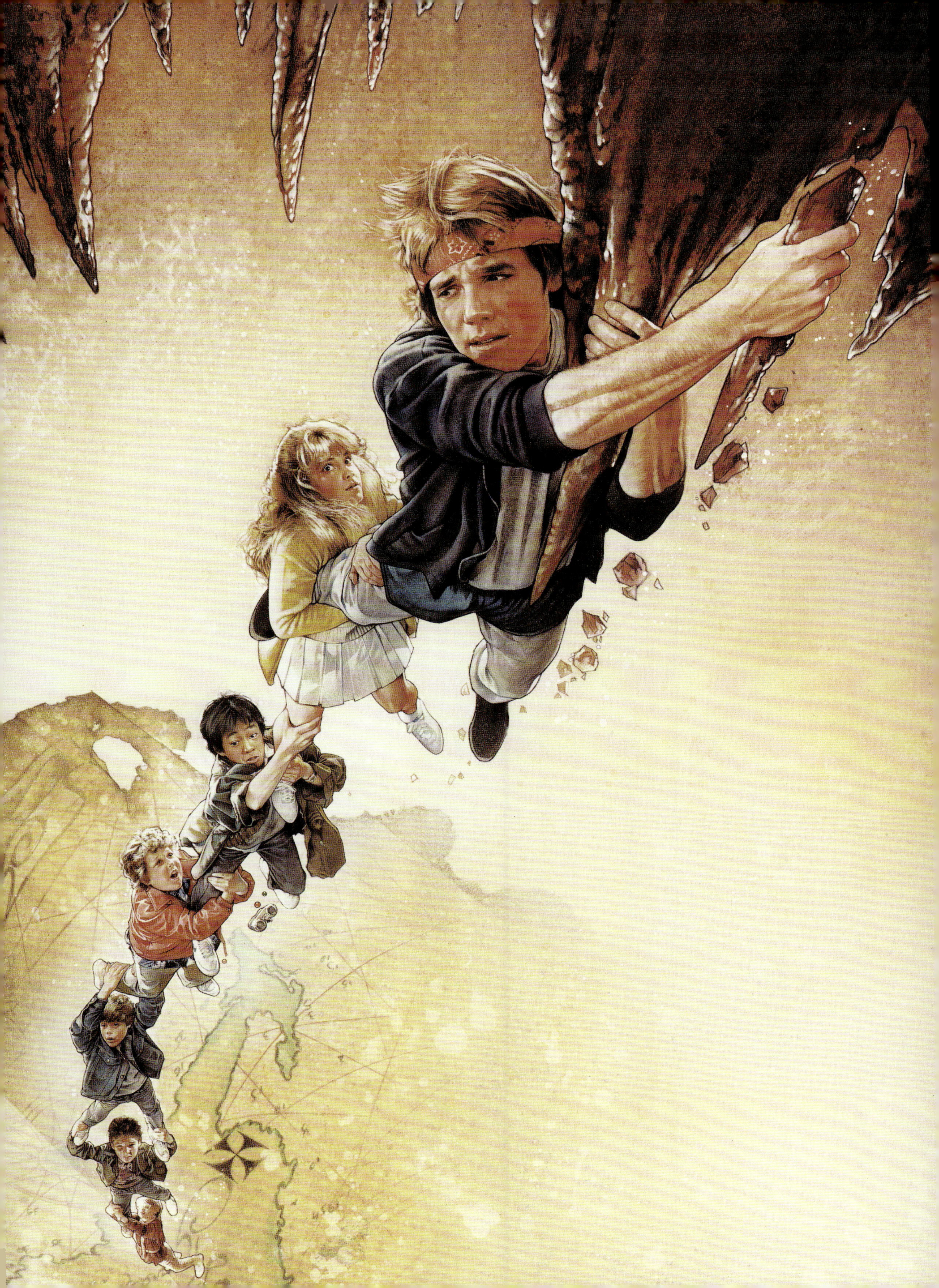

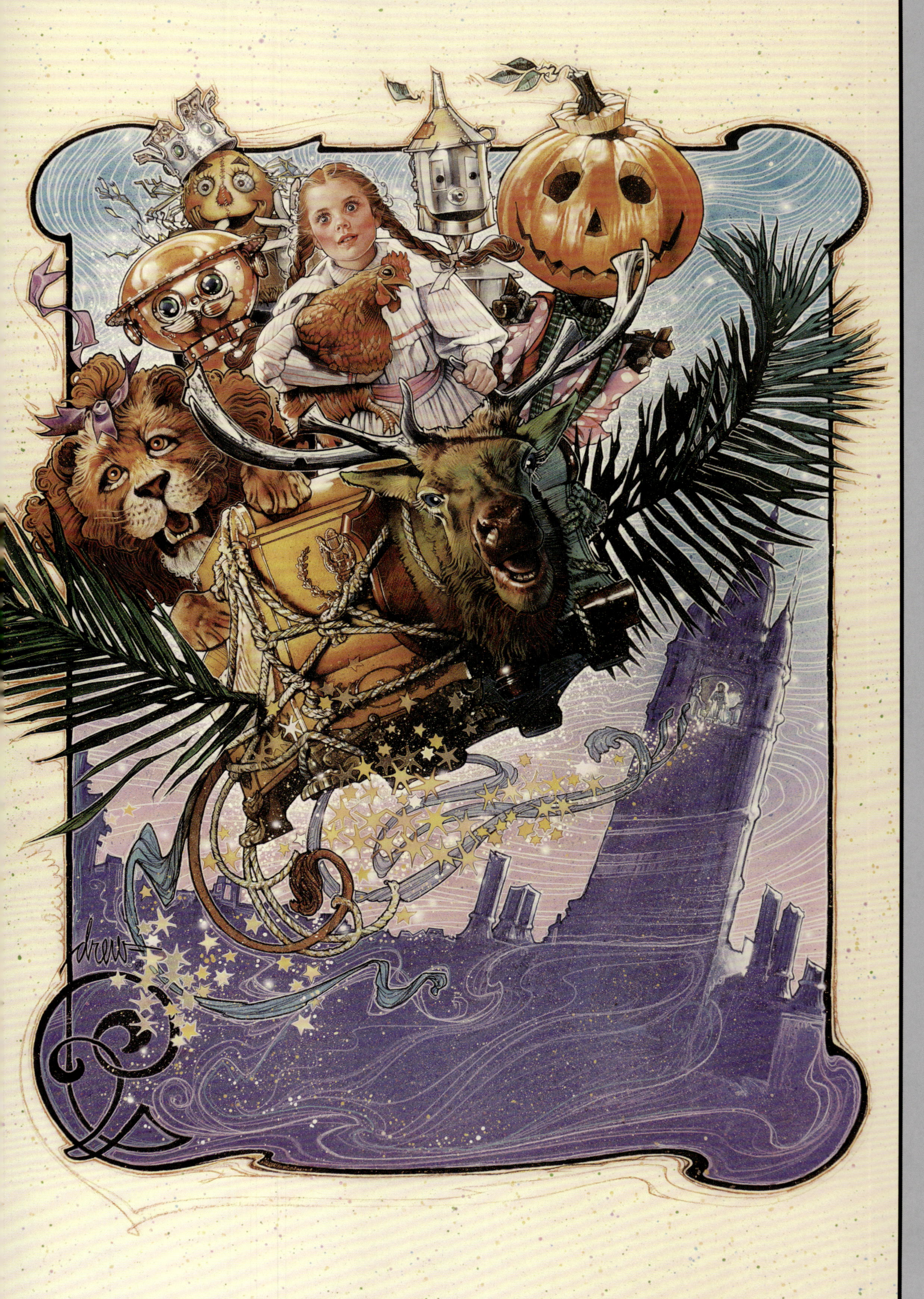
drew

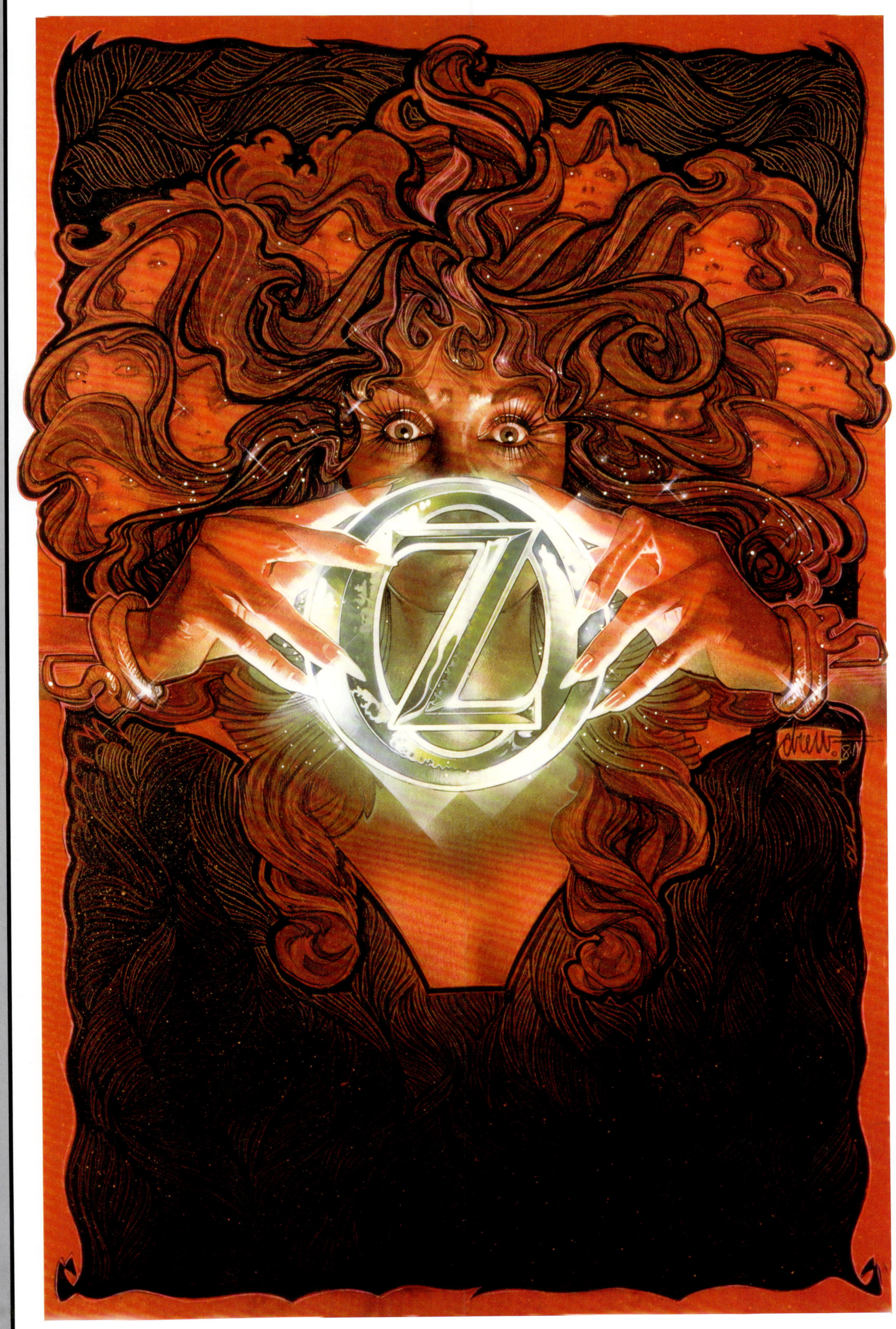

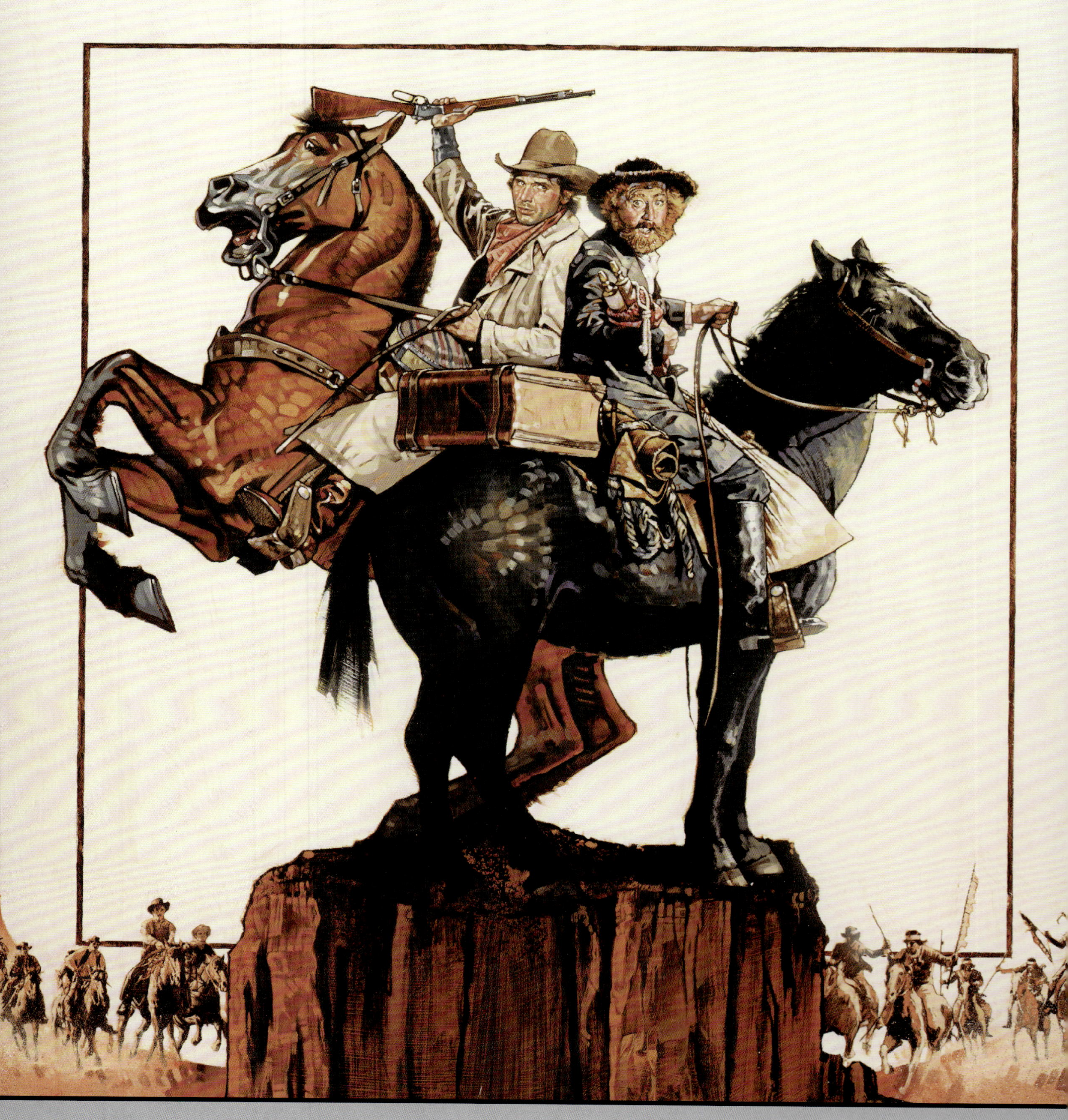

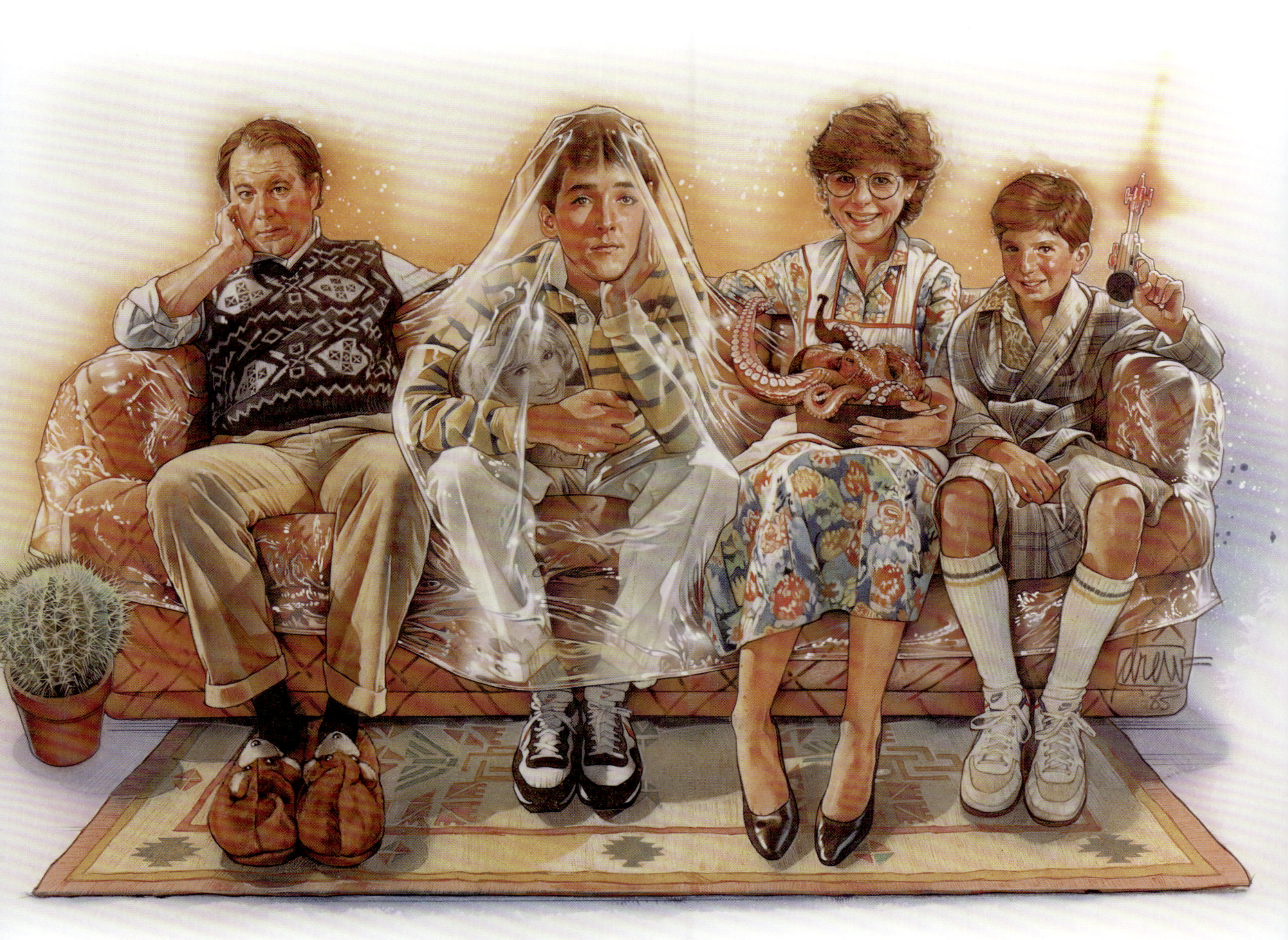

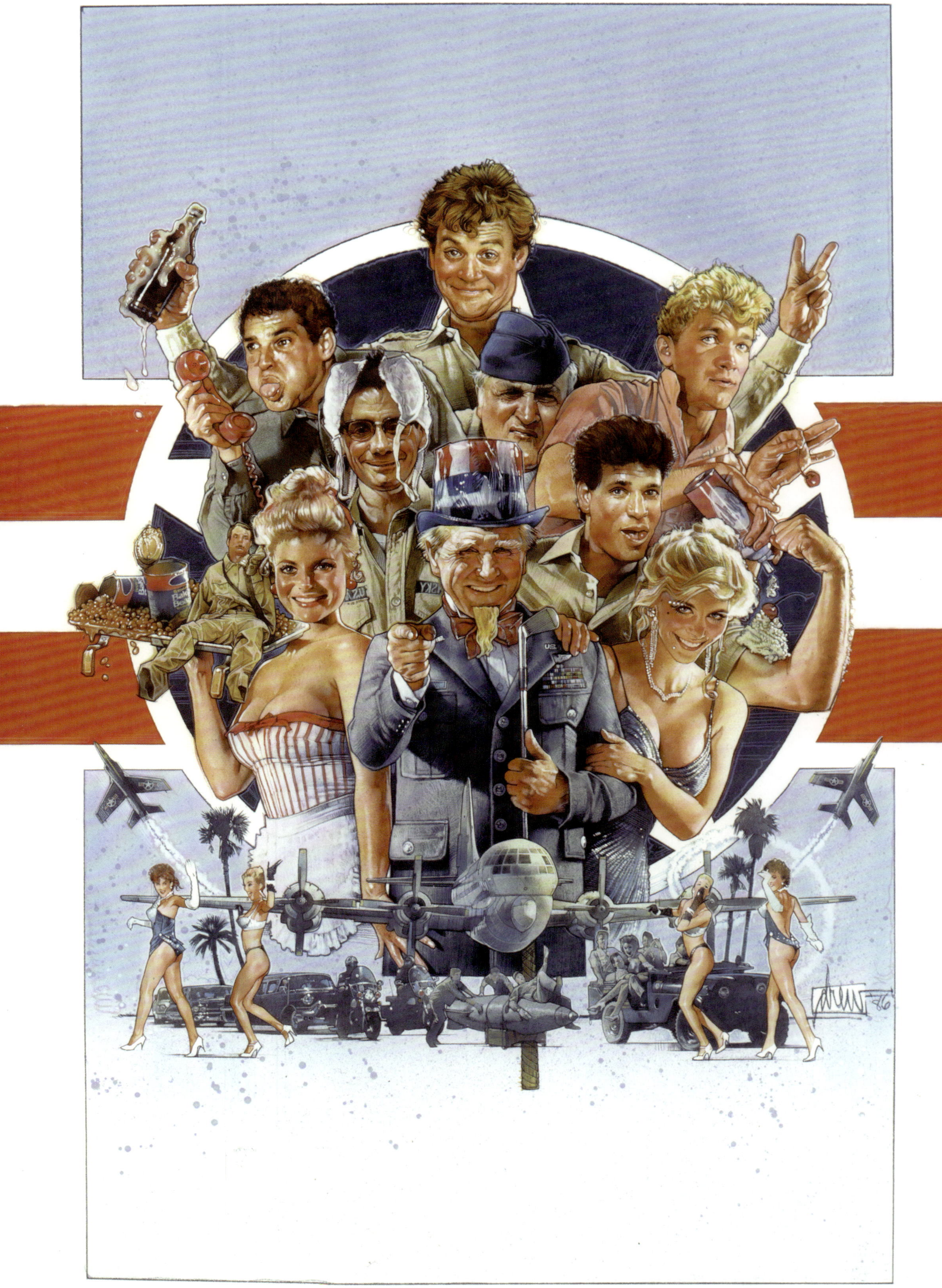

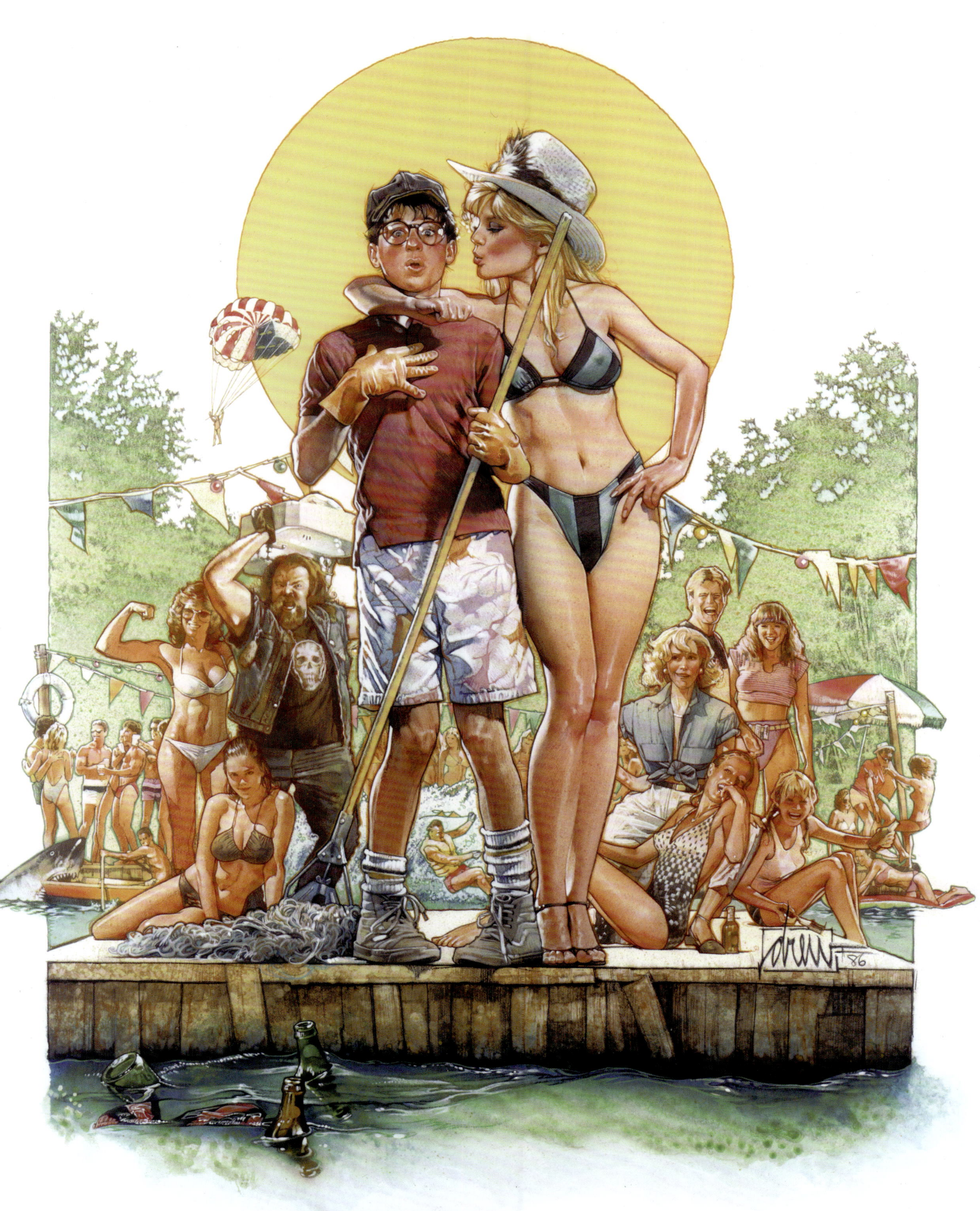
drew '86

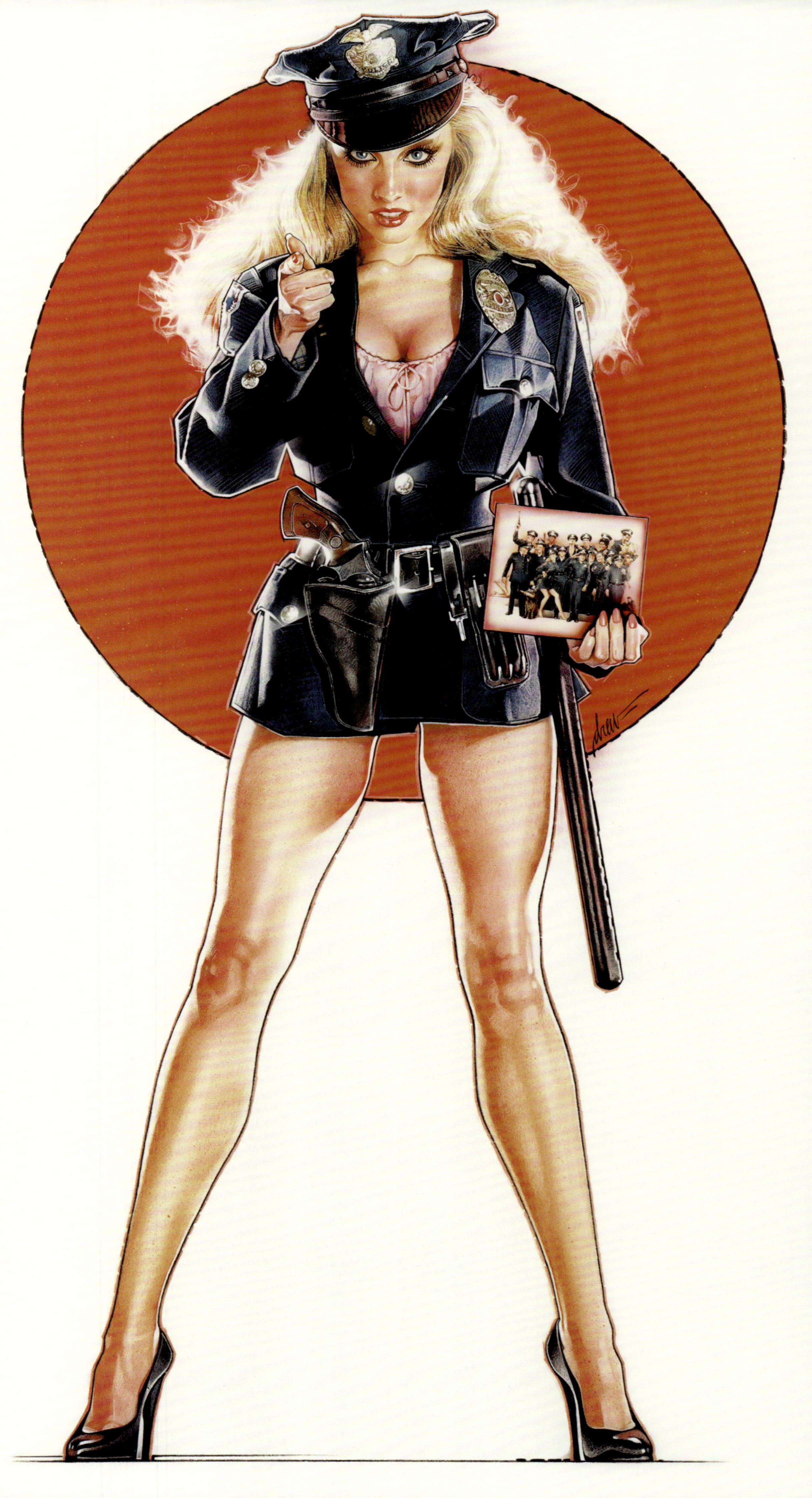

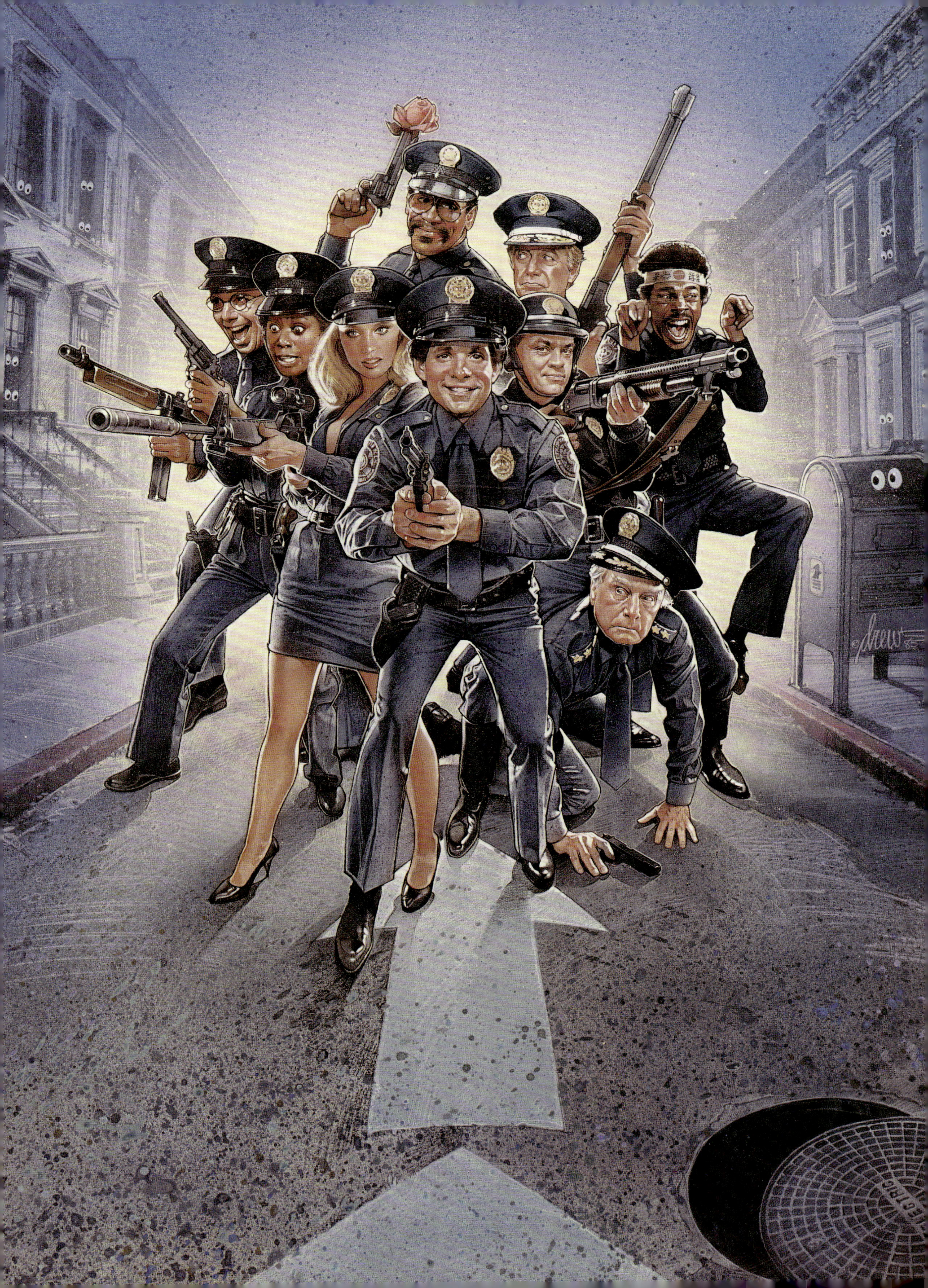

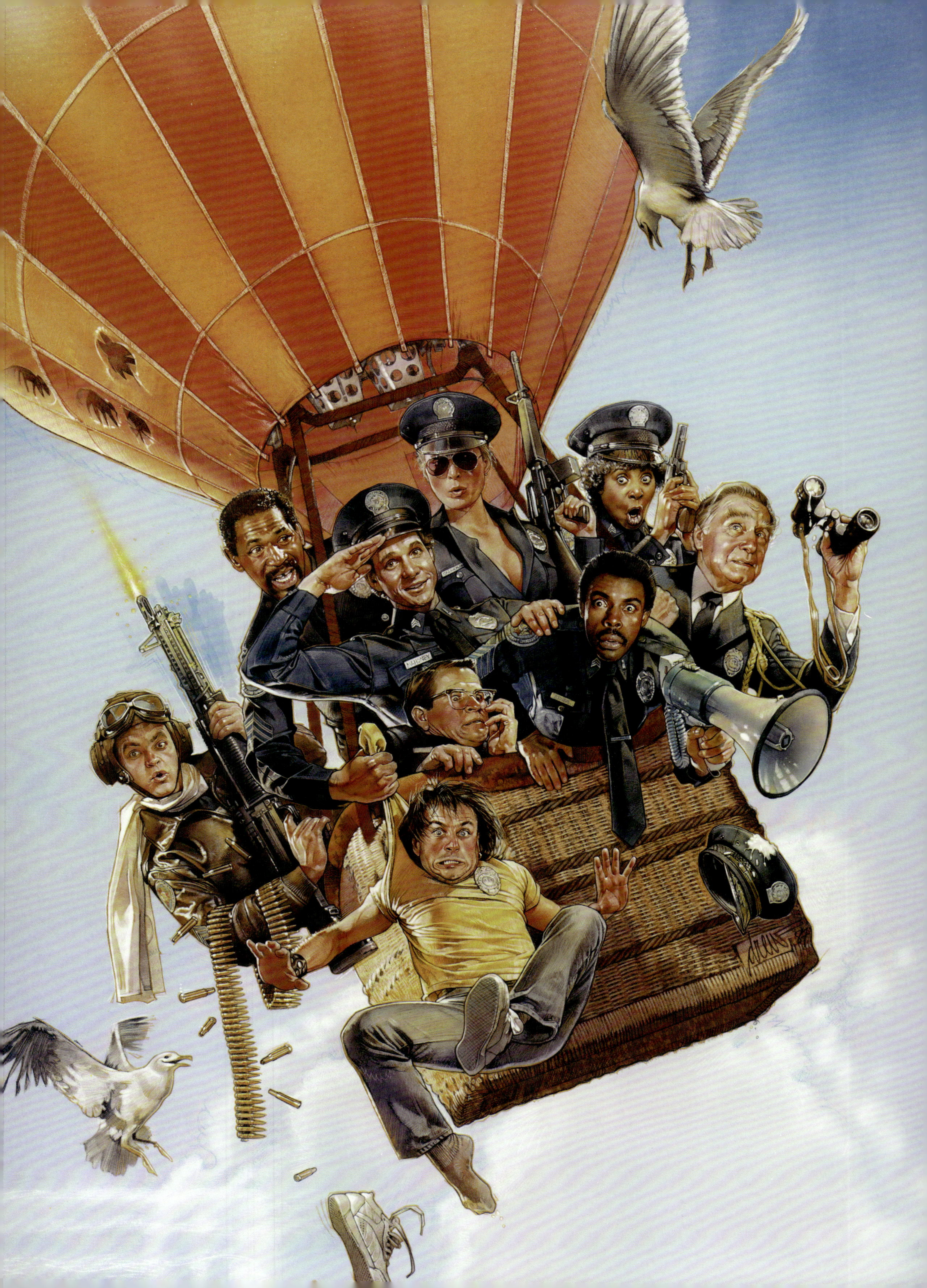

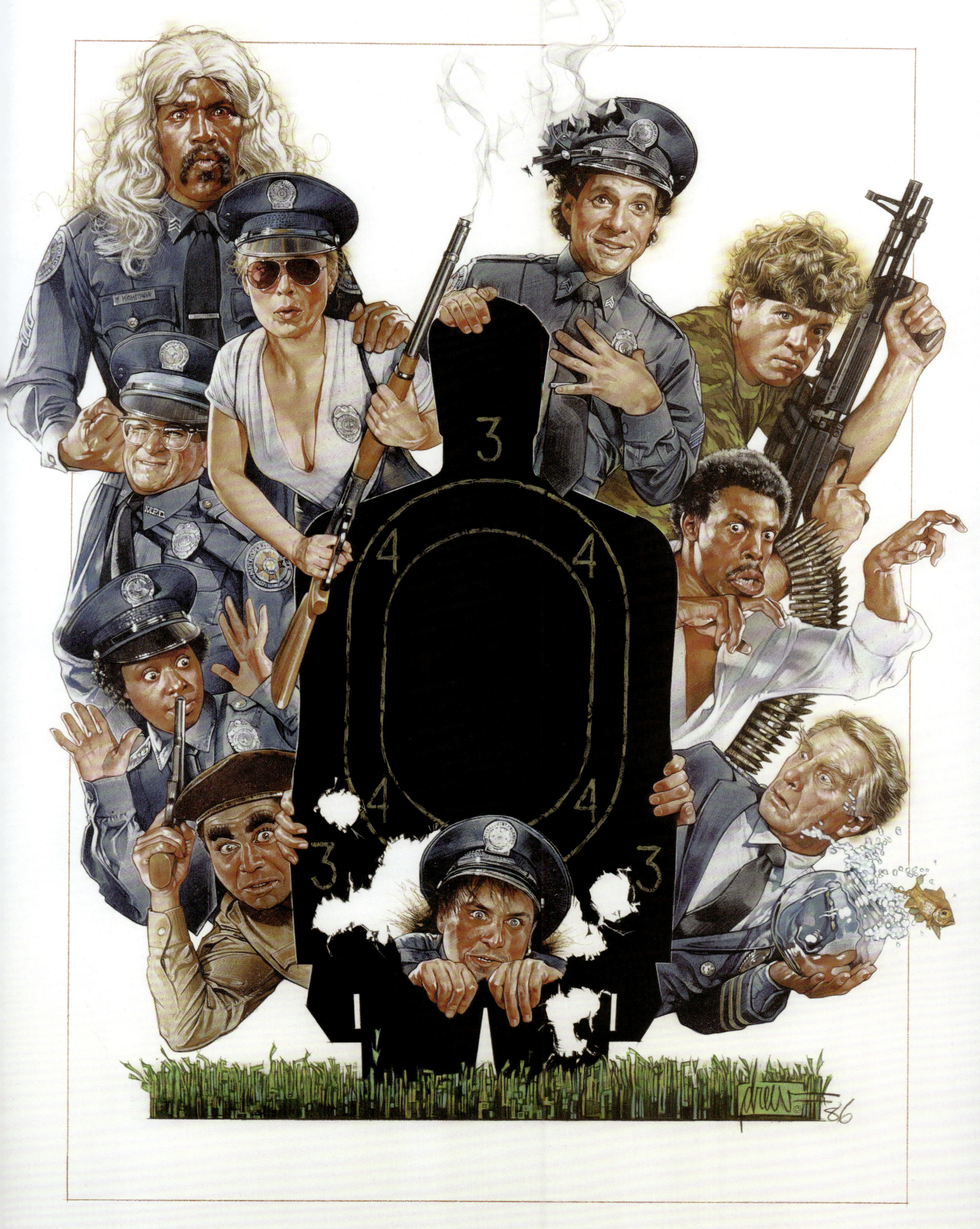
3
4
4
4
4
3
3
drew 86

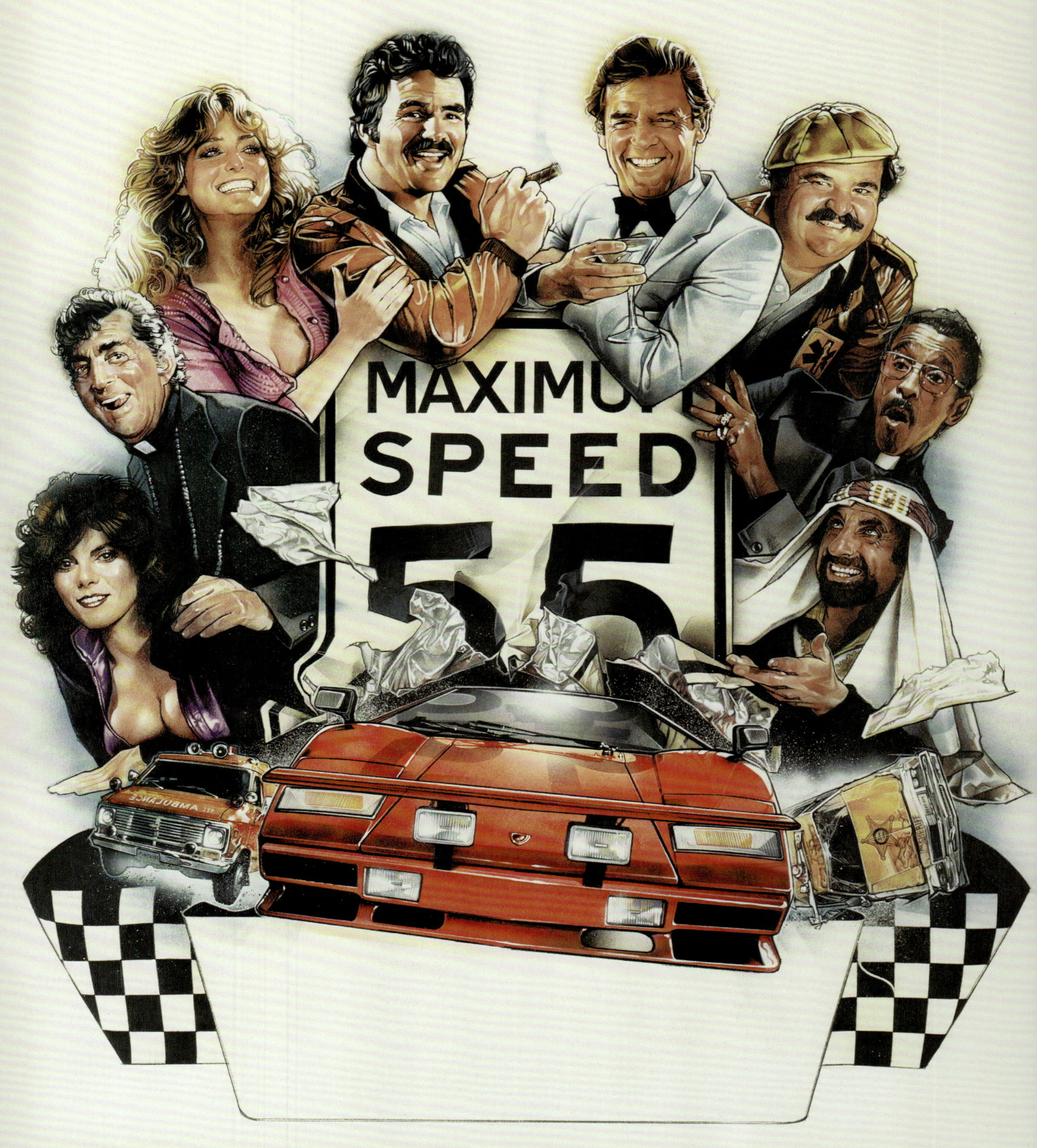
MAXIMU
SPEED
55
AMBULANCE

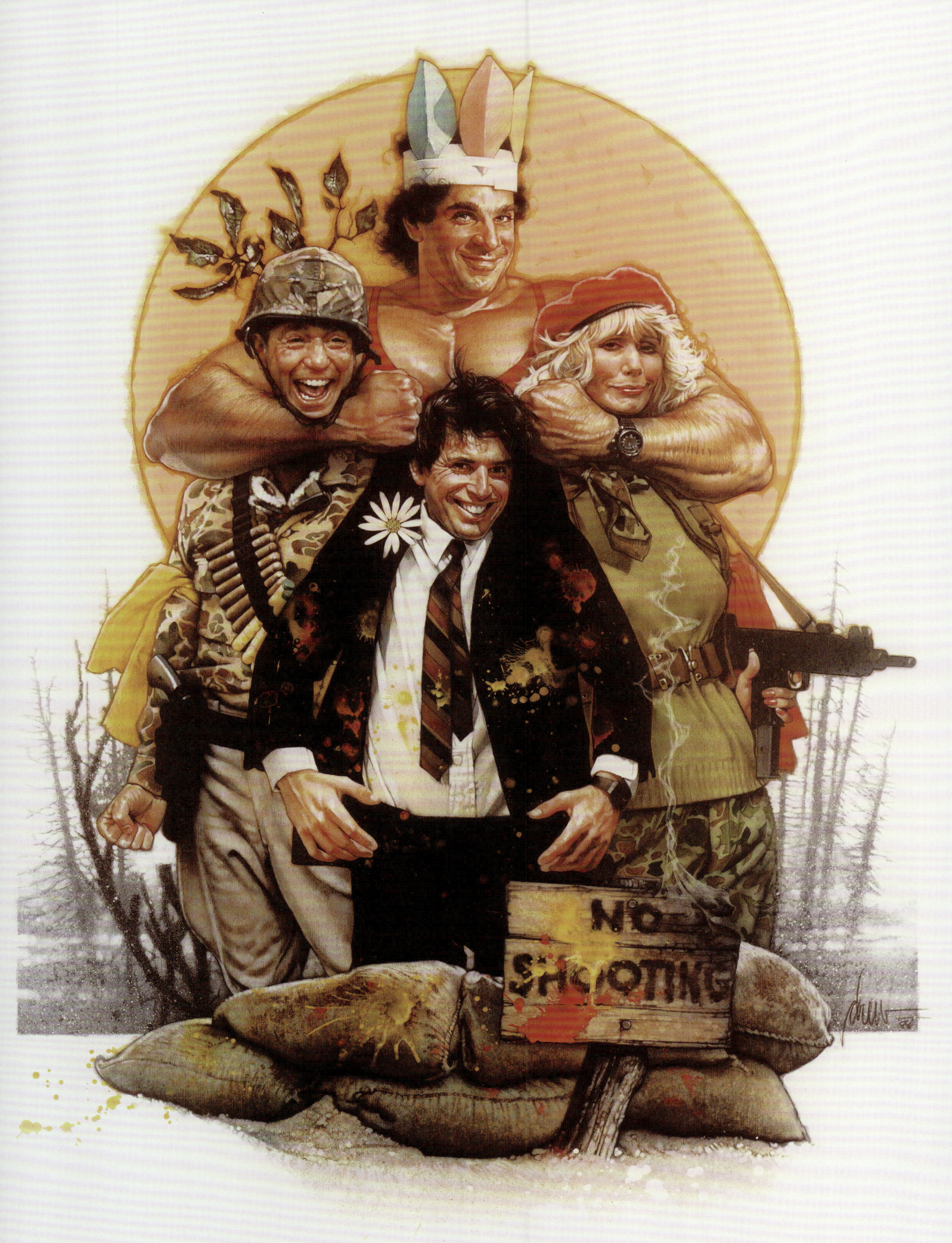

NO
SHOOTING

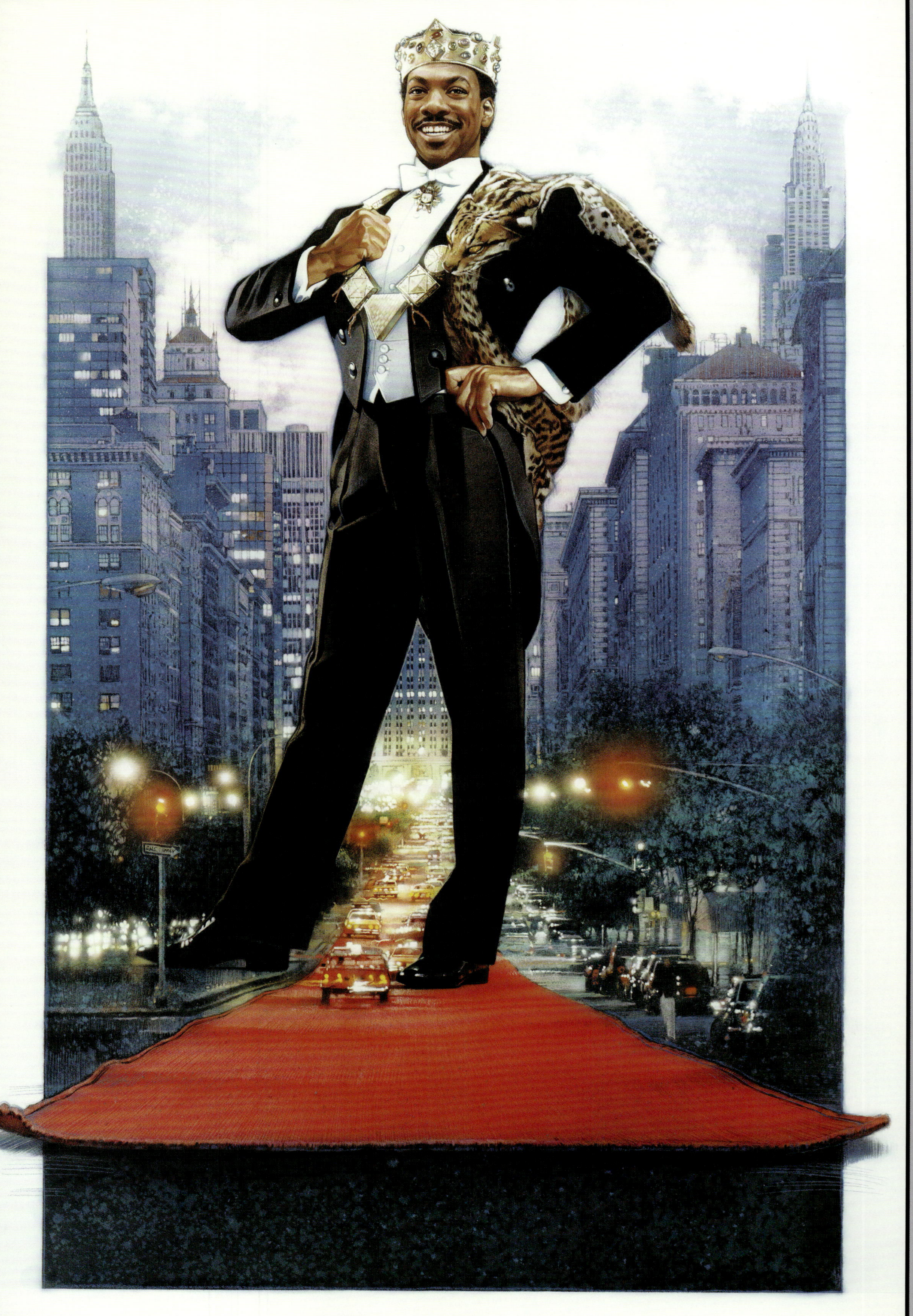

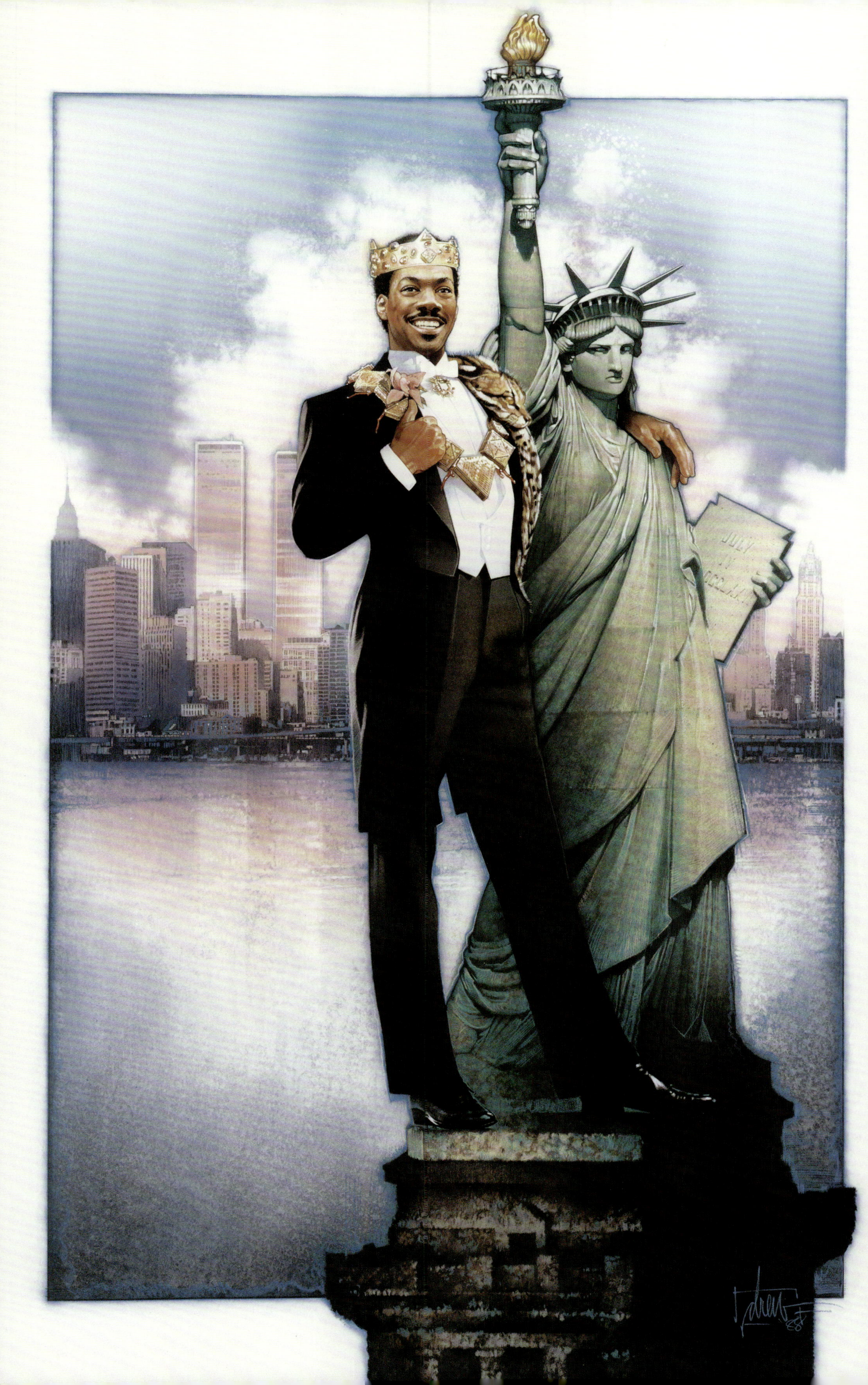

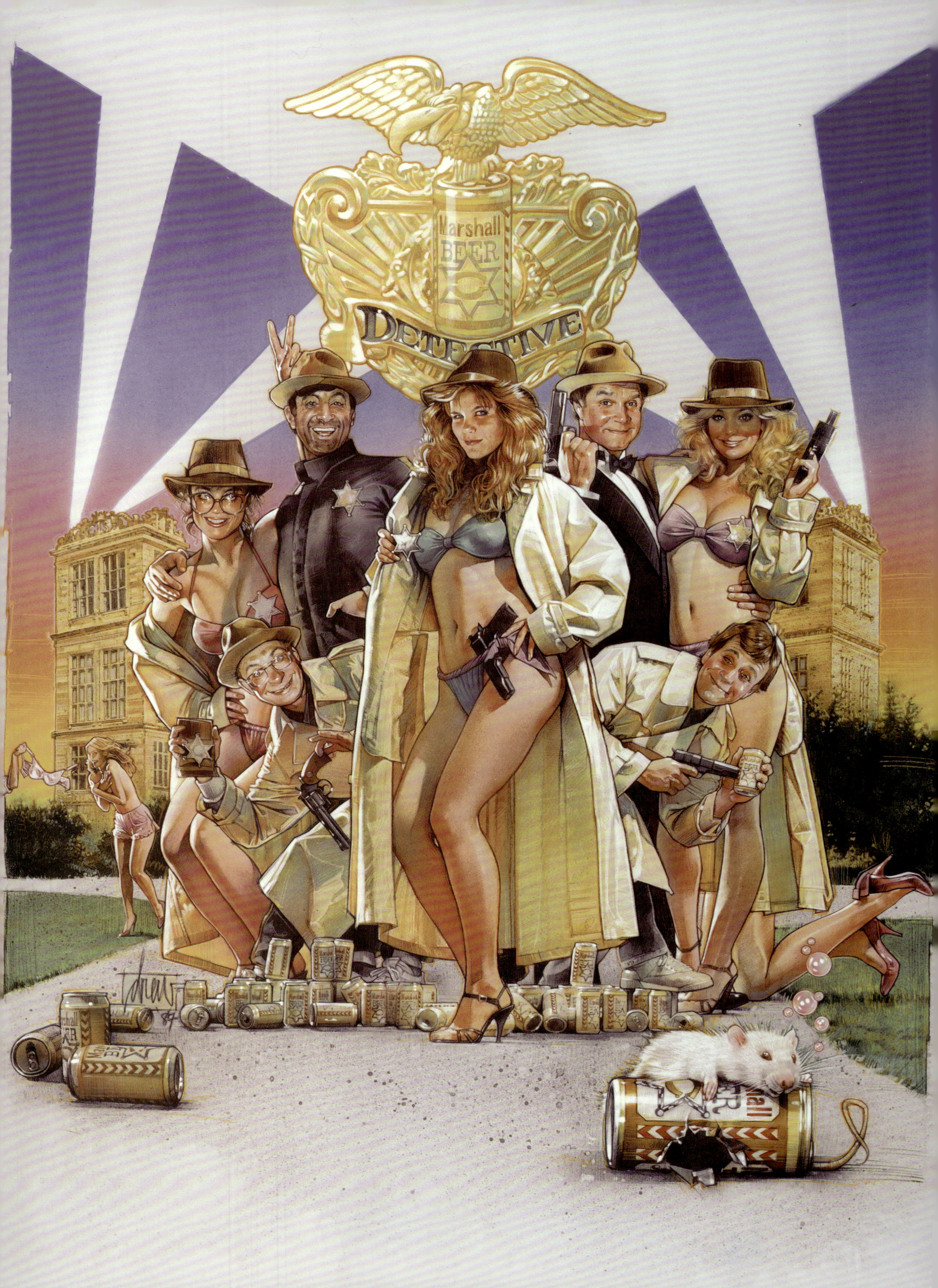
Marshall
BEER
DETECTIVE

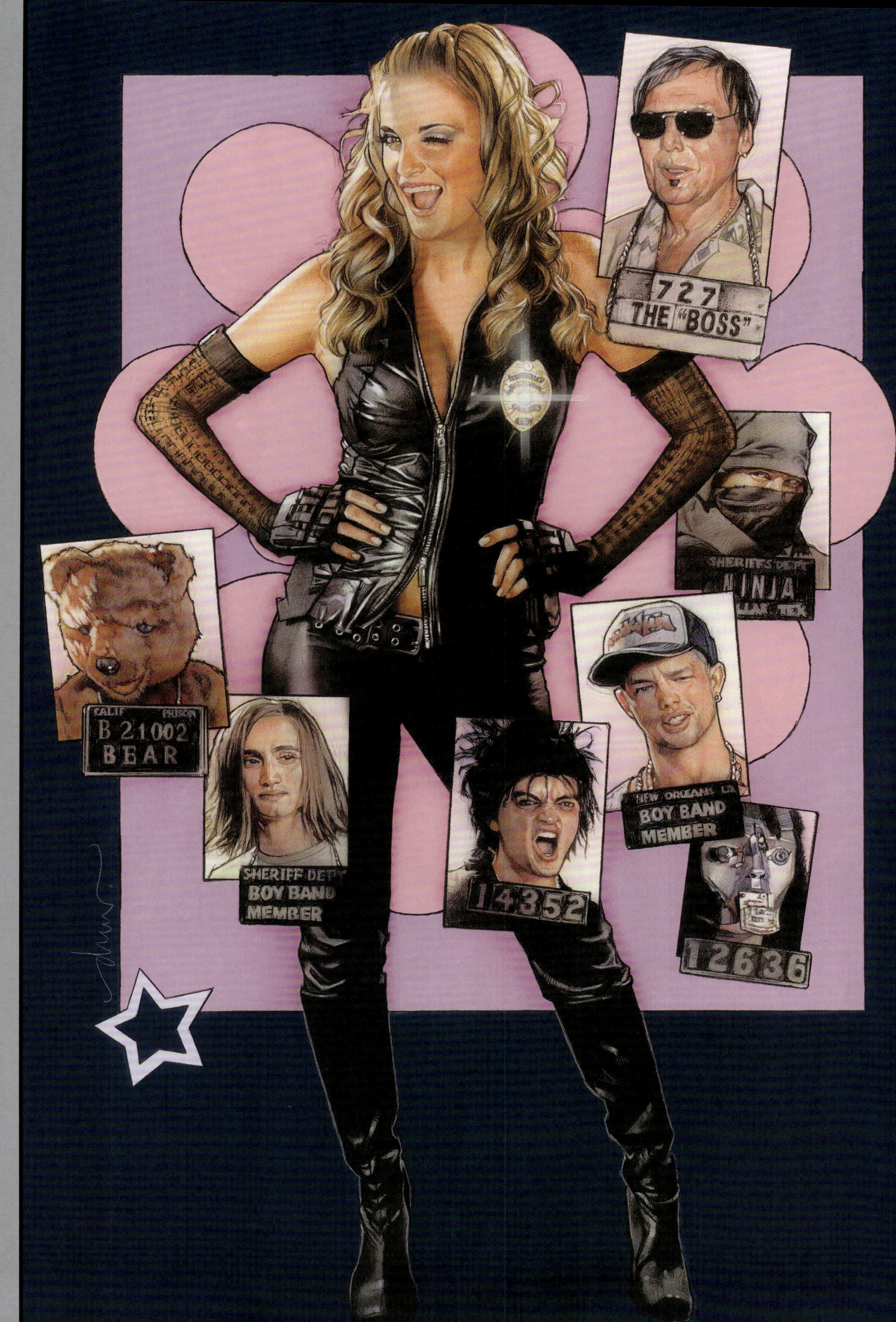
727
THE "BOSS"
SHERIFFS DEPT
NINJA
CALIF PRISON
B 21002
BEAR
SHERIFF DEPT
BOY BAND
MEMBER
14352
NEW ORLEANS LA
BOY BAND
MEMBER
12636

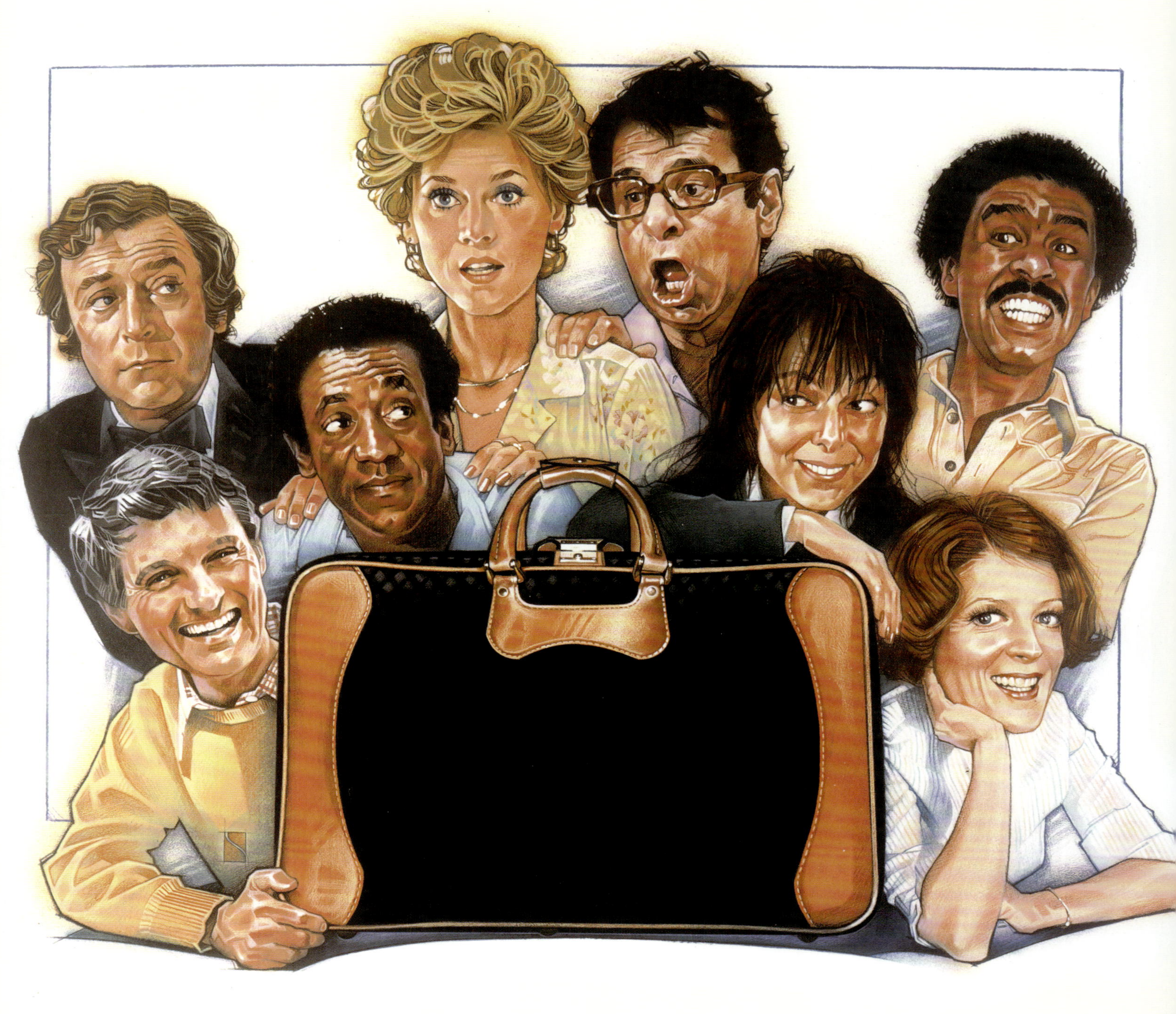

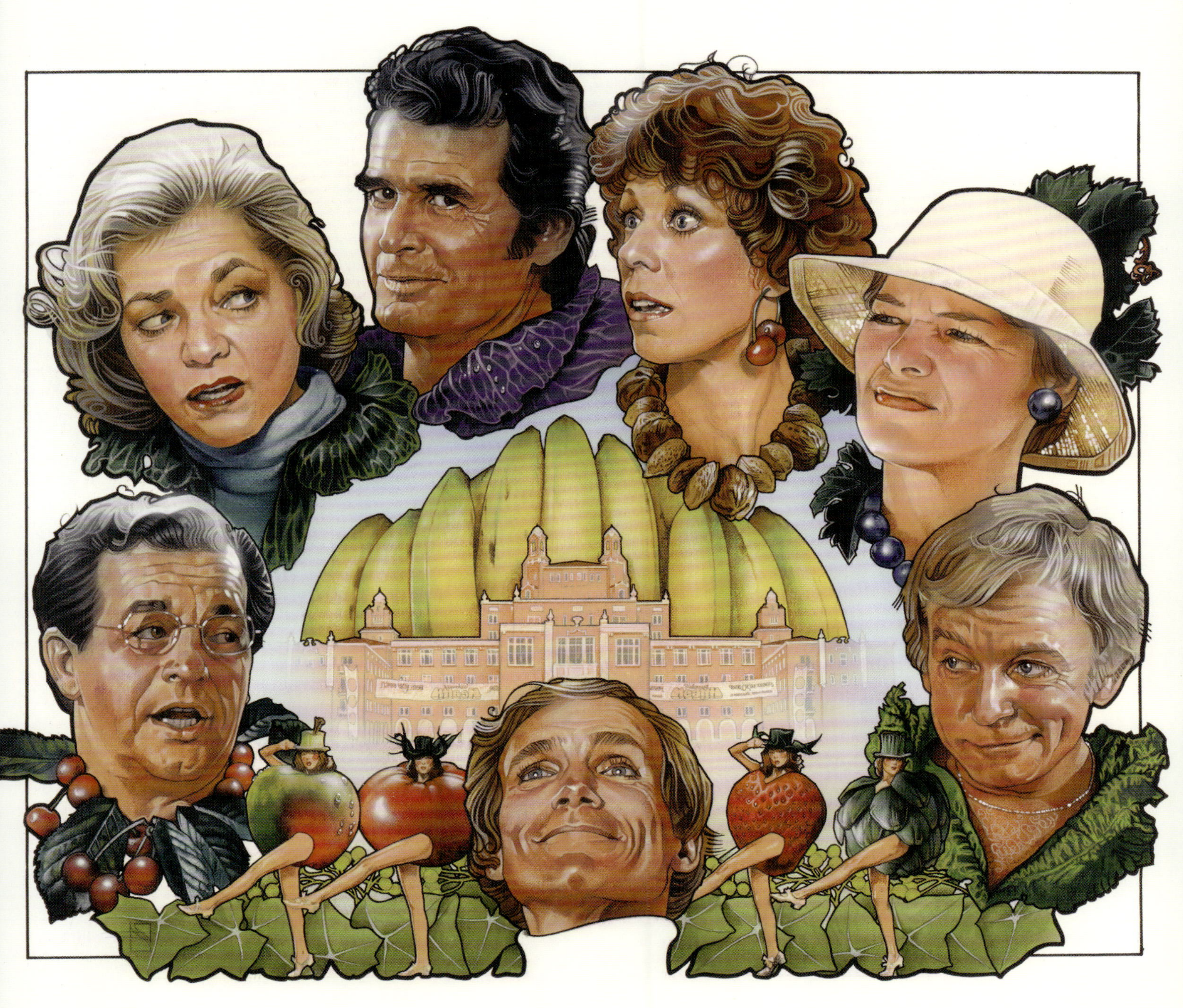

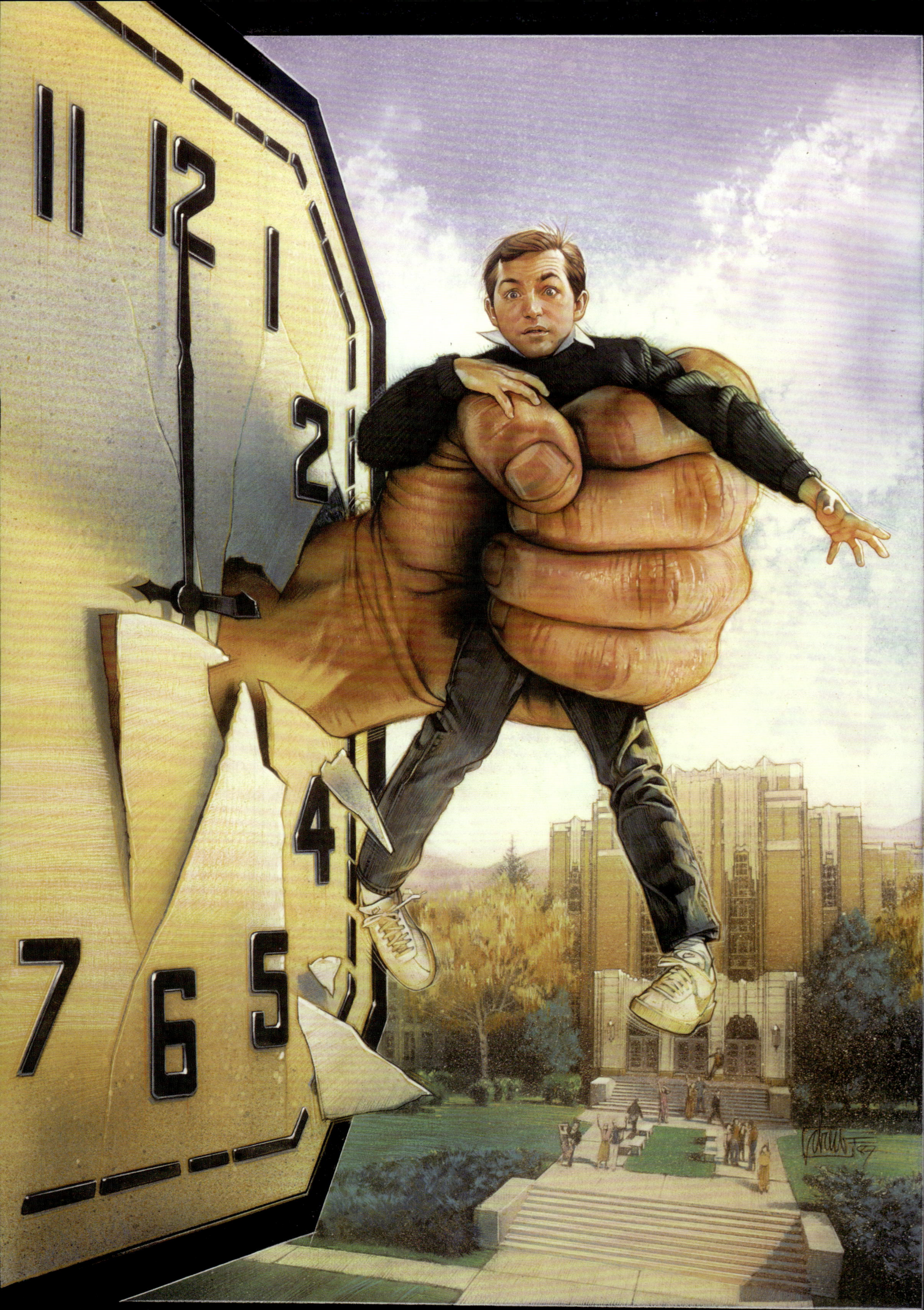

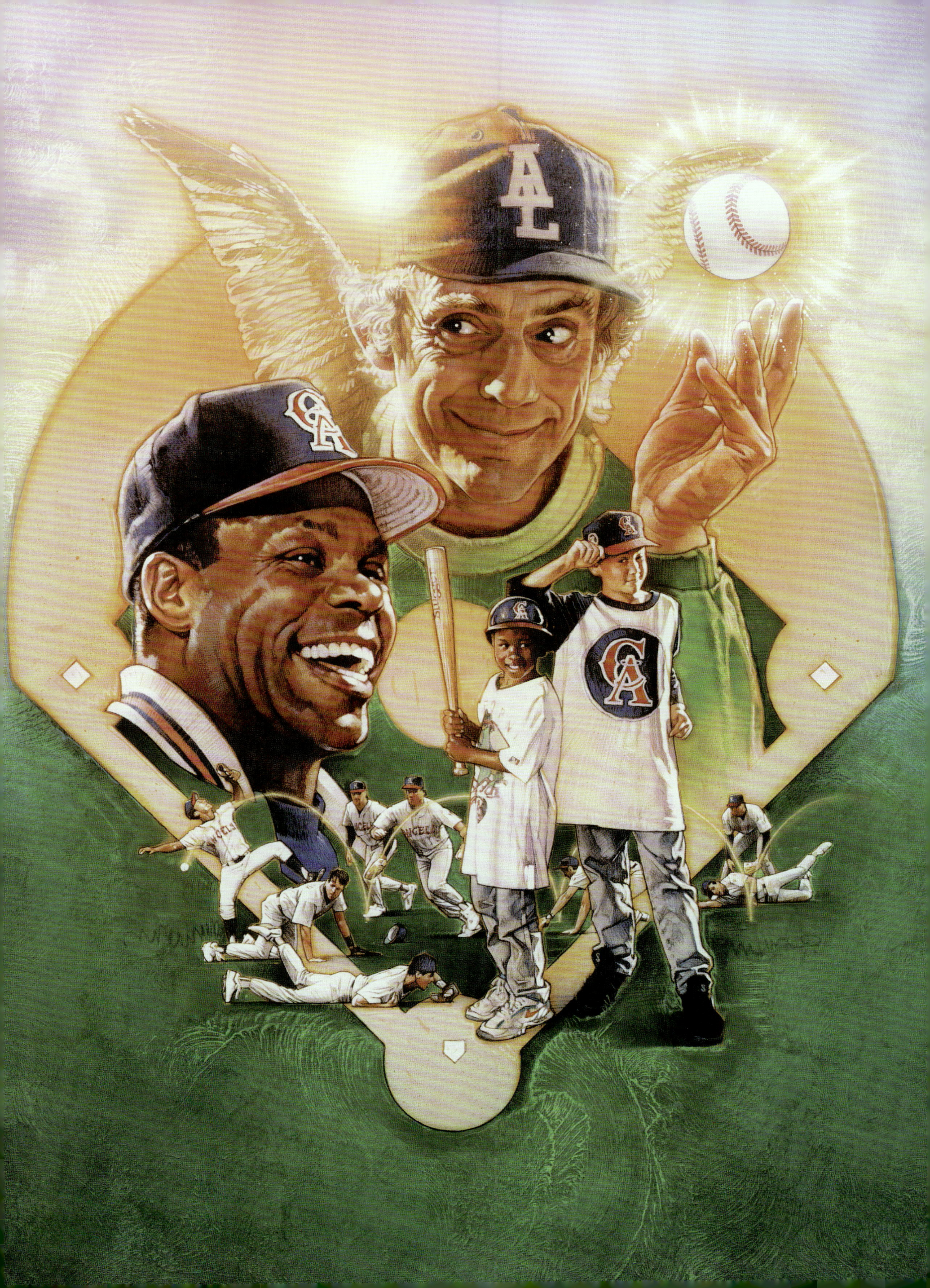

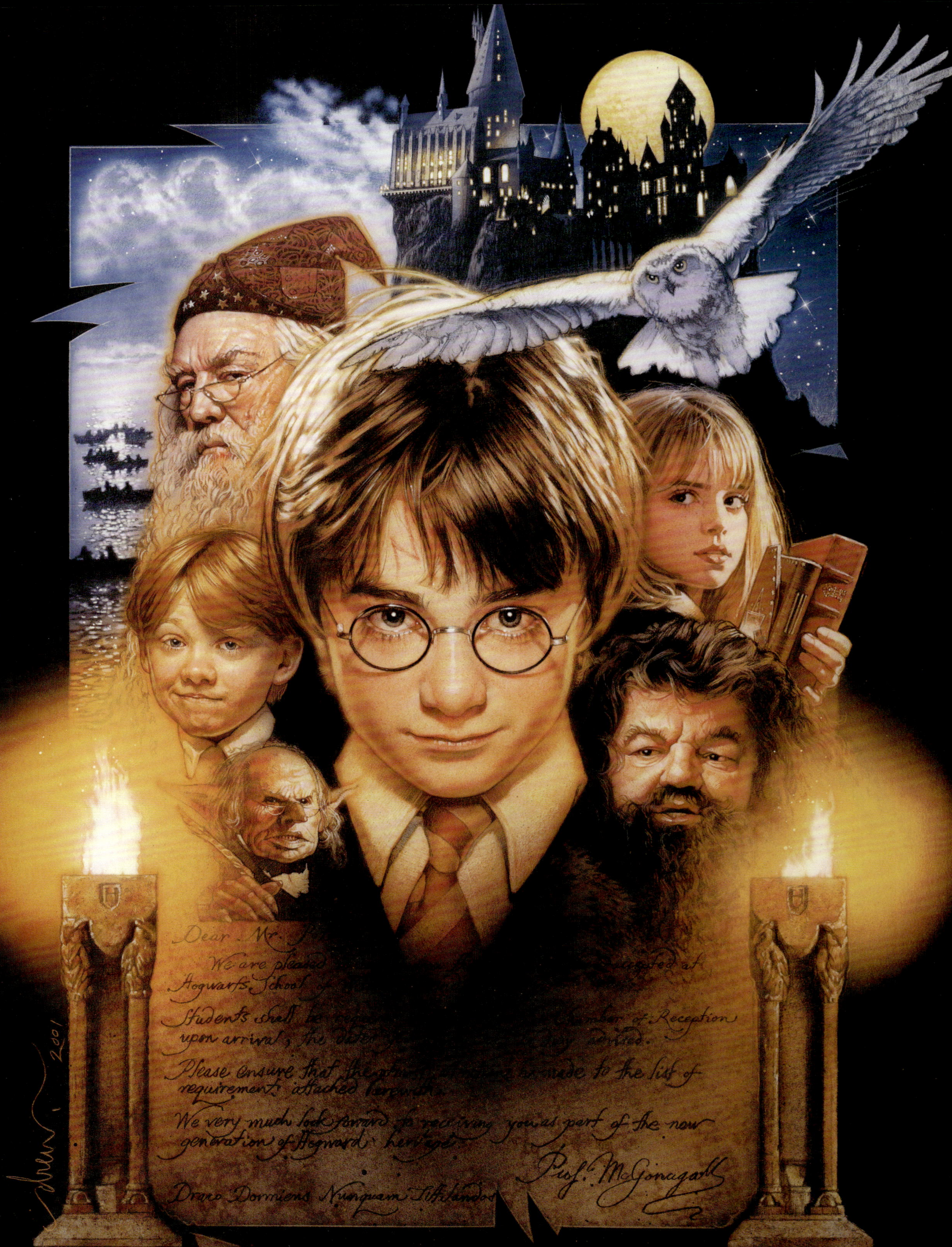

Dear Mr.
We are pleased
Hogwarts School
Students shall be
Chamber of Reception
upon arrival, the
Please ensure that
made to the list of
requirements attached
We very much look forward to receiving you as part of the new
generation of Hogwarts heritage.
Prof. McGonagall
Draco Dormiens Nunquam Titillandus
2001

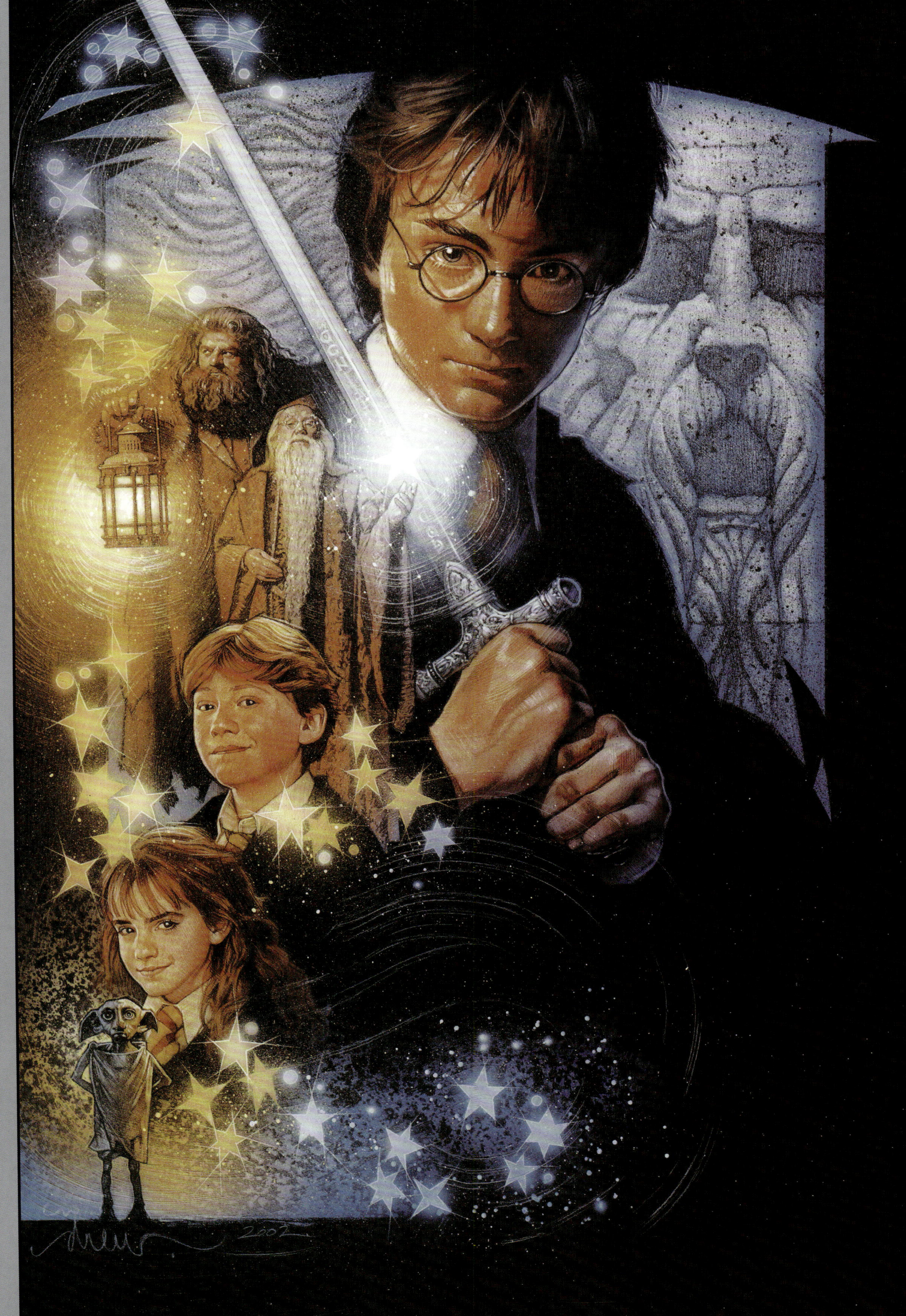
2002

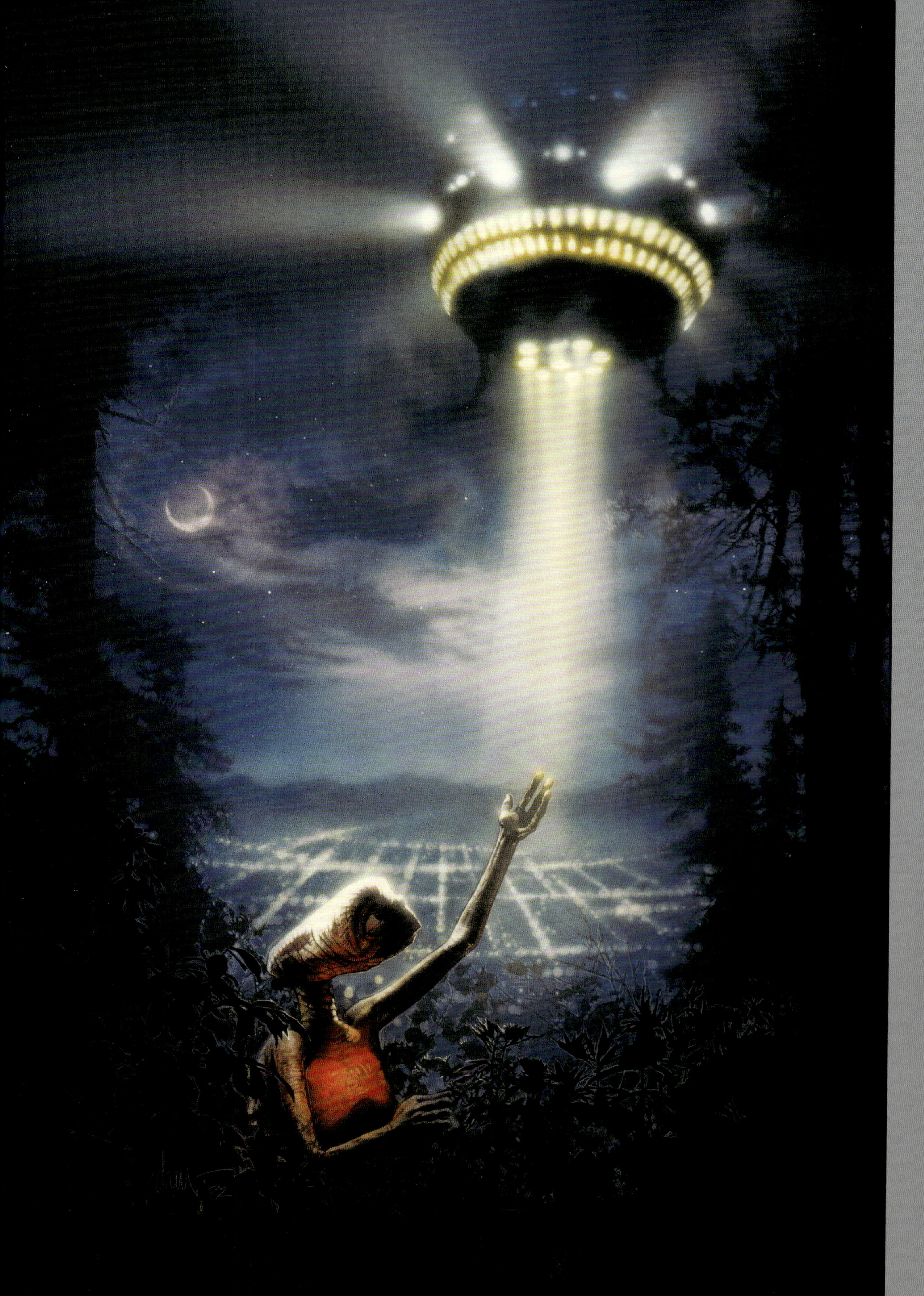

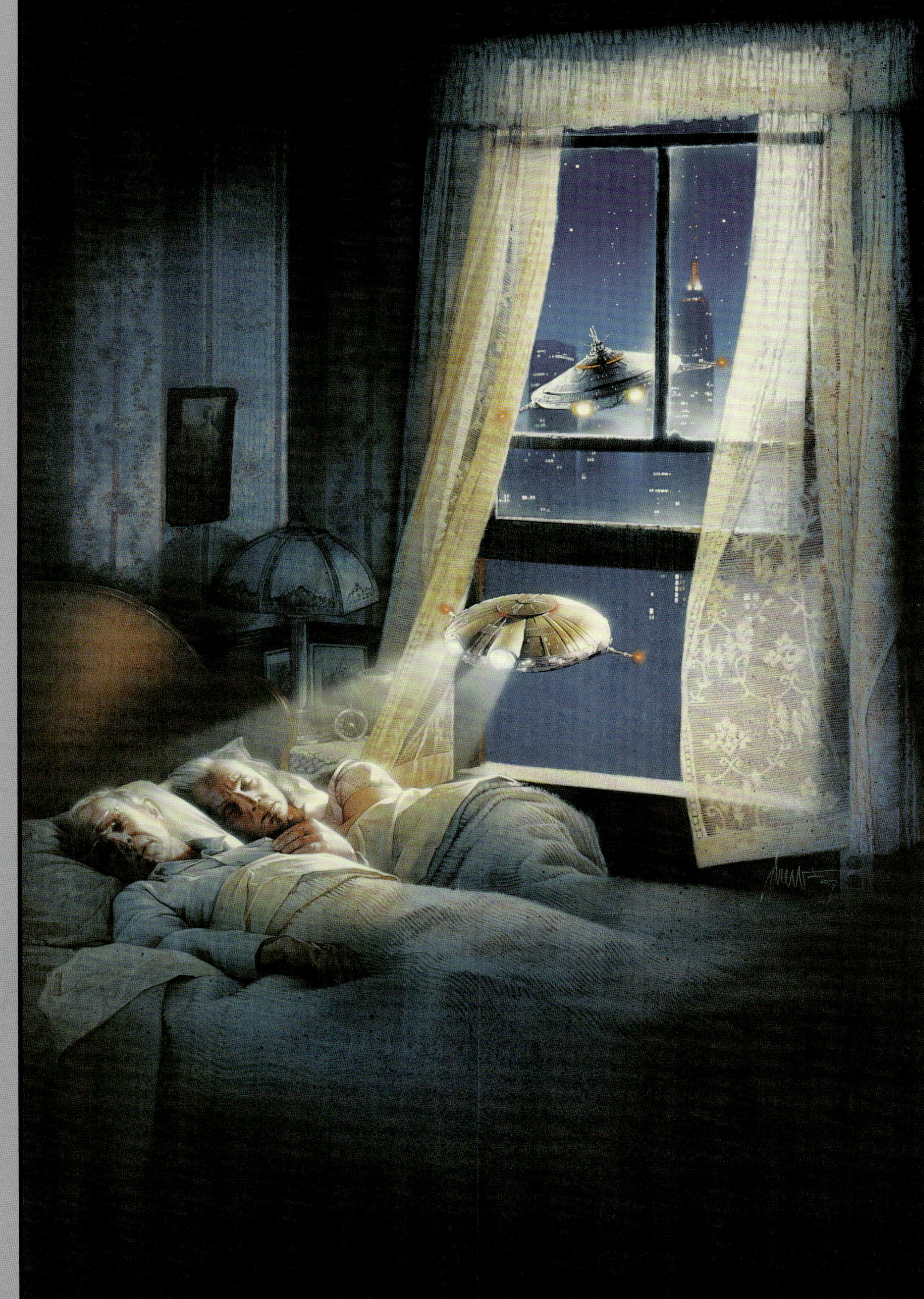

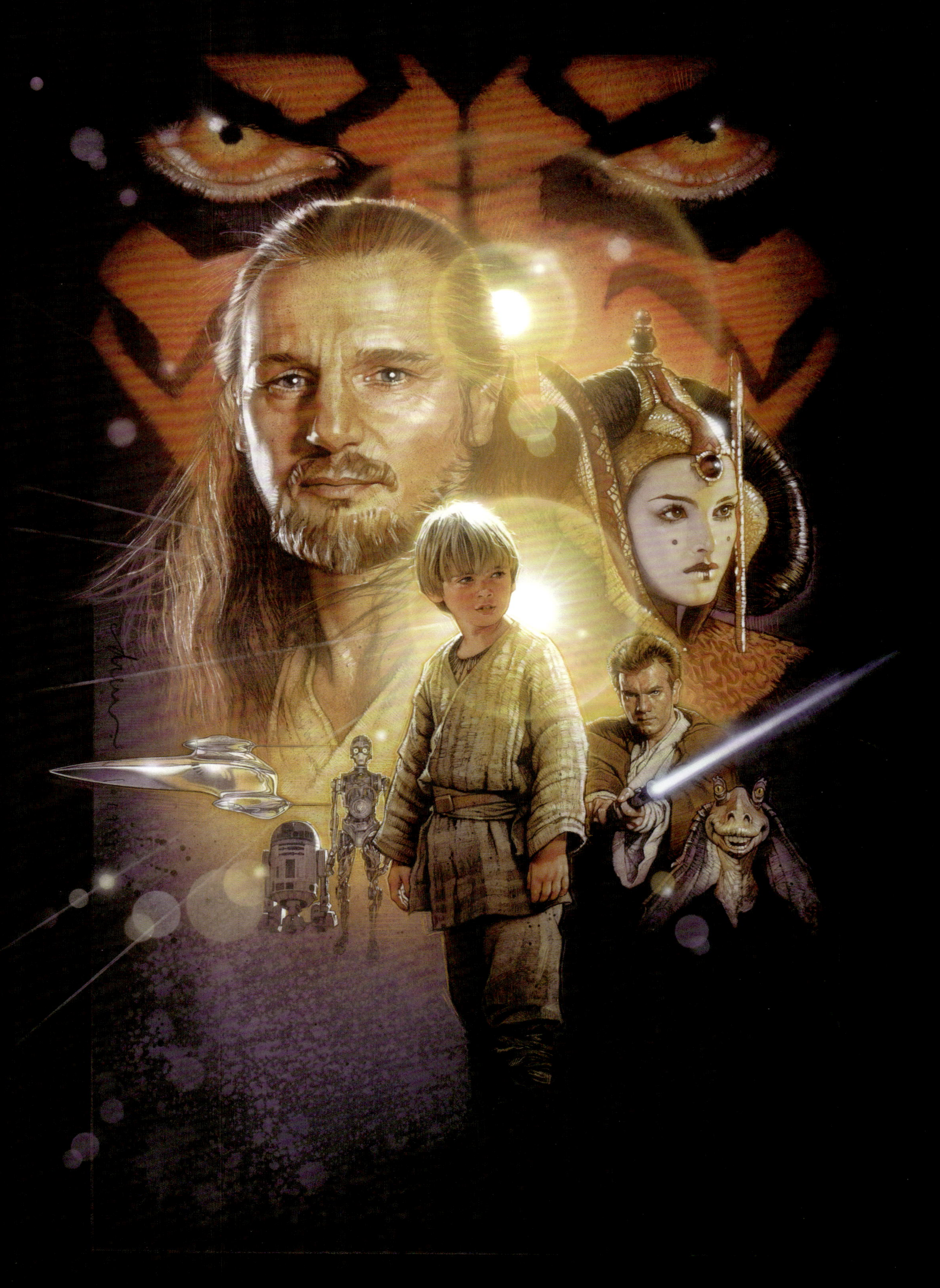

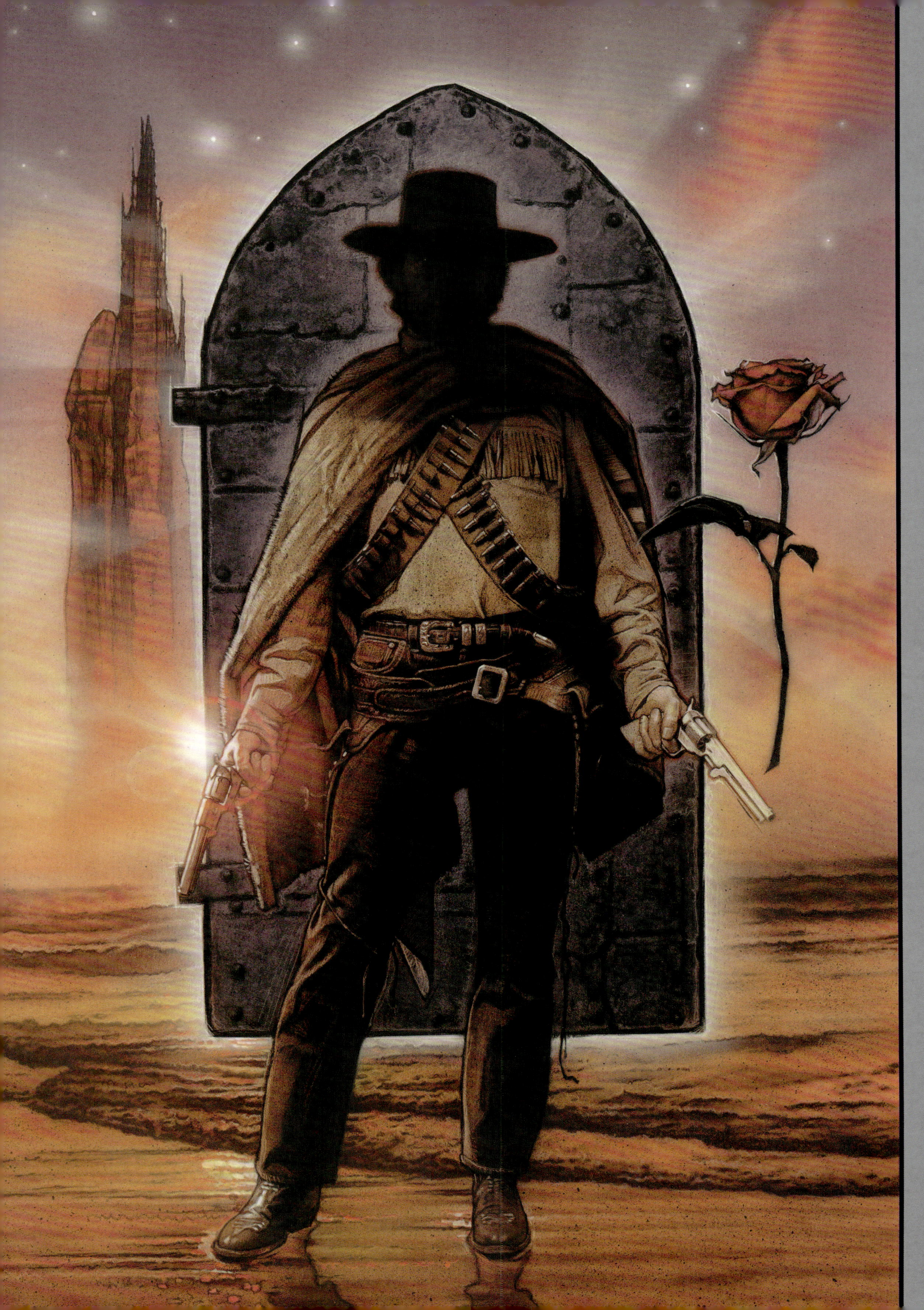

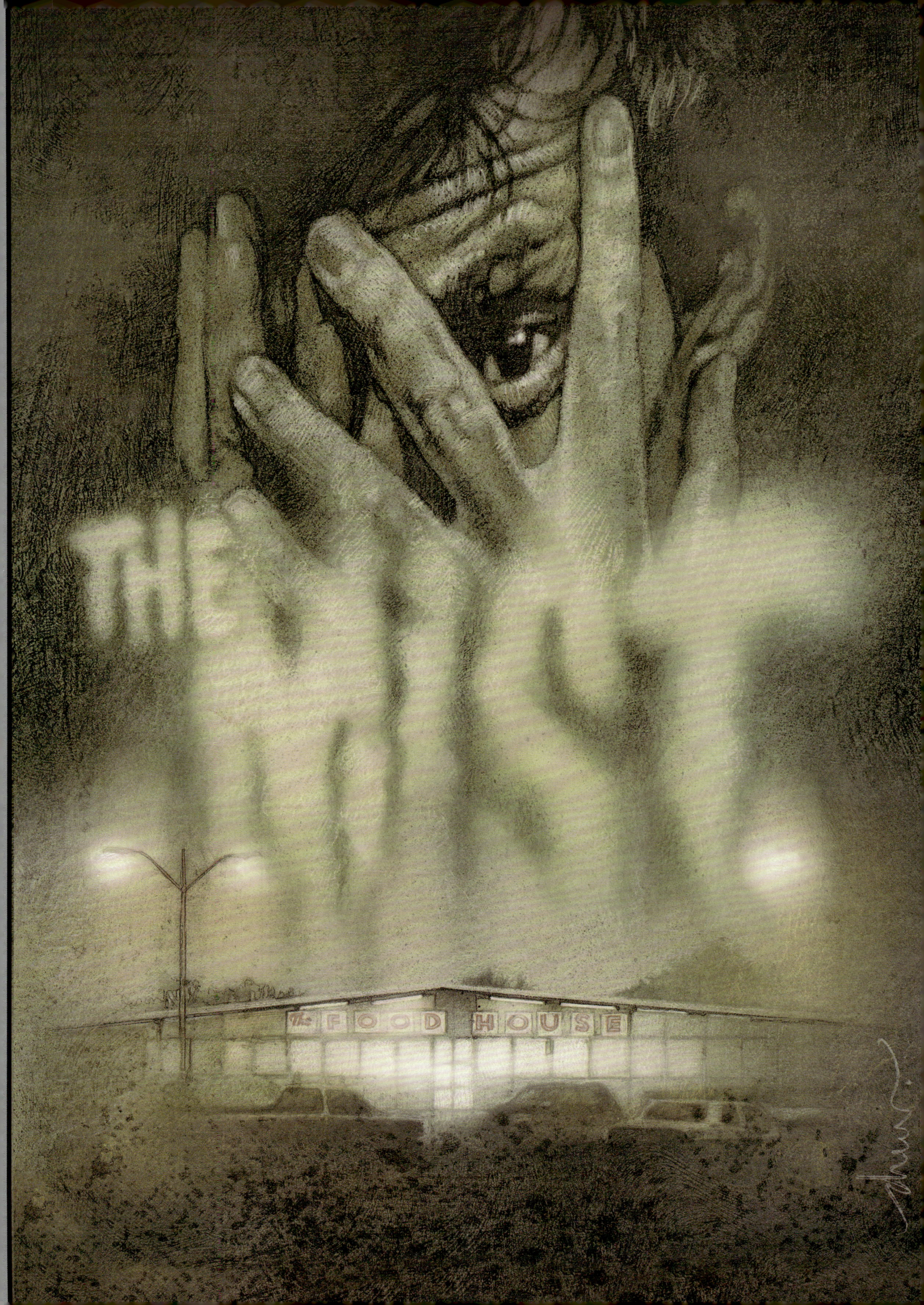
THE
the FOOD HOUSE

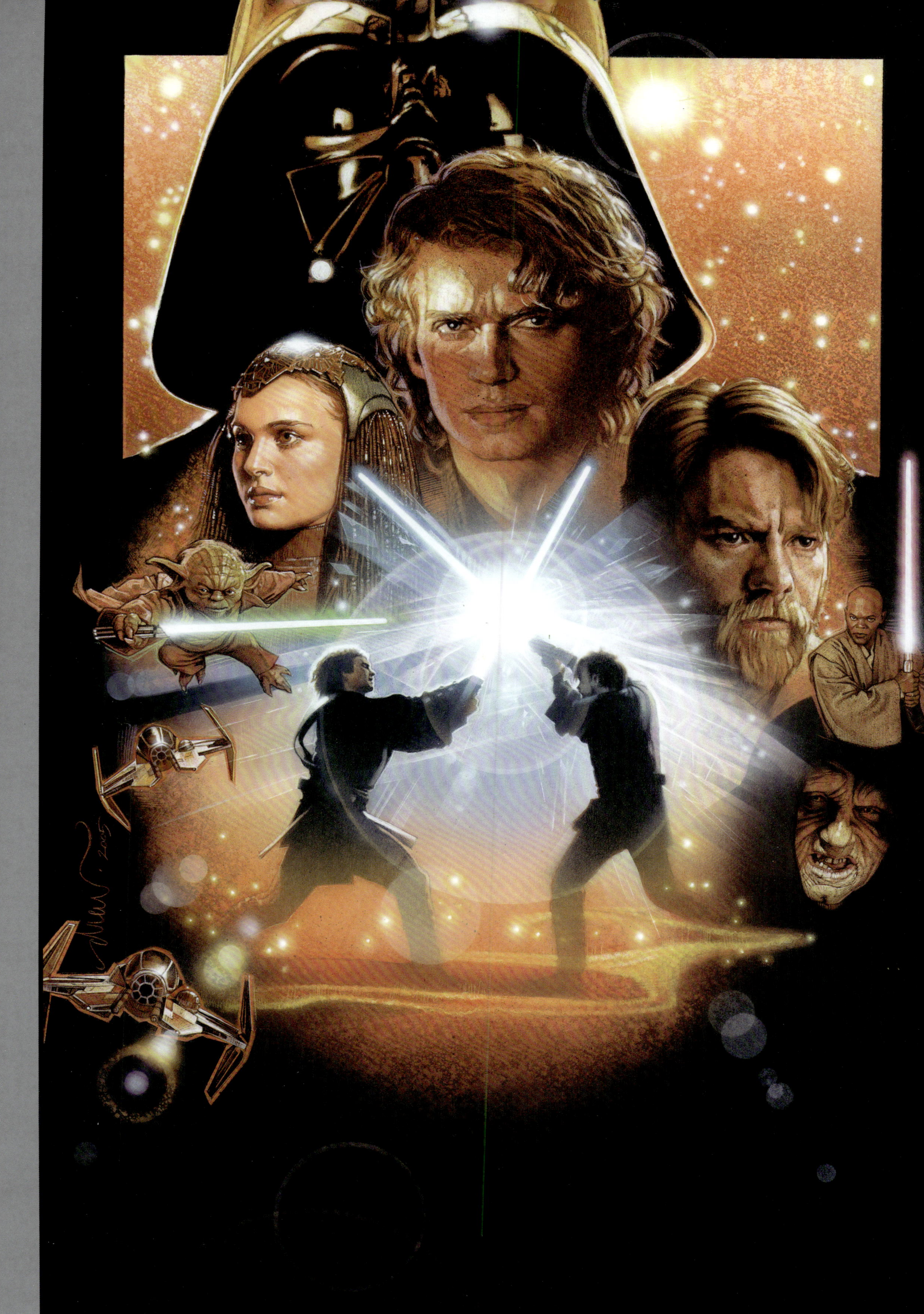

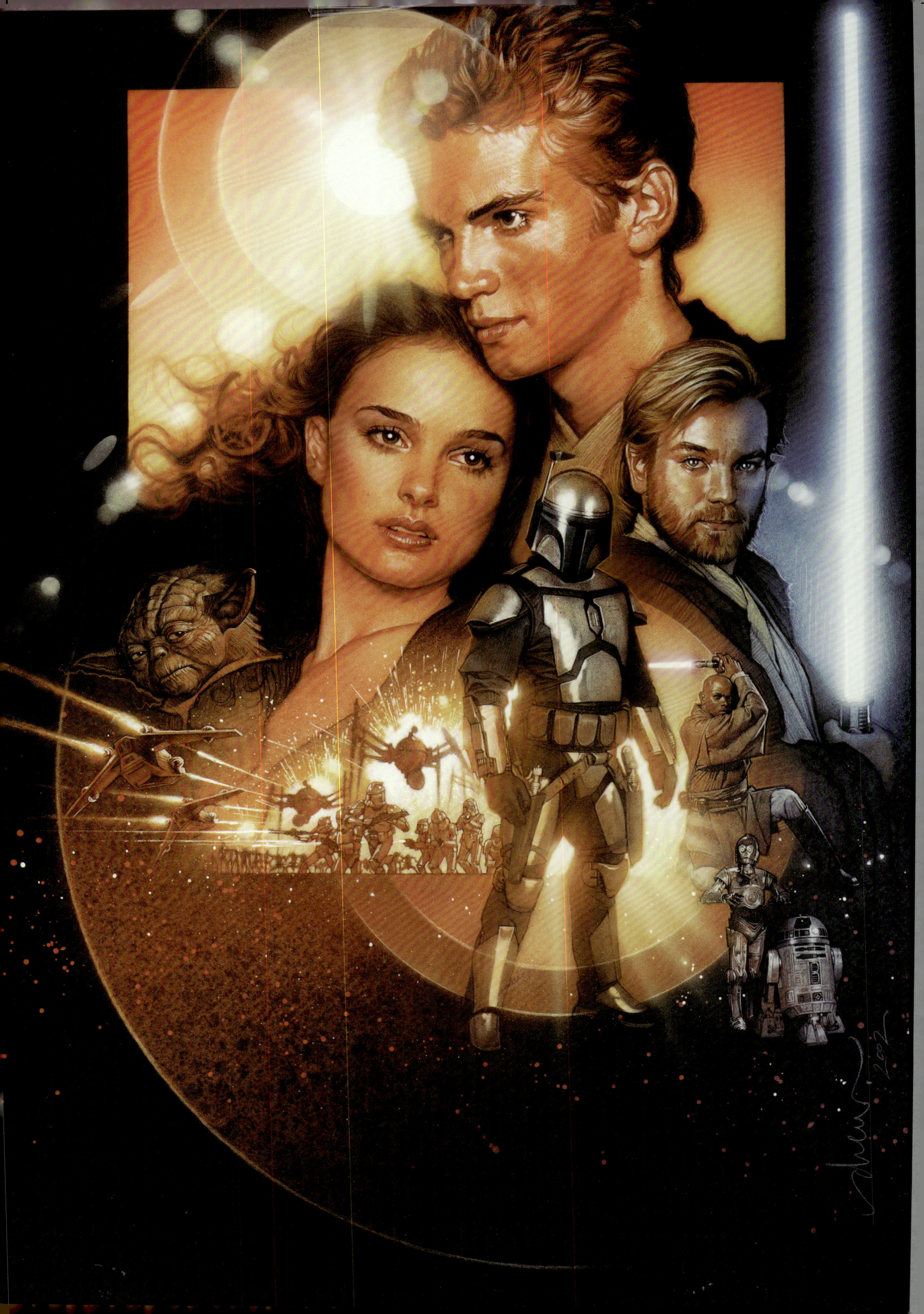

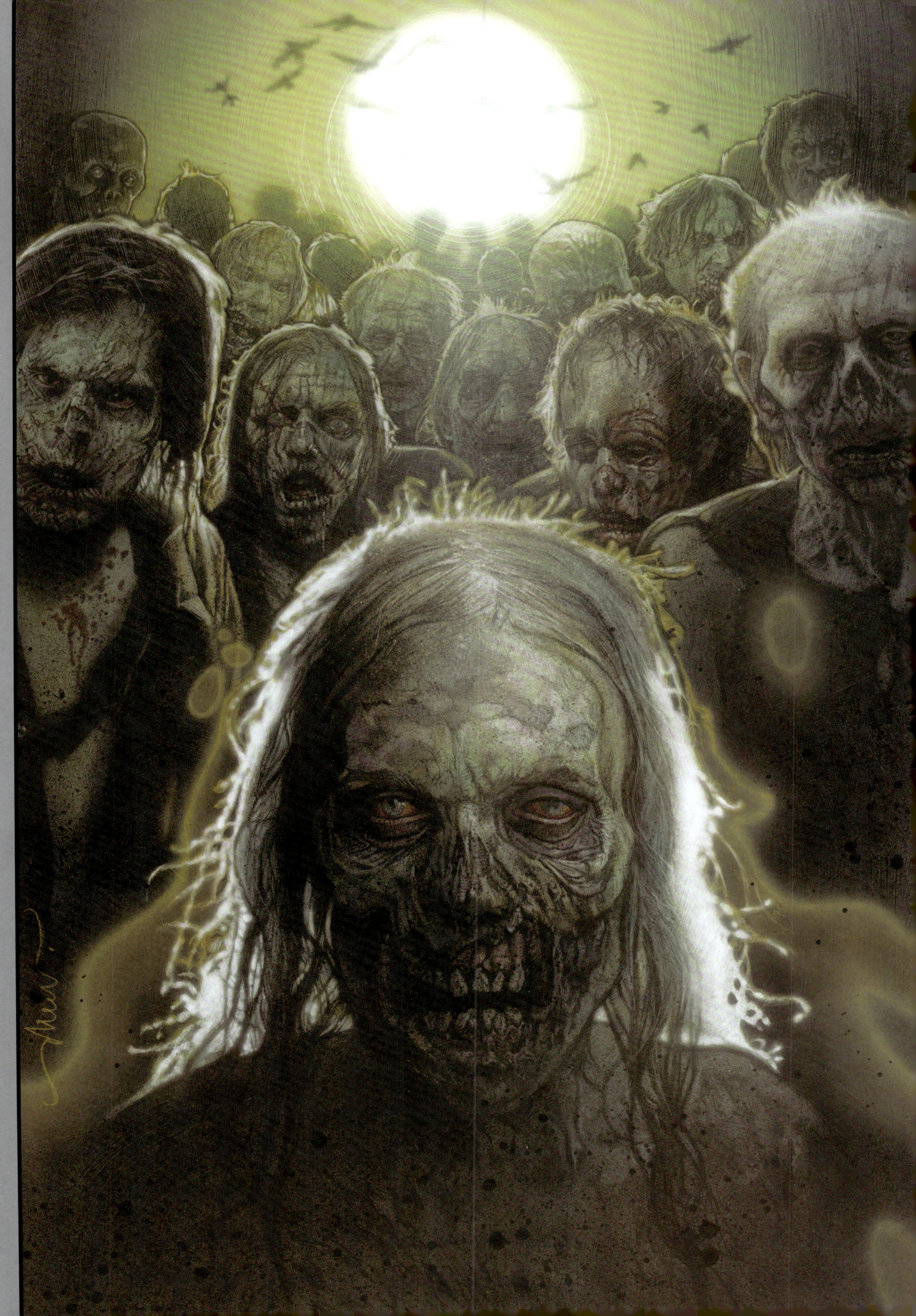

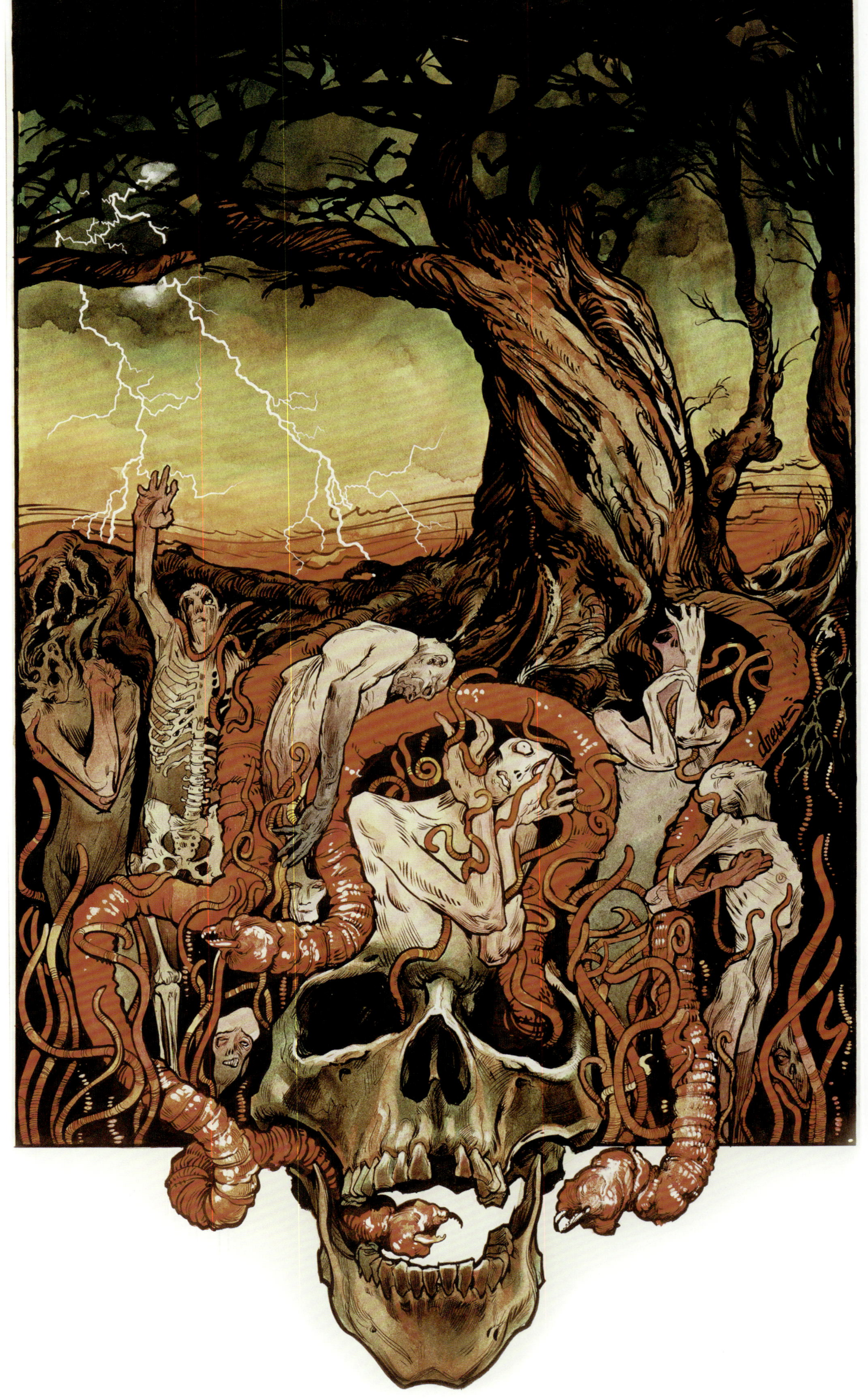

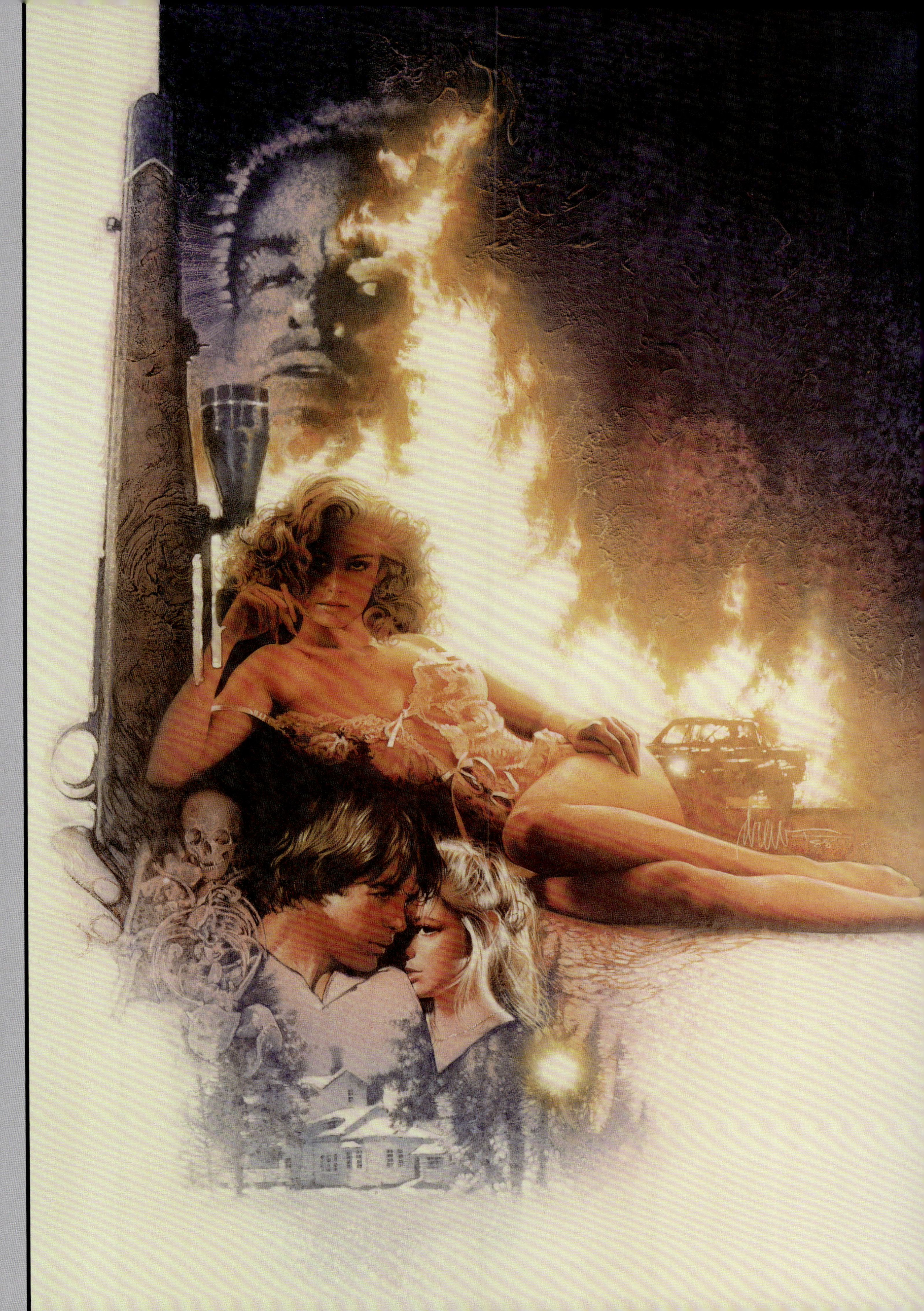

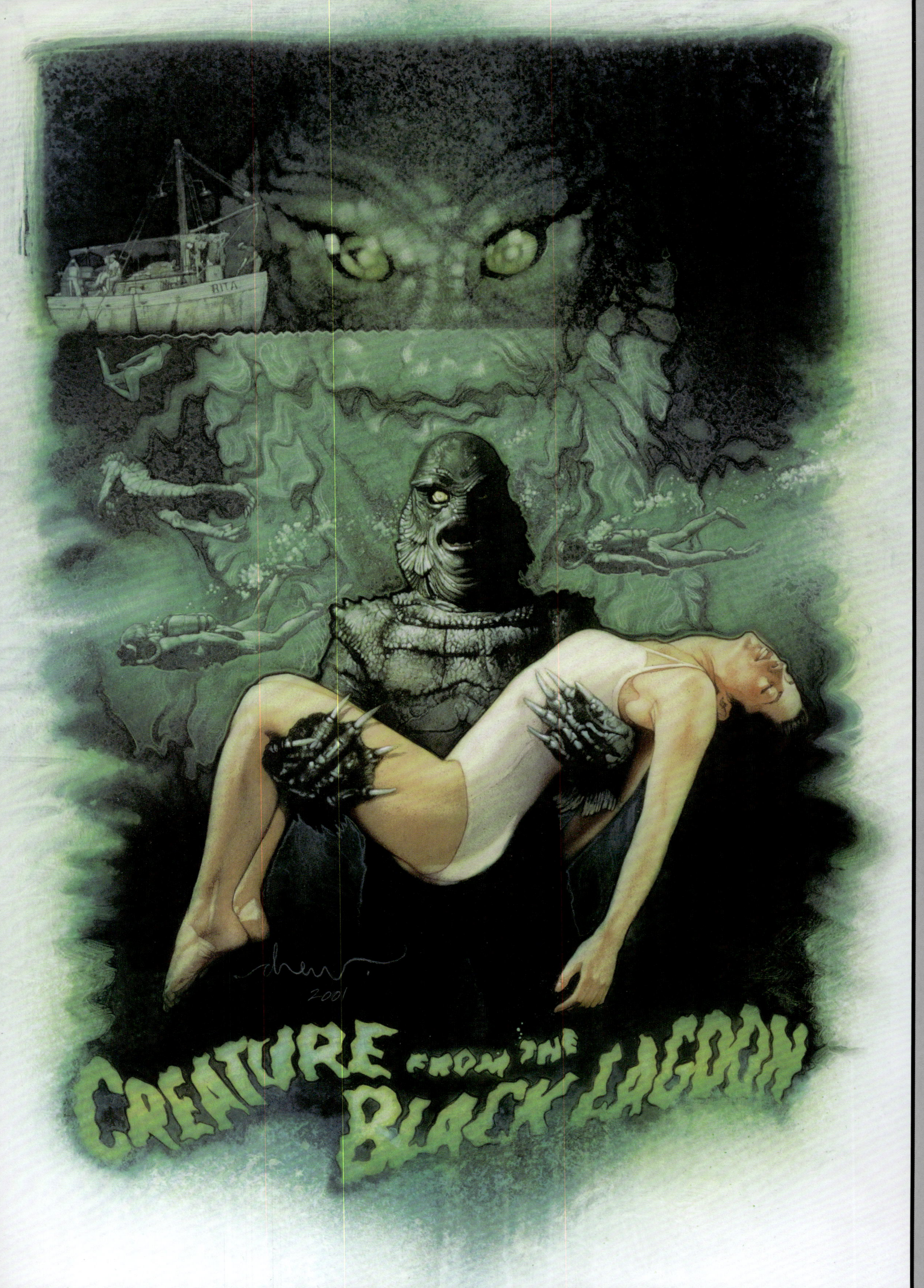
RITA
drew
2001
CREATURE FROM THE BLACK LAGOON

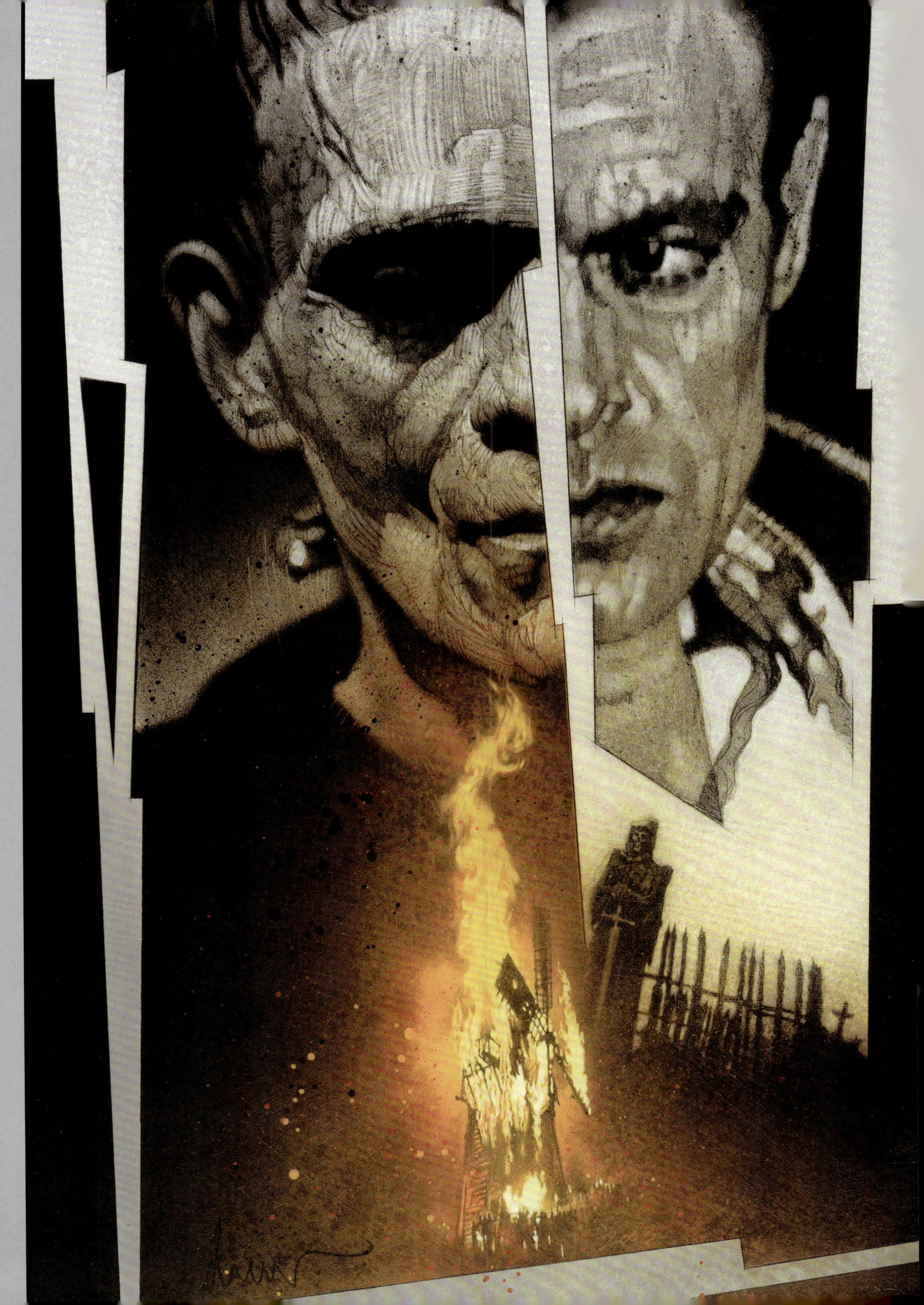

PUBLISHING

Metaphorically speaking, illustrating for books means putting on a different hat. Since books print much smaller than movie posters and are grouped and stacked on shelves, rather than prominently displayed in movie theater light boxes, the illustration must work harder in order to be noticed.

Drew's books are hard to overlook.

"The design has to be simplified," Drew says, "But the same spirit drives the design. Right off the bat, what I liked about designing for book covers was that I could do each illustration in a couple of days. With movie posters, a project can go on for weeks, sometimes months. With books, I do one day's worth of research to see what the story is about, do the drawing, send it off to the people involved, and once it was approved, do the finish in a day or two. Done. I could move on. It's nice to be able to make the statement instead of rethinking the idea a hundred thousand more times. I have never had to make a change on a book cover, never had to do more than one drawing."

Books—as is evident from looking at his *Star Wars* and "Indy" covers—came to Drew because of the movie work. When Bantam Books first started publishing the *Star Wars* novels and the issue of what to do for the cover arose, George Lucas simply said, "Get Drew."

Of course, Drew's work includes other subjects, such as book covers for *Star Trek*, comic book covers for *Masters of the Universe*, *John Carpenter's Snake Plissken Chronicles*, and Ryan Schifrin's *Spooks*, a cover for *MAD* magazine, and a cover and interiors for *TV Guide.*

In 1985, Drew was interviewed by Laura Siegel. Laura was working for a local TV news station covering an art show in which Drew was participating at the City of Brea's art gallery. Their off-screen conversation uncovered a mutual admiration between Drew and her father, Jerry Siegel, co-creator of Superman. In response, Drew got a delightful letter from "Superman."

So when the opportunity arose to do a cover for DC Comics to honor the original series with an homage to the cover art for *Action Comics* #1, "I jumped at the opportunity," Drew says. "It was a chance to actually be a part of a childhood dream. But even more so, to honor Mr. Siegel as best I could and thank Jerry for his timeless gift, his vision, insight, and creativity."

Drew's work is featured on the cover of *Action Comics* #800. Look closely in the lower left-hand corner and you will see Drew running in fear.

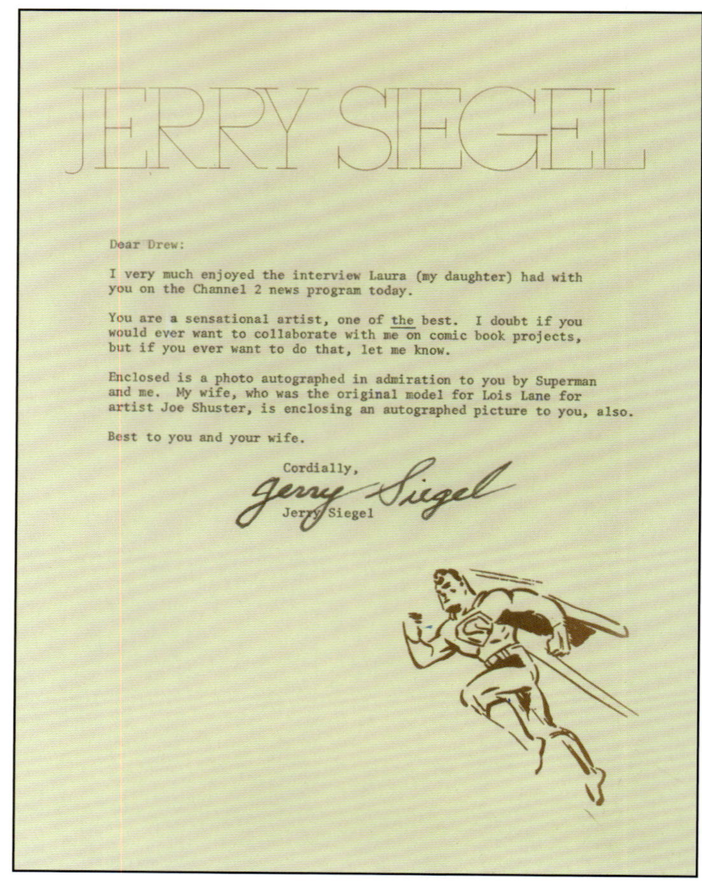

JERRY SIEGEL

Dear Drew:

I very much enjoyed the interview Laura (my daughter) had with you on the Channel 2 news program today.

You are a sensational artist, one of the best. I doubt if you would ever want to collaborate with me on comic book projects, but if you ever want to do that, let me know.

Enclosed is a photo autographed in admiration to you by Superman and me. My wife, who was the original model for Lois Lane for artist Joe Shuster, is enclosing an autographed picture to you, also.

Best to you and your wife.

Cordially,

Jerry Siegel

Jerry Siegel

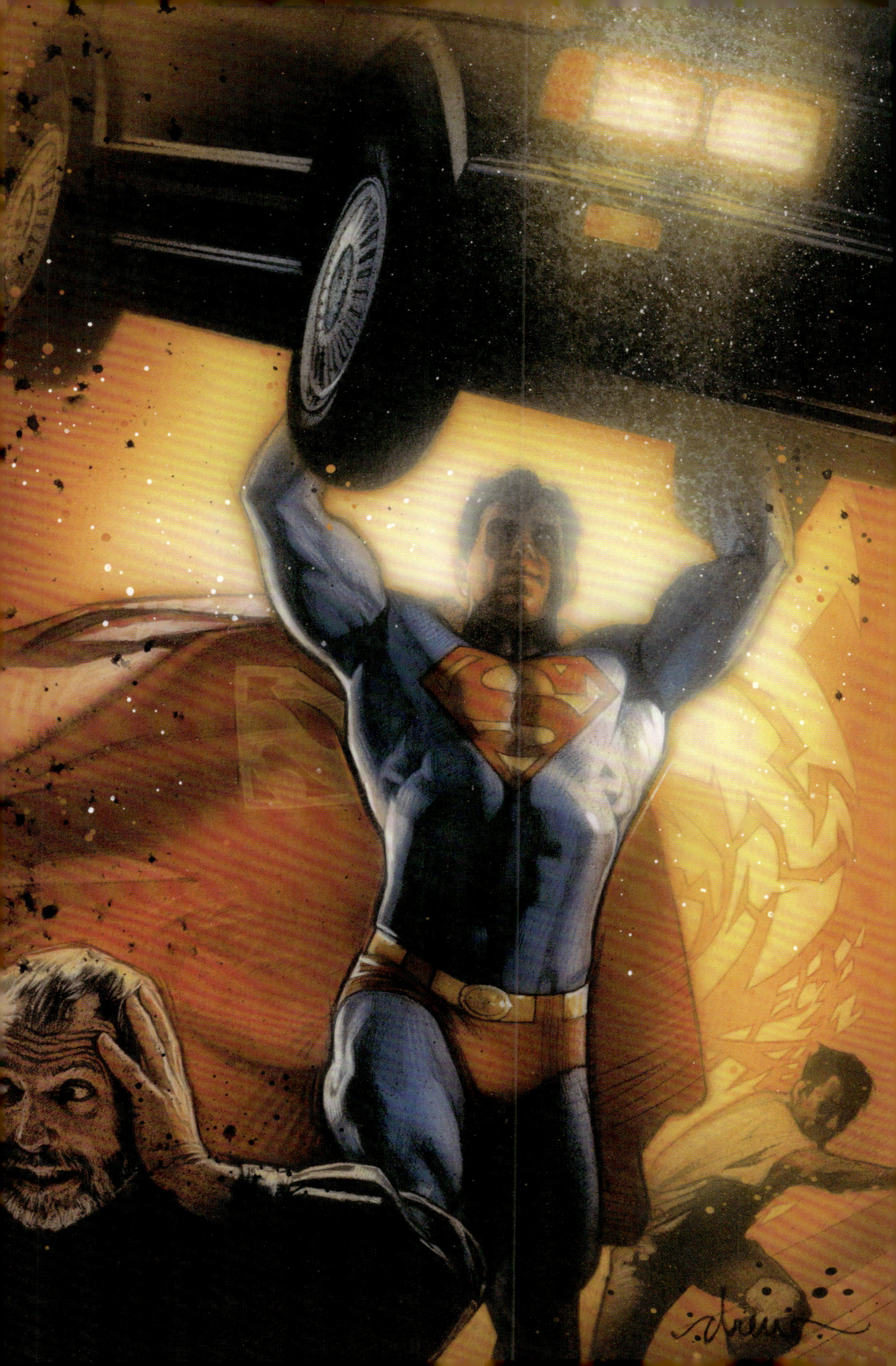

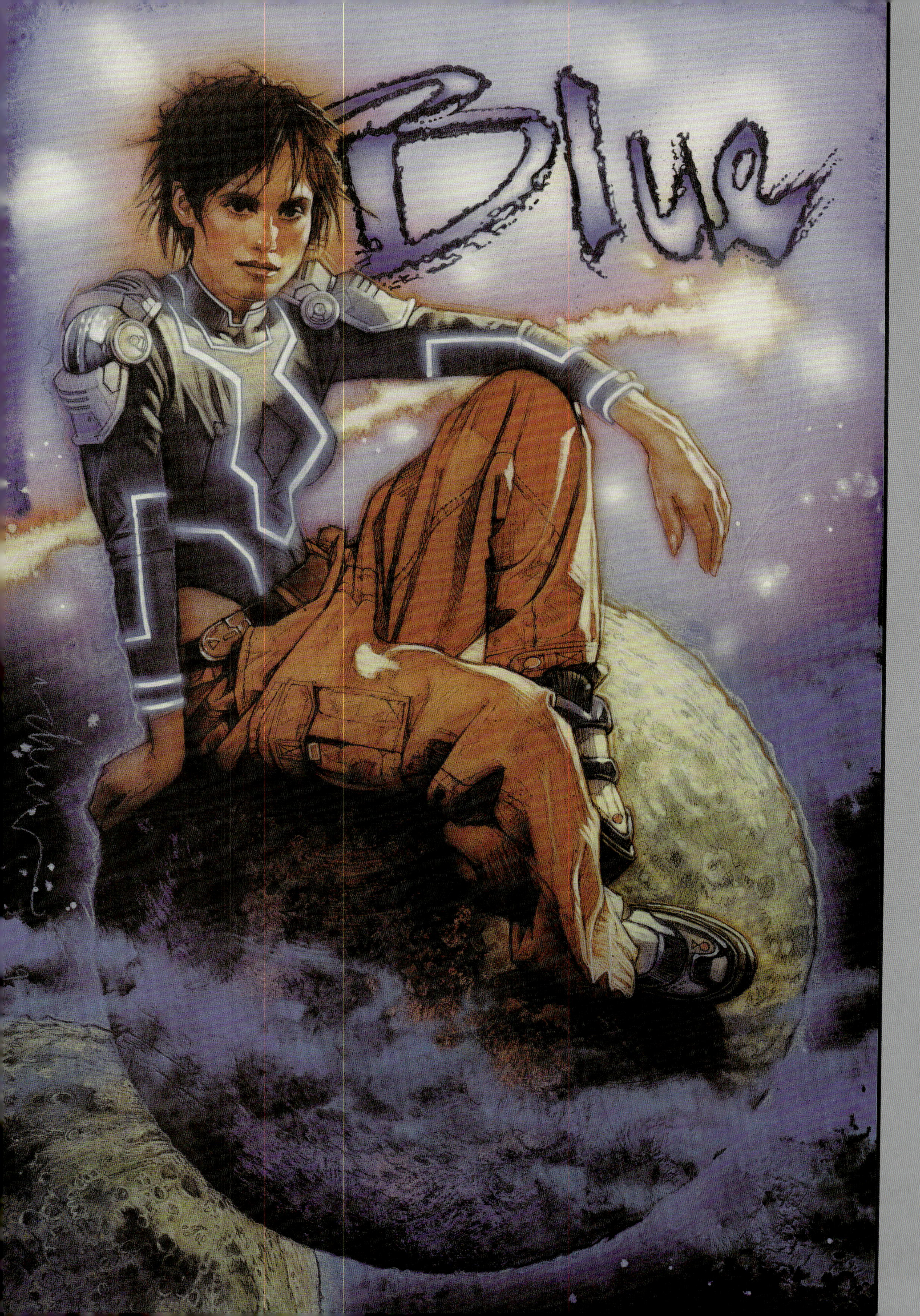
Blue

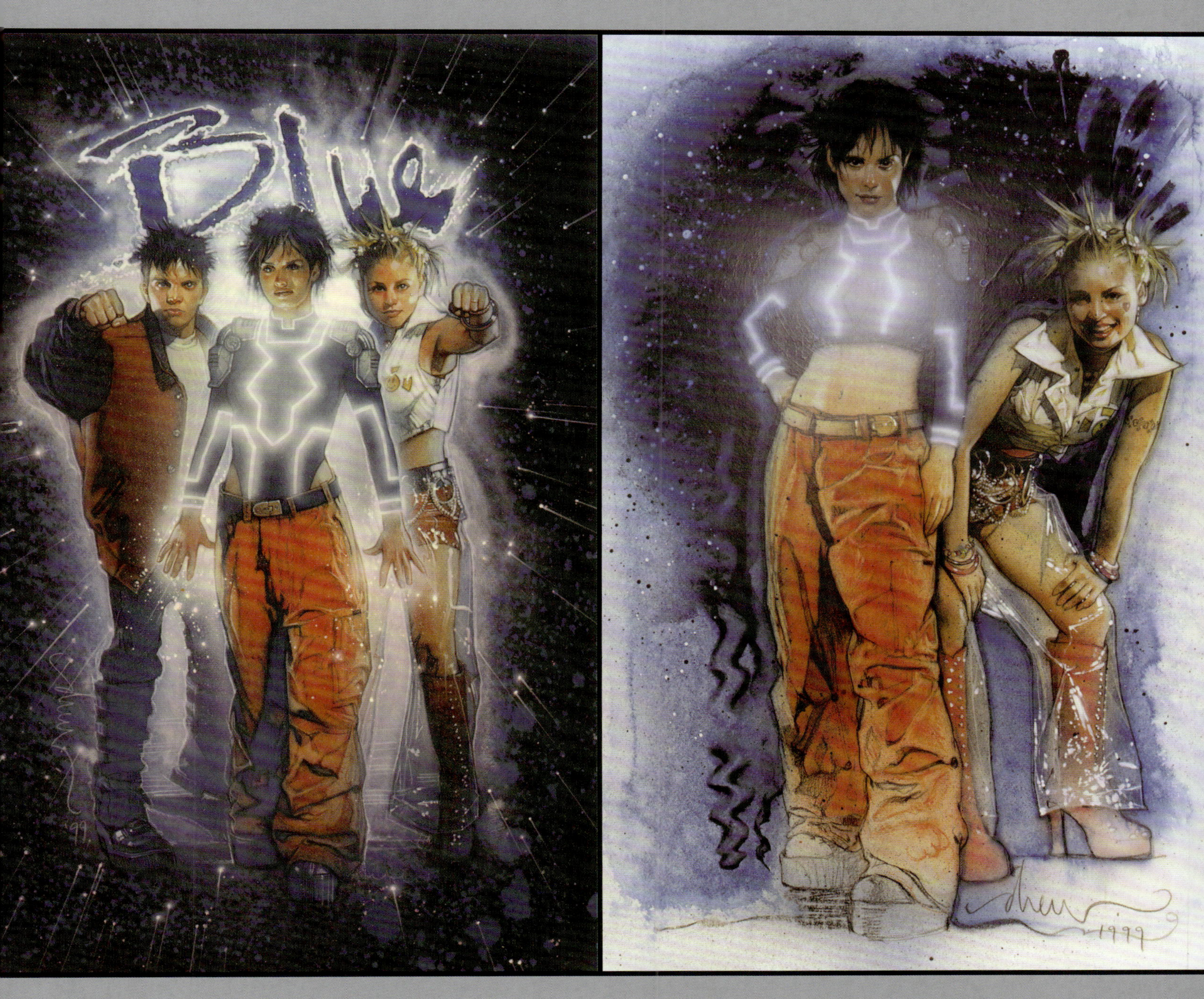
Blue
1999

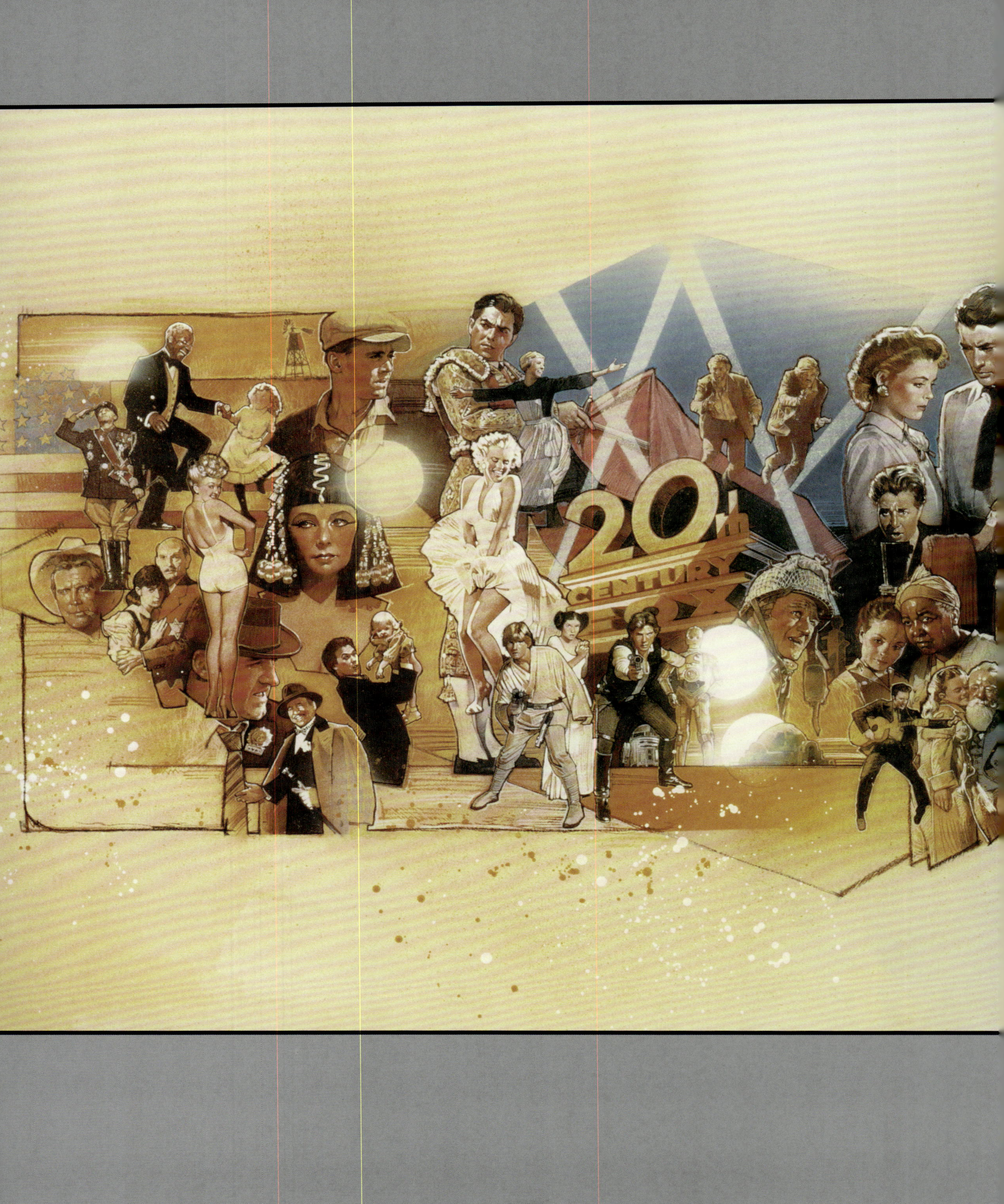
20th
CENTURY

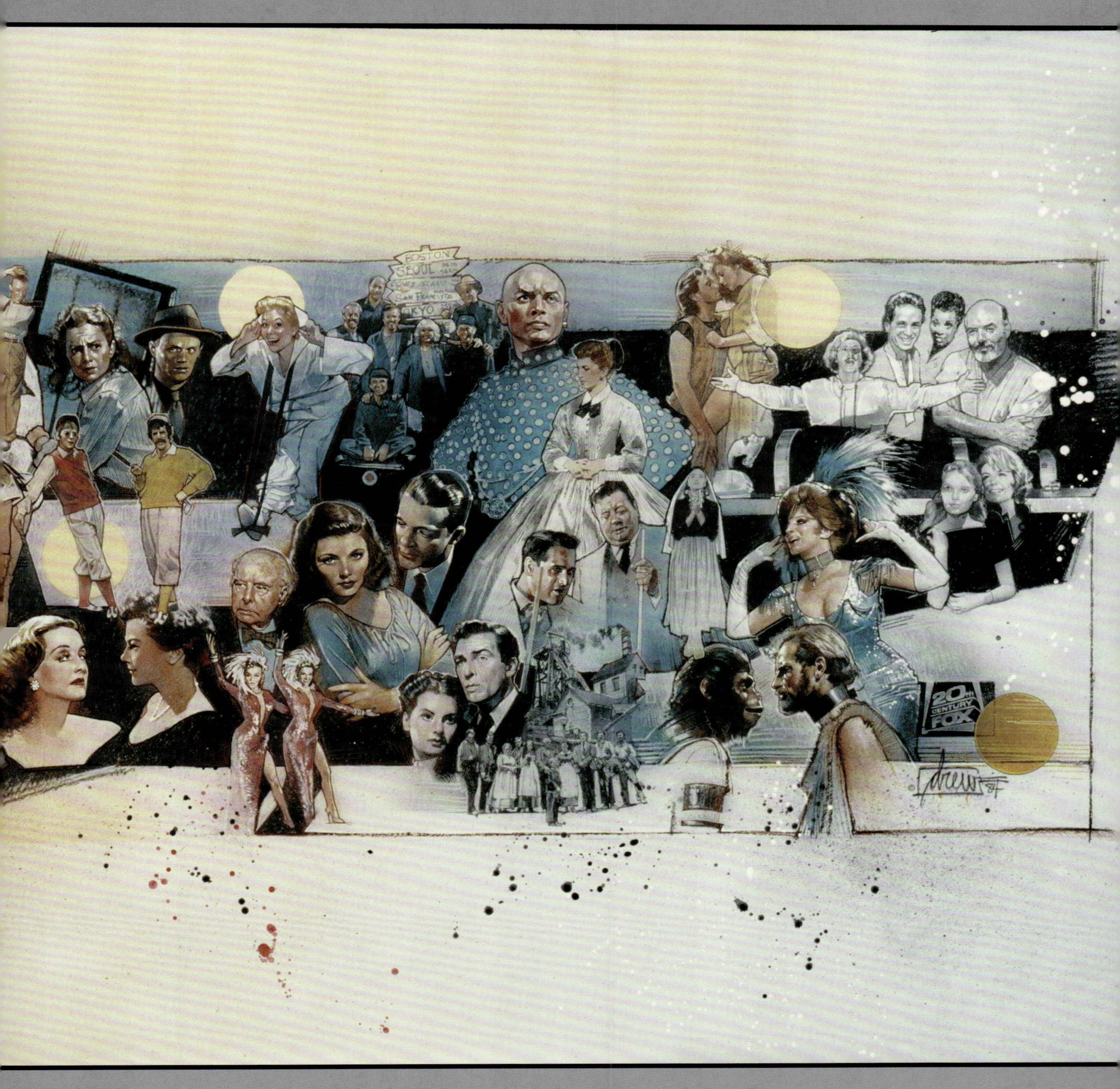
BOSTON
SEOUL
SAN FRANCISCO
20th CENTURY FOX
© drew '84

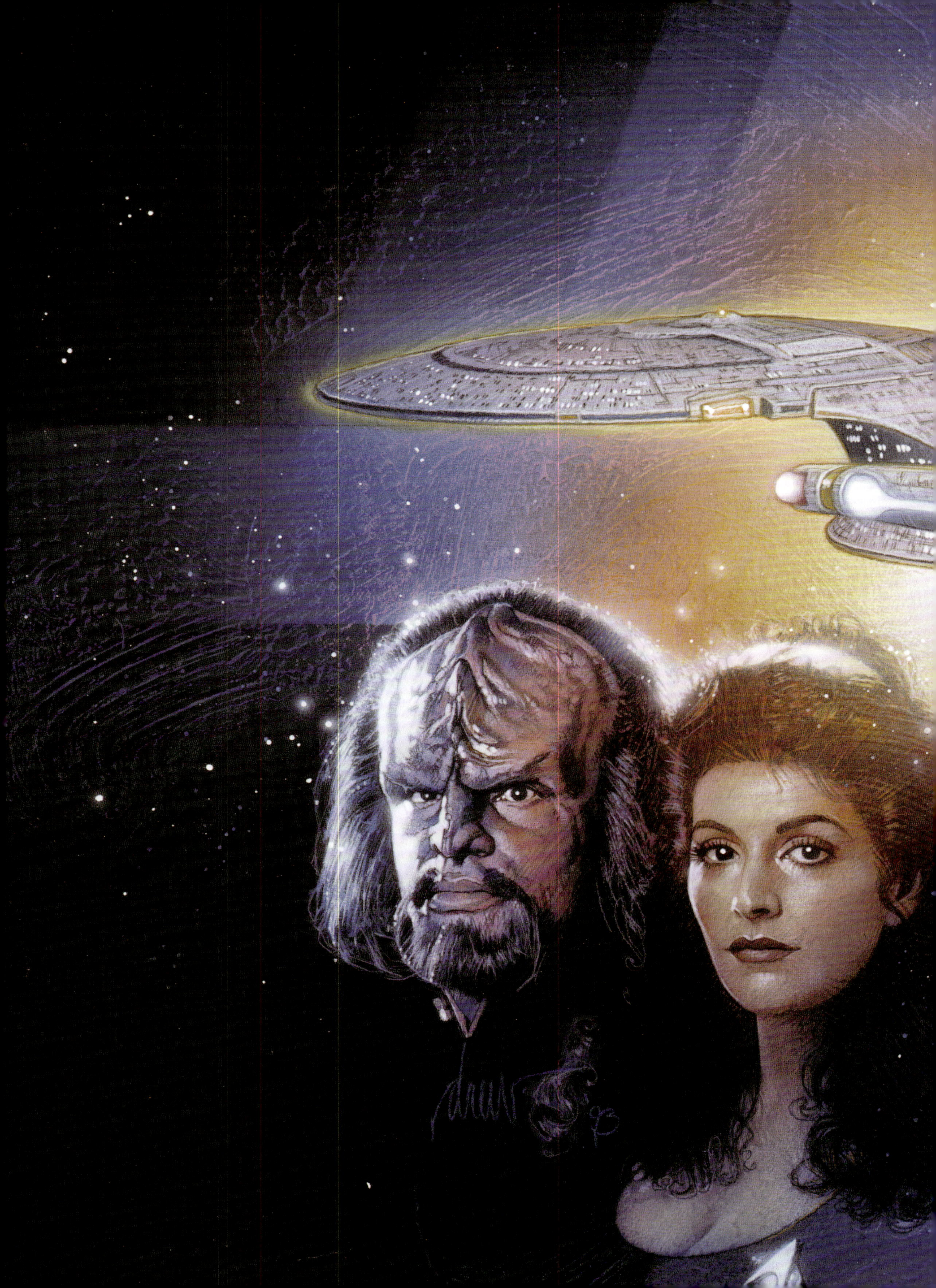

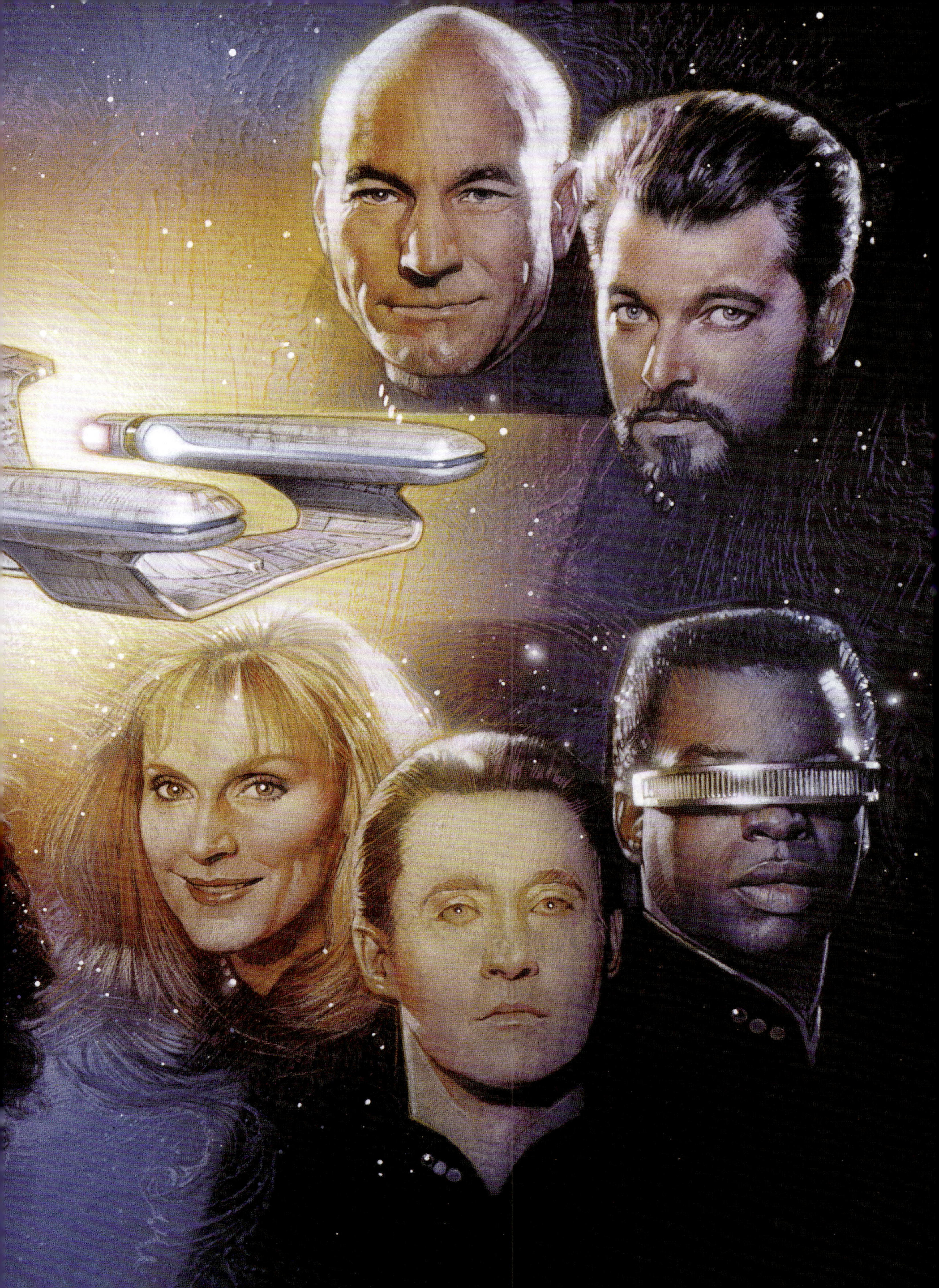

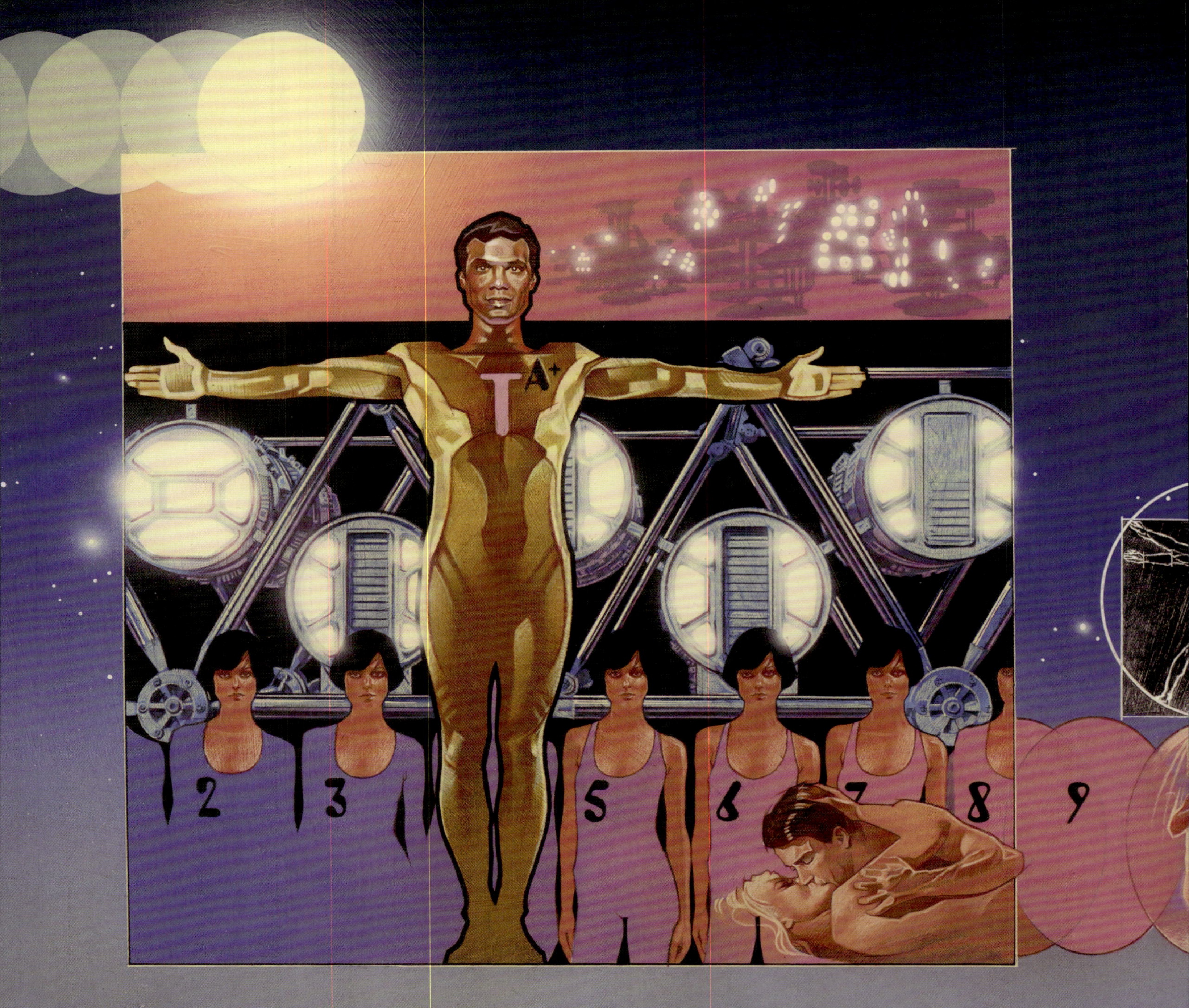
T
A+
2
3
5
6
7
8
9

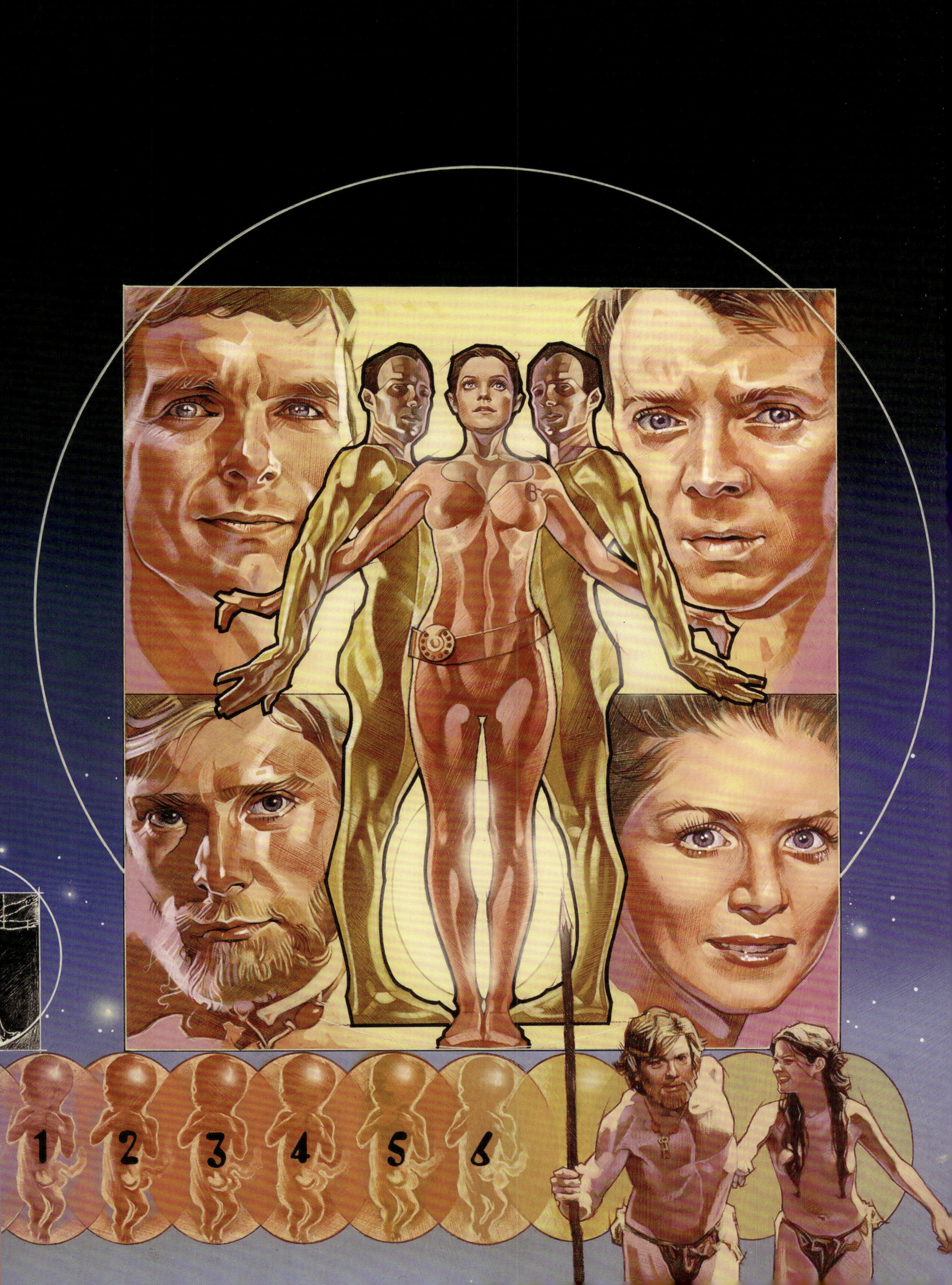
1
2
3
4
5
6

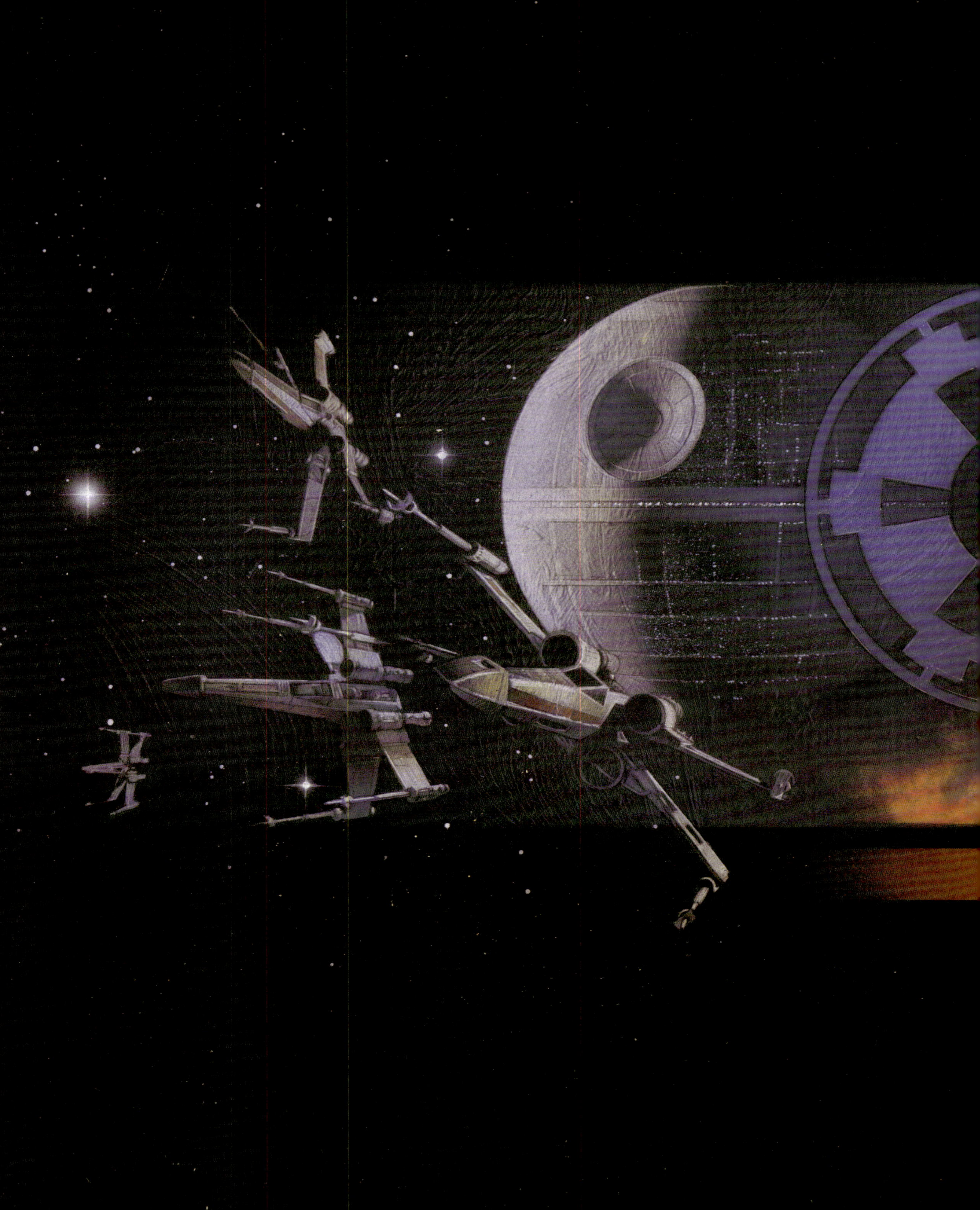

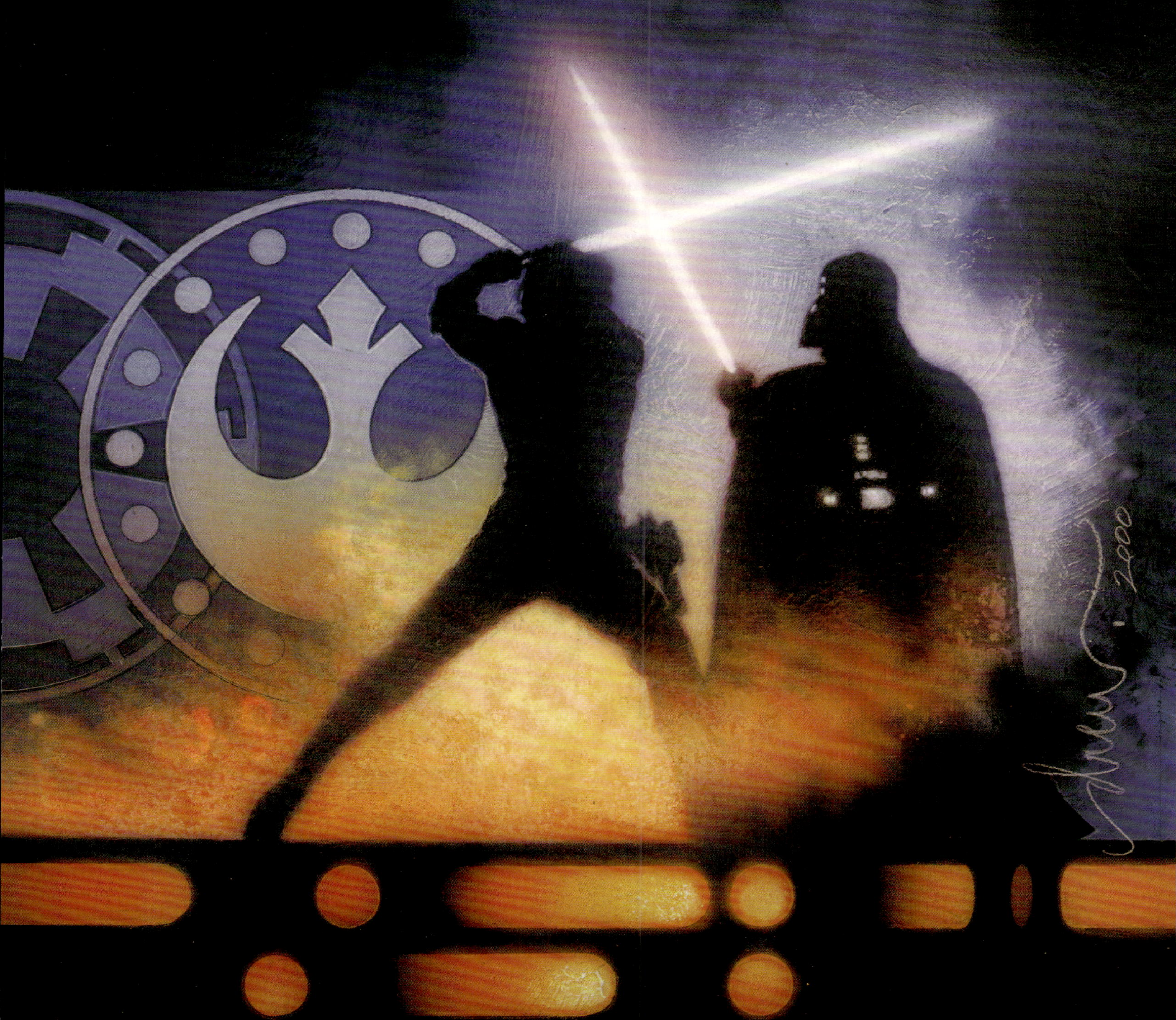

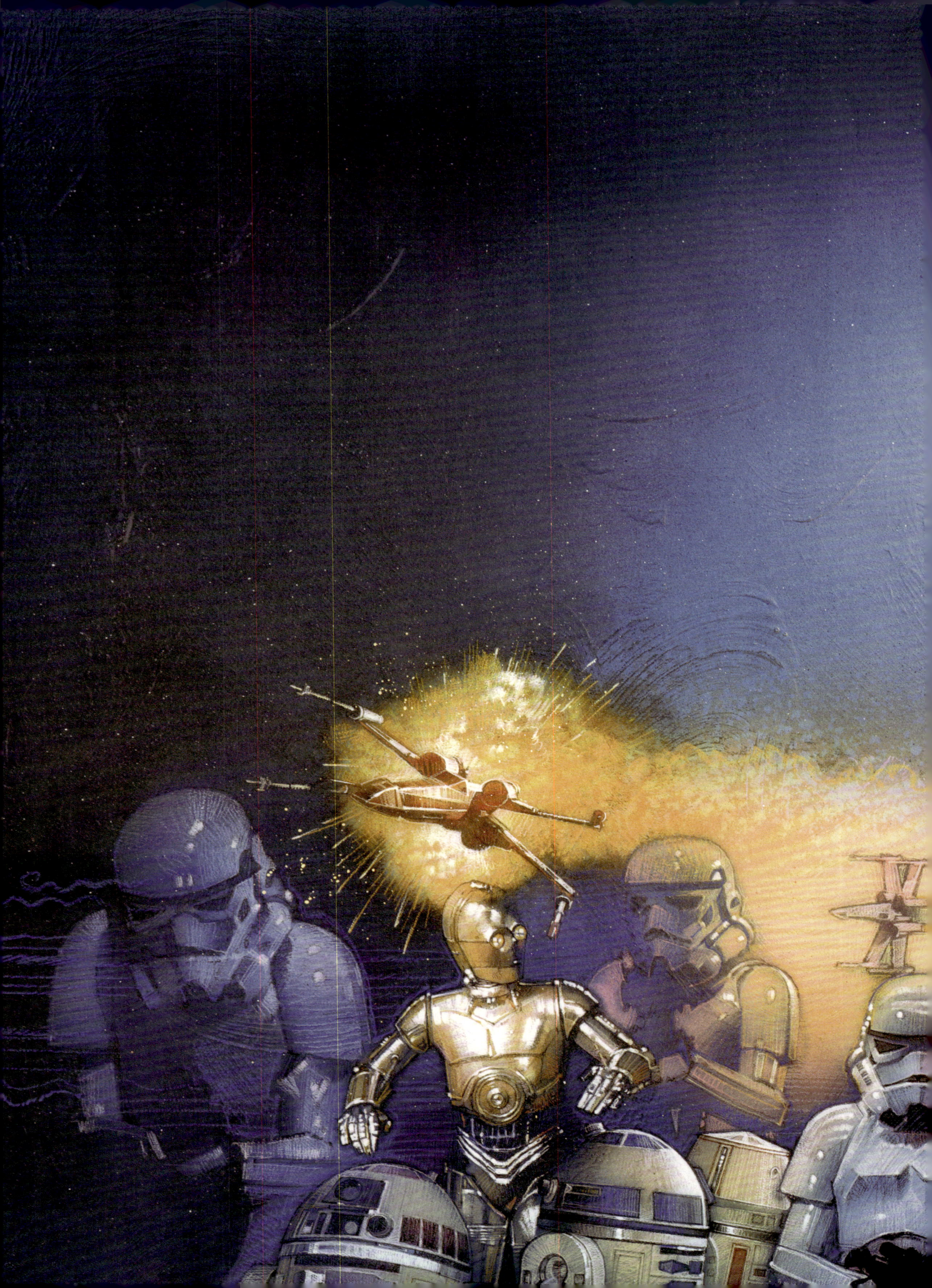

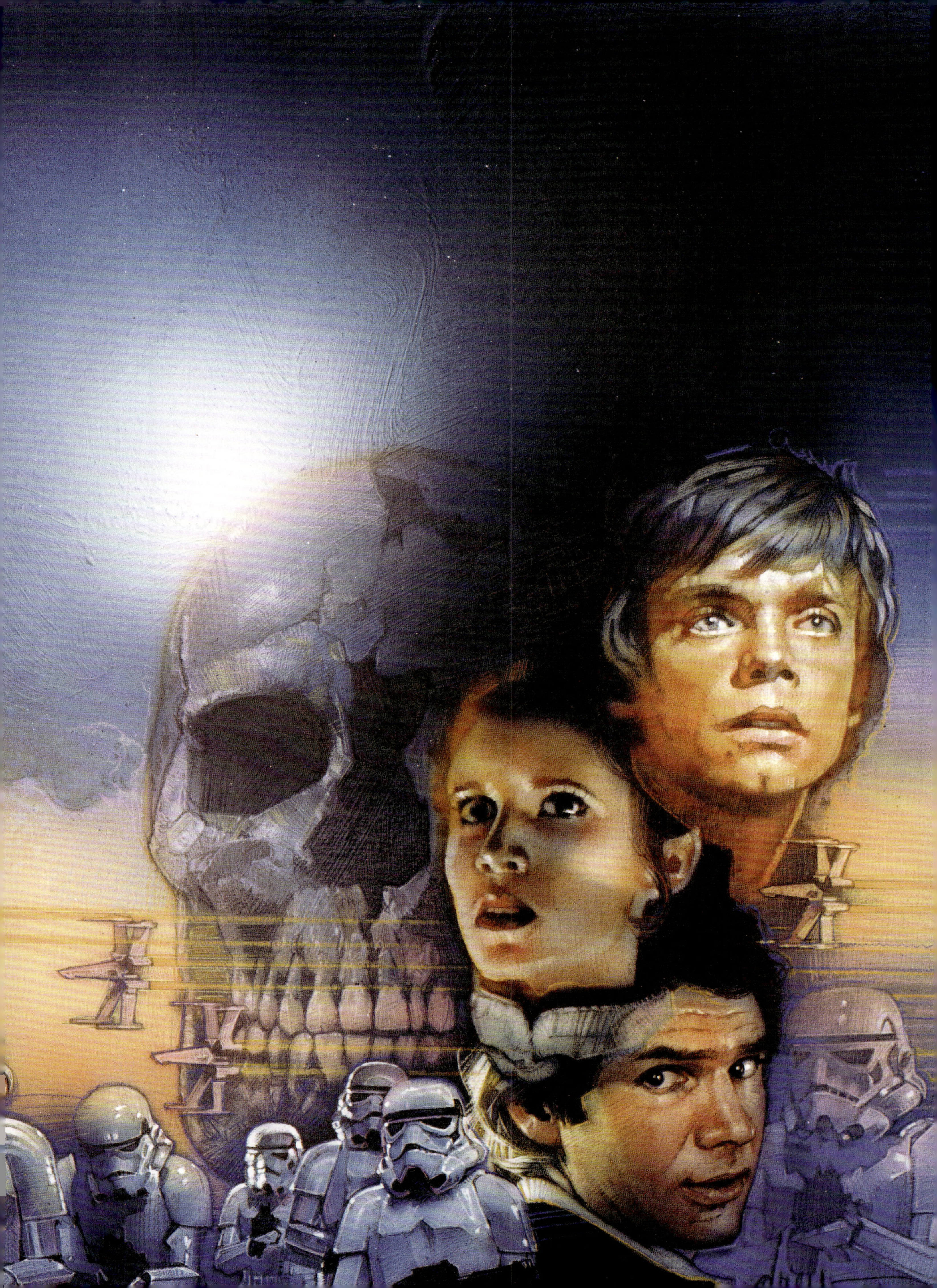

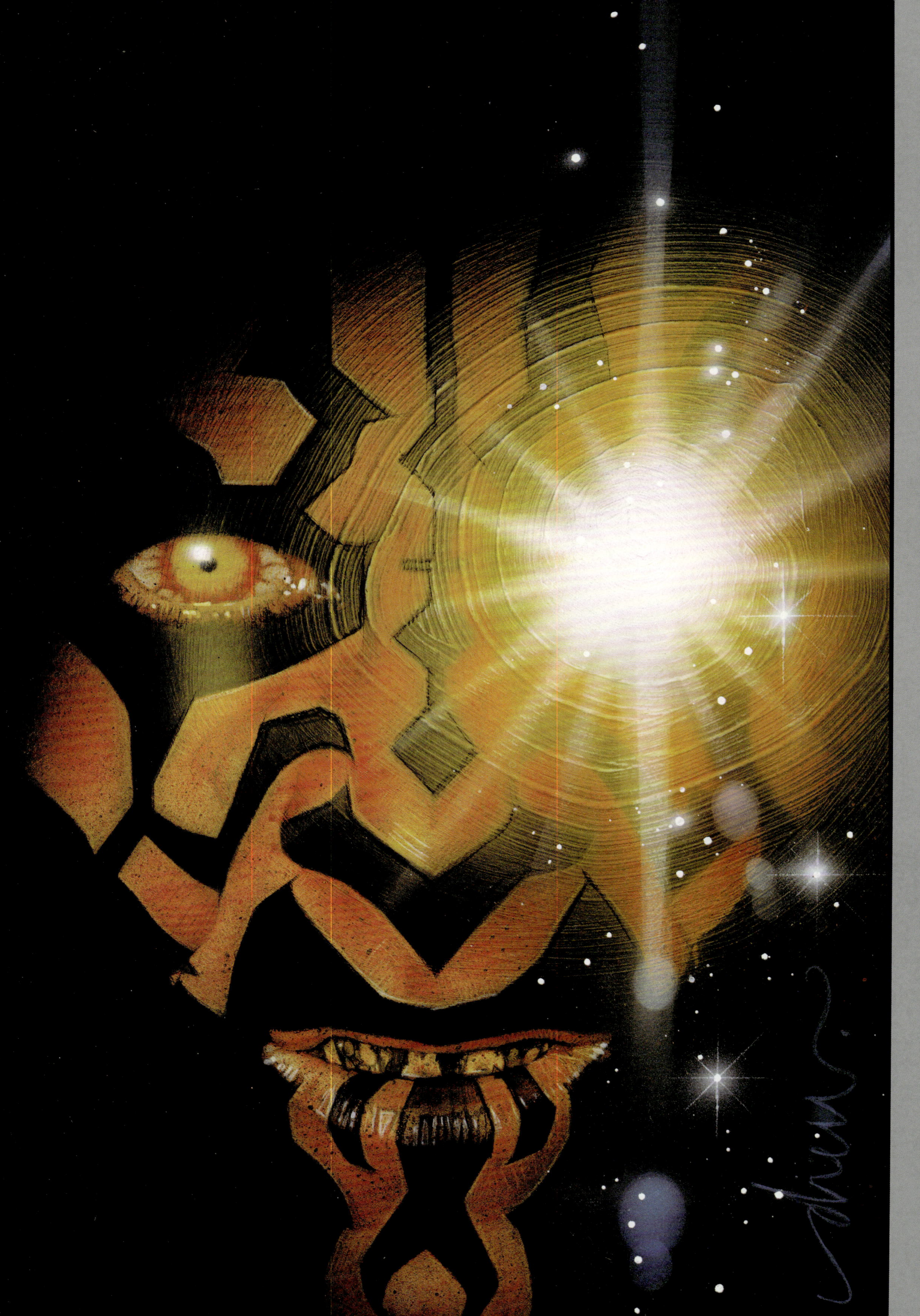

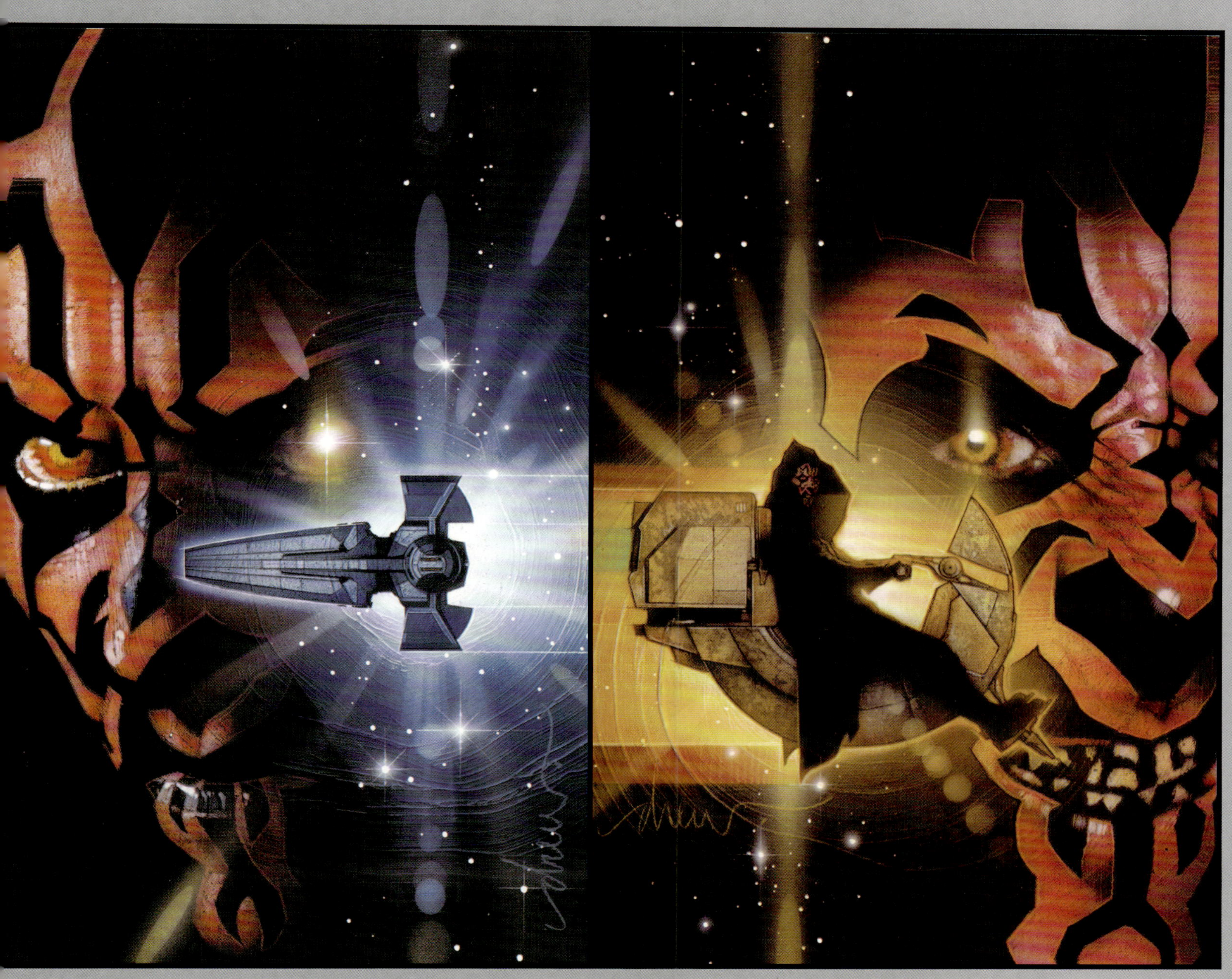

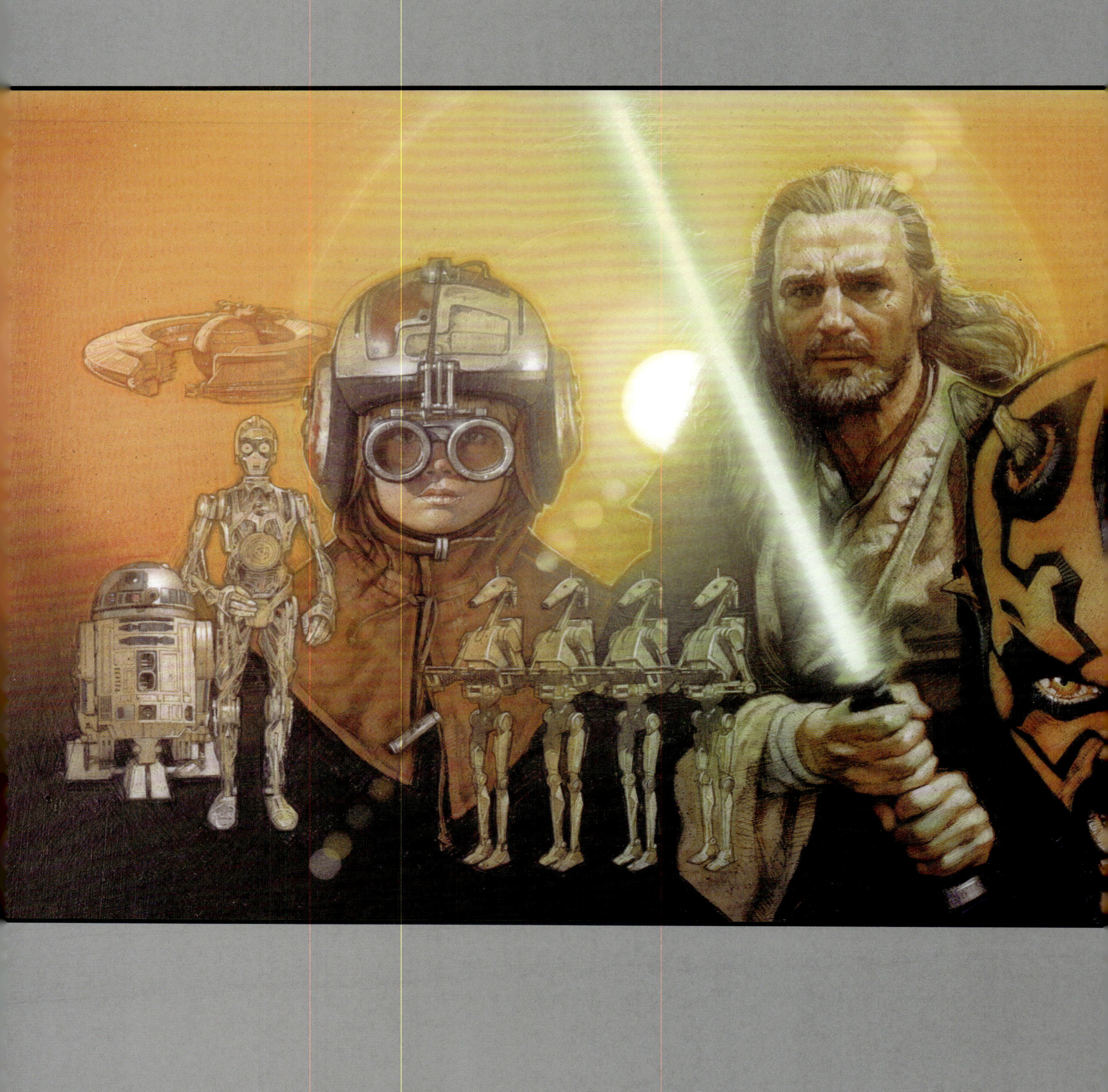

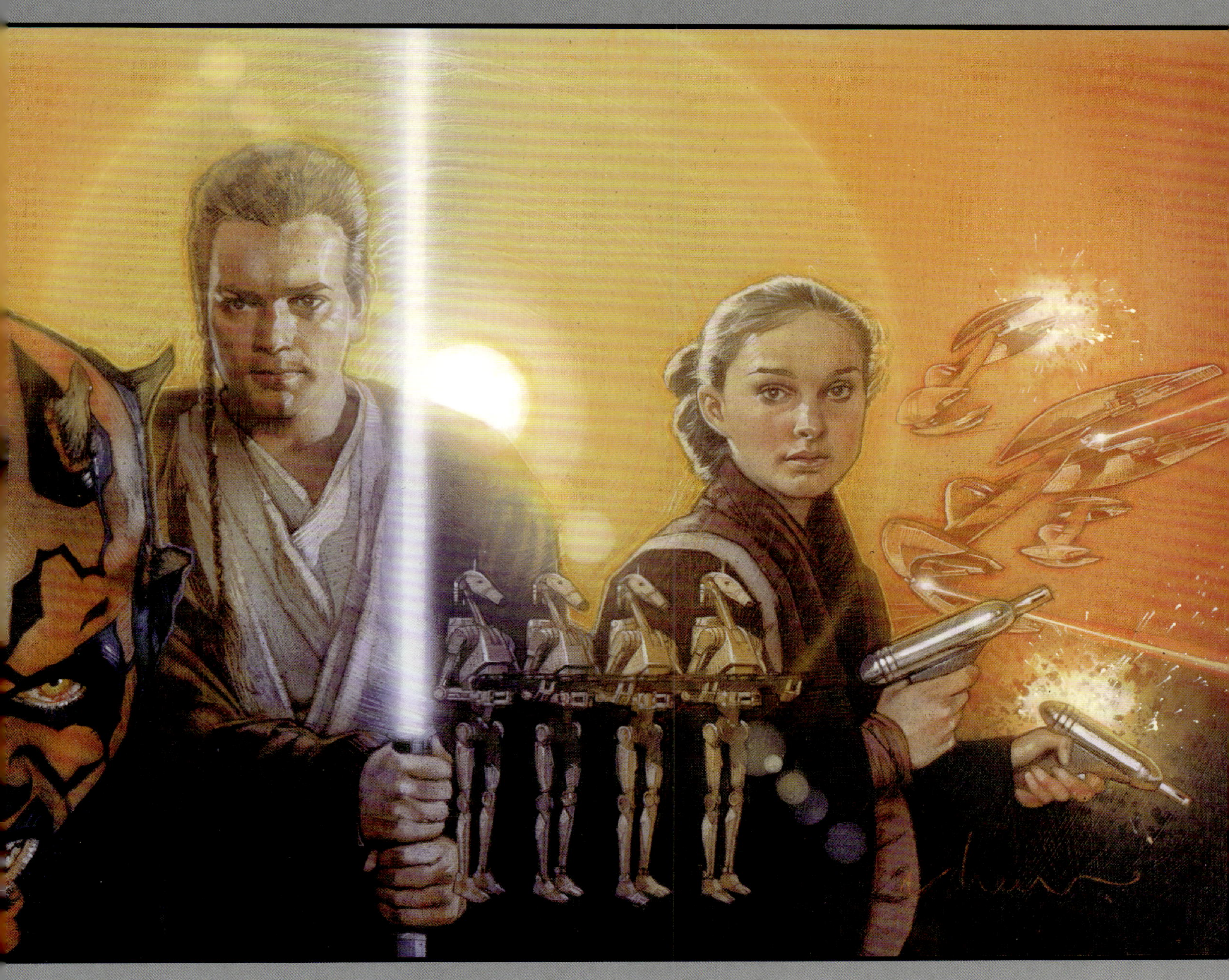

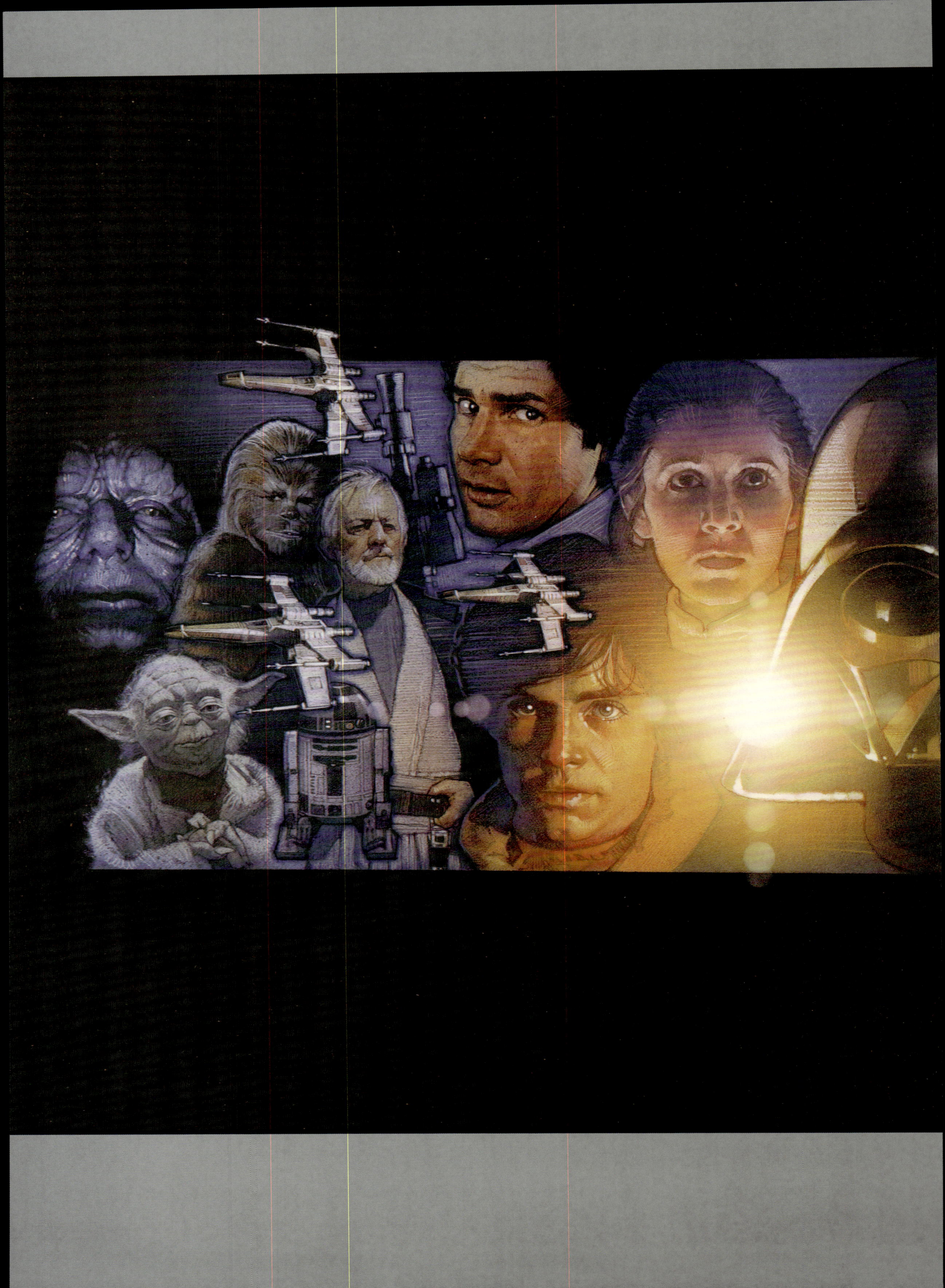

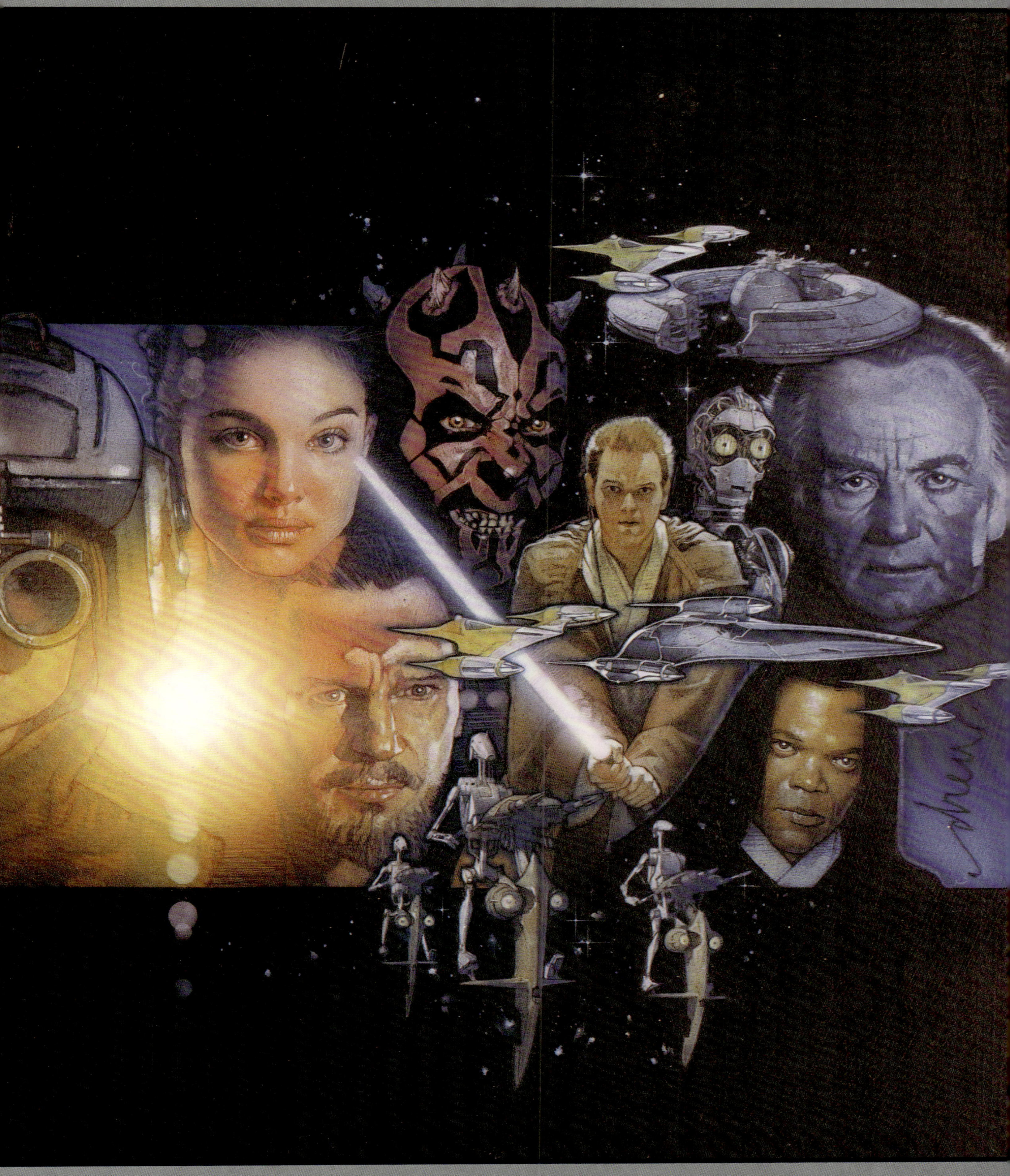

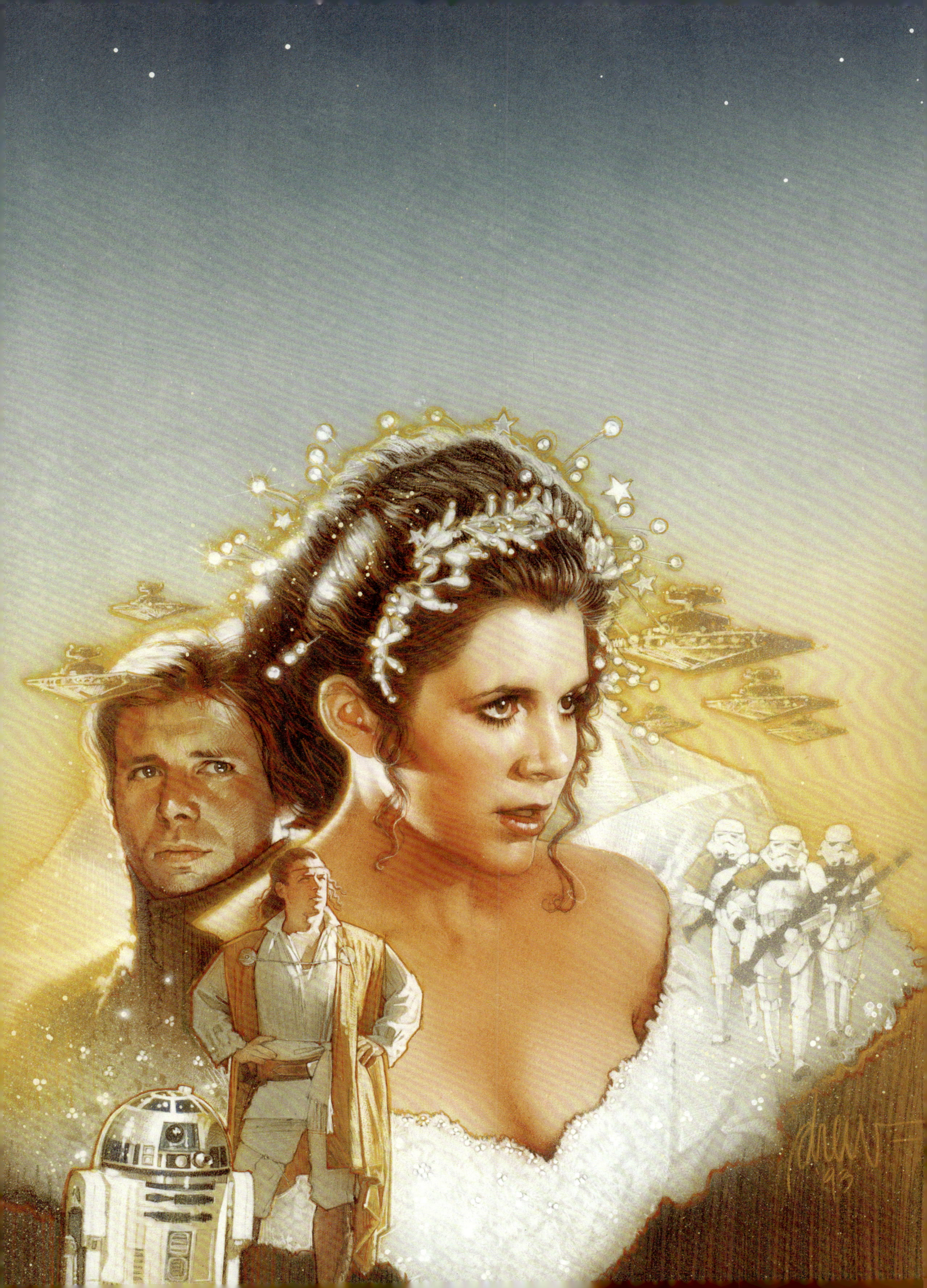

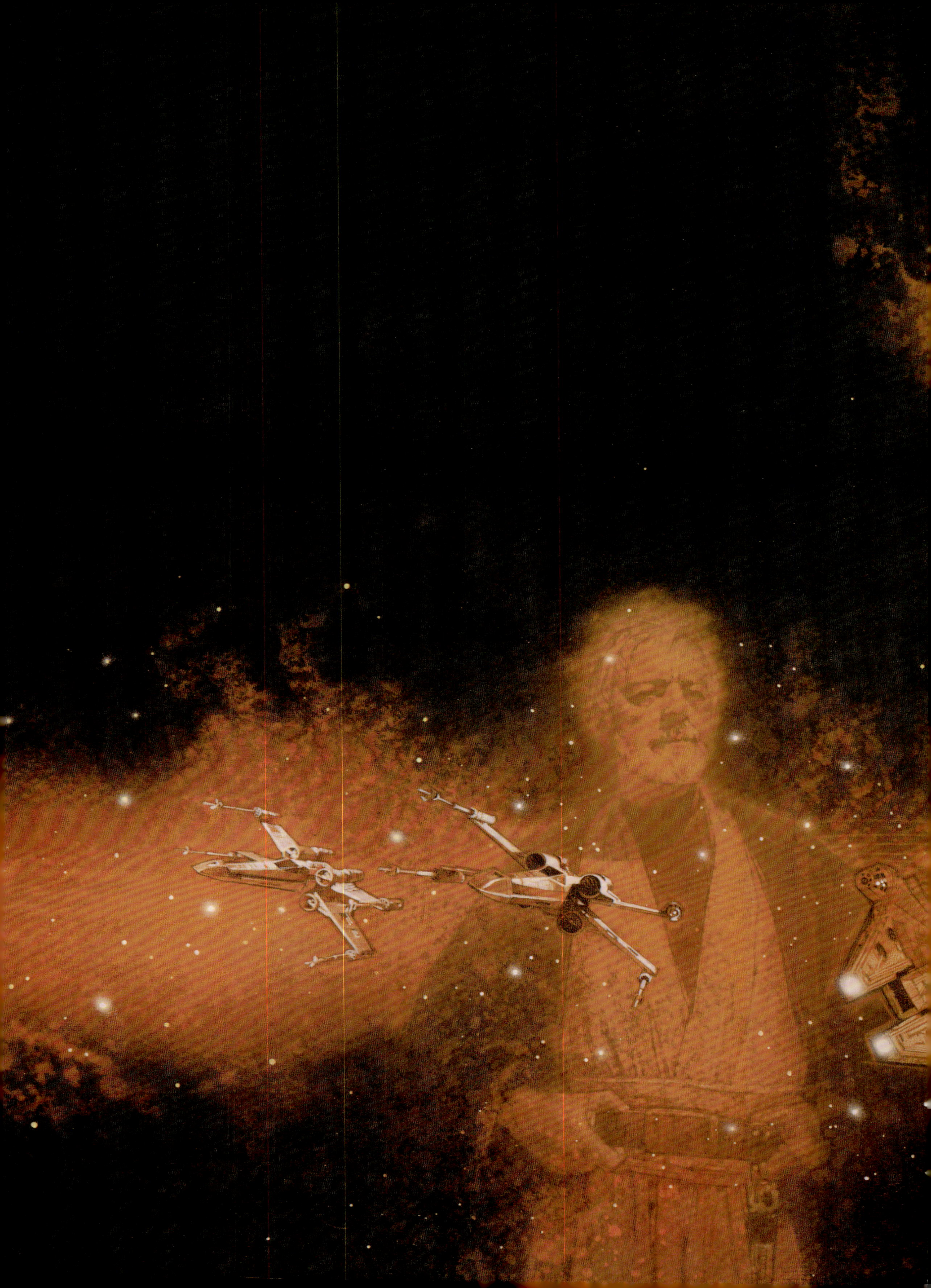

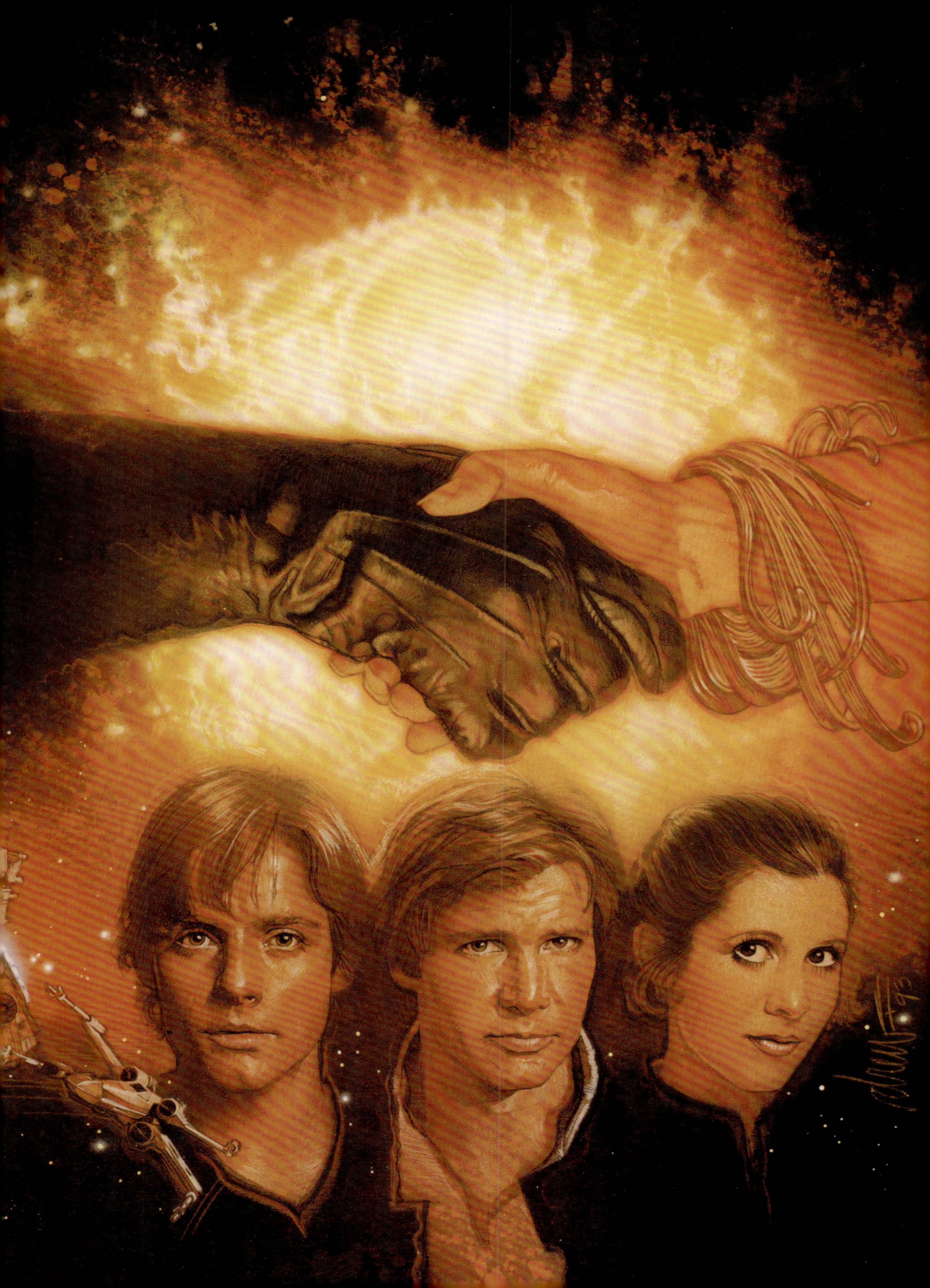

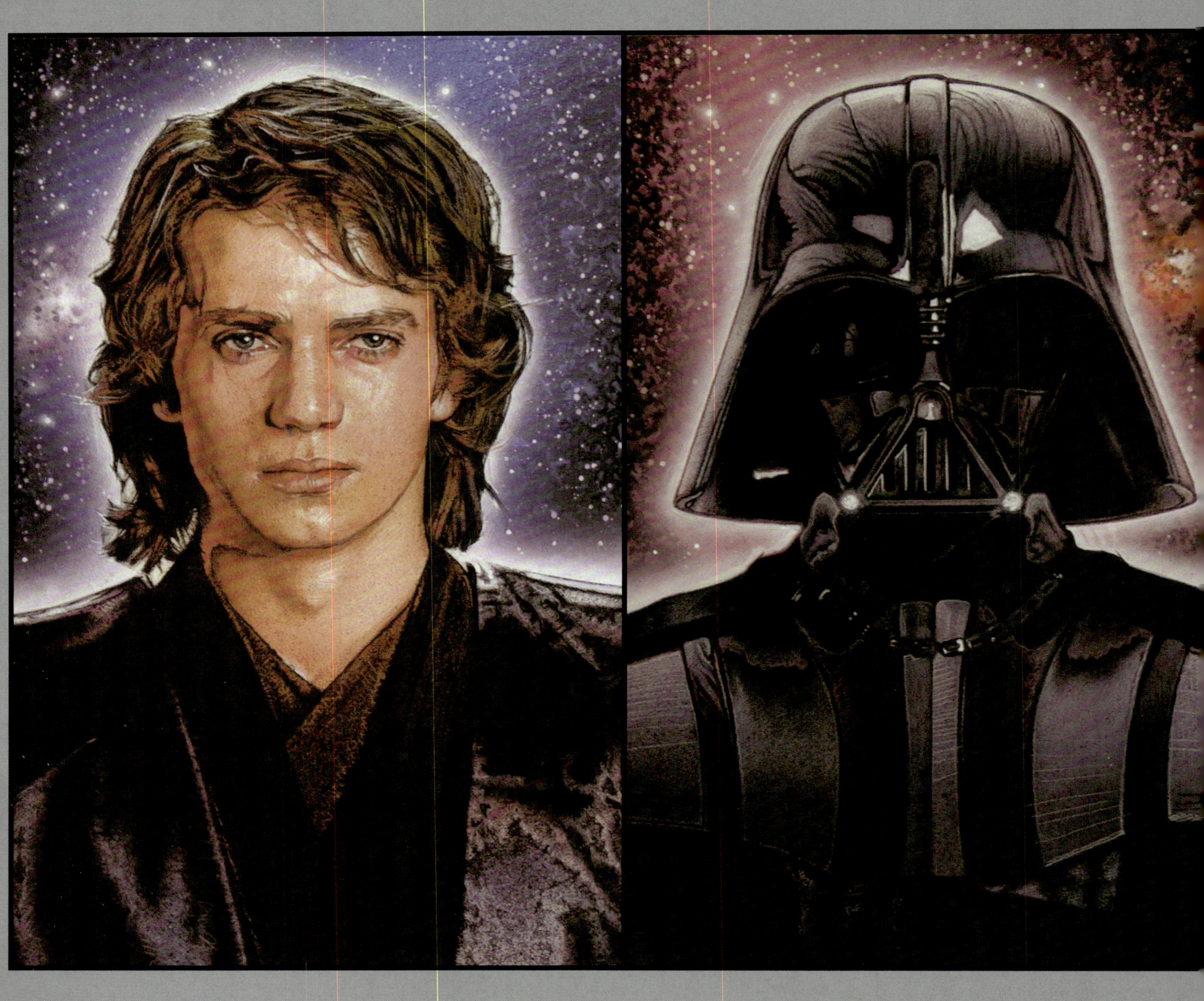

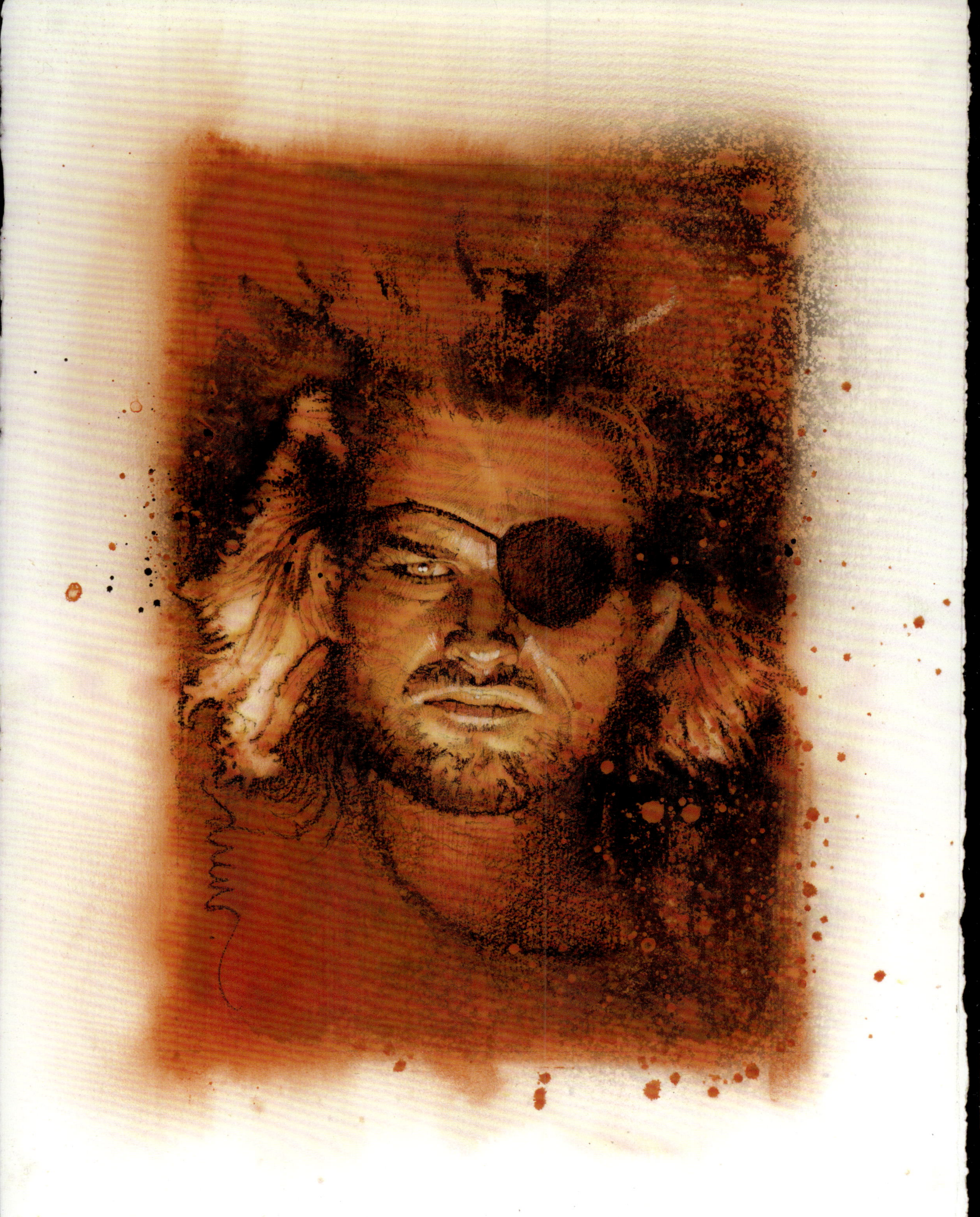

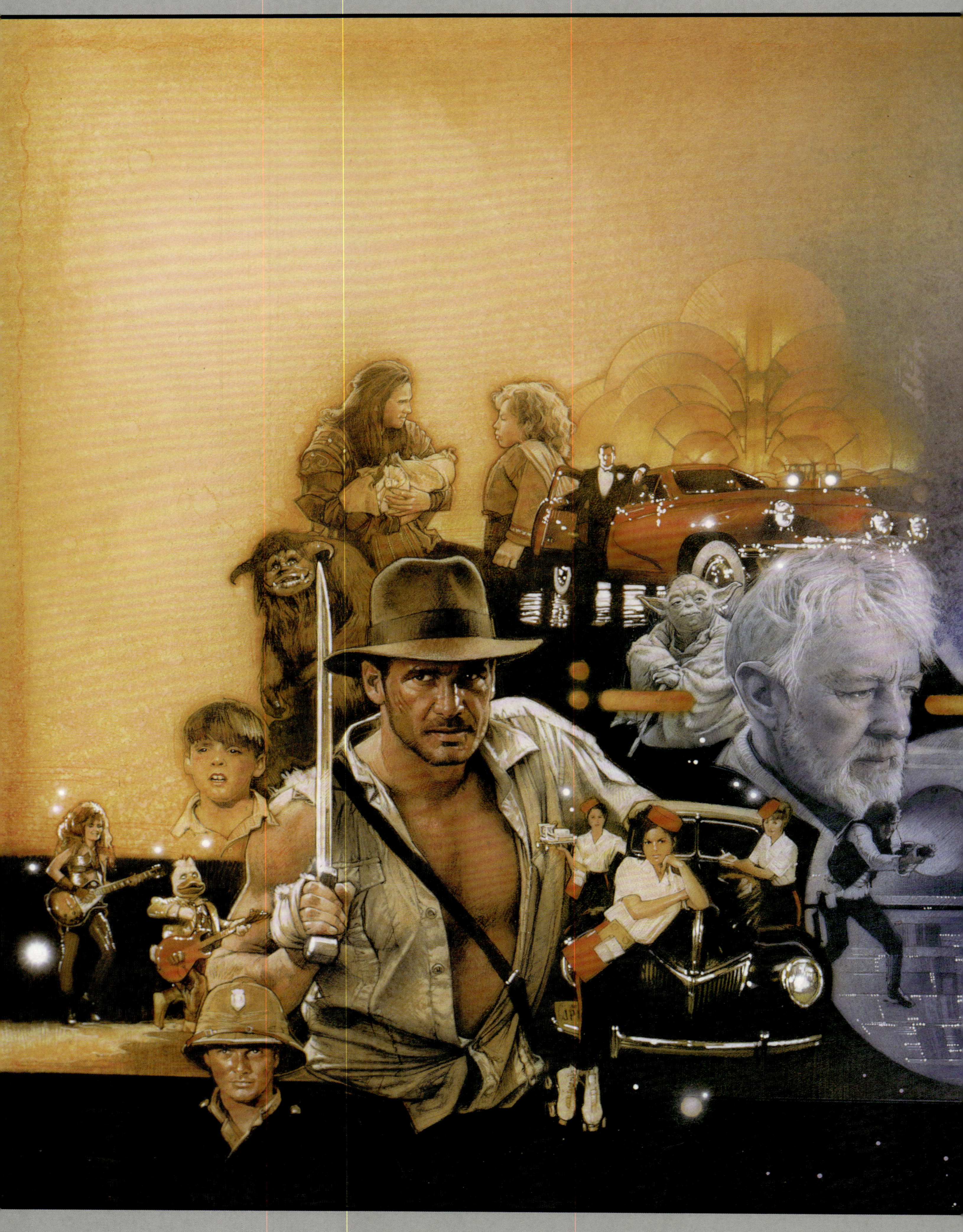

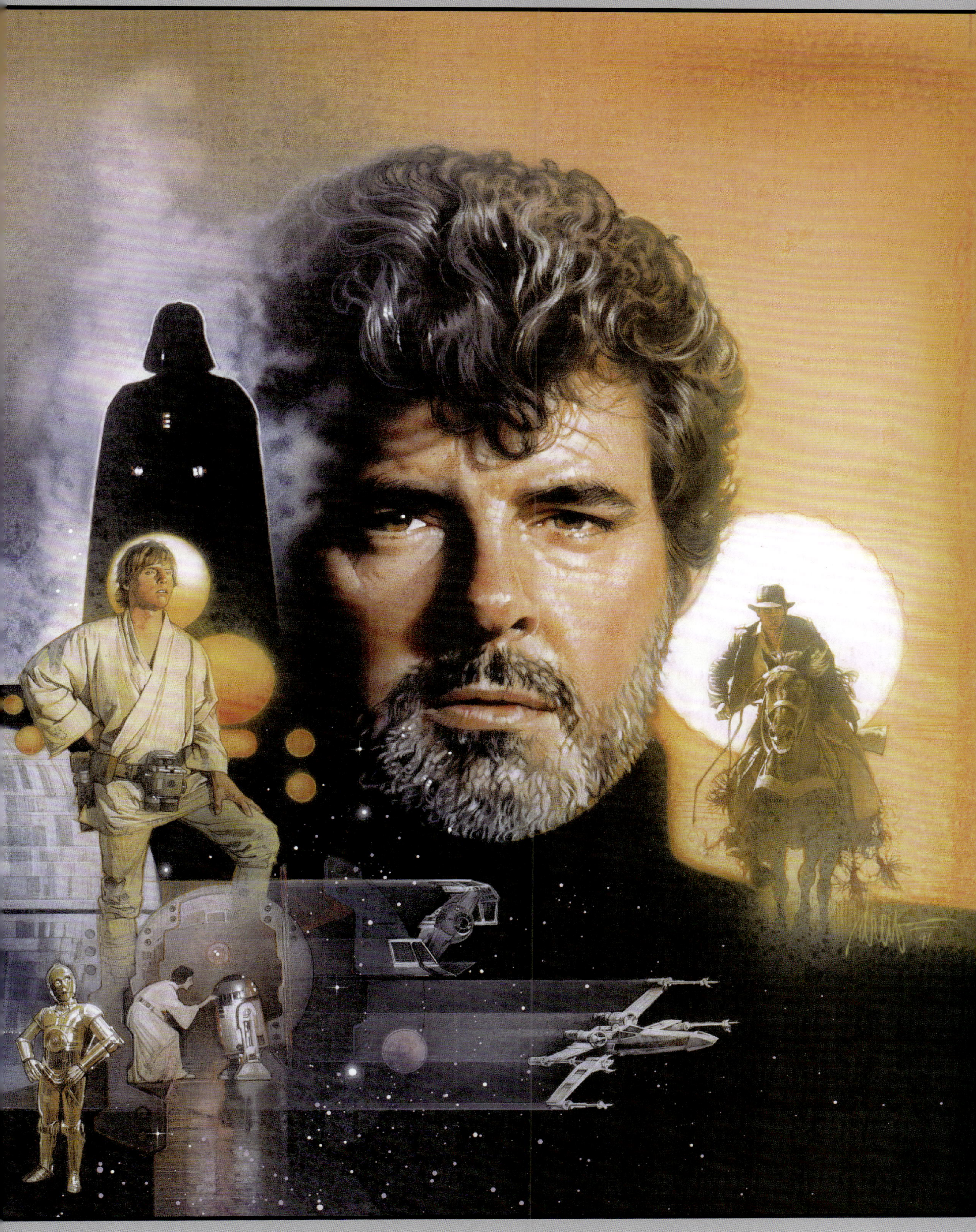

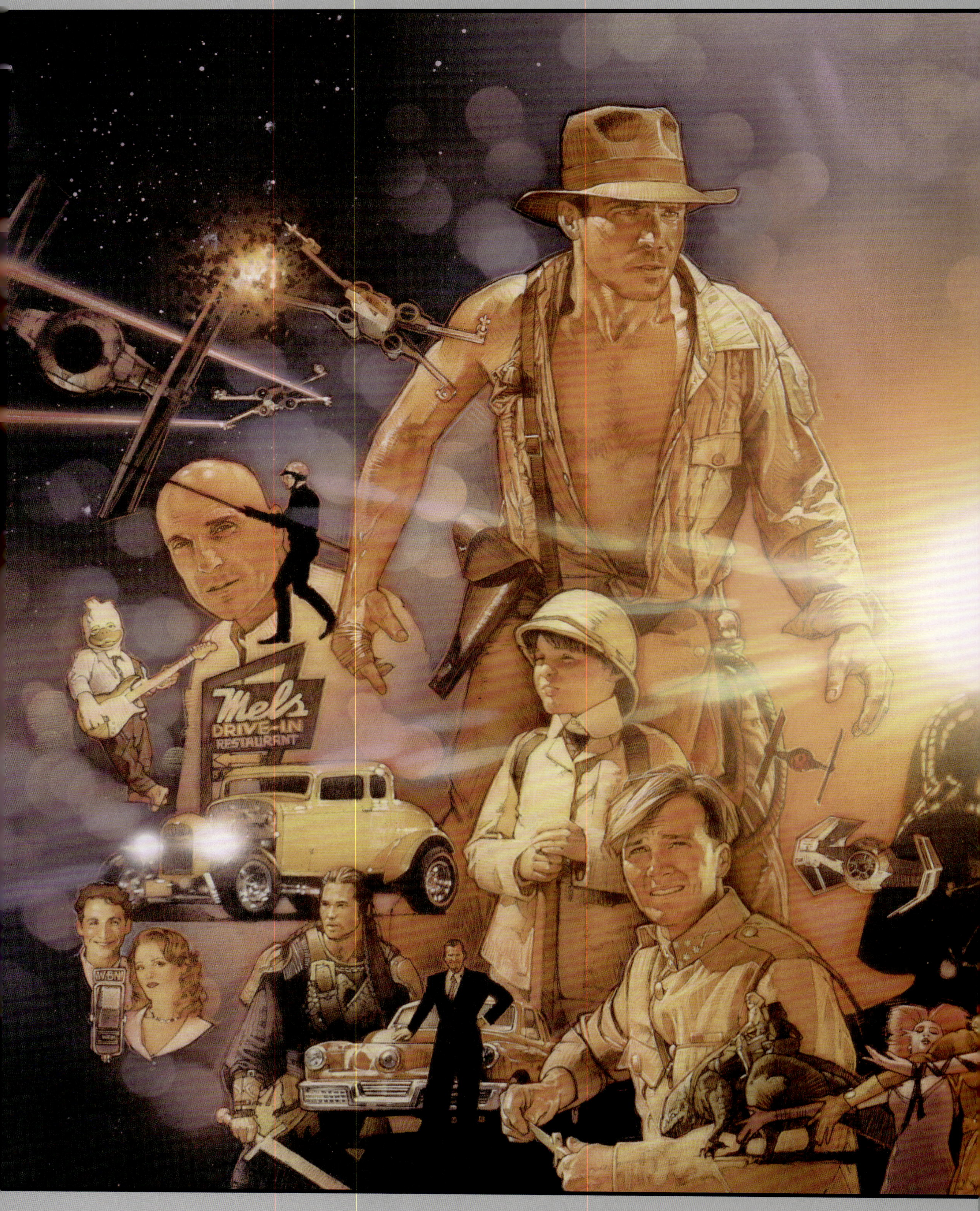
Mels
DRIVE-IN
RESTAURANT
WBN

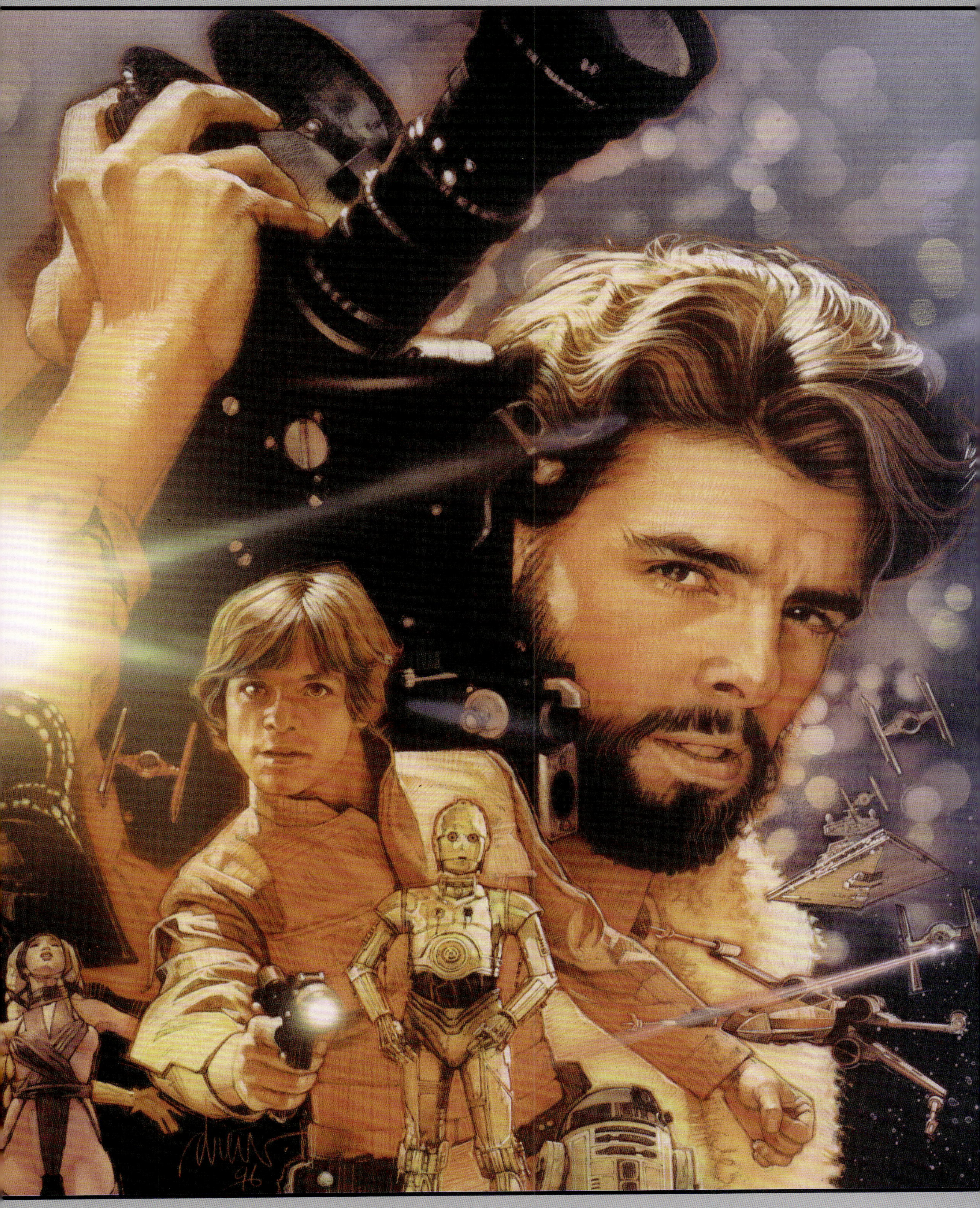

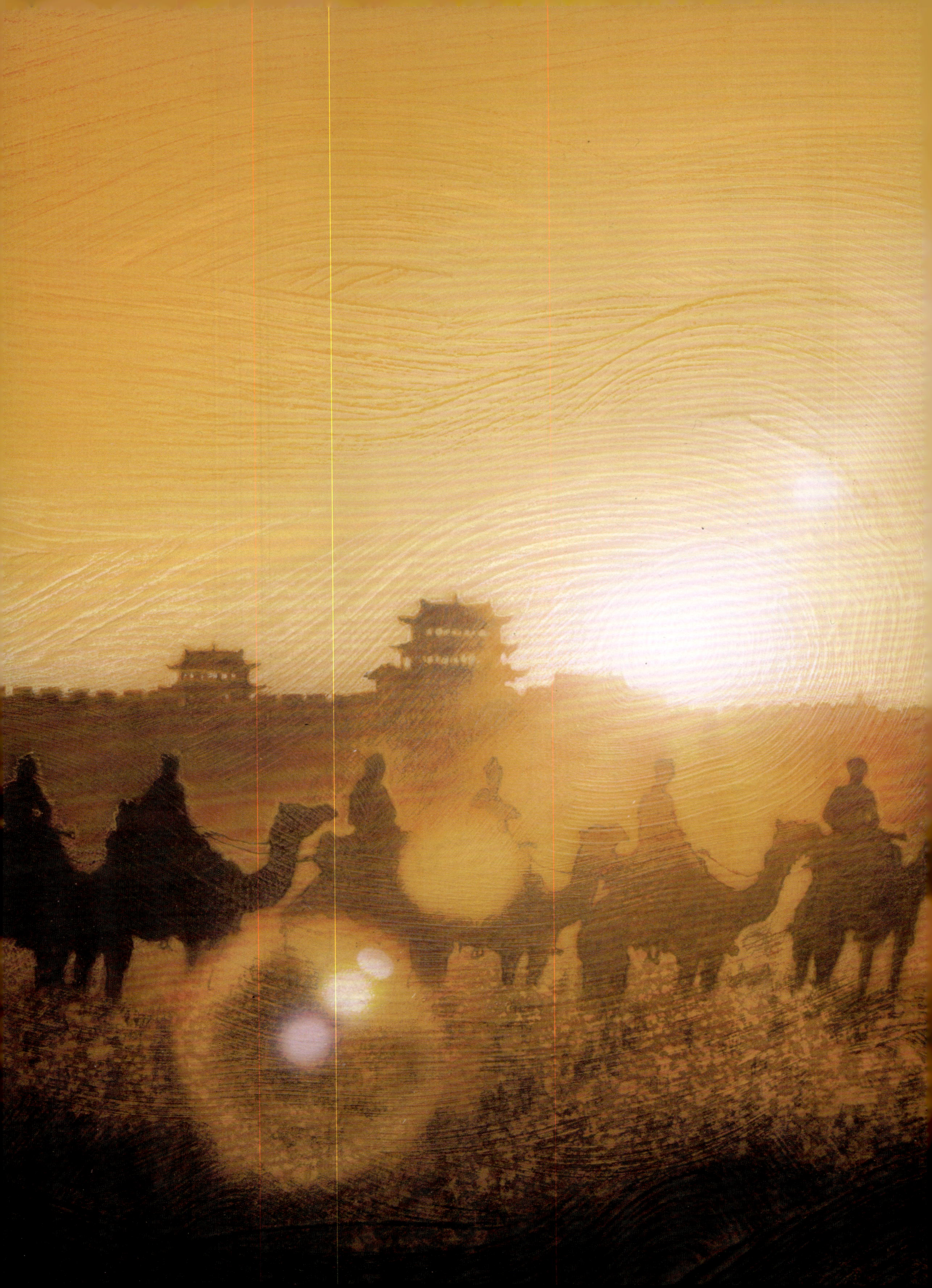

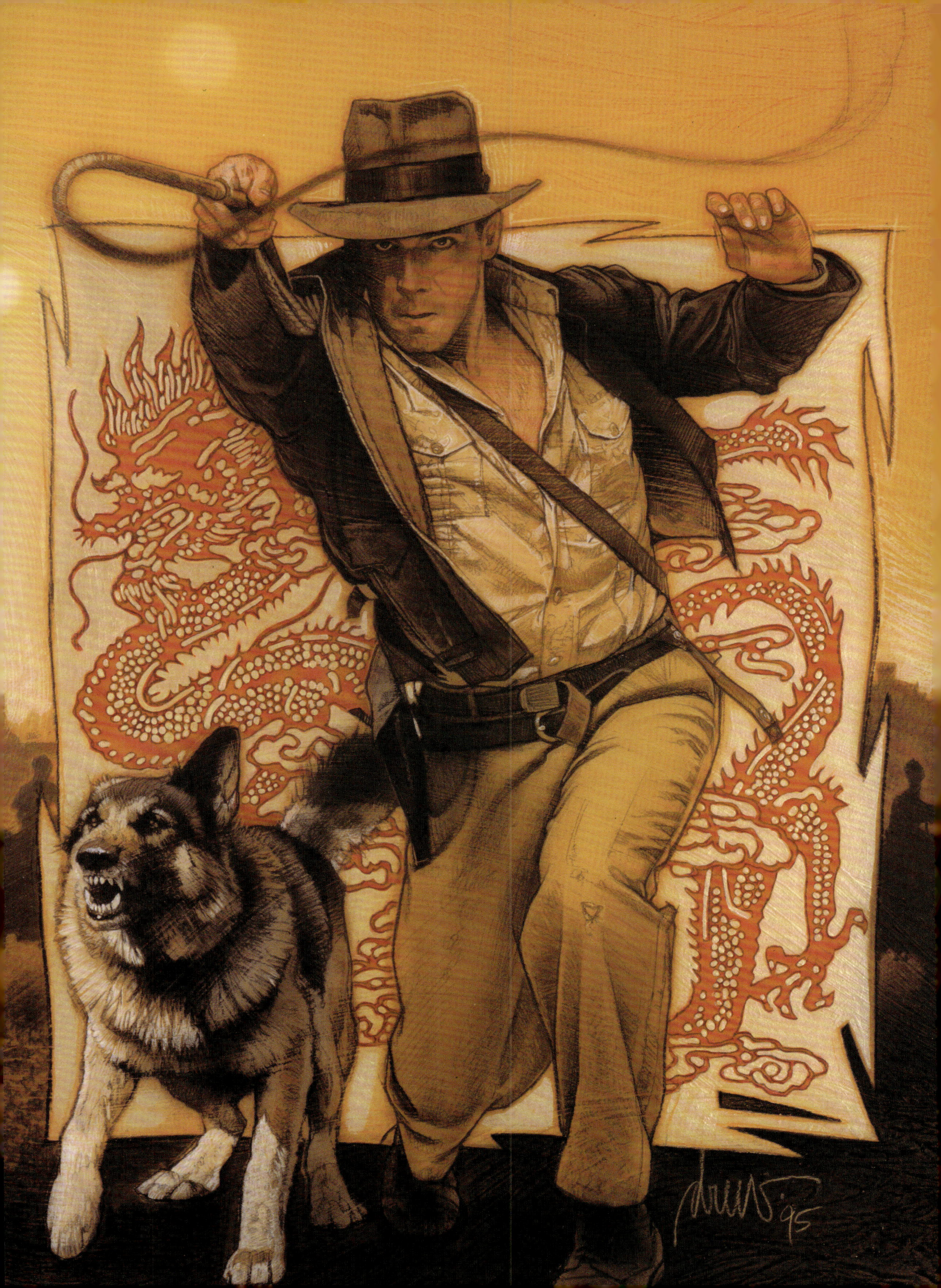

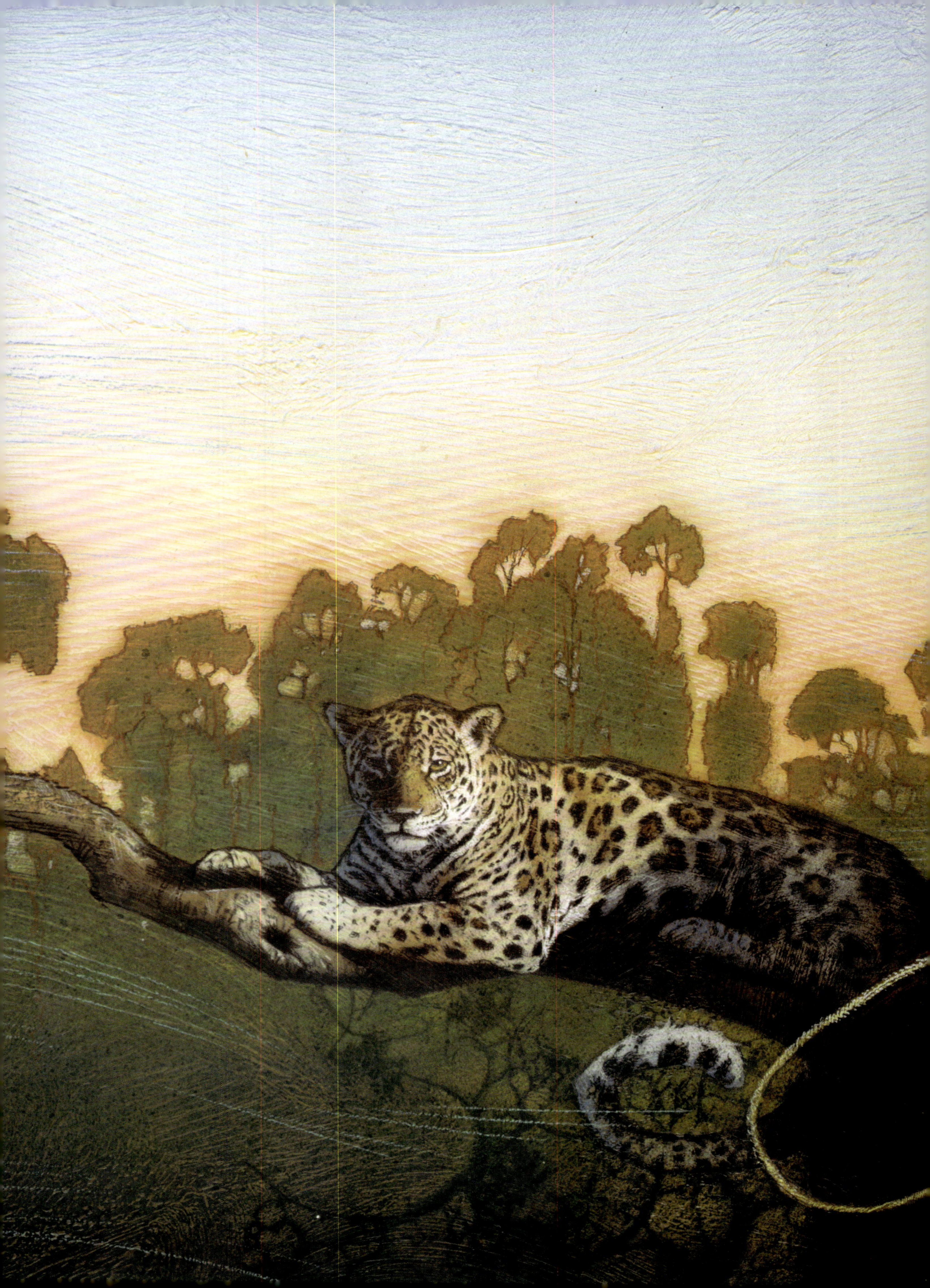

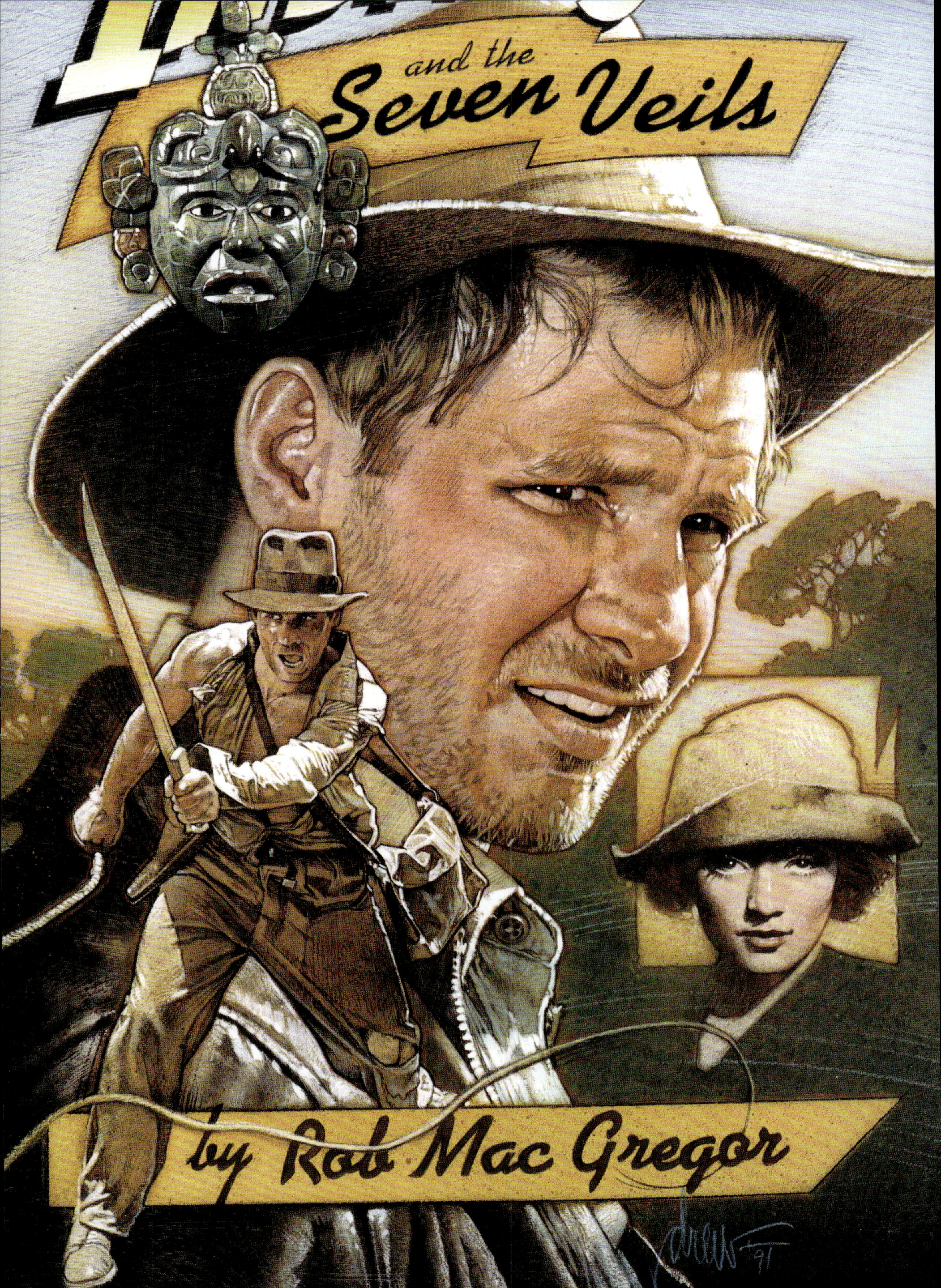
and the
Seven Veils
by Rob Mac Gregor
Drew '91

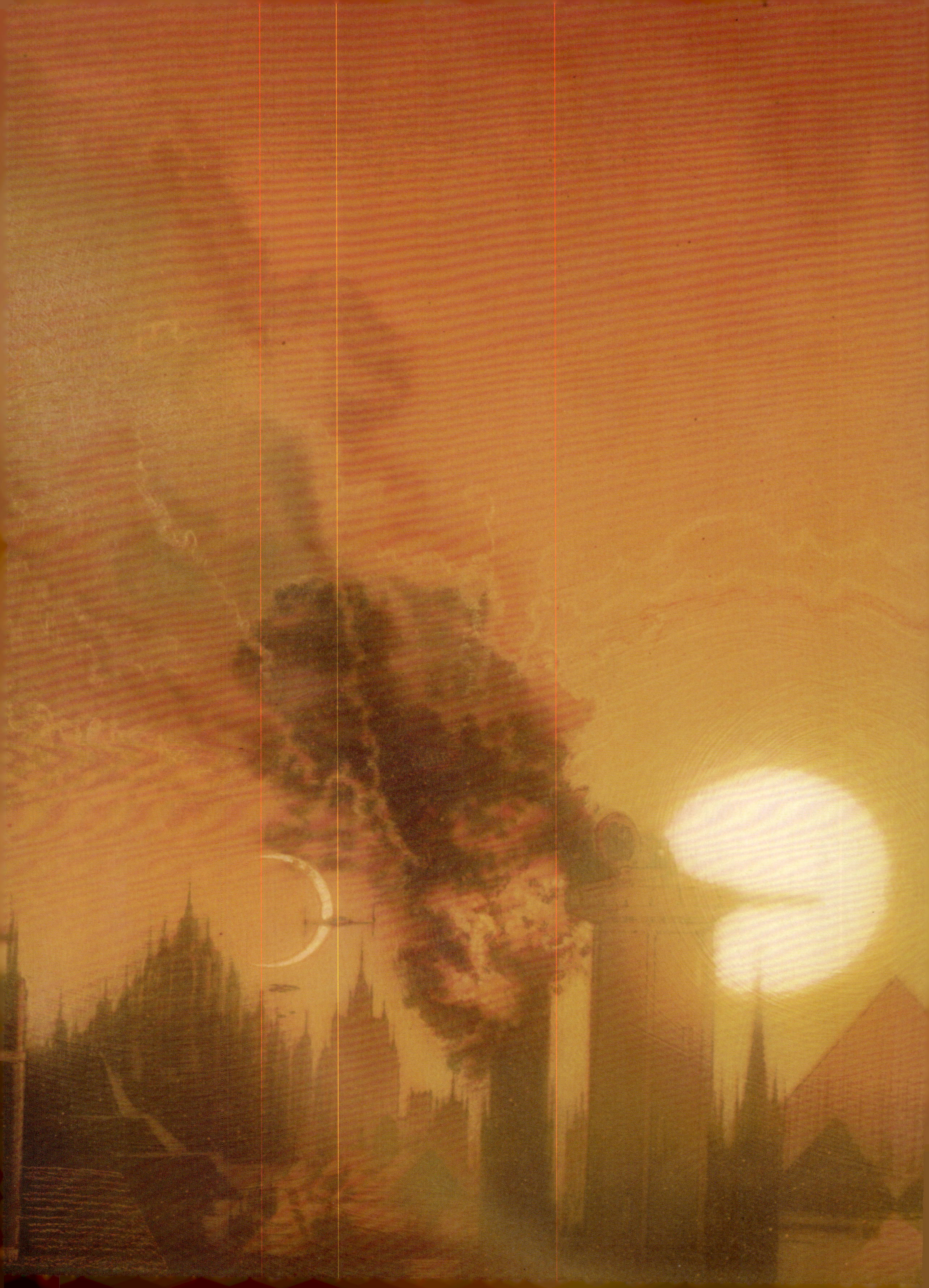

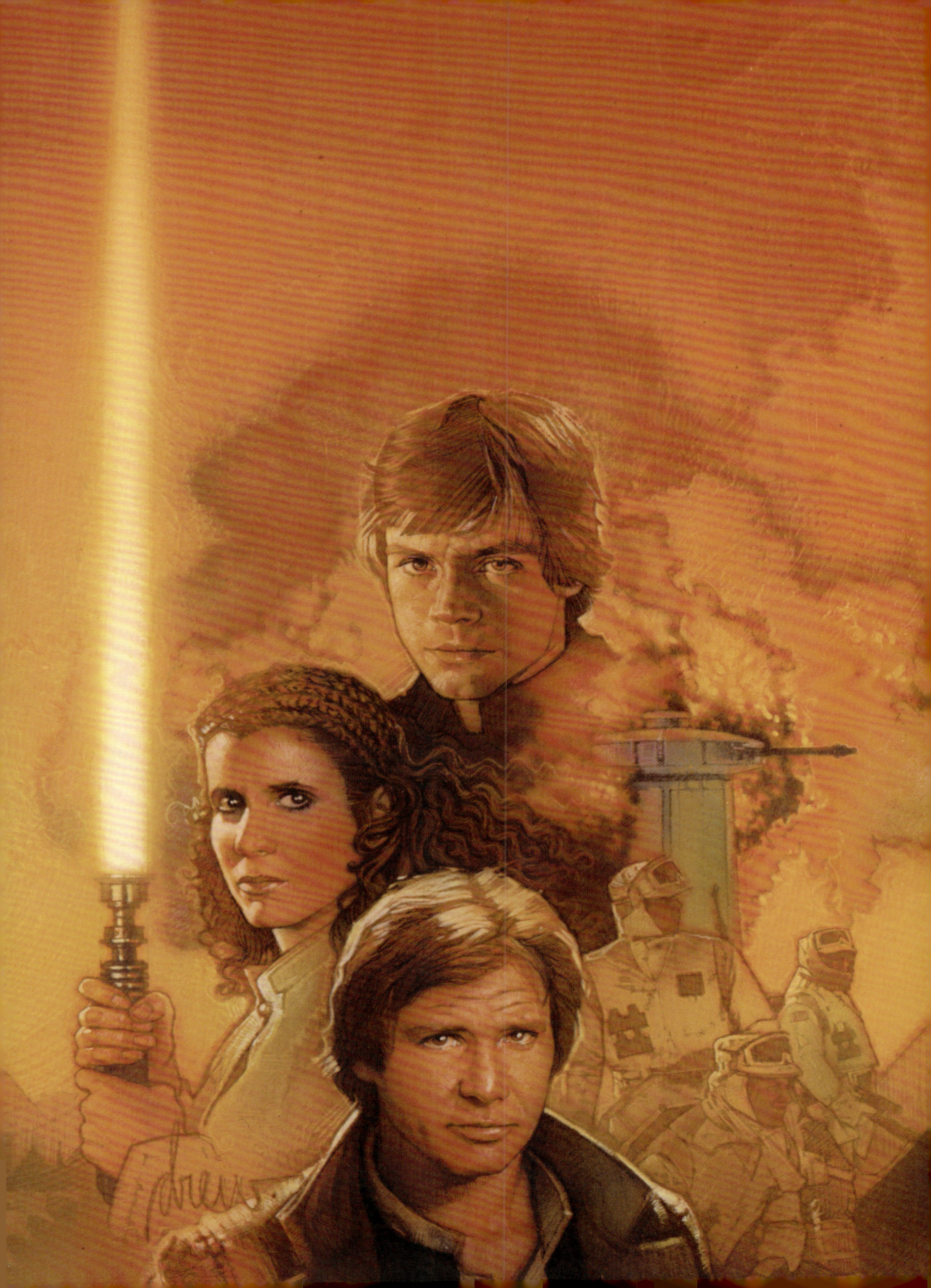

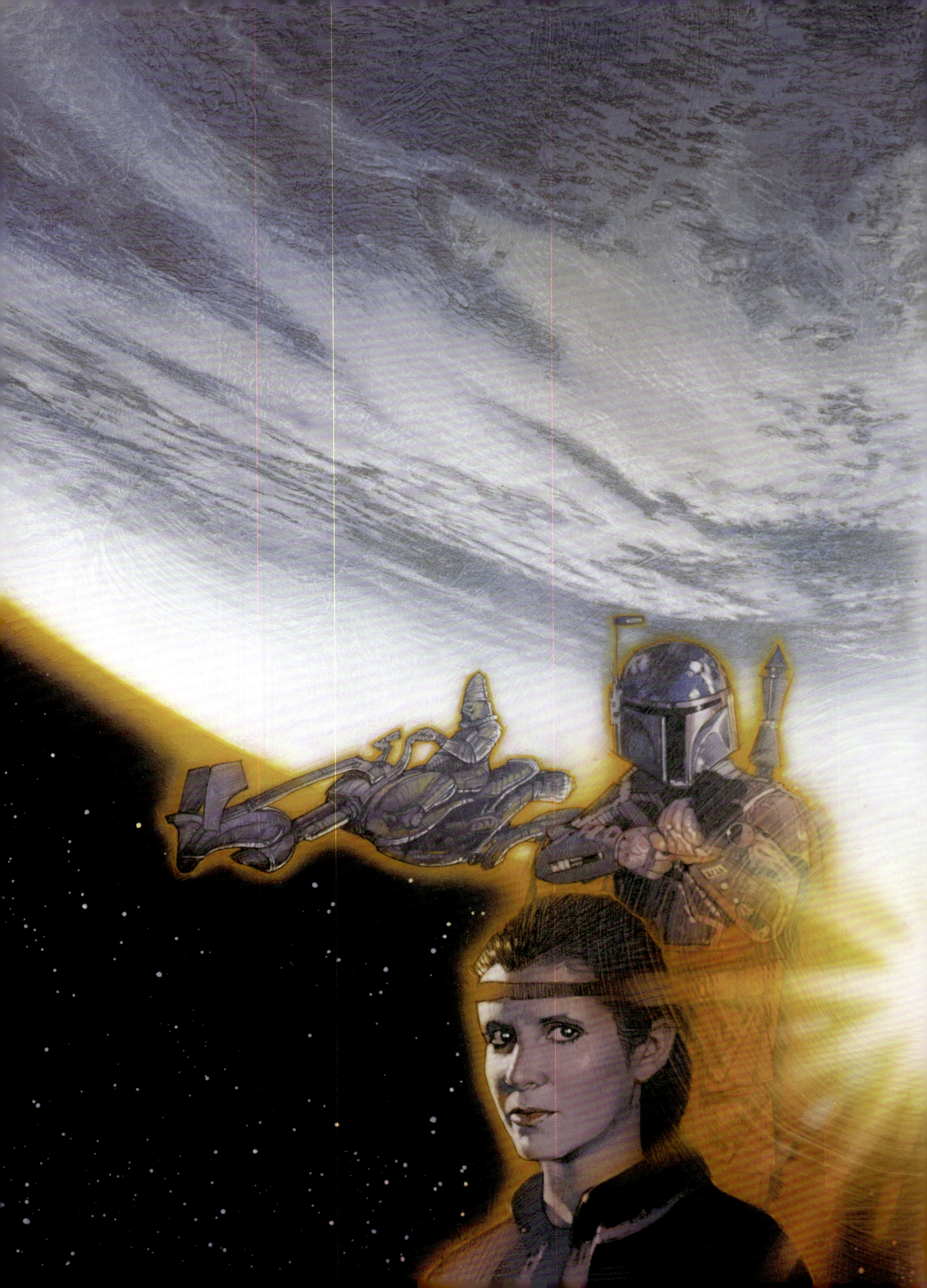

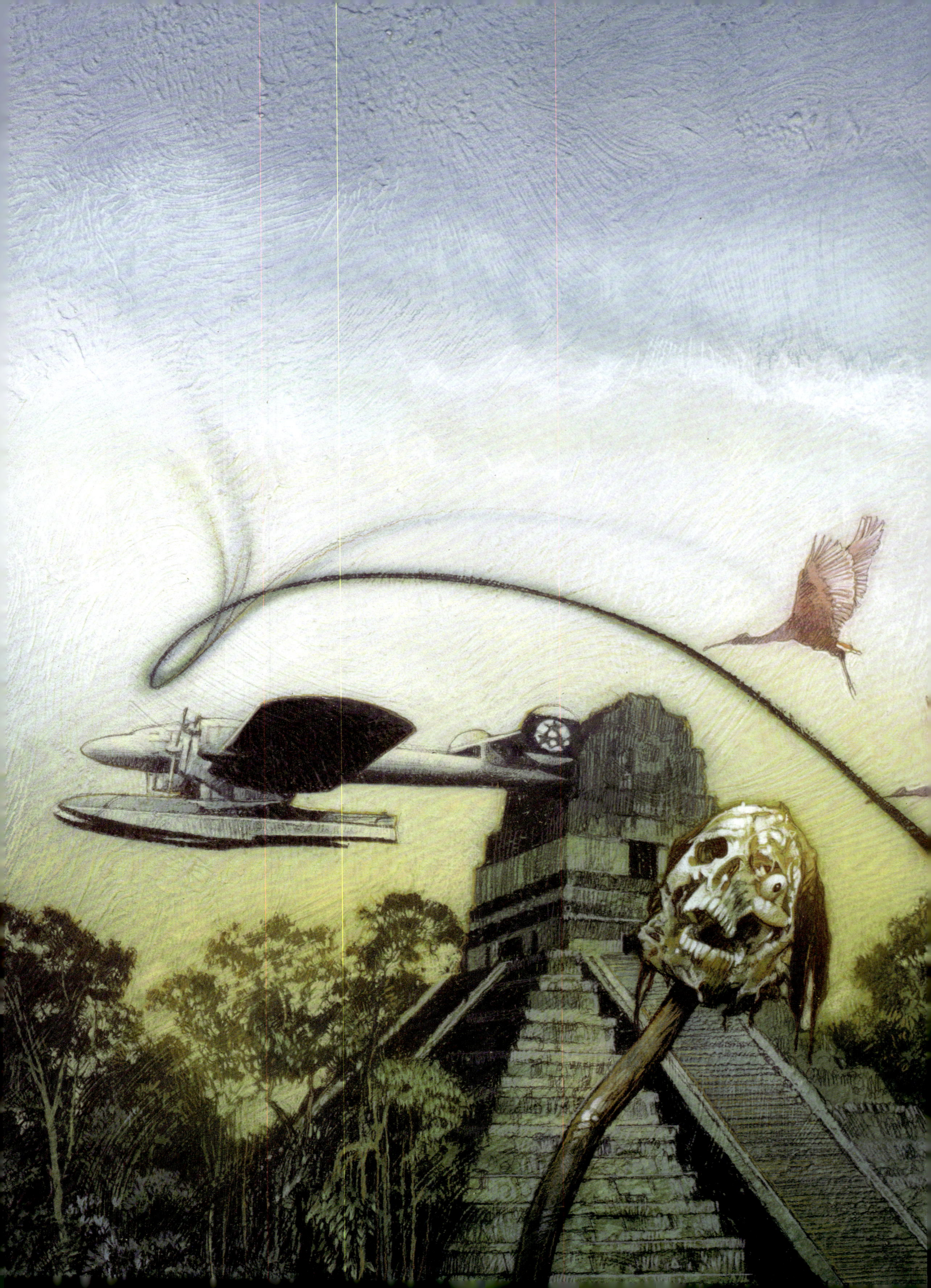

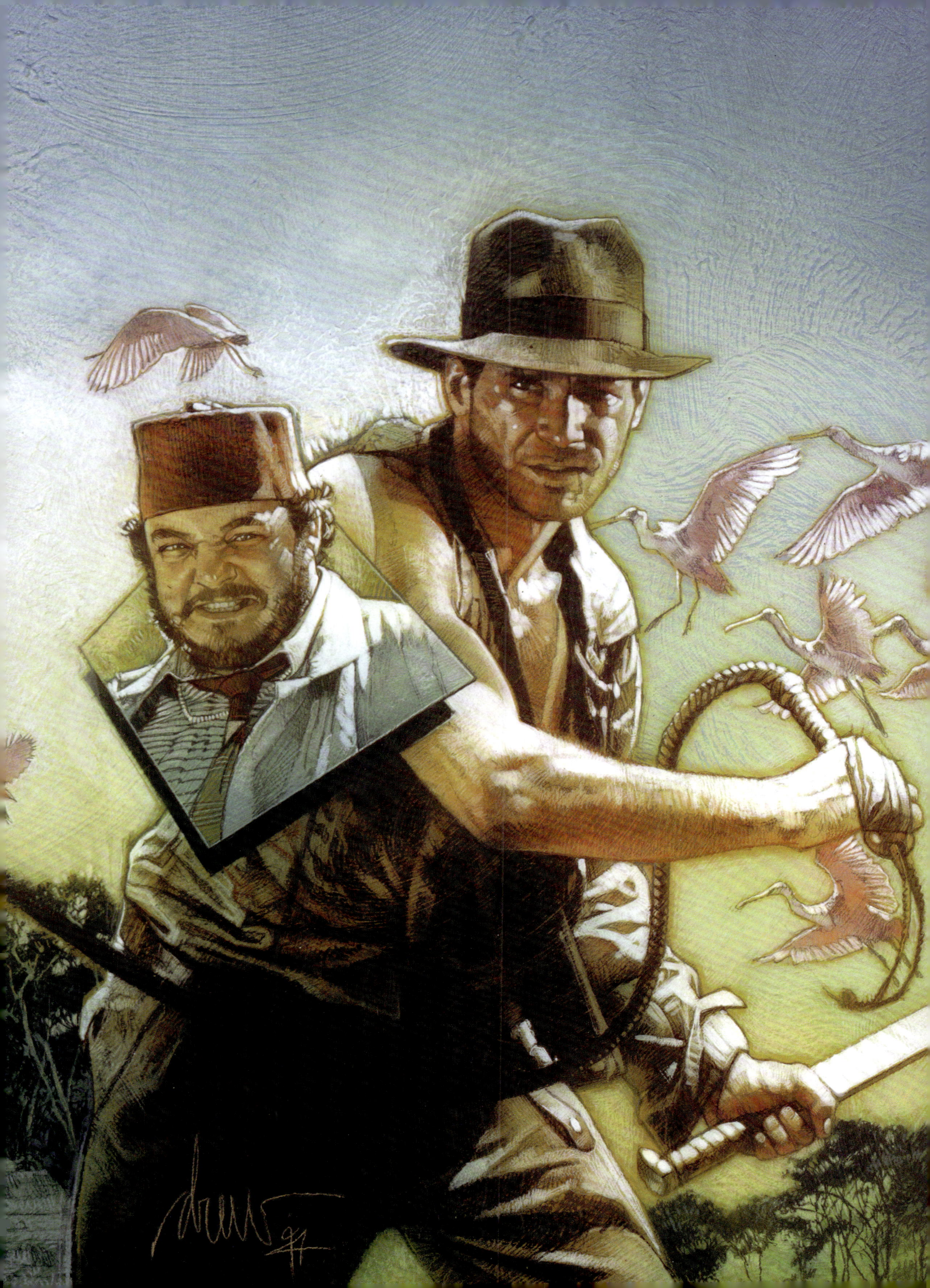

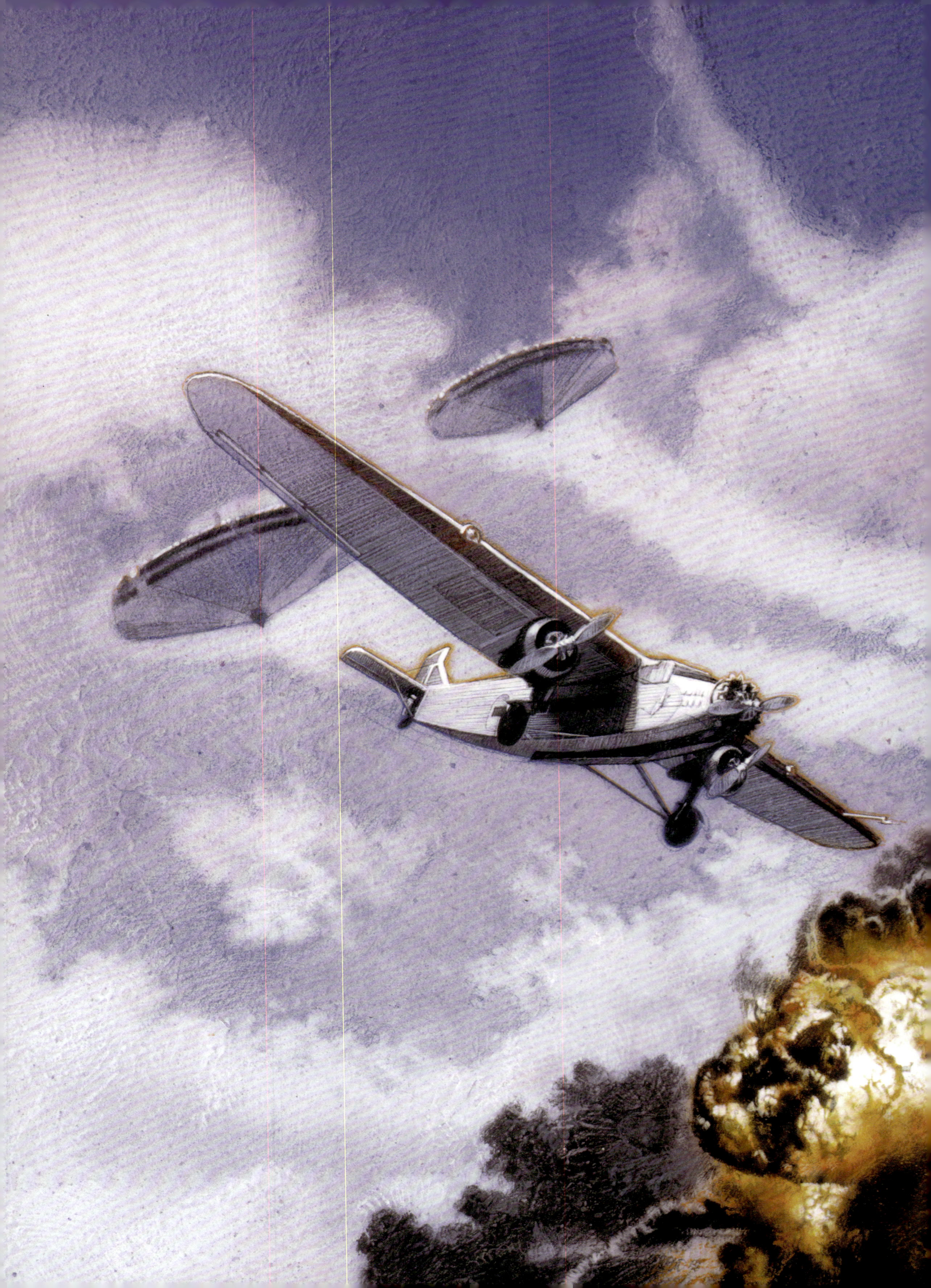

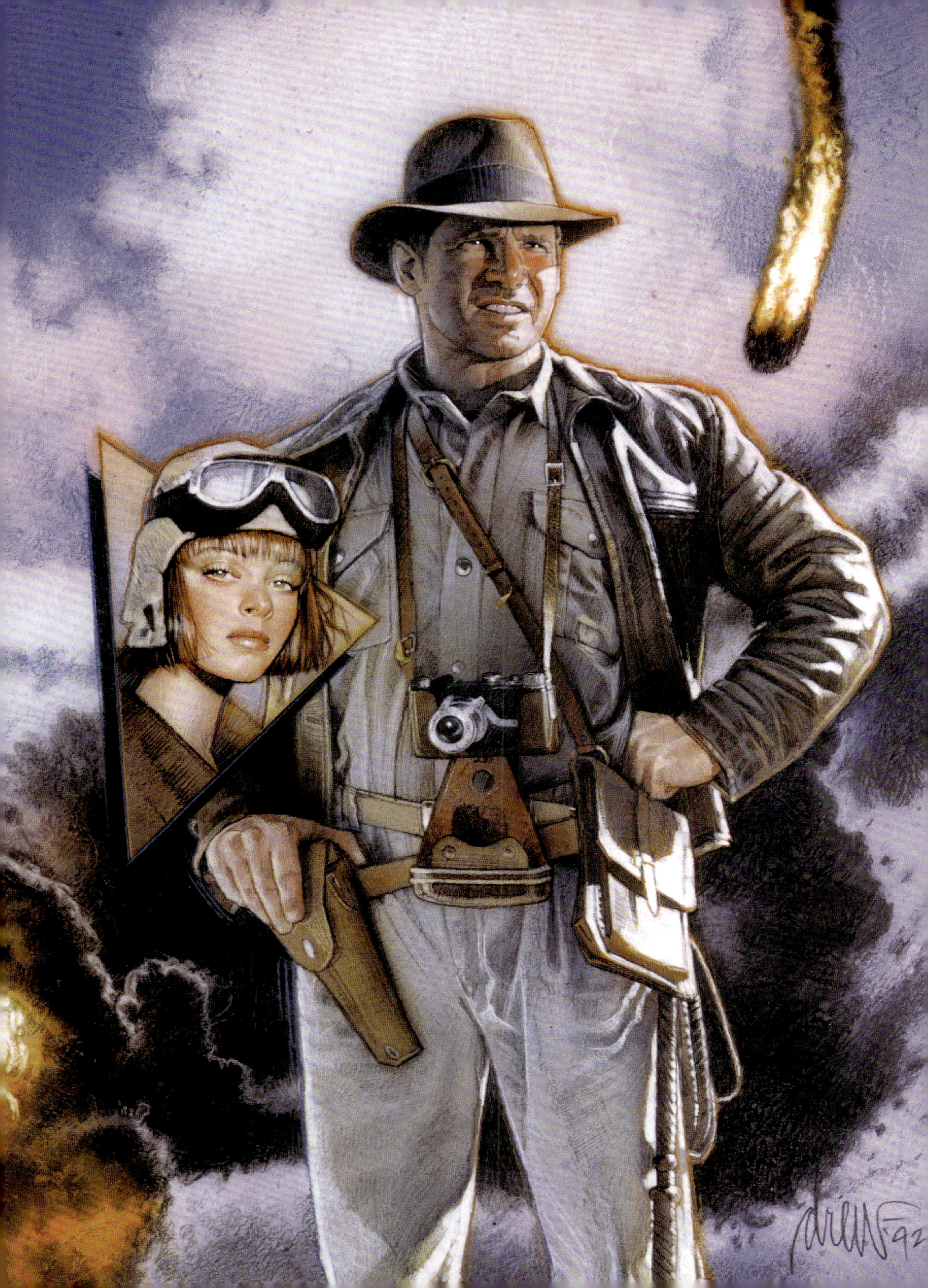

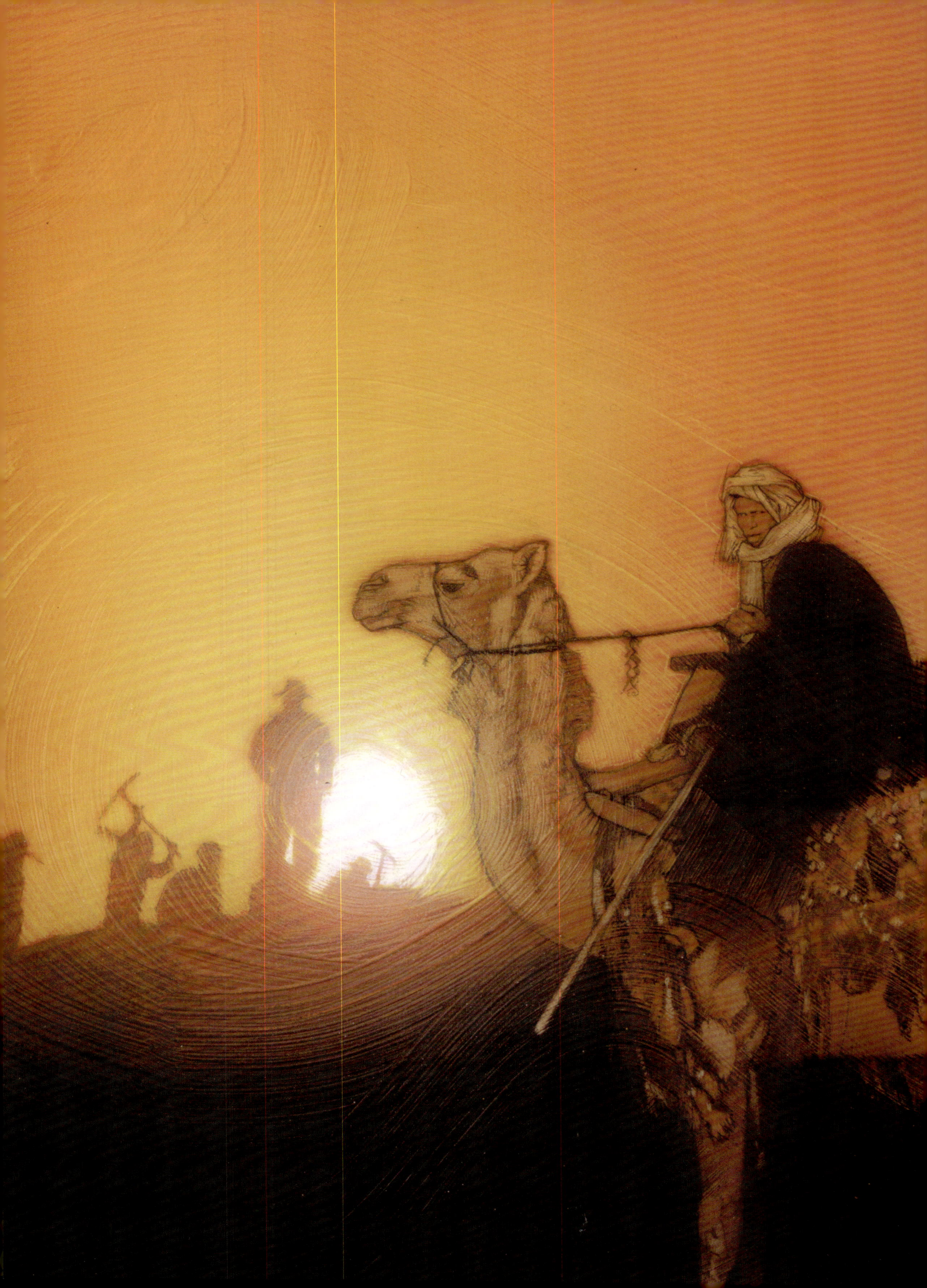

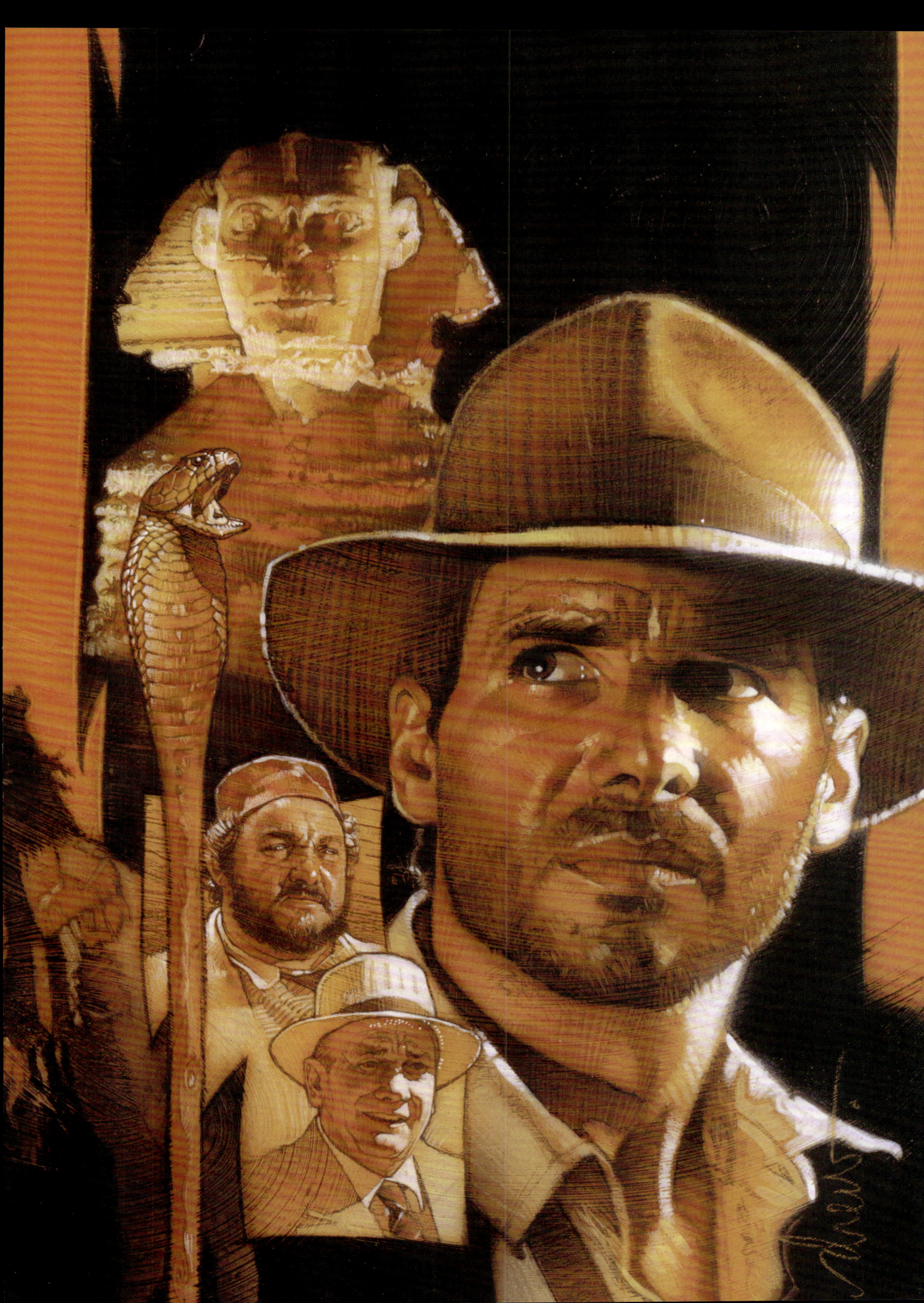

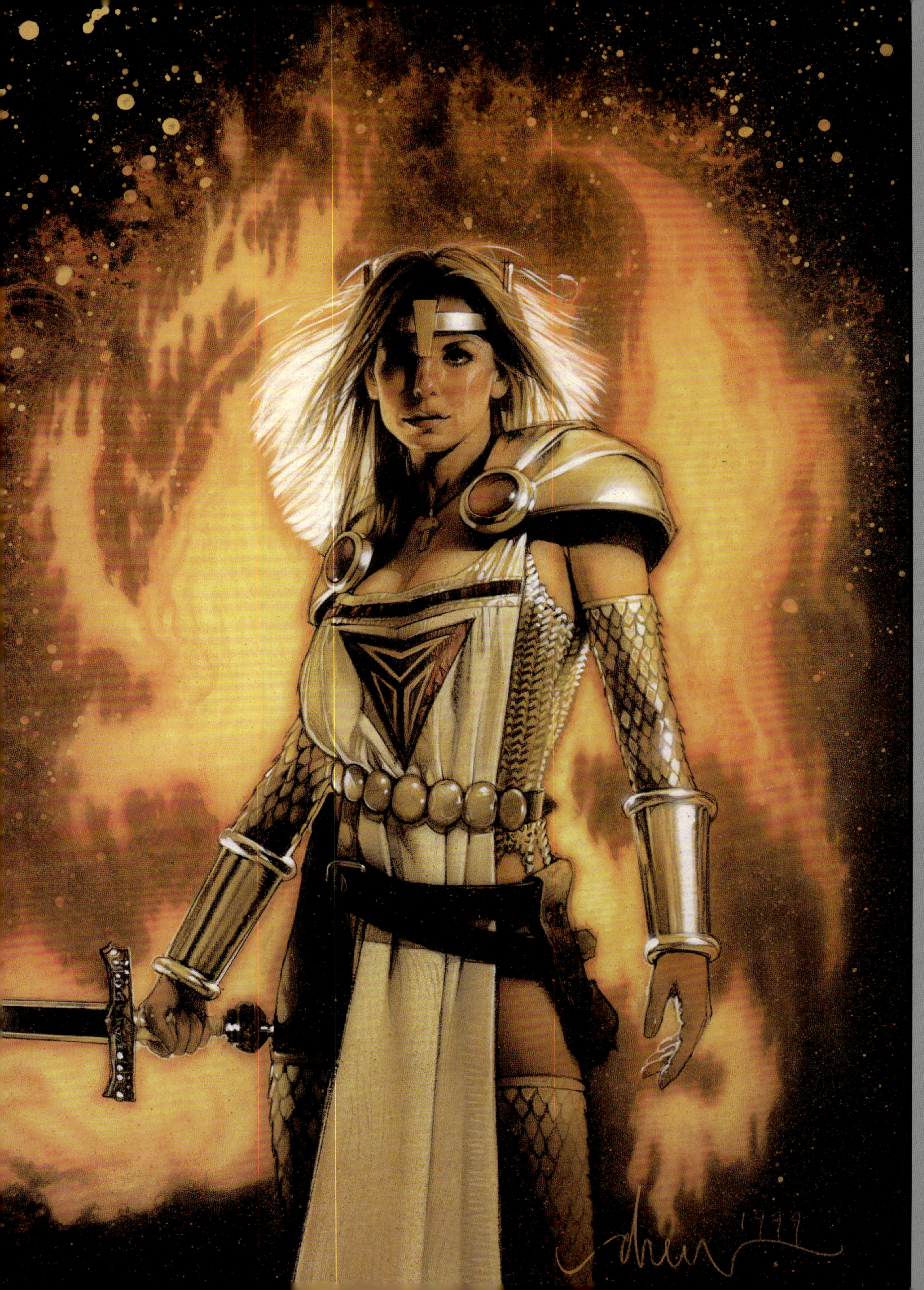

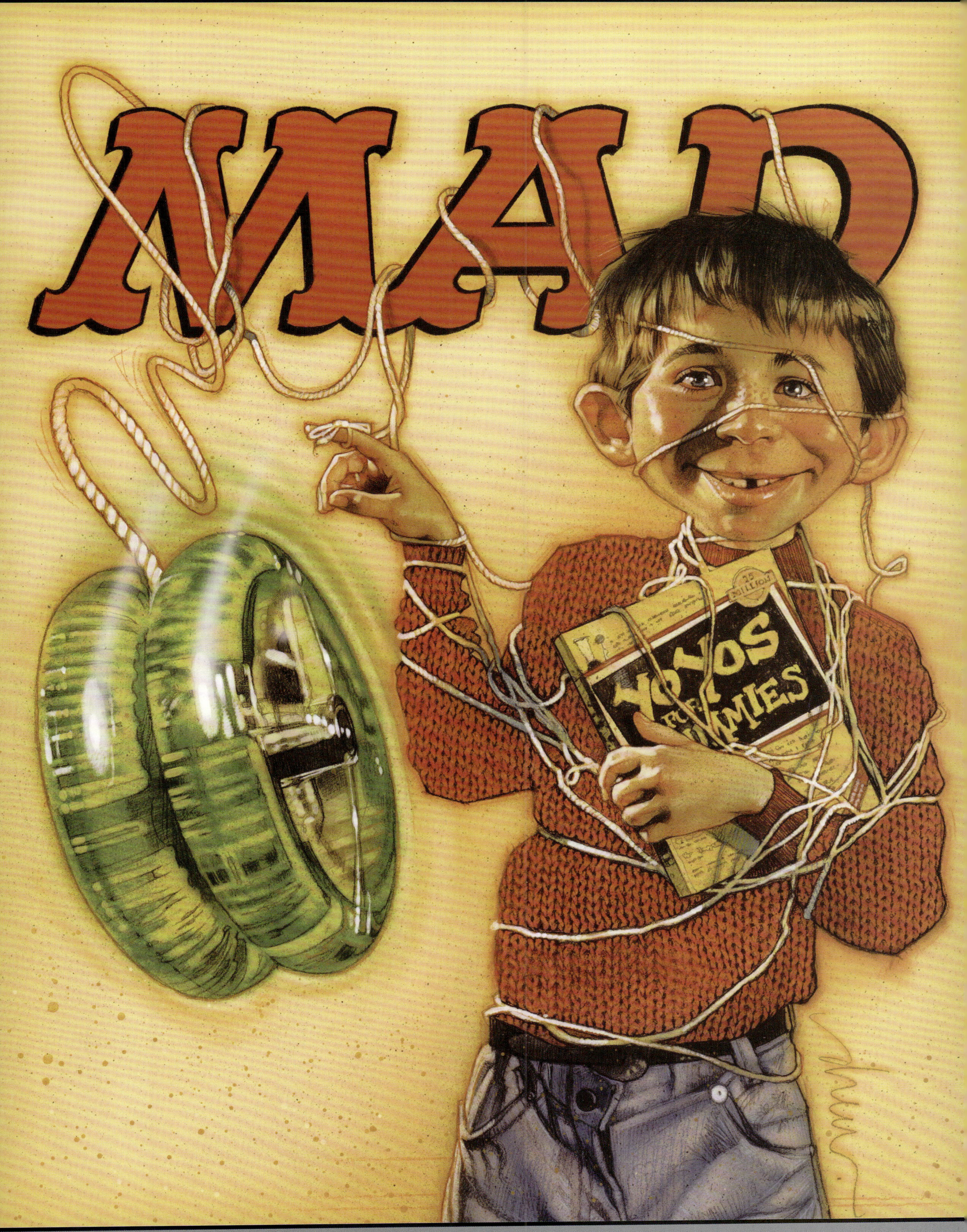
MAD

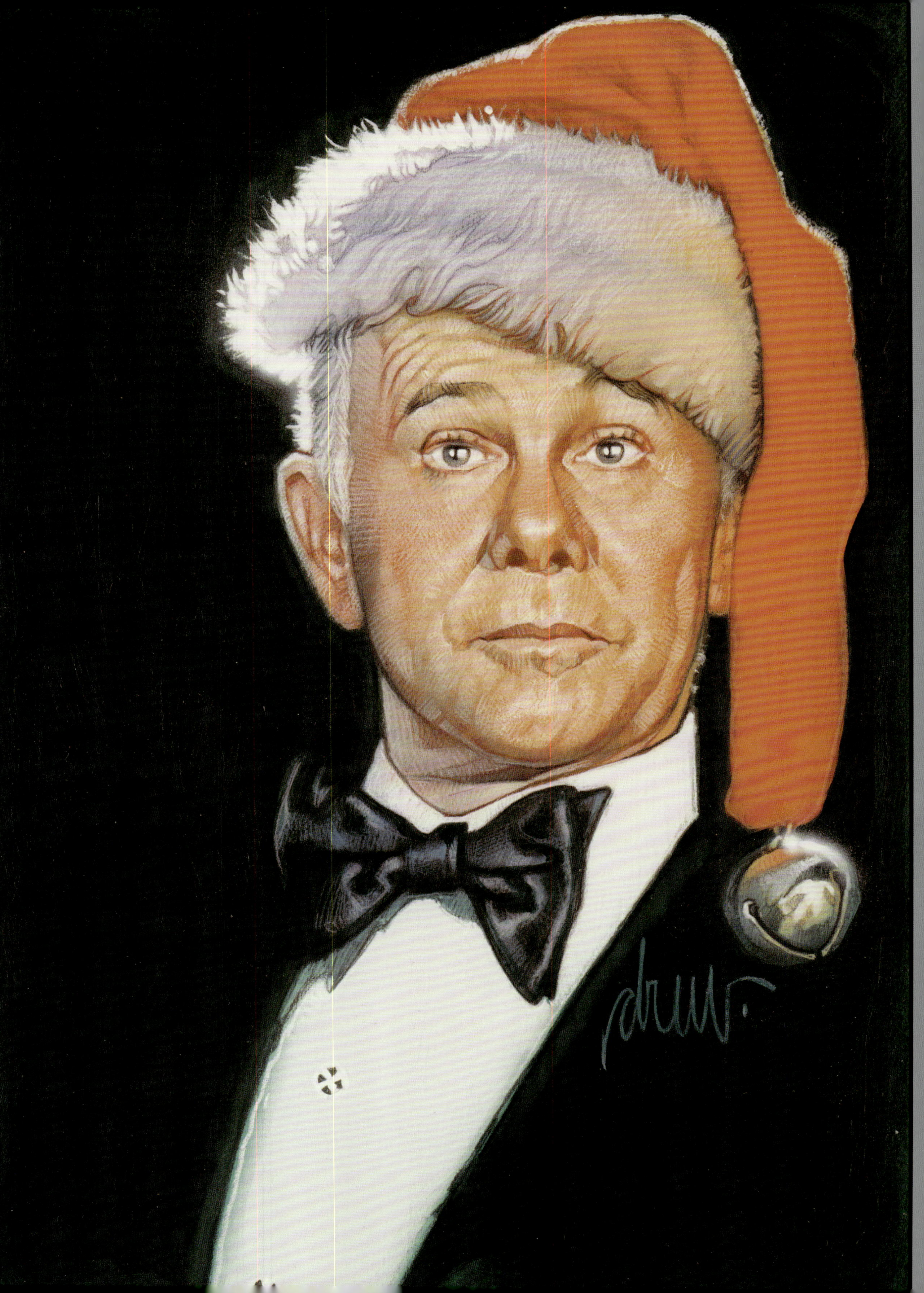

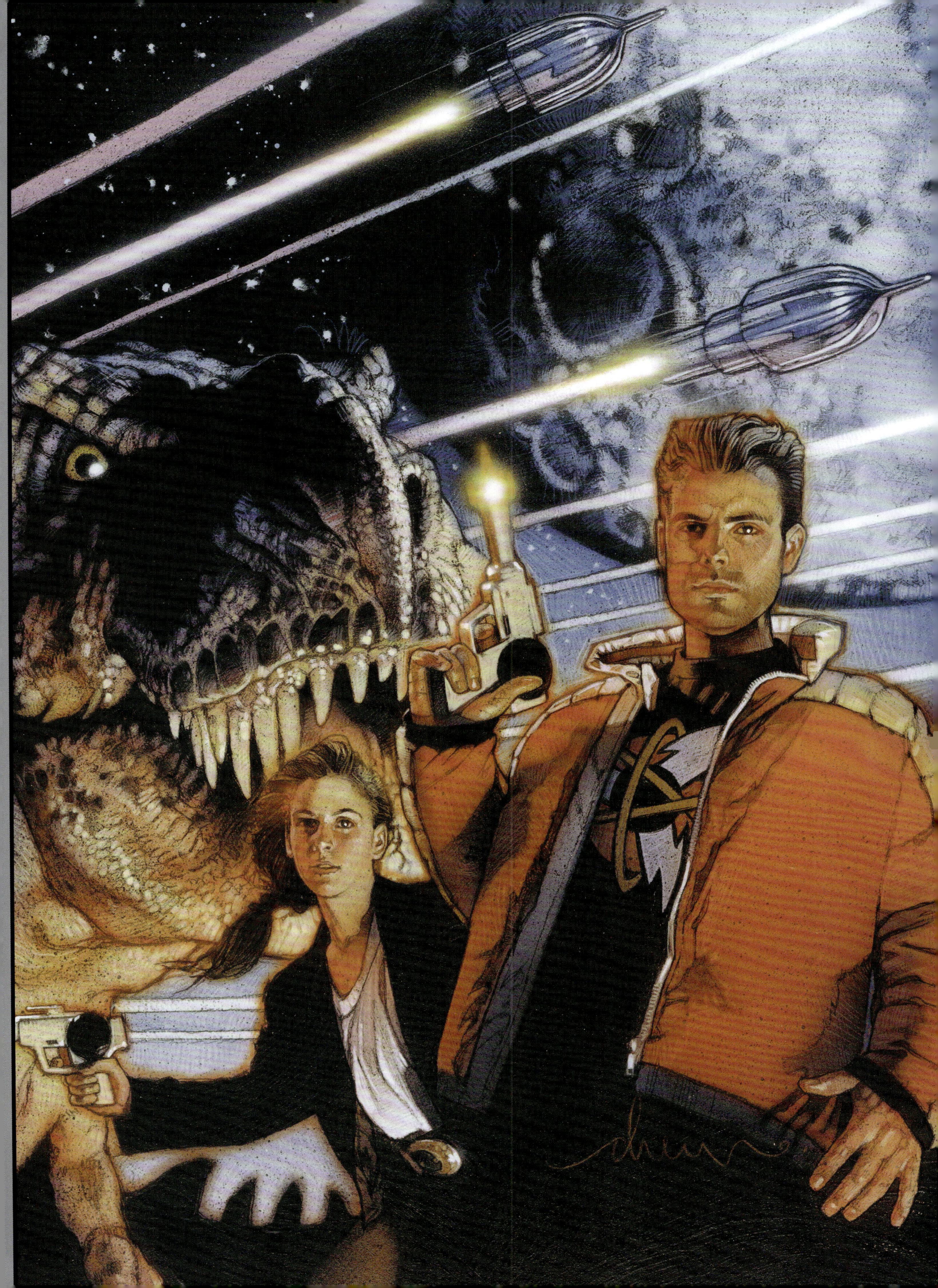

COMMERCIAL WORKS

The term "commercial" is a general heading for all kinds of things from U.S. postal stamps to collector plates and cards, game boxes, advertising, posters, packaging, logos, magazine articles, brochures, and other hard-to-categorize items.

Once you have a reputation, the work tends to flow freely. Each job represented here holds a history that often extends beyond Drew's own memory.

"One can't be immortalized on a postage stamp unless they've been dead for ten years," Drew says. "The people I was fortunate to honor were stars and heroes long gone. I never got to paint a movie poster for them, so painting legends like Henry Fonda was a great joy. When the stamps are unveiled, I often have the further privilege of meeting their families. In the tribute to Henry Fonda, his daughter Jane picked me out of the audience to publicly thank me for the portrait of her father. It was a very humbling experience.

"The unveiling of the Edward G. Robinson stamp placed me at a luncheon with both sides of his family. They were all very sweet and grateful for the work I had done. That was a special moment for me since my only real mentor in college, Lorser Feitelson, was close friends with Edward G., who was himself a passionate art collector.

"I met John Wayne's family in the same way."

If a book cover is a simplified design when compared to a movie poster, then what do we say about a postage stamp? In most cases, it is simply a portrait. The Hollywood Composers series (1999) honored men like Max Steiner, Dimitri Tiomkin, Alfred Newman, Bernard Herrmann, Franz Waxman, and Erich Wolfgang Korngold. Then came the husband and wife team of Alfred Lunt and Lynn Fontanne (1999), "Celebrate the Century 1990s" (2000), "The Broadway Composers" (2001), novelist Zora Neale Hurston (2003)—about fifty stamps in all.

Collector plates served to remind us of the Little Rascals, Frank Sinatra, The Three Stooges, Princess Diana, the Lone Ranger, and others.

In some ways, the original art created for these jobs is much like the people it represents. The job—the commercial object—is often "here today and gone tomorrow." Each set of stamps is a limited run. When they run out, they're gone. Once they've been sold, the collector plates are no longer available. Drew's Indiana Jones and *Lord of the Rings* trading cards are gone. The two *Clue* games and the computer games for which Drew illustrated the box covers are out of print. The Superman poster from the seventies (although it was altered by someone else's hand) is gone. (The version shown here is untouched.)

While the men and women and events on these stamps are part of history, their memories linger. "The life, love, and power of their art is still here. Without the collectors, owners, and appreciators, so much of art is dust-to-dust. At the least, I am grateful for this book, which is a celebration and living archive of so much that otherwise is so soon gone and forgotten."

It has been said that the earliest forms of illustration were prehistoric cave paintings. Maybe drawing on stone was one way to find permanency, one way to pass on knowledge and memory. Maybe the postal service is onto something here. We should not let our memories or our histories disappear. The Golden Age of illustration preceded us, flourishing in a world rich with the printed word. Today, technology occupies our senses.

Let's not surrender our souls completely to a digital world.

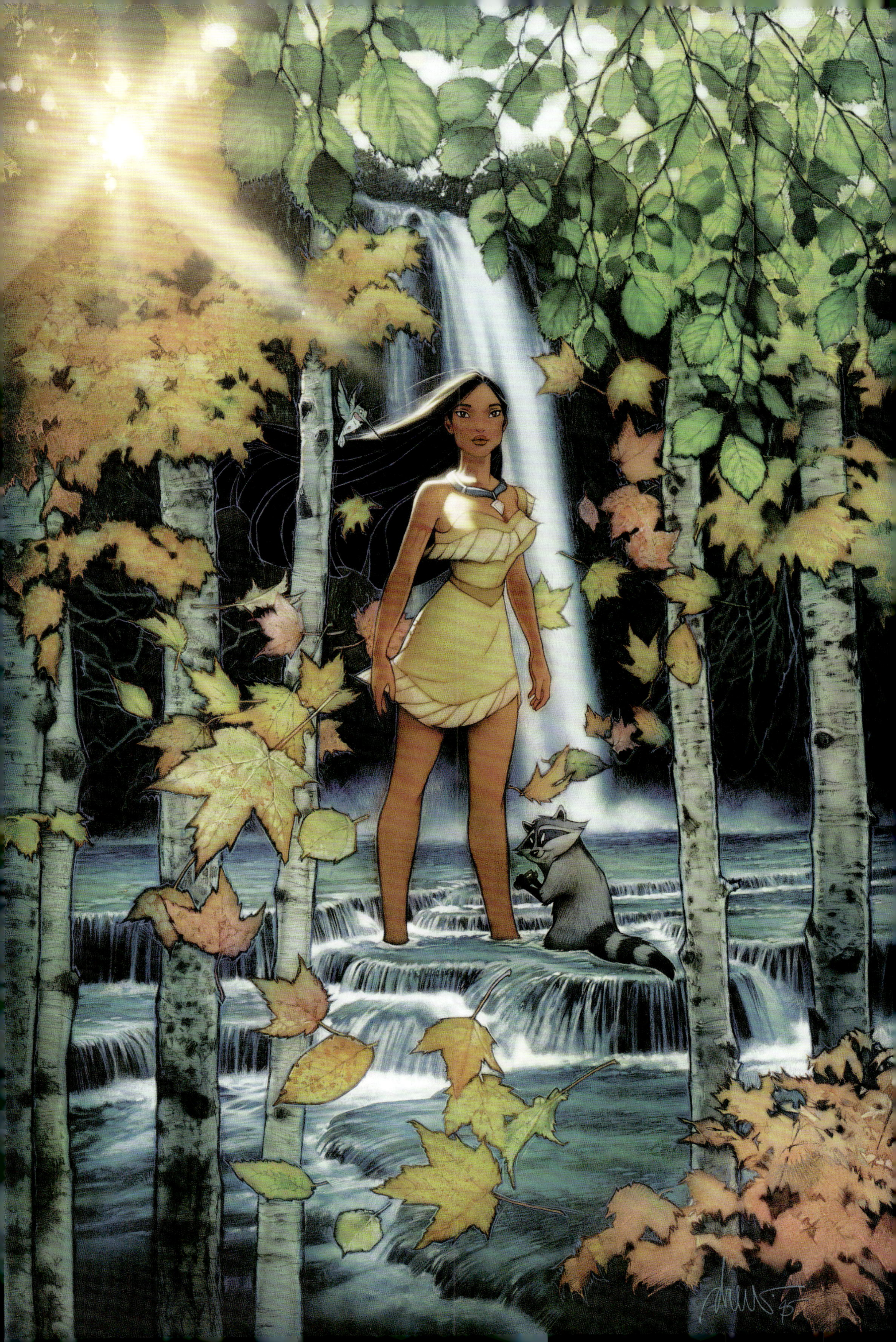

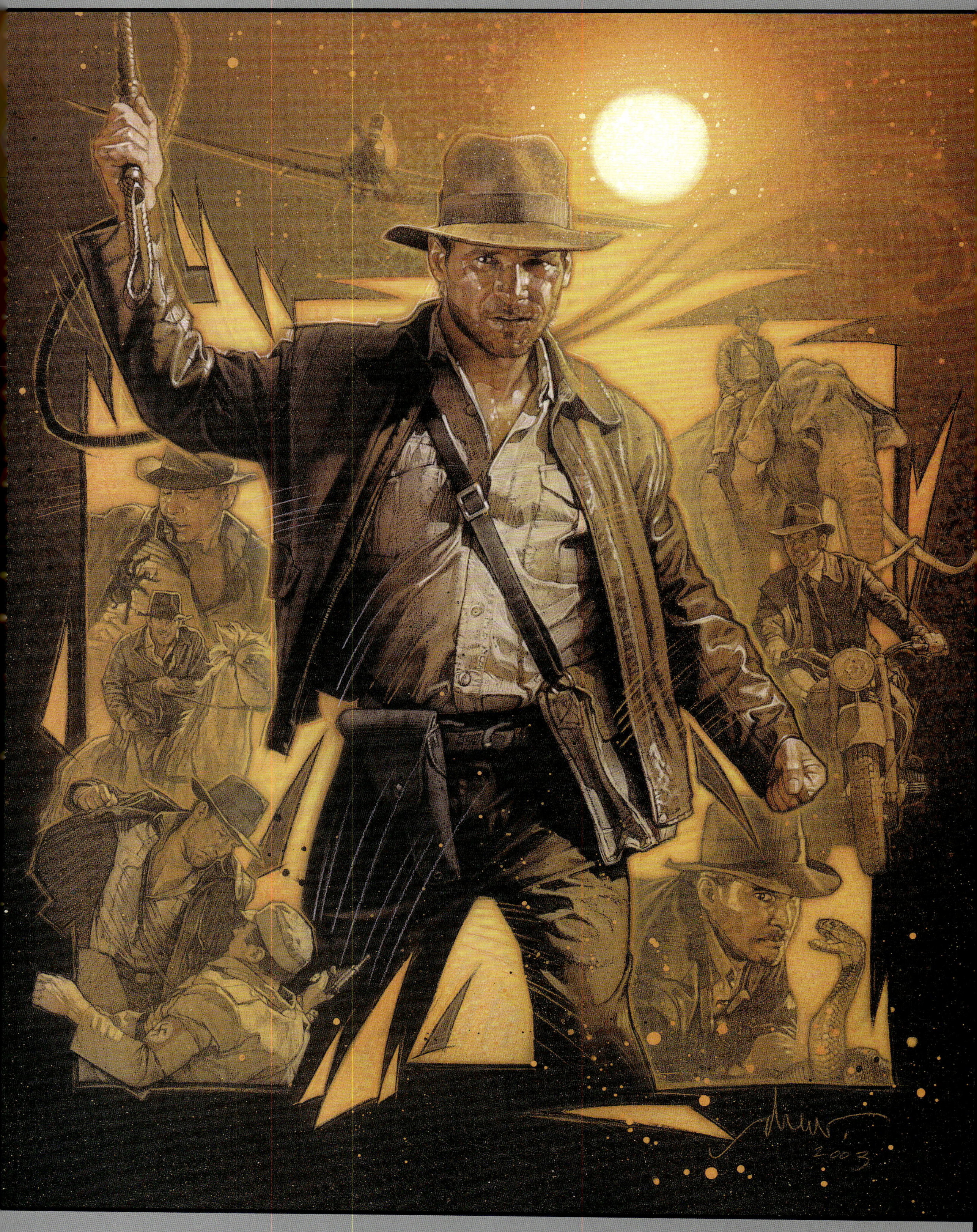

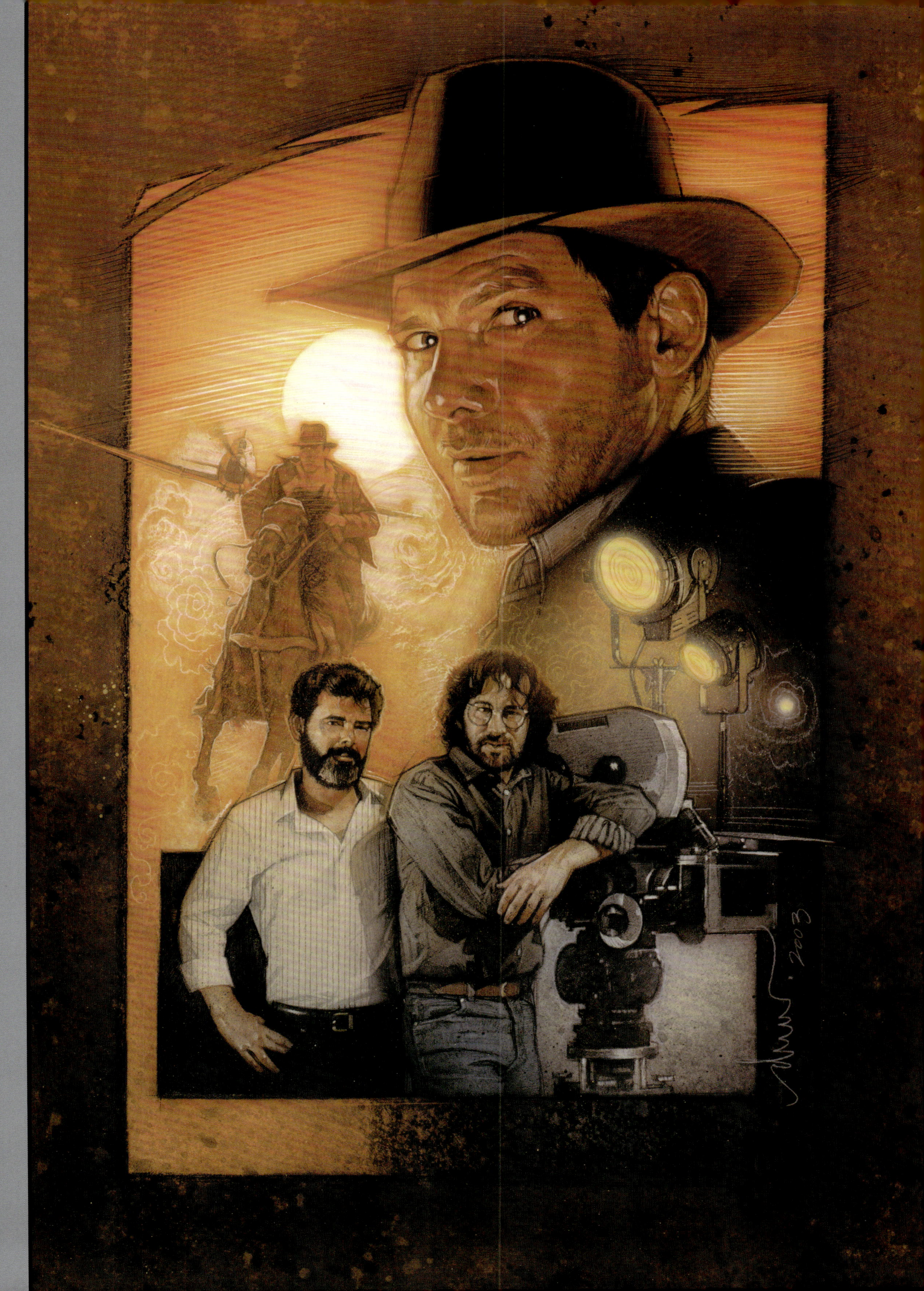
2003

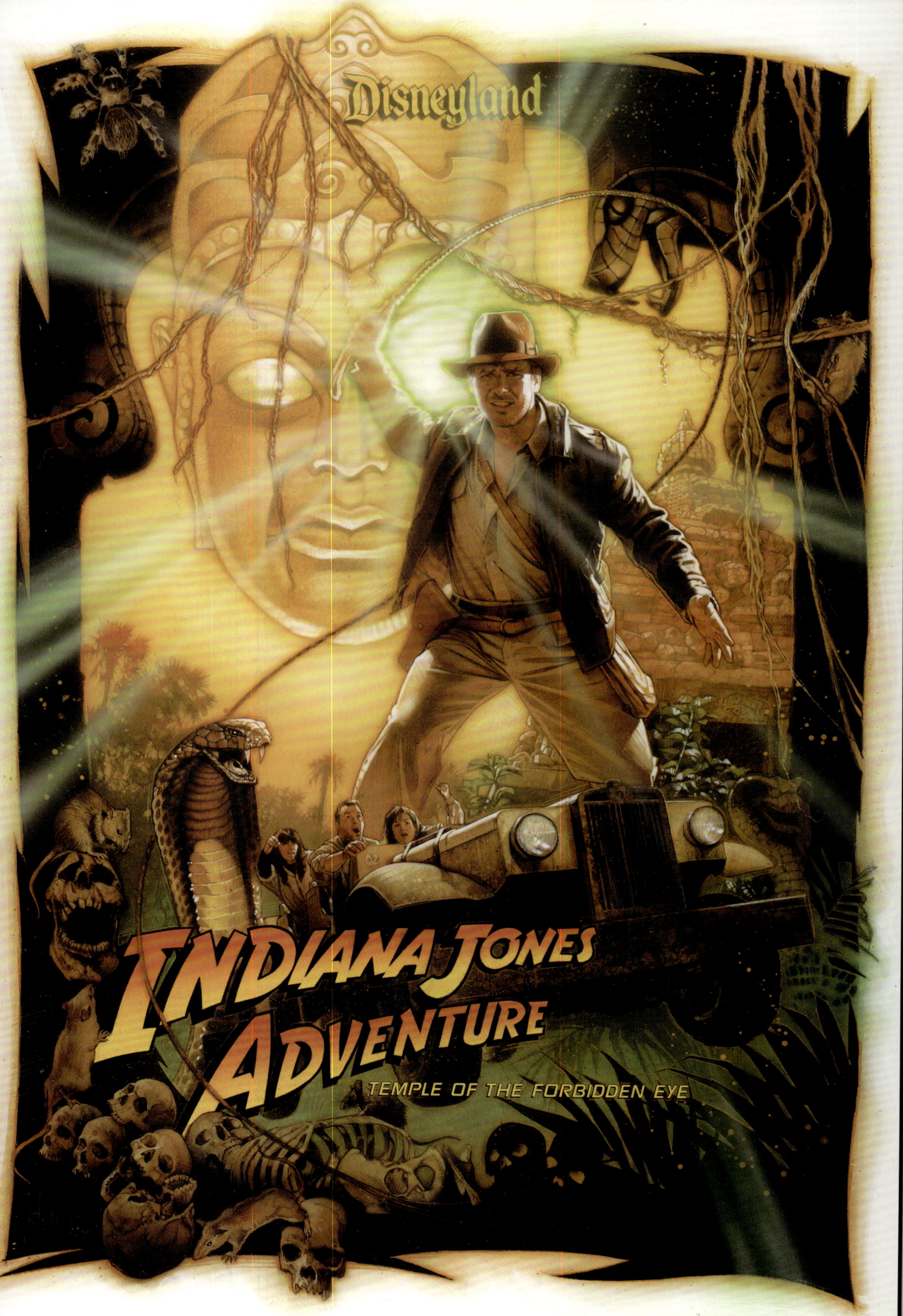

Disneyland

INDIANA JONES ADVENTURE

TEMPLE OF THE FORBIDDEN EYE

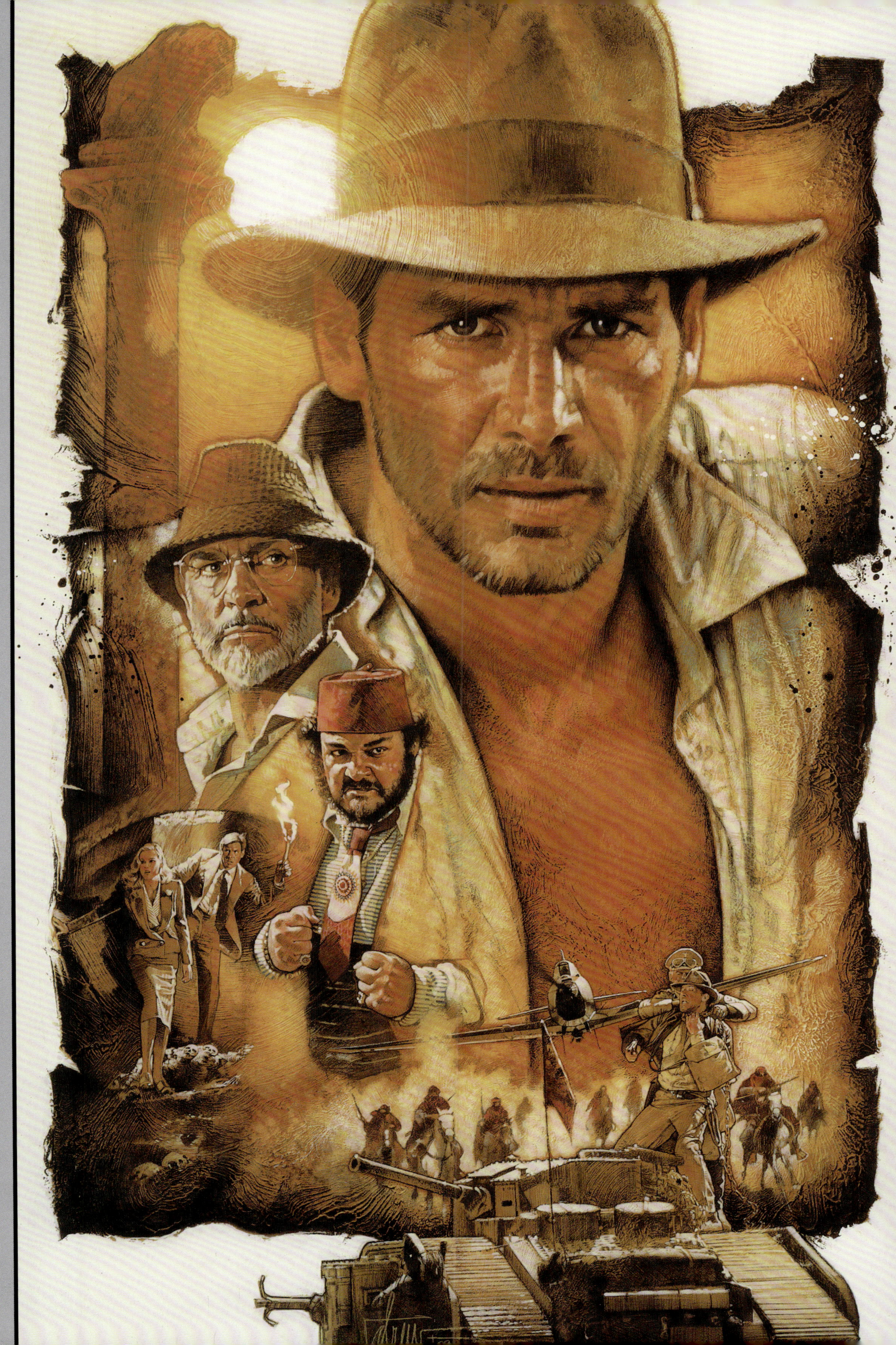

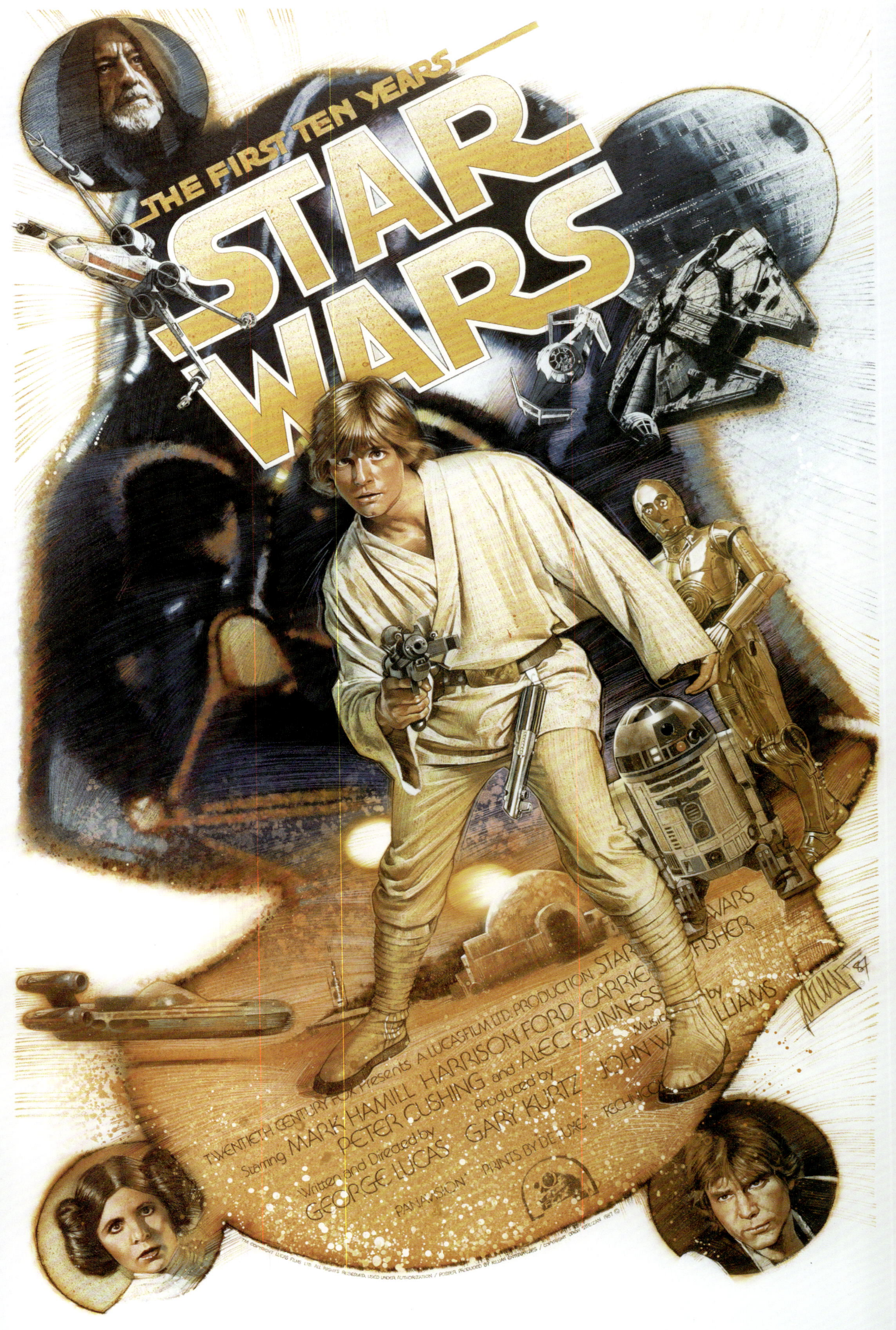
THE FIRST TEN YEARS
STAR WARS
TWENTIETH CENTURY FOX Presents A LUCASFILM LTD. PRODUCTION STAR WARS
Starring MARK HAMILL HARRISON FORD CARRIE FISHER
PETER CUSHING and ALEC GUINNESS
Written and Directed by GEORGE LUCAS
Produced by GARY KURTZ
Music by JOHN WILLIAMS
PANAVISION® PRINTS BY DE LUXE® TECHNICOLOR®
TM COPYRIGHT LUCAS FILMS LTD. ALL RIGHTS RESERVED. USED UNDER AUTHORIZATION / POSTER PRODUCED BY KILLIAN ENTERPRIZES / COPYRIGHT DREW STRUZAN 1987 ©

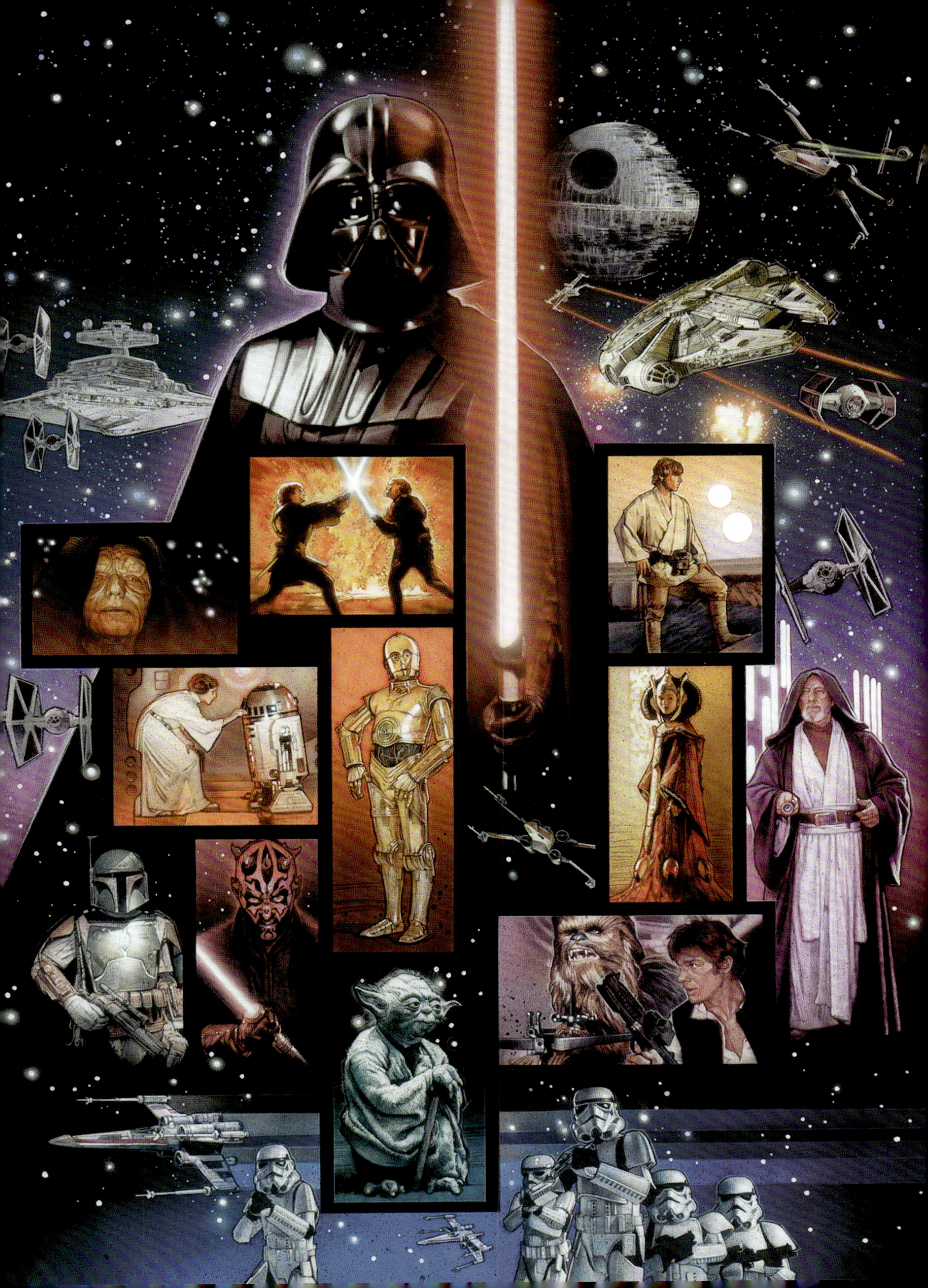

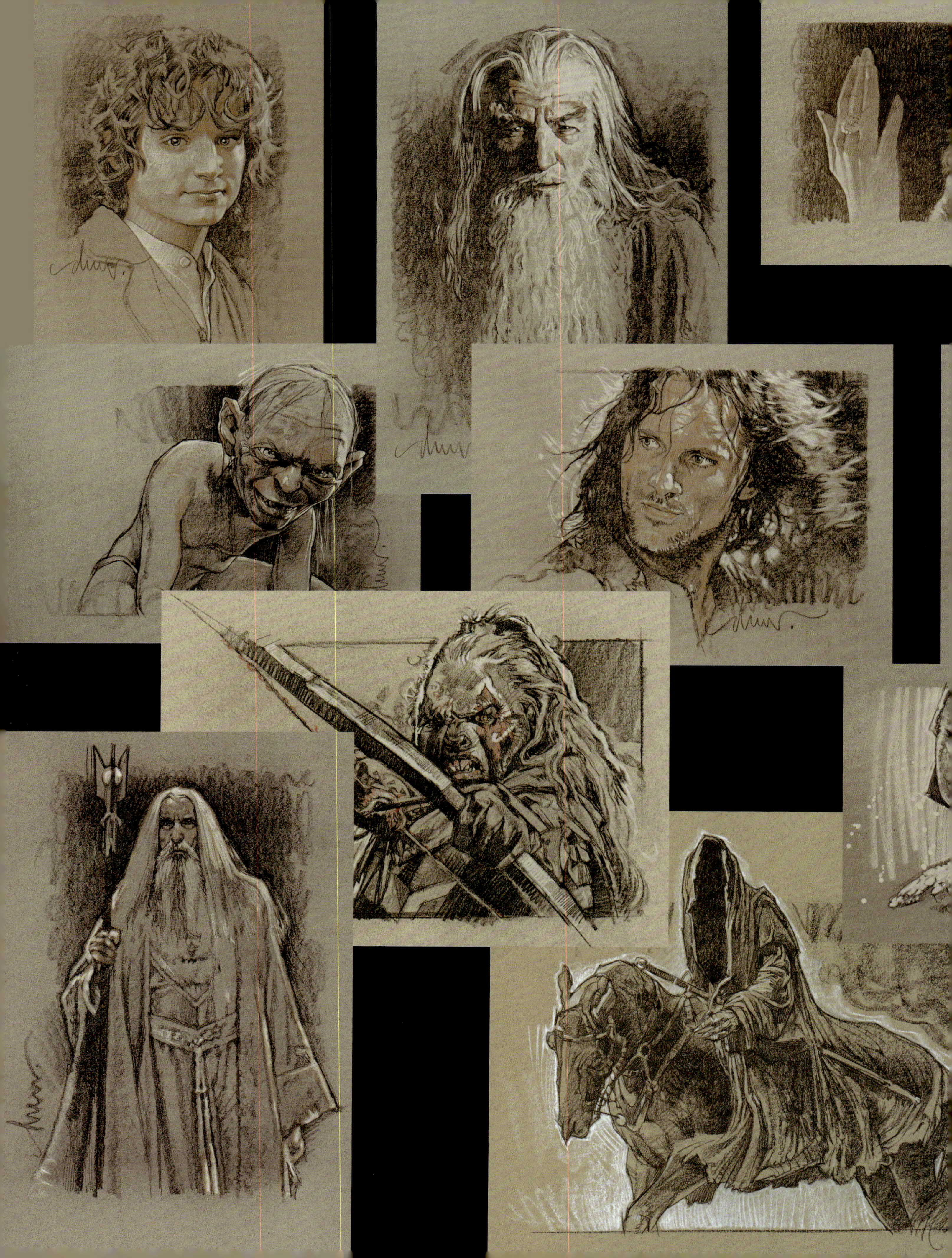

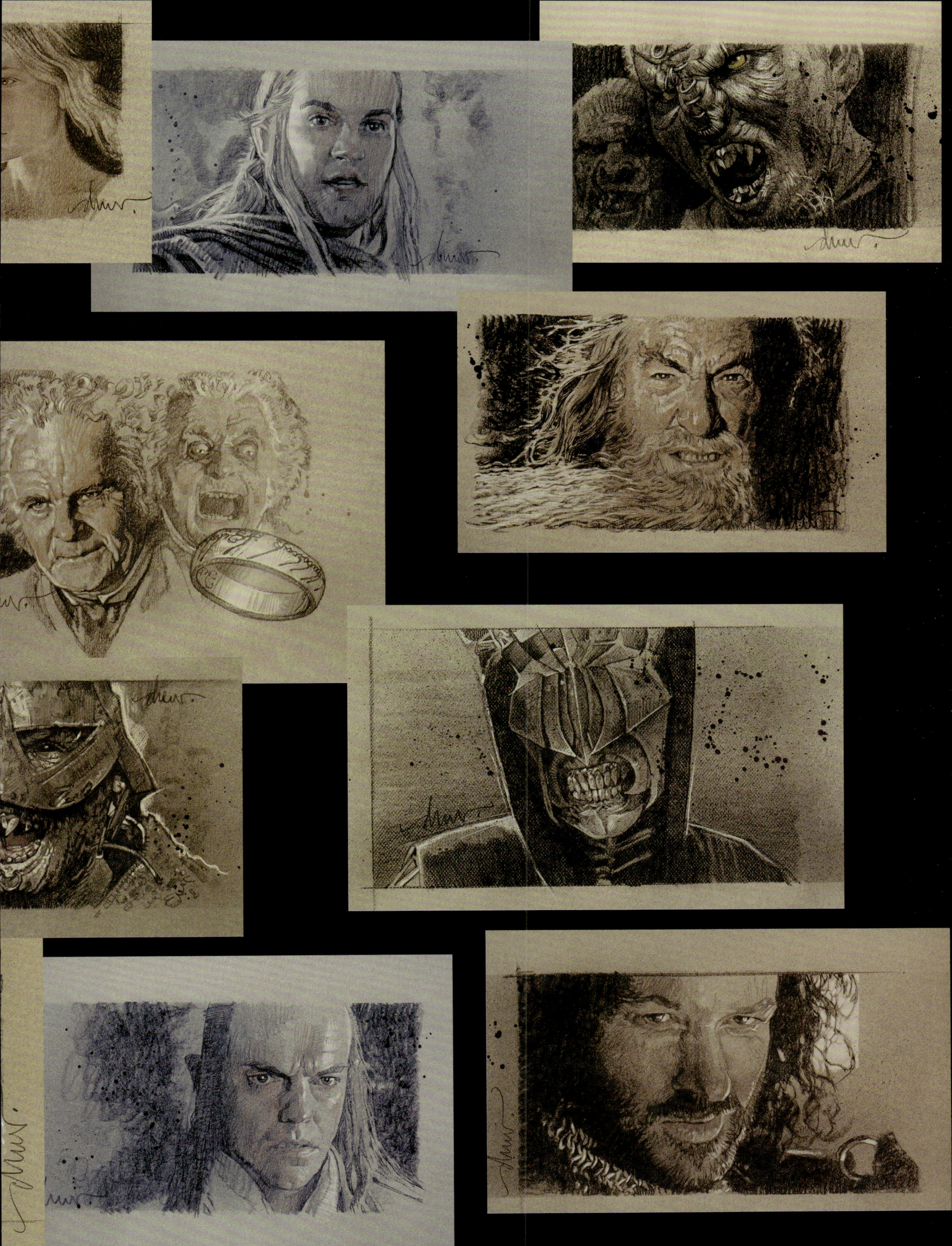

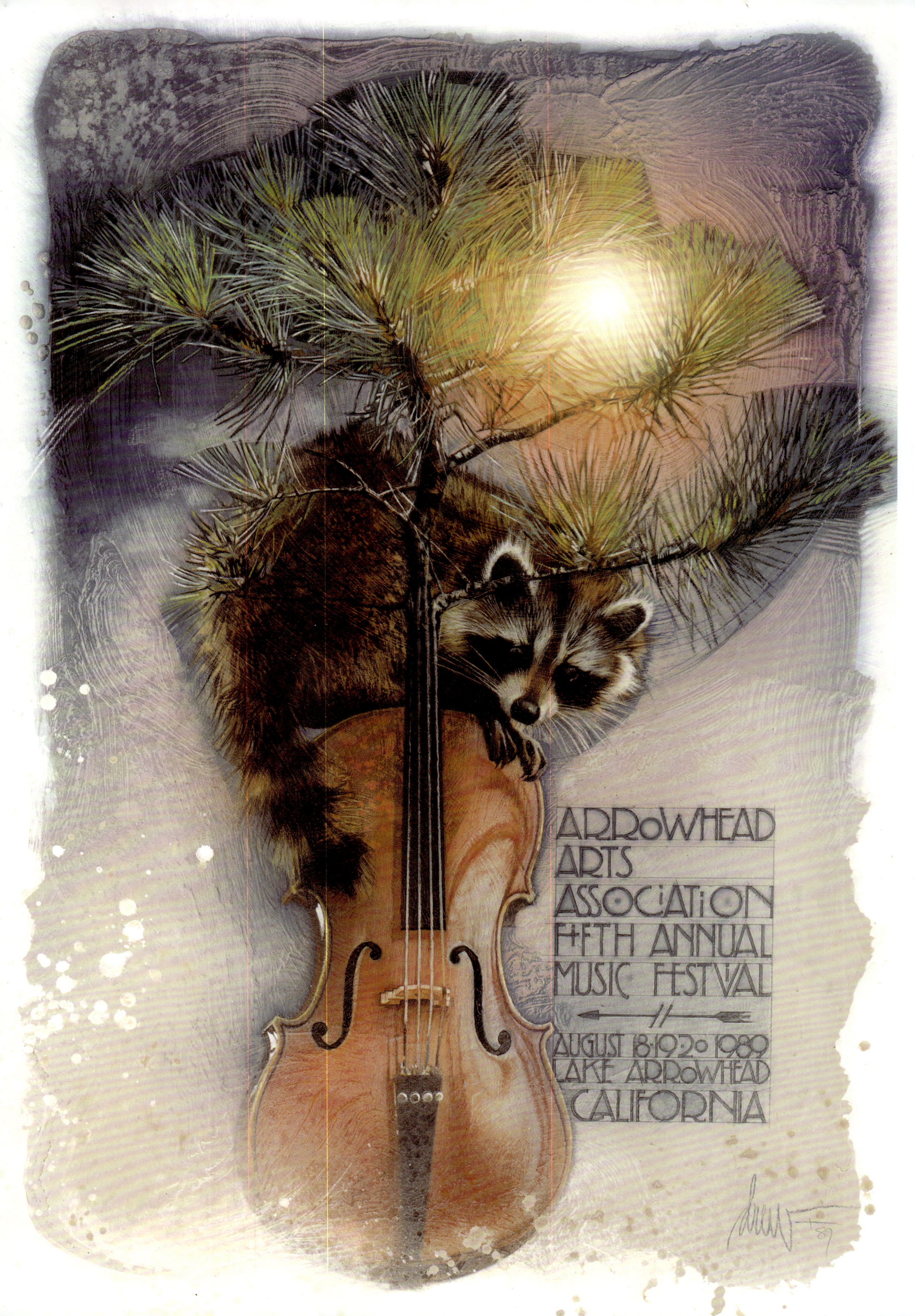
ARROWHEAD
ARTS
ASSOCIATION
FIFTH ANNUAL
MUSIC FESTIVAL
AUGUST 18·19·20 1989
LAKE ARROWHEAD
CALIFORNIA

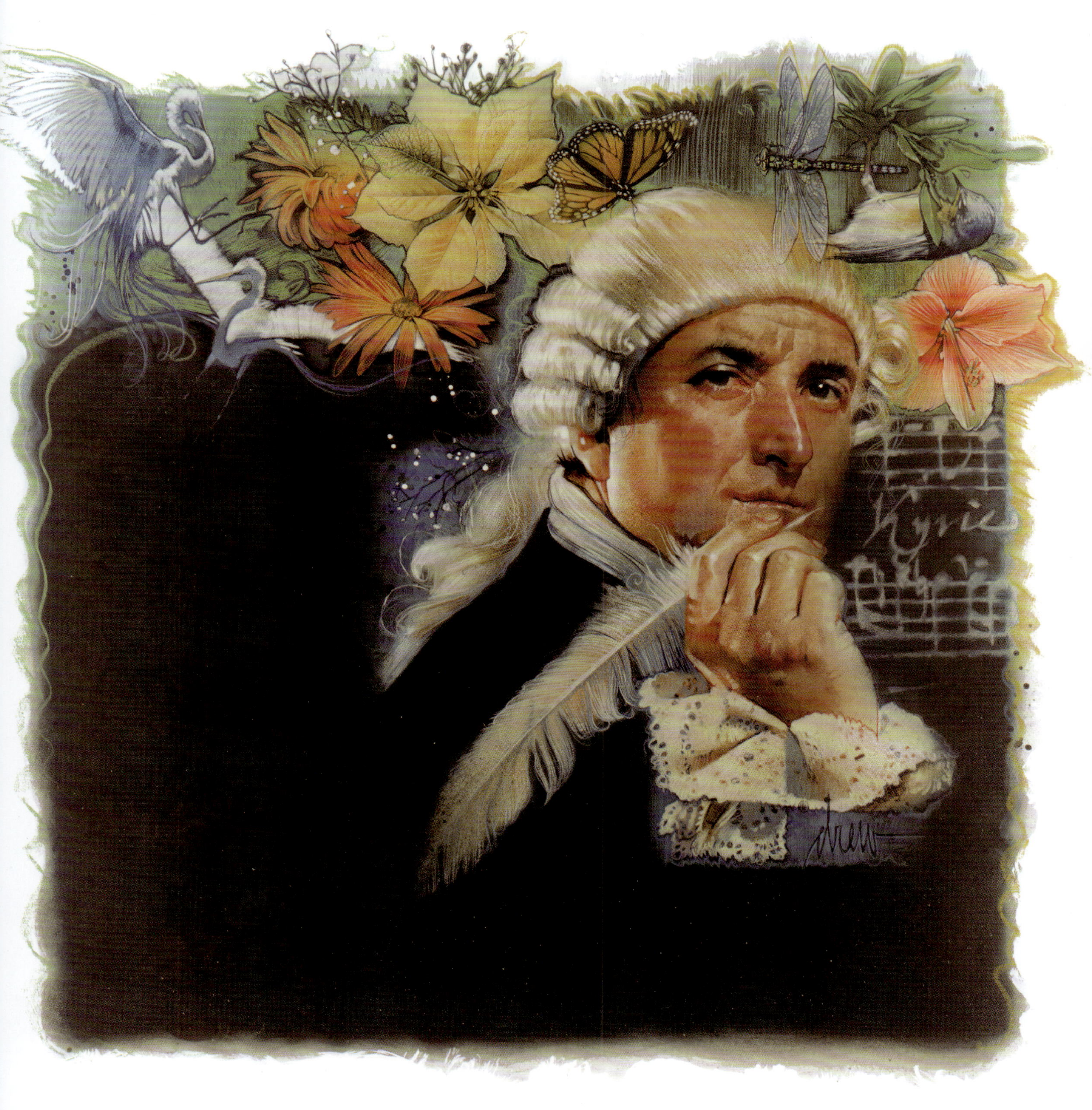
Kyrie
drew

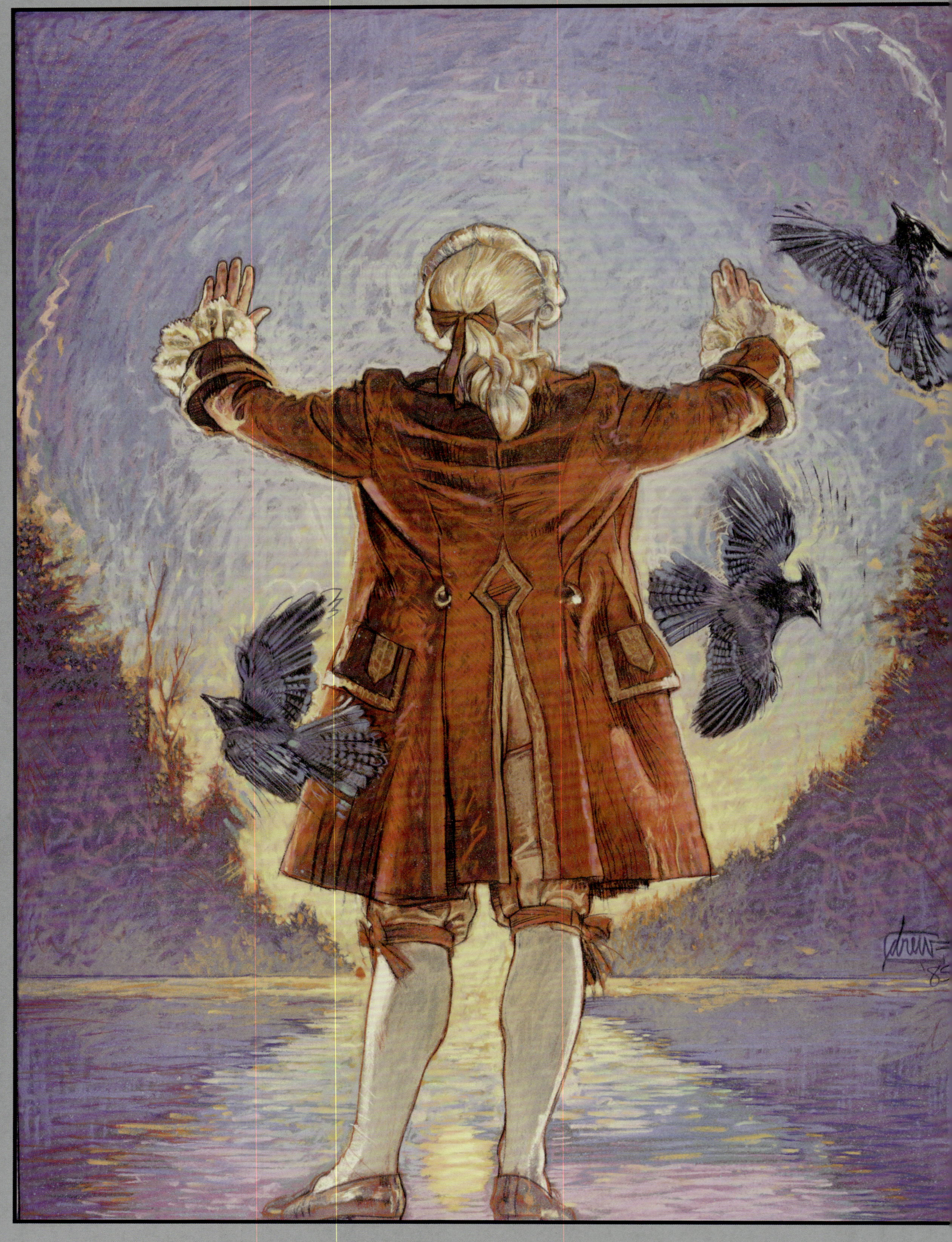

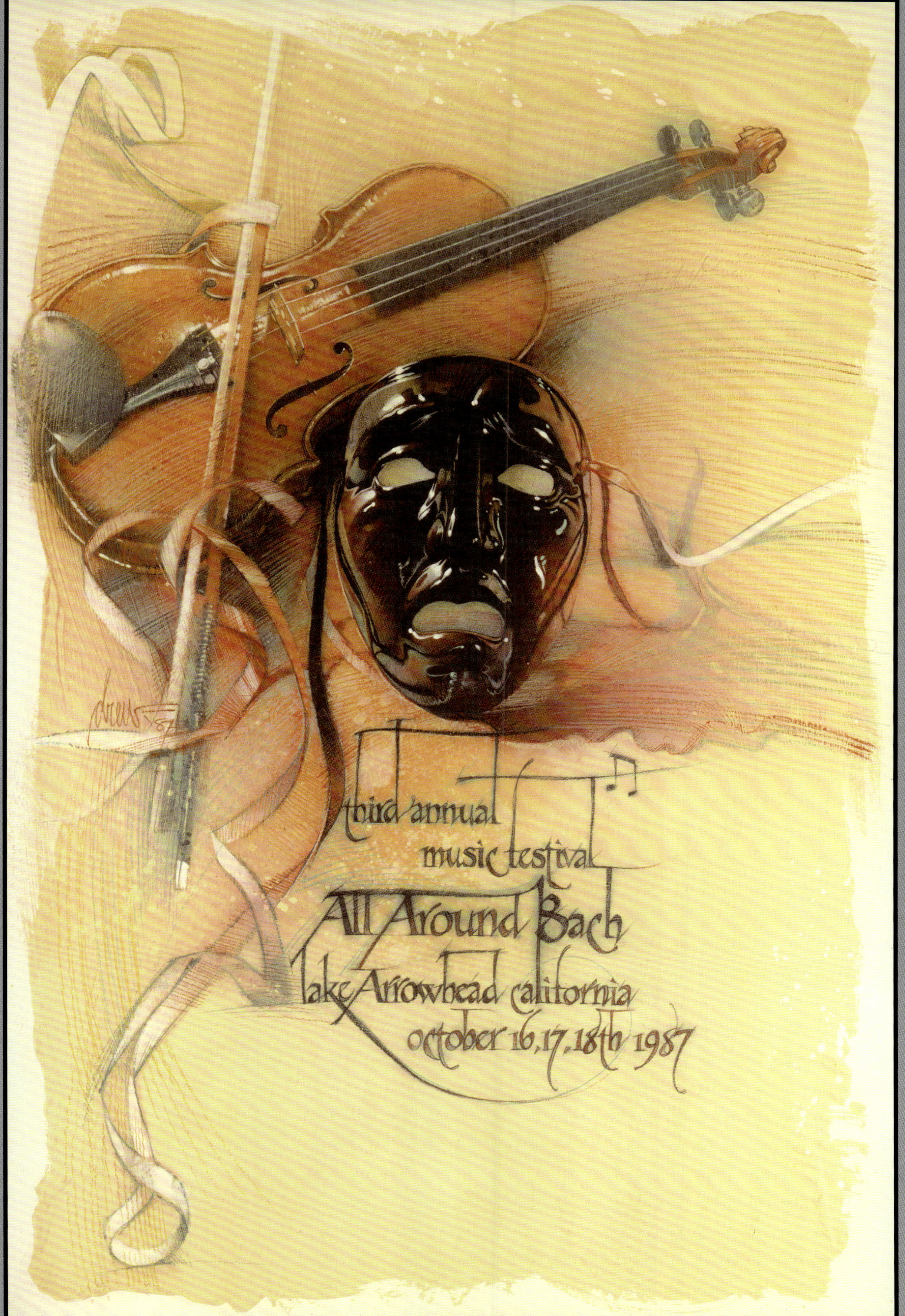
third annual
music festival
All Around Bach
Lake Arrowhead california
october 16,17,18th 1987

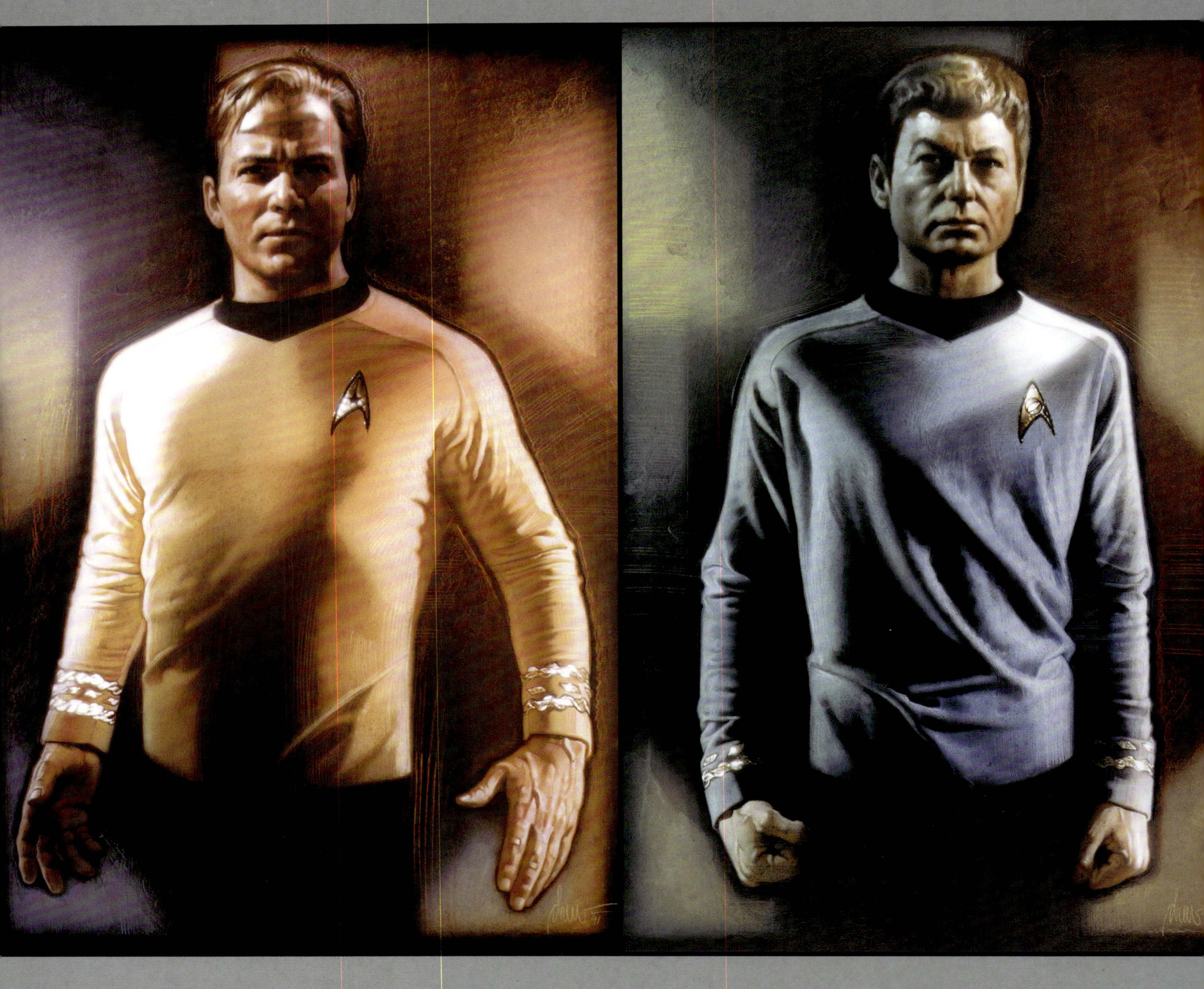

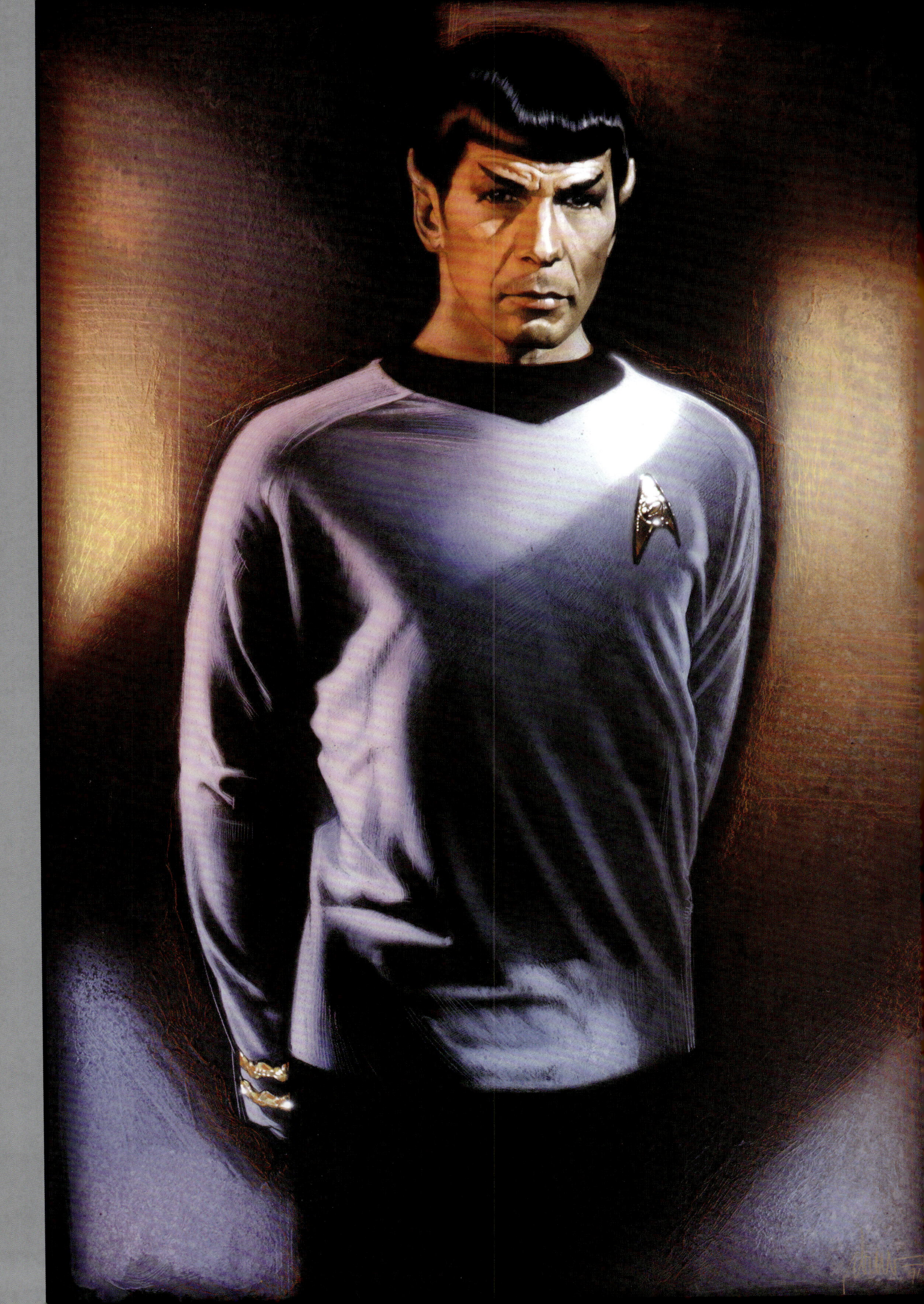

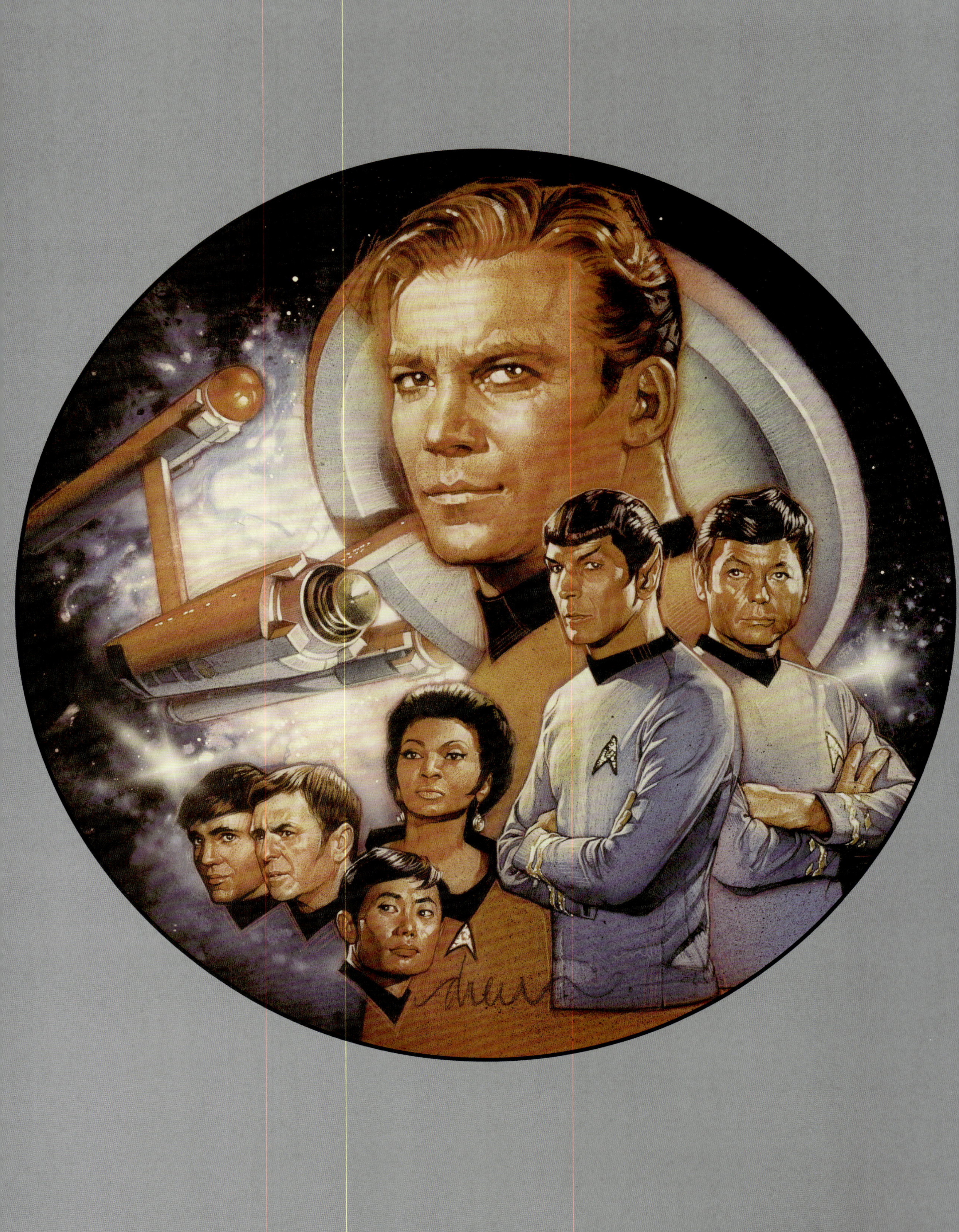

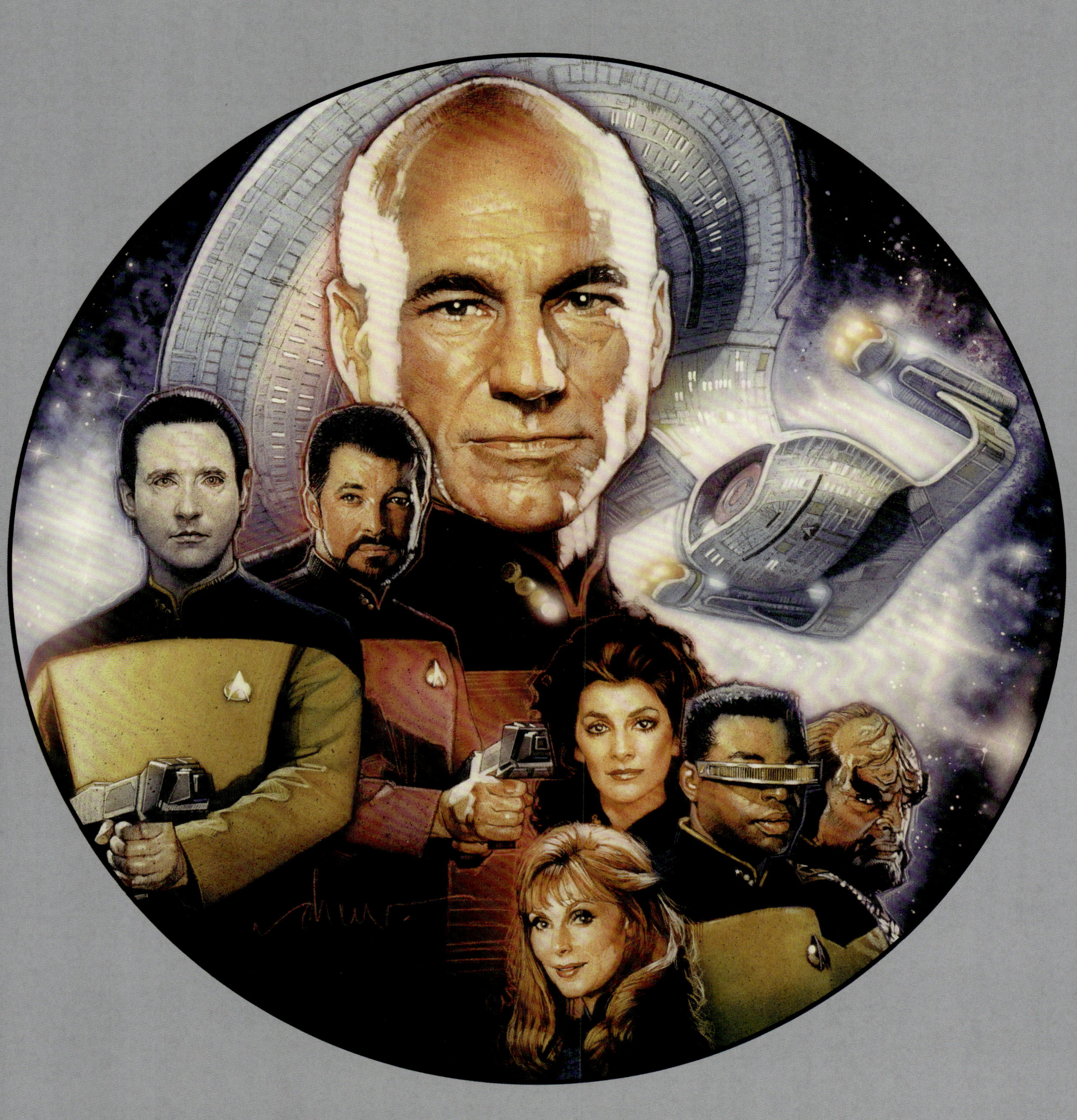

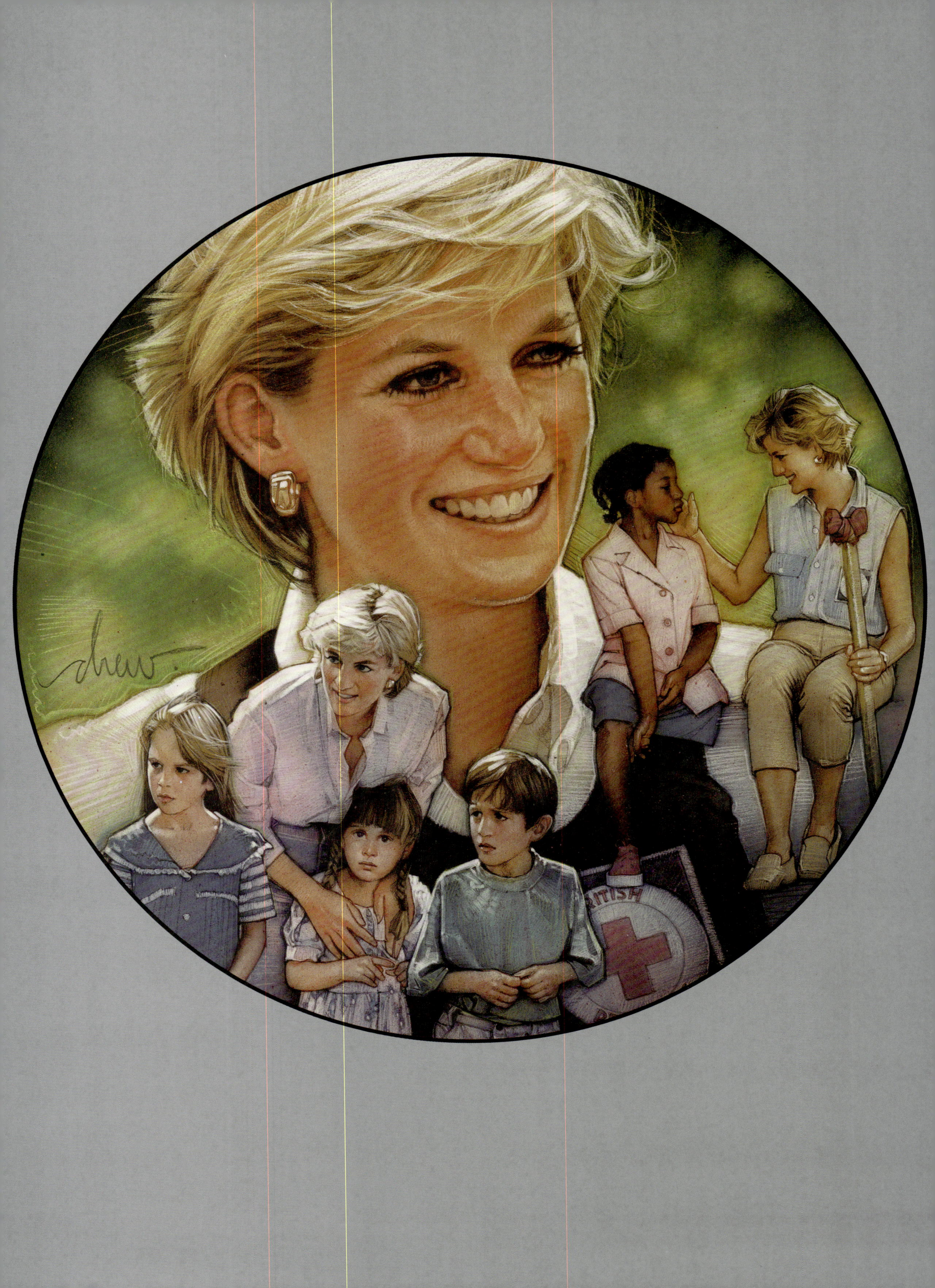

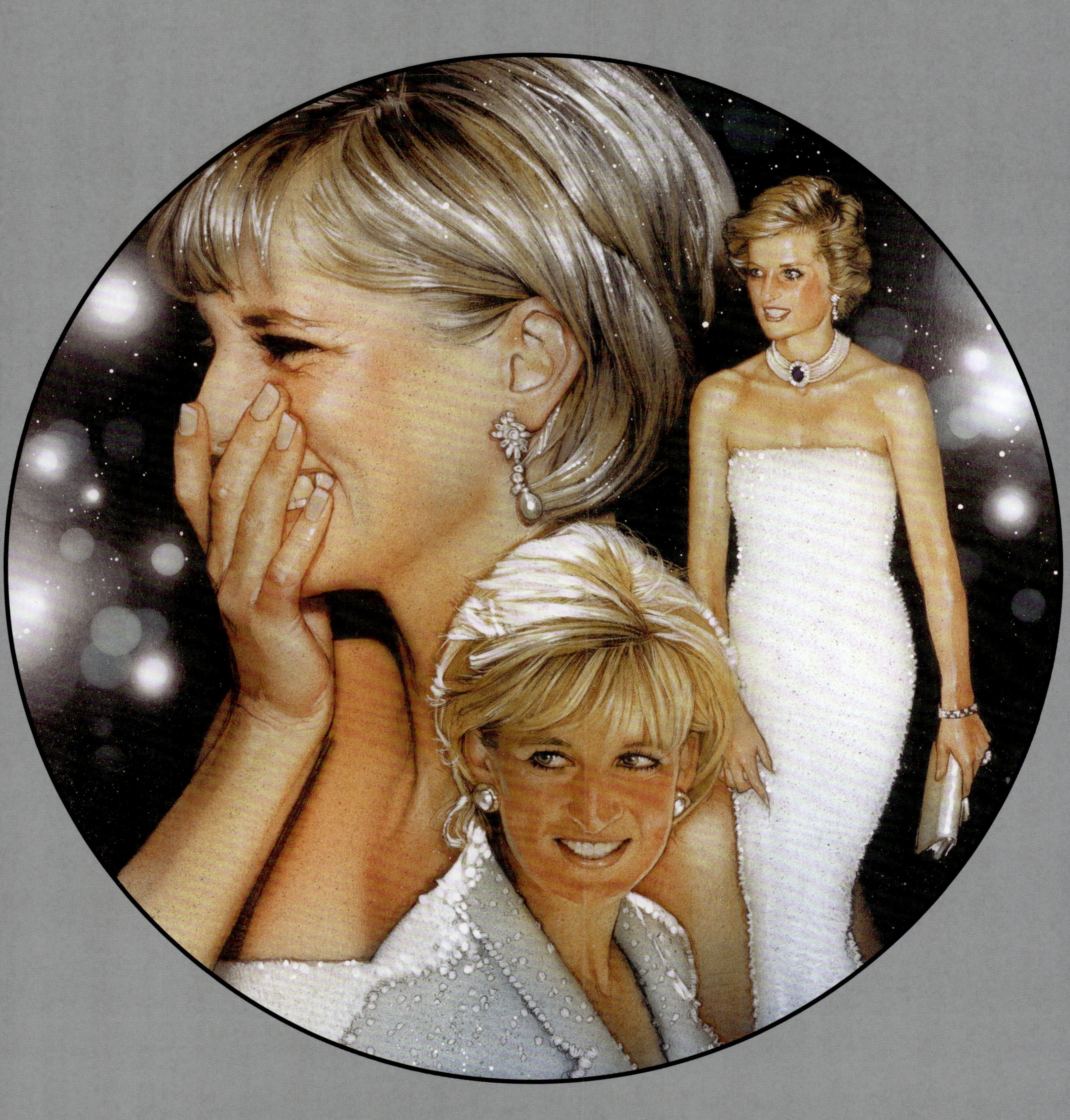

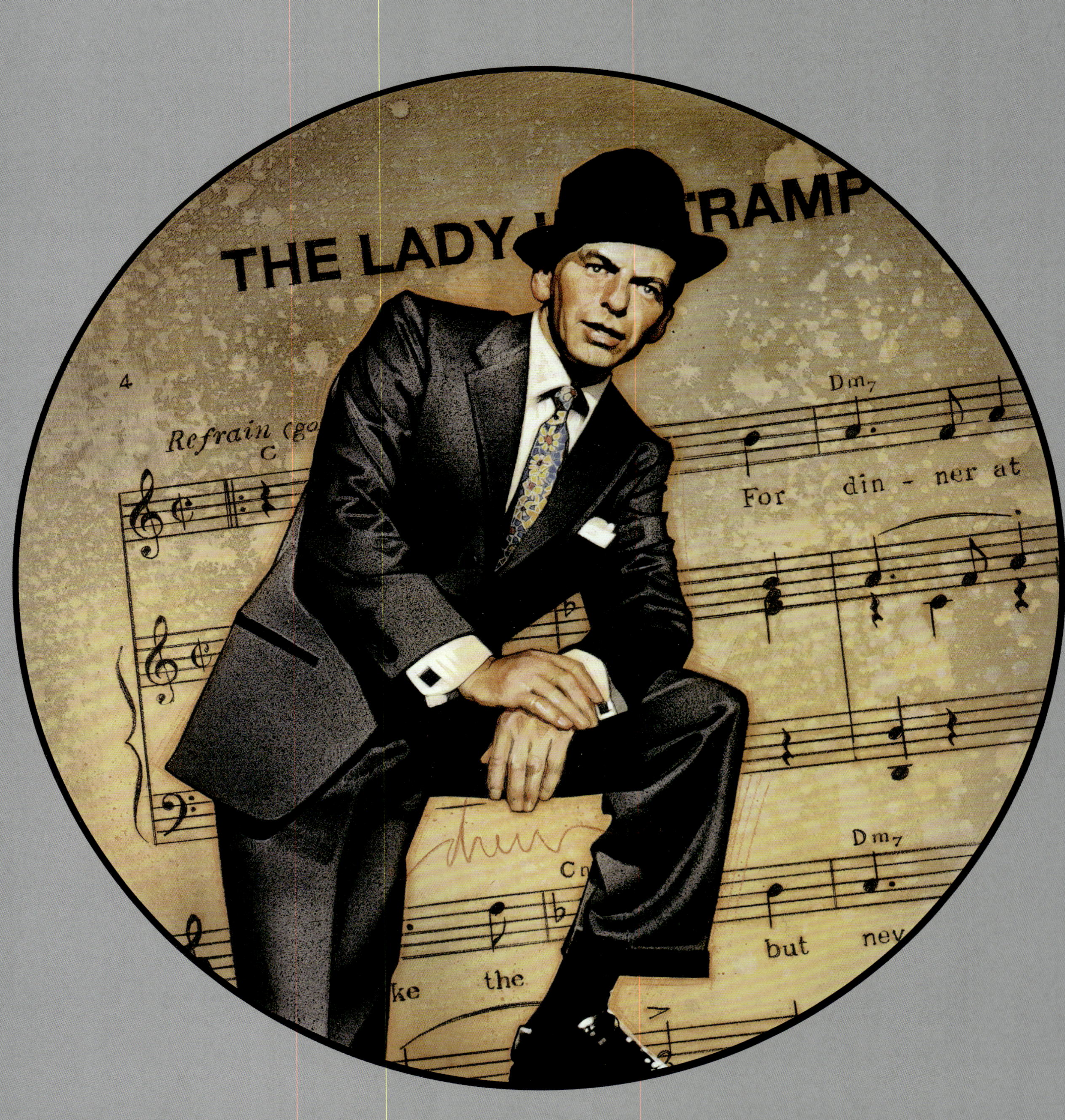
THE LADY
TRAMP
4
Refrain (go
C
Dm7
For din - ner at
Dm7
but nev
the
ke

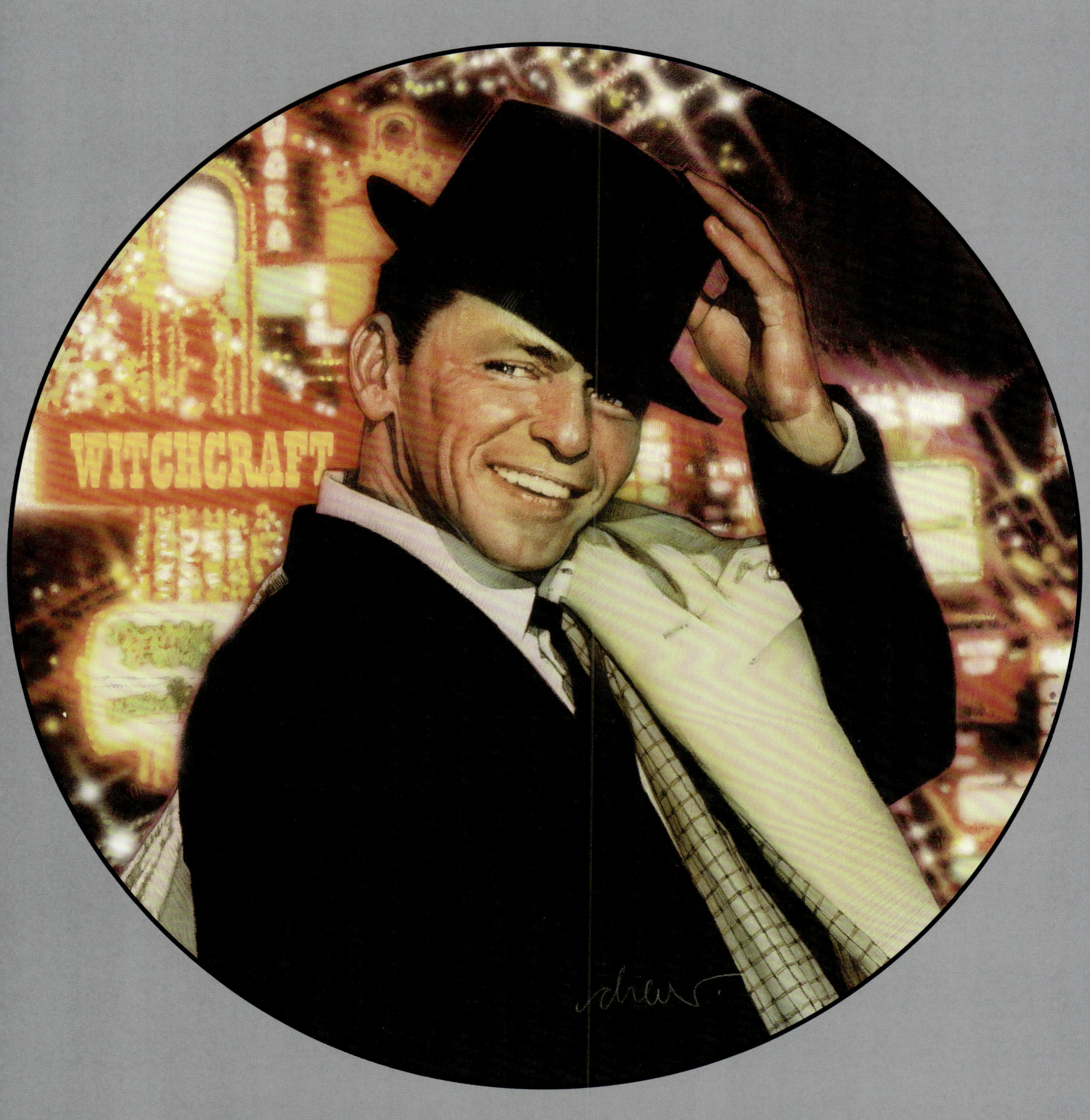
WITCHCRAFT

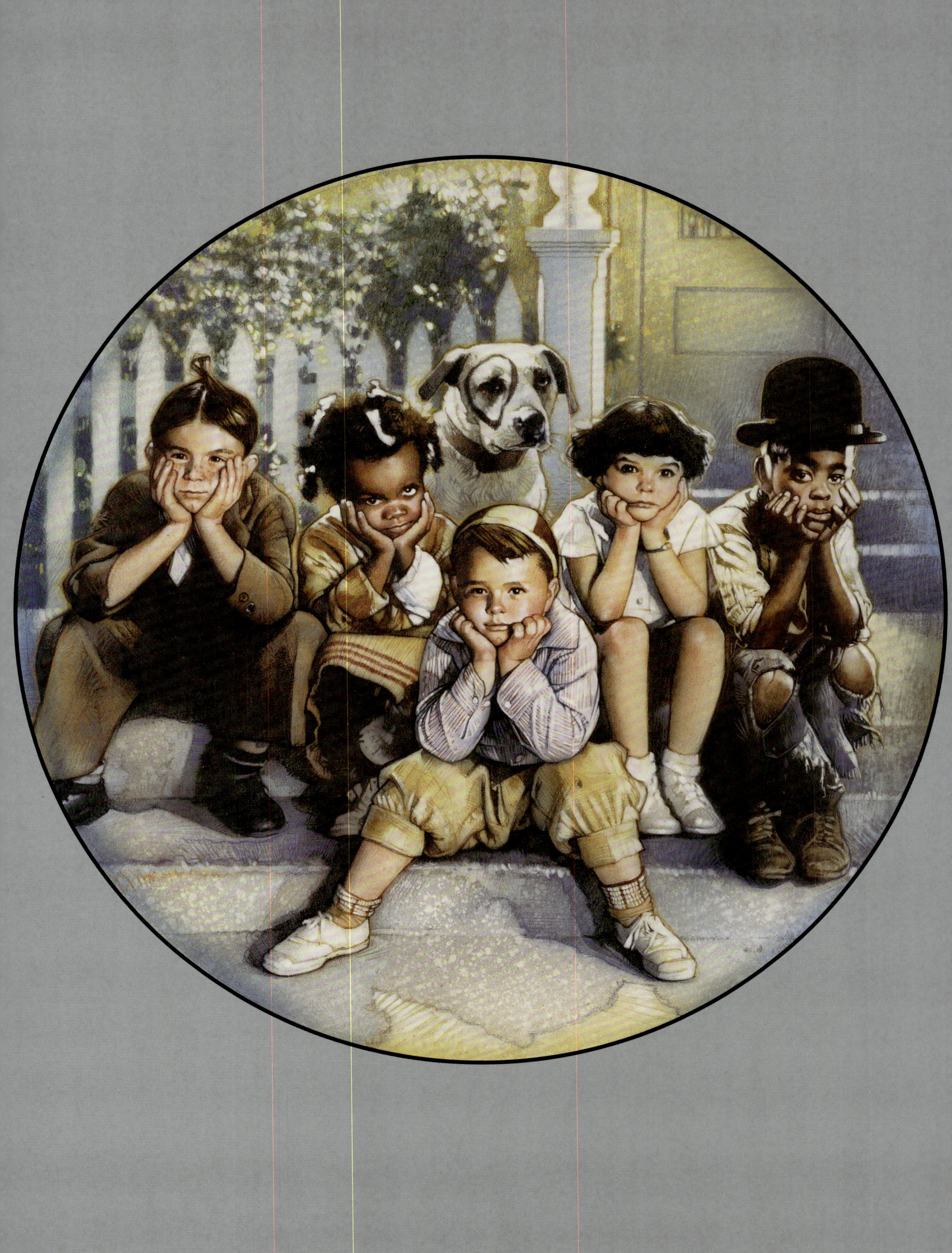

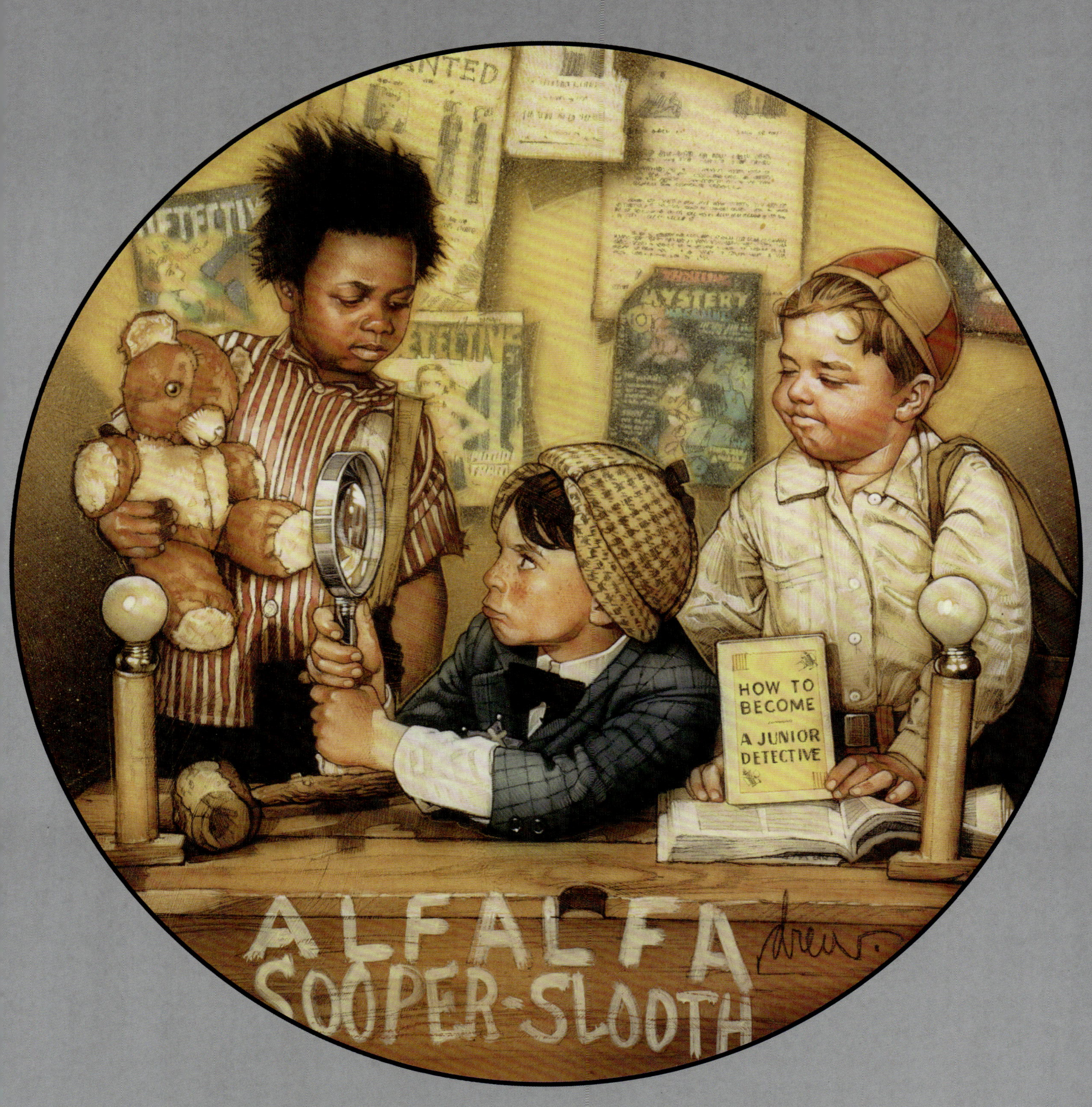
HOW TO
BECOME
A JUNIOR
DETECTIVE
MYSTERY
ALFALFA
SOOPER-SLOOTH

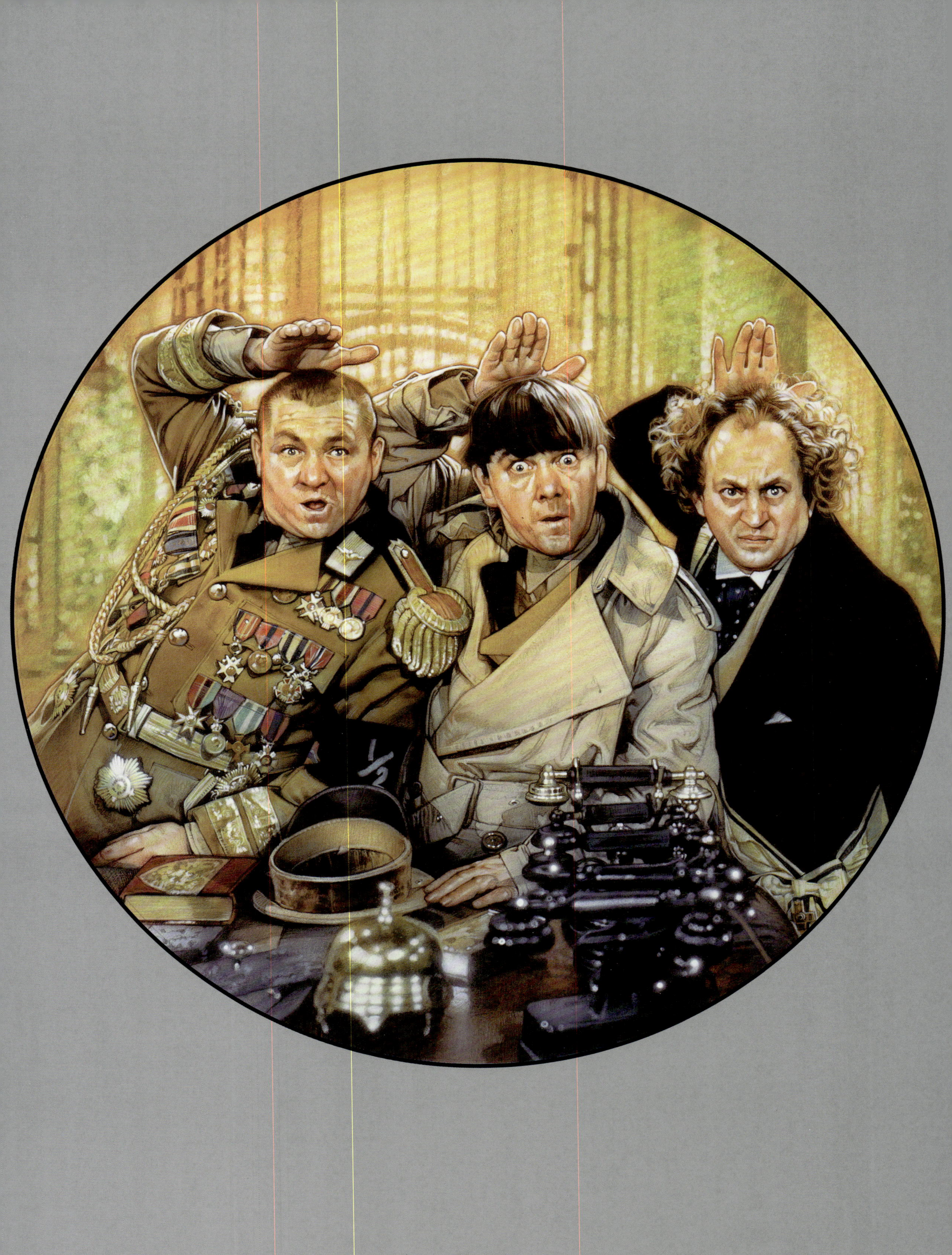

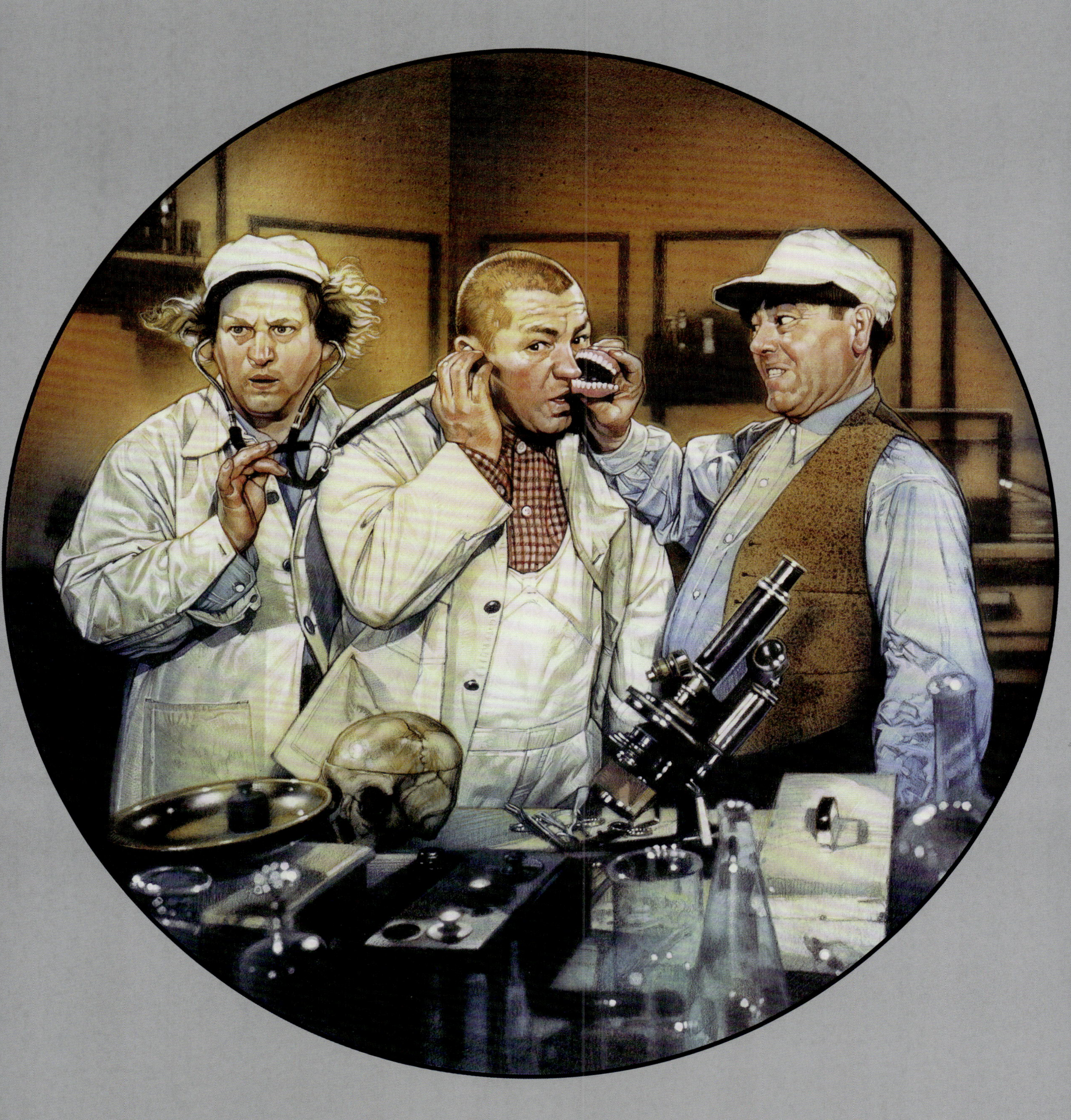

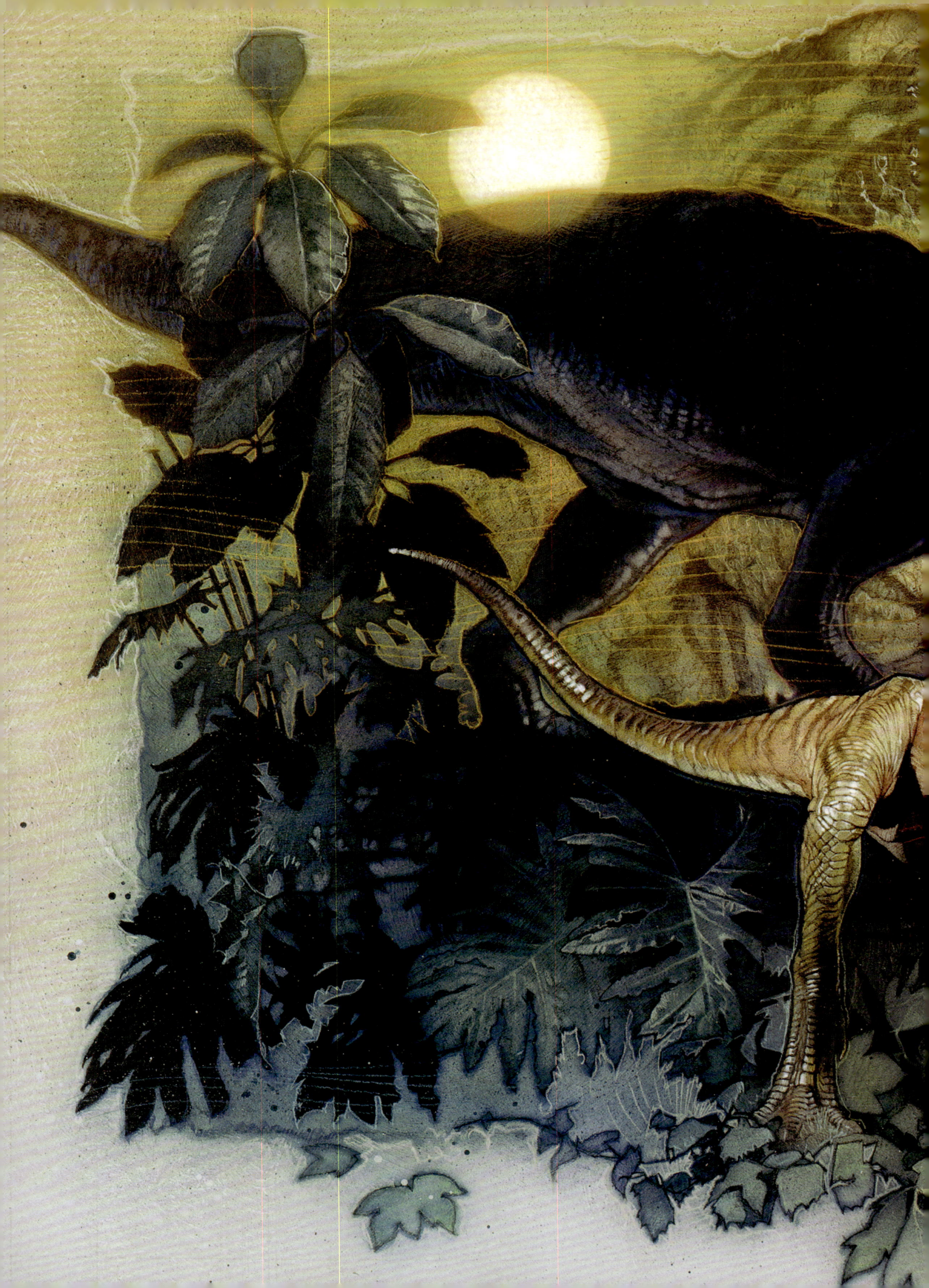

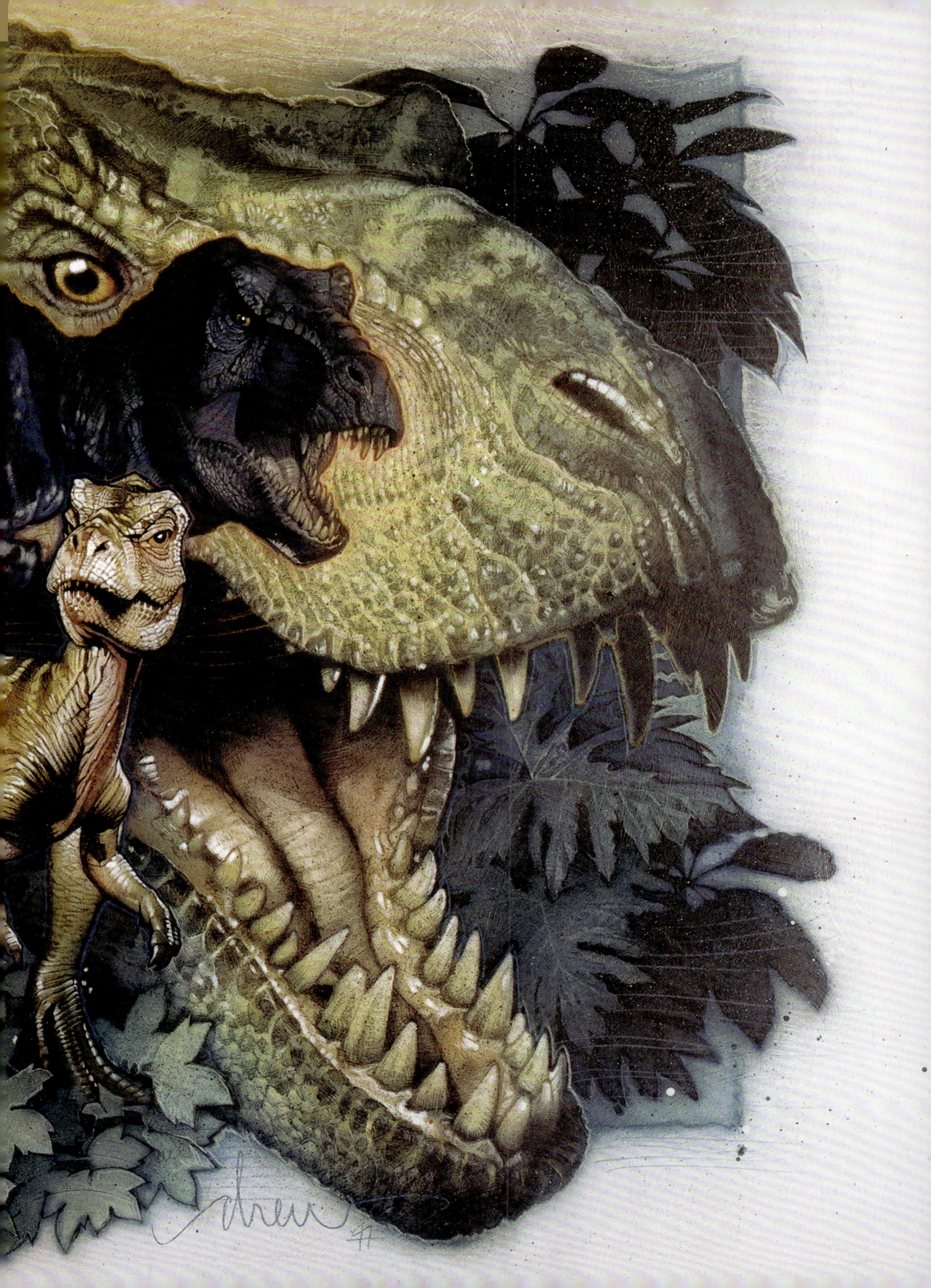

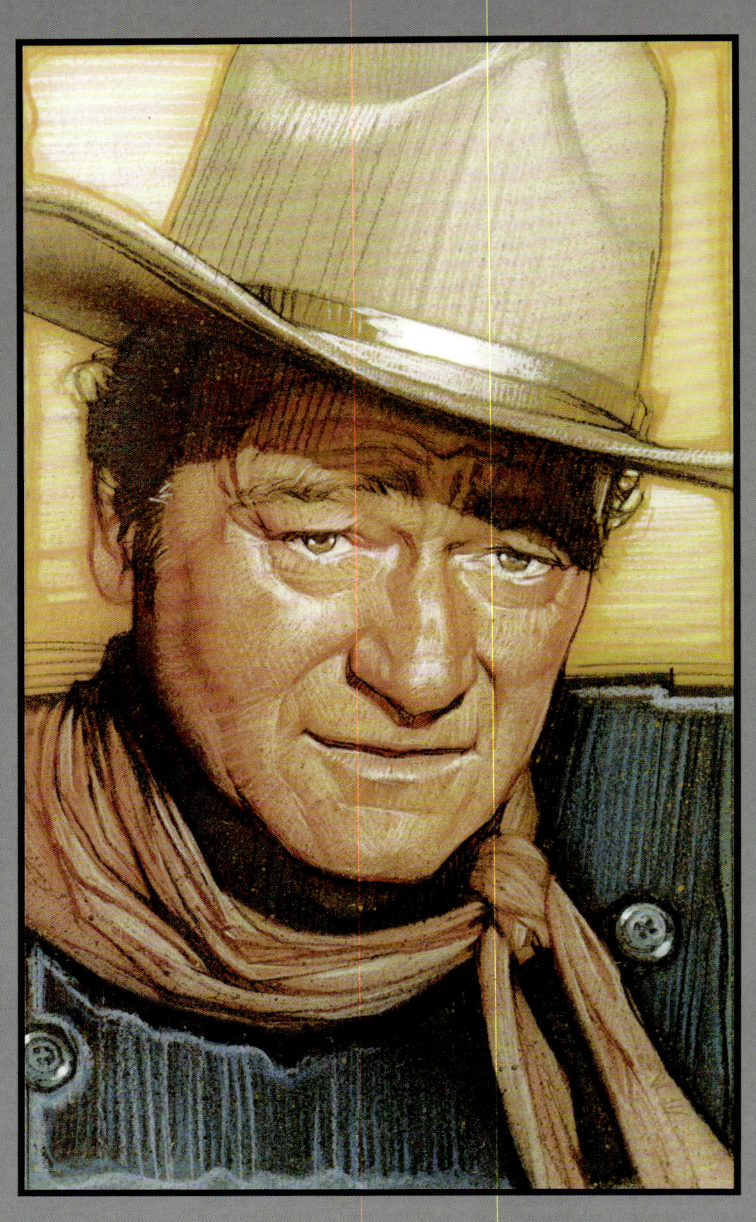

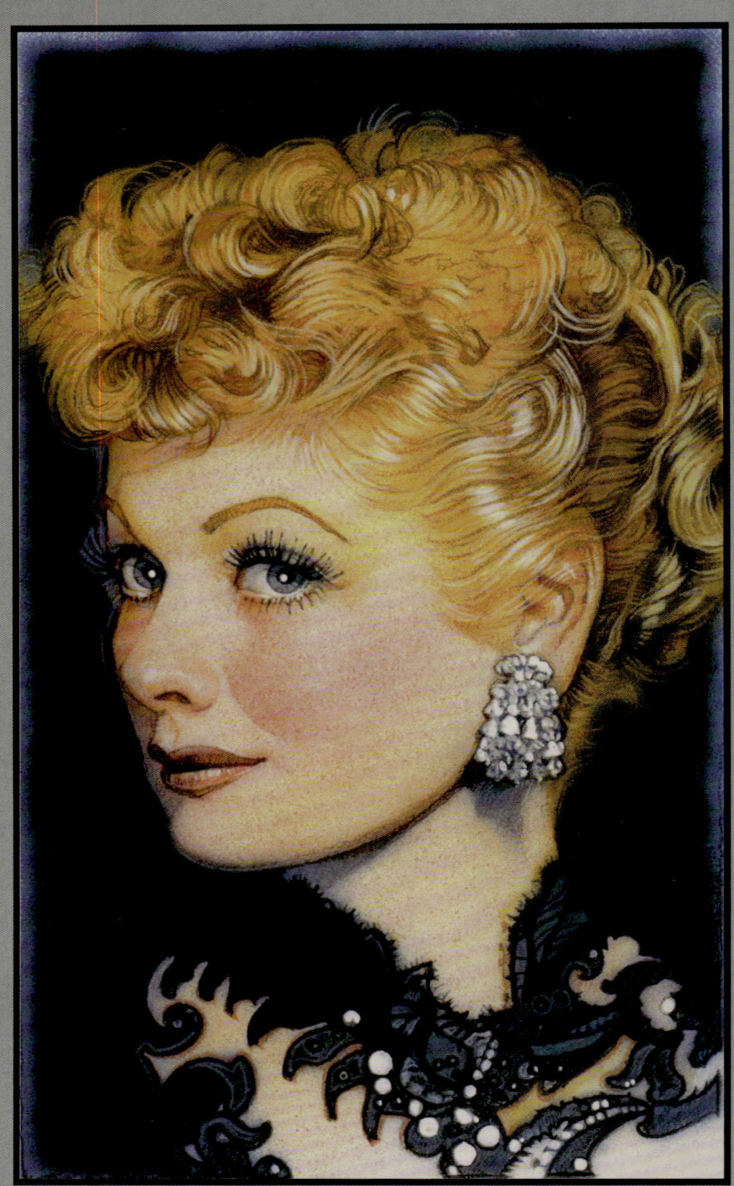

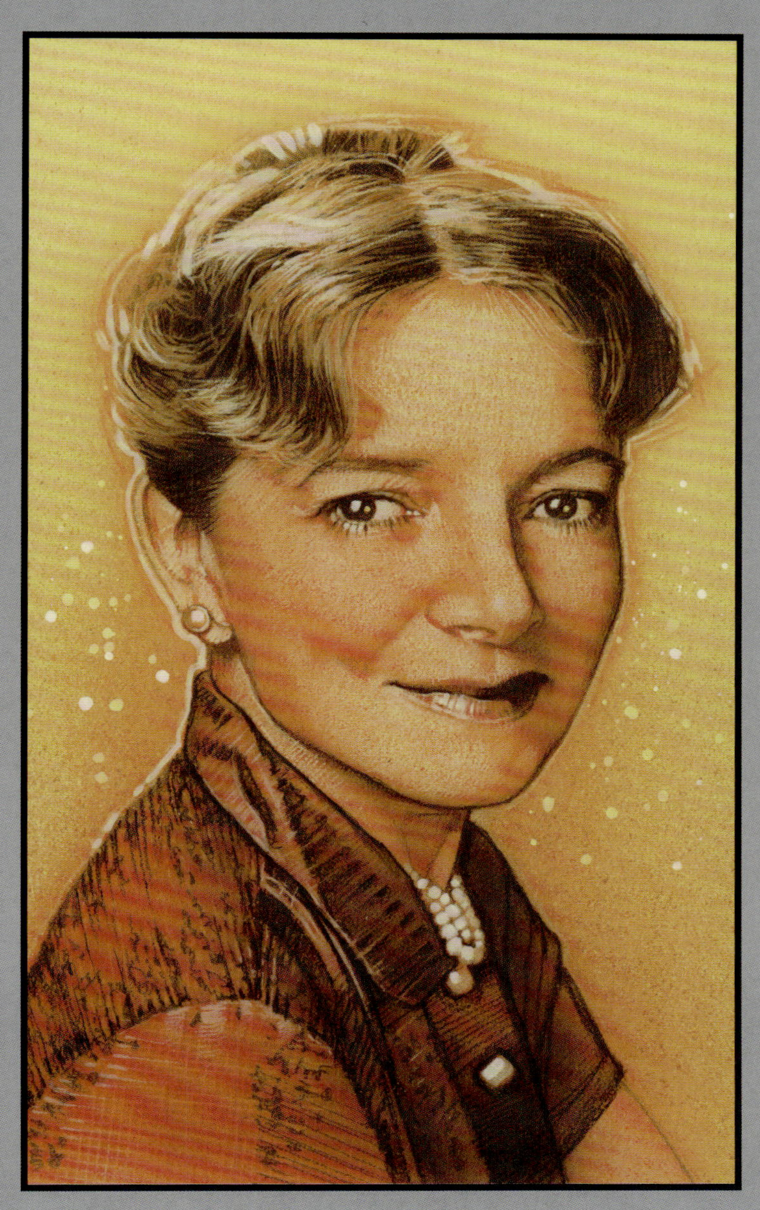

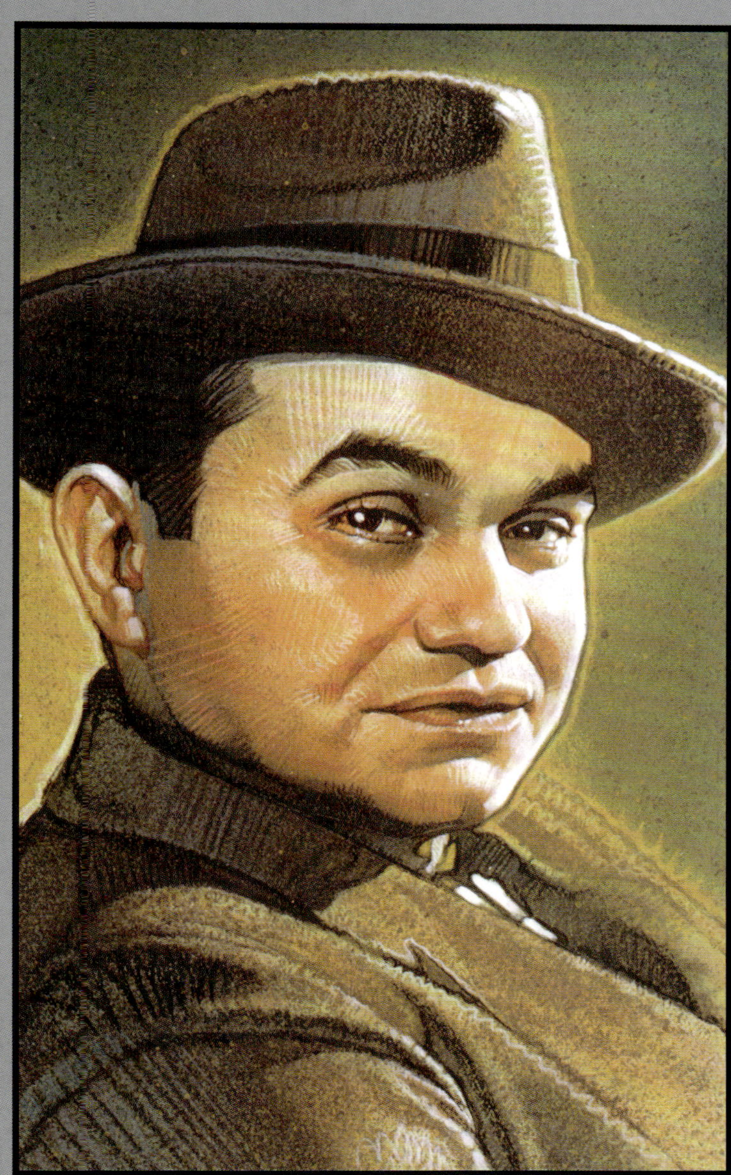

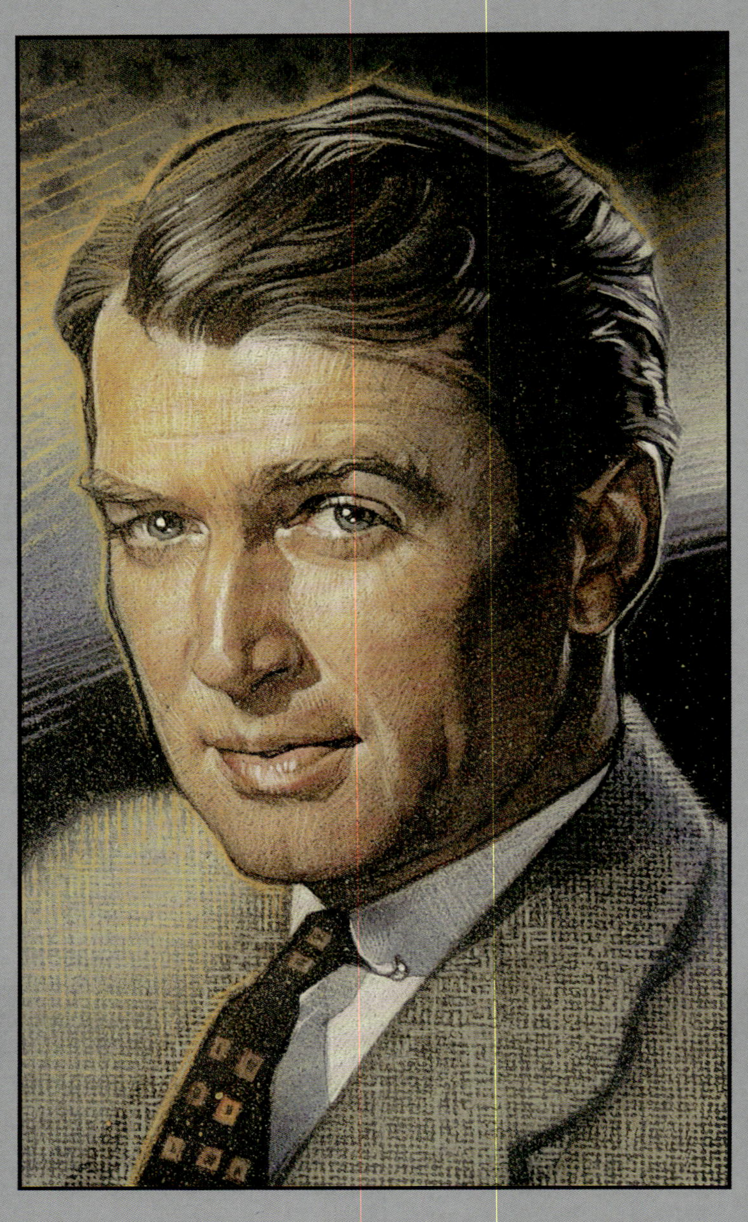

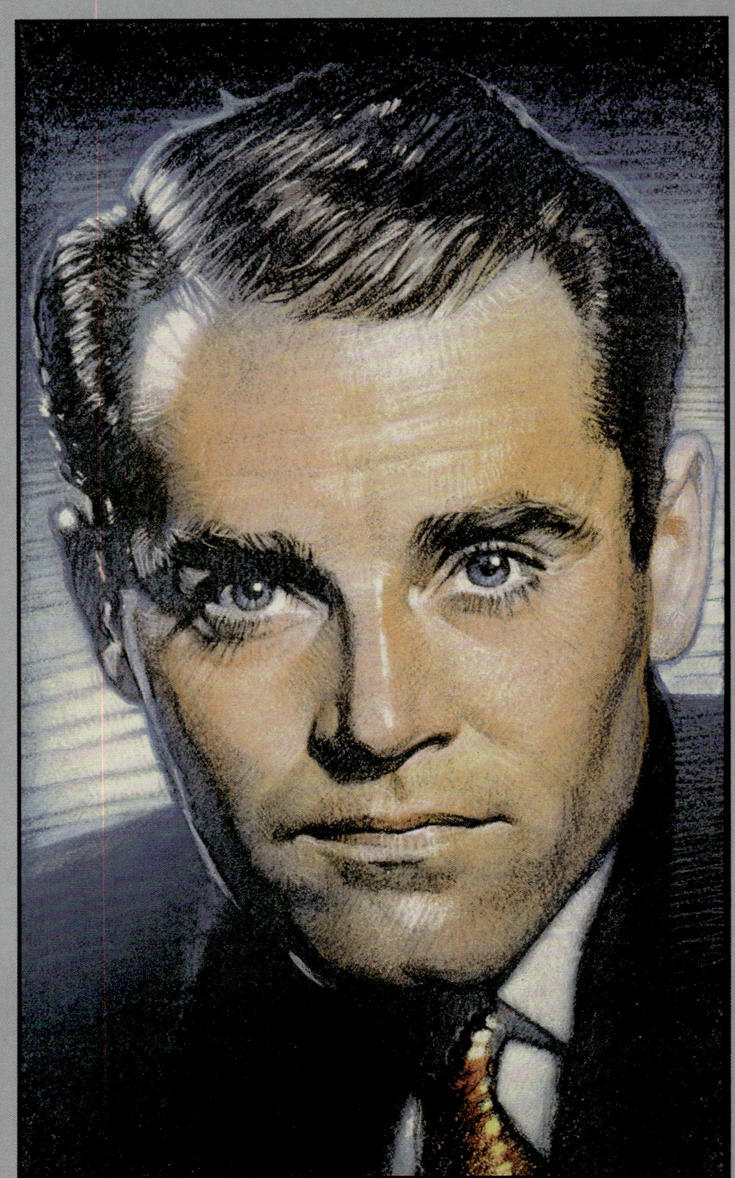

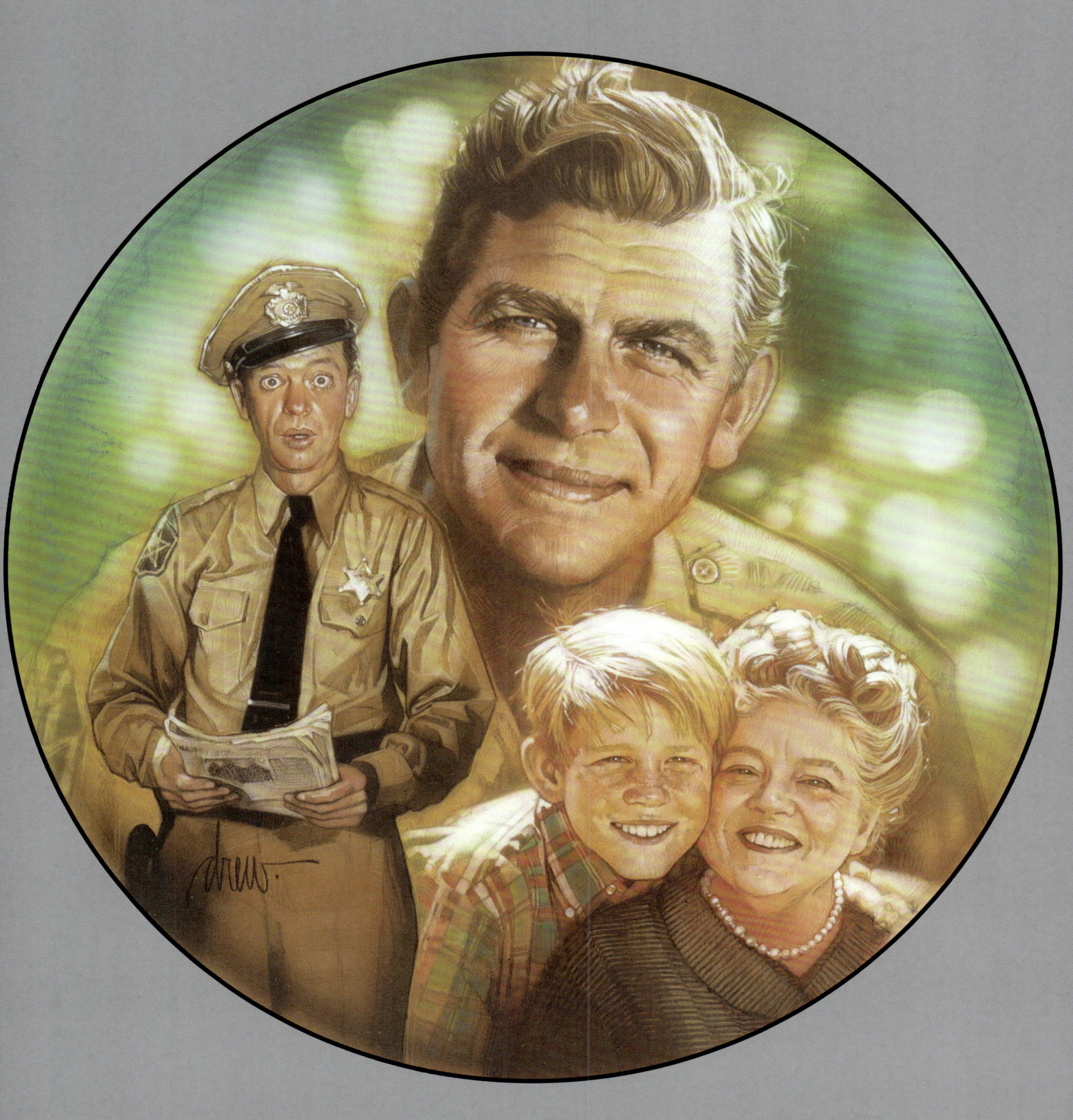
drew.

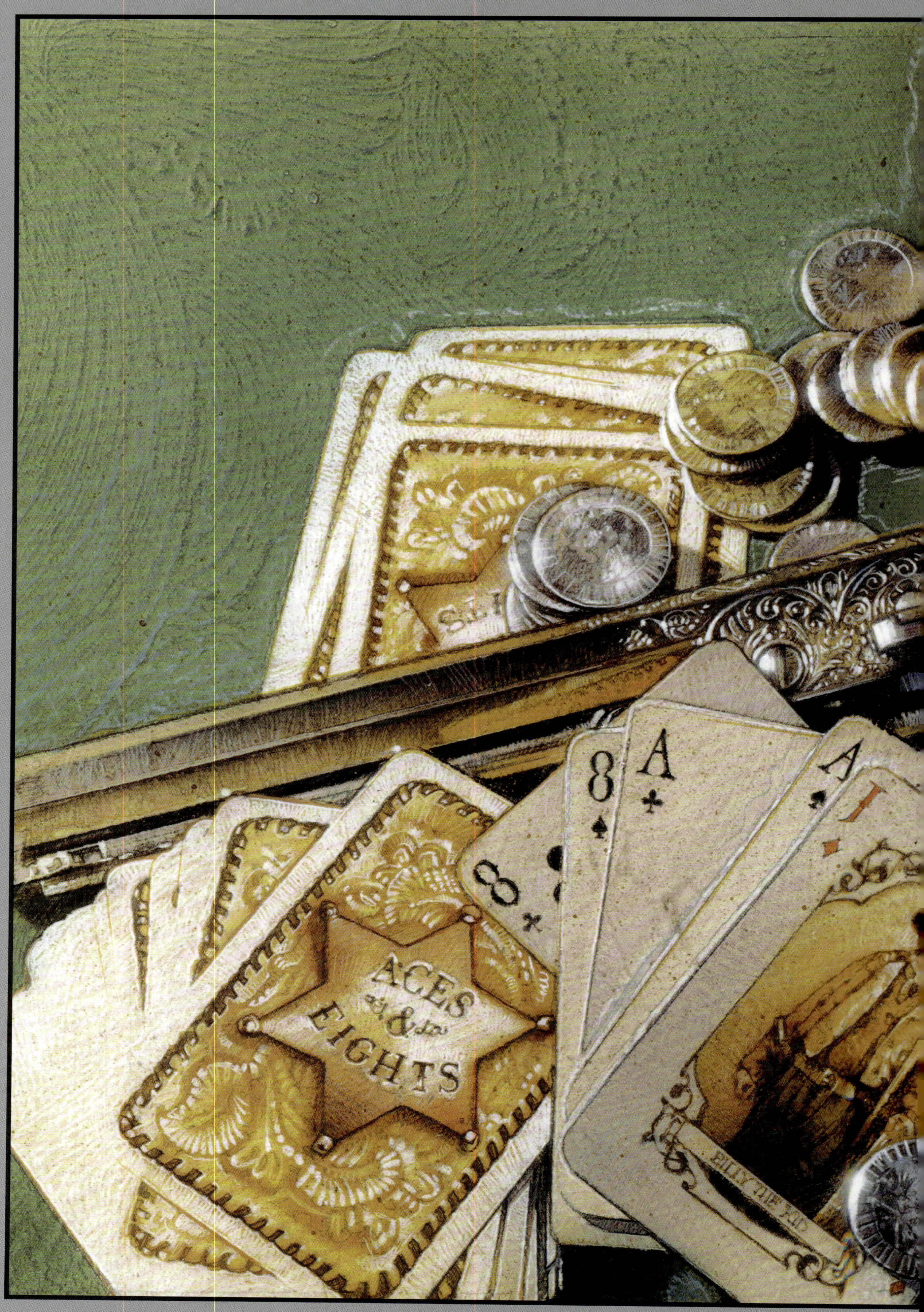
ACES
&
EIGHTS
BILLY THE KID

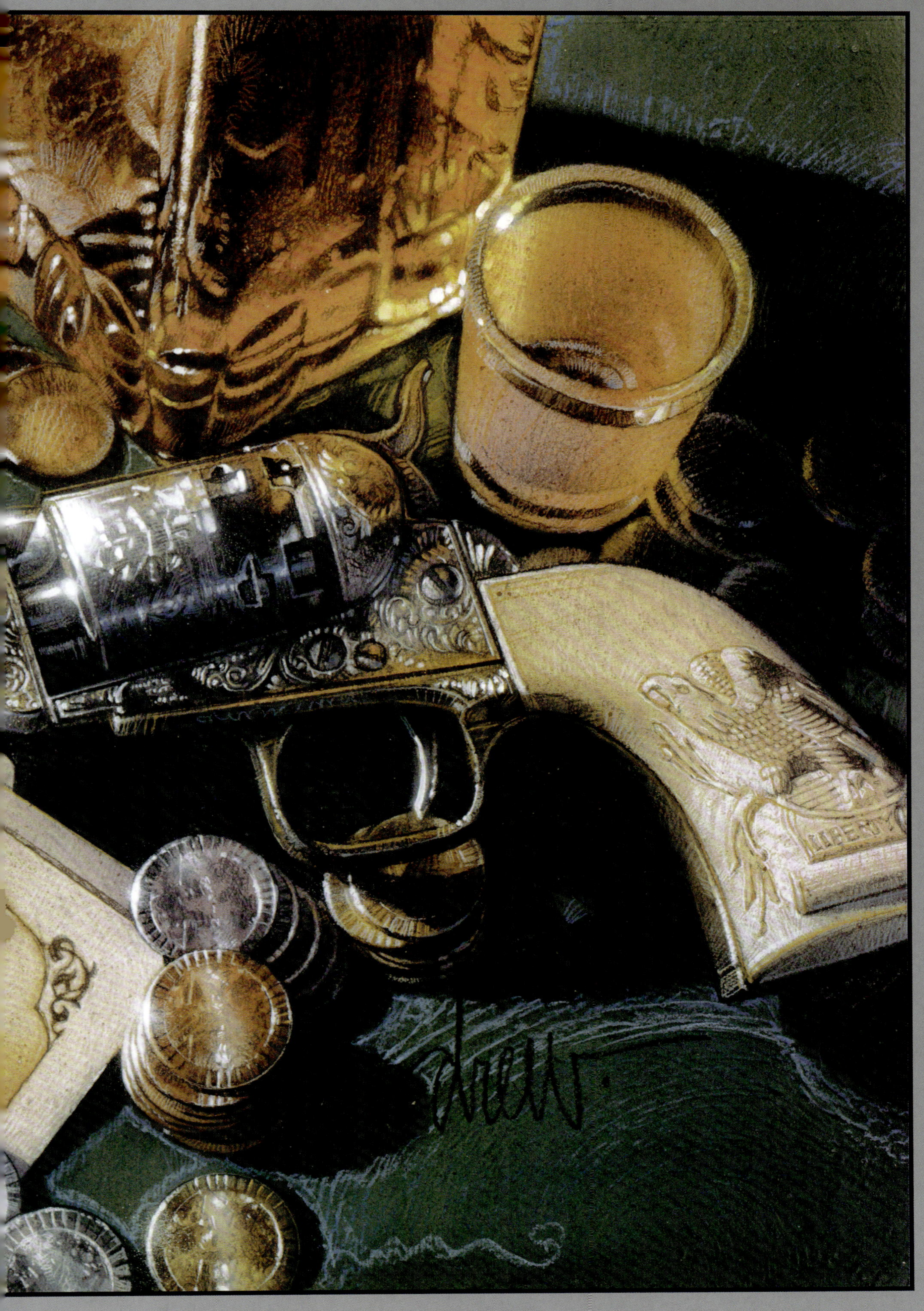

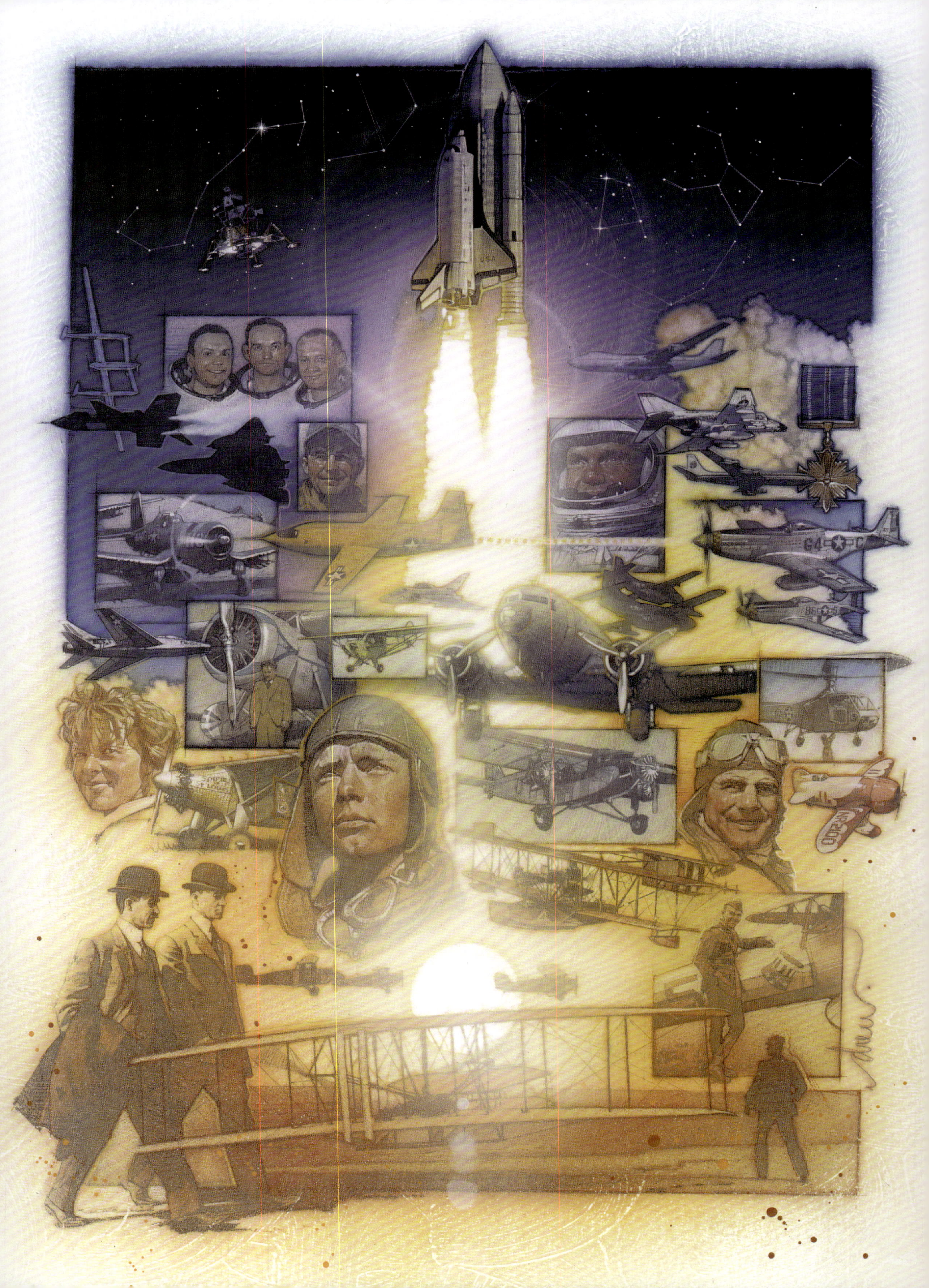

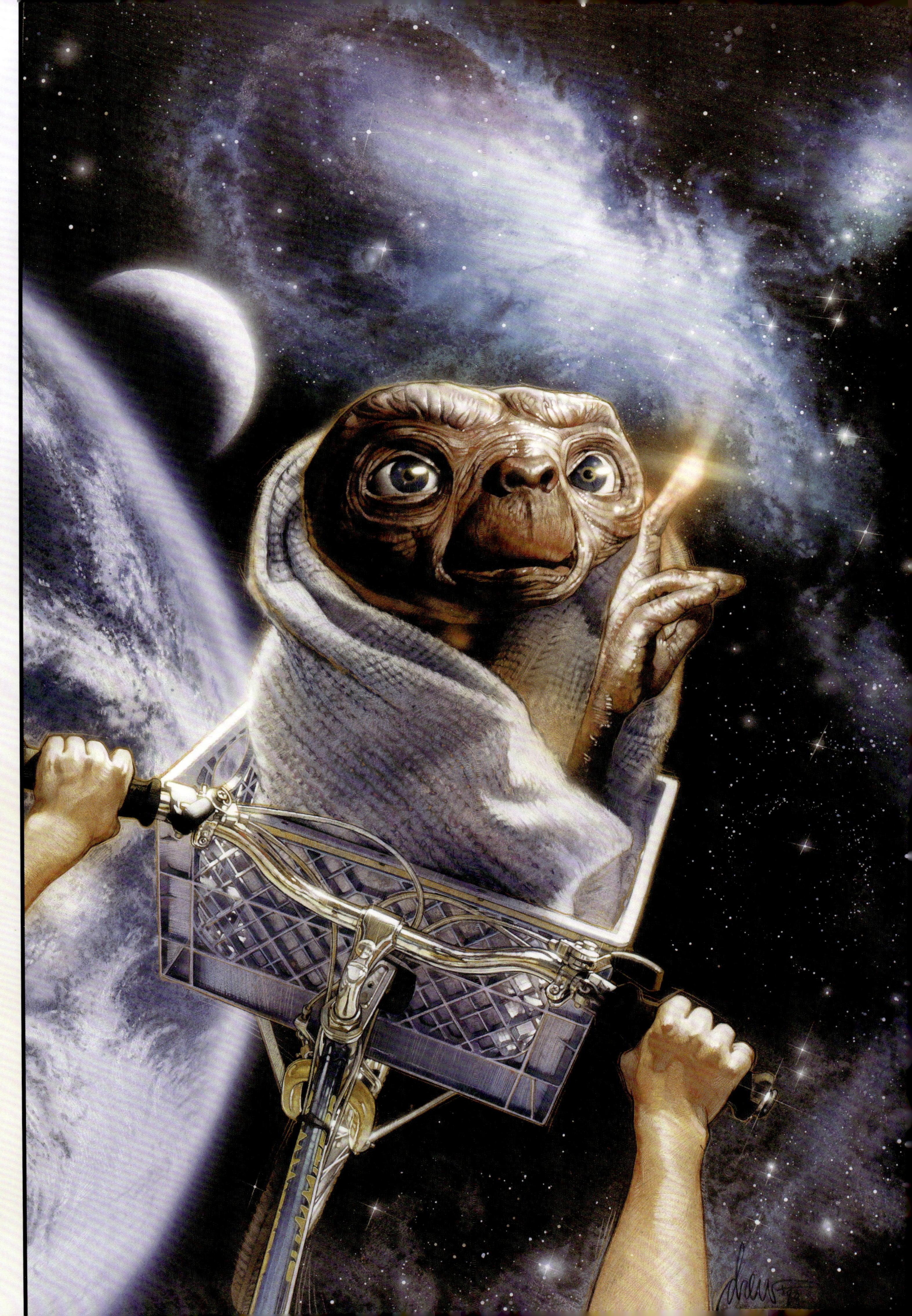

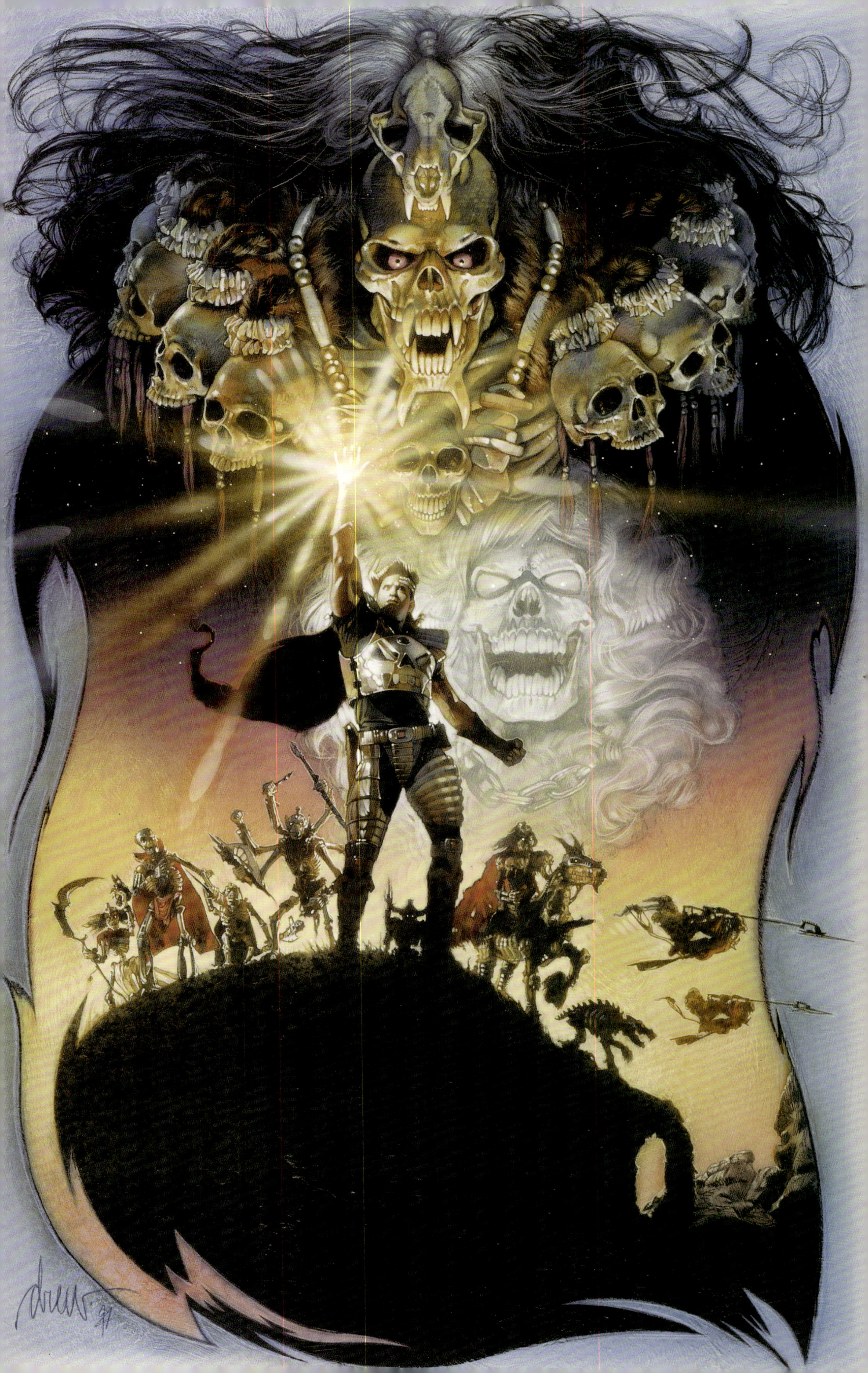

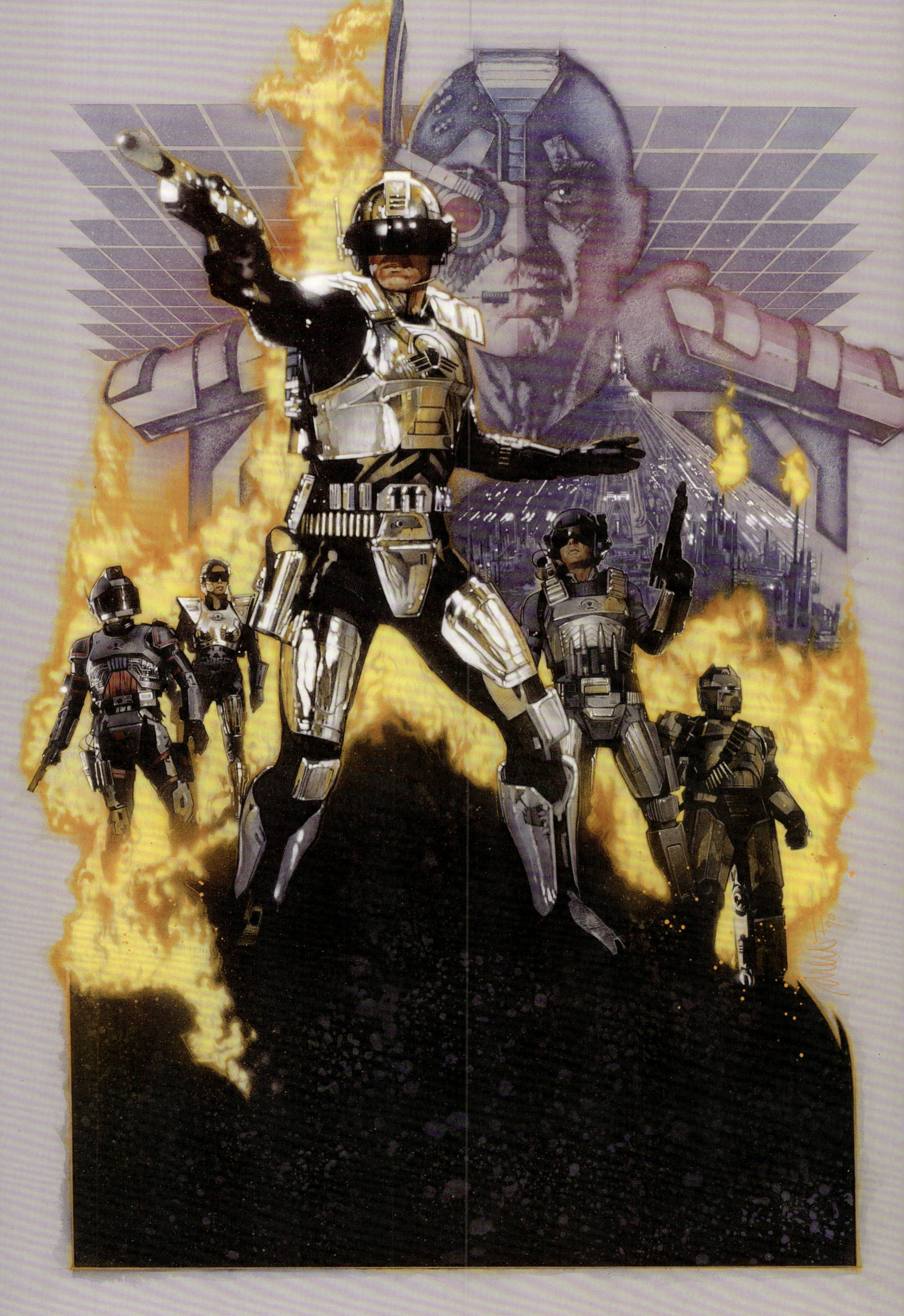

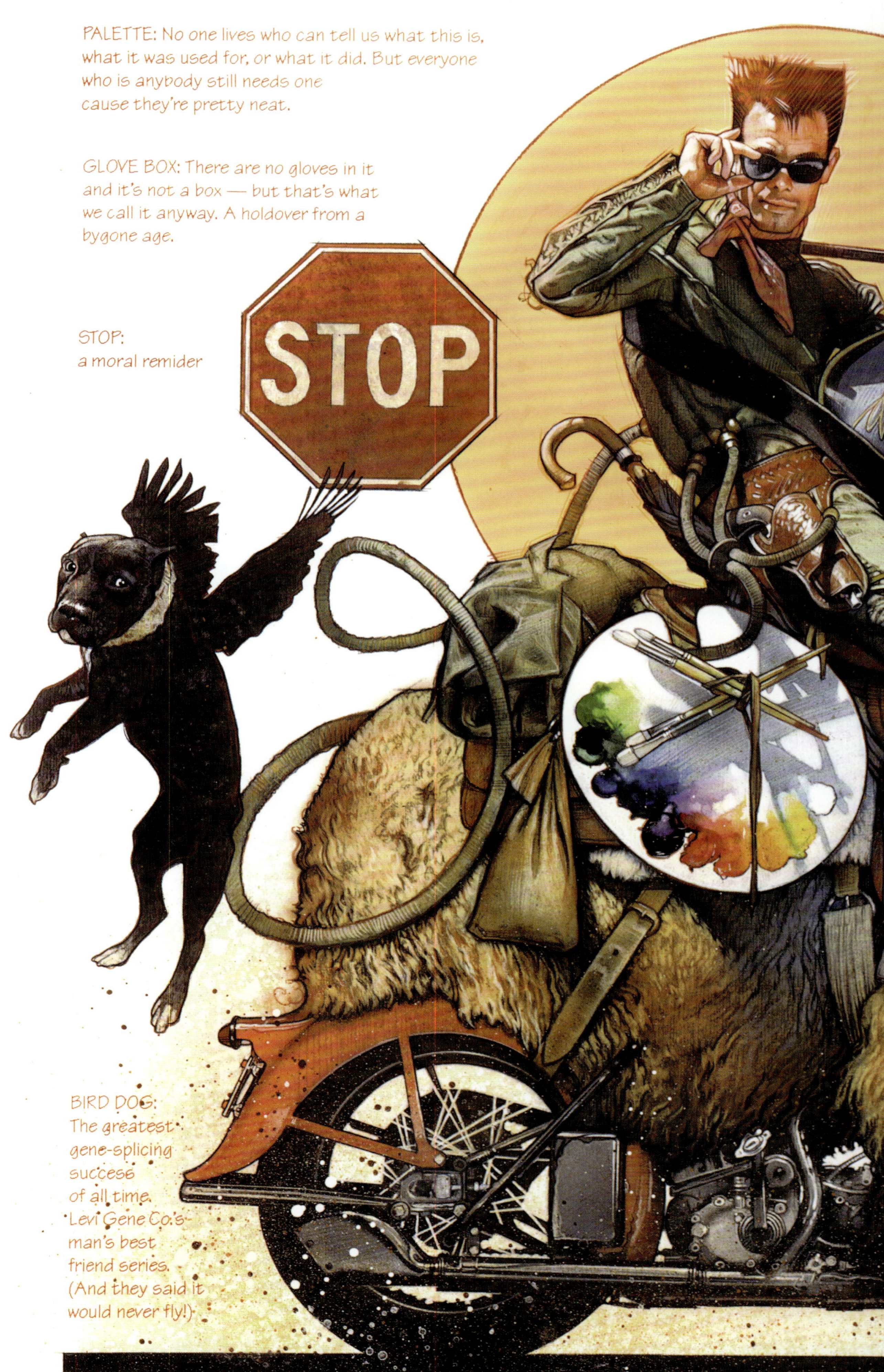

CONCEIVED AND EXECUTED BY DREW STRUZAN

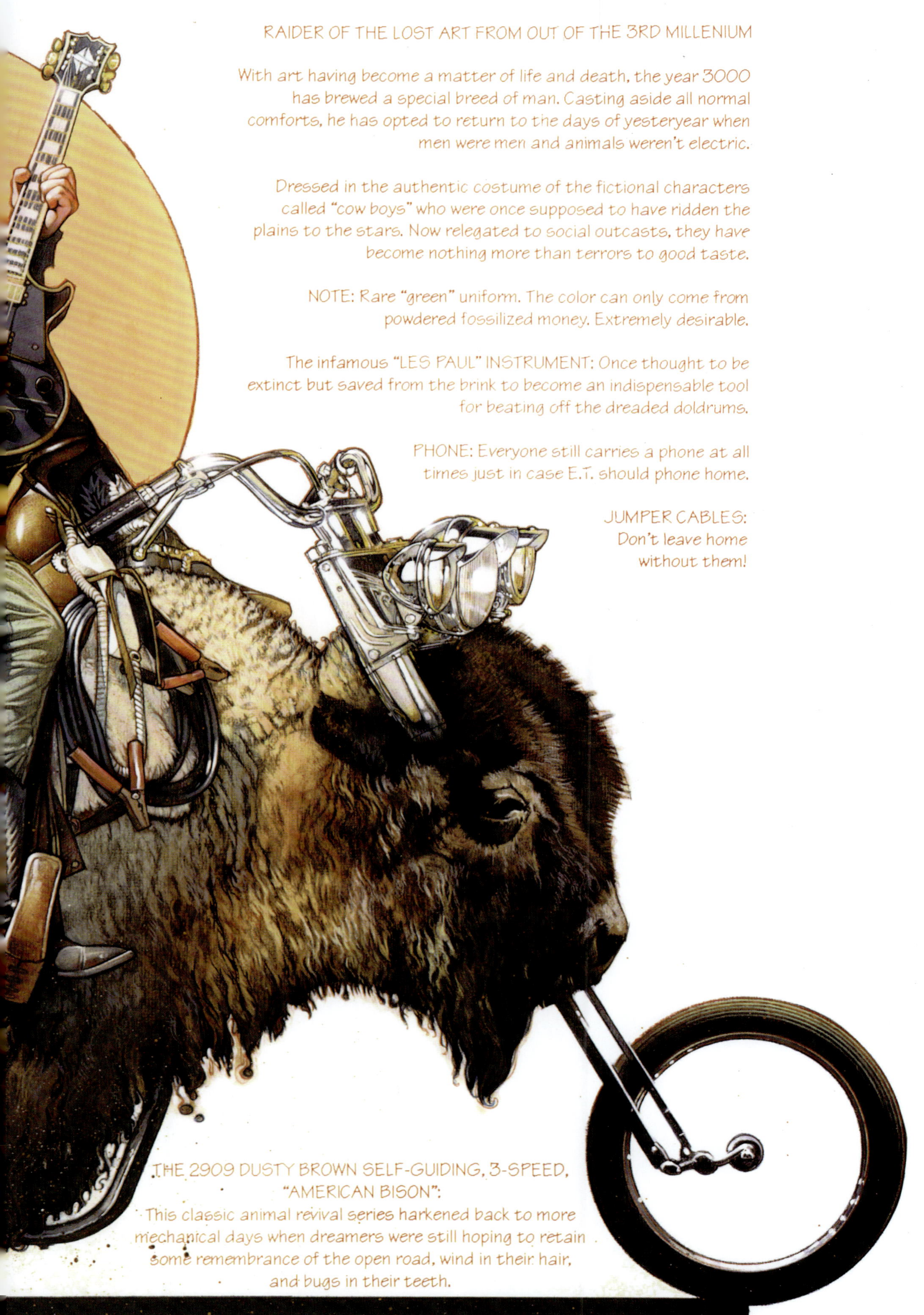

RAIDER OF THE LOST ART FROM OUT OF THE 3RD MILLENIUM

With art having become a matter of life and death, the year 3000 has brewed a special breed of man. Casting aside all normal comforts, he has opted to return to the days of yesteryear when men were men and animals weren't electric.

Dressed in the authentic costume of the fictional characters called "cow boys" who were once supposed to have ridden the plains to the stars. Now relegated to social outcasts, they have become nothing more than terrors to good taste.

NOTE: Rare "green" uniform. The color can only come from powdered fossilized money. Extremely desirable.

The infamous "LES PAUL" INSTRUMENT: Once thought to be extinct but saved from the brink to become an indispensable tool for beating off the dreaded doldrums.

PHONE: Everyone still carries a phone at all times just in case E.T. should phone home.

JUMPER CABLES: Don't leave home without them!

THE 2909 DUSTY BROWN SELF-GUIDING, 3-SPEED, "AMERICAN BISON": This classic animal revival series harkened back to more mechanical days when dreamers were still hoping to retain some remembrance of the open road, wind in their hair, and bugs in their teeth.

RAIDER OF THE LOST ART FROM OUT OF THE 3RD MILLENIUM

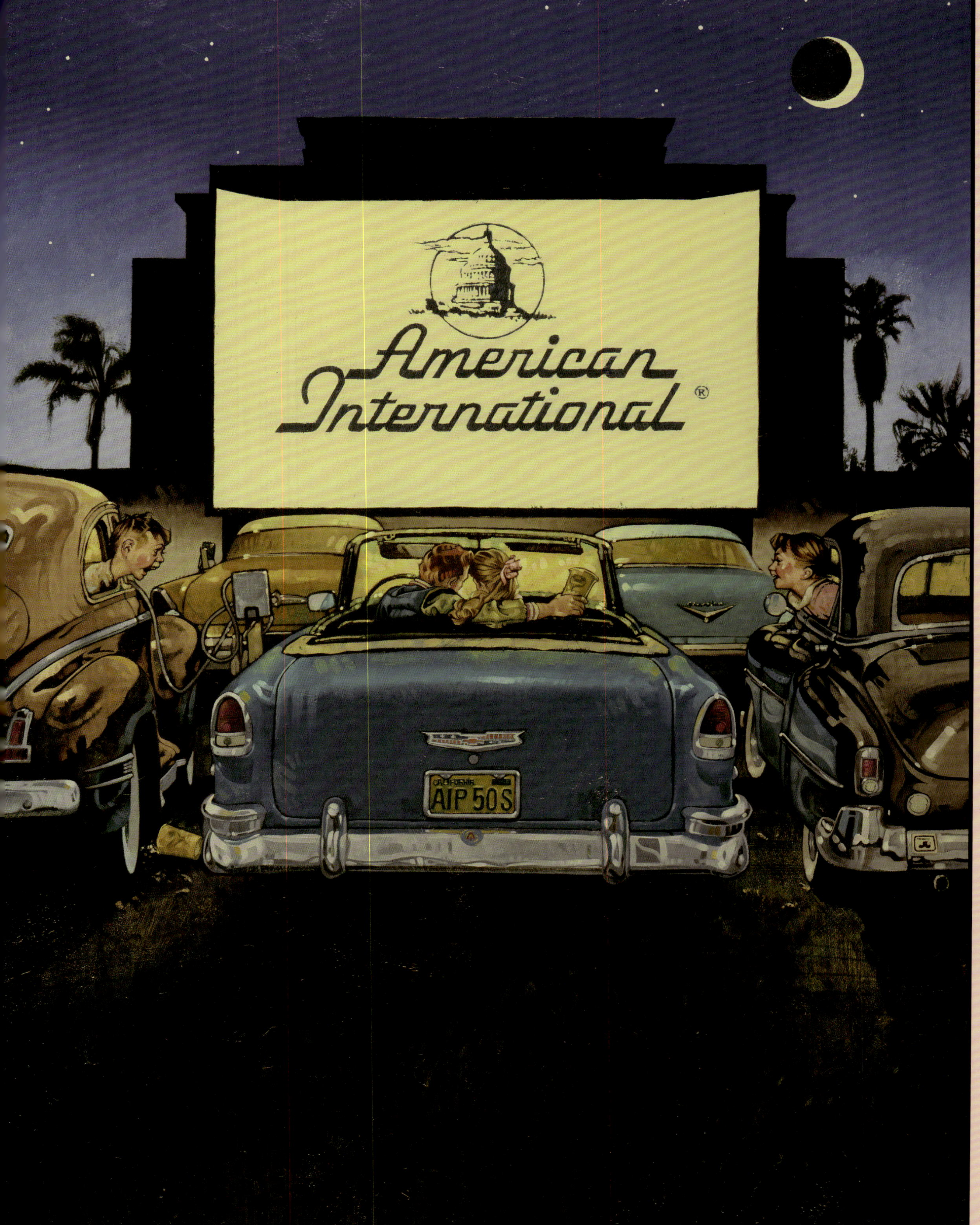
American
International
CALIFORNIA
AIP 50S

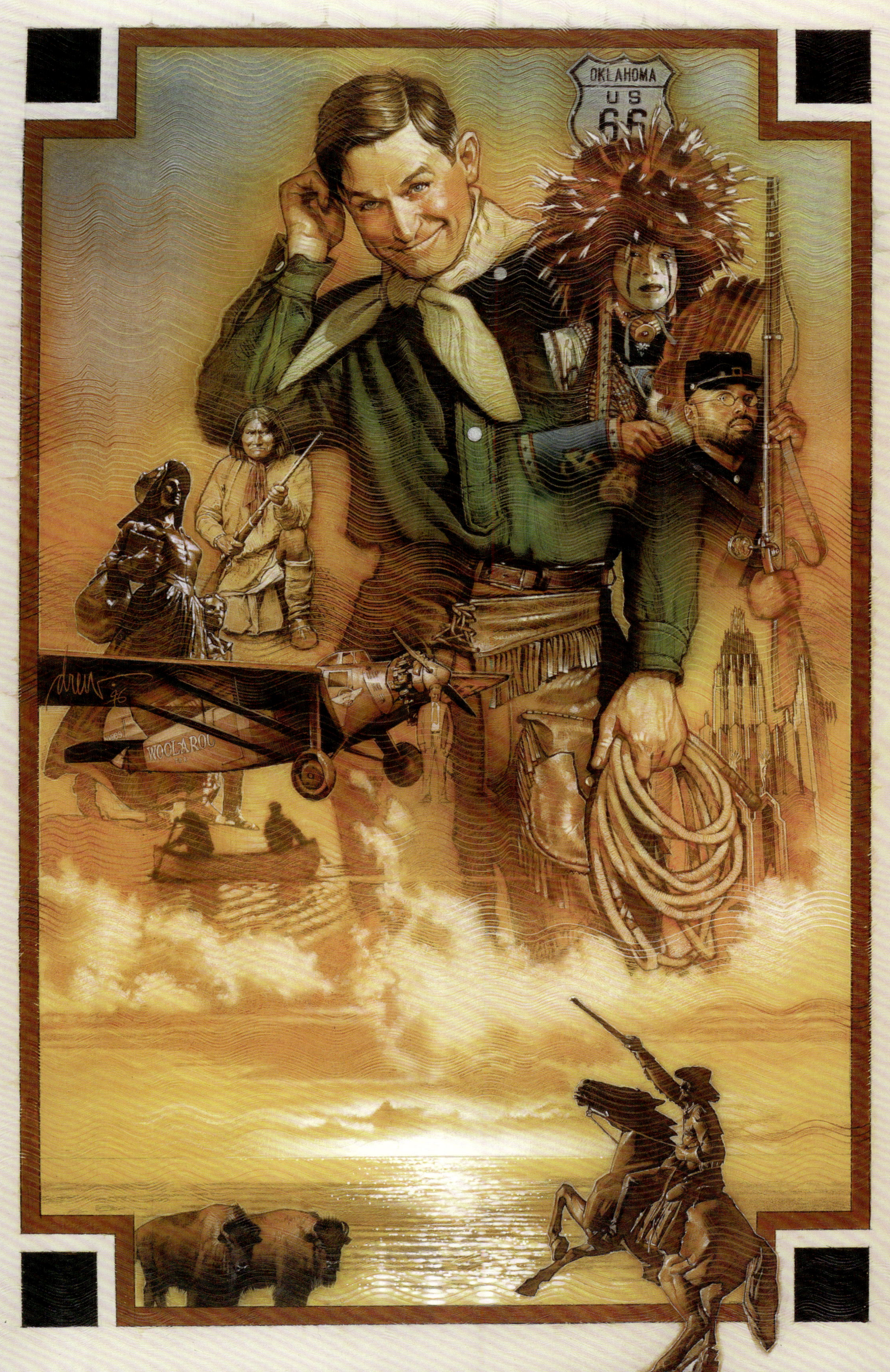
OKLAHOMA
US
66
WOOLAROC

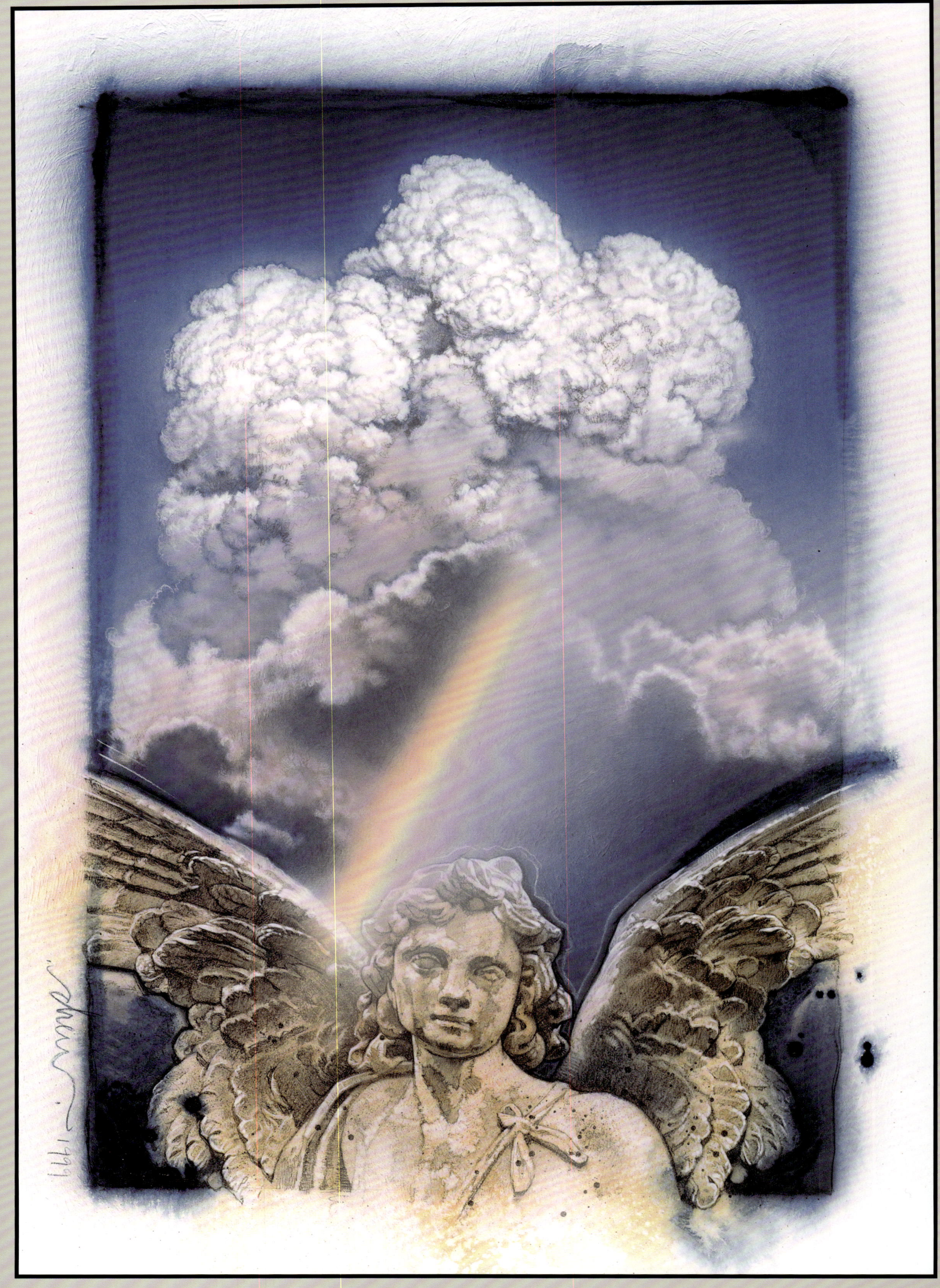

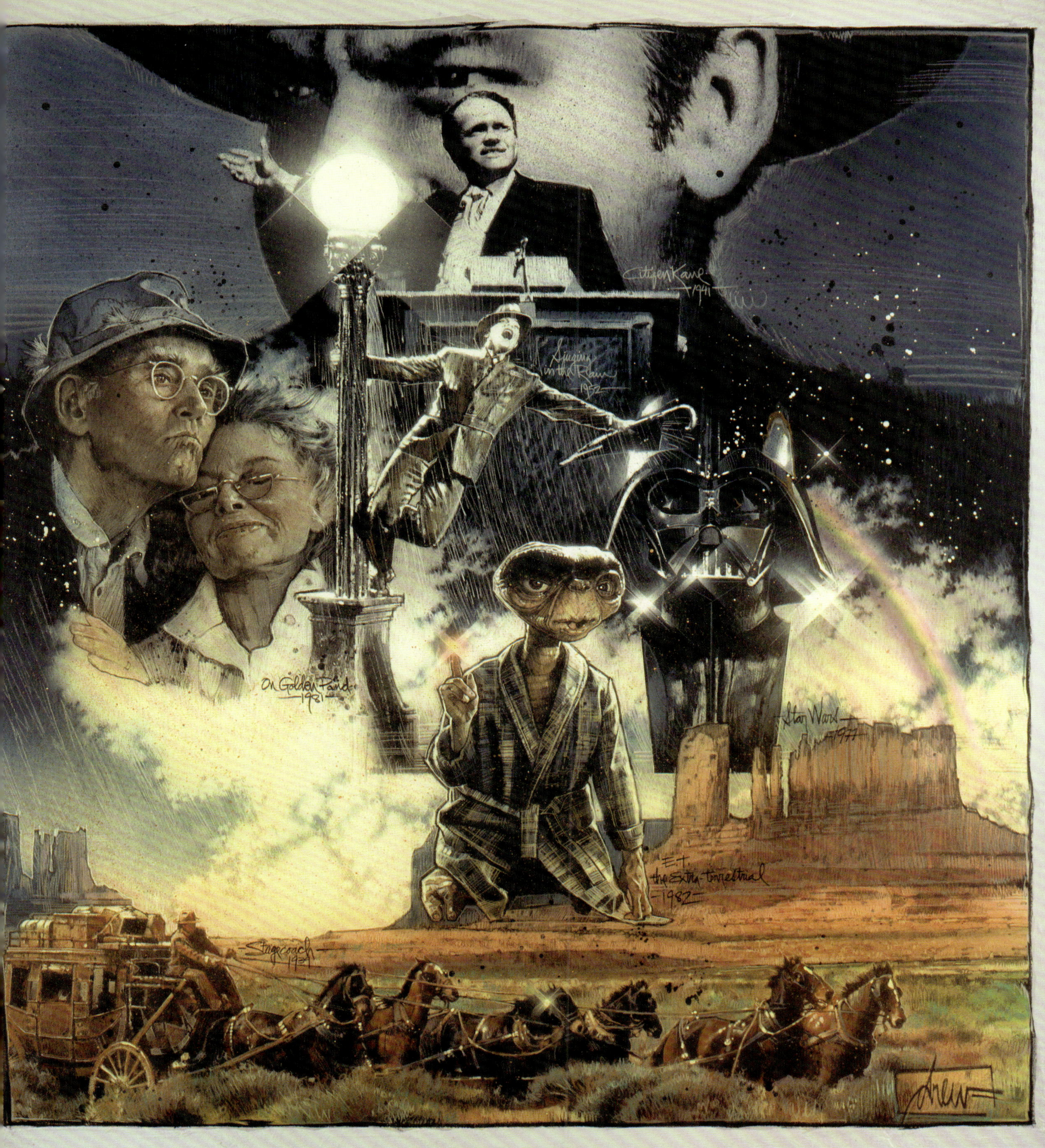

Citizen Kane 1941
Singin' in the Rain 1952
On Golden Pond 1981
Star Wars 1977
E.T. the Extra-Terrestrial 1982
Stagecoach 1939

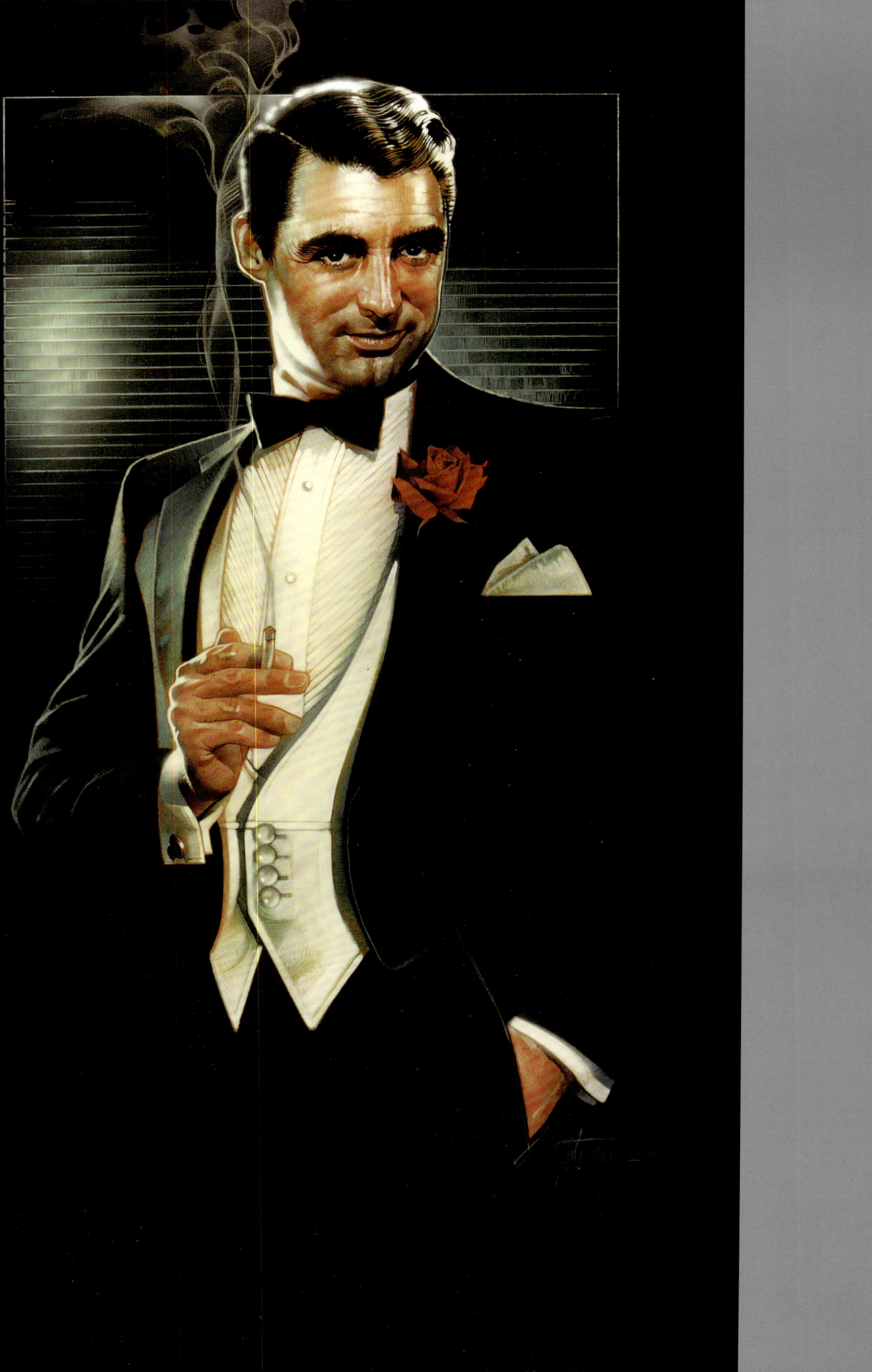

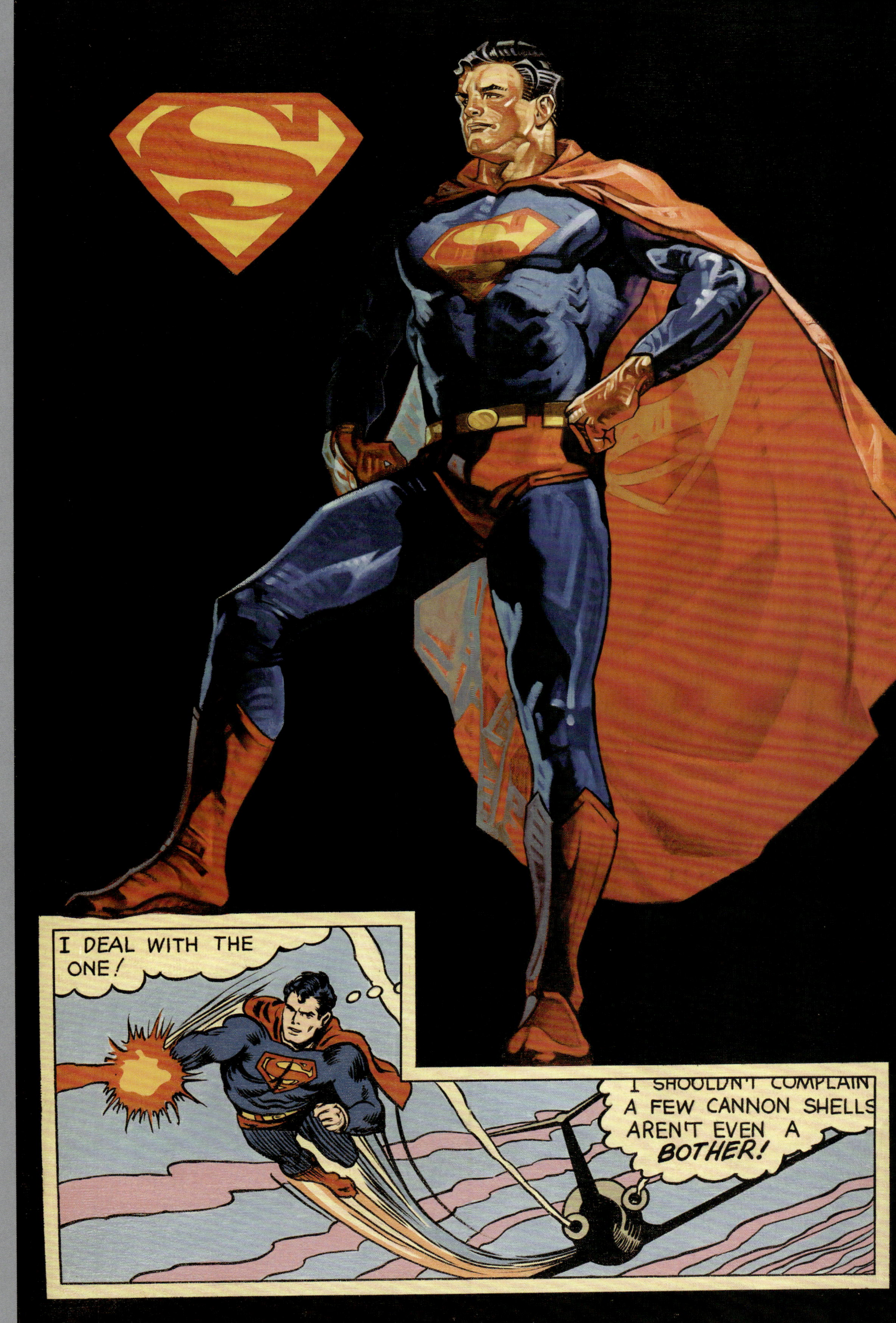
I DEAL WITH THE ONE!
I SHOULDN'T COMPLAIN A FEW CANNON SHELLS AREN'T EVEN A BOTHER!

PERSONAL WORKS

"I would have ideas," Drew says with regard to his personal paintings. "I wanted to fuss with different techniques and mediums. I never really found the time to do as much as I was thinking about, but I painted what I had the time for. I paint because I need to."

His personal work is rarely seen outside of his website. On occasion, these works have been printed in articles and in various books. Sometimes, a painting hangs in a museum show, but, by and large, few people have had the privilege of standing in front of one of his original paintings.

Quiet, reflective, and idealistic, Drew enjoys organizing the world of his canvas not so much for practical reasons, but for aesthetic expression. His orientation toward creativity moves him to transform chaos into a pleasing composition and a thing of beauty. In this way, he expresses the need to make the world a better place in which to live.

One recurring subject in Drew's personal work is the nude. In Drew's case, the nude is the portal that brings the viewer to the artistic experience.

"Historically, in most paintings, nudes are not looking directly at you. The pictures were acts of voyeurism because people were insecure. I understand that some people are still immature when it comes to a painting of a nude," Drew says. "I think of the nude as the most beautiful of creation. To cover the human figure is to repudiate its beauty. To assume the nude is immoral or unrighteous is to deny the nature of the creation."

The over-sized, full-frontal nudity of *Baba Yaga* is a bold statement of the power of the female. The tongue-clickers may attempt to besmirch his artistic reputation, but Drew remains unflappable. Perception plays a large role in the opinions people form. Drew asks the viewer to set aside subjectivity and allow the painting to speak for itself. In his interpretation of Baba Yaga–often defined as the wild woman, the dark lady, or the mistress of magic–she reflects the truth and beauty of womanhood. She has strength. She is fearless. Her physical beauty is unsurpassed. If, by extension, one can see that possibility in all women, Drew will be pleased that the painting has achieved the effect he wanted.

However, while his work speaks of powerful women, his intention is not to transform public opinion. As a mature artist he realizes he cannot please all the people all the time and so he chooses to focus on communicating with those willing to discover the power in the painting.

"The nature of the artist is to face the truth–hard or soft, accepted or not, you must face the truth. Artists often acquire a reputation for being willing to sacrifice for their principles. They don't bend with every breeze. I try to have my roots in truth. From that perspective, I will live or die according to what I perceive to be important and true. My friends are people who have like values, who are dedicated to morality and kindness. Life isn't worth living without those values. They are what make us human. If I was an orator or writer, I would speak or write of those things, but as it is, I'm a painter. As such, I show the value of those traits visually. It is of interest to me that the people who most enjoyed the painting of Baba Yaga were older women who said they loved the painting because it demonstrates that someone finally sees the power innate in women. I'm not one to paint a cuddly woman and make it another object of voyeurism. I've been married for forty-three years now and I can see the wisdom, insight, and great power in women. That power can be used or abused, but when it is used right, it is one of the grandest things in society. I'm sad to say it often goes unused or untapped.

"I've got grandkids now, so I have a new subject," Drew

continues. "My grandson is beautiful physically, probably more beautiful to me because I love him. I painted him riding a horse with the fantasies in his head swirling all around him. I'm trying to take what I feel about him and make a picture of those feelings. It isn't enough to paint his face. He's a little guy on his horse and he's dreaming. He's got power and thought and vision and hopes already. That's what makes children so beautiful. They hold the future and possibility. I also did a picture of him walking hand in hand with his father, my son. That piece is so emotional. It's just a guy and a kid walking along. It is a very small painting but the feeling is enormous. People relate to emotion.

"To express what you think and have the response be an emotional one is exactly the way it should be. The ideas expressed within my personal work are not illustrations in the sense of telling a story. I am attempting to paint a picture just for the sake of the work. The experience is purely visual, a picture about the sense our eyes relay. It is about the beauty of color, the beauty of design, line, shape, texture. The painting is made for the sake of those things.

"The paintings are not anti-illustration. Rather, they are based on personal ideas, personal aesthetics. I'm painting for the love of the paint, the joy of the design, the juxtapositions of positives and negatives, balance and imbalance... all the tools the artist works with to create emotion. It is common in modern art to just use color or shape or a line to express emotion, but that's reducing the concept down to its simplest form, a singular experience. I'm trying to take those pure visual experiences and make them very rich, expressing many things in a painting without making it illustrative. I want the work to come off as powerful and to relate a deep experience to the viewer."

Drew's experience as an artist has taught him that the visual language can definitely be universal in nature. His conclusion is borne out by the worldwide response to his commercial work that people have shared with him. "Overwhelmingly, individuals appreciate the art not just because it is *Star Wars* or Indiana Jones or Harry Potter or *The Shawshank Redemption*. They love the art."

Drew's personal work is not far afield from his commercial work. The compositions of both are strong. The sense of connection between the painted subject and the observer is penetrating. In other words, *Baba Yaga* emits as powerful a gaze as Indiana Jones. The canvas of Drew's personal work is as complete as that of his commercial work. Each painting breathes with a life of its own. Both forms of work are built on precise aesthetic principles.

When asked to define art, Drew argues that it can't be done. "To try to define in words what is a visual experience does an injustice to the power of the medium." Nonetheless, Drew eschews art created for shock value. "Once you've seen it, the shock is over." He dismisses art that relies on rhetoric to make its point, preferring instead to let the work speak for itself. The voice he implants is something he thinks everyone should appreciate, the value of love, peace, truth, and beauty.

"This is my goal. Again, looking at nudes, not everybody is going to get it. I know that, but I'm trying to say, 'Can you see this for the love of it because I see it that way?' That's what I've used in my pictures all along, but in my personal work, I'm doing it without the connection to a hit movie or a great book or beautiful music. Can I create art without that connection? Can the untrained eye appreciate the expression of an aesthetic purpose or does it need the emotional layer of another work to connect to the picture. I don't believe the latter is true. I paint the human form for the beauty of it. The figure may draw the viewer into the painting, but then, and hopefully very quickly, the focus becomes the line or texture or pure art of the painting. Other interests take over. I do think it is working. I explore a concept and then I move on.

"My commercial illustrations changed over time, too. They changed with subject matter and, if you look at the different periods, you see that they changed technically, too. Although I found a practical way of accomplishing my work as an illustrator, I still changed the way I composed or colored or even rendered."

There is little difference between Drew's commercial work and his personal work because it was never his intention to paint an illustration in the classical sense of painting a scene from a movie or book or magazine article as many illustrators before him had done. His illustrations are meant to capture something different, the spirit of the idea of the story or storytelling.

In the illustration produced for *Coming to America*, it is a given that Eddie Murphy's character is not a thousand feet tall, but his stature–straddling the streets of New York–provides an immediate glimpse at his character. Compare that with the painting of Baba Yaga. "She is the pure feeling of power and beauty," explains Drew. "I didn't set out to paint the story of Baba Yaga. The title was an afterthought that describes the final product. I'm inspired by beauty, so I started out by painting a beautiful woman. She is full-frontal and larger than life, but once I had her on the canvas my feeling was that it just wasn't enough of a statement. She sat in the garage for two years. Eventually I pulled out the painting thinking I would throw it away, but instead brought it into the studio and put it on the easel. A few minutes later, without much conscious thought, I had a tube of red paint in my hand and a big brush and within five minutes I had painted the skull right over the top of everything. It put power alongside the beauty. When I saw it, I said, 'That's it.' *Baba Yaga* took weeks to paint but only five minutes to finish."

The Gray Lady was much the same. She started as an elegant figure on a sienna background. It was pretty, but docile. One day, Drew attacked the painting. He painted squares and inserted a Mexican devil mask and suddenly there was something else going on. The spark that ignites the emotion is the relationship between the beauty and the devil mask. That catalyst prompts questioning. Something is happening in the picture, but it is up to the viewer to figure what that something is.

Drew relies on the same intuitive leaps to breathe life into his illustrations. When he meets with his clients and discusses their film, he immediately conceives the illustration that ultimately becomes the image used for the poster. "I don't go home and pound my brain and intellectually decide what to do. Even when I do dozens of comps [in-work sketches and rough illustrations], it is usually that first flash of 'that's what this is about' that winds up as the poster.

"A painting opens a door to questions that remain unanswered except in your own heart," Drew says. "An illustration sets up a possibility of events, the culmination of which is fulfilled in the movie. In a painting, I'm not telling a story or creating a concept. I'm setting up a situation that makes you want to find out what's going on here. Open the door. I say, what you find inside is who you are. I'm not telling you who you are. I'm setting up the situation that prompts questions about who you are. Whatever is set up in your mind is what will arise. The paintings are open-ended because I am open-ended. I want to set up a situation that makes people feel things and, in the feeling, start to examine their response."

Drew's strong connection to an inner value system struggles against a world of facts and figures in an effort to bring something of greater value to the world. For Drew, the expression "beauty is truth and truth is beauty" is not merely an argument put forth in a Keats poem. It is a truth that he holds dear and that he seeks to express to the world in purely visual terms. In terms of temperament (as defined by Myers/Briggs), he aims to bring peace and integrity to his world and to the world around him. In some sense, he has done just that through personal and commercial works that help us all to see the deeper, often idealized, layer of our humanity.

He insists he does not want to explain his paintings and often shies away from titling them for fear an explanation or title will remove an integral part of the viewer's experience of self-reflection. The exploration is what excites him. The painting comes alive whenever it is viewed. It changes as the person viewing it changes. "It is always giving back to you. I believe this is what life is all about. Keep moving. Keep opening new doors."

And Drew keeps moving in his pursuit of understanding. As the author Doris Lessing once suggested, "If you want to know about something, write about it." The same can be said for visual communication. The process of creation forces one to examine the issues by putting them into a context. "Give it a shot. Run it up the flagpole and see if it flies. That's why it doesn't bother me to wait and see what a painting needs, what has yet to be done. That's the nature of the job of creating.

"Every time I talk with another artist or a writer or a director, I find the actions required for creation are the same. Whether I'm painting an illustration or a personal piece, the process is the same. The spirit, the thought, the values are the same. Everything comes from the same mind. It takes intellect to do the work, but the end product is always about the beauty and power of feeling. Don't you find truth beautiful?" he argues. "It isn't teddy bears and birdies beautiful, but principles, ideas, and morals are definitely beautiful and there is power in that beauty. That's what I would like people to see in the work."

From hundreds of responses that Drew has received from people around the world, they are seeing that and more.

Perhaps Michael J. Fox put it best when he said, "You may not know Drew, but if you love his art, you love Drew."

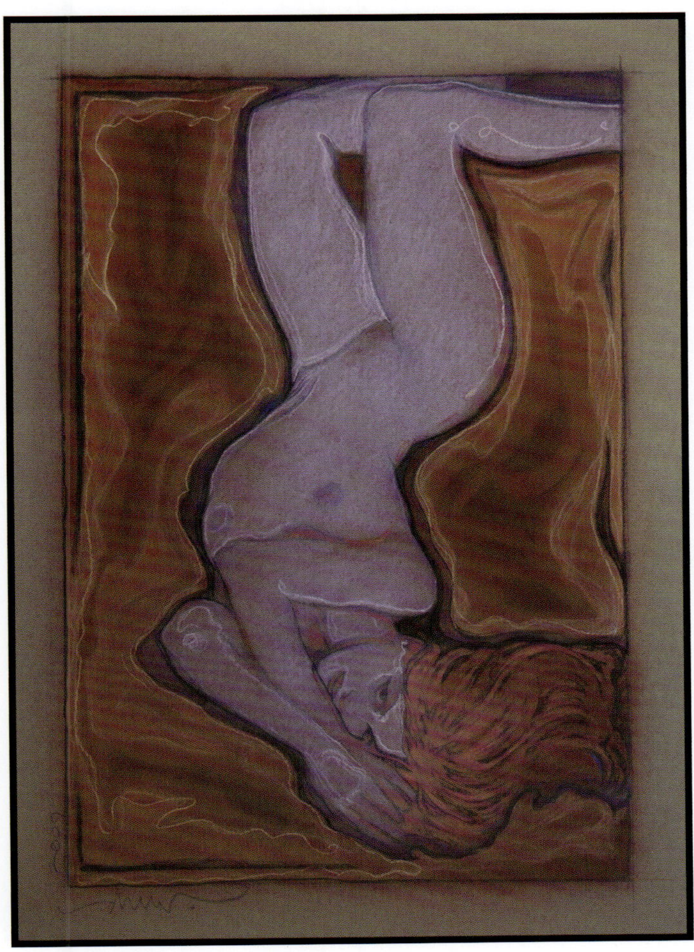

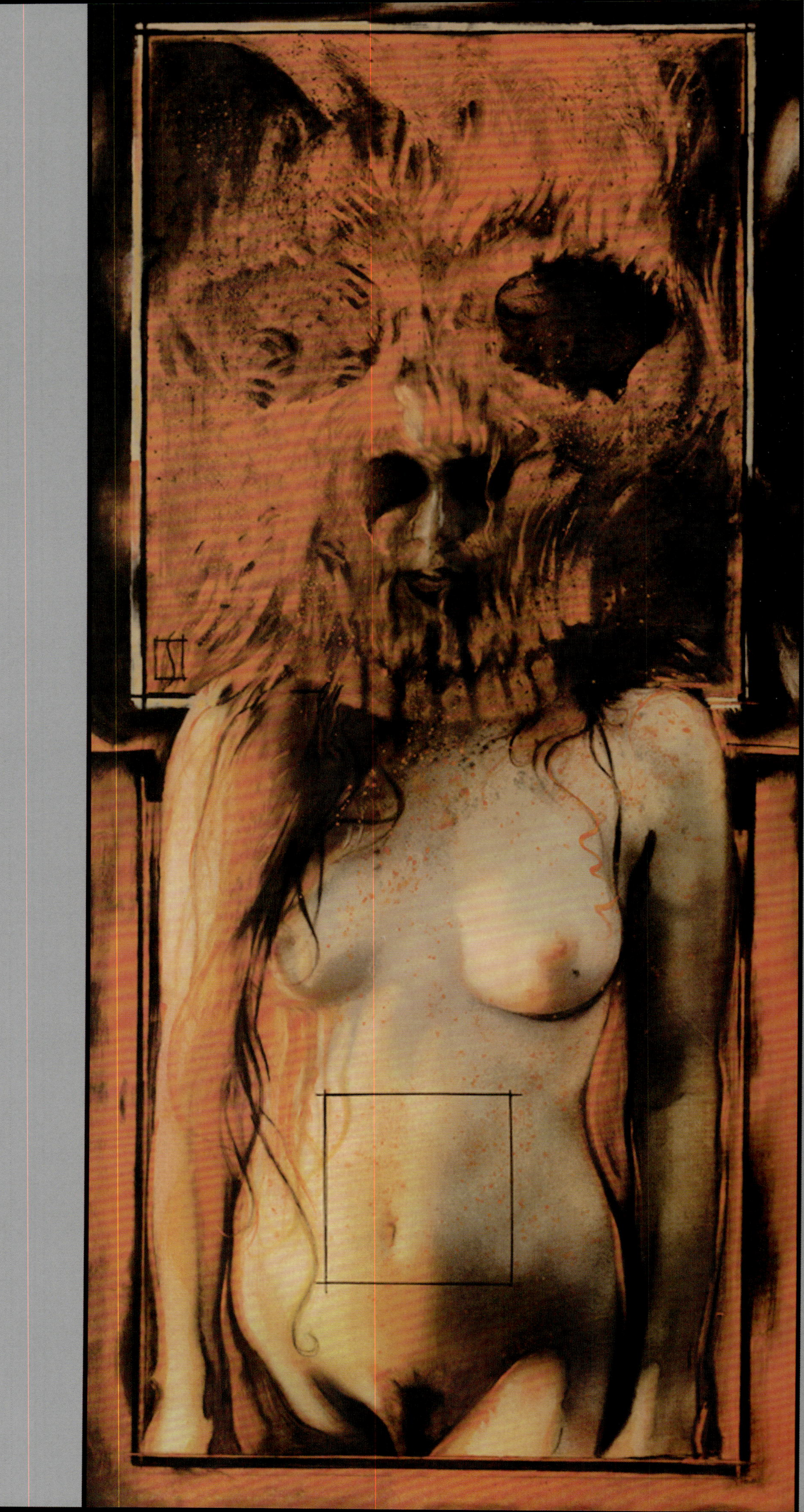

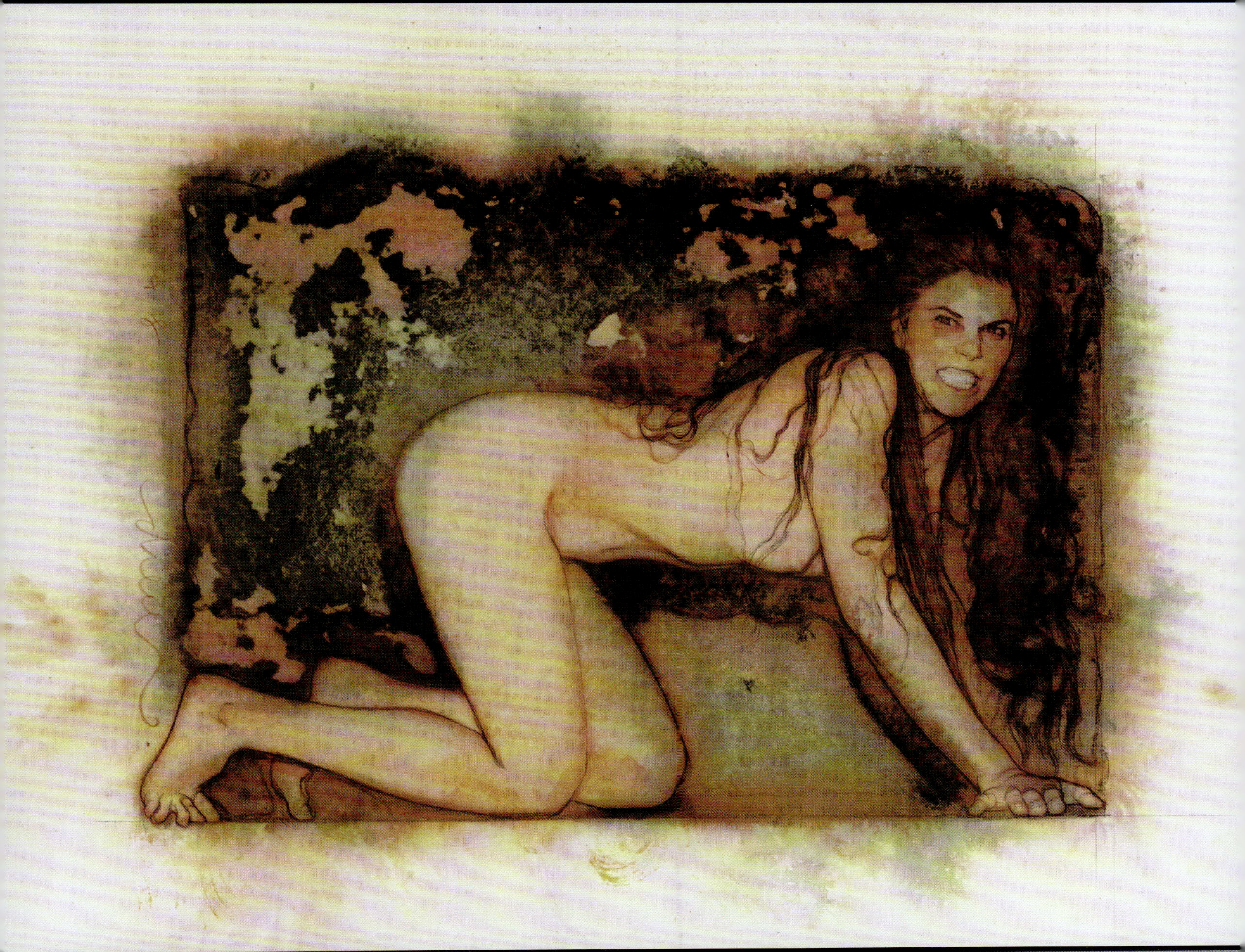

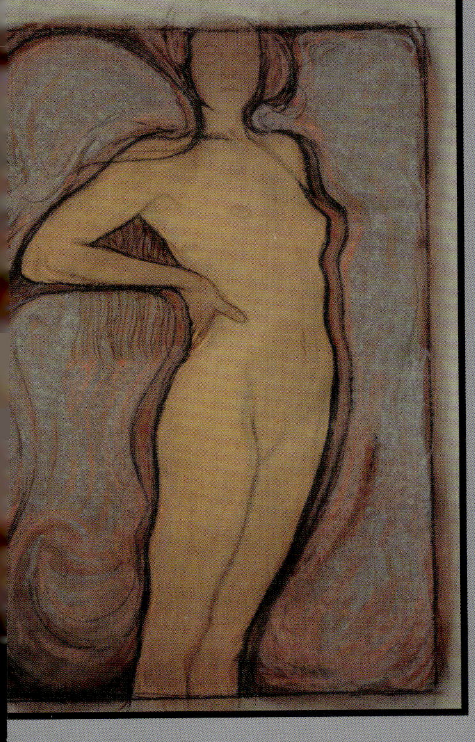

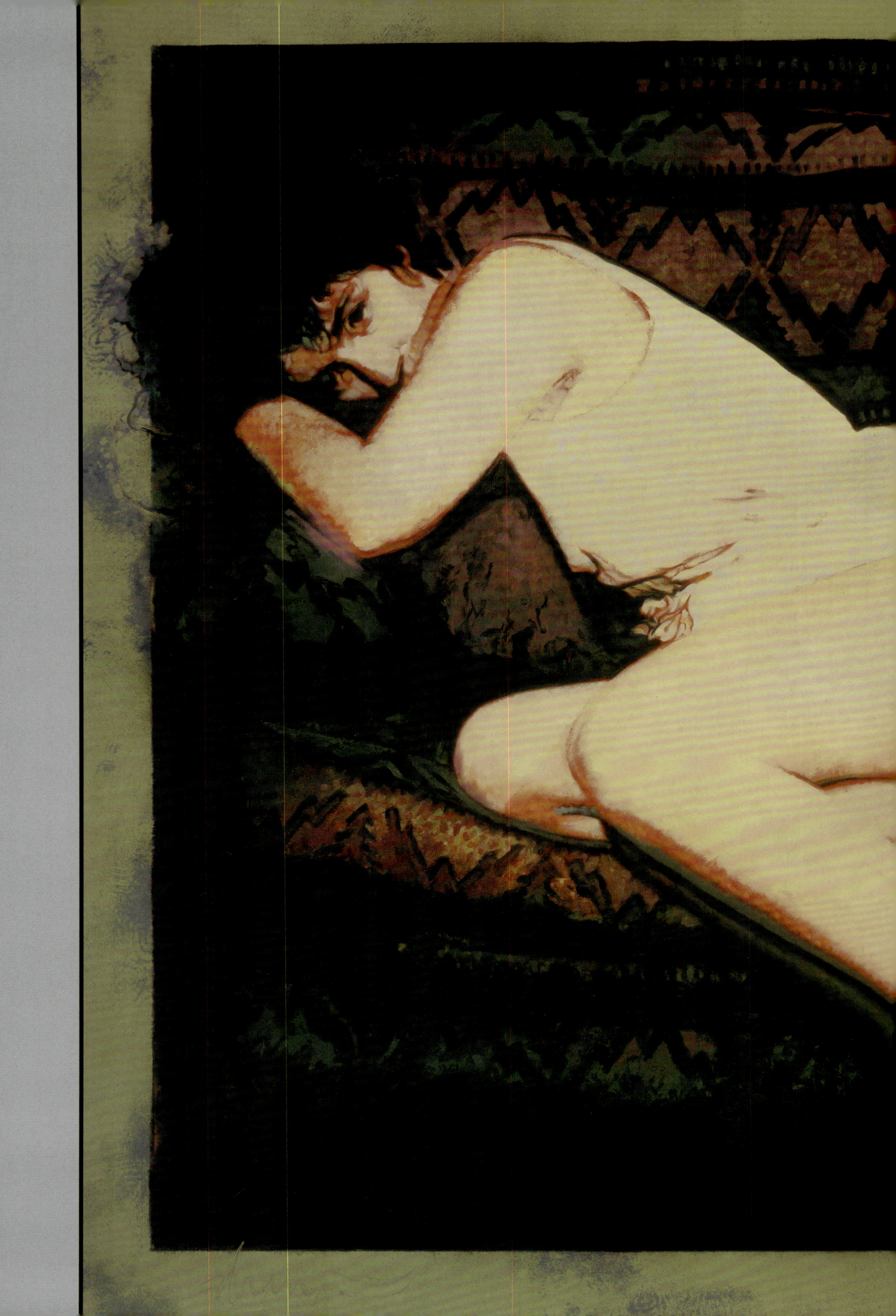

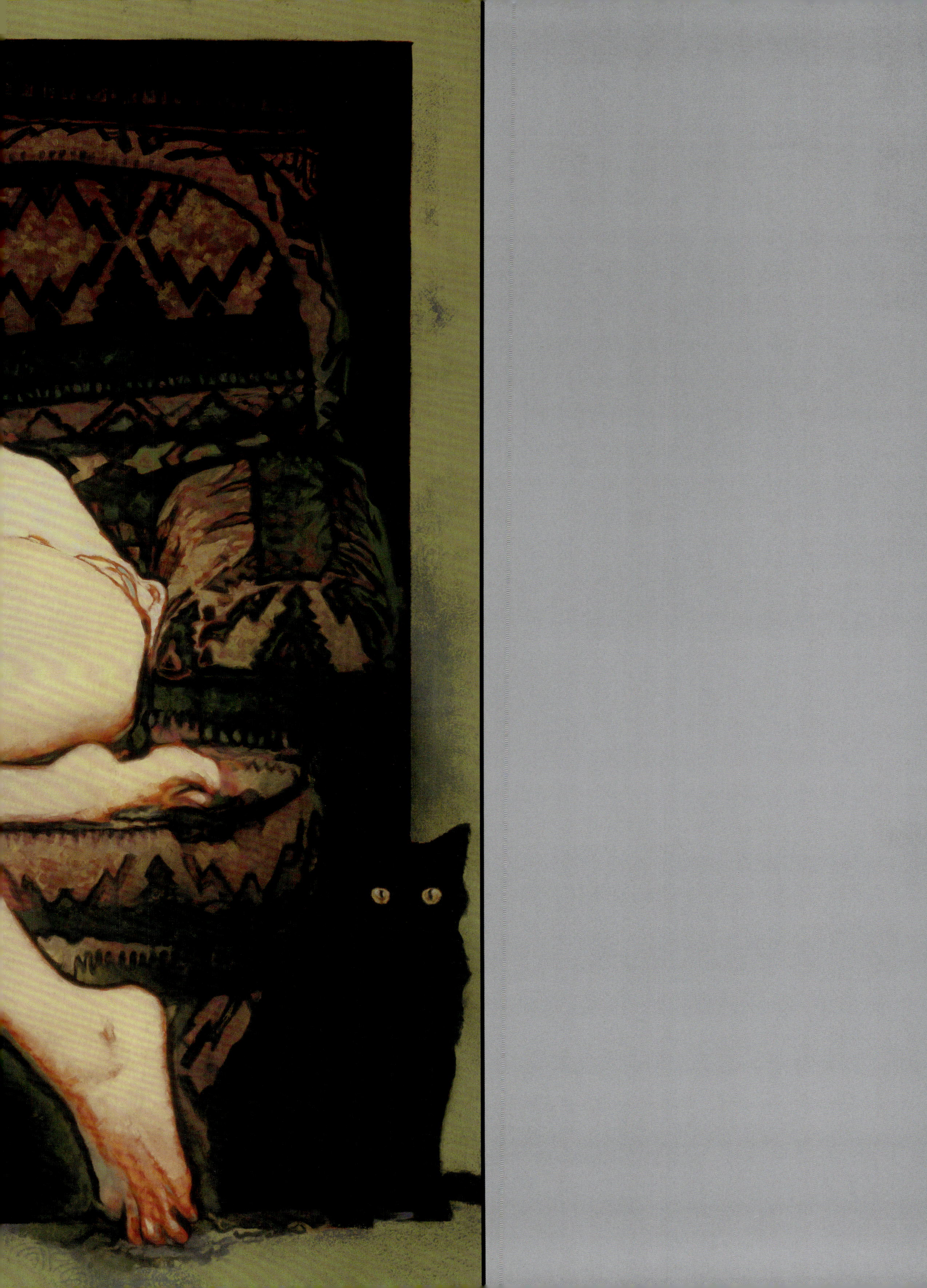

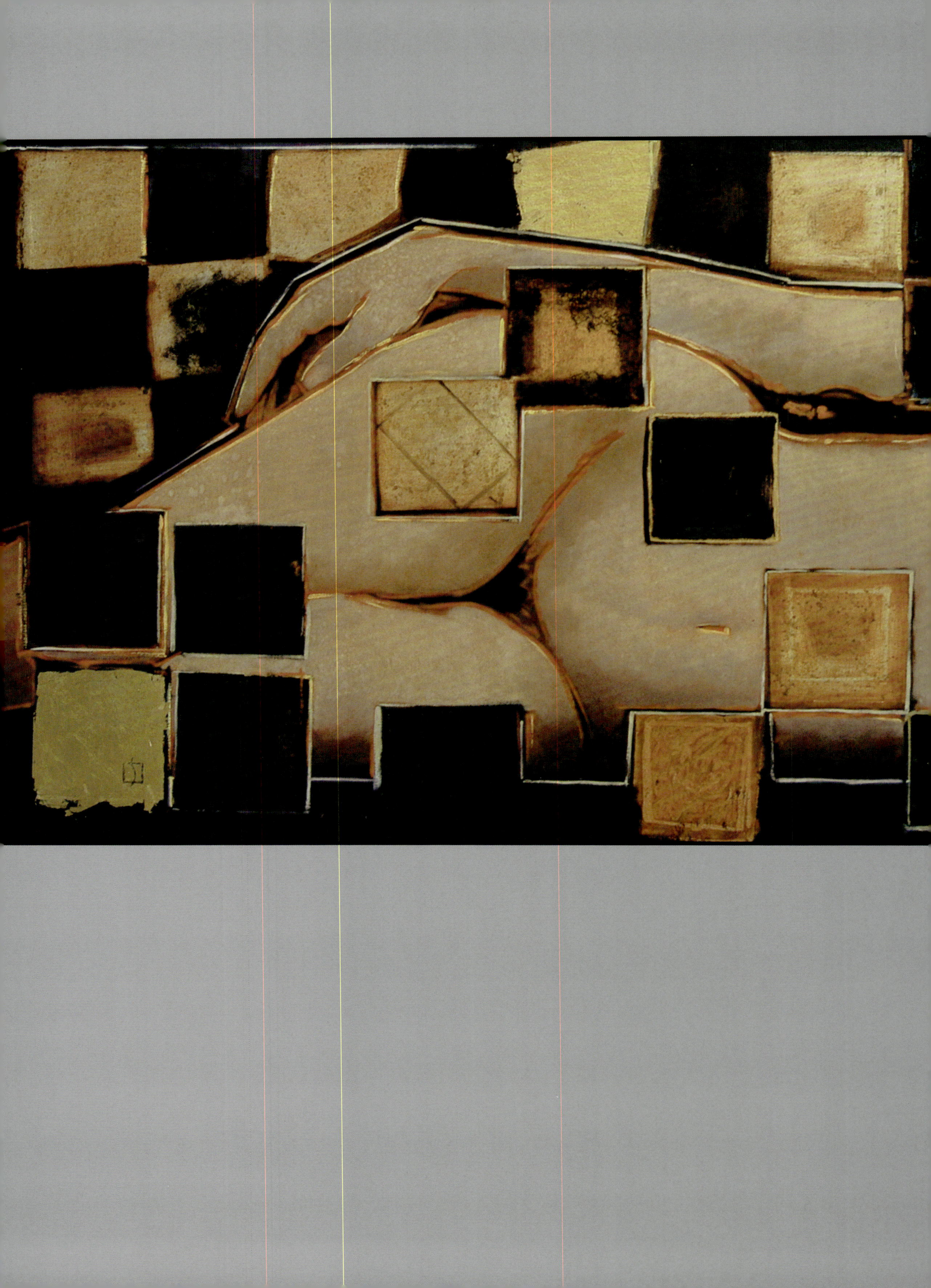

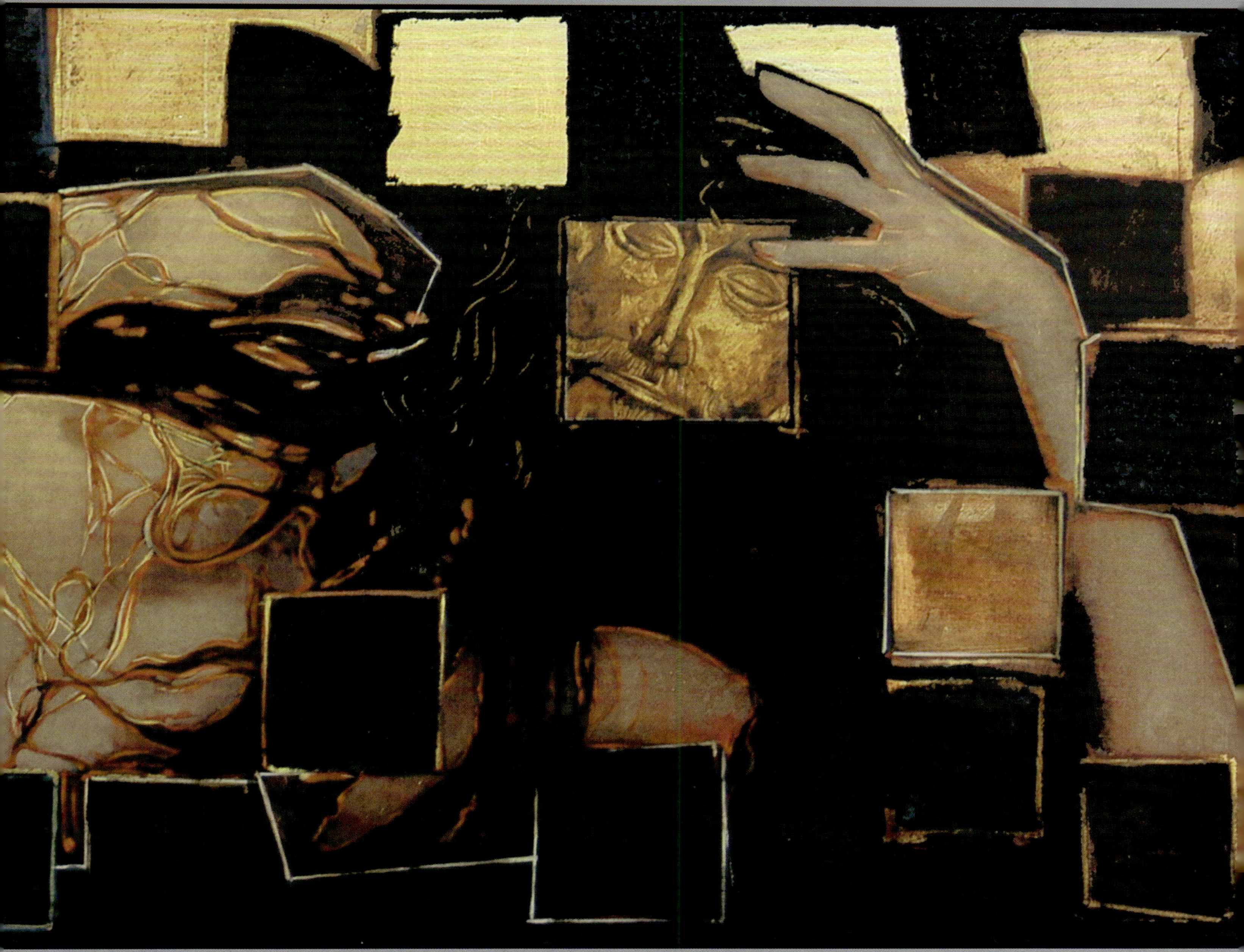

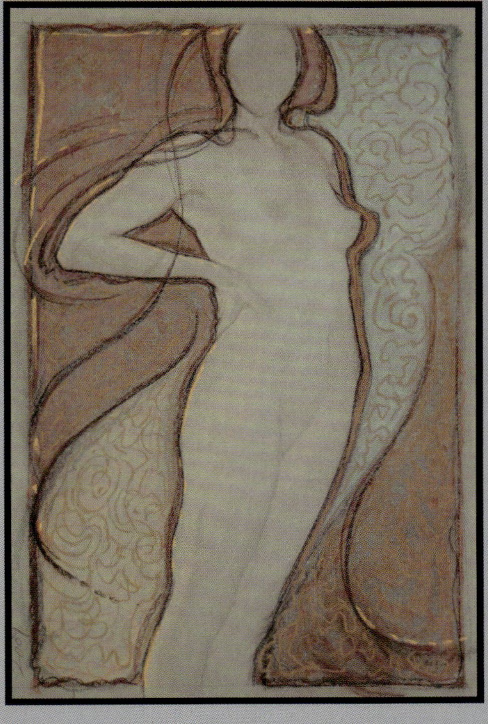

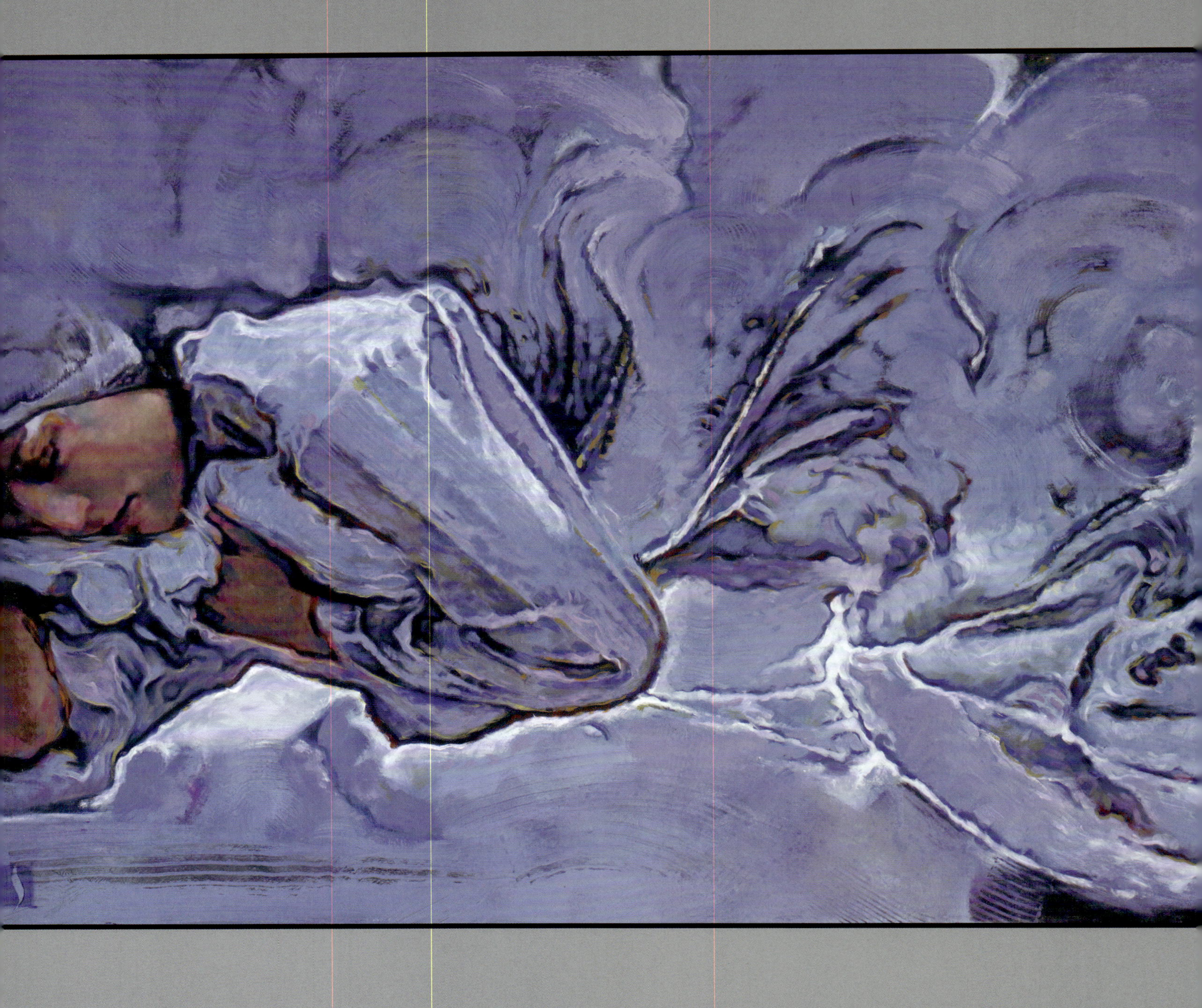

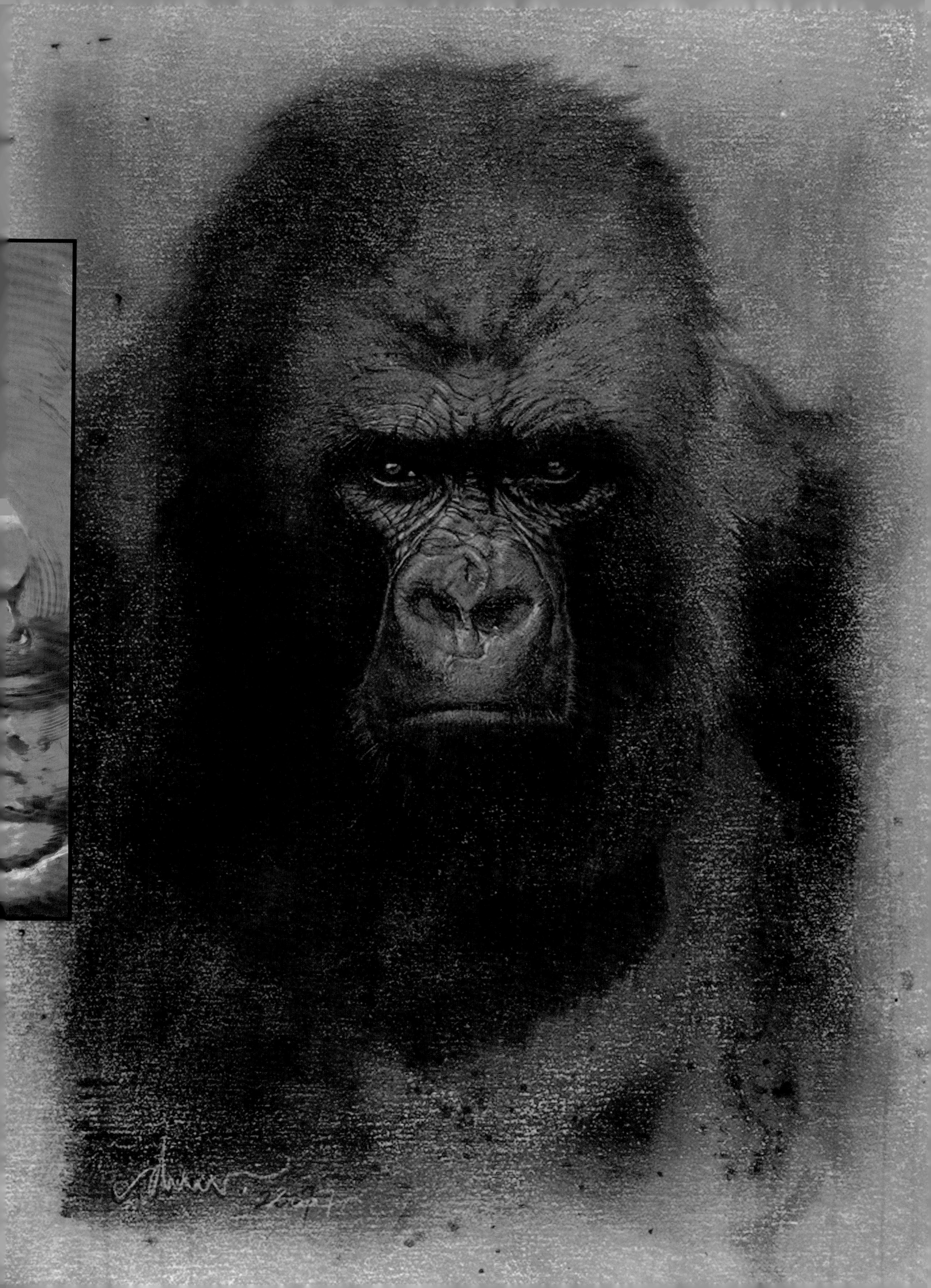

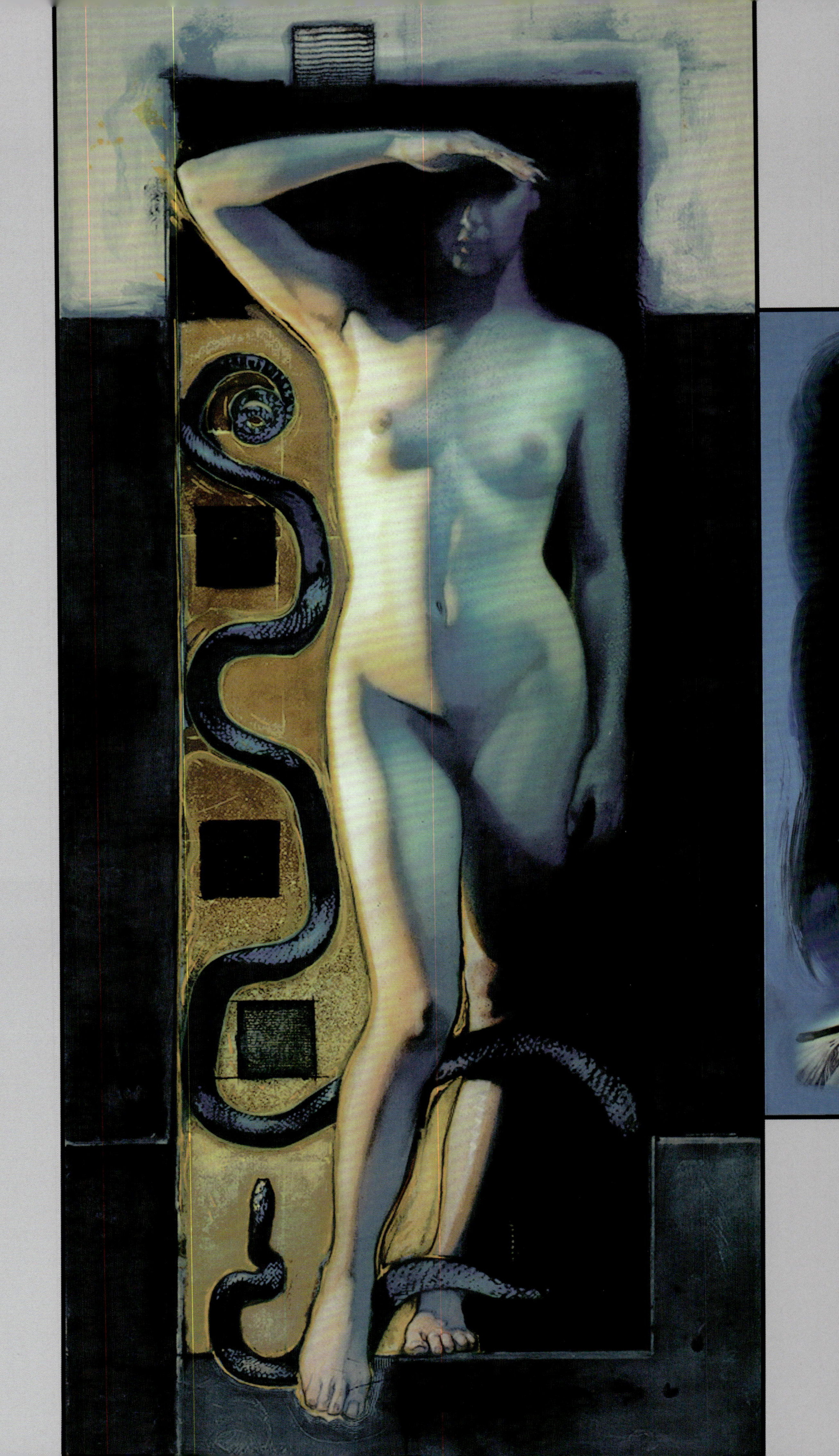

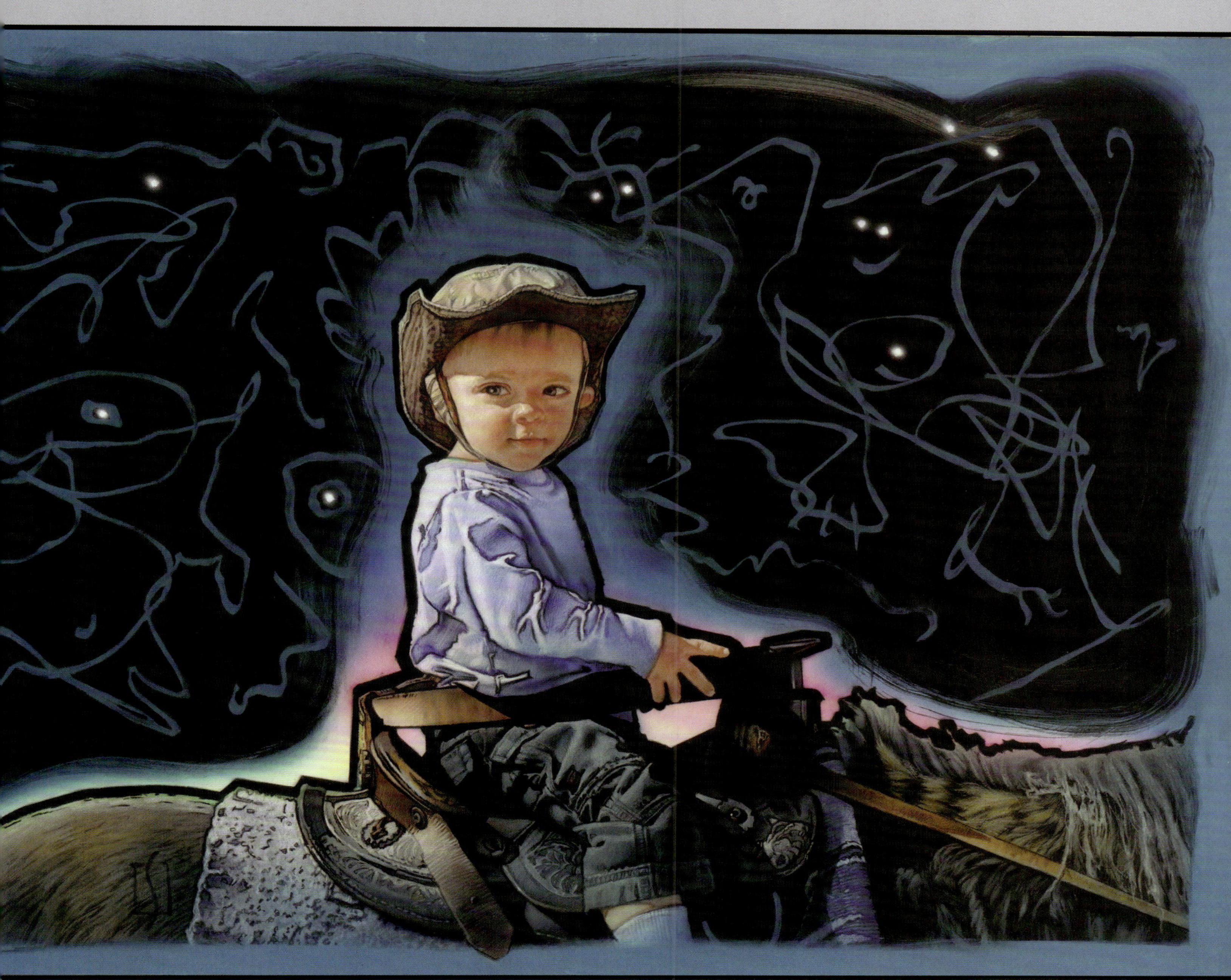

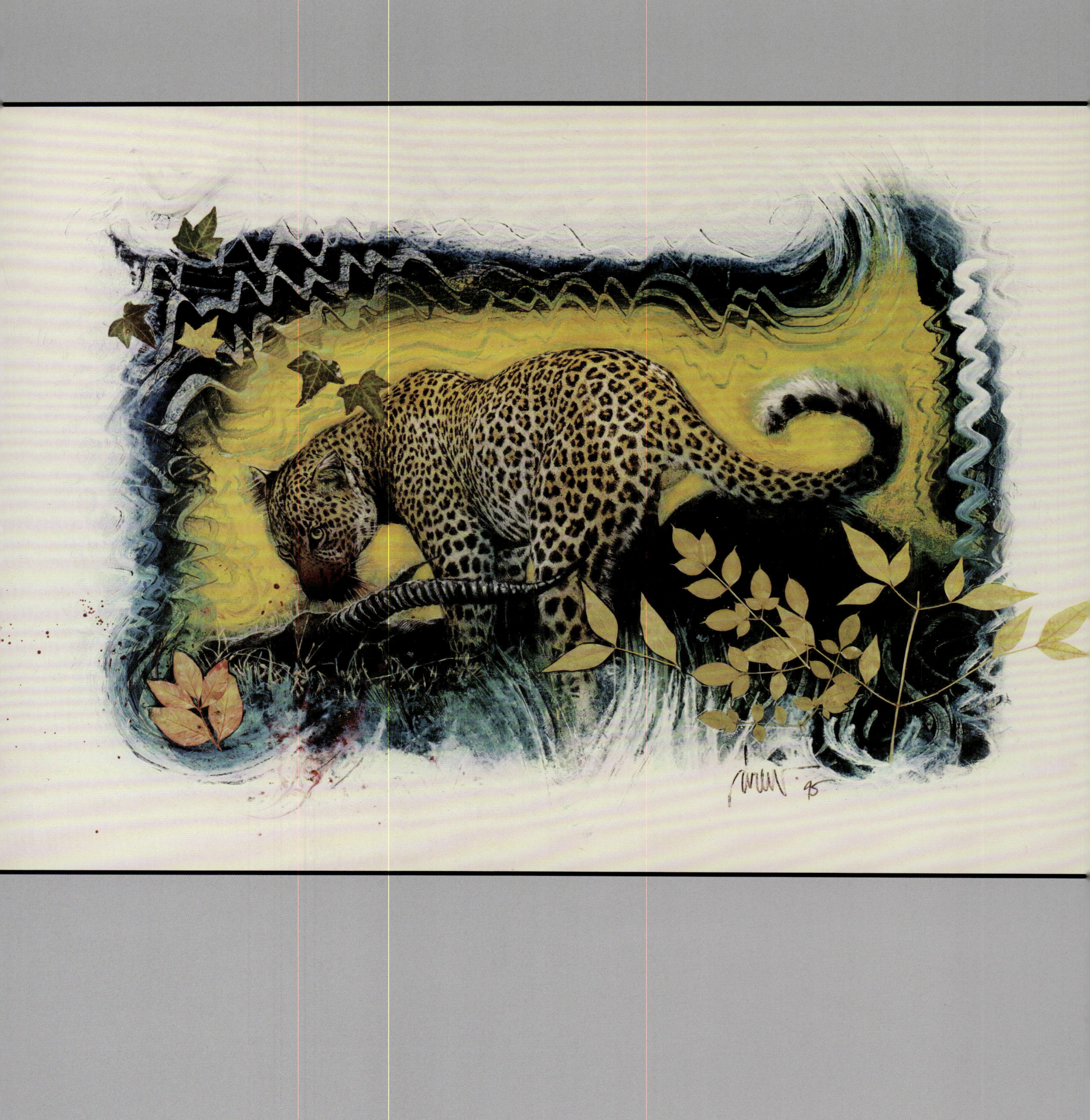

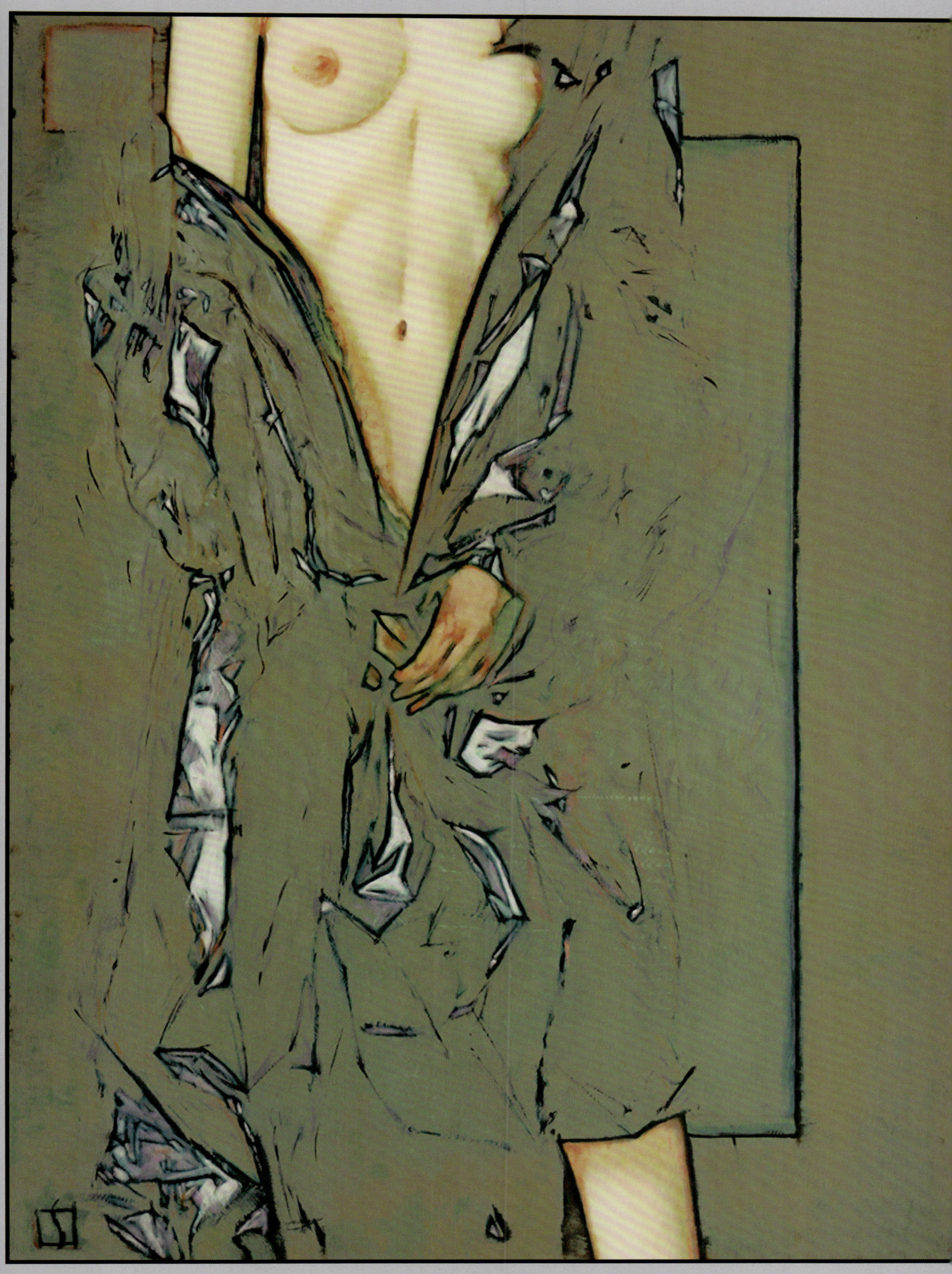

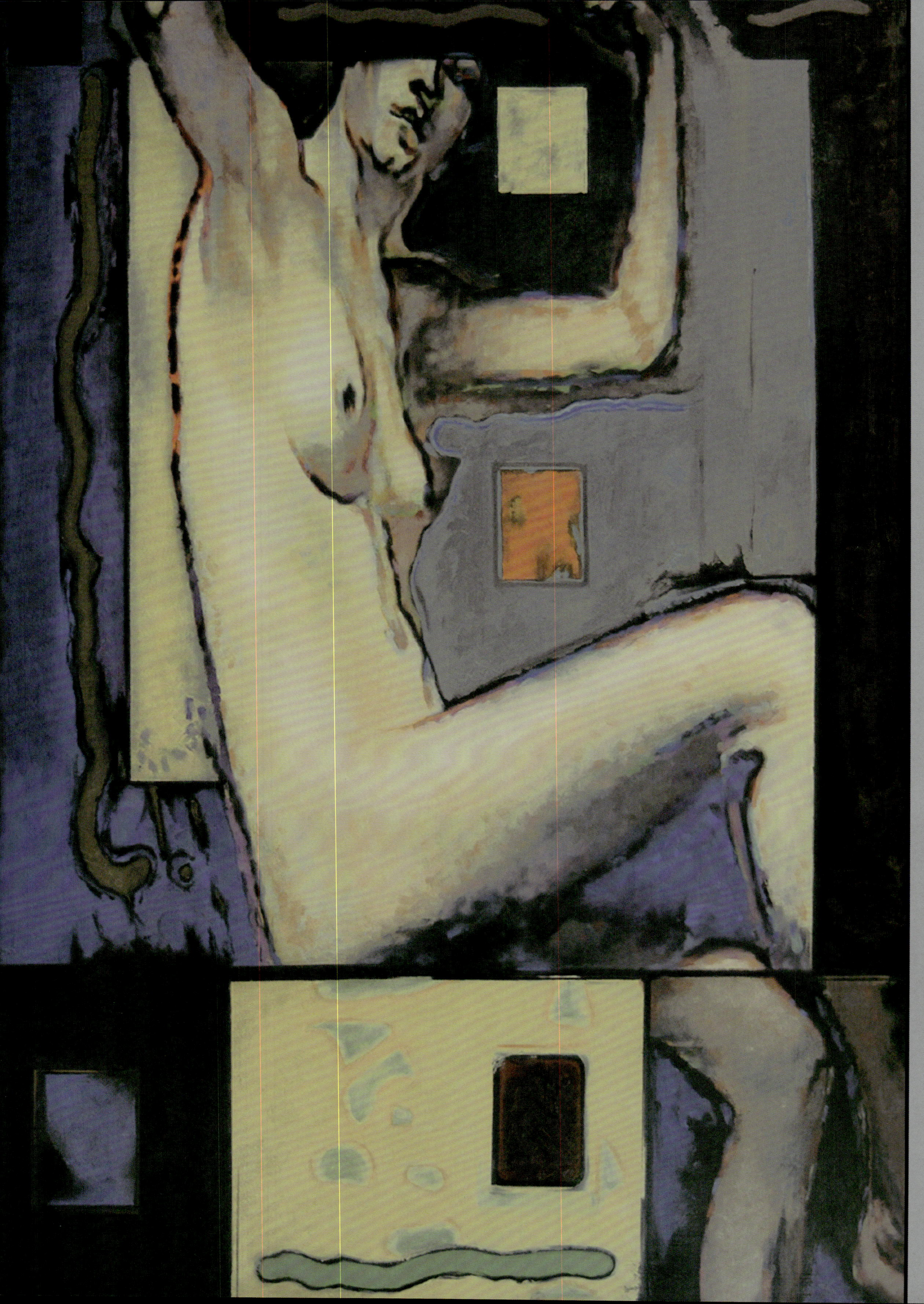

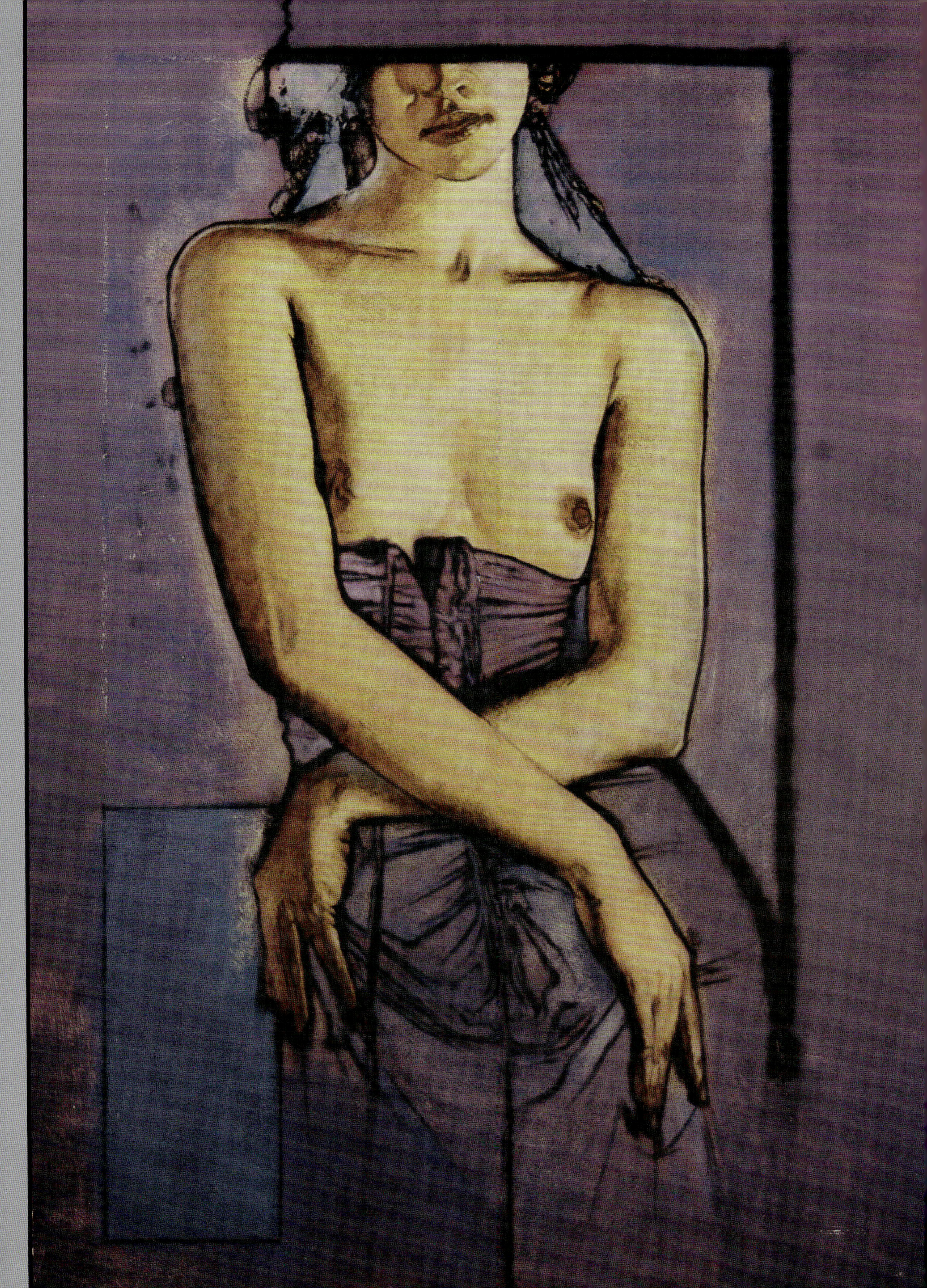

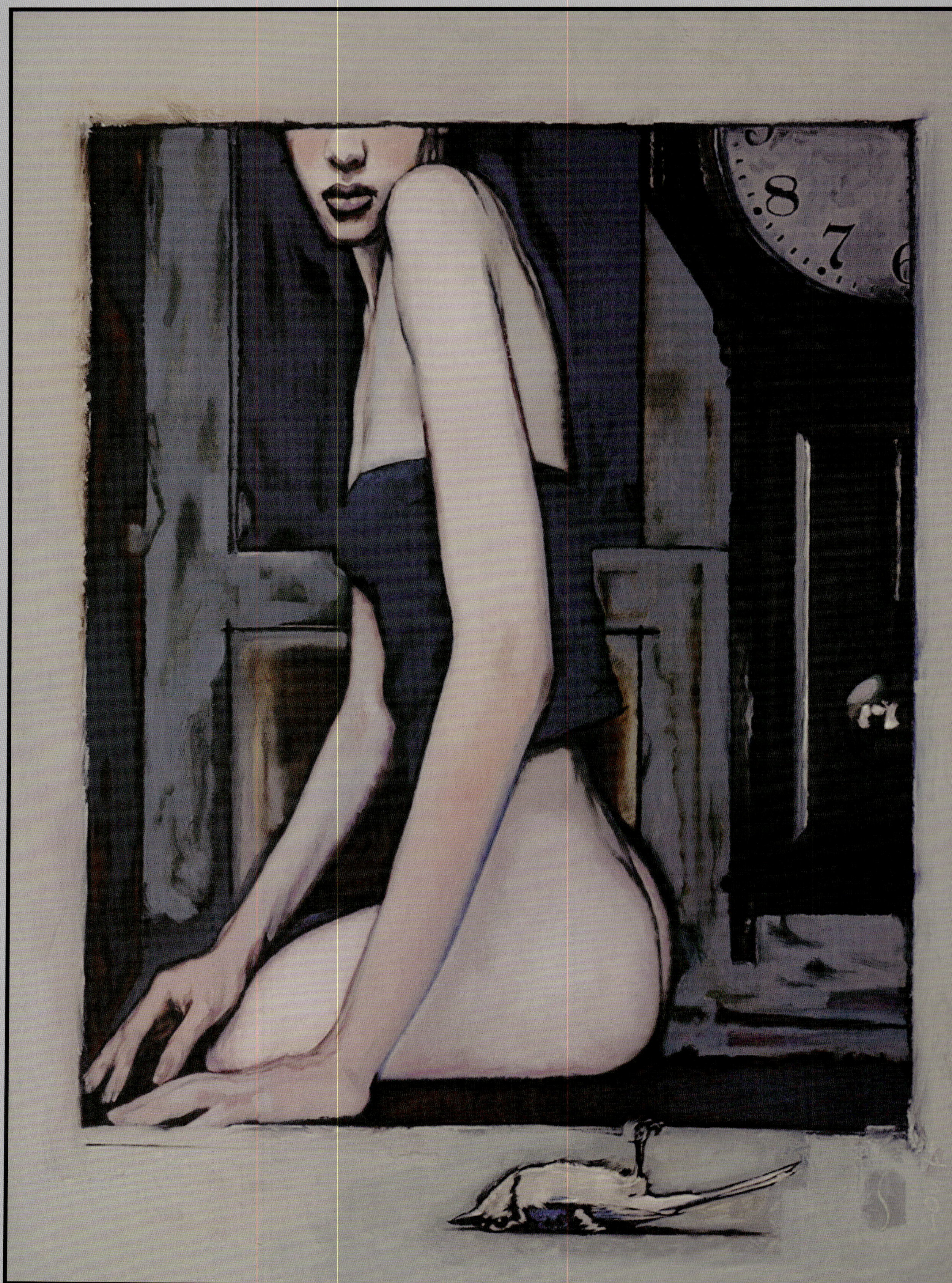

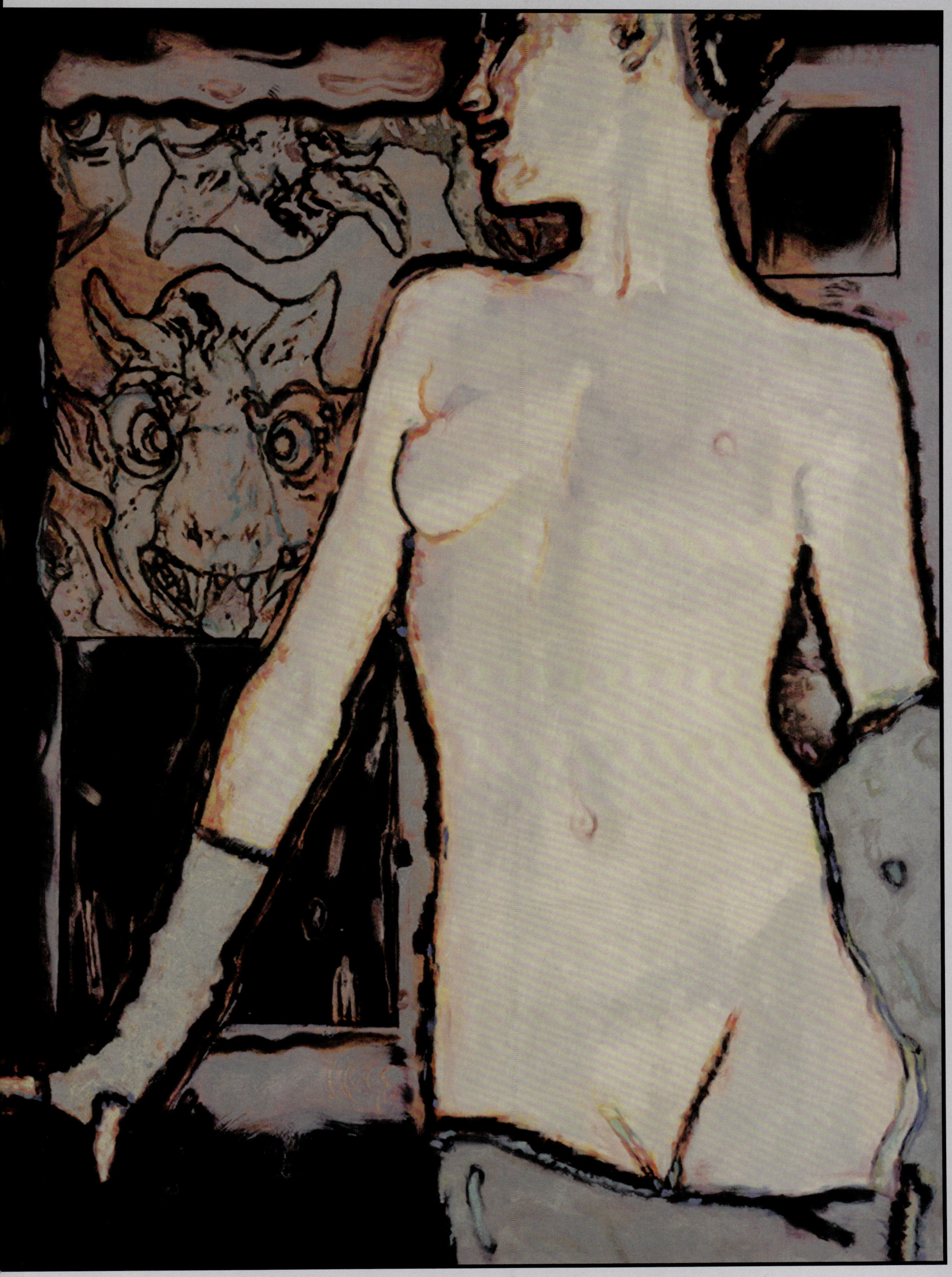

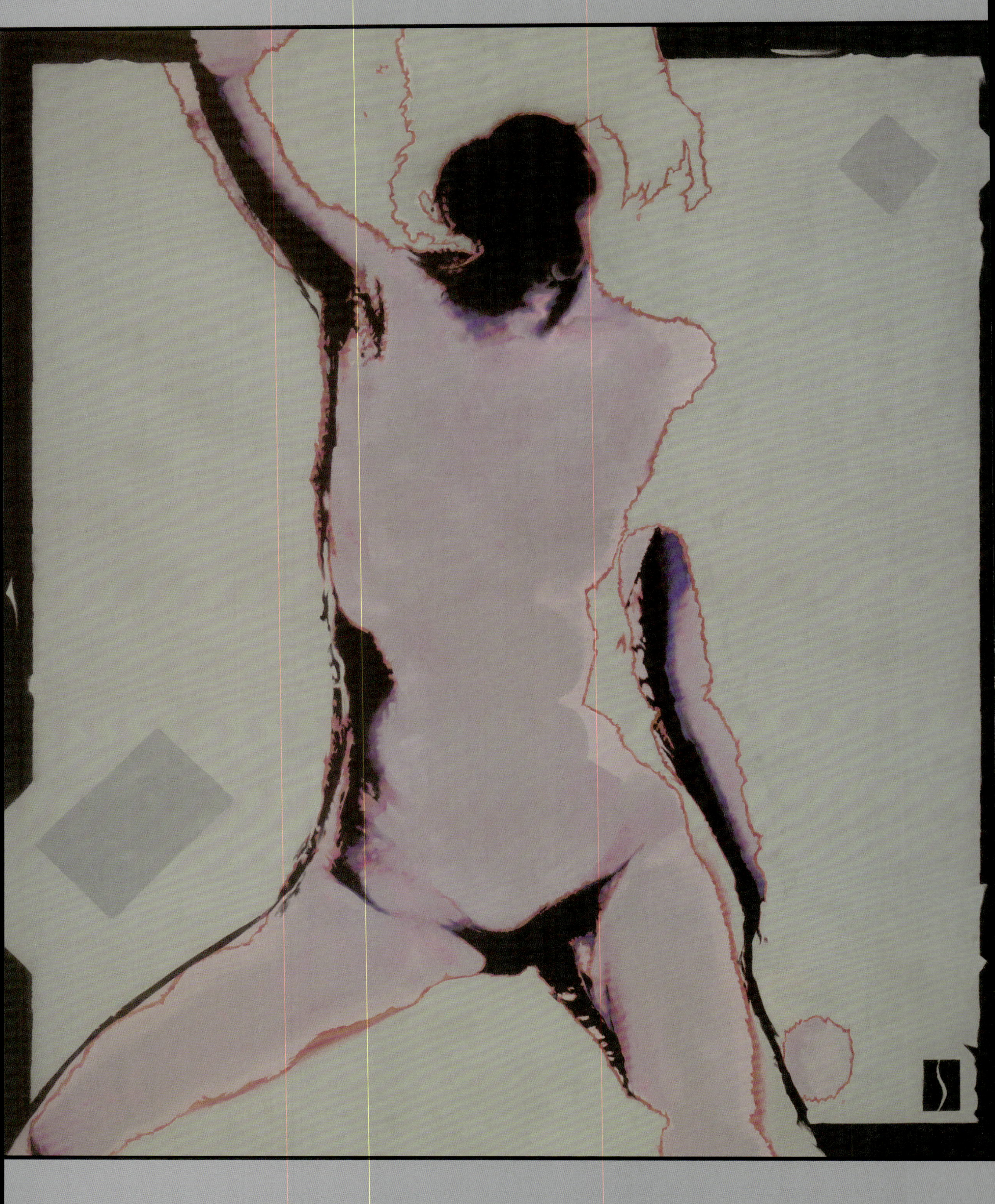

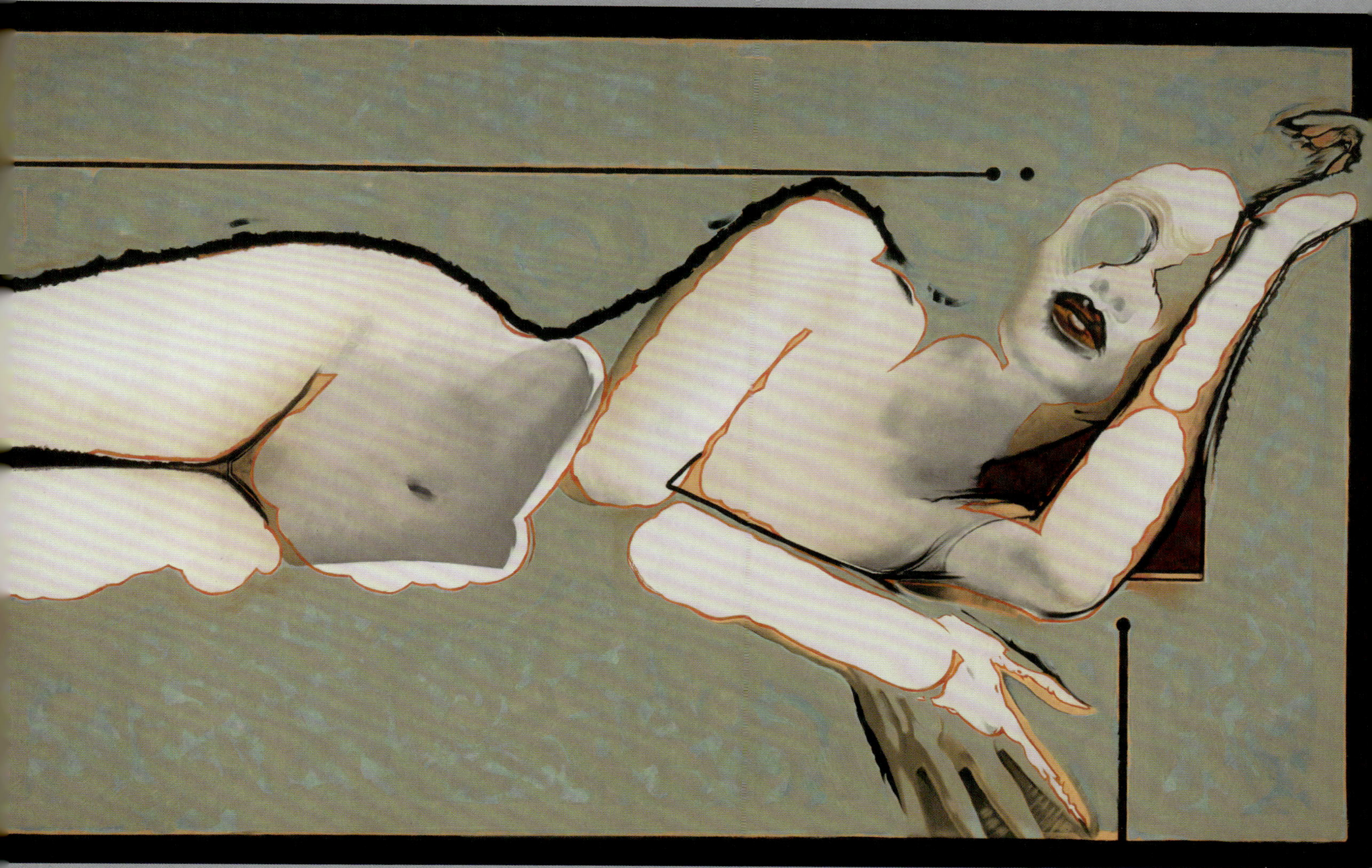

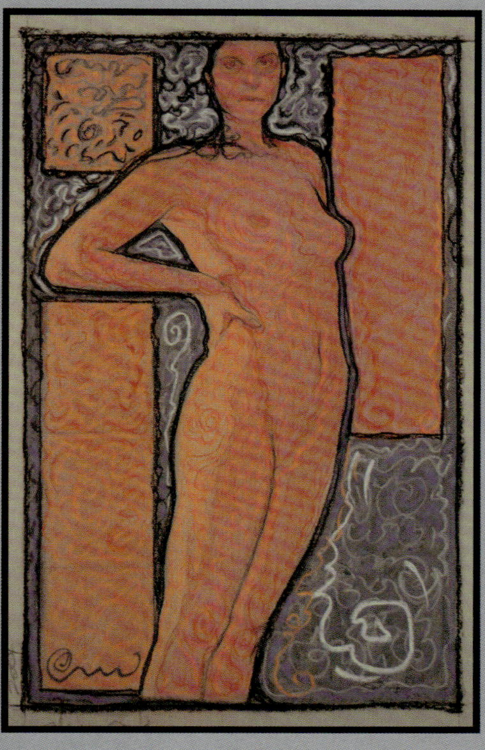

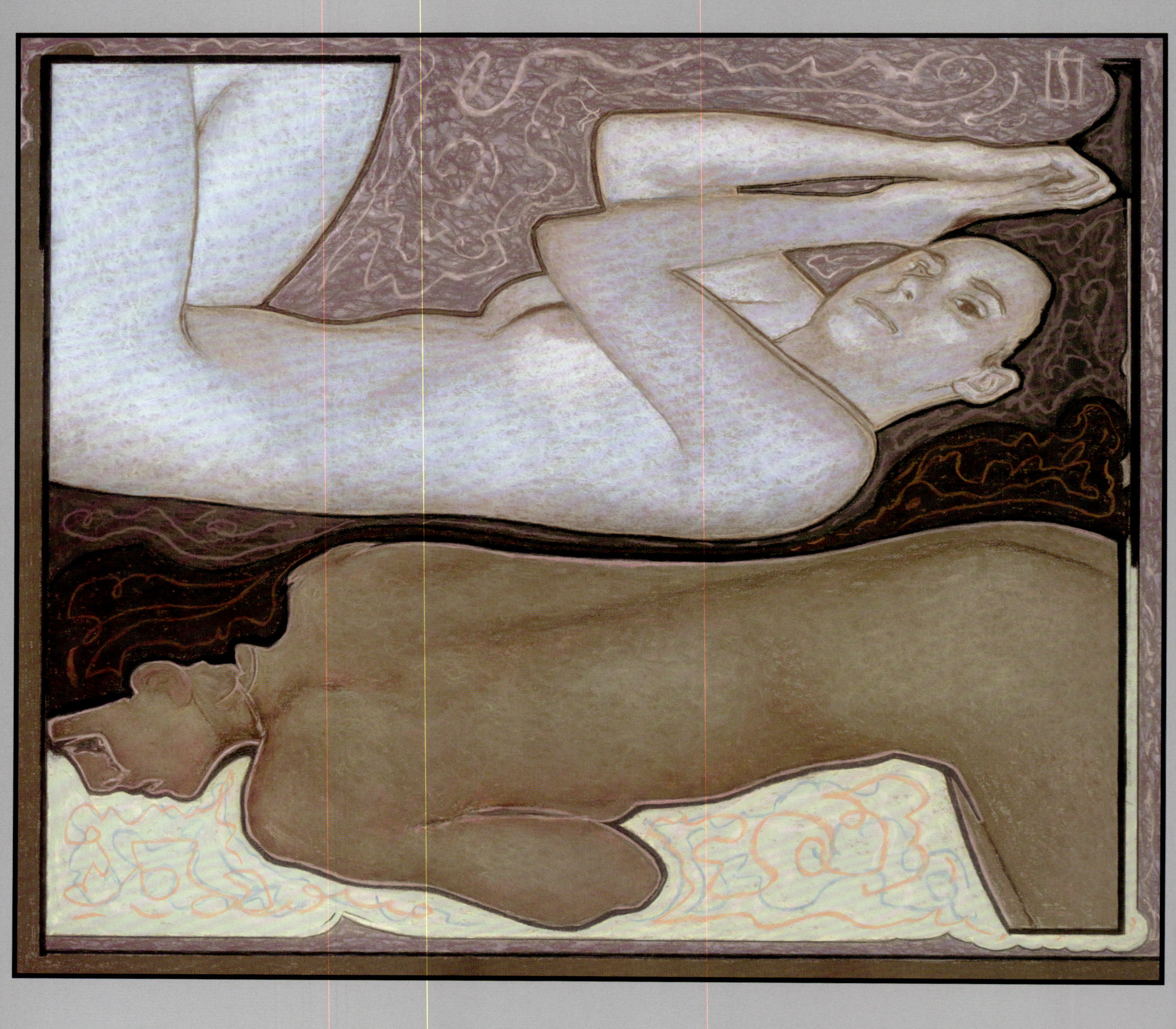

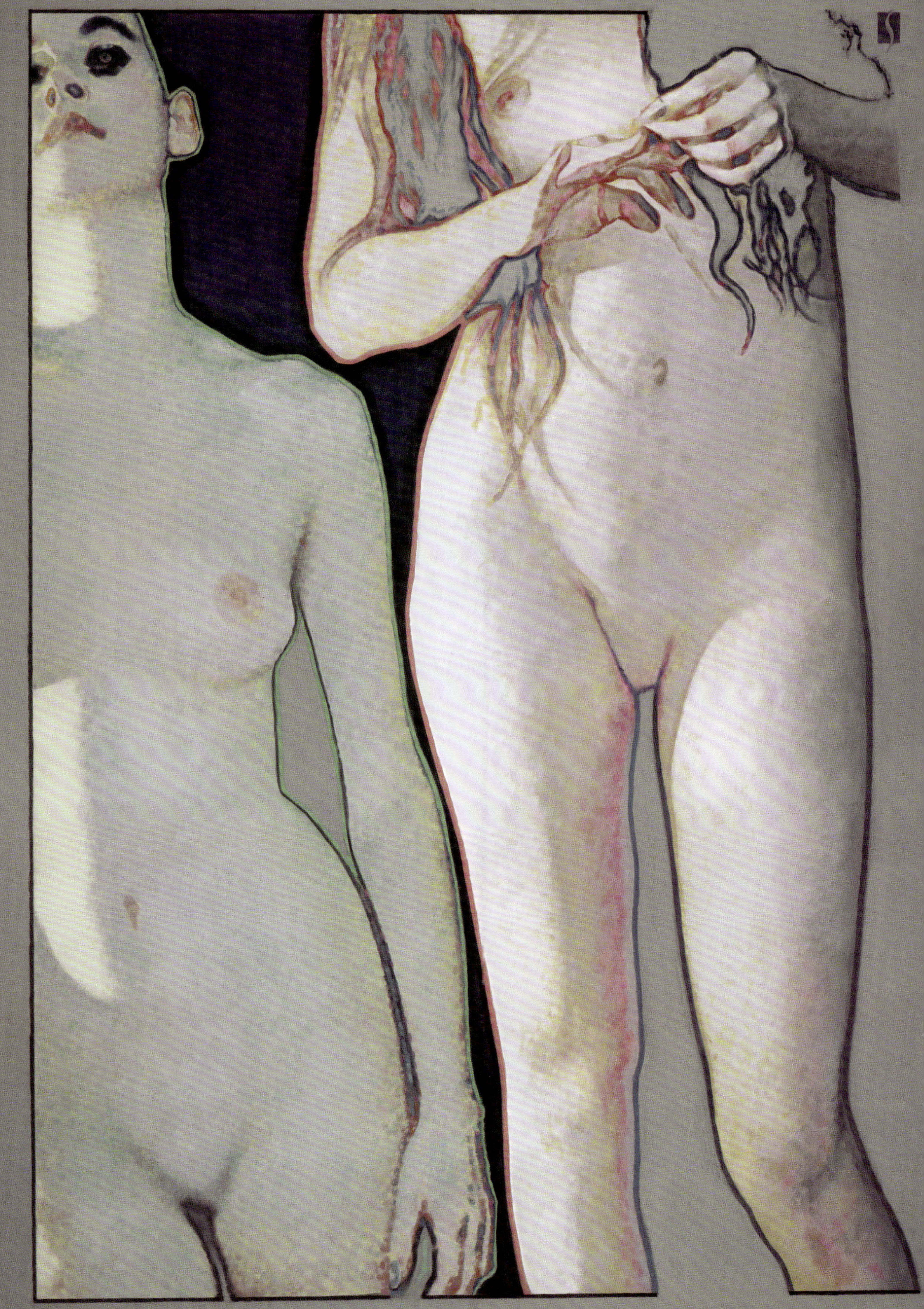

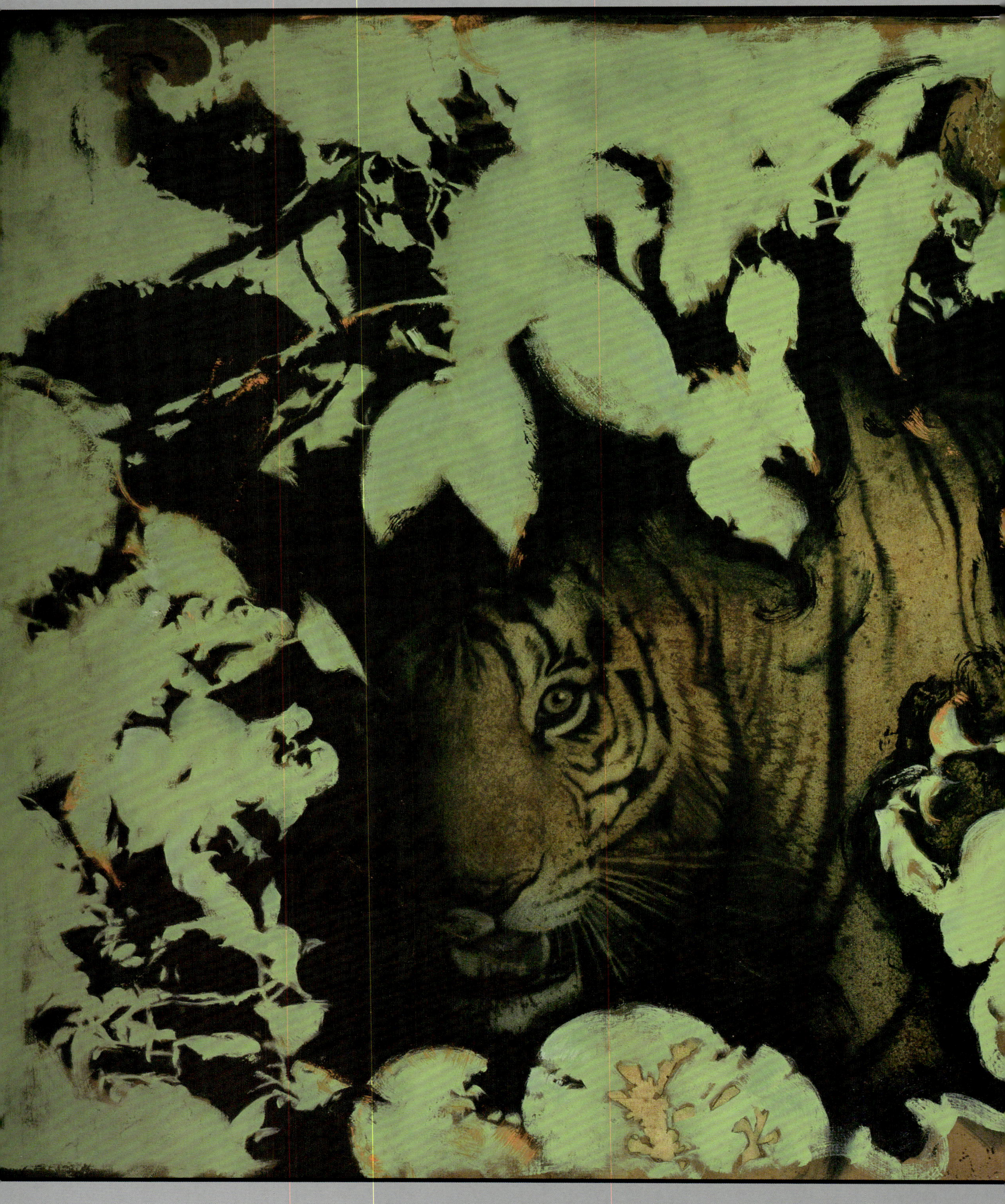

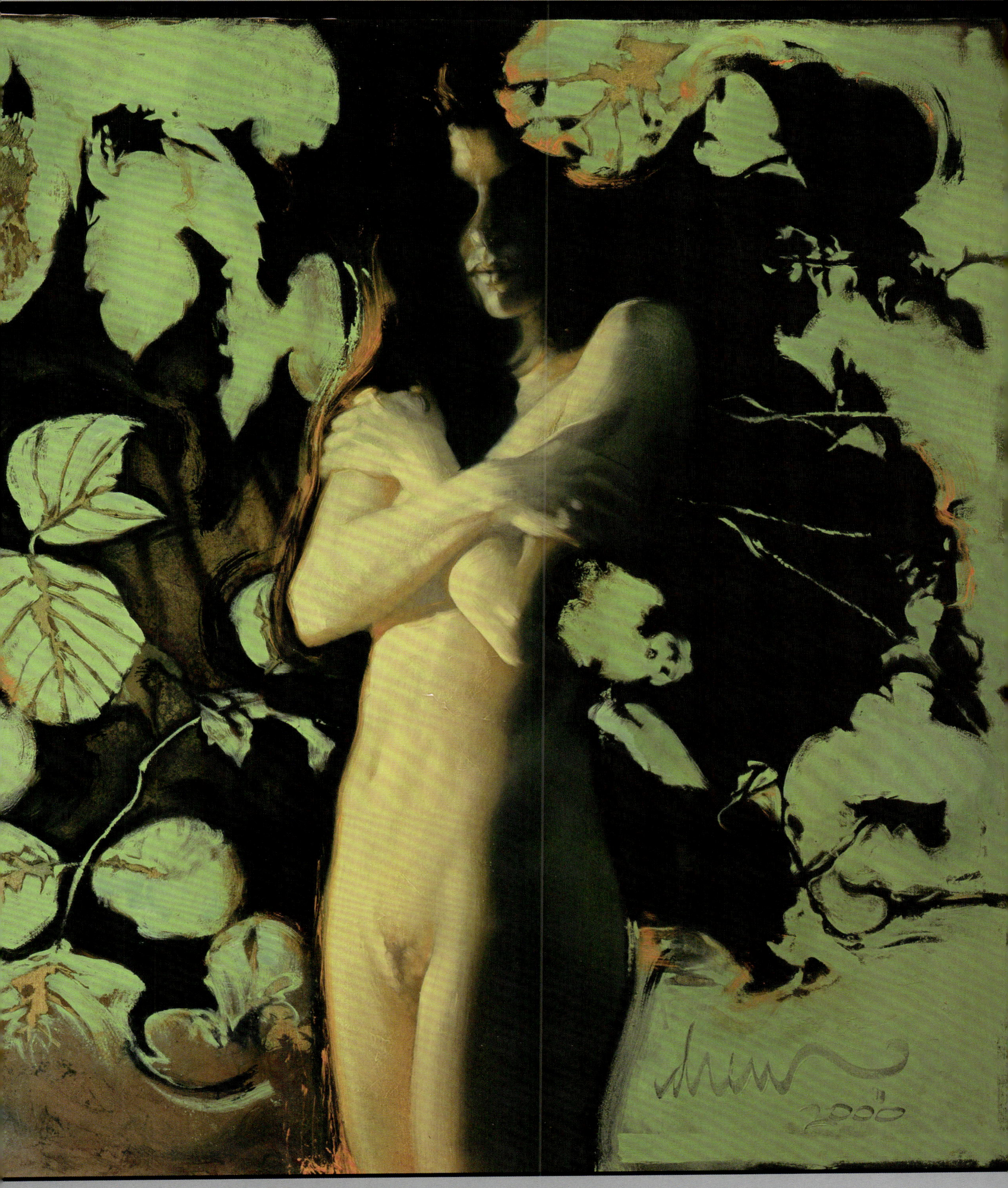

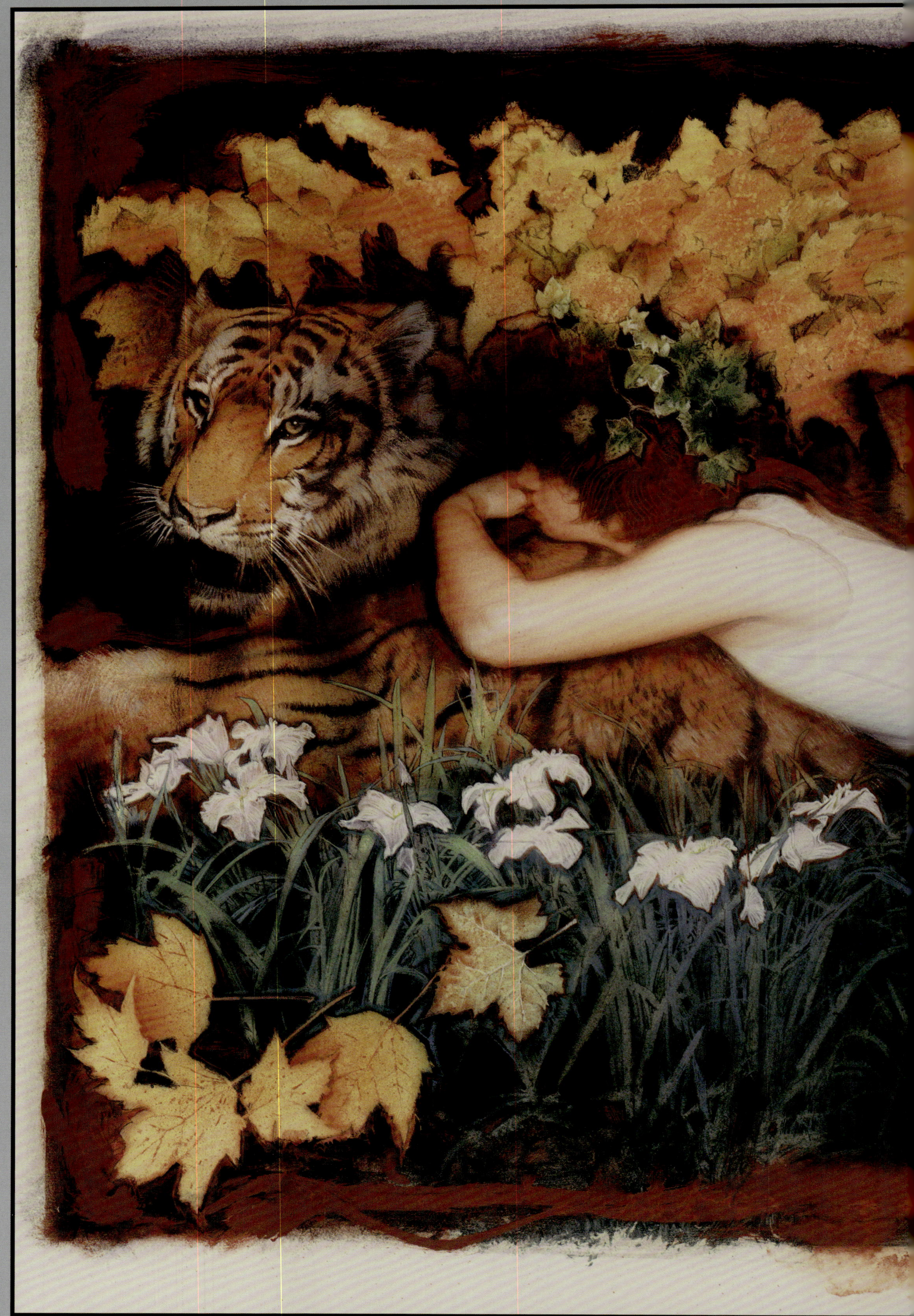

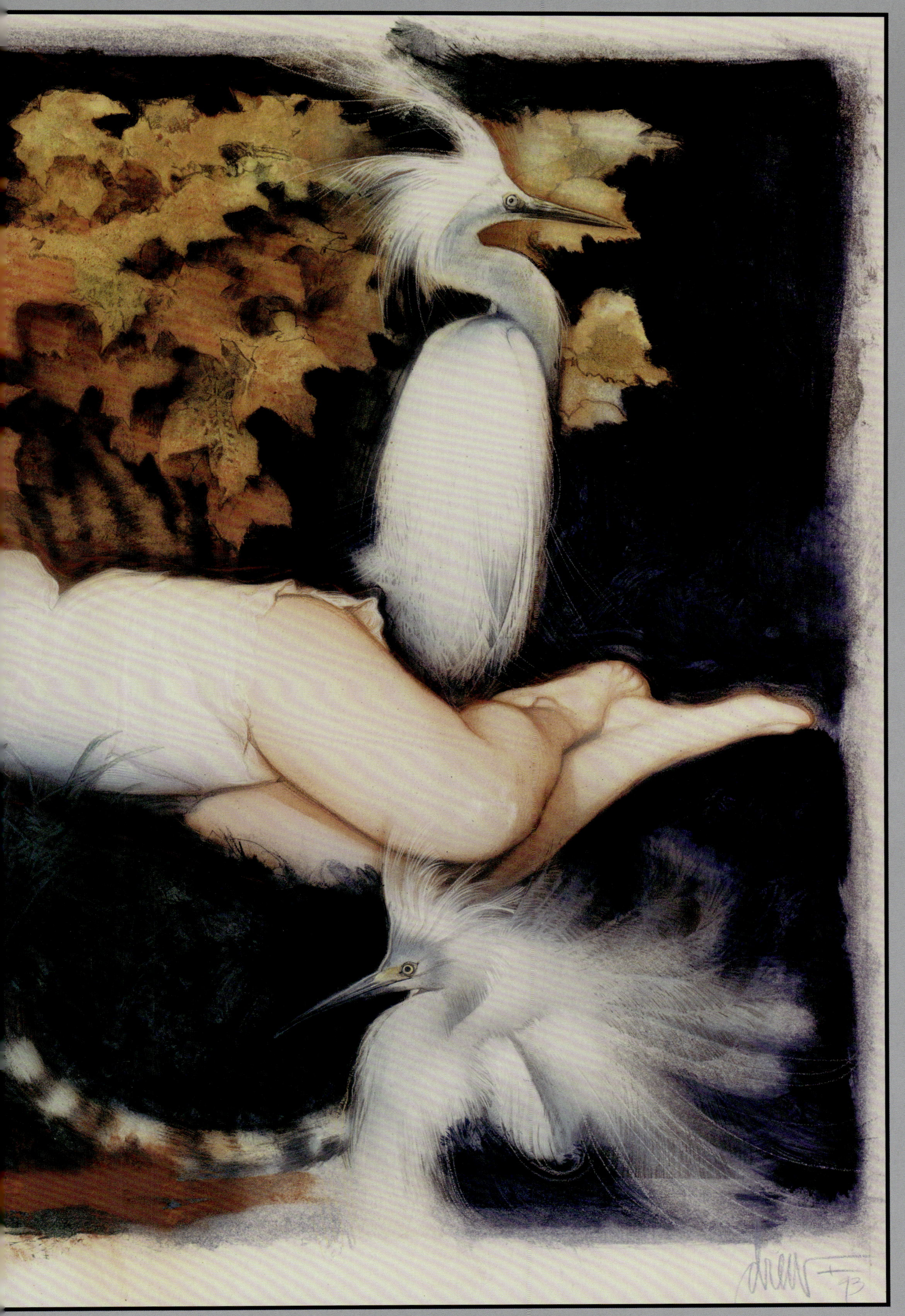

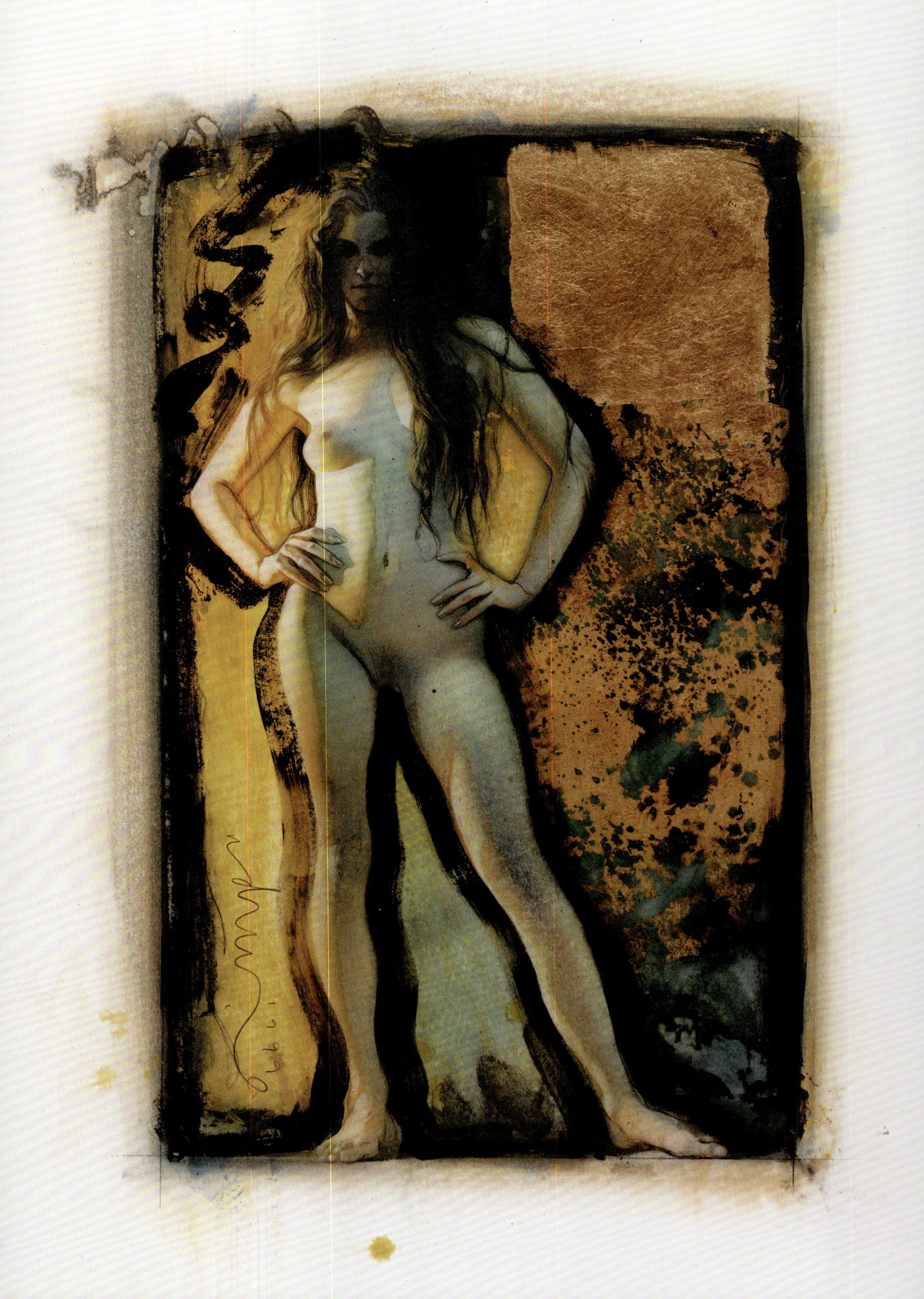

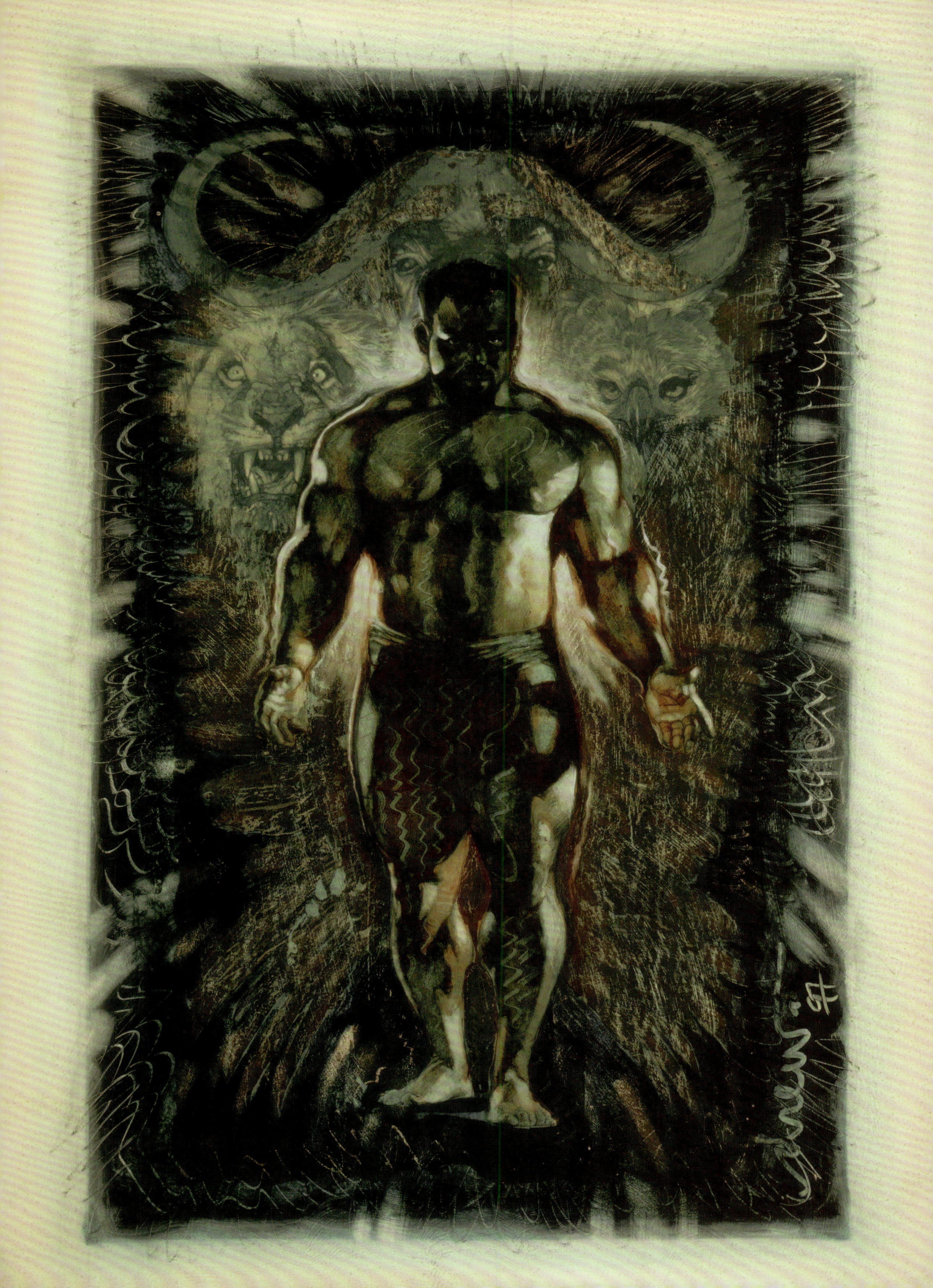

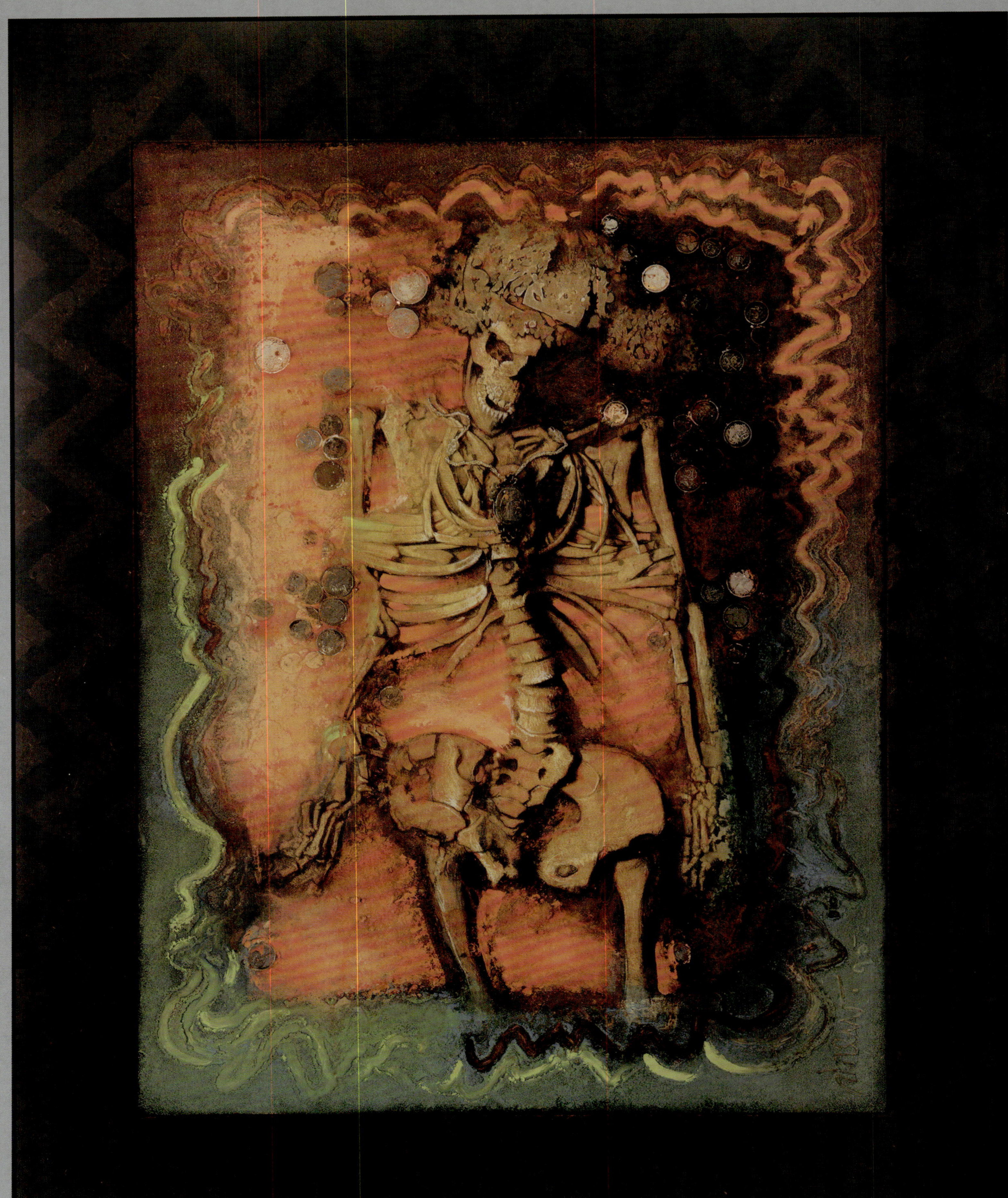

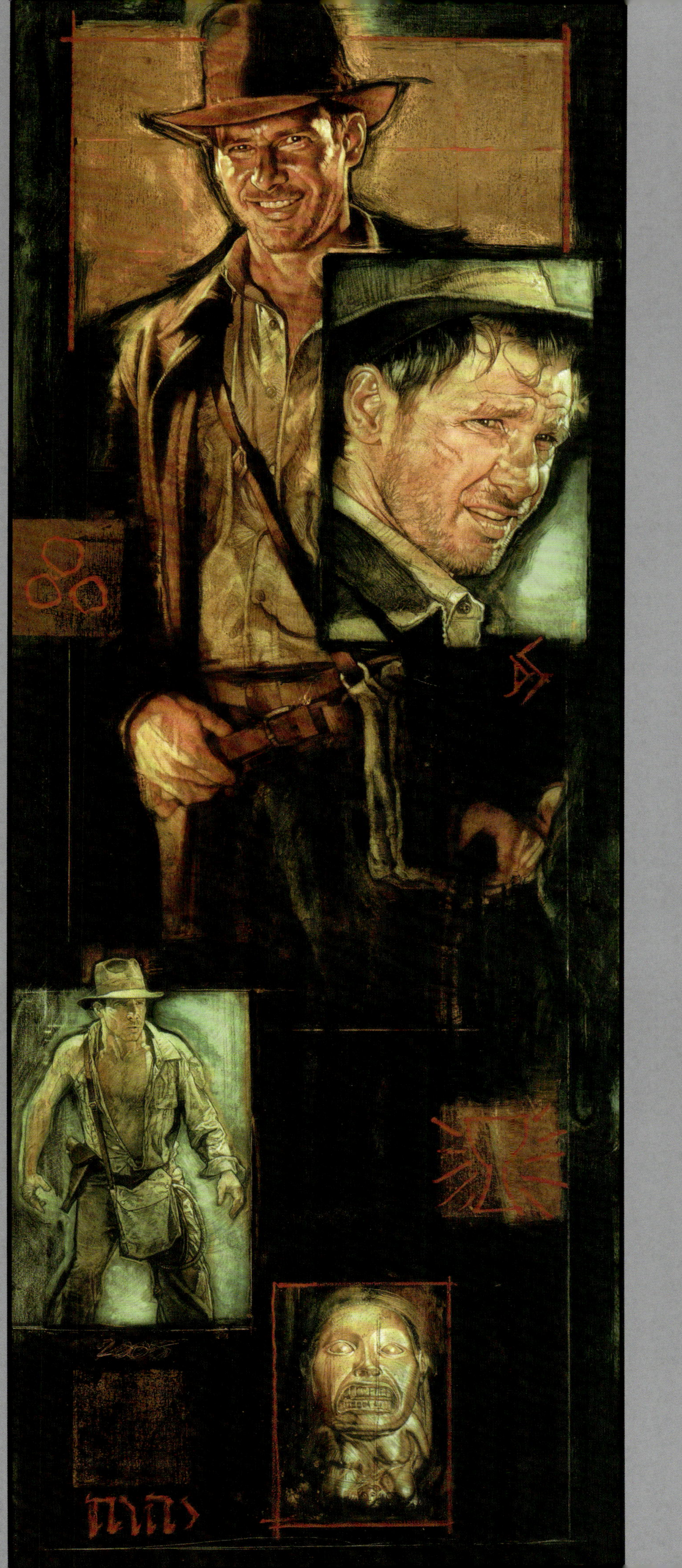

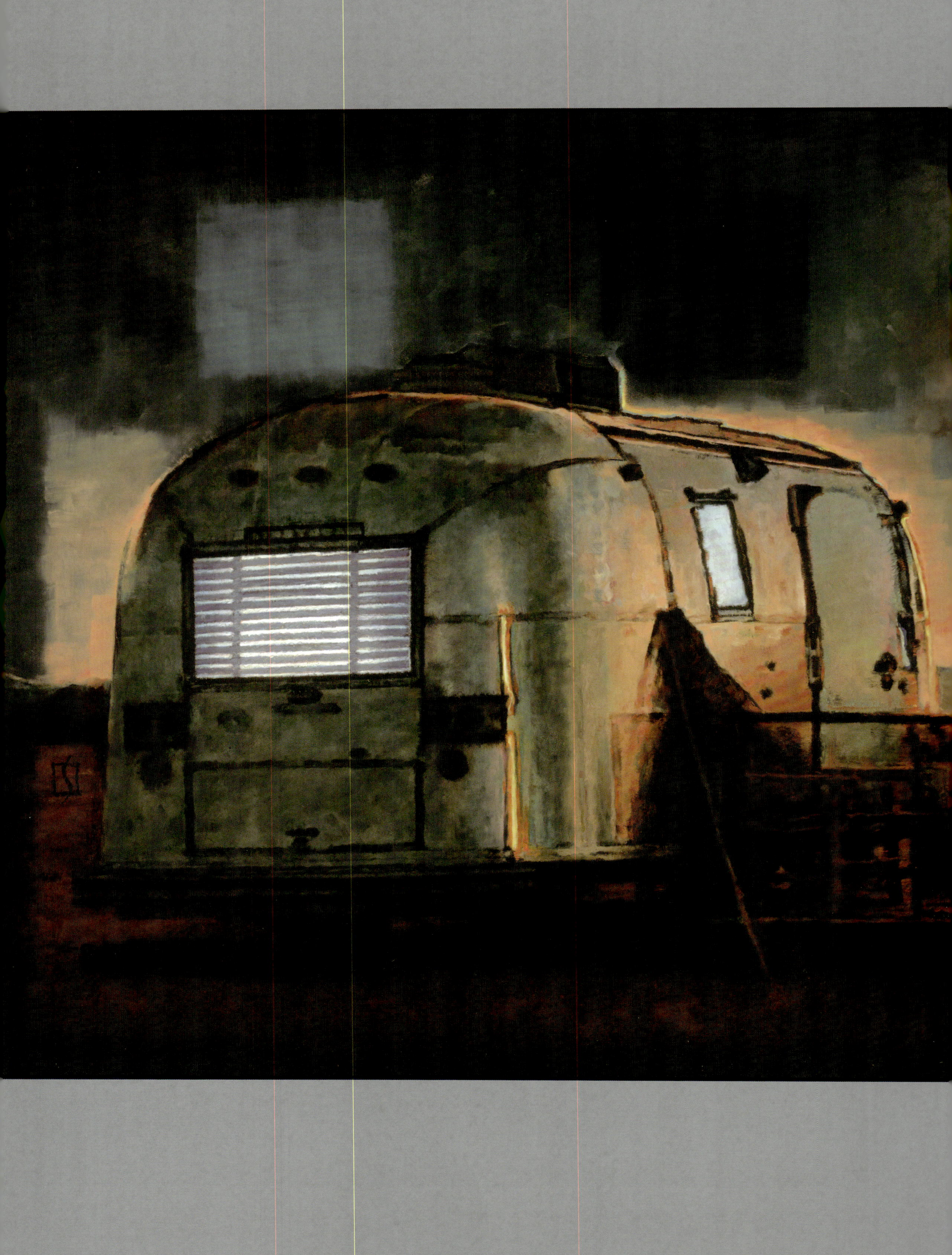

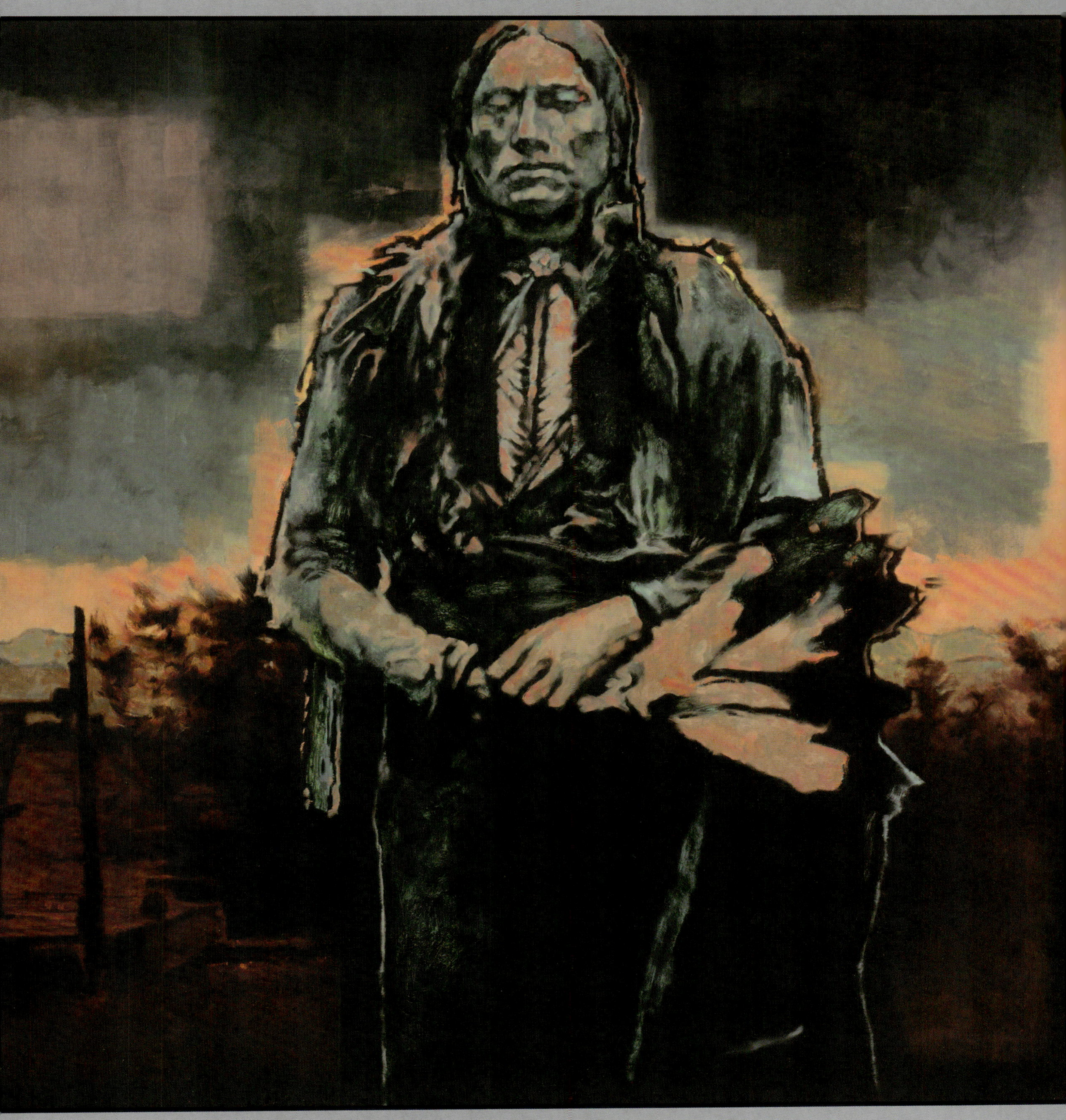

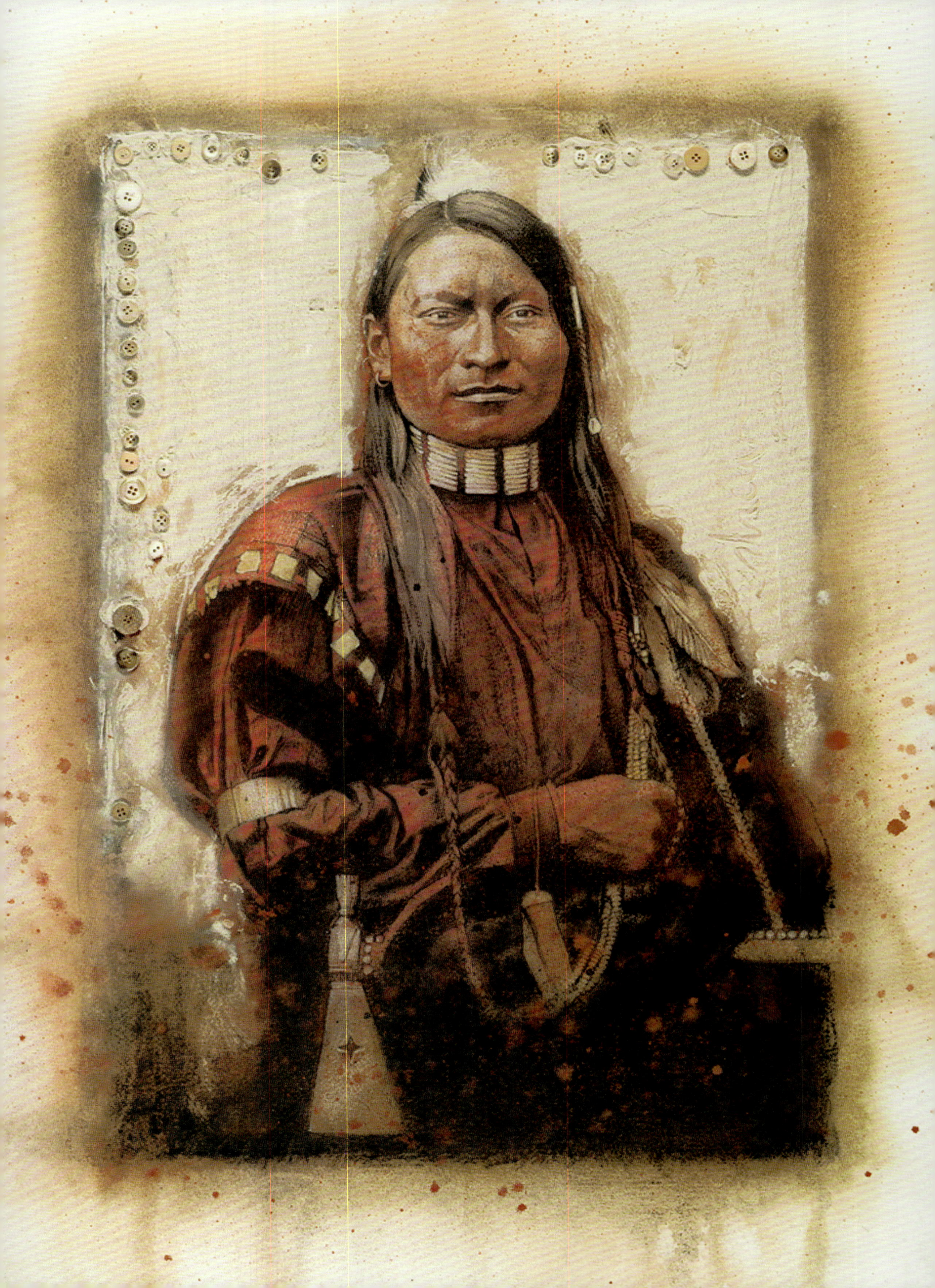

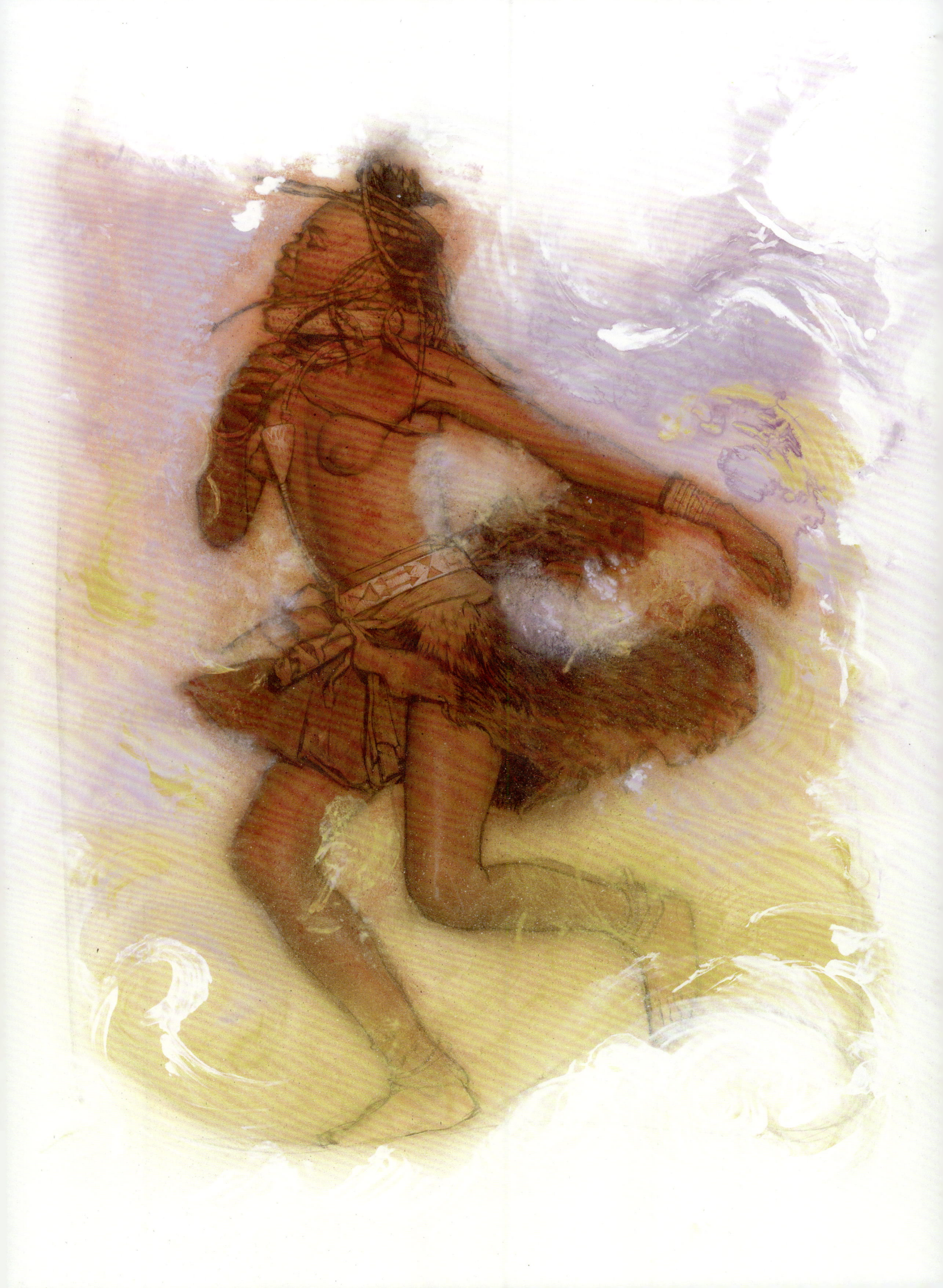

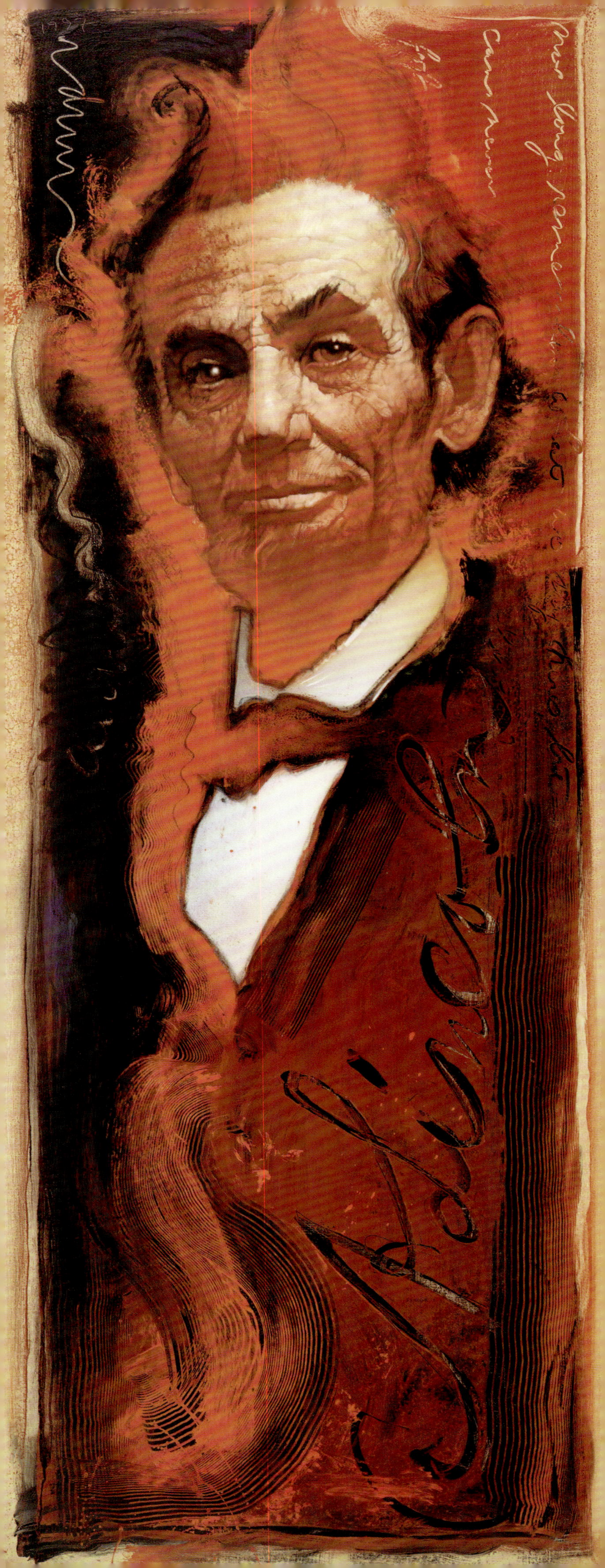

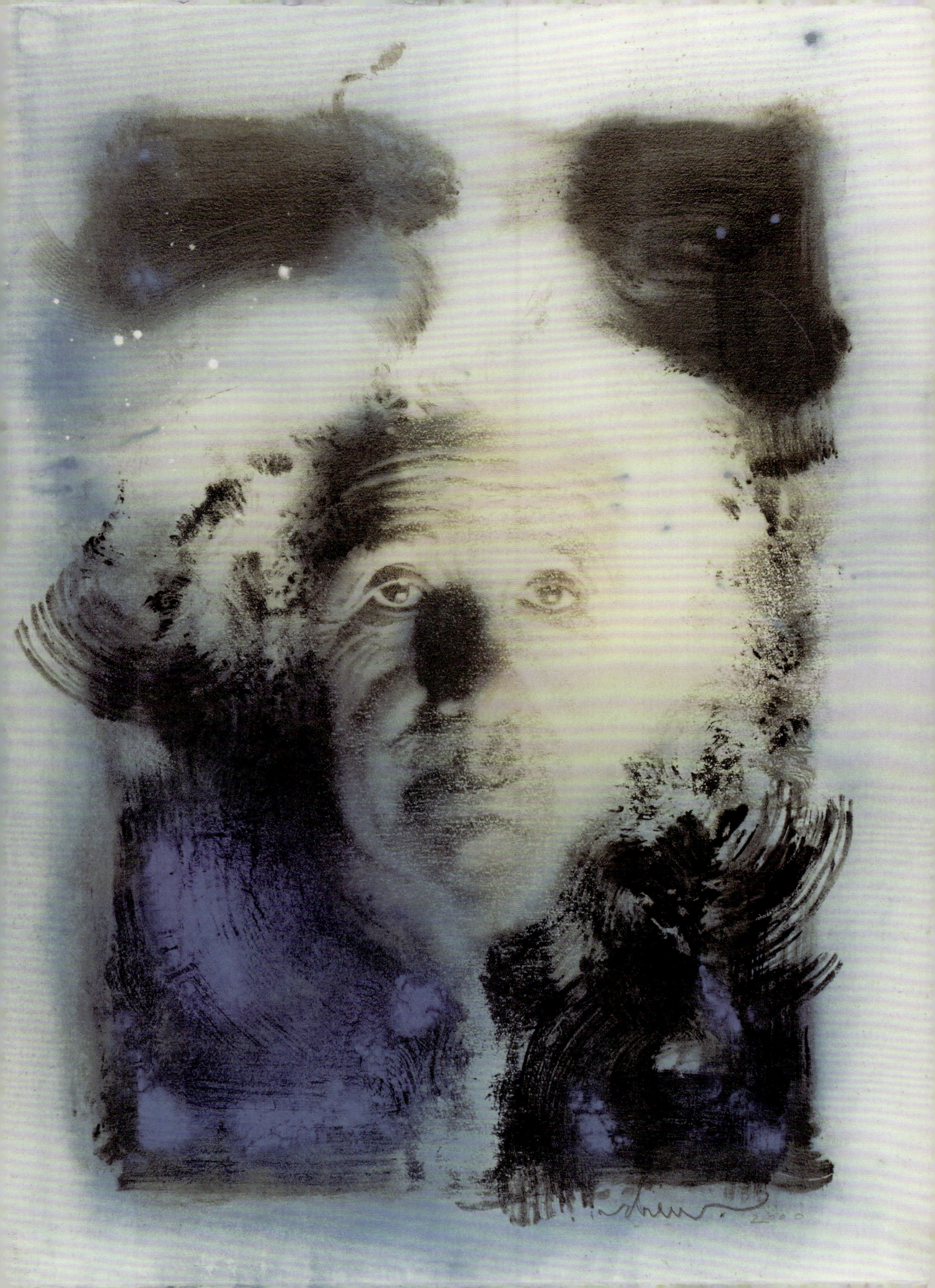

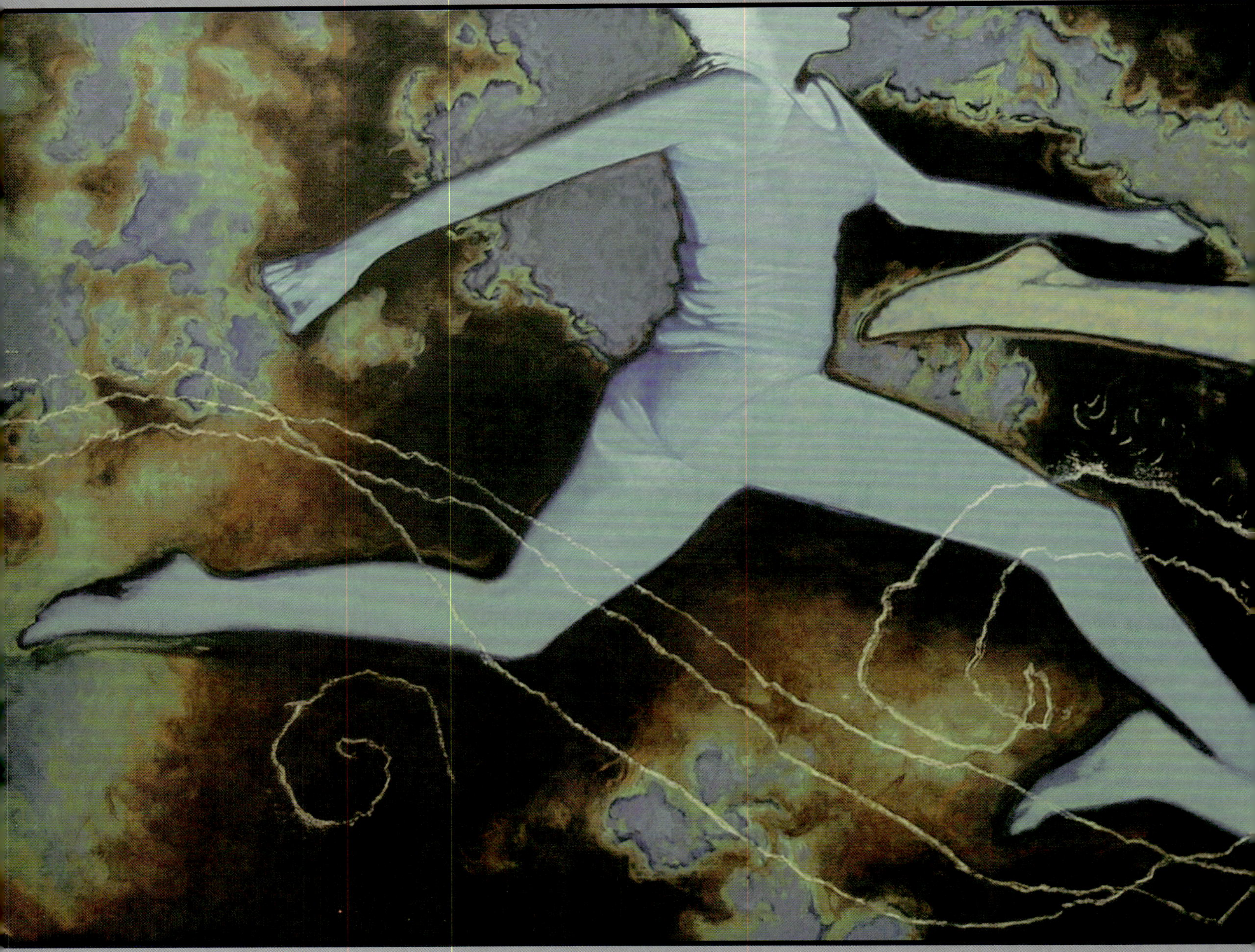

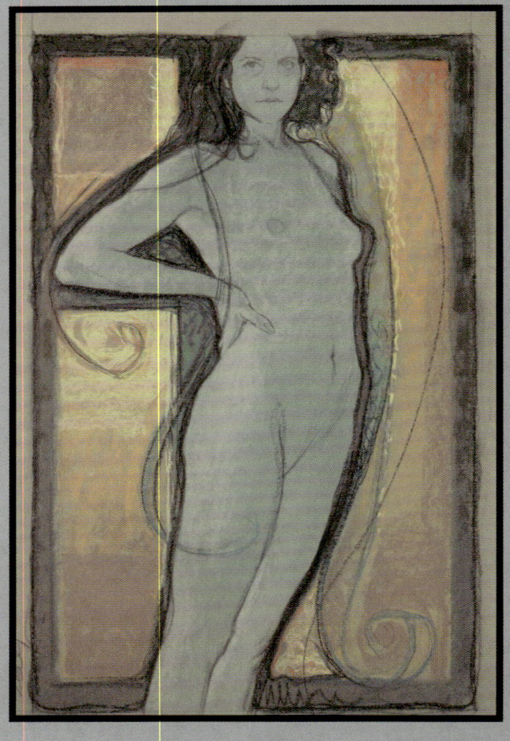

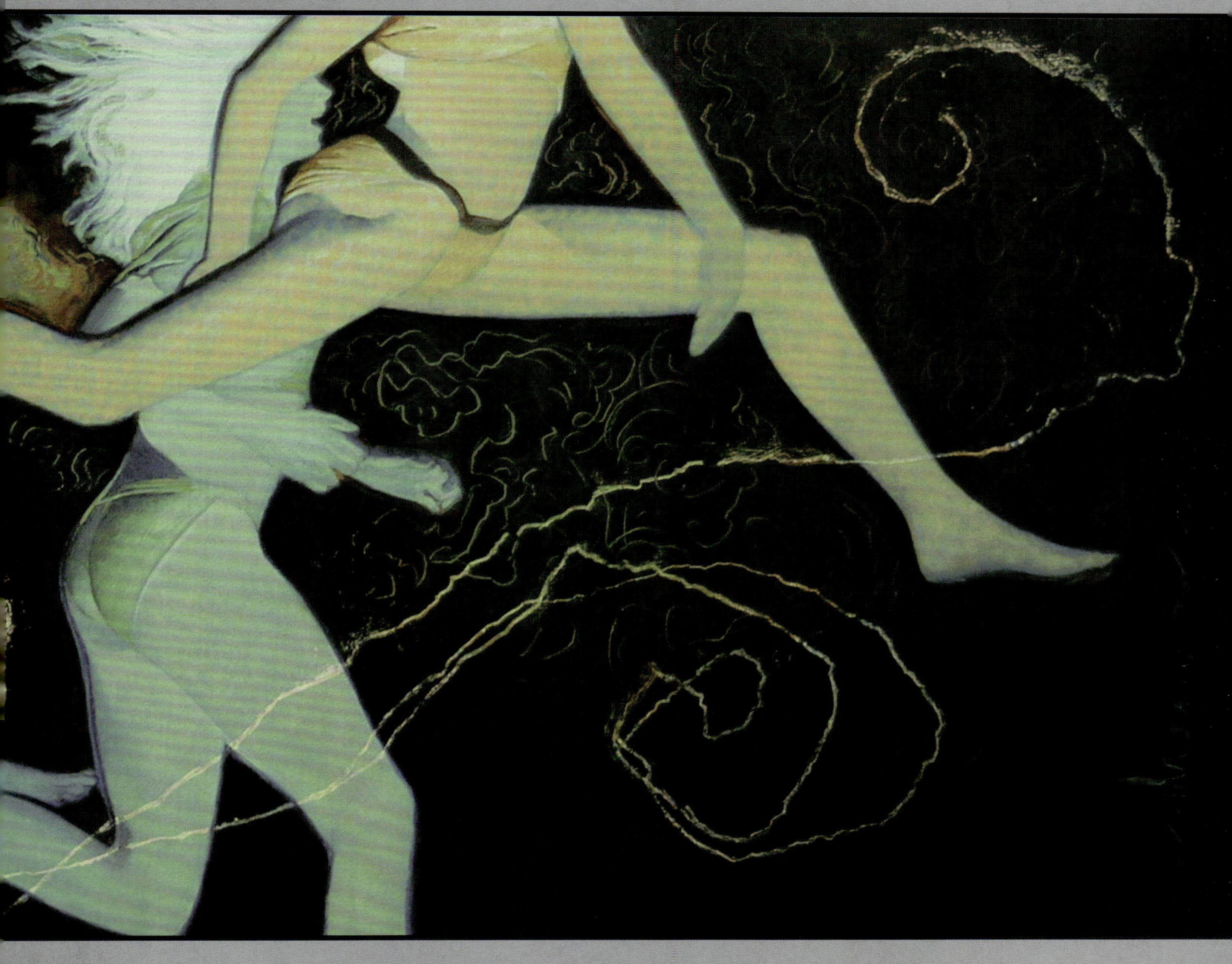

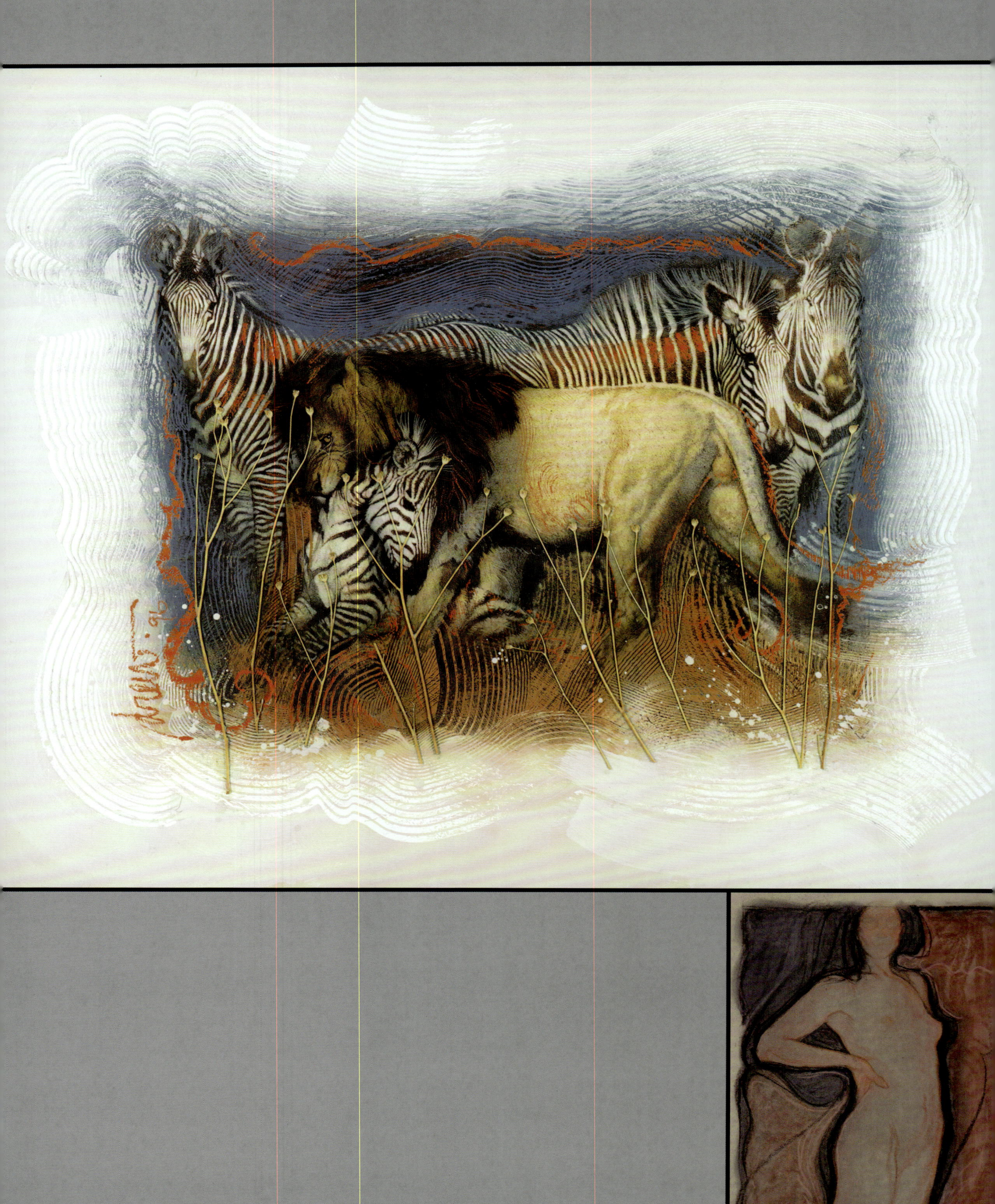

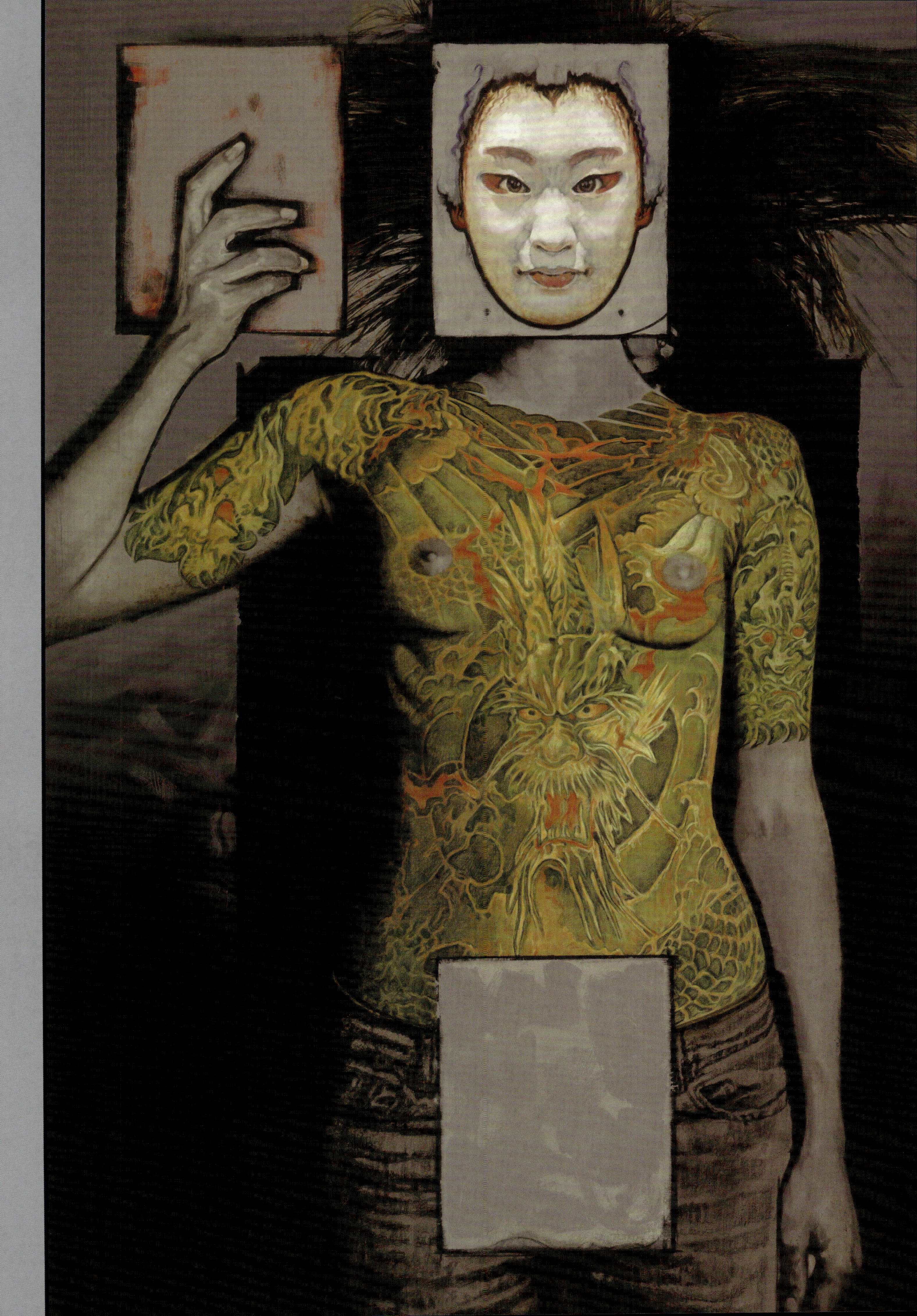

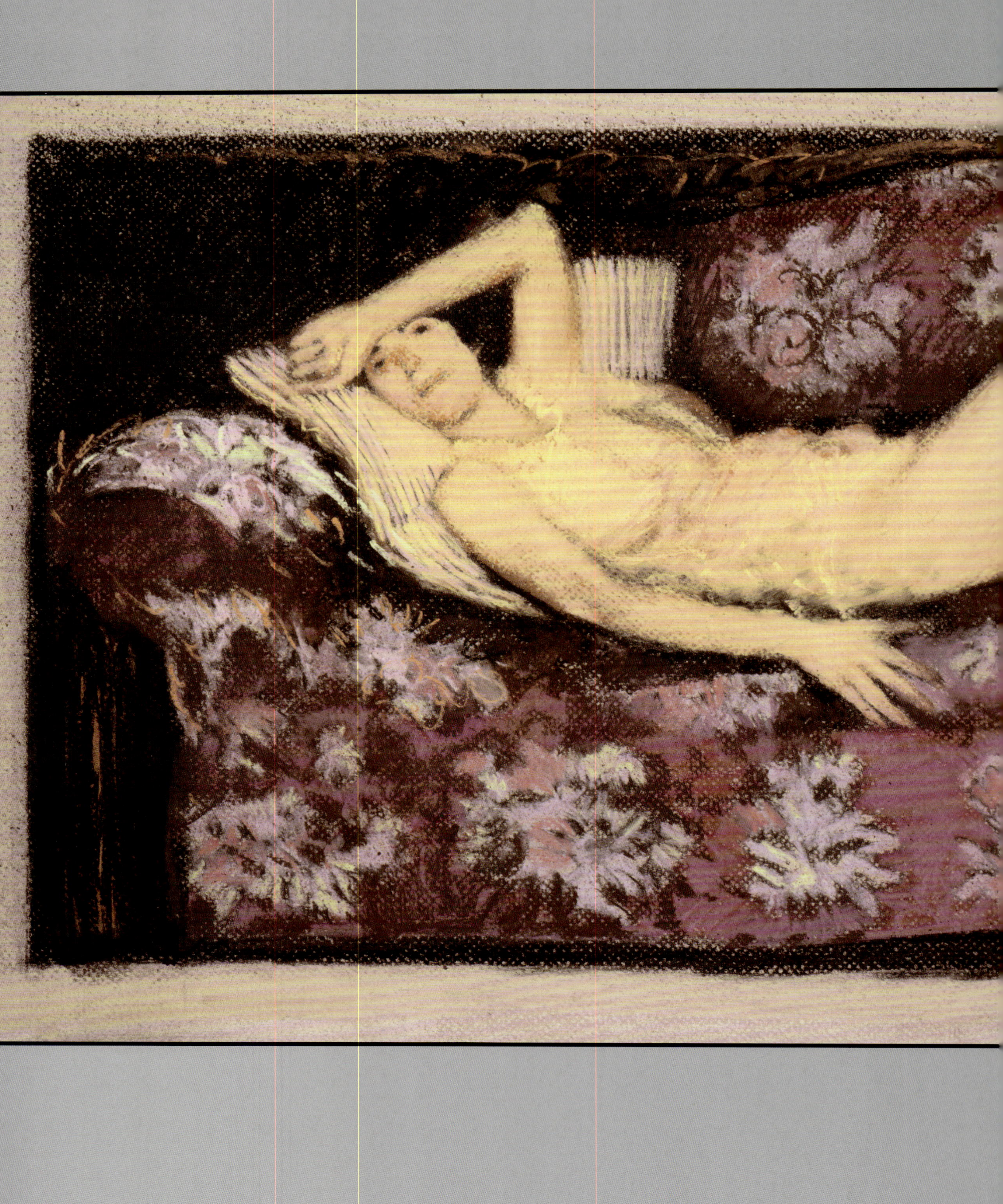

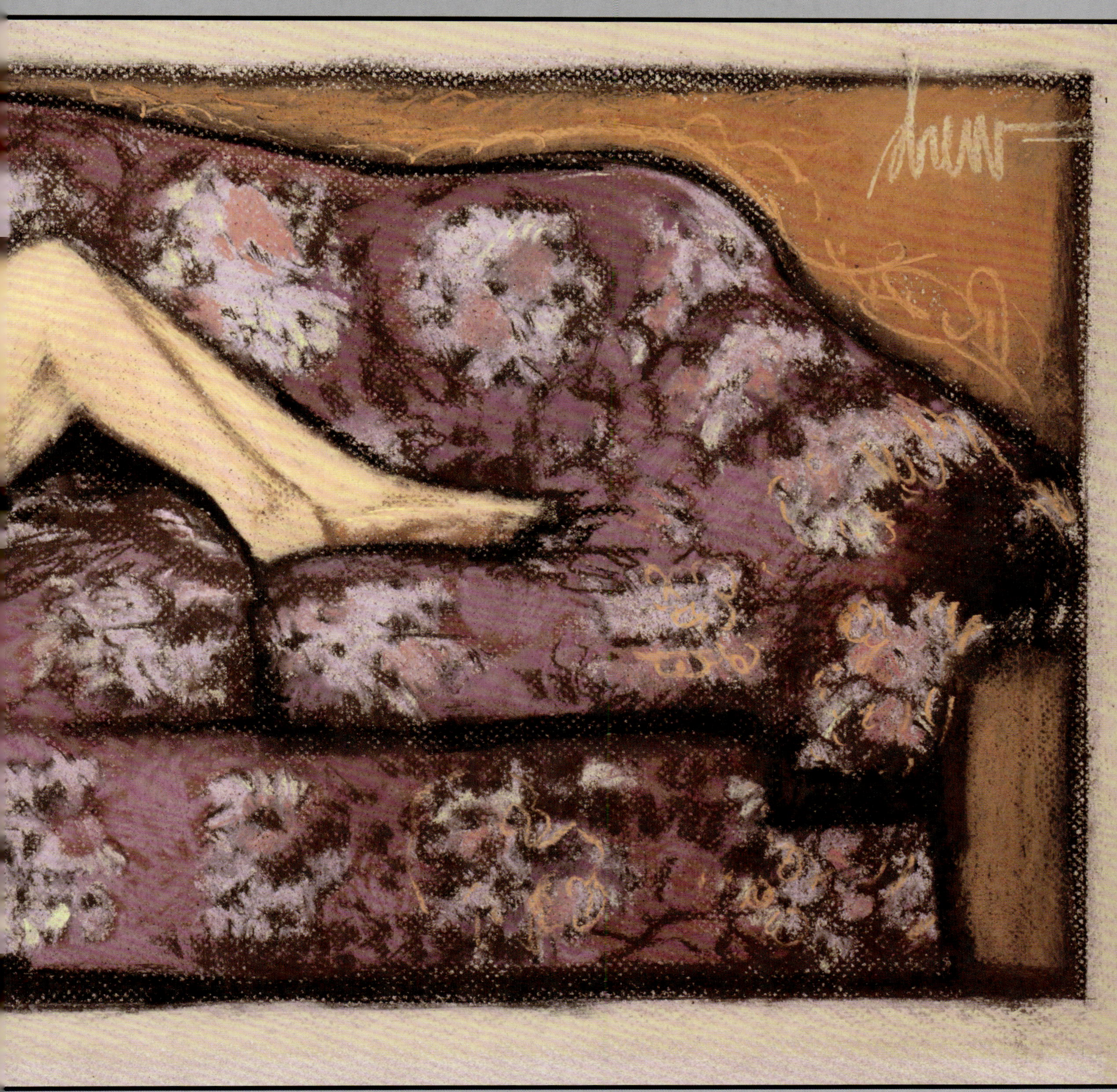

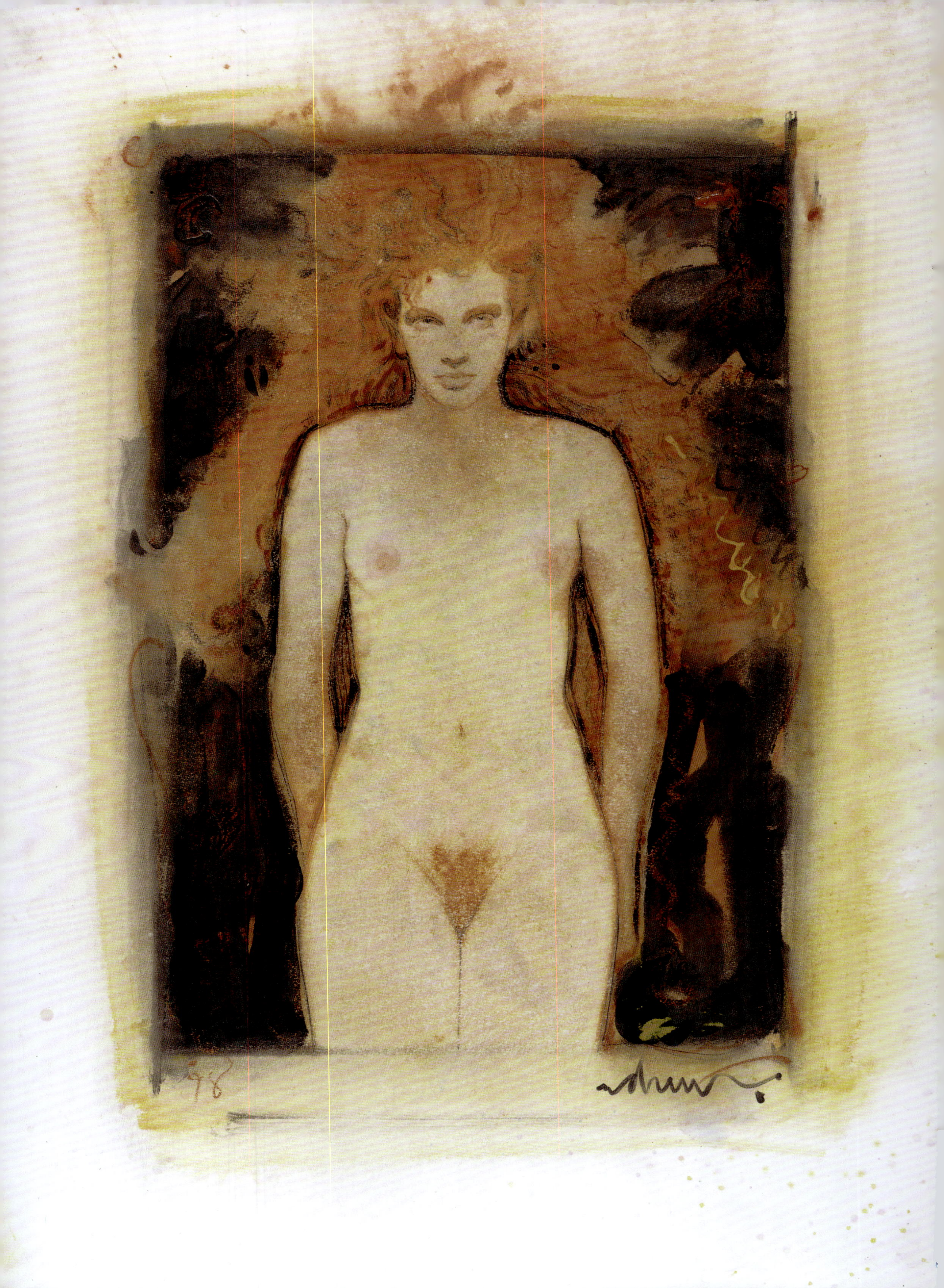

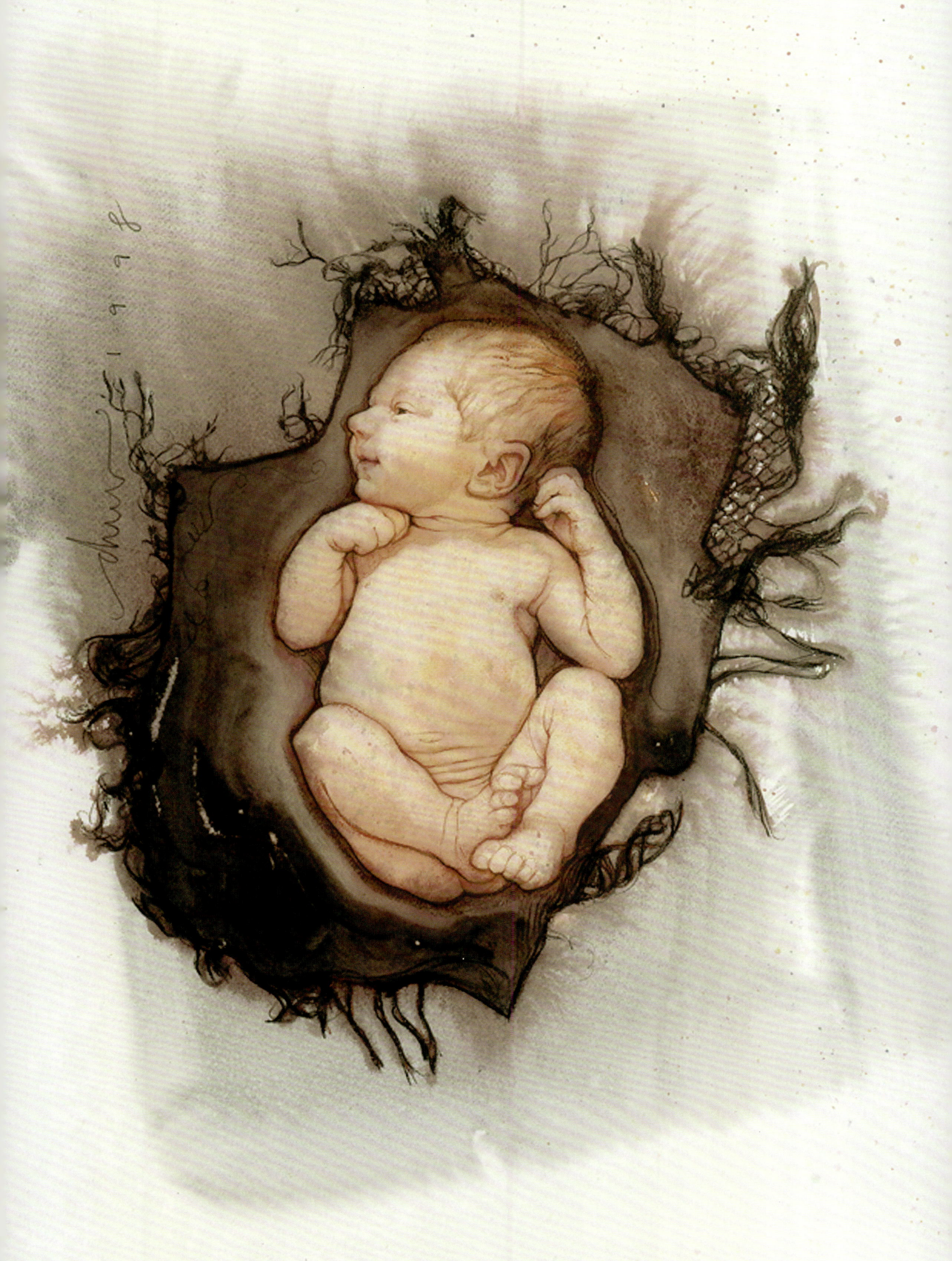

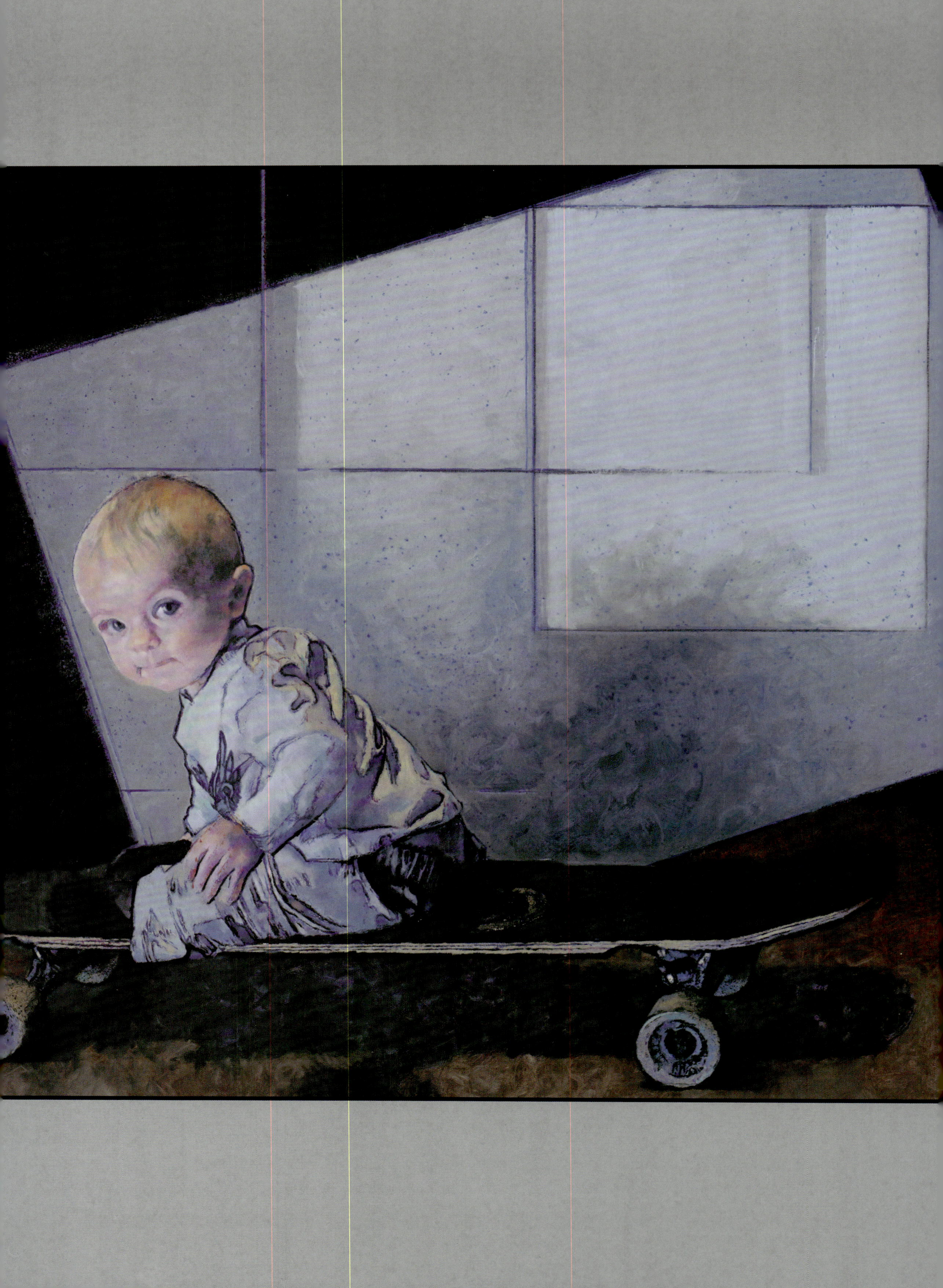

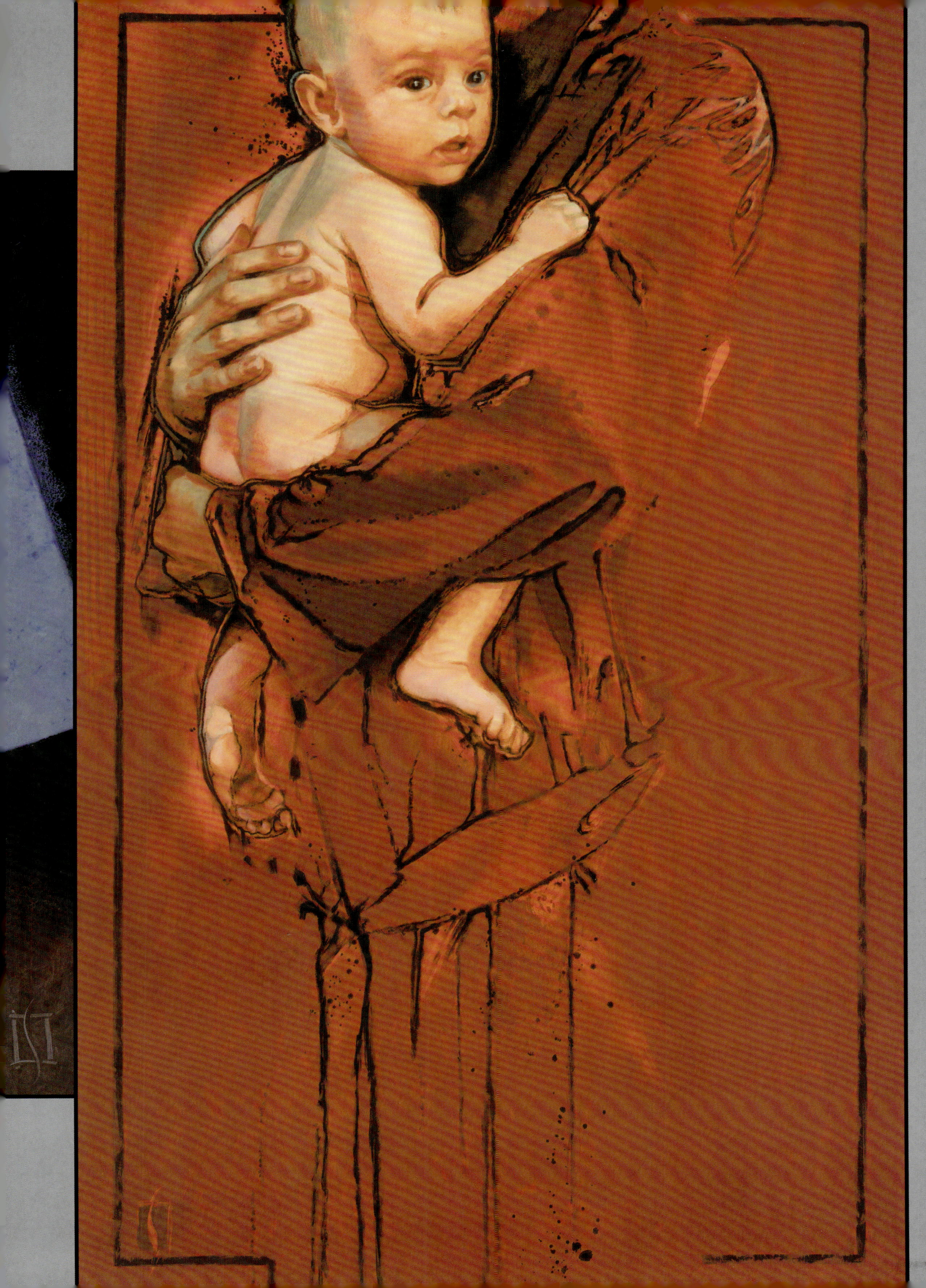

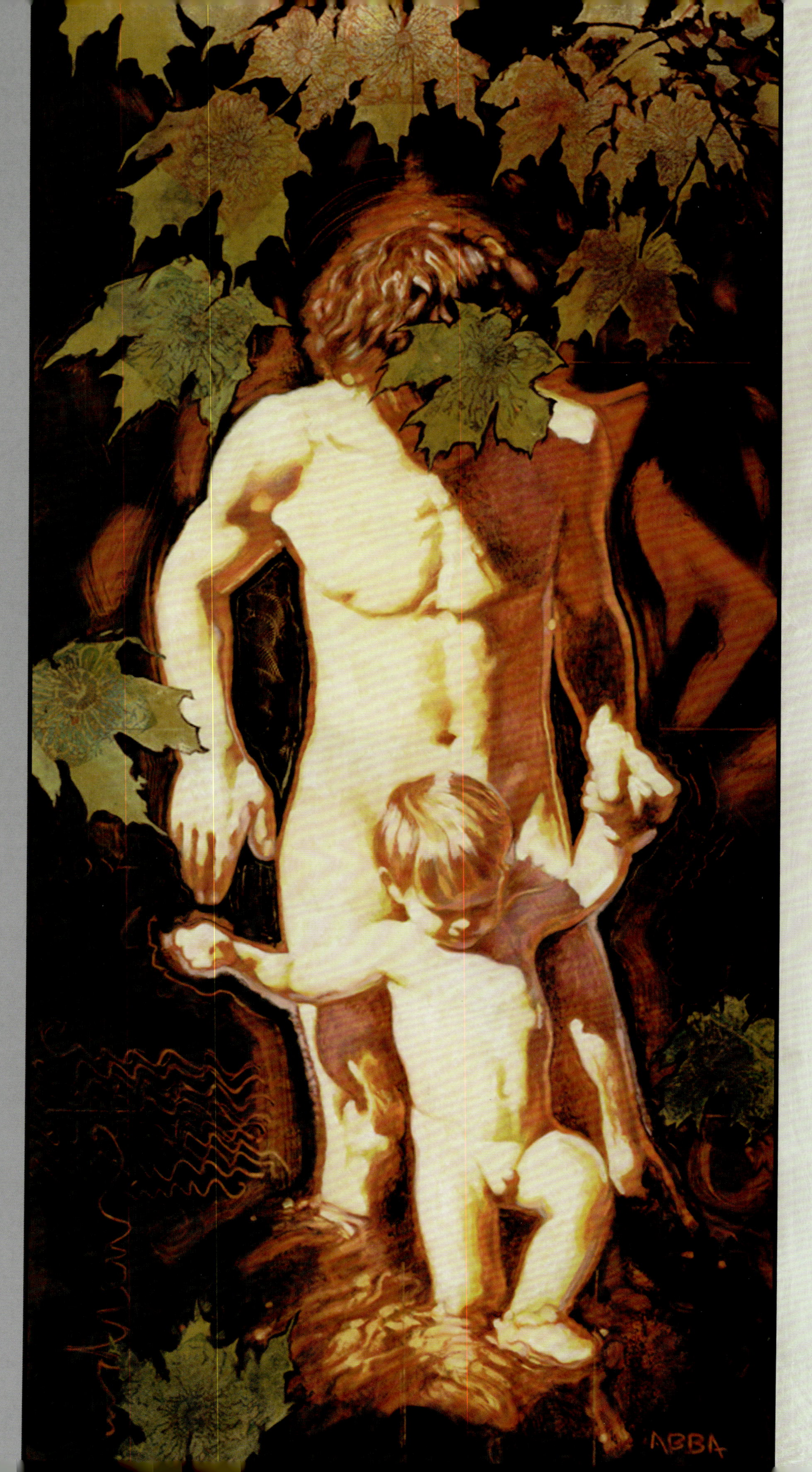
ABBA

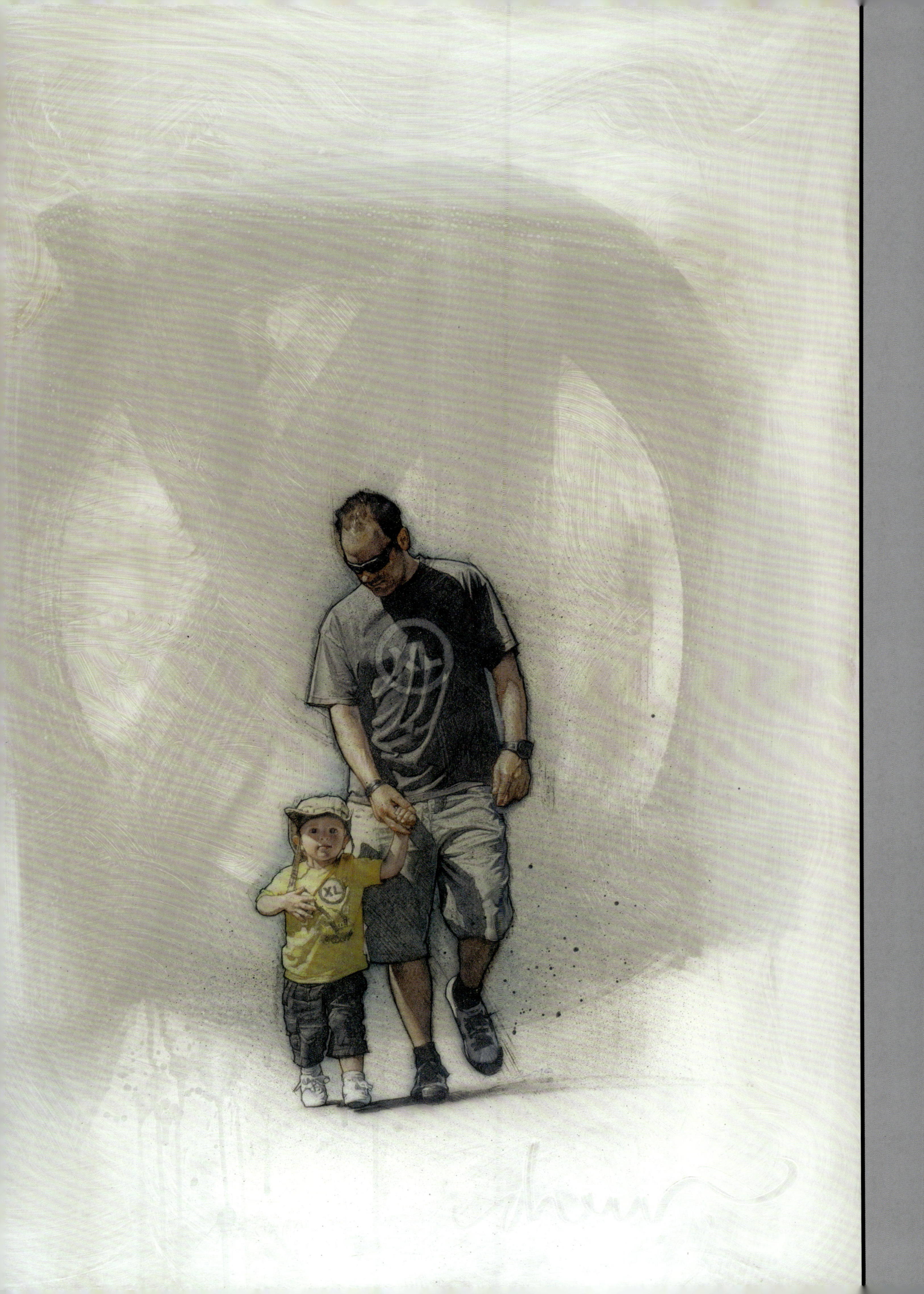
XL

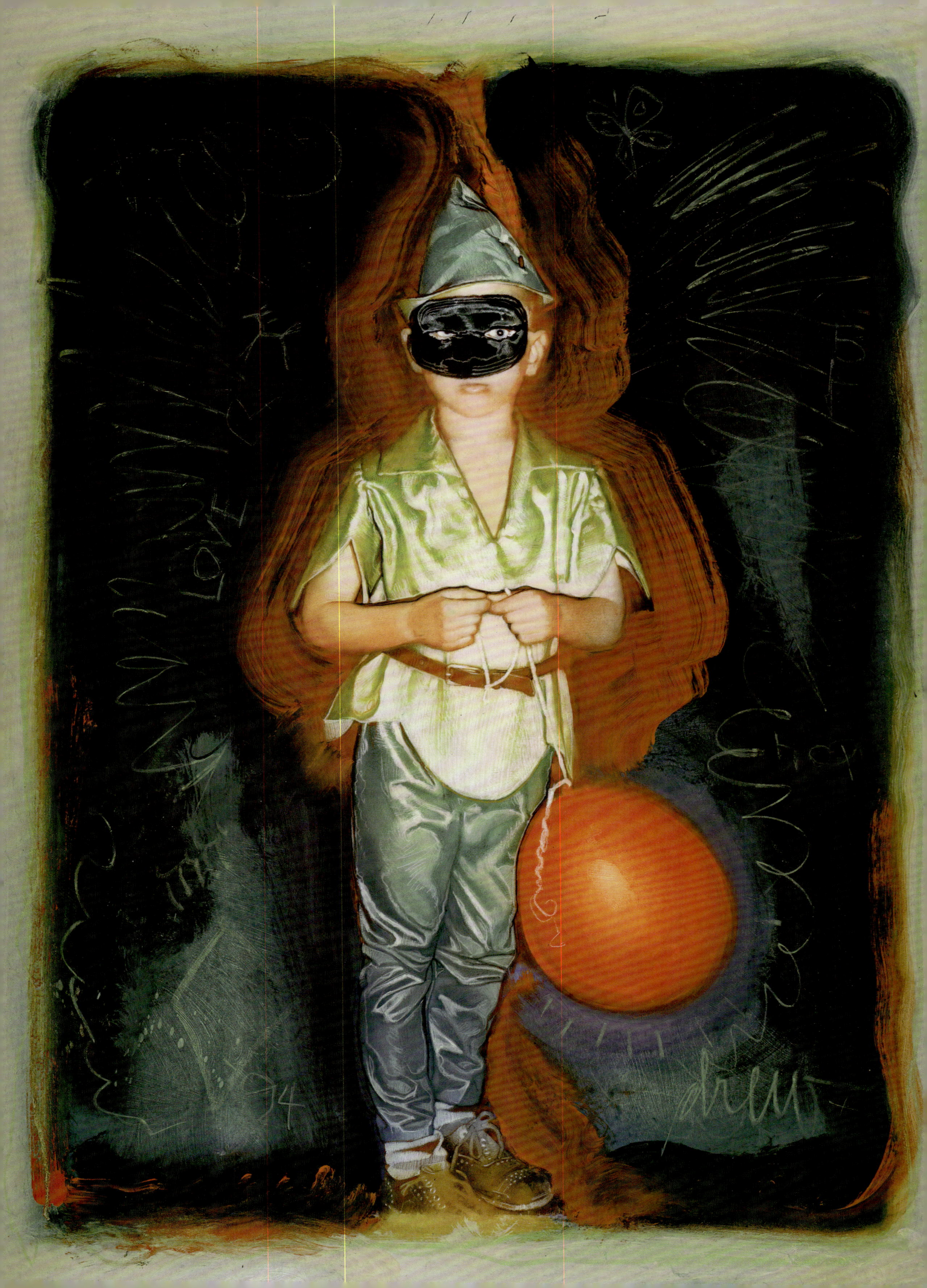

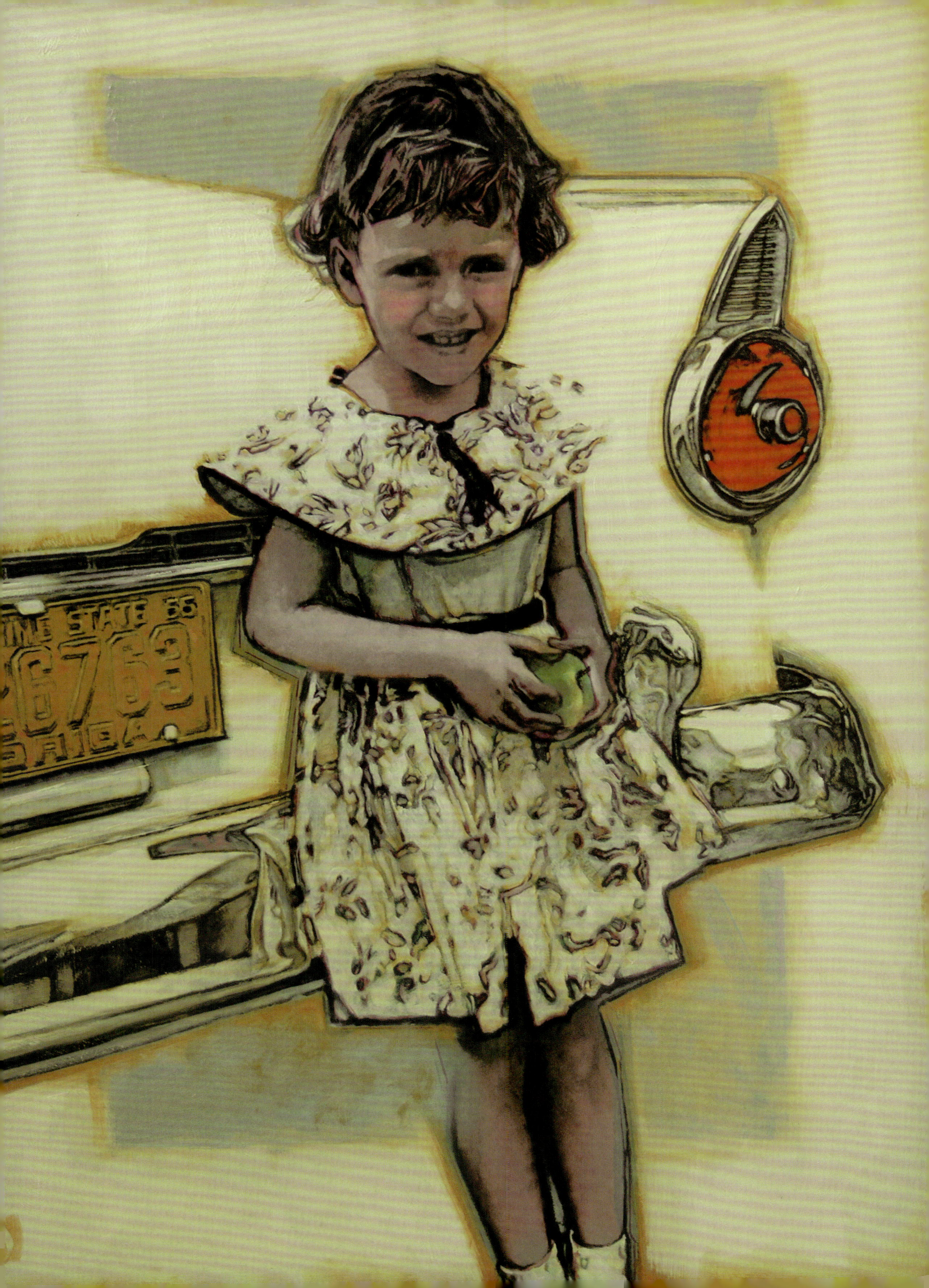
STATE 55

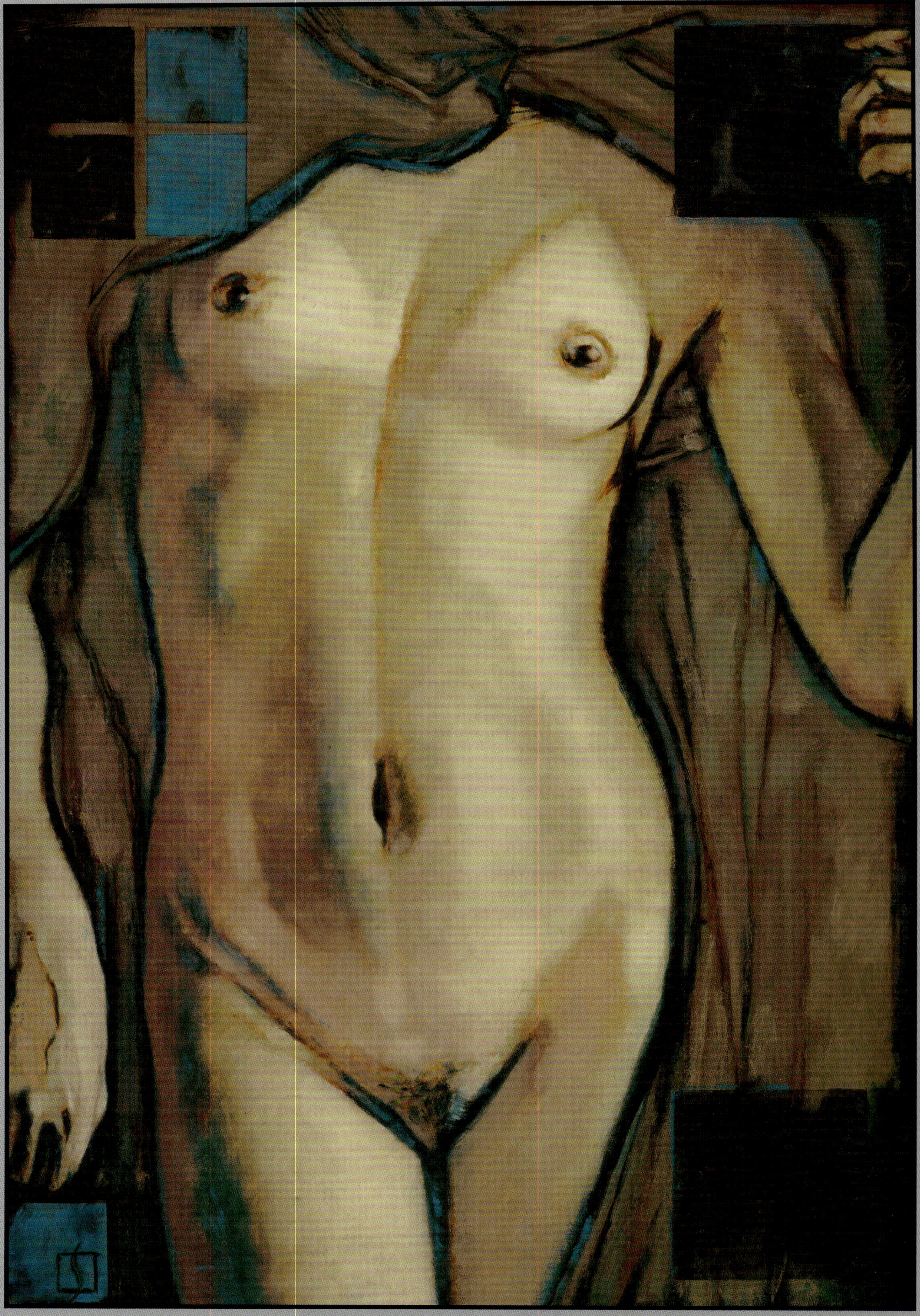

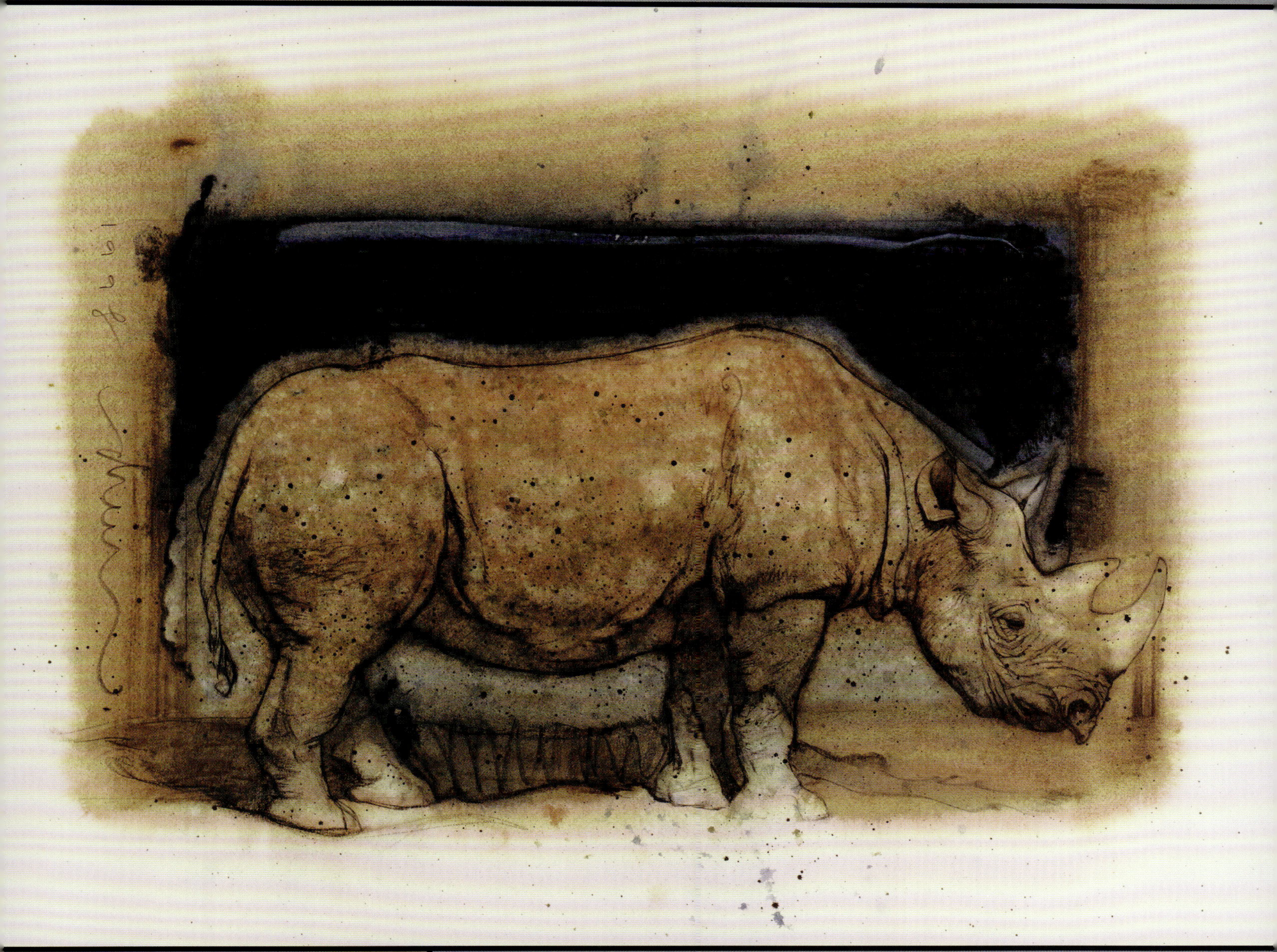

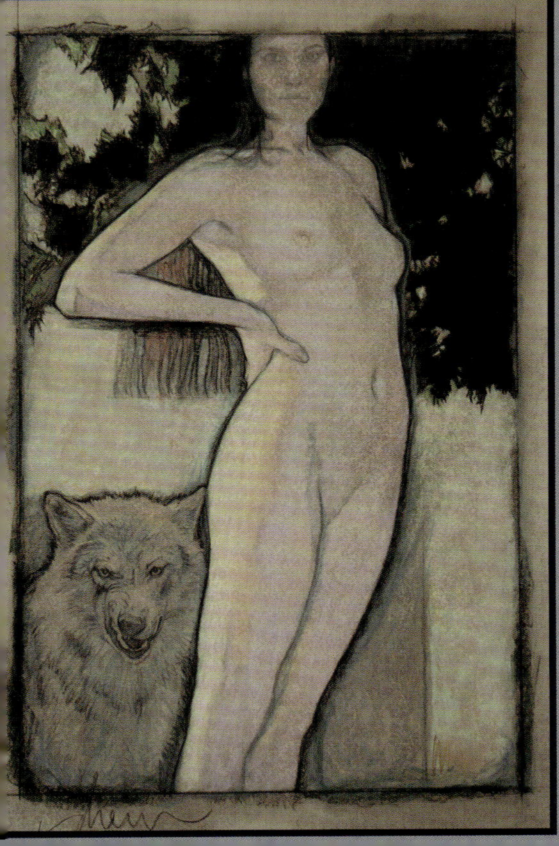

CAPTIONS

Dustjacket
Drew Struzan
8 x 11 inch art on 20 x 25 inch paper
Acrylics & colored pencils

Dustjacket
Dylan Struzan
8 x 11 inch art on 20 x 25 inch paper
Acrylics & colored pencils

Dustjacket
George Lucas
8 x 11 inch art on 20 x 25 inch paper
Acrylics & colored pencils

Page 6
Truth / Beauty
30 x 40 inches
Oils on board

Page 9
George Lucas (Foreword)
14 x 20.25 inch art on 20 x 30 inch board
Acrylics & colored pencils on board

Page 12
Self Portrait
11.5 x 18.5 inches
Acrylics & colored pencils on gessoed board

Page 15
Dylan reading
18.5 x 11.5 inches
Acrylics & colored pencils on gessoed board

Page 18
Lorser Feitelson
19 x 25 inches
Acrylics & colored pencils on paper

MUSIC

Page 21
Alice Cooper, Welcome to My Nightmare
Album Cover
24 x 30 inches
Oils on canvas

Pages 22-23
Alice Cooper, Greatest Hits
Album Cover
20 x 40 inches
Pencils on board

Pages 24-25
Mary Travers, Circles
Album Cover
20 x 40 inches
Acrylics & photo on board

Pages 26-27
Black Sabbath, Sabbath Bloody Sabbath
Album Cover (front & back)
40 x 30 inches
Colored pencils on board

Page 28
Glenn Miller
Album Cover
18 x 18 inches
Acrylics & colored pencils on board

Page 29
Beauty and the Beast
Album Cover
30 x 30 inches
Acrylics & colored pencils on gessoed board

Page 30
Tony Orlando & Dawn, To Be With You
Album Cover
24 x 24 inches
Acrylics & colored pencils on board

Page 31
The Modern Jazz Quartet, In Memoriam
Album Cover
18 x 18 inches
Oils on board

Page 32
Angels & Airwaves, I-Empire
Album Cover
30 x 40 inch board
Acrylics & colored pencils on gessoed board

Page 33
The Brothers Johnson, Blam
Album Cover
23.5 x 26 inch board
Acrylics & colored pencils on board

Pages 34-35
The Spielberg / Williams Collaboration
Album Cover (front & back)
19 x 32.375 inch art on 30 x 40 inch board
Acrylics & colored pencils on gessoed board

MOVIES

Page 37
Cowboys & Aliens
Movie Poster
24 x 36 inch art on 30 x 40 inch board
Acrylics & colored pencils on gessoed board

Page 38
First Blood
Movie Poster
31 x 40 inches
Acrylics & colored pencils on gessoed board

Page 39
The Thing
Movie Poster
24 x 23.5 inch art on 30 x 40 inch board
Acrylics & colored pencils on gessoed board

Page 40
The Outing
Movie Poster
24 x 36 inch art on 30 x 40 inch board
Acrylics & colored pencils on gessoed board

Page 41
Abominable
Movie Poster
20 x 30 inches
Acrylics & colored pencils on board

Page 42
Hellboy
Movie Poster
30 x 40 inch board
Acrylics & colored pencils on gessoed board

Page 43
Hellboy II: The Golden Army
Movie Poster
30 x 40 inch board
Acrylics & colored pencils on gessoed board

Page 44
Tarzan, the Ape Man
Movie Poster
30 x 38 inch art on 32 x 40 inch board
Acrylics & colored pencils on gessoed board

Page 45
Pan's Labyrinth
Movie Poster
30 x 40 inch board
Acrylics & colored pencils on gessoed board

Page 46
Raiders of the Lost Ark
Movie Poster (Advance)
30 x 45 inch board
Acrylics & colored pencils on gessoed board

Page 47
Indiana Jones and the Temple of Doom
Movie Poster (Advance)
25.5 x 39.5 inch art on 30 x 40 inch board
Acrylics & colored pencils on gessoed board

Page 48
Indiana Jones and the Last Crusade
Movie Poster
30 x 40 inch board
Acrylics & colored pencils on gessoed board

Page 49
Indiana Jones and the Kingdom of the Crystal Skull
Movie Poster
30 x 40 inch board
Acrylics & colored pencils on gessoed board

Page 50
Indiana Jones and the Last Crusade
Movie Poster (Advance)
30 x 40 inch board
Acrylics & colored pencils on gessoed board

Page 51
Indiana Jones and the Kingdom of the Crystal Skull
Movie Poster (Advance)
30 x 40 inch board
Acrylics & colored pencils on gessoed board

Page 52
Blade Runner
Movie Poster
30 x 40 inches
Acrylics & colored pencils on gessoed board

Page 53
Big Trouble in Little China
Movie Poster
30 x 40 inches
Acrylics & colored pencils on gessoed board

Page 54
To Be or Not To Be
Movie Poster
24.5 x 36.5 inches
Acrylics & colored pencils on gessoed board

Page 55
The Pirates of Penzance
Movie Poster
25 x 36 inches
Acrylics & colored pencils on gessoed board

Page 56
The Crocodile Hunter: Collision Course (A)
Movie Poster
22 x 34 inch art on 30 x 40 inch board
Acrylics & colored pencils on gessoed board

Page 57
The Crocodile Hunter: Collision Course (B)
Movie Poster
22 x 36 inch art on 30 x 40 inch board
Acrylics & colored pencils on gessoed board

Page 58
Hook
Movie Poster
26.5 x 40.5 inch art on 30 x 45 inch board
Acrylics & colored pencils on gessoed board

Page 59
Arabian Nights
TV Movie
20 x 31.5 inch art on 30 x 40 inch board
Acrylics & colored pencils on gessoed board

Page 60
Sahara (1)
Movie Poster
30 x 40 inch board
Acrylics & colored pencils on gessoed board

Page 61
Sahara (2)
Movie Poster
30 x 40 inch board
Acrylics & colored pencils on gessoed board

Page 62
Ladyhawke
Movie Poster
30 x 40 inch board
Acrylics & colored pencils on gessoed board

Page 63
Cutthroat Island
Movie Poster
27.5 x 39.5 inch art on 30 x 40 inch board
Acrylics & colored pencils on gessoed board

Page 64
Star Wars (Circus)
Movie Poster
30 x 40 inch board
Oils & dyes on gessoed board

Page 65
Star Wars: Revenge of the Jedi
Movie Poster
30 x 40 inch board
Acrylics & colored pencils on gessoed board

Page 66
Star Wars: Episode IV – A New Hope (Special Edition)
Movie Poster
24 x 36 inch art on 30 x 40 inch board

Acrylics & colored pencils on gessoed board

Page 67
Star Wars: Episode V – The Empire Strikes Back (Special Edition)
Movie Poster
24 x 36 inch art on 30 x 40 inch board
Acrylics & colored pencils on gessoed board

Page 68
Star Wars: Episode VI – Return of the Jedi (Special Edition)
Movie Poster
24 x 36 inch art on 30 x 40 inch board
Acrylics & colored pencils on gessoed board

Page 69
The Green Mile
Movie Poster / DVD Box Cover
24 x 36 inch art on 30 x 40 inch board
Acrylics & colored pencils on gessoed board

Page 70
The Shawshank Redemption (B)
Movie Poster
30 x 40 inch board
Acrylics & colored pencils on gessoed board

Page 71
The Shawshank Redemption (A)
Movie Poster
24 x 36 inch art on 30 x 40 inch board
Acrylics & colored pencils on gessoed board

Page 72
American Justice
Movie Poster
24 x 37.5 inches
Acrylics & colored pencils on gessoed board

Page 73
Torrente 3: El protector
Movie Poster
30 x 40 inch board
Acrylics & colored pencils on gessoed board

Page 74
Under Fire
Movie Poster
26 x 38.5 inch art on 30 x 40 inch board
Acrylics & colored pencils on gessoed board

Page 75
A Small Town in Texas
Movie Poster
30 x 40 inch board
Acrylics & colored pencils on gessoed board

Page 76
Return to Macon County
Movie Poster
30 x 30 inch board
Acrylics & colored pencils on gessoed board

Page 77
Borderline
Movie Poster
23.5 x 27 inches
Acrylics & colored pencils on gessoed board

Page 78
Champions
Movie Poster
27 x 40 inches
Acrylics & colored pencils on gessoed board

Page 79
Code Name: Emerald
Movie Poster
24 x 34 inch art on 30 x 37.5 inch board
Acrylics & colored pencils on gessoed board

Page 80
A Gift from Heaven
Movie Poster
26 x 38.75 inch art on 30 x 40 inch board
Acrylics & colored pencils on gessoed board

Page 81
Heat and Dust
Movie Poster
24 x 37 inches
Acrylics & colored pencils on gessoed board

Page 82
Cross Creek (A)
Movie Poster
40 x 20 inches
Acrylics & colored pencils on gessoed board

Page 83
Cross Creek (B)
Movie Poster
26 x 38 inches
Acrylics & colored pencils on gessoed board

Page 84
The Name of the Rose (A)
Movie Poster
26.5 x 34.25 inch art on 30 x 40 inch board
Acrylics & colored pencils on gessoed board

Page 85
The Name of the Rose (B)
Movie Poster
30 x 40 inch board
Acrylics & colored pencils on gessoed board

Page 86
Sunset
Movie Poster
27 x 36 inch art on 30 x 40 inch board
Acrylics & colored pencils on gessoed board

Page 87
Johnny Dangerously
Movie Poster
27 x 28 inch art on 32.5 x 30 inch board
Acrylics & colored pencils on gessoed board

Page 88
The Sting II (A)
Movie Poster
23.5 x 29 inch art on 30 x 40 inch board
Acrylics & colored pencils on gessoed board

Page 89
The Sting II (B)
Movie Poster
25.5 x 33.25 inch art on 30 x 40 inch board
Acrylics & colored pencils on gessoed board

Page 90
Fame
Movie Poster
23 x 29 inch art on 27 x 33 inch board
Acrylics & colored pencils on board

Page 91
Shirley Valentine

Movie Poster
23.5 x 33 inch art on 30 x 40 inch board
Acrylics & colored pencils on gessoed board

Page 92
Who's Killing the Great Chefs of Europe?
Movie Poster
25 x 33.5 inches
Acrylics & colored pencils on gessoed board

Page 93
The Seven-Per-Cent Solution
Movie Poster
30 x 30 inch board
Acrylics & colored pencils on board

Page 94
The Suit
Movie Poster
20 x 30 inch art on 30 x 40 inch board
Acrylics & colored pencils on gessoed board

Page 95
Zathura: A Space Adventure
Movie Poster
30 x 40 inches
Acrylics & colored pencils on gessoed board

Page 96
Masters of the Universe
Movie Poster
24 x 36 inch art on 30 x 40 inch board
Acrylics & colored pencils on gessoed board

Page 97
Dreamscape
Movie Poster
24 x 37.5 inch art on 30 x 40 inch gessoed board
Acrylics & colored pencils on gessoed board

Page 98
Adventures in Babysitting
Movie Poster
30 x 60 inches
Acrylics & colored pencils on board

Page 99
Hocus Pocus
Movie Poster
30 x 40 inch board
Acrylics & colored pencils on gessoed board

Page 100
Labou
Movie Poster
24 x 36 inch art on 30 x 40 inch board
Acrylics & colored pencils on gessoed board

Page 101
Harry and the Hendersons
Movie Poster
25 x 36 inch art on 30 x 40 inch board
Acrylics & colored pencils on gessoed board

Page 102
The Flintstones
Movie Poster
30 x 40 inches
Acrylics & colored pencils on gessoed board

Page 103
The Flintstones in Viva Rock Vegas
Movie Poster
30 x 40 inches
Acrylics & colored pencils on gessoed board

Page 104
Back to the Future
Movie Poster
25 x 36 inch art on 30 x 40 inch board
Acrylics & colored pencils on gessoed board

Page 105
Back to the Future Part II
Movie Poster
25 x 36 inch art on 30 x 40 inch board
Acrylics & colored pencils on gessoed board

Page 106
Back to the Future Part III
Movie Poster
25 x 36 inch art on 30 x 40 inch board
Acrylics & colored pencils on gessoed board

Page 107
The Great Muppet Caper
Movie Poster
22 x 28 inch art on 30 x 40 inch board
Acrylics & colored pencils on gessoed board

Page 108
The Muppet Movie (Studebaker)
Movie Poster
28 x 32 inch art on 30 x 35 inch board
Acrylics & colored pencils on gessoed board

Page 109
Muppet Treasure Island
Movie Poster
26 x 37 inch art on 30 x 40 inch board
Acrylics & colored pencils on gessoed board

Page 110
The Muppet Movie (rowboat)
Movie Poster
28.75 x 31.75 inch art
Acrylics & colored pencils on gessoed board

Page 111
The Muppet Christmas Carol
Movie Poster
24.75 x 32.75 inch art on 30 x 40 inch board
Acrylics & colored pencils on gessoed board

Page 112
We're Back! A Dinosaur's Story (parade)
Movie Poster
24.5 x 36 inch art on 30 x 40 inch board
Acrylics & colored pencils on gessoed board

Page 113
We're Back! A Dinosaur's Story (raft)
Movie Poster
2.5 x 30 inch art on 30 x 40 inch board
Acrylics & colored pencils on gessoed board

Page 114
An American Tail (gang plank)
Movie Poster
24 x 36 inch art on 30 x 40 inch board
Acrylics & colored pencils on gessoed board

Page 115
An American Tail (suitcases)
Movie Poster
24 x 36 inch art on 30 x 40 inch board
Acrylics & colored pencils on gessoed board

Page 116
DuckTales: The Movie – Treasure of the Lost Lamp
Movie Poster
26 x 36.5 inch art on 30 x 40 inch board
Acrylics & colored pencils on gessoed board

Page 117
The Goonies
Movie Poster
23.25 x 37 inch art on 30 x 40 inch board
Acrylics & colored pencils on gessoed board

Page 118
Return to Oz
Movie Poster
27.5 x 38.5 inch art on 30 x 40 inch board
Acrylics & colored pencils on gessoed board

Page 119
Return to Oz (Mombi)
Movie Poster (Advance)
24.75 x 38.75 inch art on 30 x 40 inch board
Acrylics & colored pencils on board

Page 120
The Frisco Kid
Movie Poster
23.5 x 25 inches
Oils on gessoed board

Page 121
Better Off Dead
Movie Poster
28 x 20 inch art on 26.5 x 36 inch board
Acrylics & colored pencils on gessoed board

Page 122
Weekend Warriors
Movie Poster
25.5 x 39 inch art on 30 x 40 inch board
Acrylics & colored pencils on gessoed board

Page 123
Meatballs III: Summer Job
Movie Poster
25 x 31.5 inch art on 30 x 40 inch board
Acrylics & colored pencils on gessoed board

Page 124
Police Academy (girl cop)
Movie Poster
32 x 55 inch board
Acrylics & colored pencils on gessoed board

Page 125
Police Academy 2: Their First Assignment
Movie Poster
26 x 40 inches
Acrylics & colored pencils on gessoed board

Page 126
Police Academy 4: Citizens on Patrol
Movie Poster
28.5 x 39 inch art on 32 x 43.5 inch board
Acrylics & colored pencils on gessoed board

Page 127
Police Academy 3: Back in Training
Movie Poster
26 x 34 inch art on 30 x 37 inch board
Acrylics & colored pencils on gessoed board

Page 128
The Cannonball Run
Movie Poster
30 x 40 inches
Acrylics & colored pencils on gessoed board

Page 129
All's Fair
Movie Poster
30 x 40 inches
Acrylics & colored pencils on gessoed board

Page 130
Coming to America
Movie Poster
30 x 40 inches
Acrylics & colored pencils on gessoed board

Page 131
Coming to America (Statue of Liberty)
Movie Poster (Advance)
30 x 40 inches
Acrylics & colored pencils on gessoed board

Page 132
Happy Hour
Movie Poster
27 x 36 inch art on 30 x 40 inch board
Acrylics & colored pencils on gessoed board

Page 133
Sexina: Popstar P.I.
Movie Poster
30 x 40 inch board
Acrylics & colored pencils on gessoed board

Page 134
California Suite
Movie Poster
30 x 40 inches
Acrylics & colored pencils on gessoed board

Page 135
Health
Movie Poster
19 x 23 inch art on 25.5 x 28.5 inch board
Acrylics & colored pencils on gessoed board

Page 136
Three O'Clock High
Movie Poster
20 x 30.5 inch art on 30 x 40 inch board
Acrylics & colored pencils on gessoed board

Page 137
Angels in the Outfield
Movie Poster
30 x 40 inches
Acrylics & colored pencils on gessoed board

Page 138
Harry Potter and the Sorcerer's Stone
Movie Poster
24 x 36 inch art on 30 x 40 inch board
Acrylics & colored pencils on gessoed board

Page 139
Harry Potter and the Chamber of Secrets
Movie Poster (unused)
24 x 36 inch art on 30 x 40 inch board
Acrylics & colored pencils on gessoed board

Page 140
E.T.: The Extra-Terrestrial
Movie Poster
27.25 x 40 inches

Acrylics & colored pencils on gessoed board

Page 141
Batteries Not Included
Movie Poster
24.5 x 31.5 inch art on 30 x 40 inch board
Acrylics & colored pencils on gessoed board

Page 142
Star Wars: Episode I – The Phantom Menace
Movie Poster
30 x 40 inch board
Acrylics & colored pencils on gessoed board

Page 143
Star Wars: Episode II – Attack of the Clones
Movie Poster
24 x 36 inch art on 30 x 40 inch board
Acrylics & colored pencils on gessoed board

Page 144
Star Wars: Episode III – Revenge of the Sith (Special Edition)
Movie Poster
30 x 40 inch board
Acrylics & colored pencils on gessoed board

Page 145
The Dark Tower
Movie Prop, Mock Movie Poster
30 x 40 inches
Acrylics & colored pencils on gessoed board

Page 146
The Mist
Movie Poster
20 x 30 inches
Acrylics & colored pencils on gessoed board

Page 147
The Walking Dead
San Diego Comic-Con Poster (TV series)
30 x 40 inch board
Acrylics & colored pencils on gessoed board

Page 148
Squirm
Movie Poster
27 x 40 inch board
Inks on board

Page 149
Into the Fire
Movie Poster
30 x 40 inch board
Acrylics & colored pencils on gessoed board

Page 150
Creature from the Black Lagoon
Collectable Print
30 x 40 inches
Oils, acrylics & colored pencils on board

Page 151
Frankenstein
Tribute Movie Poster
30 x 40 inch board
Acrylics & colored pencils on gessoed board

PUBLISHING

Page 153
Action Comics #800 (Superman)
Comic Cover
11.25 x 18 inch art on 22 x 30 inch board
Acrylics & colored pencils on gessoed board

Page 154
Blue
Poster (Convention Special)
30 x 40 inch board
Acrylics & colored pencils on gessoed board

Page 155 (left)
Blue (1)
Comic Cover
30 x 40 inch board
Acrylics & colored pencils on gessoed board

Page 155 (right)
Blue (2)
Comic Cover
30 x 40 inch board
Acrylics & colored pencils on gessoed board

Page 156-157
The Hollywood Reporter, 13 November 1984
(20th Century Fox: The First 50 Years)
Magazine Cover (5 fold)
80 x 24 inches
Acrylics & colored pencils on panel

Page 158-159
Star Trek: The Next Generation: "Future's Past"
Computer Game Box Cover
40 x 30 inch board
Acrylics & colored pencils on gessoed board

Page 160-161
Brave New World
Book Cover
24.5 x 33 inch art on 30 x 40 inch board
Acrylics & colored pencils on gessoed board

Page 162-163
Star Wars: Rebellion Era Sourcebook
Book Cover
28 x 17.5 inch art on 20 x 40 inch board
Acrylics & colored pencils on gessoed board

Page 164-165
Star Wars: The New Rebellion
Book Cover
27.5 x 18.5 inch art on 40 x 30 inch board
Acrylics & colored pencils on gessoed board

Page 166
Star Wars Darth Maul #1
Comic Cover
10 x 15.5 inch art on 20 x 30 inch board
Acrylics & colored pencils on gessoed board

Page 167 (left)
Star Wars Darth Maul #2
Comic Cover
10 x 15.5 inch art on 20 x 30 inch board
Acrylics & colored pencils on gessoed board

Page 167 (right)
Star Wars Darth Maul #3
Comic Cover
10 x 15.5 inch art on 20 x 30 inch board
Acrylics & colored pencils on gessoed board

Page 168-169
TV Guide, 15-21 May 1999 (Star Wars:
Episode I – The Phantom Menace)
Magazine Covers (4-Part Collector's Set)

20 x 40 inches
Acrylics & pencils on gessoed board

Page 170-171
Star Wars: Roleplaying Game
Box Cover
36 x 24 inch art on 40 x 30 inch board
Acrylics & colored pencils on gessoed board

Page 172-173
Star Wars: The Courtship of Princess Leia (hardback)
Book Cover
40 x 30 inch board
Acrylics & colored pencils on gessoed board

Page 174-175
Star Wars: The Truce at Bakura
Book Cover
30 x 30 inch board
Acrylics & colored pencils on gessoed board

Page 176 (left)
Star Wars: The Rise and Fall of Darth Vader (Anakin)
Book Cover (double cover)
12 x 18 inch art on 16 x 20 inch board
Acrylics & colored pencils on gessoed board

Page 176 (right)
Star Wars: The Rise and Fall of Darth Vader (Vader)
Book Cover (double cover)
12 x 18 inch art on 16 x 20 inch board
Acrylics & colored pencils on gessoed board

Page 177
John Carpenter's Snake Plissken Chronicles
Comic Cover
22 x 29.5 inches
Charcoal, acrylics & colored pencils on watercolor paper

Page 178-179
George Lucas: The Creative Impulse: Lucasfilm's First Twenty Years
Book Cover
30 x 40 inch board
Acrylics & colored pencils on gessoed board

Page 180-181
George Lucas: The Creative Impulse: Lucasfilm's First Twenty-Five Years
Book Cover
30 x 40 inch board
Acrylics & colored pencils on gessoed board

Page 182-183
Indiana Jones and the Dinosaur Eggs
Book Cover
23 x 17.5 inch art on 40 x 30 inch board
Acrylics & colored pencils on gessoed board

Page 184-185
Indiana Jones and the Seven Veils
Book Cover
23 x 17.5 inch art on 40 x 30 inch board
Acrylics & colored pencils on gessoed board

Page 186-187
Star Wars: Planet of Twilight
Book Cover
27.5 x 18.5 inch art on 40 x 30 inch board
Acrylics & colored pencils on gessoed board

Page 188-189
Star Wars: Shadows of the Empire
Book Cover
27.5 x 18.5 inch art on 40 x 30 inch board
Acrylics & colored pencils on gessoed board

Page 190-191
Indiana Jones and the Philosopher's Stone
Book Cover
23 x 17.5 inch art on 40 x 30 inch board
Acrylics & colored pencils on gessoed board

Page 192-193
Indiana Jones and the Sky Pirates
Book Cover
23 x 17.5 inch art on 40 x 30 inch board
Acrylics & colored pencils on gessoed board

Page 194-195
Indiana Jones and the Secret of the Sphinx
Book Cover
23 x 17.5 inch art on 40 x 30 inch board
Acrylics & colored pencils on gessoed board

Page 196
Lady Pendragon #1
Comic Cover
30 x 40 inches
Acrylics & colored pencils on gessoed board

Page 197
MAD #379 (YoYos for Dummies)
Magazine Cover
14 x 17 inch art on 20 x 30 inch board
Acrylics & colored pencils on gessoed board

Page 198
TV Guide, 25-31 December 1993 (Johnny Carson)
Magazine Cover
13.5 x 20.5 inches
Acrylics, oils & colored pencils on board

Page 199
Astounding Space Thrills #3
Comic Cover
14.75 x 20.25 inch art on 22 x 30 inch board
Acrylics & colored pencils on board

COMMERCIAL

Page 201
Disneyana (Pocahontas)
Collectable Print
26 x 39 inch art on 30 x 40 inch board
Acrylics & colored pencils on gessoed board

Page 202
Indiana Jones (Trilogy)
DVD Box Cover
30 x 40 inches
Acrylics & colored pencils on gessoed board

Page 203
Indiana Jones (Bonus Material)
DVD Box Cover
30 x 40 inches
Acrylics & colored pencils on gessoed board

Page 204
Disneyland, Indiana Jones Adventure
Ride Poster
30 x 40 inches
Acrylics & colored pencils on gessoed board

Page 205
Indiana Jones and the Last Crusade (Pepsi Cola)

Promotional Poster
22.25 x 34.5 inch art on 30 x 40 inch board
Acrylics & colored pencils on gessoed board

Page 206
Star Wars: The First Ten years
Collectable Poster
27 x 41 inch art on 30 x 44 inch board
Acrylics & colored pencils on gessoed board

Page 207
Star Wars
US Postage Stamps
30 x 40 inches
Acrylics & colored pencils on gessoed board

Page 208-209
The Lord of the Rings Masterpieces (Sets 1 & 2)
Tops Trading Cards
12.5 x 19.25 inches
Acrylics & colored pencils on colored paper

Page 210
Arrowhead Arts Association (5)
Event Poster
30 x 40 inches
Acrylics & colored pencils on gessoed board

Page 211
Arrowhead Bach Festival (3)
Event Poster
30 x 40 inches
Acrylics & colored pencils on gessoed board

Page 212
Arrowhead Bach Festival (1)
Event Poster
30 x 40 inches
Pastels & colored pencils on paper

Page 213
Arrowhead Bach Festival (2)
Event Poster
30 x 30 inches
Acrylics & colored pencils on gessoed board

Page 214 (left)
Star Trek (25th Anniversary, Captain Kirk)
Collectable Poster
25 x 38 inch art on 30 x 40 inch board
Acrylics & colored pencils on gessoed board

Page 214 (right)
Star Trek (25th Anniversary, Dr. McCoy)
Collectable Poster
25 x 38 inch art on 30 x 40 inch board
Acrylics & colored pencils on gessoed board

Page 215
Star Trek (25th Anniversary, Mr. Spock)
Collectable Poster
25 x 38 inch art on 30 x 40 inch board
Acrylics & colored pencils on gessoed board

Page 216
Star Trek: Captains & Crew (Star Trek)
Collector Plate
16 inch circle on 30 x 30 inch board
Acrylics & colored pencils on gessoed board

Page 217
Star Trek: Captains & Crew (The Next Generation)
Collector Plate
16 inch circle on 30 x 30 inch board
Acrylics & colored pencils on gessoed board

Page 218
Princess Diana (Princess of Hope)
Collector Plate
16 inch circle on 30 x 30 inch board
Acrylics & colored pencils on gessoed board

Page 219
Princess Diana (Princess of Style)
Collector Plate
16 inch circle on 30 x 30 inch board
Acrylics & colored pencils on gessoed board

Page 220
Frank Sinatra (Lady is a Tramp)
Collector Plate
16 inch circle on 30 x 30 inch board
Acrylics & colored pencils on gessoed board

Page 221
Frank Sinatra (Witchcraft)
Collector Plate
16 inch circle on 30 x 30 inch board
Acrylics & colored pencils on gessoed board

Page 222
The Little Rascals (Official)
Collector Plate
16 inch circle on 30 x 30 inch board
Acrylics & colored pencils on gessoed board

Page 223
The Little Rascals (Super Slooth)
Collector Plate
16 inch circle on 30 x 30 inch board
Acrylics & colored pencils on gessoed board

Page 224
The Three Stooges (The Dictators)
Collector Plate
16 inch circle on 30 x 30 inch board
Acrylics & colored pencils on gessoed board

Page 225
The Three Stooges (Dr. Howard... Dr. Fine... Dr. Howard)
Collector Plate
16 inch circle on 30 x 30 inch board
Acrylics & colored pencils on gessoed board

Page 226-227
The Lost World: Jurassic Park
Limited Edition Print
33.5 x 25.25 inch art on 30 x 4 inch board
Acrylics & colored pencils on gessoed board

Page 228 (left)
Legends of Hollywood: John Wayne
US Postage Stamp
5.525 x 7 inch art on 12 x 15 inch board
Acrylics & colored pencils on gessoed board

Page 228 (right)
Legends of Hollywood: Lucille Ball
US Postage Stamp
4 x 7 inch art on 12 x 15 inch board
Acrylics & colored pencils on gessoed board

Page 229 (left)
Legends of Hollywood: Helen Hayes
US Postage Stamp
4 x 7 inch art on 12 x 15 inch board
Acrylics & colored pencils on gessoed board

Page 229 (right)
Legends of Hollywood: Edward G. Robinson
US Postage Stamp
4 x 7 inch art on 12 x 15 inch board
Acrylics & colored pencils on gessoed board

Page 230 (left)
Legends of Hollywood: James Stewart
US Postage Stamp
4 x 7 inch art on 12 x 15 inch board
Acrylics & colored pencils on gessoed board

Page 230 (right)
Legends of Hollywood: Henry Fonda
US Postage Stamp
4 x 7 inch art on 12 x 15 inch board
Acrylics & colored pencils on gessoed board

Page 231
Andy Griffith (Mayberry RFD)
Collector Plate
16 inch circle on 30 x 30 inch board
Acrylics & colored pencils on gessoed board

Page 232-233
Aces & Eights
Playing Card Set Tin Box Cover
12 x 17 inch art on 22 x 30 inch board
Acrylics & colored pencils on gessoed board

Page 234
Celebrating 100 Years of Powered Flight
Limited Edition Print
30 x 40 inches
Acrylics & colored pencils on gessoed board

Page 235
E.T.: The Extra-Terrestrial
Parks Poster
24 x 36 inch art on 30 x 40 inch board
Acrylics & colored pencils on gessoed board

Page 236
Skeleton Warriors
Cartoon Series Marketing Poster
21 x 33 inch art on 30 x 40 inch board
Acrylics & colored pencils on gessoed board

Page 237
Captain Power
TV Series Marketing Poster
22 x 36 inch art on 30 x 40 inch board
Acrylics & colored pencils on gessoed board

Page 238-239
Raiders of the Lost Art
Promotional Poster
30 x 30 inch board
Acrylics & colored pencils on gessoed board

Page 240
Smithsonian, American International Retrospective
Poster
20 x 30 inches
Oils on canvas

Page 241
Oklahoma
Travel Poster
24.5 x 38 inch art on 30 x 40 inch board
Acrylics & colored pencils on gessoed board

Page 242
Love Endures (Columbine High School)
Limited Edition Print
20 x 30 inch art on 30 x 40 inch board
Acrylics & colored pencils on gessoed board

Page 243
America's Movies for the World's Athletes
(XXIII Olympic Games)
Poster
26 x 27.75 inches
Acrylics & colored pencils on gessoed board

Page 244
Cary Grant
Video Marketing
18 x 35 inches
Acrylics & colored pencils on board

Page 245
Superman
Poster
23 x 35 inches
Oils on canvas

PERSONAL

Page 249
Upside-down
19.25 x 28.5 inch art on 30.25 x 39 inch board
Pastels & colored pencils on gray board

Page 250
Baba Yaga
36 x 60 inches
Acrylics & oils on canvas

Page 251 (top)
Growl
30 x 22.5 inches
Acrylics, silica sand & drawing on watercolor paper

Page 251 (bottom)
X 1
14 x 22 inch art on 22 x 30 inch paper
Pastels & colored pencils on gray paper

Page 252-253
Black Cat
46 x 45 inches
Oils on canvas

Page 254-255
Black Gold
30 x 80 inches
Oils, gold leaf & copper leaf on canvas

Page 255 (bottom)
X 3
14 x 22 inch art on 22 x 30 inch paper
Pastels & colored pencils on gray paper

Page 256
Blue
29.25 x 25.5 inches
Oils on board

Page 257
Gorilla
29.5 x 41.5 inches
Drawing & acrylics on watercolor paper

Page 258
Last Eve
36 x 30 inches

Acrylics, oils & gold leaf on canvas

Page 259
Fantasize
40 x 27.5 inches
Mixed media

Page 260
Leopard
30 x 40 inches
Acrylics, oils & leaves on gessoed board

Page 261
Green
30 x 40 inches
Oils on board

Page 262
Muscles
32 x 48 inches
Oils on panel

Page 263
Purple
32 x 48 inches
Oils on panel

Page 264
Past Present Future
30 x 40 inches
Oils on board

Page 265
Gray Lady
30 x 40 inches
Oils on board

Page 266
Linear two
30 x 48 inches
Oils on panel

Page 267 (top)
Linear three
48 x 30 inches
Oils on panel

Page 267 (bottom)
X 4
14 x 22 inch art on 22 x 30 inch paper
Pastels & colored pencils on gray paper

Page 268
Chasm
29.5 x 25 inches
Pastels on board

Page 269
Channel
33 x 48 inches
Oils on panel

Page 270-271
Green Jungle
80 x 46 inches
Oils & acrylics on canvas

Page 272-273
Autumn Dream
30 x 40 inches
Acrylics & colored pencils on board

Page 274
Copper Girl
22 x 29.5 inches
Mixed media & copper leaf on watercolor paper

Page 275
Four Creatures
30 x 40 inches
Oils on board

Page 276
Hope
40 x 50 inches
Mixed media, sand, coins & jewelry on panel

Page 277
Indiana Jones
30 x 80 inches
Acrylics, oils & gold leaf on canvas

Page 278-279
Dreamtime
40 x 80 inches
Oils on panel

Page 280
Red Armed Panther
29.5 x 41.5 inches
Mixed media & silica sand on watercolor paper

Page 281
Joy
22.5 x 30 inches
Acrylics & drawing on watercolor paper

Page 282
Abe
30 x 80 inches
Acrylics & oils on canvas

Page 283
Albert
29.5 x 41.5 inches
Acrylics & charcoal on watercolor paper

Page 284-285
Soaring
80 x 30 inches
Oils on canvas

Page 284 (bottom)
X 5
14 x 22 inch art on 22 x 30 inch paper
Pastels & colored pencils on gray paper

Page 286 (top)
Sacrifice
35.25 x 42 inches
Acrylics, oils & weeds on panel

Page 286 (bottom)
X 2
14 x 22 inch art on 22 x 30 inch paper
Pastels & colored pencils on gray paper

Page 287
Tattoo
Oils on canvas
38 x 60 inches

Page 288-289
Purple Couch
31 x 14 inch art on 30 x 40 inch board
Pastels on board

Page 290
Redhead
29.5 x 41.5 inches
Drawing & acrylics on watercolor paper

Page 291
Baby
29.5 x 41.5 inches
Drawing & acrylics on watercolor paper

Page 292
Skateboard
40 x 36 inches
Oils on panel

Page 293
Madonna
24 x 40 inches
Oils on panel

Page 294
ABBA
40 x 80 inches
Oils on canvas

Page 295
XL
33 x 44 inches
Acrylics & colored pencils on panel

Page 296
Red Balloon
30 x 40 inches
Acrylics & oils on board

Page 297
'55
36 x 48 inches
Oils on panel

Page 298
Turquoise
30 x 40 inches
Oils on board

Page 299 (top)
Rhino (vignette)
41.5 x 29.5 inches
Acrylics & drawing on watercolor paper

Page 299 (bottom)
X 6
14 x 22 inch art on 22 x 30 inch paper
Pastels & colored pencils on gray paper

COPYRIGHT (IN ALPHABETICAL ORDER)

'55 © Copyright Drew Struzan 2008
ABBA © Copyright Drew Struzan 2000
Abe © Copyright Drew Struzan 1997
Abominable © Copyright Drew Struzan 2004
Aces & Eights © Copyright The Franklin Mint 1994
Action Comics #800 (Superman) © Copyright DC Comics 2002
Adventures in Babysitting © Copyright Drew Struzan 1987
Albert © Copyright Drew Struzan 2000
Alice Cooper, Greatest Hits © Copyright Warner Brothers Inc. 1974
Alice Cooper, Welcome to My Nightmare © Copyright PE&E 1975
All's Fair © Copyright TMS 1988
America's Movies for the World's Athletes (XXIII Olympic Games) © Copyright Drew Struzan 1984
American Justice © Copyright TMS 1986
An American Tail (gang plank) © Copyright Universal City Studios, Inc. 1986
An American Tail (suitcases) © Copyright Universal City Studios, Inc. 1986
Andy Griffith (Mayberry RFD) © Copyright The Franklin Mint 1994
Angels & Airwaves, I-Empire © Copyright Angels & Airwaves 2006
Angels in the Outfield © Copyright The Walt Disney Company 1994
Arabian Nights © Copyright ABC 2000
Arrowhead Arts Association (5) © Copyright Drew Struzan 1989
Arrowhead Bach Festival (1) © Copyright Drew Struzan 1985
Arrowhead Bach Festival (2) © Copyright Drew Struzan 1986
Arrowhead Bach Festival (3) © Copyright Drew Struzan 1987
Astounding Space Thrills #3 © Copyright Day 1 Comics 1998
Autumn Dream © Copyright Drew Struzan 1993
Baba Yaga © Copyright Drew Struzan 1998
Baby © Copyright Drew Struzan 1998
Back to the Future © Copyright Universal City Studios, Inc. 1985
Back to the Future Part II © Copyright Universal City Studios, Inc. 1989
Back to the Future Part III © Copyright Universal City Studios, Inc. 1990
Batteries Not Included © Copyright Universal City Studios, Inc. 1987
Beauty and the Beast © Copyright The Walt Disney Company 1991
Better Off Dead © Copyright Warner Brothers Inc. 1985
Big Trouble in Little China © Copyright 20th Century Fox Picture Corp. 1986
Black Cat © Copyright Drew Struzan 2008
Black Gold © Copyright Drew Struzan 2004
Black Sabbath, Sabbath Bloody Sabbath © Copyright Warner Brothers Records 1973
Blade Runner © Copyright Drew Struzan 2003
Blue (1) © Copyright Drew Struzan 1999
Blue (2) © Copyright Drew Struzan 1999
Blue [poster] © Copyright Drew Struzan 1999
Blue © Copyright Drew Struzan 2007
Borderline © Copyright AFD 1980
Brave New World © Copyright Drew Struzan 1978
The Brothers Johnson, Blam © Copyright Drew Struzan 1978
California Suite © Copyright Columbia Pictures 1979
The Cannonball Run © Copyright Warner Brothers Inc. 1980
Captain Power © Copyright Landmark Entertainment 1990
Cary Grant © Copyright The Nostalgia Merchant 1975
Celebrating 100 Years of Powered Flight © Copyright Drew Struzan 2000
Champions © Copyright Embassy 1984
Channel © Copyright Drew Struzan 2010
Chasm © Copyright Drew Struzan 2010
Code Name: Emerald © Copyright MGM / UA 1985
Coming to America (Statue of Liberty) © Copyright Paramount Pictures Corporation 1988
Coming to America © Copyright Paramount Pictures Corporation 1988
Copper Girl © Copyright Drew Struzan 1999
Cowboys & Aliens © Copyright Universal Studios 2011
Creature from the Black Lagoon © Copyright Hollywood on Paper 2001
The Crocodile Hunter: Collision Course (A) © Copyright MGM Pictures, Inc. 2002
The Crocodile Hunter: Collision Course (B) © Copyright MGM Pictures, Inc. 2002
Cross Creek (A) © Copyright Universal City Studios, Inc. 1983
Cross Creek (B) © Copyright Universal City Studios, Inc. 1983
Cutthroat Island © Copyright MGM / Carolco 1996
The Dark Tower © Copyright Drew Struzan 2007
Deception © Copyright Drew Struzan 2010
Disneyana (Pocahontas) © Copyright The Walt Disney Company 1995
Disneyland, Indiana Jones Adventure © Copyright The Walt Disney Company 1994
Dreamscape © Copyright 20th Century Fox Picture Corp. 1984
Dreamtime © Copyright Drew Struzan 2007
Drew Struzan © Copyright Drew Struzan 2010
DuckTales: The Movie – Treasure of the Lost Lamp © Copyright The Walt Disney Company 1990
Dylan Reading © Copyright Drew Struzan 1988
Dylan Struzan © Copyright Drew Struzan 2011
E.T.: The Extra-Terrestrial © Copyright Universal City Studios, Inc. 1983
E.T.: The Extra-Terrestrial [Parks Poster] © Copyright Universal City Studios, Inc. 1990
Fame © Copyright MGM 1979
Fantasize © Copyright Drew Struzan 2010
First Blood © Copyright Orion Pictures 1982
The Flintstones © Copyright Universal City Studios, Inc. 1994
The Flintstones in Viva Rock Vegas © Copyright Universal City Studios, Inc. 2000
Four Creatures © Copyright Drew Struzan 1997
Frank Sinatra (Lady is a Tramp) © Copyright The Franklin Mint 1998
Frank Sinatra (Witchcraft) © Copyright The Franklin Mint 1996
Frankenstein © Copyright Drew Struzan 2003
The Frisco Kid © Copyright Warner Brothers Inc. 1980
Galidor © Copyright Lego Systems, Inc. 2001
George Lucas © Copyright Drew Struzan 1997
George Lucas [Foreword] © Copyright Drew Struzan 2011
George Lucas: The Creative Impulse: Lucasfilm's First Twenty Years ™ & © 1991 Lucasfilm Ltd. All rights reserved. Used under authorization.
George Lucas: The Creative Impulse: Lucasfilm's First Twenty-Five Years ™ & © 1996 Lucasfilm Ltd. All rights reserved. Used under authorization.
A Gift from Heaven © Copyright Hatchwell / Lucarelli Prod. 1994
Glenn Miller © Copyright Readers Digest 1986
The Goonies © Copyright Warner Brothers Inc. 1985
Gorilla © Copyright Drew Struzan 2007
Gray Lady © Copyright Drew Struzan 2006
The Great Muppet Caper © Copyright Henson & Associates 1981
Green © Copyright Drew Struzan 2006
Green Jungle © Copyright Drew Struzan 2000
The Green Mile © Copyright Warner Brothers Inc. 2006
Growl © Copyright Drew Struzan 1998
Happy Hour © Copyright TMS 1987
Harry and the Hendersons © Copyright Universal City Studios, Inc. 1986
Harry Potter and the Chamber of Secrets © Copyright Drew Struzan 2002
Harry Potter and the Sorcerer's Stone © Copyright Warner Brothers Inc. 2001
Health © Copyright Drew Struzan 1980
Heat and Dust © Copyright Universal City Studios, Inc. 1983
Hellboy © Copyright Columbia Tristar 2003
Hellboy II: The Golden Army © Copyright Drew Struzan 2008

Hocus Pocus © Copyright The Walt Disney Company 1993
The Hollywood Reporter, 13 November 1984 (20th Century Fox: The First 50 Years) © Copyright 20th Century Fox 1984
Hook © Copyright Sony / Tristar 1991
Hope © Copyright Drew Struzan 1995
Indiana Jones (Bonus Material) ™ & © 2003 Lucasfilm Ltd. All rights reserved. Used under authorization.
Indiana Jones (Trilogy) ™ & © 2003 Lucasfilm Ltd. All rights reserved. Used under authorization.
Indiana Jones © Copyright Drew Struzan 2005
Indiana Jones and the Dinosaur Eggs ™ & © 1995 Lucasfilm Ltd. All rights reserved. Used under authorization.
Indiana Jones and the Kingdom of the Crystal Skull [Advance]™ & © 2008 Lucasfilm Ltd. All rights reserved. Used under authorization.
Indiana Jones and the Kingdom of the Crystal Skull ™ & © 2008 Lucasfilm Ltd. All rights reserved. Used under authorization.
Indiana Jones and the Last Crusade (Pepsi Cola) © Copyright Lucasfilm Ltd. 1989
Indiana Jones and the Last Crusade [Advance] ™ & © 1998 Lucasfilm Ltd. All rights reserved. Used under authorization.
Indiana Jones and the Last Crusade ™ & © 1998 Lucasfilm Ltd. All rights reserved. Used under authorization.
Indiana Jones and the Philosopher's Stone ™ & © 1994 Lucasfilm Ltd. All rights reserved. Used under authorization.
Indiana Jones and the Secret of the Sphinx ™ & © 1997 Lucasfilm Ltd. All rights reserved. Used under authorization.
Indiana Jones and the Seven Veils ™ & © 1991 Lucasfilm Ltd. All rights reserved. Used under authorization.
Indiana Jones and the Sky Pirates ™ & © 1992 Lucasfilm Ltd. All rights reserved. Used under authorization.
Indiana Jones and the Temple of Doom ™ & © 1984 Lucasfilm Ltd. All rights reserved. Used under authorization.
Indiana Jones and the Unicorn's Legacy ™ & © 1991 Lucasfilm Ltd. All rights reserved. Used under authorization.
Into the Fire © Copyright TMS 1988
John Carpenter's Snake Plissken Chronicles © Copyright Drew Struzan 2003
Johnny Dangerously © Copyright 20th Century Fox Picture Corp. 1985
Joy © Copyright Drew Struzan 1999
Labou © Copyright Drew Struzan 2006
Lady Pendragon #1 © Copyright Drew Struzan 2000
Ladyhawke © Copyright Warner Brothers Inc. 1985
Leopard © Copyright Drew Struzan 1995
Last Eve © Copyright Drew Struzan 1998
Legends of Hollywood: Edward G. Robinson © Copyright US Postal Service 1999
Legends of Hollywood: Helen Hayes © Copyright US Postal Service 2001
Legends of Hollywood: Henry Fonda © Copyright US Postal Service 2005
Legends of Hollywood: James Stewart © Copyright US Postal Service 2006
Legends of Hollywood: John Wayne © Copyright US Postal Service 2000
Legends of Hollywood: Lucille Ball © Copyright US Postal Service 1998
Linear three © Copyright Drew Struzan 2010
Linear two © Copyright Drew Struzan 2010
The Little Rascals (Official) © Copyright The Franklin Mint 1993
The Little Rascals (Super Slooth) © Copyright The Franklin Mint 1996
The Lord of the Rings Masterpieces (1) © Copyright Drew Struzan 2006
The Lord of the Rings Masterpieces (2) © Copyright Drew Struzan 2007
Lorser Feitelson © Copyright Drew Struzan 2004
The Lost World: Jurassic Park © Copyright Drew Struzan 1997
Love Endures (Columbine High School) © Copyright Drew Struzan 1999
MAD #379 (YoYos for Dummies) © Copyright Drew Struzan 1998
Madonna © Copyright Drew Struzan 2009
Mary Travers, Circles © Copyright Warner Brothers Inc. 1975
Masters of the Universe © Copyright Cannon Group 1987
Meatballs III: Summer Job © Copyright TMS 1986
The Mist © Copyright Drew Struzan 2007
The Modern Jazz Quartet, In Memoriam © Copyright Little David Records 1974
The Muppet Christmas Carol © Copyright The Walt Disney Company 1992
The Muppet Movie (rowboat) © Copyright AFD 1979
The Muppet Movie (Studebaker) © Copyright AFD 1979
Muppet Treasure Island © Copyright The Walt Disney Company 1996
Muscles © Copyright Drew Struzan 2006
The Name of the Rose (A) © Copyright 20th Century Fox Picture Corp. 1986
The Name of the Rose (B) © Copyright 20th Century Fox Picture Corp. 1986
Oklahoma © Copyright Oklahoma Tourism Board 1996
The Outing © Copyright TMS 1986
Pan's Labyrinth © Copyright Drew Struzan 2006
Past Present Future © Copyright Drew Struzan 2007
The Pirates of Penzance © Copyright Universal City Studios, Inc. 1982
Police Academy (girl cop) © Copyright Warner Brothers Inc. 1984
Police Academy 2: Their First Assignment © Copyright Warner Brothers Inc. 1984
Police Academy 3: Back in Training © Copyright Warner Brothers Inc. 1986
Police Academy 4: Citizens on Patrol © Copyright Warner Brothers Inc. 1987
Princess Diana (Princess of Hope) © Copyright The Franklin Mint 1997
Princess Diana (Princess of Style) © Copyright The Franklin Mint 1997
Purple © Copyright Drew Struzan 2008
Purple Couch © Copyright Drew Struzan 1989
Raiders of the Lost Ark ™ & © 1982 Lucasfilm Ltd. All rights reserved. Used under authorization.
Raiders of the Lost Art © Copyright Drew Struzan 1990
Red Armed Panther © Copyright Drew Struzan 2000
Red Balloon © Copyright Drew Struzan 1994
Redhead © Copyright Drew Struzan 1998
Return to Macon County © Copyright AIP 1976
Return to Oz © Copyright The Walt Disney Company 1984
Return to Oz (Mombi) © Copyright Buena Vista Pictures 1984
Rhino (vignette) © Copyright Drew Struzan 1998
Sacrifice © Copyright Drew Struzan 1996
Sahara (1) © Copyright MGM / UA 1984
Sahara (2) © Copyright MGM / UA 1984
Self Portrait © Copyright Drew Struzan 1988
The Seven-Per-Cent Solution © Copyright Universal City Studios, Inc. 1976
Sexina: Popstar P.I. © Copyright Sharkey Productions 2007
The Shawshank Redemption (A) © Copyright Warner Brothers Inc. 2004
The Shawshank Redemption (B) © Copyright Drew Struzan 2004
Shirley Valentine © Copyright Paramount Pictures Corporation 1989
Skateboard © Copyright Drew Struzan 2009
Skeleton Warriors © Copyright Landmark Entertainment 1994
A Small Town in Texas © Copyright AIP 1976
Smithsonian, American International Retrospective © Copyright American International Pictures 1979
Soaring © Copyright Drew Struzan 2004
The Spielberg / Williams Collaboration © Copyright Sony Music Corp. 1991
Squirm © Copyright American International Pictures 1976
Star Trek (25th Anniversary, Captain Kirk) © Copyright Paramount Pictures Corporation 1991

Star Trek (25th Anniversary, Dr. McCoy) © Copyright Paramount Pictures Corporation 1991
Star Trek (25th Anniversary, Mr. Spock) © Copyright Paramount Pictures Corporation 1991
Star Trek: Captains & Crew (Star Trek) © Copyright The Franklin Mint 1999
Star Trek: Captains & Crew (The Next Generation) © Copyright The Franklin Mint 1999
Star Trek: The Next Generation: "Future's Past" © Copyright Paramount Pictures Corporation 1993
Star Wars (Circus) ™ & © 1977 Lucasfilm Ltd. All rights reserved. Used under authorization.
Star Wars © Copyright US Postal Service 2006
Star Wars Darth Maul #1 ™ & © 2000 Lucasfilm Ltd. All rights reserved. Used under authorization.
Star Wars Darth Maul #2 ™ & © 2000 Lucasfilm Ltd. All rights reserved. Used under authorization.
Star Wars Darth Maul #3 ™ & © 2000 Lucasfilm Ltd. All rights reserved. Used under authorization.
Star Wars: Episode I – The Phantom Menace ™ & © 1999 Lucasfilm Ltd. All rights reserved. Used under authorization.
Star Wars: Episode II – Attack of the Clones ™ & © 2002 Lucasfilm Ltd. All rights reserved. Used under authorization.
Star Wars: Episode III – Revenge of the Sith (Special Edition) ™ & © 2005 Lucasfilm Ltd. All rights reserved. Used under authorization.
Star Wars: Episode IV – A New Hope (Special Edition) ™ & © 1996 Lucasfilm Ltd. All rights reserved. Used under authorization.
Star Wars: Episode V – The Empire Strikes Back (Special Edition) ™ & © 1997 Lucasfilm Ltd. All rights reserved. Used under authorization.
Star Wars: Episode VI – Return of the Jedi (Special Edition) ™ & © 1997 Lucasfilm Ltd. All rights reserved. Used under authorization.
Star Wars: Planet of Twilight ™ & © 1996 Lucasfilm Ltd. All rights reserved. Used under authorization.
Star Wars: Rebellion Era Sourcebook ™ & © 2000 Lucasfilm Ltd. All rights reserved. Used under authorization.
Star Wars: Revenge of the Jedi ™ & © 1983 Lucasfilm Ltd. All rights reserved. Used under authorization.
Star Wars: Roleplaying Game ™ & © 2000 Lucasfilm Ltd. All rights reserved. Used under authorization.
Star Wars: Shadows of the Empire ™ & © 1995 Lucasfilm Ltd. All rights reserved. Used under authorization.
Star Wars: The Courtship of Princess Leia (hardback) ™ & © 1993 Lucasfilm Ltd. All rights reserved. Used under authorization.
Star Wars: The First Ten years ™ & © 1987 Lucasfilm Ltd. All rights reserved. Used under authorization.
Star Wars: The New Rebellion ™ & © 1996 Lucasfilm Ltd. All rights reserved. Used under authorization.
Star Wars: The Rise and Fall of Darth Vader (Anakin) ™ & © 2007 Lucasfilm Ltd. All rights reserved. Used under authorization.
Star Wars: The Rise and Fall of Darth Vader (Vader) ™ & © 2007 Lucasfilm Ltd. All rights reserved. Used under authorization.
Star Wars: The Truce at Bakura ™ & © 1993 Lucasfilm Ltd. All rights reserved. Used under authorization.
The Sting II (A) © Copyright Universal City Studios, Inc. 1983
The Sting II (B) © Copyright Universal City Studios, Inc. 1983
The Suit © Copyright Drew Struzan 2008
Sunset © Copyright Tristar 1988
Superman © Copyright The Thought Factory 1978
Tarzan, the Ape Man © Copyright Drew Struzan 1981
Tattoo © Copyright Drew Struzan 2007
The Thing © Copyright Universal City Studios, Inc. 1982
Three O'Clock High © Copyright Universal City Studios, Inc. 1987
The Three Stooges (Dr. Howard... Dr. Fine... Dr. Howard) © Copyright The Franklin Mint 1993
The Three Stooges (The Dictators) © Copyright The Franklin Mint 1993
To Be or Not To Be © Copyright 20th Century Fox Picture Corp. 1984
Tony Orlando & Dawn, To Be With You © Copyright PE&E 1976
Torrente 3: El protector © Copyright Drew Struzan 2005
Truth / Beauty © Copyright Drew Struzan 2010
Turquoise © Copyright Drew Struzan 2006
TV Guide, 15-21 May 1999 (Star Wars: Episode I – The Phantom Menace) ™ & © 1999 Lucasfilm Ltd. All rights reserved. Used under authorization.
TV Guide, 25-31 December 1993 (Johnny Carson) © Copyright Drew Struzan 1993
Under Fire © Copyright Orion Pictures 1983
Upside-down © Copyright Drew Struzan 2009
The Walking Dead © Copyright AMC 2010
We're Back! A Dinosaur's Story (parade) © Copyright Universal City Studios, Inc. 1993
We're Back! A Dinosaur's Story (raft) © Copyright Universal City Studios, Inc. 1993
Weekend Warriors © Copyright TMS 1986
Who's Killing the Great Chefs of Europe? © Copyright Warner Brothers Inc. 1976
X 1 © Copyright Drew Struzan 2009
X 2 © Copyright Drew Struzan 2009
X 3 © Copyright Drew Struzan 2009
X 4 © Copyright Drew Struzan 2009
X 5 © Copyright Drew Struzan 2009
X 6 © Copyright Drew Struzan 2010 XL © Copyright Drew Struzan 2011
Zathura: A Space Adventure © Copyright Columbia Pictures 2005